Critical Writings on

COMMONWEALTH LITERATURES:

A Selective Bibliography to 1970,
with a List of Theses and Dissertations

Compiled by
William H. New

The Pennsylvania State University Press
University Park and London

Library of Congress Cataloging in Publication Data

New, William H
   Critical writings on Commonwealth literatures.

   Includes index.
   1. English literature--Commonwealth of Nations
authors--History and criticism--Bibliography.
I. Title.
Z2000.9.N48   016.82'09   74-15195
ISBN 0-271-01166-1

Contents

Foreword

Bibliographers are harried by the individuality of every problem they look
at and constantly on the watch for yet another elusive but useful reference.
Minor authors vie with major authors for recognition; books and articles vie
with notes, reviews, and review articles; and lines of demarcation blur. A
compiler must react to each entry pragmatically in order to make his work
clear and helpful, but the selectivity that inevitably results, though it
has its own logic, will seem inconsistent to one reader, arbitrary to
another, perhaps even cavalier to a third. This book is ultimately neither
more nor less than a guide and aid to research, in a field of literary study
that is only just recently attracting serious international critical attention.

The term "Commonwealth" poses a problem. My solution might seem at first
to suggest that (whatever political and cultural ties may exist) "Commonwealth"
is a bibliographer's term of convenience. The United Kingdom and the
Mediterranean Commonwealth (Cyprus, Malta, Gibraltar) are not included; South
Africa and the Philippines are. Yet the apparent arbitrariness of such an
apolitical division makes critical sense. What India shares with Australia,
South Africa, the Philippines, and the others--and not with the United
Kingdom--is its endeavour in the twentieth century still to devise its
English-language literary culture.

Language, of course, raises even more questions, for the Asian and African
nations are multilingual; Canada and South Africa each use two major European
languages; Australia and New Zealand, like the others, have strong indigenous
oral literatures which are gradually being recorded. Where studies of these
other literatures seem significantly to bear on the English ones, I have
included them here, and otherwise left them out. The problem of translations
into English is thornier still. The basic criterion in these situations
seemed not to be the significant influence of the translated writers on their
English-language compatriots, and certainly not their intrinsic worth, but
rather the active participation of the writers themselves in translating
their own works, and/or the extent to which, in translation, they have
attracted serious English-language criticism. Hence writers like Gabrielle

Roy, Roger Lemelin, Ingrid Jonker, Uys Krige, and Rabindranath Tagore appear here, while many less translated but no less talented writers do not. While I have attempted, moreover, to list French and Afrikaans criticism of the respective writers, I have had no access to criticism written in any of the Asian languages. (The extensive Swedish criticism of Commonwealth writers, incidentally, has been written in English, and much of the German criticism of African and Canadian literature has been translated, though the work of Russian, Polish, and Czech critics--who have focussed primarily on Africa-- remains for the most part in the original.)

Two other groups of writers raise special problems: first, those like Northrop Frye, Marshall McLuhan, and Walter Murdoch, whose writings have influenced literature more than been strictly literary, and second, the travellers and émigrés whose attachment to the land of their adoption may seem slight. The first group has been kept; the second has not. D.H. Lawrence, Rudyard Kipling, Samuel Butler, Anthony Trollope, and Joyce Cary do not appear here, therefore, unless the general studies of their work or sojourn illuminate in some way the literary milieux in which Commonwealth writers were writing. The South African emigrants to England, the U.S.A., Canada, and the Caribbean, however--like Dan Jacobson, Ezekiel Mphahlele, John Peter, and Peter Abrahams--are listed as South Africans still; V.S. Naipaul remains Trinidadian and Katherine Mansfield a New Zealander; David Martin becomes an Australian, and Malcolm Lowry is classified as the Canadian, which in his letters he affirmed himself (in all but the legal sense) to be. It is a question of emphasis in the works of the individual writer, which proves as workable a basis as any on which to make such distinctions. The grouping together of several East and West African nationalities under the one title "African," and the several nations of the West Indies under another single title obviously works even more militantly against growing nationalist sentiments. It is only acceptable if critics recognize the genuine differences between, say, Guyanese and Jamaican points of view, while acknowledging the practicality of bibliographically bringing them together.

Malta and Cyprus are omitted because no substantial criticism has yet been directed towards their English literatures. In time, writers like Francis Ebejer and Taner Baybars, and others elsewhere, will attract more attention; and essays will explore such topics as the Mediterranean impact on the English language, or the link between the native Mediterranean writers' responses to their world and those of writers (Roy Campbell or Robert Graves, for example) who have been transplanted to it. Indeed, one of the most serious gaps that this bibliography exposes is the very lack of criticism

directed towards some of the significant writers. Govind Desani, Sylvia
Wynter, George Johnston, Charles Madge, Lee Kok Liang, Gloria Rawlinson, Dan
Davin, Louis Johnson, Andrew Salkey, Samuel Selvon--all have been too much
ignored.

Criticism, furthermore, tends frequently to be clouded by national issues
(politics in South Africa, for example, or identity crises in Canada and
New Zealand), or by the nationality and perspective of the critic himself,
often to the detriment of objectivity. As though in response to such a
charge, Australian criticism has been paramountly historical in nature,
attempting to preserve judicious objectivity though sometimes sacrificing
imaginative spontaneity for it. Much of the best Australian criticism
therefore appears in notes, whereas much of the best New Zealand criticism
appears in reviews. But as the shortness of the "COMMONWEALTH: GENERAL"
section indicates, there has been too little comparative criticism altogether
Perhaps at this stage such a situation is inevitable. Although in Africa,
Southeast Asia, the West Indies, and even New Zealand, there are too few
commentaries on the local scene, criticism in the new nations does at first
accompany each society's attempt to discover and enunciate its distinctive
culture. Only later, when that is somewhat secured, do observers look
beyond their region. Paradoxically what they sometimes discover then are
parallels, differences, innovations, and trends that can illuminate their
own culture and another at the same time.

Still, a substantial body of critical writing has already accumulated. If
I have not in most cases listed short notices, I have tried to include those
that added to critical knowledge. (One publishing company in Canada is
performing a valuable service by collecting and reprinting reviews of major
writers' works.) The fact that much of the extended criticism concerns
"general" topics creates another predicament, for significant comments on
individual writers are frequently ensconced in discussions of thematic or
technical or other large critical topics. I have not attempted to isolate
all of these under "INDIVIDUAL AUTHORS," assuming that any student of a
particular figure will automatically consult the relevant passages of books
like D.G. Jones' Butterfly on Rock, Kendrick Smithyman's A Way of Saying,
Gerald Moore's The Chosen Tongue, and the works listed under "COMMONWEALTH:
GENERAL."

Major statements are not, of course, always made in long books, nor in
connection with major writers, and, in any event, "major" is a subjective,
critically quarrelsome term. In identifying "major writers" (for the
"INDIVIDUAL AUTHORS" sections) I have used the term loosely and widely, in
order that research in Commonwealth writing may generally be aided. The

term is applied most narrowly to Canadian literature, which is already well
served by enumerative bibliographies edited by R.E. Watters and others. On
some occasions (on Frances Brooke and Malcolm Lowry, for example), I have
been able to add to that work; for the rest, the task has largely been one
of updating and selecting from it. The literatures without such extensive
research aids already in existence presented different kinds of challenge--
but they are the areas that created the real need for the present volume.
Standard indices to book reviews and periodicals aided in the search for
relevant material, and the other extant bibliographical references (published
variously in book, serial, and pamphlet form, and listed under "RESEARCH
AIDS" or "INDIVIDUAL AUTHORS" in the appropriate places) also proved
invaluable preliminary guides.

The increasing coverage given to Commonwealth literatures by current serial
bibliographies (Australian Literary Studies, Journal of Canadian Fiction,
Journal of Commonwealth Literature, and African Literature Today) and by the
MLA International Bibliography makes 1970 a reasonable cutoff date. There
have, of course, been various changes since 1970 which bear upon the study
of Commonwealth literatures. Some of these have been critical and bibliographic. Two large bibliographic projects still in progress--the retrospective
Canadiana project at the National Library in Ottawa and the nineteenth-
century Australian newspaper indexing project under the directorship of
Leonie Kramer at Sydney University--will undoubtedly locate more nineteenth-
century items than have been located here; and similar work remains to be
done elsewhere. More dramatic has been the discovery that the Canadian
writer Frederick Philip Grove was the same person as the nineteenth-century
German writer Felix Paul Greve, which has opened new directions for study.
Douglas Spettigue's biography, FPG: The European Years (Ottawa: Oberon,
1973), broaches some of those possibilities, and future researchers on Grove
will be aided by the useful bibliography of German criticism on Greve, not
itemized here, which appears at the end of his book.

The classification system for authors with pseudonyms varies. Writers
known more by their pseudonyms than by their given names--Katherine Mansfield,
Henry Handel Richardson, Rolf Boldrewood, Han Suyin--are listed under their
pseudonyms, using the following format: BOLDREWOOD, Rolf [T.A. Browne].
Writers who by 1970 had surrendered their pseudonyms or whose real names had
acquired equal currency with their pseudonyms are listed under their given
names. Hence "Brent of Bin Bin" appears under Miles Franklin, "Tom Collins"
under Joseph Furphy, "Martin Mills" under Martin Boyd, with this format:
BOYD, Martin [pseud. Martin Mills].

While the format of the individual entries in the bibliography has been governed by standard MLA style, it has also been affected by the idiosyncrasies of the works being itemized. Though a degree of clarity is gained, the distinctive flavour of some of the journals is lost when names are reduced to volume and issue numbers. The tropical "seasons" which the Guyanese periodical Kyk-over-al adopted--"midyear," "cropover," "yearend"--gave it a particular character. The Australian journal Quadrant similarly adapted season names to its own situation; its issue called "Summer 1960-61," for example, makes Southern Hemisphere sense, but that perspective disappears under the anonymity of "5, no. 1 (1960-61)." Some journals (e.g., Drylight) are annuals; others (e.g., Swarajya) publish annual unnumbered supplements to their numbered volumes; Westerly every year renumbers its issues as 1, 2, and 3; some fortnightly and monthly magazines (e.g., Maclean's) can be referred to more easily if one lists their date rather than their issue number; the South African Railways and Harbours Magazine ceased its numbering system with vol. 26, no. 1 (Jan 1932); and several French journals are published by date only, with no volume number. In that context Les Lettres nouvelles is another anomaly, for it went through three numbered series (in such a way as to allow two issues numbered 5 within the space of four years, 1957-1960) before it began an unnumbered series in 1964.

Some other apparent inconsistencies in the listings in this bibliography are explained by changes in the format of particular journals. When the WLWE Newsletter became WLWE (for World Literature Written in English), it changed its numbering from "number numbers" to volume and issue numbers, with separate pagination each issue. The Journal of Commonwealth Literature used number numbers from 1 to 10 (1965-1970), then shifted to volume and issue numbers beginning 6, no. 1 (1971). Black Orpheus numbered 1-22 (1957-1967), then began volume 2 and issue numbers. Encounter abandoned its number numbers in 1963, but because, like Présence Africaine, Landfall, and Overland, it had concurrently employed volume numbers, its system does not in this bibliography appear to break down. The question of pagination raises other complications. Some journals used no pagination at all. Pagination data for some newspaper entries is incomplete. Transition (Kampala), which used both volume numbers and number numbers, paginated by the latter. Articles which appeared on the inside front cover of the Bulletin (Sydney) are listed as being on the "Red Page." Southern Review (Adelaide) paginated each issue in volume 1 separately, then paginated continuously throughout each subsequent volume. Canadian Bookman continuously paginated vol. 4 nos. 1-2, and vols. 5-17, but separately paginated each issue of vols. 1-3, vol. 4 no. 3, and vol. 18 on.

Probably the most complicated history, worth recording in some detail, is

that of the Canadian Author & Bookman, which took this title in April 1940
with vol. 17, no. 1. The succeeding issues of the volume appeared in July,
November, and the following February. Vol. 18, no. 1 appeared as April-July
1941; vol. 18, nos. 2, 3 & 4 appeared in December 1942. With vol. 19 a more
regular pattern developed, with issues appearing in March, June, September,
and December, until vol. 22, nos. 3 & 4 (December 1946). Vol. 23, nos. 1-3
appeared as Spring, Fall, and December 1947, with a supplement (also called
Fall 1947) given the same number as the December issue (23, no. 3). The
cover of the March 1948 issue calls it vol. 24, no. 1; inside the magazine
the issue is called vol. 24, no. 2, which is a printing error, since the
June 1948 issue is consistently called vol. 24, no. 2. Nos. 3 and 4 of that
year appeared in September and December as usual, with another Fall supplement
also called vol. 24, no. 4. In 1949, the four issues of vol. 25 appeared
as March, Summer, Autumn, and Christmas; in 1950, the four seasons were used
consistently as names; in 1951, the seasons again were used, except that
there was no Spring issue, and the Winter issue was a double one (27, no.
3 & 4). Vol. 28 began a different kind of uncertainty about dating; nos. 1-4
are called Spring 1952, Summer 1952, Autumn 1952, and Winter 1952-53. But
volume 29 has Spring, Summer, and Autumn issues dated 1953, with no. 4 dated
solely 1954. That inconsistency about the date of the Winter issue was to
continue through most of the next decade, as was an irregular alternation
between "Autumn" and "Fall". In 1955-1956, the Spring, Summer, Fall, and
Winter issues are respectively called vol. 31, no. 1, vol. 32, no. 1, vol. 32,
no. 3, and vol. 31, no. 4; as a complete vol. 32 then followed in 1956-1957,
it is safe to assume the Summer and Fall issues were misnumbered. Similarly,
as the Winter 1958-59 and the Spring 1959 issues are both called vol. 35,
no. 1, the Winter issue should be corrected to read vol. 34, no. 4, which
would otherwise be missing. In 1960 and 1961 the journal was going through
another transitional phase. Vol. 36, nos. 1 & 2 appeared in Spring and
Summer 1961; no. 3 is called Winter 1960-61, and no. 4 Spring 1961. With
volumes 37 and 38, Summer-Fall-Winter-Spring and Summer-Winter-Spring-Summer
labels were used, with vol. 37, no. 3 and vol. 38, no. 2 both being called
Winter 1962. In 1963, however, there began another regular phase. Vol. 39,
nos. 1 & 2 appeared in Autumn and Winter 1963, nos. 3 & 4 in Spring and
Summer 1964. This pattern continued through 1970. If such inconsistencies
make enumerative bibliography frustrating, rehearsing them here makes
obvious one of the reasons it is necessary.

For information concerning the section on theses and dissertations, I have
relied not only on the standard reference works (e.g., Dissertation Abstracts
and Aslib), but also on a questionnaire I sent to universities throughout

the Commonwealth and the U.S.A. I am indebted to the many people who
responded to it, but the results must be considered essentially preliminary.
Records at some universities could provide only inadequate data on early
research; European theses are not universally listed. One of the interesting
sidelights the compilation threw on Commonwealth literature studies, however,
is the fact that Canadian universities have long accepted research in Canadian
literature as satisfying higher degree requirements, while Australian
universities have only recently acknowledged the academic legitimacy of
Australian literature. And whereas, throughout the Commonwealth, comparative
studies are in their infancy, criticism in the United States has largely
adopted the comparative approach. Still, much research in all aspects of
Commonwealth literature remains to be done, and it is my hope that this
checklist will facilitate and encourage it.

I want to thank my research assistants, Penelope Connell and Stanley Fogel,
for their help with preliminary work; Carole Gerson, for her help with
journals; and Rosalyn Alexander, for the skill and energy with which she
checked references and helped locate titles. My colleague, Dr. Adrian
Mitchell, and Dr. Peter Alcock of Massey University, offered helpful advice;
and librarians at the University of the West Indies (Cave Hill and Mona),
the National Library of South Africa, the Turnbull Library (Wellington), the
National Library of Australia, the Fryer Library (Brisbane), the Commonwealth
Institute and the Royal Commonwealth Society (London), Harvard University,
the University of Malaya (Kuala Lumpur), and the Bibliothèque Nationale
(Paris) helped confirm titles that were unavailable locally; all that
assistance was much appreciated. I should like to thank the University of
British Columbia for a grant in aid of the project; Joan Sandilands, Jennifer
Gallup, and the staff of the U.B.C. Library Humanities Division for their
encouragement and willing assistance, and for the professional expertise
they brought to bear upon countless problems; Dr. Jayne K. Kribbs, at The
Pennsylvania State University Press, for her skilful editorial guidance; and
Gale Dawson and Rosemary Leach for their patient and efficient typing. I
want also to thank R.E. Watters, Donald Stephens, A.N. Jeffares, Anthony
Alpers, Nissim Ezekiel, and Carl Klinck, who introduced to me the literatures
of the Commonwealth.

W.H.N

University of British Columbia
Vancouver, Canada
May 1974

Master List and Table of Abbreviations

AAPSS   Annals of the American Academy of Political and Social Science (Philadelphia)

AATB   Afro-Asian Theatre Bulletin (Lawrence, Kan.)

AAW   Afro-Asian Writings (Later Lotus, Cairo)

AAWA   Afro-Asian and World Affairs (New Delhi)

Abbia (Yaoundé, Cameroun)

ABC   American Book Collector (Chicago)

ABOB   Association of British Orientalists Bulletin (London)

Academy and Literature (London)

Acadie (Fredericton, N.B.)

ActaUCP   Acta Universitatis Carolinae-Philologica (Prague)

ActaV   Acta Victoriana (Toronto)

Adam   Adam International Review (London)

Adelphi (London)

ADHSJP   Armidale and District Historical Society Journal and Proceedings (Armidale, N.S.W.)

Adult Education (Melbourne)

Advent (Pondicherry)

Advocate (Melbourne)

AForum   African Forum (New York)

AfrA   African Arts/Arts d'Afrique (Los Angeles)

AfrAff   African Affairs (London)

AfrD   African Drum (London)

Africa (London)

AfricaR   Africa Report (Washington)

AfricaSE   Africa South in Exile (Cape Town)

Afrika Heute (Bonn, Rhein, Germany)

Afrique Actuelle (Paris)

AfrN   African Notes (Ibadan)

Afro-Caribbean Heritage (London)

AfrQ   Africa Quarterly (New Delhi)

AfrR   African Review (Accra)

AfrSt   African Statesman (Lagos)

AfrW   African World (London)

AfrWr   African Writer (Onitsha)

Age (Melbourne)

AgraUJ   Agra University Journal of Research

AHR   Alberta Historical Review (Edmonton)

Airways (Sydney)

AL   American Literature (Durham, N.C.)

ALA   L'Afrique littéraire et artistique (Paris)

Alaska Review (Anchorage)

ALS   Australian Literary Studies (Hobart)

ALT   African Literature Today (Freetown & London)

Americana (New York)

American Review (New York)

Amity (Bombay)

AmPM   American Poetry Magazine (Milwaukee)

AngloAmR   Anglo-American Review (New York)

ANSSR   Akademija Nauk SSSR (Moscow)

ANZY   Arts in New Zealand Yearbook (Wellington)

AQ   American Quarterly (Minneapolis)

AR   Antioch Review (Yellow Springs, Ohio)

Arena (Wellington)

ArielE   Ariel: A Review of International English Literature (Calgary)

ArO   Archiv Orientální (Prague)

ArQ   Arizona Quarterly (Tucson)

ArtL   Art and Letters (later Indian Art and Letters, London)

Arts (Sydney)

Aryan Path (Bombay)

ASACN   American Society for African Culture Newsletter (New York)

ASch   American Scholar (Washington)

AsH   Asian Horizon (London)

AsHum   Asia and the Humanities (Bloomington, Ind.)

AsR   Asian Review (London)

AsRev   Asiatic Review (formerly Asian Review, London)

AssamQ   Assam Quarterly (Dighali Pukhuri, Gauhati)

AsSt   Asian Student (San Francisco)

AT   Africa Today (Denver, Colo.)

Athenaeum (later New Statesman and Nation, London)

Atlantic   Atlantic Monthly (Boston)

AtlanticA   Atlantic Advocate (Fredericton, N.B.)

Atlas (Marion, Ohio)

AUMLA   Journal of the Australasian Universities Language and Literature
                Association (Christchurch, N.Z.)

Aussenpolitik (Stuttgart)

AustA   Australian Author (Mosman, N.S.W.)

AustBR   Australian Book Review (Kensington Park, S.A.)

AustCM   Australian Country Magazine (Sydney)

AustH   Australian Highway (Sydney)

AustJPH   Australian Journal of Politics and History (Brisbane)

AustL   Australian Letters (Adelaide)

AustLJ   Australian Library Journal (Sydney)

AustLR   Australian Left Review (Sydney)

AustQ   Australian Quarterly (Sydney)

Australian (Sydney)

Australian Teacher (Sydney)

AustT	Australian Tradition (Melbourne)
AustU	Australian University (Parkside, Victoria)
AustWW	Australian Women's Weekly (Sydney)
BA	Books Abroad (Norman, Okla.)
BAALE	Bulletin of the Association for African Literature in English (Freetown)
BACLALS	Bulletin of the Association of Commonwealth Literature and Language Studies (Leeds & Ottawa)

Balcony (Sydney)

BANQ	Biblionews and Australian Notes and Queries (Surrey Hills, N.S.W.)

Bantu (Pretoria)

BARev	Black Academy Review (Buffalo, N.Y.)
BB	Bulletin of Bibliography (Boston)
BBBull	B'nai B'rith Bulletin (Sydney)
BCLQ	British Columbia Library Quarterly (Vancouver)
BCM	British Columbia Monthly (Vancouver)
Beaver	(Winnipeg)

Bengali Literature (Calcutta)

Bhavan's Journal (Bombay)

BIASLIC	Bulletin of the Indian Association of Special Libraries and Information Centres (Calcutta)

Bim (Barbados)

Bird Lore (later Audubon Magazine, New York)

BITC	Bulletin of the Institute of Traditional Cultures (Madras)
BJA	British Journal of Aesthetics (London)
BlackW	Black World (formerly Negro Digest, Chicago)
BLM	Bonniers Litterära Magasin (Stockholm)

Bluestocking (Cape Town)

BNYPL	Bulletin of the New York Public Library
BO	Black Orpheus (Ibadan)

Bookfellow (Sydney)

Bookman (later American Review, New York)

Bookman (later London Mercury, London)

Book News (Philadelphia)

Books (London)

Books and Bookmen (London)

Bookseller (London)

BORIA   Bhandarkar Oriental Research Institute Annals (Poona)

Boston Transcript

BP   Banasthali Patrika (Rajasthan)

Brandwag (Johannesburg)

Bridge (Sydney)

BritAL   British Annual of Literature (London)

BRMIC   Bulletin of the Ramakrishna Mission Institute of Culture
                   (Calcutta)

Broadside (Sydney)

BSCP   Bibliographical Society of Canada Papers (Toronto)

Bulletin (Sydney)

Bulletin (later South African Bookman, Pretoria)

Busara (Nairobi)

BUSE   Boston University Studies in English

CA   Cuadernos Americanos (Mexico)

Cahiers du Sud (Marseille)

Caliban (Toulouse)

CalR   Calcutta Review

CanA   Canadian Author (later Canadian Author & Bookman, Toronto)

CanAB   Canadian Author & Bookman (Toronto)

Canada Month (Montreal)

CanB   Canadian Bookman (later Canadian Author & Bookman, Toronto)

Canberra Times

CanC   Canadian Commentator (later Commentator, Toronto)

CanF   Canadian Forum (Toronto)

CanFN   Canadian Field Naturalist (Ottawa)

CanGJ   Canadian Geographical Journal (Ottawa)

CanHR   Canadian Historical Review (Toronto)

CanJEPS   Canadian Journal of Economics and Political Science (Toronto)

CanL   Canadian Literature (Vancouver)

CanLAB   Canadian Library Association Bulletin (later Canadian Library
                Journal, Ottawa)

CanLJ   Canadian Library Journal (Ottawa)

CanM   Canadian Magazine (Montreal)

CanMenn   Canadian Mennonite (Altona, Manitoba)

CanMerc   Canadian Mercury (Toronto)

CapeIM   Cape Illustrated Magazine (later South African Illustrated
                Magazine, Cape Town)

CapeMM   Cape Monthly Magazine (later Cape Quarterly Review, Cape Town)

CAR   Central Asian Review (London)

CarQ   Caribbean Quarterly (Mona, Jamaica)

CarSt   Caribbean Studies (Rio Piedras, Puerto Rico)

CarV   Caribbean Voices (radio transcripts on file at the University
                of the West Indies, Mona, Jamaica)

Cataract (Montreal)

CathW   Catholic World (New York)

CE   College English (Champaign, Ill.)

CentM   Centennial Magazine (Sydney)

CentR   Centennial Review (East Lansing, Mich.)

Century (New York)

CenturyM   Century Magazine (New Delhi)

Ceylon Observer Ceylon Observer Pictorial Annual (Colombo)

Chamber's Journal (Edinburgh & London)

Chap-Book (later Dial, Chicago)

ChinL   Chinese Literature (Peking)

CIL   Contemporary Indian Literature (New Delhi)

CitWR   Citizen and Weekend Review (formerly Weekend Review, New Delhi)

Civilitá Cattolica (Rome)

CLAJ   College Language Association Journal (Baltimore)

Classic (Johannesburg)

CLS   Comparative Literature Studies (College Park, Md.)

CMis   Carleton Miscellany (Northfield, Minn.)

CMLR   Canadian Modern Language Review (Toronto)

CO   Current Opinion (New York)

Comentário (Rio de Janeiro)

Comment (Wellington)

Commentary (New York)

Commentator (Toronto)

Commonweal (New York)

Commonwealth Journal (London)

Communist Review (London)

Community (Colombo)

CompD   Comparative Drama (Kalamazoo, Mich.)

Conch (Paris)

Congo-Afrique (Kinshasa)

ConL   Contemporary Literature (Madison, Wis.)

Conspectus (New Delhi)

Contact (Toronto)

Contemporary (Lahore)

ContR   Contemporary Review (London)

Contrast (Cape Town)

ContV   Contemporary Verse (Victoria, B.C.)

Convivium (Bologna)

Cornhill (London)

Correspondant (Paris)

Cosmic Society (New Delhi)

Country Guide   Country Guide and Northwest Farmer (Winnipeg)

CP   Concerning Poetry (Bellingham, Wash.)

CPM   Canadian Poetry Magazine (Toronto)

CR   Critical Review (Melbourne & Sydney)

CraneR   Crane Review (Medford, Mass.)

Critic (Cape Town)

Critic (London)

Critic (Perth)

Criticism (Detroit)

Critique (Minneapolis)

Critique (Paris)

CritQ   Critical Quarterly (Hull, Eng.)

CRL   College and Research Libraries (Menasha, Wis.)

CUF   Columbia University Forum (Washington)

CulEA   Cultural Events in Africa (London)

Cultural Forum (New Delhi)

Culture (Quebec)

CurAB   Current Affairs Bulletin (Sydney)

Current Opinion (New York)

Daily Worker (London)

Darshana International (Banaras Hindu University, Varansi)

Delta (Cambridge)

Delta (Montreal)

Delta (Palmerston North, N.Z.)

Devoir   Le Devoir (Montreal)

DHLR   D.H. Lawrence Review (Fayetteville, Ark.)

Dial (Chicago)

Dickensian (London)

DilR   Diliman Review (Quezon City, Philippines)

Diogenes (Hobart)

Diogenes (Montreal)

Diogenes (New York)

Discourse (Moorhead, Minn.)

Dispute (Wellington)

Dissent (Melbourne)

DomI   Dominion Illustrated Monthly (Montreal)

Douglas Library Notes (supp. to Queen's Review, Kingston, Ont.)

DR   Dalhousie Review (Halifax, N.S.)

Drama   Drama: Quarterly Theatre Review (London)

Drum (London)

Drylight (Sydney)

Dubliner (Dublin)

DUJ   Durham University Journal

EA   Etudes Anglaises (Paris)

EAJ   East Africa Journal (Nairobi)

E&S   Essays and Studies by Members of the English Association (London)

Economic Times (Bombay)

Ecrits du Canada Français (Montreal)

Edinburgh Review

EdR   Educational Record (Quebec)

Education (Sydney)

Education (Wellington)

Educational Miscellany (Agartala, Tripura)

Education Gazette (Sydney)

EF   Etudes Françaises (Montreal)

EFT   English Fiction in Transition (later ELT, Lafayette, Ind.)

EH   Eastern Horizon (Hong Kong)

EIC   Essays in Criticism (Oxford)

EigoS   Eigo Seinen [The Rising Generation] (Tokyo)

Éire (St. Paul, Minn.)

EJ   English Journal (Champaign, Ill.)

ELit   Etudes Littéraires (Quebec)

Ellipse (Sherbrooke, P.Q.)

ELT   English Literature in Transition (1880-1920 (Lafayette, Ind.)

Encounter (London)

EngA   English in Australia (Melbourne)

English (London)

EngQ   English Quarterly (Waterloo, Ont.)

EngR   English Review (later National Review, London)

Enlite (Baroda)

ERM   Empire Review and Magazine (London)

ES   English Studies (Amsterdam)

ESA   English Studies in Africa (Johannesburg)

Esprit   L'Esprit (Paris)

Ethics (Chicago)

ETJ   Educational Theatre Journal (Washington)

Etruscan (Sydney)

Etudes   Etudes: Revue Catholique d'intérêt générale (Paris)

Européen   L'Européen (Paris)

Evidence (Toronto)

EWR   East-West Review (Doshisha University, Kyoto)

Expl   Explicator (Columbia, S.C.)

Expression (Brisbane)

FAZ   Frankfurter Allgemeine Zeitung

FdL   Forum der Litteren (Leiden, Netherlands)

Fellowship (Nyack, N.Y.)

Femina   Femina and Woman's Life (Bloemfontein)

FfT   Food for Thought (Toronto)

FGB   France Grande Bretagne (Paris)

Fiddlehead (Fredericton, N.B.)

Figaro   Le Figaro (Paris)

First Statement (Montreal)

FL   Figaro Littéraire (Paris)

Folio (London)

Folklore (Calcutta)

FortR   Fortnightly Review (later Contemporary Review, London)

Forum (Johannesburg)

Forum (New York)

FPt   Far Point (Winnipeg)

France-Amérique (Paris)

France-Asia (Saigon)

Fredomways (Boston)

Freeman (New York)

Frontiers (Christchurch, N.Z.)

Fulbright News Letter (New Delhi)

Galmahra (Brisbane)

Gazette   Le Gazette Littéraire (Lausanne)

GdC   Gants du Ciel (Montreal)

Geste (Leeds)

Ghana Teachers Journal (Saltpond, Ghana)

Graphic (London)

Great Auk (Gruyere, Victoria)

GrR   La Grande Revue (Paris)

Guardian (Manchester)

HAB   Humanities Association Bulletin (Canada)

Harper's   Harper's Magazine (New York)

Hasifrut (Tel Aviv)

HBg   Home and Building (Auckland)

Helikon (Budapest)

Helikon (Johannesburg)

Hemisphere (Canberra)

HER   Harvard Educational Review (Cambridge, Mass.)

Here and Now (Auckland)

Here and Now (Toronto)

HibJ   Hibbert Journal (London)

Hindustan Times (New Delhi)

Hochland (Munich)

Holiday   Holiday Magazine (Philadelphia)

HSANZ   Historical Studies: Australia and New Zealand (Melbourne)

HudR   Hudson Review (New York)

Huis   Huisgenoot (Kaapstad, South Africa)

Humanist Review (later Quest, Bombay)

IAC   Indo-Asian Culture (New Delhi)

IAL   Indian Art and Letters (London)

Ibadan

IEY   Iowa English Yearbook (Iowa City)

IFR   Indian and Foreign Review (Delhi)

ILit   Iaşul Literar (Jassy, Romania)

Independent Woman (Washington)

Index (Toronto)

Indian Express (New Delhi)

Indian P.E.N. (Bombay)

Indian Railways (New Delhi)

IndL   Indian Literature (New Delhi)

Indo Asia (Tübingen)

Insight (Lagos)

InstAM   Institut für Ausland Mitt (Stuttgart)

IntFR   International Forum Review (Vancouver)

IntLA   International Literary Annual (London)

ISE   Ibadan Studies in English

Islands Review (Townsville, Queensland)

IWI	Illustrated Weekly of India (Times of India, Bombay)
IWT	Indian Writing Today (Bombay)
JAAC	Journal of Aesthetics and Art Criticism (New York)
JAf	Jewish Affairs (Johannesburg)
JapQ	Japan Quarterly (Tokyo)
JASt	Journal of Asian Studies (Ann Arbor, Mich.)
JCanS	Journal of Canadian Studies (Peterborough, Ont.)
JCH	Journal of Contemporary History (London)
JCL	Journal of Commonwealth Literature (Leeds)
JdD	Journal of des Débats (Paris)
JDLUC	Journal of the Department of Letters, University of Calcutta
JdP	Journal des Poètes (Brussels)
Jewish Frontier (New York)	
JIBSA	Journal of the Institute of Bankers of South Africa (Cape Town)
JJ	Jamaica Journal (Kingston)
JJCL	Jadavpur Journal of Comparative Literature (Calcutta)
JKU	Journal of the Karnatak University (Humanities)
JKUR	Jammu and Kashmir University Review
JMAS	Journal of Modern African Studies (London)
JMSUB	Journal of the Maharaja Sayajirao University of Baroda
JMU	Journal of the Mysore University
JNAA	Journal of the National Academy of Administration (Mussoorie)
JNALA	Journal of the New African Literature and the Arts (Stanford)
JNESA	Journal of the Nigerian English Studies Association
JOIB	Journal of the Oriental Institute (Baroda)
JOLW	John O'London's Weekly
JPS	Journal of the Polynesian Society (Auckland)
JPU	Journal of the Patna University
JRAHS	Journal of the Royal Australian Historical Society (Sydney)
JRQHS	Journal of the Royal Queensland Historical Society (Brisbane)

JRSA   Journal of the Royal Society of Arts (London)

JSSB   Journal of the Siam Society (Bangkok)

JUJK   Journal of the University of Jammu and Kashmir

JUP   Journal of the University of Poona

Kaie (Georgetown, Guyana)

Kivung   Kivung: Journal of the Linguistic Society of the University of
                Papua and New Guinea (Port Moresby)

Kiwi (Auckland)

Klasgids (Pretoria)

KR   Kenyon Review (Gambier, Ohio)

Kriterium (Cape Town)

KURJ   Kurukshetra University Research Journal

KUY   Kerala University Youth (Trivandrum)

Kyk-over-al (Georgetown, Guyana)

Landfall (Christchurch, N.Z.)

L&I   Literature and Ideology (Montreal)

L&L   Life and Letters (London)

L&P   Literature and Psychology (West Hartford, Conn.)

Language and Learning [Harvard Educational Review]

LanM   Les Langues Modernes (Paris)

Lantern (Pretoria)

LaTrobeLJ   La Trobe Library Journal (Melbourne)

LCrit   Literary Criterion (Mysore)

LE&W   Literature East and West (New Paltz, N.Y.)

Lectures (Montreal)

LetN   Les Lettres Nouvelles (Paris)

LHY   Literary Half-Yearly (Mysore)

LibAR   Library Association Record (London)

Liberté (Montreal)

Liberty (Toronto)

LibW   Library World (London)

Life and Letters Today (later London Mercury and Bookman)

Limi (Pretoria)

Lines Review (Edinburgh)

Link (Castries, St. Lucia)

Link (New Delhi)

Listener (London)

LitD   Literary Digest (New York)

LitEcho   Literarischen Echo (later Literatur, Berlin)

Literary Miscellany (New York)

Literary Review (London)

Literatur (Stuttgart)

LitR   Literary Review (Teaneck, N.J.)

Living Age (New York)

LMag   London Magazine

London Evening Standard

London Mercury

Looking Back (Port Elizabeth, South Africa)

LuganoR   Lugano Review (Switzerland)

Maclean's   Maclean's Magazine (Toronto)

Mahfil (East Lansing, Mich.)

MahP   Maharashtra Parichaya (New Delhi).

Mainstream (New Delhi)

Makar (Brisbane)

MakJ   Makerere Journal (later Mawazo, Kampala)

MalR   Malahat Review (Victoria, B.C.)

ManAR   Manitoba Arts Review (Winnipeg)

Mankind (Sydney)

Manuscripts (Geelong, Victoria)

MarxQ   Marxist Quarterly (Toronto)

Masque (Sydney)

Massey's (Toronto)

Mate (Auckland)

Mawazo (Kampala)

McMaster University Monthly (Hamilton, Ont.)

MCR   Melbourne Critical Review (later CR)

MD   Modern Drama (Lawrence, Kan.)

Meanjin (Melbourne)

MelbR   Melbourne Review

MFS   Modern Fiction Studies (Lafayette, Ind.)

Midstream (New York)

Mirror (Bombay)

Miscellany (Calcutta)

MLN   Modern Language Notes (Baltimore)

MLQ   Modern Language Quarterly (Seattle)

MLR   Modern Language Review (Cambridge, Eng.)

Moderna Språk (Stockholm)

ModR   Modern Review (Calcutta)

Month (London)

Mosaic (Winnipeg)

Mother India (Pondicherry)

MP   Modern Philology (Chicago)

MQR   Michigan Quarterly Review (East Lansing)

MR   Massachusetts Review (Amherst)

MUM   Melbourne University Magazine

Mysterious East (Fredericton, N.B.)

Nada   Nada: Rhodesia Ministry of Internal Affairs Annual (Salisbury)

N&Q   Notes and Queries (London)

NAR   North American Review (Mount Vernon, Iowa)

Narrative (later Biologia Culturale, Rome)

NatEd   National Education (Wellington)

NatER   National and English Review (London)

Nation (New York)

Nation (Sydney)

Nation and Athenaeum (later New Statesman and Nation, London)

NatM   National Monthly (Toronto)

NatR   National Review (New York)

Nature   Nature Magazine (Washington)

Nederlandse Post (Pretoria)

NegroD   Negro Digest (Chicago)

NEHGR   New England Historical and Genealogical Register (Boston)

NEM   New England Magazine (Boston)

NEQ   New England Quarterly (Baltimore)

NewA   New African (London)

New Age (New Delhi)

New Campus Review (Denver, Colo.)

New Criterion (later, Criterion, London)

New Frontier (Toronto)

New Leader (New York)

New Nation (Pretoria)

New Republic (Marion, Ohio)

New Society (London)

New Statesman [and Athenaeum] (London)

New Statesman and Nation (London)

Nexus (Nairobi)

Nieuwe Stem (Armheim, South Africa)

NigM   Nigeria Magazine (Lagos)

Nigrizia (Verona)

Nimrod (Newcastle, N.S.W.)

Nine (London)

NL   Nouvelles Littéraires (Paris)

NLR   New Left Review (London)

NMon   Neuphilologische Monatsschrift (Leipzig)

NOB   New Orient Bimonthly (Prague)

North (Townsville North, Queensland)

Northern Folk (Cairns, Queensland)

Northland Magazine (Whangarei, N.Z.)

Northwest Review (Eugene, Ore.)

Nova (London)

Novel (Providence, R.I.)

Now (Calcutta)

NR   Northern Review (Toronto)

NRF   Nouvelle Revue Française (Paris)

NRJ   Northern Rhodesian Journal (later Zambia Journal, Livingstone)

NS   Die Neueren Sprachen (Frankfurt-am-Main)

NTM   New Theatre Magazine (Bristol)

Numbers (Wellington)

Nuova Presenza (Rome)

NWF   New World Fortnightly (Georgetown, Guyana)

NWQ   New World Quarterly (Mona, Jamaica)

NY   New Yorker

NYRB   New York Review of Books

NYTBR   New York Times Book Review

NYTM   New York Times Magazine

NZEA   New Zealand Exporter Annual (Auckland)

NZG   New Zealand Geographer (Christchurch)

NZL   New Zealand Listener (Wellington)

NZLi   New Zealand Libraries (Wellington)

NZM   New Zealand Magazine (Wellington)

NZMR   New Zealand Monthly Review (Christchurch)

NZNW   New Zealand New Writing (Wellington)

NZPC   New Zealand Parent and Child (Wellington)

NZPY   New Zealand Poetry Yearbook (Wellington)

NZRM   New Zealand Railways Magazine (Wellington)

Observer (London)

Odu (Ibadan)

OJES   Osmania Journal of English Studies (Hyderabad)

Okyeame (Legon)

OL   Orbis Litterarum (Copenhagen)

Ons Eie Boek (Cape Town)

Ontario History (Toronto)

OntHSP   Ontario Historical Society Papers (Toronto)

OntLR   Ontario Library Review (Toronto)

Opinion (Burnside, S.A.)

Opinion (Paris)

Optima (Johannesburg)

Orbis (Louvain)

OrientR   Orient Review [and Literary Digest] (Calcutta)

Ouderni   Ouderni dell'instituto de Glottologia (Bologna)

Outlook (London)

Outspan (Bloemfontein)

Overland (Melbourne)

Oxford Review

PA   Présence Africaine (Paris)

Pacific Spectator (Stanford)

PakQ   Pakistan Quarterly (Karachi)

PakR   Pakistan Review (Lahore)

Paris Review (Paris)

Pegaso (Florence)

Performing Arts (Toronto)

Personalist (Los Angeles)

Personality (formerly Outspan, Johannesburg)

Perspective (Karachi)

Phoenix (Seoul)

PHum   Przeglad Humanistyczny (Warsaw)

Phylon (Atlanta)

Poet Lore (Boston)

Poetry (Chicago)

Poetry Australia (Fivedock, N.S.W.)

Poetry Magazine (Sydney)

PoetryR   Poetry Review (London)

Pol (Sydney)

Political Science Review (Jaipur)

PolP   Polish Perspectives (Warsaw)

PPSB   Post Primary School Bulletin (Wellington)

PQ   Philological Quarterly (Iowa City)

PR   Partisan Review (New Brunswick, N.J.)

Prabuddha Bharata (Calcutta)

Prajna (Varanasi)

PRen   Purple Renoster (Johannesburg)

Presenza (Rome)

Preuves (Paris)

Progressive Worker (Vancouver)

Prospect (Melbourne)

PrS   Prairie Schooner (Lincoln, Neb.)

PrzO   Przeglad Orientalistyczny (Warsaw)

PrzS   Przeglad Socjologiczny (Lodz)

PTRSC   Proceedings and Transactions of the Royal Society of Canada
                 (Ottawa)

Public Affairs (Bangalore)

Public Servant (Pretoria)

Publisher's Monthly (Taipei)

QBSAL   Quarterly Bulletin of the South African Library (Cape Town)

QQ   Queen's Quarterly (Kingston, Ont.)

QTJ   Queensland Teachers Journal (Brisbane)

Quadrant (Sydney)

Quarry (Kingston, Ont.)

Quarterly Review (London)

Queen's Review (Kingston, Ont.)

Quest (Bombay)

Quill and Quire (Toronto)

RAA   Revue Anglo-Americaine (later Etudes Anglaises, Paris)

Race (London)

Radical Humanist (Calcutta)

RAL   Research in African Literatures (Austin)

Rassegna Italiana (Rome)

RCSLN   Royal Commonwealth Society Library Notes (London)

RDM   Revue des Deux Mondes (Paris)

Realist (Sydney)

Realist Writer (later Realist, Melbourne)

Reality (Pietermaritzburg)

Recherches Sociographiques (Quebec)

REL   Review of English Literature (Leeds)

Rélations (Montreal)

Renascence (Milwaukee)

Reporter (Dayton, Ohio)

ResRev   Research Review (Legon, Ghana)

RevB   Revue Blanche (Paris)

RevBl   Revue Bleue (Paris)

RevH   Revue Hebdomadaire (Paris)

RevL   Revue de l'université Laval (Quebec)

RevN   La Revue Nouvelle (Paris)

Revolution (Carlton, Victoria)

RevP   Revue de Paris

RevT   Revue Théâtrale (Paris)

RevUM   Revista de la Universidad de México (Mexico City)

RGB   Revue Générale Belge (Brussels)

RIB   Revista Interamericana di Bibliografia (Washington)

RIE   Revista de Ideas Estéticas (Madrid).

RLC   Revue de Littérature Comparée (Paris)

RLMC   Rivista di Letterature Moderne e Comparate (Florence)

RLV   Revue des Langues Vivantes (Brussels)

RLz   Radyans'ske Literaturosnavstvo (Kiev)

Rooi Rose (Johannesburg)

Rythmes du Monde (Paris)

SafB   South African Bookman (Pretoria)

SafM   South African Magazine (Cape Town)

SafP   South African Publisher (Johannesburg)

SafQ   South African Quarterly (Johannesburg)

SafRHM   South African Railways & Harbours Magazine (Johannesburg)

SAIA   South Africa: Information and Analysis (Paris)

SAJS   South African Journal of Science (Cape Town)

SALi   South African Libraries (Johannesburg)

Sameeksha (Madras)

SAMNB   Sahitya Akademi Monthly News Bulletin (New Delhi)

SAP   Studia Anglica Posnaniensia (Poznán)

SAPEN   South African P.E.N. Yearbook (Johannesburg)

SAQ   South Atlantic Quarterly (Durham, N.C.)

Sarie Marais (Cape Town)

Sassar (formerly South African Railways Magazine, Johannesburg)

SatN   Saturday Night (Toronto)

SatR   Saturday Review (New York)

SatRL   Saturday Review of Literature (later SatR, New York)

Savacou (Mona, Jamaica)

SBL   Studies in Black Literature (Fredericksburg, Va.)

Scholastic (Pittsburgh)

SchP   Scholarly Publishing (Toronto)

Science and Culture (Calcutta)

Scintilla (Karachi)

Scotland's Magazine (Edinburgh)

SELit   Studies in English Literature (Tokyo)

Seminar (New Delhi)

Shenandoah (Lexington, Va.)

Sikh Review (Calcutta)

SIR   Studies in Romanticism (Boston)

SJ   Silliman Journal (Dumaquete City, Philippines)

Solidarity (Manila)

SoR   Southern Review (Baton Rouge)

SoRA   Southern Review (Adelaide)

Soundings (New Haven, Conn.)

South Australiana (Adelaide)

Southerly (Sydney)

SovL   Soviet Literature (Moscow)

Spear   Spear Magazine (Lagos)

Spectator (London)

Spotlight (Cape Town)

SR   Sewanee Review (Sewanee, Tenn.)

Sri Aurobindo Circle (Bombay)

Srinvantu (Calcutta)

SSF   Studies in Short Fiction (Newberry, S.C.)

Stand (Newcastle-upon-Tyne)

Standpunte (Cape Town)

Statesman (Delhi)

Stem   De Stem (Arnhem, Netherlands)

StN   Studies in the Novel (Denton, Tex.)

Story (New York)

Stride (Leeds)

Studiekamraten (Lund)

Studies (Dublin)

Suid-Afrika (Johannesburg)

Sunday Mail (Kuala Lumpur)

Sussex County Magazine (Eastbourne)

Swarajya (Madras)

SWR   Southwest Review (Dallas)

Sydney Morning Herald

Synthèses (Brussels)

Taalgenoot (Johannesburg)

TableR   La Table Ronde (Paris)

TamR   Tamarack Review (Toronto)

TasE   Tasmanian [Journal of] Education (Hobart)

TC   Twentieth Century (London)

TC (Melbourne) Twentieth Century (Melbourne)

TCL   Twentieth Century Literature (Los Angeles)

Teangadóir (Toronto)

TeaterSA (Cape Town)   Teater Suid Afrika: Quarterly for South African Theater

Tempo (Rome)

Temps   Le Temps (Paris)

TEng   Teaching of English (Sydney)

Tenggara (Kuala Lumpur)

TES   Times Educational Supplement (London)

Theoria (Pietermaritzburg)

THM   Tien Hsia Monthly (Shanghai)

Thought (Delhi)

Thought (New York)

THRA   Tasmanian Historical Research Association, Papers and
                      Proceedings (Hobart)

Threshold (Belfast)

Thyrse   Le Thyrse (Brussels)

Time and Tide (London)

Times   London Times

Times of India (Bombay)

Tirade (Amsterdam)

TLR   Turnbull Library Record (Wellington)

TLS   Times Literary Supplement (London)

TN   Theatre Notebook (London)

TQ   Texas Quarterly (Austin)

Transition (Kampala)

Trek (Johannesburg)

Tribune (Sydney)

TriQ   Tri-Quarterly (Evanston, Ill.)

Triveni (Masulipatam)

TSE   Tulane Studies in English (New Orleans)

TSLL   Texas Studies in Literature and Language (Austin)

TTDJ   Triumala Tirupati Devasthanams Journal (Tirupati)

TUELA   Transactions of the United Empire Loyalists' Association
                (Brampton, Ont.)

Tumasek (Singapore)

T.Wetenskap Kuns   Tydskrif vir Wetenskap en Kuns (Pretoria)

Twórczość (Warsaw)

UA   United Asia (Bombay)

UAHSA   University of Auckland Historical Society Annual

UBCAC   University of British Columbia Alumni Chronicle (Vancouver)

UCQ   University College Quarterly (East Lansing, Mich.)

UCWCA   University College of the Western Cape, Annals (Bellville,
                South Africa)

UDQ   University of Denver Quarterly

UES   Unisa English Studies (Pretoria)

UKCR   University of Kansas City Review (later UR)

Unilit (Secunderabad)

UNISA (Pretoria)

Unitas (Manila)

United College Journal (Hong Kong)

Unity (Chicago)

Universitas (Stuttgart)

UnivM   University Magazine (Montreal)

UnivS   University Studies (Karachi)

UR   University Review (Kansas City, Mo.)

URSE   University of Rajasthan Studies in English

USH   University Studies in History (Perth)

UTQ   University of Toronto Quarterly

UWIRST   University of the West Indies Radio Service Transcripts (on
               file at the University, Mona, Jamaica)

UWR   University of Windsor Review (Windsor, Ont.)

Valósag (Budapest)

Vancouver Life

Veldtrust (Bloemfontein)

Venture (Karachi)

Verve (Adelaide)

Vestes (Sydney)

VHM   Victorian Historical Magazine (Melbourne)

Vinduet (Oslo)

Vision (Karachi)

Visvabharati News (Santiniketan, Birbhum, West Bengal)

VLit   Voprosy Literarury (Moscow)

VLU   Vestnik Leningradskogo U. Ser. Istorii, Jasyka i Literatury

Voice of St. Lucia (Castries)

Voices (Port-of-Spain, Trinidad)

Voorslag (Durban)

VQ   Visvabharati Quarterly (Santiniketan, Birbhum, West Bengal)

VQR   Virginia Quarterly Review (Charlottesville, Va.)

WA   West Africa (London)

WAL   Western American Literature (Fort Collins, Colo.)

Walkabout (Melbourne)

WAR   West African Review (Liverpool, later Spear, Lagos)

WasR   Wascana Review (Regina)

WATJ   Western Australia Teachers' Journal (Perth)

WCR   West Coast Review (Burnaby, B.C.)

WCSMLL   Western Canadian Studies in Modern Languages and Literature
                (Regina)

Week (Toronto)

Week News (Auckland)

WeekR   Weekend Review (later Citizen, New Delhi)

Westerly (Perth)

WestH   Westminster Hall (Vancouver)

WHR   Western Humanities Review (Salt Lake City)

Will   Willison's Monthly (later CanF, Toronto)

WLB   Wilson Library Bulletin (New York)

WLWE Newsletter   World Literature Written in English (later WLWE, Arlington,
                Tex.)

Women on the March (New Delhi)

World Wide (Montreal)

WR   Western Review (Iowa City)

WrW   Writer's Workshop (Calcutta)

WSCL   Wisconsin Studies in Contemporary Literature (Madison)

Wurm (Johannesburg)

WuW   Welt und Wort (Bad Woerishofen)

WWG   Weekly Westminster Gazette (later Weekly Westminster, London)

WWR   Walt Whitman Review (Detroit)

WZUG   Wissenschaftliche Zeitschrift der Ernst Moritz Arndt-Universität
                (Griefswald)

WZUL   Wissenschaftliche Zeitschrift der Karl-Marx-Universität (Leipzig)

WZUR   Wissenschaftliche Zeitschrift der Universität Rostock

XUS   Xavier University Studies (New Orleans)

YCGL   Yearbook of Comparative and General Literature (Chapel Hill, N.C.)

Yes (Montreal)

YR   Yale Review (New Haven, Conn.)

Zaire (Brussels)

Zeit   Die Zeit (Hamburg)

ZFEU   Zeitschrift für französische und englische Unterricht (Berlin)

Zuka (Nairobi)

Commonwealth General

Research Aids

1 Annual Serial Bibliographies
   Commonwealth and South Africa: Journal of Commonwealth Literature
   [See also MLA International Bibliography.]
   Africa: African Literature Today
   Australia: Australian Literary Studies
   Canada: Canadian Literature; Journal of Canadian Fiction (after 1972)

2 Flint, John E. Books on the British Empire and Commonwealth: A Guide
   for Students. London: Oxford Univ. Press, 1968. [Books on history.]

3 Goode, Stephen H. Index to Commonwealth Little Magazines, 1964-1965.
   New York: Johnson Repr. Corp., 1966. Vol. 2, 1966-1967. New York:
   Johnson Repr. Corp., 1968. Vol. 3, 1968-1969. Troy, N.Y.: Whitston,
   1970.

4 Hamner, Robert D. "Literary Periodicals in World-English." WLWE
   Newsletter, 14, supp. (1968), 22 pp.

5 Jones, Joseph. Terranglia: The Case for English as World Literature.
   New York: Twayne, 1965.

General

6 Adcock, A. St. John. "Literature of Greater Britain." Bookman (London),
   42 (1912), 233-53.

7 Baudet, Henri. Paradise on Earth: Some Thoughts on European Images of
   Non-European Man. Trans. Elizabeth Wentholt. New Haven and London:
   Yale Univ. Press, 1965.

8 Bolt, Christine. Victorian Attitudes to Race. London: Routledge &
   Kegan Paul, 1971.   .

9 Bowra, C. M. Primitive Song. London: Weidenfeld & Nicolson, 1962.

10 Brent, P. L. "Introduction" to Young Commonwealth Poets '65. London:
   Heinemann, 1965, 13-14.

11 Burgess, Anthony. The Novel Today. London: Longmans, Green, 1963.

12 Churchill, R. C. "[Commonwealth Literature]." In George Sampson, The
   Concise History of English Literature. 3rd ed. Cambridge: Cambridge
   Univ. Press, 1970, 734-65.

13 The Commonwealth in Books. London: National Book League, 1964.

14 Day, Paul W. "Commonwealth Poems of Today." FPt, 3 (1969), 69-74.

15 "English as Highway or as Barrier." TLS, 16 Sept. 1965, p. 796.

16 Gil'dena, Z.M., et al., eds. Problemy Lingvistiki i zarubežnoj literatury. Riga: Zinatne, 1968.

17 Goodwin, Kenneth, ed. National Identity. London: Heinemann, 1970.

18 Greene, Margaret Lawrence. The School of Femininity. Toronto: Nelson, 1936; repr. Toronto: Musson, 1972. [Also appeared as We Write as Women. London: Joseph, 1937.]

19 Gunasinghe, Siri. "Commonwealth Poetry Conference, Cardiff: A Commentary." JCL, 2 (1966), 148-51.

20 Helps, E. A. "Preface" to Songs and Ballads of Greater Britain. London and Toronto: Dent; New York: Dutton, 1913, v-xii.

21 "An Interest and Its Future." TLS, 16 Sept. 1965, p. 808.

22 Iyengar, K. R. Srinivasa. Two Cheers for the Commonwealth. London: Asia, 1970.

23 Jeffares, A. Norman. "The Author in the Commonwealth." NigM, 95 (1967), 351-55.

24 ____ "Role of the Author in the Commonwealth." Commonwealth Journal, 9 (1966), 205-10.

25 ____ "The Study of Commonwealth Writing." WLWE Newsletter, 15, supp. (1969), 1-15.

26 Jones, Joseph. "British Commonwealth Literature." In Education and Our Expanding Relations. Durban: Univ. of Natal Press, 1962, 401-11.

27 ____ "Commonwealth Literature: Developments and Prospects." In Robin W. Winks, ed., The Historiography of the British Empire--Commonwealth. Durham, N.C.: Duke Univ. Press, 1966, 493-522.

28 McLeod, A. L., ed. The Commonwealth Pen: An Introduction to the Literature of the British Commonwealth. Ithaca: Cornell Univ. Press, 1961.

29 Naipaul, V. S. "Images." New Statesman, 70 (1965), 452-53.

30 New, William H. "The Commonwealth in Print." CanL, 30 (1966), 53-58. [Repr. in WLWE Newsletter, 12, supp. (1967), 53-58.]

31 ____ "Introduction" to Four Hemispheres. Toronto: Copp Clark, 1971, v-ix.

32 ____ "The Island and the Madman: Recurrent Imagery in the Major Novelists of the Fifties." ArQ, 22 (1966), 328-37.

33 Oaten, Edward Farley, et al. Chapters 10-13 of The Cambridge History of English Literature, Vol. 14. Cambridge: Cambridge Univ. Press, 1916.

34 O'Donnell, Margaret J. "Introduction" to An Anthology of Commonwealth Verse. London: Blackie, 1963, xvii-xxi.

35 Povey, John F. "Poor Waifs Upon Creation's Skirts." DR, 47 (1967), 213-21.

36 Press, John, ed. Commonwealth Literature: Unity and Diversity in a Common Culture. London: Heinemann Educational, 1965.

37 Rajan, B. "Looking for Poetic Character." JCL, 2 (1966), 155-57.

38 Ratcliffe, Michael. The Novel Today. London: Longmans, Green, 1968.

39 Rutherford, Anna, Donald Hannah, and Hena Maes-Jelinek. Introductory notes to Commonwealth Short Stories. London: Edward Arnold, 1971, passim.

40   Sandison, A. "The Imperial Idea and English Fiction: Its Form and
     Function." In The Theory of Imperialism and the European Partition
     of Africa. Edinburgh: Centre for African Studies, 1967, 1-26.

41   _____   The Wheel of Empire: A Study of the Imperial idea in Some Late
     Nineteenth and Early Twentieth-Century Fiction. London: Macmillan,
     1967.

42   Sergeant, Howard. "Introduction" to Commonwealth Poems of Today. London:
     John Murray, 1967, 13-25.

43   _____   "Introduction" to New Voices of the Commonwealth. London: Evans,
     1968, 11-17.

44   _____   "Poetry of the Commonwealth." English, 15 (1965), 208-11.

45   Simpson, D. H. "English Language and the Arts in the Commonwealth."
     Commonwealth Journal, 10 (1967), 207-08.

46   _____   "Pens of Empire." RCSLN, 128 (1967), 1-4.

47   Smithyman, Kendrick. "The Common Experience, the Common Response." JCL,
     6, no. 1 (1971), 6-18.

48   "Sounding the Sixties--2. The Commonwealth." TLS, 16 Sept. 1965,
     pp. 786-813.

49   Stevenson, Lionel. "Literature in Emerging Nations." SAQ, 64 (1965),
     394-400.

50   Turner, Arlin. "Scholars Discover the Commonwealth Literatures." ALS, 1
     (1964), 203-05.

51   Walsh, William. "Commonwealth Writing in English." TLS, 27 Nov. 1970,
     p. 1379.

52   _____   A Manifold Voice: Studies in Commonwealth Literature. London:
     Chatto & Windus, 1970.

53   Watters, Reginald Eyre. "Original Relations, a Genographic Approach to
     the Literatures of Canada and Australia." CanL, 7 (1961), 6-17.

54   _____   "A Quest for National Identity." In Proceedings of the 3rd Congress
     of the International Comparative Literature Association. The Hague:
     Mouton, 1962, 224-41.

See also: 840, 2648, 4307, 4324, 5818, 6064-6072.

Africa (East and West)

Research Aids

55 Abrash, Barbara. Black African Literature in English since 1952: Works and Criticism. Introd. by John F. Povey. New York: Johnson Repr. Corp., 1967.

56 Amosu, Margaret. Creative African Writing in the European Languages: A Preliminary Bibliography. Ibadan: Inst. of African Studies, 1964.

57 Jahn, Janheinz. A Bibliography of Neo-African Literature from Africa, America and the Caribbean. London: Andre Deutsch, 1965.

58 Lang, D. M., ed. "African." In The Penguin Companion to Literature. Vol. IV. Harmondsworth: Penguin, 1969, 333-60.

59 Nitecki, A. Onitsha Publications. Syracuse, N. Y.: Syracuse Univ. Press, 1967.

60 Páricsy, Pál. A New Bibliography of African Literature. Budapest: Center for Afro-Asian Research of the Hungarian Academy of Sciences, 1969.

61 ____ "Selected International Bibliography of Negritude, 1960-1969." SBL, 1, no. 1 (1970), 103-15.

62 Porter, Dorothy. "African and Caribbean Creative Writings: A Bibliographic Survey." AForum, 1, no. 4 (1966), 107-11.

63 Zell, H. M., et al. The Literature of Africa: An Annotated Bibliographical Guide to Creative Writing by Black African Authors. New York: Africana Pub. Corp., 1969.

See also: 5793.

General

64 Abraham, W. E. The Mind of Africa. London: Weidenfeld & Nicolson, 1962.

65 Achebe, Chinua. "The African Writer and the Biafran Cause." Conch, 1, no. 1 (1969), 8-14.

66 ____ "The Black Writer's Burden." PA, 59 (1966), 135-40.

67 ____ "English and the African Writer." Transition, 18 (1965), 27-30.

68 ____ "The Novelist as Teacher." In item 36, pp. 201-05.

69 ____ "The Role of the Writer in a New Nation." NigM, 81 (1964), 157-60.

70 _____ "Where Angels Fear to Tread." NigM, 75 (1962), 61-62.

71 Aig-Imokhuede, M. "On Being a West African Writer." Ibadan, 12 (1961), 11-12.

72 Asalache, K. "After Tigritude, What?" EAJ, 5, no. 7, Ghala supp. (1968), 50-53.

73 Astrachan, Anthony M. "Creative Writing." NigM, 79 (1963), 290-94.

74 Awoonor-Williams, George. "Fresh Vistas for African Literature." AfrR, 1, no. 1 (1965), 35, 48.

75 Bahoken, J. C. "Revolution and Development of an African Cultural Consciousness." AAW, 1, nos. 2-3 (1968), 135-41.

76 Balandier, Georges. Ambiguous Africa: Cultures in Collision. Trans. by Helen Weaver. London: Chatto & Windus, 1966. [Orig. pub. 1957.]

77 Bame, K. N. "Comic Plays in Ghana." AfrA, 1, no. 4 (1968), 30-34, 101.

78 _____ "The Popular Theatre in Ghana." ResRev, 3, no. 2 (1968), 34-39.

79 Banham, Martin. "African Literature II: Nigerian Dramatists in English and the Traditional Nigerian Theatre." JCL, 3 (1967), 92-102.

80 _____ "The Beginnings of a Nigerian Literature in English." REL, 3, no. 2 (1962), 88-99.

81 _____ "Drama in the Commonwealth: Nigeria." NTM, 4 (1960), 18-21.

82 _____ "Nigerian Dramatists and the African Oral Tradition." JNALA, 5-6 (1968), 10-19.

83 _____ "Notes on Nigerian Theatre: 1966." BAALE, 4 (1966), 31-36.

84 _____ "A Piece That We May Fairly Call Our Own." Ibadan, 12 (1961), 15-18.

85 _____, and J. A. Ramsaran. "West African Writing." BA, 36 (1962), 371-74.

86 Barba, H. "Image of the African in Transition." UKCR, 29 (1963), 215-21.

87 Bastide, Roger. "Variations on Negritude." PA, 36 (1961), 83-91.

88 Beier, Ulli. "The Conflict of Cultures in West African Poetry." BO, 1 (1957), 17-21.

89 _____ "Public Opinion on Lovers." BO, 14 (1964), 4-16. [Market Literature.]

90 _____ "Some Nigerian Poets." PA, 32-33 (1960), 50-63.

91 _____, ed. Introduction to African Literature: An Anthology of Critical Writing from "Black Orpheus." London: Longmans, 1967.

92 Bilen, Max. "The African Poet as Bard of His People." PA, 54 (1965), 141-45.

93 Biobaku, S. Religion in Contemporary African Literature. Ndola, Zambia: C. C. S. Press, 1966.

94 Bischofberger, Otto. Tradition und Wandel aus der Sicht der Romanschriftsteller Kameruns und Nigerias. Einsiedeln, Switzerland: Etzel-Druck, 1968.

95 Blair, Dorothy S. "Negritude." Parts I and II. Contrast, 1, no. 2 (1961), 38-48; 1, no. 3 (1961), 38-49.

96 Bodurin, A. "What Is African Literature?" AfrSt, 1, no. 1 (1965), 33-42.

97 Böttcher, K.-H. "Zwischen zwei Kulturen." FAZ, supp., 31 May 1969.

98 Boucquey, E. "Présence du 'Cahier d'un retour au pays natal' d'Aimé Césaire dans la littérature de la négritude." Zaire, 15, no. 1 (1961), 95-106.

99   Bown, Lalage, and Michael Crowder, eds. First International Congress
     of Africanists. Evanston, Ill.: Northwestern Univ. Press, 1964.

100 Brench, A. C. The Novelists' Inheritance in French Africa. London:
     Oxford Univ. Press, 1967.

101 ____   Writing in French from Senegal to Cameroon. London: Oxford Univ.
     Press, 1967.

102 Carpenter, P. "East and West: A Brief View of Theatre in Ghana and
     Uganda since 1960." MakJ, 8 (1963), 33-39.

103 Cartey, Wilfred, ed. Whispers from a Continent: The Literature of
     Contemporary Black Africa. New York: Random House, 1969.

104 Catrice, Paul. "L'Afrique noire au miroir de ses écrivains." Rhythmes
     du Monde, 8 (1960), 101-07.

105 Chimenti, E. "Culture and Criticism: African Critical Standards for
     African Literature and the Arts." JNALA, 3 (1967), 1-7.

106 Chukwukere, B. I. "African Novelists and Social Change." Phylon, 26
     (1965), 228-39.

107 ____   "The Problem of Language in Creative Writing." ALT, 3 (1969),
     15-26.

108 Clark, John Pepper. "Another Kind of Poetry." Transition, 25 (1966),
     17-22.

109 ____   "Aspects of Nigerian Drama." NigM, 89 (1966), 118-26.

110 ____   "The Communication Line Between Poet and Public." AForum, 3, no. 1
     (1967), 42-53.

111 ____   "The Legacy of Caliban." BO, 2 (1968), 16-39.

112 ____   "A Note on Nigerian Poetry." PA, 58 (1966), 55-64.

113 ____   "Poetry in Africa Today." Transition, 18 (1965), 20-26.

114 ____   "Themes of African Poetry of English Expression." PA, 54 (1965),
     70-89.

115 Collins, Harold R. The New English of the Onitsha Chapbooks.
     Athens, Ohio: Ohio Univ. Center for Internat. Studies, 1968.

116 Cook, Mercer, and Stephen E. Henderson. The Militant Black Writer in
     Africa and the United States. Madison: Univ. of Wisconsin Press, 1969.

117 Cordeaux, Shirley. "The BBC African Service's Involvement in African
     Theatre." RAL, 1 (1970), 147-55.

118 Crowder, Michael. "Tradition and Change in Nigerian Literature." BAALE, 3
     (1965), 1-17.

119 Crowley, D. J. "Symbolism in African Verbal Art." AfrA, 1, no. 4 (1968),
     14-16, 116-17.

120 Curtin, Philip D., ed. Africa Remembered: Narratives by West Africans
     from the Era of the Slave Trade. Madison: Univ. of Wisconsin Press,
     1968.

121 Dathorne, O. R. "The African Novel--Document to Experiment." BAALE,
     3 (1965), 18-39.

122 ____, ed. African Poetry for Schools and Colleges. London: Macmillan,
     1969.

123 ____   "African Writers of the Eighteenth Century." In item 91, pp. 234-40.
     [Also in LMag, 5, no. 6 (1965), 51-58.]

124 ____   "Ibo Literature: The Novel as Allegory." AfrQ, 7 (1967), 365-68.

125 ___ "Pioneer African Drama: Heroines and the Church." BAALE, 4 (1966), 19-23.

126 ___ "Tradition and the African Poet." PA, 67 (1968), 202-06.

127 Davidson, B. "African Literature Now." WA, 27 June 1964, p. 711.

128 Dei-Anang, Michael F. Africa Speaks. Accra: Guinea Press, 1959.

129 Diakhaté, L. "Valeurs de la négritude et convergence." PA, 68 (1968), 149-52.

130 Drayton, Arthur D. "The Return of the Past in the Nigerian Novel." Ibadan, 10 (1960), 27-30.

131 Echeruo, M. J. C. "Incidental Fiction in Nigeria." AfrWr, 1, no. 1 (1962), 10-11.

132 ___ "Traditional and Borrowed Elements in Nigerian Poetry." NigM, 89 (1966), 142-55.

133 Edwards, Paul, and David Carroll. "Approach to the Novel in West Africa." Phylon, 23 (1962), 319-31.

134 Ekwensi, C. "African Literature." NigM, 83 (1964), 294-99.

135 ___ "Literary Influences on a Young Nigerian." TLS, 4 June 1964, pp. 475-76.

136 ___ "Problems of Nigerian Writers." NigM, 78 (1963), 217-19.

137 Ferguson, J. "Nigerian Drama in English." MD, 11 (1968), 10-26.

138 ___ "Nigerian Poetry in English." Insight, 13 (1966), 7-8.

139 Finnegan, Joan. Oral Literature in Africa. Oxford: Clarendon, 1970.

140 Fischer, S. L. "Africa: Mother and Muse." AR, 21 (1961), 305-17.

141 Franklin, Albert. "La négritude: réalité ou mystification--reflexions sur Orphée Noir." PA, 14 (1952), 287-303.

142 Furay, Michael. "Africa in Negro American Poetry to 1929." ALT, 2 (1969), 32-41.

143 Geering, K. "Modern Poetry in Africa." Revolution, 1 (1962), 3-4.

144 Gérard, Albert. "Nigéria: naissance d'une littérature." Congo-Afrique, 8 (1968), 66-70.

145 Gleason, Judith. "Out of the Irony of Words." Transition, 18 (1965), 34-38.

146 ___ This Africa: Novels by West Africans in English and French. Evanston, Ill.: Northwestern Univ. Press, 1965.

147 Gordimer, Nadine. The Interpreters: Theme as Communication in the African Novel. Johannesburg: Univ. of the Witwatersrand, 1969; also in KR, 32 (1970), 9-26.

148 Hammond, Dorothy, and Alta Jablow. The Africa That Never Was: Four Centuries of British Writing About Africa. New York: Twayne, 1970.

149 Hanshell, Deryck. "African Writing Today." Month, 32 (1964), 246-54.

150 Hopkinson, T. "Deaths and Entrances: The Emergence of African Writing." TC, 165 (1959), 332-39.

151 Hughes, B. "Filling the Literary Vacuum." EAJ, 5, no. 1 (1968), 5-8.

152 Irele, Abiola. "Negritude--Literature and Ideology." JMAS, 3 (1965), 499-526.

153 ___ "Negritude or Black Cultural Nationalism?" JMAS, 3 (1965), 321-48.

154   ____   "A New Mood in the African Novel." WA, 20 Sept. 1969, pp. 1113-115.

155   Ita, J. M. "Negritude: Some Popular Misconceptions." NigM, 97 (1968),
      116-20.

156   Izevbaye, D. S. "African Literature Defined." ISE, 1, no. 1 (1969),
      56-69.

157   Jaffe, H. "African Literary Studies." NewA, 5, no. 9 (1963), 13-14.

158   Jahn, Janheinz. Muntu: An Outline of the New African Culture. Trans.
      Marjorie Grene. New York: Grove, 1961. [Orig. pub. 1958.]

159   ____   A History of Neo-African Literature. Trans. Oliver Coburn and
      Ursula Lehrburger. London: Faber & Faber, 1968. [Orig. pub. 1966.]

160   ____   "The Scope of Modern African Literature." RAL, 1 (1970), 167-75.

161   James, A. "African Literature: Definition and Function." JNESA, 2,
      no. 2 (1969), 129-39.

162   Jeanpierre, W. A. "'Negritude'--Its Development and Significance." PA,
      39 (1961), 32-49.

163   Jetha, Abdul. "A Consideration of Modern African Poetry in English."
      Nexus, 1, no. 2 (1967), 29-30, 33-35.

164   Jones, Eldred. "African Literature 1966-1967." AForum, 3, no. 1 (1967),
      5-25.

165   ____   "Jungle Drum and Wailing Piano: West African Fiction and Poetry
      in English." AForum, 1, no. 4 (1966), 93-106.

166   ____   Othello's Countrymen: The African in English Renaissance Drama.
      London: Oxford Univ. Press, 1965.

167   Jones-Quartey, K. A. B. "The Problem of Language in the Development
      of the African Theatre." Okyeame, 4, no. 1 (1969), 95-102.

168   ____   "Tragedy and the African Audience." Okyeame, 3, no. 1 (1968), 50-56.

169   Kane, Mohamadou. "The African Writer and His Public." PA, 58 (1966),
      10-32.

170   Kariuki, J. "Relating Literature and Life." NegroD, 15, no. 9 (1966),
      39-46.

171   Kemoli, A., and D. K. Mulwa. "The European Image of Africa and the
      African." Busara, 2, no. 2 (1969), 51-53.

172   Kennard, P. "Recent African Drama." BAALE, 2 (n. d.), 11-19.

173   Kennedy, J. S. "Language and Communication Problems in the Ghanaian
      Theatre." Okyeame, 4, no. 1 (1969), 103-09.

174   ____   "The National Theatre in Ghana." EAJ, 6, no. 7 (1969), 38-45.

175   Kesteloot, Lilyan. Les écrivains noirs de langue française: naissance
      d'une littérature. Brussels: Université Libre de Bruxelles, 1963.

176   ____   Négritude et situation coloniale. Yaoundé: Editions CLE, 1969.

177   Killam, G. D. Africa in English Fiction 1874-1939. Ibadan: Ibadan Univ.
      Press, 1968.

178   ____   "Recent African Fiction." BAALE, 2 (1965), 1-10.

179   Klíma, Vladimír. Modern Nigerian Novels. Prague: Academia, 1969.

180   Kolade, Christopher. "Looking at Drama in Ghana." AForum, 1, no. 3
      (1966), 77-79.

181   Korostovtsev, M. A., ed. Essays on African Culture. Moscow: Nauka,
      1966.

182   Kunene, Daniel P.   "Deculturation: The African Writer's Response."   AT,
      15, no. 4 (1968), 19-24.

183   Kunene, M.   "Background to African Literature."   AAW, 1 (1968), 35-40.

184   Lagneau-Kesteloot, Lilyan.   "Problems of the Literary Critic in Africa."
      Abbia, 8 (1965), 29-44.

185   Lamming, George.   "The African Writer in the Contemporary World."   AfrA,
      2, no. 4 (1969), 38-39.

186   Langbaum, R.   "Autobiography and Myth in and out of Africa."   VQR, 40
      (1964), 64-80.

187   Larson, C. R.   "African-Afro-American Literary Relations: Basic
      Parallels."   NegroD, 19, no. 2 (1969), 35-42.

188   _____   "The Search for the Past: East and Central African Writing."
      AT, 15, no. 4 (1968), 12-15.

189   Laurence, Margaret.   Long Drums and Cannons.   London: Macmillan, 1968.

190   Le Baron, B.   "Négritude: A Pan-African Ideal."   Ethics, 76 (1966),
      267-76.

191   Leopold, W.   "Jezyk i literature Afryki Wschodniej."   PrzS, 20 (1967),
      153-84.

192   Lewis, L. P.   "Some Aspects of the African Novel."   Nexus, 1, no. 1
      (1967), 26-28.

193   Lienhardt, Peter.   "Tribesmen and Cosmopolitans: On African Literature."
      Encounter, 25, no. 5 (1965), 54-57.

194   Lindfors, Bernth.   "Five Nigerian Novels."   BA, 39 (1965), 411-13.

195   _____   "African Vernacular Styles in Nigerian Fiction."   CLAJ, 9 (1966),
      265-73.

196   Literatura stran Afriki.   Moscow: Nauka, 1964.

197   Litto, Frederic M.   "Introduction" to Plays from Black Africa.   New York:
      Hill & Wang, 1968, vii-xvii.

198   Long, R. A.   "Négritude."   NegroD, 18, no. 7 (1969), 11-15, 57-59.

199   Lucas, Walter.   "Drums and Drama in Central Africa."   Drama, 82 (1966),
      38-41.

200   McDowell, R. E.   "African Drama, West and South."   AT, 15, no. 4 (1968),
      25-28.

201   McHardy, Cecile.   "The Performing Arts in Ghana."   AForum, 1, no. 1
      (1965), 113-17.

202   Mahood, M. M.   Joyce Cary's Africa.   London: Methuen, 1964.

203   Mazrui, Ali.   "Africa and the Crisis of Relevance in Modern Culture."
      PA, 72 (1969), 9-20.

204   _____   "The English Language and the Origins of African Nationalism."
      Mawazo, 1, no. 1 (1967), 14-22.

205   _____   "Meaning Versus Imagery in African Poetry."   PA, 66 (1968), 49-57.

206   _____   "Négritude and Negrology."   AT, 16, no. 3 (1969), 11-12.

207   Mazrui, M.   "Religion in African Fiction: A Consideration."   EAJ, 5,
      no. 1 (1968), 32-36.

208   Mbiti, John S.   African Religions and Philosophy.   London: Heinemann,
      1969.

209 Melone, Thomas. "The Theme of Negritude and Its Literary Problem."
     PA, 48 (1963), 166-81.

210 Mensah, A. A. "The Popular Song and the Ghanaian Writer." Okyeame, 4,
     no. 1 (1969), 110-19.

211 Mezu, S. Okechukwu. "The Origins of African Poetry." JNALA, 2 (1966),
     16-23.

212 Mohome, P. M. "Négritude: Evaluation and Elaboration." PA, 68 (1968),
     122-40.

213 Moore, Gerald, ed. African Literature and the Universities. Ibadan:
     Ibadan Univ. Press, 1965.

214 _____ "The Imagery of Death in African Poetry." Africa, 38, no. 1 (1968),
     57-70.

215 _____ "English Words, African Lives." PA, 54 (1965), 90-101.

216 _____ "Macbeth and African Drama." Transition, 4 (1962), 27-28.

217 _____ Seven African Writers. London: Oxford Univ. Press, 1962.

218 _____ "Time and Experience in African Poetry." Transition, 26 (1966),
     18-22.

219 _____ "Poetry and the Nigerian Crisis." BO, 2, no. 3 (1969), 10-13.

220 _____, and Ulli Beier. "Introduction" to Modern Poetry from Africa.
     Harmondsworth: Penguin, 1963, 13-29.

221 Morriseau-Leroy, F. "African National Theatre." Okyeame, 4, no. 1
     (1969), 91-94.

222 Mphahlele, Ezekiel. "African Literature: What Traditions?" UDQ, 2,
     no. 2 (1967), 36-68.

223 _____ "The Cult of Négritude." Encounter, 16, no. 3 (1961), 50-52.

224 _____ "The Language of African Literature." HER, 34 (1964), 298-306.

225 _____ "Out of Africa." Encounter, 14, no. 4 (1960), 61-63.

226 _____ "Realism and Romanticism in African Literature." AT, 15, no. 4
     (1968), 4.

227 _____ "Writers in Search of Themes." WAR, 32, no. 416 (1962), 40-41.

228 Nicol, Abioseh. "The Soft Pink Palms." PA, 8-10 (1956), 107-21.

229 Nicol, Davidson S. H. Africa, A Subjective View. London: Longmans,
     1964.

230 _____ "Négritude in West Africa." New Statesman, 60 (1960), 353-54.

231 _____ "West African Poetry." AfricaSE, 5, no. 3 (1961), 115-22.

232 Nketia, J. H. K. "The Language Problem and the African Personality."
     PA, 67 (1968), 157-71.

233 _____ "The Poetry of Akan Drums." BO, N. S. 2, no. 2 (1968), 27-35.

234 Nwoga, Donatus. "Onitsha Market Literature." Transition, 19 (1965),
     25-33.

235 Obiechina, Emmanuel N. "Cultural Nationalism in Modern African Creative
     Literature." ALT, 1 (1968), 24-35.

236 _____ "Growth of Written Literature in English-Speaking West Africa."
     PA, 66 (1968), 58-78.

237 _____ "Transition from Oral to Literary Tradition." PA, 63 (1967),
     140-61.

238 ____ Understanding Modern African Poetry. Enugu: Citadel Books, 1967.

239 Obumselu, Ben. "The Background of Modern African Literature." Ibadan, 22 (1966), 46-59.

240 Ogot, Grace. "The African Writer." EAJ, 5, no. 11 (1968), 35-37.

241 Ogunba, Oyin. "Theatre in Nigeria." PA, 58 (1966), 63-88.

242 Okot p'Bitek. "The Self in African Imagery." Transition, 15 (1964), 32-35.

243 Okpaku, J. "Tradition, Culture and Criticism." PA, 70 (1969), 137-46.

244 Okwu, E. C. "A Language of Expression for Nigerian Literature." NigM, 91 (1966), 289-92, 313-15.

245 Ower, John. "Manichean Metaphor: The Black African in Modern Literature." Mosaic, 2, no. 2 (1969), 1-12.

246 Paden, J. N., and E. W. Soja. The African Experience. Evanston, Ill.: Northwestern Univ. Press, 1968.

247 Páricsy, Pál. "Gondolatok as Afrikai Irodalomról." Valósag, 10, no. 11 (1968), 96-101.

248 Parry, J. "Nigerian Novelists." ContR, 200 (1961), 377-81.

249 Picterse, Cosmo, and Donald Munro, eds. Protest and Conflict in African Literature. London: Heinemann Educational, 1969.

250 Potexina, G. I. Ocerki sovremennoj literatury zapadnoj Afriki. Moscow: Nauka, 1968.

251 Povey, John F. "Changing Themes in the Nigerian Novel." JNALA, 1 (1966), 3-11.

252 ____ "Contemporary West African Writing in English." BA, 40 (1966), 253-60.

253 ____ "The English Language of the Contemporary African Novel." Critique (Minneapolis), 1, no. 3 (1969), 79-96.

254 ____ "The Political Theme in South and West African Novels." AfrQ, 9, no. 1 (1969), 33-39.

255 ____ "The Quality of African Writing Today." LitR, 11 (1968), 403-21.

256 ____ "West African Drama in English." CompD, 1 (1967), 110-22.

257 ____ "West African Poetry: Tradition and Change." AT, 15, no. 4 (1968), 5-7.

258 Prichard, N. S. "The Terrible Storm of Growth: A Theme in African Poetry." CP, 1, no. 2 (1968), 27-36.

259 Proceedings of the Conference on African Writing in English. Ife: Univ. Dept. of African Studies, 1968.

260 Ramsaran, J. A. "African Twilight: Folktale and Myth in Nigerian Literature." Ibadan, 15 (1963), 17-19.

261 ____ "Literature in West Africa and the West Indies." NegroD, 11, no. 1 (1962).

262 ____ New Approaches to African Literature. Ibadan: Ibadan Univ. Press, 1956.

263 Redding, Saunders. "Modern African Literature." CLAJ, 7 (1964), 191-201.

264 Reed, John. "Between Two Worlds: Some Notes on the Presentation by African Novelists of the Individual in Modern African Society." MakJ, 7 (1963), 1-14.

265 _____ "Poetry in East Africa." Mawazo, 1, no. 4 (1968), 31-36.

266 Rive, Richard. "Images of Drums and Tom-Toms." Contrast, 3 (1964), 48-54.

267 _____ "Race and Poetry." Contrast, 16 (1967), 49-61.

268 Rubadiri, D. "Why African Literature?" Transition, 15 (1964), 39-42.

269 Sartre, Jean-Paul. Black Orpheus. Trans. S. W. Allen. Paris: Présence Africaine, n.d.

270 Schmidt, Nancy J. "Nigeria: Fiction for the Average Man." AfricaR, 10, no. 8 (1965), 39-41.

271 Senanu, K. E. "The Literature of West Africa." In item 27, pp. 167-84.

272 Senghor, Leopold Sedar. "Negritude and the Concept of Universal Civilization." PA, 46 (1963), 9-13.

273 _____ "On Negrohood: Psychology of the African Negro." Diogenes (New York), 37 (1962), 1-15.

274 Shelton, Austin J., ed. The African Assertion. New York: Odyssey, 1968.

275 _____ "Behaviour and Cultural Value in West African Stories: Literary Sources for the Study of Culture Contact." Africa, 34 (1964), 353-59.

276 _____ "The Black Mystique: Reactionary Extremes in 'negritude.'" AfrAff, 63 (1964), 115-28.

277 _____ "Critical Criteria for the Study of African Literature." LE&W, 12 (1968), 1-12.

278 _____ "Some Problems of Inter-Communication." JMAS, 2 (1964), 395-403.

279 Shore, Herbert. "Drums, Dances and Then Some." TQ, 7, no. 2 (1964), 225-31.

280 Simon, Erica. "Negritude and Cultural Problems of Contemporary Africa." PA, 47 (1963), 122-46.

281 Soyinka, Wole. "And After the Narcissist?" AForum, 1, no. 4 (1966), 53-64.

282 _____ "The Fourth Stage." In The Morality of Art: Essays Presented to G. Wilson Knight, ed. D. W. Jefferson. London: Routledge & Kegan Paul, 1969, 119-34.

283 _____ "From a Common Backcloth: A Reassessment of the African Literary Image." ASch, 32 (1963), 387-96.

284 _____ "Terrible Understanding." Atlas, 15 (1968), 36-39.

285 _____ "Towards a True Theatre." Transition, 8 (1963), 21-30.

286 Standa, E. "Thoughts on African Culture." Busara, 2, no. 2 (1969), 54-57.

287 Sterling, Thomas. "Africa's Black Writers." Holiday, 41, no. 2 (1967), 131-40.

288 Taban lo Liyong. The Last Word: Cultural Synthesism. Nairobi: East Africa Pub. House, 1969.

289 _____ "Meditations in Limbo." Busara, 2, no. 2 (1969), 32-36.

290 _____ "The Role of the Creative Artist in Contemporary Africa." EAJ, 6, no. 1 (1969), 29-39.

291 Taiwo, Oladele. An Introduction to West African Literature. London: Nelson, 1967.

292 Theroux, Paul. "Voices Out of the Skull." BO, 20 (1966), 41-58.

293 Thomas, L. V. "Senghor and Négritude." PA, 54 (1965), 102-32.

294 Thomas, P. D. "A Touch of Négritude." PA, 71 (1969), 26-34.

295 Tibble, Anne. African-English Literature. London: Peter Owen, 1965.

296 Treadgold, Mary. "Writers in Search of Themes." WAR, 32, no. 413 (1962), 57-61.

297 Tregidgo, P. S. "West African Novels." Ghana Teachers Journal, 39, no. 3 (1963), 17-23.

298 Tucker, Martin. Africa in Modern Literature: A Survey of Contemporary Writing in English. New York: Frederick Ungar, 1967.

299 ____ "West African Literature: The Second Decade." AT, 13, no. 5 (1967), 7-9; 13, no. 6, (1967), 7-8.

300 Wake, Clive H. "African Literary Criticism." CLS, 1 (1964), 197-205.

301 Wali, Obiajunwa. "The Dead End of African Literature?" Transition, 10 (1963), 13-15.

302 ____ "The New African Novelists." Freedomways, 6, no. 2 (1966), 163-71.

303 ____ "The Individual and the Novel in Africa." Transition, 18 (1965), 31-33.

304 Warner, Alan. "A New English in Africa?" REL, 4, no. 2 (1963), 45-54.

305 Wästberg, Per. Afrikas moderna Litteratur. Stockholm: Wahlström & Widstrand, 1969.

306 ____ The Writer in Modern Africa. Uppsala: Scandinavian Inst. of African Studies, 1968.

307 Wauthier, Claude. The Literature and Thought of Modern Africa. Trans. Shirley Kay. London: Pall Mall, 1966.

308 Whiteley, Wilfred H. "The Concept of an African Prose Literature." Diogenes (New York), 37 (1962), 28-49.

309 Wonodi, Okogbule. "The Creative Process in Poetry." Conch, 1, no. 2 (1969).

310 Wright, Edgar. "African Literature I: Problems of Criticism." JCL, 2 (1966), 103-12.

311 "Writing in West Africa: A Chance to Adapt and Experiment." TLS, 10 Aug. 1962, p. 570.

312 Young, Peter. "A Note from Onitsha." BAALE, 4 (1966), 37-40.

See also: 2325, 2358, 2521, 4324, 4416, 5834, 5837, 5884, 5885, 5897, 6073-6095.

Individual Authors

ACHEBE, Chinua

313 Adejumo, M. A., and O. Adelusi. Notes and Essays on Chinua Achebe's "Things Fall Apart." Ibadan: Onibonoje Press, 1966.

314 Carroll, David. Chinua Achebe. New York: Twayne, 1970.

315 Dale, J. "Chinua Achebe, Nigerian Novelist." QQ, 75 (1968), 460-75.

316 Irele, Abiola. "The Tragic Conflict in Achebe's Novels." BO, 17 (1965), 24-32.

317 ____ "Chinua Achebe: The Tragic Conflict in His Novels." In item 91, pp. 167-78.

318 Jones, Eldred. "[Review of Achebe]." REL, 5, no. 4 (1964), 39-43.

319 Jordan, J. O. "Culture Conflict and Social Change in Achebe's Arrow of God." Critique (Minneapolis), 13, no. 1 (1970), 66-82.

320 Killam, G. D. The Novels of Chinua Achebe. London: Heinemann Educational, 1969.

321 Klíma, Vladimír. "Chinua Achebe's Novels." ActaUCP, 12, no. 1 (1969), 32-34.

322 Lindfors, Bernth. "Achebe's African Parable." PA, 66 (1968), 130-36.

323 ____ "The Folktale as Paradigm in Chinua Achebe's Arrow of God." SBL, 1, no. 1 (1970), 1-15.

324 ____ "The Palm Oil with which Achebe's Words Are Eaten." ALT, 1 (1968), 3-18.

325 Meyers, J. "Culture and History in Things Fall Apart." Critique (Minneapolis), 11, no. 1 (1968), 25-31.

326 Mezu, Okechukwu. "Littérature biafraise: les tragique héros de Chinua Achebe." ALA, 4 (1969), 22-25.

327 Moody, H. L. B. "Shrewd Foreknowledge or Prophetic Guess?" NigM, 89 (1966), 129-31.

328 Mpondo, S. "L'univers existentiel de l'intellectuel africain chez Chinua Achebe." PA, 70 (1969), 172-80.

329 Ngugi, James. "Satire in Nigeria: Chinua Achebe, T. M. Aluko and Wole Soyinka." In item 249, pp. 56-69.

330 Nwoga, Donatus. "The Chi Offended." Transition, 15 (1964), 5.

331 Okafor, C. A. "The Inscrutability of the Gods: Motivation of Behaviour in Chinua Achebe's Arrow of God." PA, 63 (1967), 207-14.

332 Okunaga, Y. "The Tragic Conflict in Achebe's No Longer at Ease." JNESA, 2 (1969), 141-42.

333 Ravenscroft, Arthur. "African Literature V: Novels of Disillusion." JCL, 6 (1969), 120-37.

334 ____ Chinua Achebe. London: Longmans, Green, 1969.

335 Riddy, Felicity. "Language as Theme in No Longer at Ease." JCL, 9 (1970), 38-47.

336 Serumaga, Robert. "Interview with Chinua Achebe." CulEA, 28 (1967), 1-4.

337 Shelton, Austin J. "The Offended Chi in Achebe's Novels." Transition, 13 (1964), 36-37.

338 ____ "The 'Palm Oil' of Language: Proverbs in Chinua Achebe's Novels." MLQ, 30 (1969), 86-111.

339 Stock, A. G. "Yeats and Achebe." JCL, 5 (1968), 105-11.

340 Weinstock, D. J. "Achebe's Christ-Figure." JNALA, 5-6 (1968), 20-26.

341 ____, and C. Ramadan. "Symbolic Structure in Things Fall Apart." Critique (Minneapolis), 11, no. 1 (1968), 33-41.

342 Wren, Robert M. "Anticipation of Civil Conflict in Nigerian Novels: Aluko and Achebe." SBL, 1, no. 2 (1970), 21-32.

See also: 52, 189, 217, 254, 6096-6099.

ARMAH, Ayi Kwei

343 Aidoo, Christina Ama Ata. "Introduction" to The Beautyful Ones Are Not Yet Born. New York: Collier-Macmillan, 1969, vii-xii.

344 Armah, Ayi Kwei. "African Socialism: Utopian or Scientific?" PA, 64 (1967), 6-30.

AWOONOR, Kofi [George Awoonor-Williams]

345 Interview with George Awoonor-Williams. CulEA, 29 (1967), 1-3.

346 Mphahlele, Ezekiel. "Introduction" to Kofi Awoonor, Night of My Blood. Garden City, N. Y.: Doubleday (Anchor), 1971, 9-20.

347 Tolson, Melvin. "Three African Poets." AForum, 1, no. 3 (1966), 121-23.

BREW, Kwesi

348 Thumboo, Edwin. "Kwesi Brew: The Poetry of Statement and Situation." ALT, 4 (1969), 19-36.

CLARK, John Pepper

349 Ademola, Frances. "J. P. Clark and His Audience." AForum, 1, no. 2 (1965), 84-85.

350 Anozie, Sunday O. "Two Nigerian Poets." AfrWr, 1, no. 1 (1962), 3-4.

351 Astrachan, Anthony M. "Like Goats to the Slaughter." BO, 16 (1964), 21-24.

352 Nnoka, B. G. "Authenticity in John Pepper Clark's Early Poems and Plays." LE&W, 12 (1968), 56-67.

353 Povey, John F. "'Two hands a man has': The Poetry of J. P. Clark." ALT, 1 (1968), 36-47.

354 Thumboo, Edwin. "J. P. Clark: Two Seedlings and the Iroko." Mawazo, 1, no. 2 (1967), 70-72.

See Also: 189, 214, 257, 369, 394, 404, 6077.

EKWENSI, Cyprian

355 Lindfors, Bernth. "Cyprian Ekwensi: An African Popular Novelist." ALT, 3 (1969), 2-14.

356 Povey, John F. "Cyprian Ekwensi and Beautiful Feathers." Critique (Minneapolis), 8, no. 1 (1965), 63-69.

357 Shelton, Austin J. "Pan-Africanism and Beautiful Feathers." BA, 39 (1965), 34-36.

358 _____ "'Rebushing' or Ontological Recession to Africanism: Jagua's Return to the Village." PA, 46 (1963), 49-58.

See also: 189, 4627.

NGUGI, James [Ngugi wa Thiong'o]

359 Cook, David. "A New Earth." EAJ, 6, no. 12 (1969), 13-20.

360 Knipp, T. R. "Two Novels from Kenya." BA, 41 (1967), 393-97.

361 Reed, John. "James Ngugi and the African Novel." JCL, 1 (1965), 117-21.

See also: 249, 333, 6099.

NICOL, Abioseh [Davidson Nicol]

362 Cobb, Robert P. "The Fiction of Abioseh Nicol." AForum, 2, no. 2
     (1966), 122-23.

NZEKWU, Onuora

363 Povey, John F. "The Novels of Onuora Nzekwu." LE&W, 12 (1968), 68-84.

See also: 4627.

OKARA, Gabriel

364 Anozie, Sunday O. "The Theme of Alienation and Commitment in Okara's
     The Voice." BAALE, 3 (1965), 54-67.

365 Brambilla, C. "Okara." Nigrizia, 86 (1969), 17-21.

366 Roscoe, A. A. "Okara's Unheeded Voice: Explication and Defence."
     Busara, 2, no. 1 (1969), 16-22.

See also: 333.

OKIGBO, Christopher

367 Anozie, Sunday O. "Christopher Okigbo: A Creative Itinerary 1957-1961."
     PA, 64 (1967), 158-67.

368 ____ "A Structural Approach to Okigbo's Distances." Conch, 1, no. 1
     (1969), 19-29.

369 Beier, Ulli. "Three Mbari Poets." BO, 12 (1963), 46-50.

370 Dathorne, O. R. "African Literature IV: Ritual and Ceremony in Okigbo's
     Poetry." JCL, 5 (1968), 79-91.

371 ____ "Limits by Christopher Okigbo." BO, 15 (1964), 59-60.

372 ____ "Okigbo Understood: A Study of Two Poems." ALT, 1 (1968), 19-23.

373 Etherton, M. J. "Christopher Okigbo and African Tradition: A Reply to
     Professor Ali A. Mazrui." Zuka, 2 (1968), 48-52.

374 Ikiddeh, Ime. "Dathorne on Okigbo: A Comment." ALT, 2 (1969), 55-56.

375 Mazrui, Ali. "Abstract Verse and African Tradition." Zuka, 1 (1968),
     47-49.

376 Povey, John F. "Epitaph for Christopher Okigbo." AT, 14, no. 6 (1967),
     22-23.

377 Theroux, Paul. "Christopher Okigbo." Transition, 22 (1965), 18-20.

378 Thomas, Peter. "'Ride me Memories': A Memorial Tribute to Christopher
     Okigbo." AfrA, 1, no. 5 (1968), 68-70.

379 Thumboo, Edwin. "Dathorne's Okigbo: A Dissenting View." ALT, 3 (1969),
     44-49.

380 Whitelaw, Marjory. "Interview with Christopher Okigbo, 1965." JCL, 9
     (1970), 28-37.

381 "The Writer in Politics . . . Christopher Okigbo, Wole Soyinka and the
     Nigerian Crisis." JNALA, 4, (1967), 1-13.

See also: 259.

SOYINKA, Wole

382 Aidoo, Ama Ata. "Poets and Ostriches." WA, 13 Jan. 1968, pp. 40-41.

383 Akaraogun, Alan. "Wole Soyinka." Spear, 5 (1966), 13-19.

384 Allen, S. "Two Writers: Senghor and Soyinka." NegroD, 16, no. 2 (1967),
     54-67.

385 Anon. "Our Authors and Performing Artists I." NigM, 88 (1966), 57-64.

386 ____ "Portrait: National Dramatist." WA, 19 Dec. 1964, p. 1417.

387 Asalache, K. "The Making of a Poet: Wole Soyinka." PA, 67 (1968),
     172-74.

388 Berry, Boyd M. "Review of Kongi's Harvest." Ibadan, 27 (1966), 53-55.

389 Bodurin, A. "Wole Soyinka: Poet, Satirist, and Political Neophyte."
     AfrSt, 2, no. 3 (1967), 19-27.

390 Brambilla, C. "Wole Soyinka, l'anti-Senghor." Nigrizia, 86 (1969),
     19-24.

391 Collings, R. "A propos . . ." AfrA, 2, no. 3 (1969), 82-84.

392 Cook, David. "Of the Strong Breed." Transition, 13 (1964), 38-40.

393 "The Detention of Wole Soyinka." AATB, 3, no. 2 (1968), 27.

394 Esslin, Martin. "Two Nigerian Playwrights." In item 91, pp. 255-62.

395 Iyengar, K. R. Srinivasa. "Wole Soyinka's The Road." In item 22,
     pp. 148-62.

396 Jones, Eldred. "Interpreting The Interpreters." BAALE, 4 (1966), 13-18.

397 ____ "Wole Soyinka's The Interpreters: Reading Notes." ALT, 2 (1969),
     42-50.

398 Laburthe, Tolra P. "Soyinka ou la Tigritude." Abbia, 19 (1968), 55-67.

399 MacLean, Una. "Wole Soyinka." BO, 15 (1964), 46-51.

400 Mahood, M. M., et al. "Three Views of The Swamp Dwellers." Ibadan,
     6 (1959), 27-28.

401 Ogunba, Oyin. "Traditional Content of the Plays of Wole Soyinka." ALT,
     4 (1970), 2-18.

402 Povey, John F. "Wole Soyinka and the Nigerian Drama." TriQ, 5 (1966),
     129-35.

403 ____ "Wole Soyinka: Two Nigerian Comedies." CompD, 3 (1969), 120-32.

404 Reckord, Barry. "Notes on Two Nigerian Playwrights." NewA, 4, no. 7
     (1965), 171.

405 Soyinka, Wole. "Salutations to the Gut." In Frances Ademola, ed.,
     Reflections. Lagos: African Univ. Press, 1962, 109-15.

406 ____ "Wole Soyinka." New Statesman, 77 (1969), 740.

407 Stewart, J. "Return to His Native Village." Busara, 2, no. 1 (1969),
     37-39.

408 Watson, Ian. "Soyinka's International Drama." Transition, 27 (1967),
     24-26.

409 Yankowitz, Susan. "The Plays of Wole Soyinka." AForum, 1, no. 4 (1966),
     129-33.

See also: 189, 216, 249, 259, 333, 6077, 6100, 6101.

TUTUOLA, Amos

410 Armstrong, Robert P. "The Narrative and Intensive Continuity: The
     Palm-Wine Drinkard." RAL, 1 (1970), 9-34.

411   Awoonor-Williams, George. "Tutuola and His Fantasy World." WA, 27 April
      1968, pp. 490-91.

412   Collins, Harold R. Amos Tutuola. New York: Twayne, 1969.

413   ____ "Founding a New National Literature: The 'Ghost' Novels of Amos
      Tutuola." Critique (Minneapolis), 4, no. 1 (1960), 17-28.

414   Jones, Eldred. "Turning Back the Pages III: Amos Tutuola--The Palm-Wine
      Drinkard Fourteen Years On." BAALE, 4, (1966), 24-30.

415   Klíma, Vladimír. "Tutuola's Inspiration." ArO, 35 (1967), 556-62.

416   Leslie, Omolara. "The Palm-Wine Drinkard: A Reassessment of Amos
      Tutuola." JCL, 9 (1970), 48-56. [Repr. from PA, 71 (1969), 99-108,
      where it appeared with Mrs. Leslie's maiden name, M. Ogundipe.]

417   Lindfors, Bernth. "Amos Tutuola and D. O. Fagunwa." JCL, 9 (1970),
      57-65.

418   ____ "Amos Tutuola and His Critics." Abbia, 22 (1969), 109-18.

419   ____ "Amos Tutuola's The Palm-Wine Drinkard and Oral Tradition."
      Critique (Minneapolis), 11, no. 1 (1968), 42-50.

420   ____ "Amos Tutuola's Television-Handed Ghostess." ArielE, 2, no. 1
      (1971), 68-77.

421   Moore, Gerald. "Amos Tutuola." BO, 1 (1957), 27-35. [Repr. in item 91,
      pp. 179-87.

422   Obiechina, Emmanuel N. "Amos Tutuola and the Oral Tradition." PA, 65 (1968),
      85-106.

423   Olubummo, A. "D. O. Fagunwa--A Yoruba Novelist." Odu, 9 (1963), 26-30.

424   Schmidt, Nancy J. "Tutuola Joins the Mainstream of Nigerian Novelists."
      AT, 15, no. 3 (1968), 22-24.

425   Taban lo Liyong. "Tutuola, Son of Zinjanthropus." Busara, 1, no. 1
      (1968), 3-8.

See Also: 189, 217, 259.

Australia

Research Aids

426 Australian Periodical Index. Sydney: Mitchell Library. 1956-1959
(cumulated 1961). [Cont. of Index to Periodicals. 3 vols., 1944-1955.]

427 Borchardt, D. H. Australian Bibliography: A Guide to Printed Sources
of Information. Melbourne: Cheshire, 1963.

428 ____ "Australian Bibliography: An Essay." CRL, 23 (1961), 207-12,
251-54.

429 Cuthbert, Eleonora Isabel. Index of Australian and New Zealand Poetry.
New York: Scarecrow, 1963.

430 Dornbusch, C. E. The Australian Military Bibliography. Cornwallville,
N. Y.: Hope Farm Press, 1964. [See comments in BANQ, 17 (1964), 7-8.]

431 Eagleson, Robert D. Bibliography of Writings on Australian English.
(Univ. of Sydney Australian Lang. Research Centre Occas. Paper, 11.)
Sydney: Univ. of Sydney, 1968.

432 Edwards, Ron. Index of Australian Folk Song, 1857-1970. Holloways Beach,
Queensland: Rams Skull Press, 1971.

433 Ferguson, John. Bibliography of Australia, 1851-1900. 7 vols. Sydney:
Angus & Robertson, 1941-69.

434 Hubble, G. V., ed. Modern Australian Fiction: A Bibliography, 1940-1965.
Perth: Winmarley Street, G. V. Hubble, 1969.

435 Johnston, Grahame. Annals of Australian Literature. Melbourne: Oxford
Univ. Press, 1970.

436 Laird, J. T. "A Checklist of Australian Literature of World War I."
ALS, 4 (1969), 148-63.

437 Leeson, Ida. A Bibliography of Bibliographies of the South Pacific.
Melbourne: Oxford Univ. Press, 1954.

438 Miller, E. Morris. Australian Literature: A Bibliography to 1938.
Extended to 1950 with historical outline and descriptive commentaries
by Frederick T. Macartney. Sydney: Angus & Robertson, 1956.

439 Muir, Marcie. A Bibliography of Australian Children's Books. London:
Deutsch, 1970.

440 Stone, Graham. Australian Science Fiction Index, 1939-1962. Sydney:
Futurian Soc., 1964.

441 A Subject Index to Current Literature. Canberra: Commonwealth National
Library, 1945-d., ann.

442 Tipping, Marjorie, ed. 'Meanjin Quarterly' Index, 1940-1965. Melbourne:
Meanjin, 1969.

443   Tregenza, John. *Australian Little Magazines, 1923-1954*. Adelaide: Libraries Board of South Australia, 1964.

General

444   Adams, J. D. "Australian Children's Literature: A History to 1920." *VHM*, 38 (1967), 6-28.

445   Aldous, Allan. *The Theatre in Australia*. Melbourne: Hawthorn, 1947.

446   Alexander, John C. "Australian Image: Vision and Depth." *Meanjin*, 21 (1962), 328-35.

447   Allan, J. Alex. *Men and Manners in Australia: Being a Social and Economic Sketch History*. Melbourne: Cheshire, 1945.

448   Allen, H. C. *Bush and Backwoods: A Comparison of the Frontier in Australia and the United States*. Sydney: Angus & Robertson, 1959.

449   Allen, John. "The Australian Seminar on Drama." *AustQ*, 30, no. 4 (1958), 44-51.

450   ____ "A Message from the Human Body." *Masque*, 8 (1969), 28-32.

451   ____ "The Theatre in Australia." *ETJ*, 13 (1961), 99-102.

452   Anchen, John Oscar. *The Australian Novel: A Critical Survey*. Melbourne: Whitcombe, 1940.

453   Anderson, Hugh. *Colonial Ballads*. Melbourne: Cheshire, 1962.

454   ____ *Farewell to Old England, a Broadside History of Early Australia*. Adelaide: Rigby, 1964.

455   ____ *A Guide to Ten Australian Poets*. Melbourne: Melbourne Univ. Press, 1953.

456   ____ *The Singing Roads: A Guide to Australian Children's Authors and Illustrators*. Sydney: Wentworth, 1965.

457   Anon. "Australian Drama and Theatre." *CurAB*, 22, no. 7 (1958), 115-28.

458   ____ "Australian Literature." *Southerly*, 2, no. 2 (1941), 23-26.

459   ____ "The Australian Novel." *CurAB*, 22, no. 13 (1958), 195-208.

460   ____ "Australian Writing: A Sequel." *QQ*, 67 (1960), 105-10.

461   ____ "The Characteristics of Australian Literature [1890]." In item 479, pp. 44-49.

462   ____ "End of a Hero?" *Meanjin*, 16 (1957), 298-99.

463   ____ "Modern Australian Poetry." *CurAB*, 15, no. 7 (1955), 98-112.

464   ____ "Myths in Antipodean Writing." *TLS*, 14 June 1963, p. 144.

465   ____ "Novelists and Poets: The Decade in Australia." *CurAB*, 39, no. 3 (1966), 35-48.

466   ____ "Standards in Australian Literature." *CurAB*, 19, no. 3 (1956), 35-47.

467   Argyle, Barry. "The German Element in Australian Fiction." *WasR*, 5, no. 2 (1970), 5-22.

468   ____ "Problems in Studying Nineteenth-Century Australian Fiction." In item 36, pp. 48-63.

469 Auchterlonie, Dorothy, ed. Australian Poetry, 1968. Sydney: Angus &
     Robertson, 1968.

470 "Australian Humour: A Symposium." AustL, 2, no. 1 (1957), 32-45.

471 "Australian Literature: Education Broadsheet 21, English 5." Australian,
     16 July 1969, pp. 12-13.

472 Baker, Sidney J. The Australian Language. Sydney: Currawong, 1966.

473 _____ Australia Speaks. Sydney: Shakespeare Head, 1953.

474 _____ The Drum: Australian Character and Slang. Sydney: Currawong, 1959.

475 Barker, Uther. The Emotional Life: Literature and Art. Sydney: Wentworth,
     1969.

476 Barnes, John. "Australian Books in Print: Filling Some Gaps." Westerly,
     2 (1967), 60-63.

477 _____ "Australian Poetry: Time of Hope." Westerly, 1 (1969), 57-61.

478 _____ "Counting the Swans." Westerly, 2 (1963), 81-85.

479 _____, ed. The Writer in Australia: A Collection of Literary Documents
     1856-1964. Melbourne: Oxford Univ. Press, 1969.

480 Bartlett, Norman. "The Need for Criticism: The Australian Tradition."
     Southerly, 2, no. 1 (1941), 12-16.

481 _____ "Winds of Change in the Australian Novel." AustQ, 32, no. 4 (1960),
     75-85.

482 Barton, G. B. Literature in New South Wales. Sydney: T. Richards, Govt.
     Printer, 1866.

483 _____, ed. The Poets and Prose Writers of New South Wales. Sydney: Gibbs,
     Shallard, 1866.

484 Baxter, J. "Who Was Ned Kelly?" AustB, 4 (1965), 51-52.

485 _____ "World of Inner Space." Nation (Sydney), 6 March 1956, pp. 15-17.

486 Beasley, Jack. Socialism and the Novel: A Study of Australian Literature.
     Petersham, N. S. W.: The Author, 1958.

487 Beatty, Bill. Tales of Old Australia. Sydney: Ure Smith, 1966.

488 Beaver, Bruce. "Australian Letter." Landfall, 18 (1964), 348-53.

489 _____ "Younger Poets of Australia." Hemisphere, 12, no. 11 (1968), 13-15.

490 _____, and Ian Turner. "Australian Letters." Landfall, 19 (1965), 368-74.

491 Beckett, Jeremy. "John Greenway and the Aborigines: A Rejoinder." ALS,
     2 (1967), 298-99. [See item 657.]

492 Bernard, J. R. L. "Australian Pronunciation and Australian Attitudes."
     TEng, 15 (1969), 4-17.

493 _____ "Length and Identification of Australian English Vowels." AUMLA,
     27 (1967), 37-58.

494 _____ "On the Uniformity of Spoken Australian English." Orbis, 18 (1969),
     62-73.

495 Blake, Leslie J. Australian Writers. Adelaide: Rigby, 1968.

496 _____ "The Speewa Legends." Meanjin, 24 (1965), 239-43.

497 Boldrewood, Rolf. [T. A. Browne]. Old Melbourne Memories. Rev. ed.
     London and New York: Macmillan, 1896.

498 Boyd, Robin. "The Australian Prettiness." AustL, 3, no. 3 (1961), 17-20.

499 _____ The Australian Ugliness. Melbourne: Cheshire, 1960; Melbourne: Penguin, 1963.

500 Bradish, C. R. "The 'Ned Kelly' Literature." Southerly, 18 (1957), 45-47.

501 Bradley, Jeana. "Recent Australian Fiction." Westerly, 2 (1965), 51-53.

502 Braham, Noni. "'Writers' Retreat': Armidale 1968." TC (Melbourne), 23 (1968), 39-43.

503 Brereton, John Le Gay. Knocking Around. Sydney: Angus & Robertson, 1930.

504 Brisbane, Katharine. "Where Have Our Playwrights Gone?" Australian, 20 Sept. 1967, p. 8.

505 Brissenden, R. F. "Old Mates and New Conspirators." Quadrant, 12, no. 1 (1968), 8-13. [A discussion of Patrick Morgan's "The Misuse of Australian Literature." See item 857.]

506 _____ "Some Recent Australian Plays." TQ, 5, no. 2 (1962), 185-92.

507 _____, ed. Southern Harvest. Melbourne: Macmillan, 1964.

508 Brown, Cyril. Writing for Australia: A Nationalist Tradition in Australian Literature? Melbourne: Hawthorne, 1950.

509 Buckley, Vincent. Essays in Poetry, Mainly Australian. Melbourne: Melbourne Univ. Press, 1957.

510 _____ "New Bulletin Poets." Bulletin (Sydney), 22 June 1963, pp. 30-32.

511 _____ "The Search for an Australian Identity." LCrit, 6, no. 3 (1964), 12-20. [Repr. in item 866, pp. 12-20.]

512 _____ "Towards an Australian Literature." Meanjin, 18 (1959), 59-68.

513 _____ "Utopianism and Vitalism in Australian Literature." Quadrant, 3, no. 2 (1959), 39-51.

514 Burgess, O. N. "Fifty Years of 'Granny.'" AustQ, 36, no. 3 (1964), 78-85.

515 Burke, Iris. "Some References of Special Literary Interest in Vols. IV, V and VI (1859-1860) of the Australian Home Companion and Band of Hope Journal." App. I, Foreshadowings. Sydney: Australian Documentary Facsimile Soc., 1963.

516 Burns, Bob. "A Novel Chronicle." Prospect, 7, no. 1 (1964), 27-29.

517 Byrne, Desmond. Australian Writers. London: Bentley, 1896. ["Introduction" repr. in item 479, pp. 50-61.]

518 Byrnes, John V. "Barren Fields--Recultivated." Southerly, 21, no. 3 (1961), 6-18.

519 _____ "The Cause of Literature--and Howe." Southerly, 20 (1959), 122-38.

520 _____ "Our Literature in Chains." Southerly, 21, no. 3 (1961), 2-17.

521 _____ "William Charles Wentworth--and the Continuity of Australian Literature." AustL, 5, no. 3 (1963), 10-18.

522 _____ "Writers and Historians." AustL, 6, no. 2 (1964), 24-29.

523 Byrnes, R. S., and Val Vallis, eds. The Queensland Centennial Anthology. London: Longmans, [1959].

524 Callaghan, J., and R. E. Smythe. A Critical Survey of Australian Short Stories. Sydney: College Press, 1966.

525 Casey, Gavin. The Writing of Novels and Short Stories. Canberra: Australian National Univ., 1964.

526 Castle, Edgar. "Kangaroo with Flowers." SoRA, 1, no. 2 (1964), 24-29.

527 Charlesworth, M. J. "Australian Letter: Land of Hope and Glory."
    Comment, 1, no. 1 (1959), 24-26.

528 Chisholm, A. R. "Celeste de Chabrillan and the Gold Rush." Meanjin,
    28 (1969), 197-201.

529 ____ "The Changing Image of Europe in Australian Poetry." In Folklore
    Studies in Honour of Arthur Palmer Hudson. NCarF, 13, nos. 1-2 (1965),
    181-92.

530 ____ The Familiar Presence. Melbourne: Melbourne Univ. Press, 1967.

531 ____ The Making of a Sentimental Bloke. Melbourne: Melbourne Univ. Press,
    1964. [On C. J. Dennis.]

532 ____ Men Were My Milestones. Melbourne: Melbourne Univ. Press, 1958.

533 Christesen, C. B., ed. On Native Grounds: Australian Writing from
    "Meanjin Quarterly." Sydney: Angus & Robertson, 1968.

534 ____ "The Twenty-One Lives of Meanjin Quarterly." TQ, 5, no. 2 (1962),
    84-93.

535 Clancy, L. J. "Fiction Chronicle." Meanjin, 28 (1969), 413-25.

536 ____ "Max Harris and the Academics." Dissent, 20 (1967), 43-45.

537 Clark, Manning. "Good Day to You Ned Kelly." Quadrant, 11, no. 4 (1967),
    64-69.

538 ____, et al. Ned Kelly: Man and Myth. Melbourne: Cassell, 1969.

539 Clarke, Donovan. "The Image of Australian Man." AustQ, 37, no. 2 (1965),
    67-78.

540 Cleverly, J. F. "Tutors and Governesses in Australian Literature."
    Education (Sydney), 8 April 1964, p. 3.

541 Coleman, Peter, ed. Australian Civilisation. London: Angus & Robertson,
    1962.

542 Coles, Frederick G. Australiana Collection. Melbourne: Gaston Renard,
    1965.

543 Conlon, Anne. "'Mine Is a Sad yet True Story': Convict Narratives,
    1818-1850." JRAHS, 55 (1969), 43-82.

544 Connell, R. W. "Images of Australia." Quadrant, 12, no. 2 (1968), 9-19.

545 "A Controversy: Australian Poets Reply to Their English Critics." AustL,
    1, no. 1 (1957), 17-23.

546 Coombes, A. J. Some Australian Poets. Sydney: Angus & Robertson, 1938.

547 Covell, Roger. Australia's Music: Themes of a New Society. Melbourne:
    Sun Books, 1967.

548 ____ "How Our Playwrights See Us." Hemisphere, 7, no. 5 (1963), 3-7.

549 Cowan, Peter. "Writer and Teacher." EngA, 1 (1965), 13-16.

550 Cox, P. B. "Charles Harpur and the Early Australian Poets." JRAHS, 24
    (1939), 249-67.

551 Craig, Alexander. "Australian Poetry--Nobody's Rocking the Boat."
    Bulletin (Sydney), 16 Sept. 1967, pp. 31-32.

552 Crick, Don. "A Critical Comment." Overland, 38 (1968), 35-37.

553 Cross, Gustav. "Australian Poetry in the Sixties." Poetry Australia, 5
    (1965), 33-38.

554 ____ "Little Magazines in Australia." REL, 5, no. 4 (1964), 20-28.

555 Cross, Zora Bernice May. An Introduction to the Study of Australian Literature. Sydney: Teachers College and Angus & Robertson, 1922.

556 Cummins, Eric. "Drama Is Successful When It Helps the Community to an Understanding of What Is Significant in Its Life." Australian, 17 Feb. 1967, p. 7.

557 Curran, Greg. "Into the Urban Sprawl . . . Some New Australian Plays." Masque, 12 (1969), 27-30.

558 Cusack, Dymphna. "First Writers' Association." AustA, 1, no. 2 (1969), 33-35.

559 ____ "Unfair for Writers." Australian, 19 Nov. 1968, p. 8.

560 Cusack, Frank, ed. "Introduction" to The Australian Christmas. Melbourne: Heinemann, 1966, v-xii.

561 Davies, M. Bryn. "English Novelists in Australia." LCrit, 6, no. 3 (1964), 113-25. [Repr. in item 866, pp. 113-25.]

562 Davison, P. H. "Three Australian Plays: National Myths Under Criticism." Southerly, 23 (1963), 110-27.

563 Dawe, Bruce. "Recent Trends in Australian Poetry." TC (Melbourne), 19 (1964), 59-63.

564 Day, A. Grove. Australian Fiction: The First Hundred Years. (Univ. of Hawaii Occas. Paper, 55.) Honolulu: Univ. of Hawaii, 1951.

565 Delbridge, Arthur. "The Australian Accent and Articulatory Method." EngA, 4 (1967), 21-26.

566 ____ "The Use of English in Australian Literature." HER, 34 (1964), 306-11.

567 Denat, A. "Note sur la littérature australienne." RLC, 40 (1966), 129-31.

568 Devaney, James. Poetry in Our Time. Melbourne: Melbourne Univ. Press, 1952.

569 Dickson, Suzy. "Culture in North Queensland." North, 2 (1967), 3-6.

570 Diesendorf, Margaret. "Australia: sept pains et quelques poissons." Liberté, 9, no. 4 (1967), 15-28.

571 Dobbie, James M. "Australian Newsletter." Arena, 26 (1951), 25-26.

572 Dobson, Rosemary. "Modern Australian Poetry--A Personal View." TEng, 5 (1964), 6-20.

573 Douglas, Dennis. "Mini-mags and the Poetry Explosion." Overland, 41 (1969), 46-47.

574 Drake-Brockman, Henrietta. "The First Private Letter." Westerly, 3 (1963), 29-36.

575 ____ "[The International Symposium on the Short Story. Part I] Australia." KR, 30 (1968), 478-85.

576 ____ "The Thirties." Quadrant, 11, no. 5 (1967), 21-33.

577 Dugan, Michael. "Poetry: A New Scene." Great Auk, 8 (1969), n. pag. [See also "Various Editorial Notes." Great Auk, 8 (1969), n. pag.]

578 Dunlevy, Maurice. "End of the Road for a Quarterly [Southerly]." Canberra Times, 21 Sept. 1968, p. 15.

579 ____ "A Plea for a Most Unprofitable Venture." Canberra Times, 25 Oct. 1969, p. 16.

580 Dunstan, Keith. Wowsers. Melbourne: Cassell, 1968.

581 Dutton, Geoffrey. "Australian Letter." Landfall, 14 (1960), 373-77.

582 ____ "Australian Letter." Landfall, 15 (1961), 381-86.

583 ____ "Australian Letter." Landfall, 16 (1962), 371-76.

584 ____ "Australian Poetic Diction." AustL, 1, no. 1 (1957), 12-16.

585 ____ "Culture: Artists and Flat-Landers." In Craig McGregor and David
      Beal, eds., Life in Australia. Sydney: Southern Cross International,
      1968, 179-93.

586 ____ "The Essential Rivals." AustBR, 7 (1969), 239-40.

587 ____, ed. The Literature of Australia. Harmondsworth: Penguin, 1964.

588 ____, ed. Modern Australian Writing. Manchester: Collins, 1967.

589 ____ "The Struggle for Prose." Bulletin (Sydney), 31 Dec. 1966, pp. 28-29.

590 ____, and Max Harris, eds. The Vital Decade: Ten Years of Australian
      Life and Letters. Melbourne: Sun Books, 1968.

591 ____, and Nancy Cato. "Blokes and Sheilahs." AustL, 1, no. 4 (1958),
      13-18.

592 Eagleson, Robert D. "Convict Jargon and Euphemism." ALS, 2 (1965),
      141-46. [See item 660.]

593 ____ "In Pursuit of Australian English." AustH, 47, no. 3 (1967), 2-4.

594 Earnshaw, John. "An Excursion into Vague Realms of Australiana: What
      Happened to Surgeon Bass's Library?" BANQ, 3, no. 2 (1969), 14-17.

595 ____ "A Further Note on Billy Barlow." Meanjin, 15 (1956),
      422-23.

596 Eldershaw, M. Bernard. Essays in Australian Fiction. Melbourne: Melbourne
      Univ. Press, 1938.

597 Elkin, P. K. "The Lower Slopes." Poetry Magazine, 1 (1964), 2-6.

598 Elliott, Brian. "Antipodes: An Essay in Attitudes." AustL, 7, no. 3
      (1967), 51-70.

599 ____ "An American-Australian Novelist of the Nineteenth Century: W. H.
      Thomes." AustQ, 29, no. 3 (1957), 79-93.

600 ____ "Birds Without Song and Flowers Without Smell." Southerly, 18 (1957),
      155-60.

601 ____ "Faute de Mieux Criticism." AustBR, 8 (1969), 247-48.

602 ____ James Hardy Vaux: A Literary Rogue in Australia. Adelaide: Wakefield,
      1944.

603 ____ The Landscape of Australian Poetry. Melbourne: Cheshire, 1967.

604 ____ "Literature in Australia: A Comparison with America." Geste, 6,
      no. 5 (1961), 1-5.

605 ____ Singing to the Cattle. Melbourne: Georgian House, 1947.

606 ____ "Tailpiece on the Primrose." Southerly, 18 (1957), 104-07.

607 ____, and A. C. W. Mitchell. "Introduction" to Bards in the Wilderness:
      Australian Colonial Poetry to 1920. Melbourne: Nelson, 1970, xv-xxvii.

608 Engel, S. "Political Novels in Australia." HSANZ, 7 (1956), 303-13.

609 Esson, Louis. "Introduction" to Australian Writers Speak. Sydney:
      Angus & Robertson, 1943, 7-10.

610 ____ "A National Drama?" Adult Education, 4, no. 4 (1965), 12-14.
      [Repr. from Fellowship (August 1921).]

611 Ewers, John K. Creative Writing in Australia. Melbourne: Georgian House, 1955; rev. ed. 1959.

612 ____ The Great Australian Paradox. Perth: Carroll's, 1940.

613 ____ "Introduction" to Modern Australian Short Stories. Melbourne: Georgian House, 1965, ix-xiv.

614 ____ "A Question of Standards." Meanjin, 16 (1957), 434-36.

615 ____ Tell the People! Sydney: Currawong, 1943.

616 ____ "A Writer in Perth." Westerly, 4 (1967), 63-71.

617 Fabinyi, Andrew. "The Australian Book." TQ, 5, no. 2 (1962), 77-81.

618 ____ "The Australian Book." Meanjin, 17 (1958), 312-18.

619 ____ "The Australian Book: A Sketch of the Economic and Social Background." Vestes, 8 (1965), 153-64.

620 ____ "The Australian Publisher." Meanjin, 21 (1962), 198-203.

621 ____ "On Australian Publishing." Meanjin, 28 (1969), 398-401.

622 ____ "The Literary Link." Hemisphere, 11, no. 4 (1967), 23-27.

623 Farmer, Geoffrey A. J. "Australiana." BANQ, 3, no. 2 (1969), 5-13.

624 Fellowship of Australian Writers. Australian Writers Speak: Literature and Life in Australia. Sydney: Angus & Robertson, 1943

625 Ferguson, G. A. "Recognition for the Writer." Australian, 30 Sept. 1968, p. 8.

626 Finch, Alan. Pens and Ems. Adelaide: Rigby, 1965.

627 Fischer, Gerald. "The Professional Theatre in Adelaide, 1838-1922." AustL, 2, no. 4 (1960), 79-97.

628 Fitzgerald, R. D. The Elements of Poetry. Brisbane: Univ. of Queensland Press, 1963.

629 ____ "Narrative Poetry." Southerly, 26 (1966), 11-24.

630 ____ "Nationalism and Internationalism." Southerly, 27 (1967), 260-65.

631 ____ "A Poet on Poetry." Australian, 10 Sept. 1969, pp. 12-13.

632 Forrest, David. "The Split-Level Culture." In item 962, pp. 34-50.

633 Foster, I. M., et al. "South Australian Literature, 1836-1900." AustL, 2, no. 4 (1960), 43-53.

634 Foster, John Wilson. "John Greenway on Folksong--A Reply." ALS, 3 (1967), 63-65. [See item 657.]

635 Franklin, Miles. Laughter Not for a Cage: Notes on Australian Writing, with Biographical Emphasis on the Struggles, Function and Achievement of the Novel in Three Half-Centuries. Sydney: Angus & Robertson, 1956.

636 Fredman, L. E. "Melbourne Bohemia in the Nineteenth Century." Southerly, 18 (1957), 83-91.

637 Freehill, Norman. "Anti-Nationalism in Australian Criticism." Realist, 29 (1968), 63-66.

638 Friederich, Werner P. Australia in Western Imaginative Prose Writing 1600-1960. Chapel Hill: Univ. of N. C. Press, 1967.

639 Garnsey, Wanda. "Influences on Australian Poetry." EH, 4, no. 2 (1967), 18-20.

640 Gaskin, Howard. "How It Strikes a Contemporary." Westerly, 2 (1968), 67-69.

641 Gibbs, A. M. "Meanjin and the Australian Literary Scene." JCL, 4 (1967), 130-38.

642 Gifford, K. H. Jindyworobak: Towards an Australian Culture. Melbourne: Jindyworobak, 1944.

643 Glaskin, G. M. "Creative Art Down Under." EH, 2, no. 1 (1961), 41-46.

644 Goodwin, Kenneth. "Recent Australian Poetry: A Survey." LHY, 10, no. 1 (1969), 74-83.

645 Gorelik, Mordecai. "Gorelik in Australia." Masque, 7 (1968), 19-25.

646 Grattan, C. Hartley. Australian Literature. Seattle: Univ. of Wash. Book Store, 1929.

647 ____ "Australia's 10 for UNESCO." BA, 31 (1957), 237-42.

648 ____ "A Garrulity About Australian Literature since 1927." Meanjin, 26 (1965), 405-16.

649 Green, H. M. Australian Literature, 1900-1950. Parkville, Victoria: Melbourne Univ. Press, 1963; London: Cambridge Univ. Press, 1964.

650 ____ "Australian Literature, 1938." Southerly, 1, no. 1 (1939), 37-41; "Australian Literature, 1939-40." 2, no. 2 (1941), 17-22; "Australian Literature, 1941." 3, no. 2 (1942), 11-16; "Australian Literature, 1942." 4, no. 2 (1943), 34-39; "Australian Literature, 1943." 5, no. 3 (1944), 26-28; "Australian Literature, 1944." 6, no. 4 (1945), 20-26; "Australian Literature, 1945." 7, no. 4 (1946), 211-16; "Australian Literature, 1946." 8, no. 4 (1947), 212-17.

651 ____ Fourteen Minutes. Sydney: Angus & Robertson, 1944.

652 ____ A History of Australian Literature. Vol. I (1789-1923), Vol. II (1923-1950). Sydney: Angus & Robertson, 1962.

653 ____ An Outline of Australian Literature. Sydney: Whitcombe & Tombs, 1930.

654 ____ "What Is Australian Literature?" Southerly, 1, no. 2 (1940), 15-17.

655 Greenop, Frank S. History of Magazine Publishing in Australia. Sydney: Murray, 1947.

656 Greenway, John. "Anything Like Waltzing Matilda: Observations on Folksong in Australia." Quadrant, 1, no. 2 (1957), 45-51.

657 ____ "Folksong--A Protest." ALS, 2 (1967), 179-92. [See items 491, 634.]

658 Gronowski, Irene. "Modern Australian Drama." Quadrant, 5, no. 2 (1961), 67-74.

659 Gunn, John. "Level of English Usage in a Letter from Australia, 1798." TC, (Melbourne) 22 (1968), 239-51.

660 Gunson, Niel. "'Bushranger' and 'Croppy': A Footnote to 'Convict Jargon and Euphemism'." ALS, 2 (1966), 214-16. [See item 592.]

661 Hadgraft, Cecil. Australian Literature: A Critical Account to 1955. London: Heinemann, 1960.

662 ____ "Charles Rowcroft, for Example." ALS, 2 (1966), 171-78.

663 ____ "Histories of Australian Literature." LCrit, 6, no. 3 (1964), 102-06. [Repr. in item 866, pp. 102-06.]

664 ____ Queensland and Its Writers: 100 Years . . . 100 Authors. Brisbane: Univ. of Queensland Press, 1959.

665 ____, and Elizabeth Webby. "More Substance of Fisher's Ghost." ALS, 3 (1968), 190-200.

666   ____, and Richard Wilson, eds. "Introduction" to A Century of Australian
      Short Stories. London: Heinemann, 1963, pp. ix-xvi.

667   Hagan, J. Printers and Politics: A History of the Australian Printing
      Unions, 1850-1950. Canberra: Australian National Univ. Press, 1966.

668   Hall, David, and H. Winston Rhodes. "Books from Australia." Landfall, 8
      (1954), 26-35.

669   Hall, Rodney, and Thomas W. Shapcott. "Introduction" to New Impulses in
      Australian Poetry. St. Lucia: Univ. of Queensland Press, 1968, pp. 1-13.

670   Hall, Sandra. "Out to Spot the Writers." Bulletin (Sydney), 1 March 1969,
      pp. 41-44.

671   ____ "Taking the Plunge into Publishing." Bulletin (Sydney), 10 Aug.
      1966, pp. 39-40.

672   Hamer, Clive. "Anthony Trollope's Australian Novels." BANQ, 1, no. 4
      (1966), 24-29.

673   ____ "Fifty Years Ago--An Overlooked Novel." Southerly, 18 (1957), 41-44.

674   ____ "Novels of 'The System.'" Southerly, 18 (1957), 206-11.

675   ____ "The Surrender to Truth in the Early Australian Novel." ALS, 2
      (1965), 103-16.

676   Hanger, Eunice. "Australian Drama Now." MD, 8 (1965), 73-81. [Also in
      LCrit, 6, no. 3 (1964), 76-82; Repr. in item 866, pp. 76-82.]

677   ____ "Australian Plays in the Fryer Library at the University of
      Queensland." Southerly, 23 (1963), 132-36.

678   ____ "David Burn in Sydney, 1844-1845." Southerly, 24 (1964), 232-41.

679   ____ "Introduction" to Three Australian Plays. Minneapolis: Univ. of
      Minnesota Press, 1968, pp. 7-22.

680   ____ "Place in Australian Plays." AustQ, 34, no. 2 (1962), 67-73.

681   ____ "Queensland Drama." Southerly, 20 (1959), 216-25.

682   Hardy, Frank. "Environment and Ideology in Australian Literature: A
      Personal View." In item 962, pp. 69-80.

683   Harris, Max. "Angry Penguins and After." Quadrant, 7, no. 1 (1963), 5-10.

684   ____ "Conflicts in Australian Intellectual Life, 1940-1964." In item 962,
      pp. 16-33.

685   ____ "The Dirtiest Word to Call a Writer." Australian, 16 April 1967,
      p. 10.

686   ____ "Good and Not-so-Good Books Lately." Australian, 28 Dec. 1968, p. 9.

687   ____ "In Search of a New Breed of Writers." Australian, 30 March 1967,
      p. 9.

688   ____ "Recent Publishing and the Australian Identity." Hemisphere, 10,
      no. 2 (1967), 2-6.

689   ____ "To Define True Mateship." Geste, 6, no. 5 (1961), 6-9.

690   ____ "What the Professionals Read and Liked in 1967." Australian,
      30 Dec. 1967, p. 9.

691   Harrison-Ford, Carl. "Poetics Before Politics." Meanjin, 29 (1970),
      226-31. [Reply to item 696.]

692   Harrower, Elizabeth. "[The International Symposium on the Short Story,
      Part 3] Australia." KR, 31 (1969), 479-85.

693   Harvey, Frank R. Theatre. Melbourne: Longmans, 1965.

694   Heddle, Enid Moodie. Australian Literature Now. A Reader's Survey.
      London and New York: Longmans Green, 1949.

695   Helping Literature in Australia: The Work of the Commonwealth Literary
      Fund. Canberra: Government Printer, 1967.

696   Hemensley, Kris. "First Look at 'the New Australian Poetry.'" Meanjin,
      29 (1970), 118-21. [See item 691.]

697   Heney, Thomas. "On Some Australian Poems [1888]." In item 479, pp. 38-43.

698   Heseltine, H. P. "Australian Image: The Literary Heritage." Meanjin,
      21 (1962), 35-49.

699   ____   "The Australian Nineties: An Experiment in Critical Method." TEng,
      6 (1965), 17-32.

700   ____   "Brereton, the Bulletin and A. G. Stephens." ALS, 1 (1963), 16-31.

701   ____   "C. Hartley Grattan in Australia: Some Correspondence, 1937-1938."
      Meanjin, 29 (1970), 356-64. [With K. S. Prichard, Vance Palmer, Mary
      Gilmore, Miles Franklin.]

702   ____   "Deep Spring Rising--A Note on Modern Australian Poetry." Poetry
      Magazine, 4-5 (1964), 52-57.

703   ____   "Poetry Chronicle, 1962." Meanjin, (1962), 495-504.

704   ____   "Thoughts from an Ivory Tower." Dissent, 14 (1965), 36-39.

705   ____   "Towards an 'Inside Narrative': John Barnes' The Writer in Australia."
      Meanjin, 28 (1969), 541-49.

706   ____, ed. Australian Idiom: An Anthology of Contemporary Prose and
      Poetry. Melbourne: Cheshire, 1963; London: Angus & Robertson, 1964.

707   Heuzenroeder, John. "D. H. Lawrence's Australia." ALS, 4 (1970), 319-33.

708   ____   "Havelock Ellis's Australian Idyll." ALS, 3 (1967), 3-17.

709   Hewett, Dorothy. "The Writer in Australia." Westerly, 4 (1969), 69-74.

710   Hiener, W. and J. E. "Literary Composition on Board a Convict Ship: The
      Pestonjee Bomanjee Journal." ALS, 4 (1969), 164-69.

711   Higham, Charles. "The Fictionaries." Bulletin (Sydney), 25 Feb. 1967,
      pp. 17-20.

712   ____   "Letter from Sydney." HudR, 19 (1967), 645-52.

713   ____, ed. Australian Writing Today. Harmondsworth: Penguin, 1968.

714   Hill, R. "Assembling Evidence for Early Australian Pronunciation." EngA,
      8 (1968), 21-27.

715   ____   "Prospects of the Study of Early Australian Pronunciation." ES, 48
      (1967), 43-52.

716   Hiramatsu, Mikio. "A Japanese Approach to Australian Literature."
      Hemisphere, 11, no. 2 (1967), 7-10.

717   Hollis, Christopher. "Art et littérature en Australie." La Table Ronde,
      183 (1963), 100-04. [Trans. from English by Marcelle Sibon.]

718   Holroyd, John. George Robertson of Melbourne, 1825-1898: Pioneer
      Bookseller and Publisher. Melbourne: Robertson & Mullens, 1968.

719   Holt, Edgar. "Thunder Without Lightening." Southerly, 18 (1957), 182-85.

720   Hope, A. D. "Australian and Canadian Poetry." DR, 42 (1963), 99-102.

721   ____   Australian Literature, 1950-1962. Melbourne: Melbourne Univ. Press,
      1963.

722 ____ "English in England and Australia." Opinion, 10, no. 2 (1967),
    14-19.

723 ____ "H. M. Green: The Man and the Work." Meanjin, 20 (1961), 431-34.

724 ____ "The Literary Pattern in Australia." UTQ, 26 (1957), 122-32.

725 ____ "Meanjin Comes of Age." Landfall, 16 (1962), 376-80.

726 ____ "A Note on the Ballads." LCrit, 6, no. 3 (1964), 47-51. [Repr. in
    item 866, pp. 47-51.]

727 ____ "Payments for Poets." AustA, 1, no. 4 (1969), 7-9.

728 ____ "Perception and Poetry; or, the New Cratylus." Meanjin, 26 (1967),
    385-95.

729 ____ "T. Inglis Moore: A Pioneer in Australian Literary Studies."
    Meanjin, 26 (1967), 177-79.

730 Horne, C. J. "Australian Literature in the University Libraries of the
    United Kingdom: A Survey." AustU, 2, no. 2 (1964), 162-81.

731 Horner, J. C. "The Themes of Four Convict Novels." THRA, 15 (1967),
    18-32.

732 Hort, Greta. "The Australian Folksong and the Origin of the Folksong."
    REL, 6, no. 4 (1965), 81-99.

733 Howarth, R. G. "'The Great Australian Adjective.'" Southerly, 8 (1947),
    34-36.

734 ____ Literary Particles. Sydney and London: Angus & Robertson, 1946.

735 ____ Notes on Modern Poetic Technique, English and Australian. Sydney:
    Angus & Robertson, 1949.

736 Hunt, Hugh. The Making of Australian Theatre. Melbourne: Cheshire, 1960.

737 Ingamells, Rex. "Archives and Authors: Australians Form Commemorative
    Association." NZL, 16 (14 March 1947), 26-27.

738 ____ Conditional Culture. Commentary by Ian Tilbrook. Adelaide:
    F. W. Preece, 1938. [Repr. in item 467, pp. 245-65.]

739 ____ Handbook of Australian Literature. Melbourne: Jindyworobak, 1949.

740 Inglis, K. S. "The Anzac Tradition." Meanjin, 24 (1965), 25-54.

741 Irvin, Eric. "Australia's 'First' Dramatists." ALS, 4 (1969), 18-30.

742 ____ "Australia's First Hamlet." TC (Melbourne), 22 (1967), 56-67.

743 ____ "Drama Comes to Australia." Quadrant, 11, no. 1 (1967), 33-38.

744 ____ "From the London Theatres." TN, 22 (1968), 169-73.

745 ____ "Georgian Theatre in Sydney." Quadrant, 10, no. 4 (1966), 55-59.

746 ____ "Laura Keene and Edwin Booth in Australia." TN, 23 (1969), 95-100.

747 ____ "The Stage Discovers Australia." TC (Melbourne), 21 (1967), 170-75.

748 James, Brian. "Introduction" to Australian Short Stories, Second Series.
    London: Oxford Univ. Press, 1963, pp. ix-xv.

749 James, G. F. "Anthony Trollope in Australia." Age, 19 March 1966, p. 22.

750 Johnston, George. "Why Buy Books?" AustBR, 8 (1969), 241.

751 Johnston, Grahame, ed. Australian Literary Criticism. Melbourne: Oxford
    Univ. Press, 1962.

752 ____ "The Language of Australian Literature." ALS, 3 (1967), 18-27.

753 Jones, Evan. "The Poet in the University." AustA, 1, no. 4 (1969), 21-25.

754 Jones, Joseph and Johanna. Authors and Areas of Australia. Austin:
     Steck-Vaughn, 1970.

755 Jose, A. W. The Romantic Nineties. Sydney: Angus & Robertson, 1933.

756 Kardoss, John. "The Australian Theatre: Retrospect and Prospect."
     Quadrant, 1, no. 1 (1957), 77-81.

757 ____ A Brief History of the Australian Theatre. Sydney: Univ. Dramatic
     Society, 1954.

758 ____ Theatre Arts in Australia. Sydney: Wentworth, 1961.

759 Keesing, Nancy. "Australian Primitive Poets." Opinion, 9, no. 1 (1965),
     22-34.

760 ____ "Australia's 'Unlucky' Novelists: Some Considerations Upon Recent
     Fiction." Southerly, 22, no. 2 (1962), 84-89.

761 ____ "Out of Print--Out of Mind." Arts, 3 (1966), 18-36.

762 Kellow, Henry Arthur. Queensland Poets. London: Harrop, 1930.

763 Kelly, Gwen. "Some Modern Trends and Old Traditions in Australian
     Literature." Culture, 23 (1962), 266-80.

764 Kemeny, P. "Notes on the Development of Australian Fiction: III, IV,
     V." WATJ, 55 (1965), 14-15, 67-69, 110-12.

765 ____ "The Search for an Australian Conscience in Her Literature, Parts
     1 and 2." WATJ, 54 (1964), 281-82, 351-60.

766 Keneally, Thomas. "As If a Man Had Never Loved It." EngA, 2 (1967),
     5-11.

767 ____ "The Australian Novel." Age, 3 Feb. 1968, p. 22.

768 King, Alec. "Australian Poet and Settler--Tough or Sentimental."
     Westerly, 1 (1962), 93-96.

769 ____ "The Look of Australian Poetry in 1967." Meanjin, 27 (1968), 171-83.

770 ____, and Douglas Stewart. "Contemporary Australian Poetry, I [&] II."
     LCrit, 6, no. 3 (1964), 52-75. [Repr. in item 866, pp. 52-75.]

771 Kippax, H. G. "Introduction" to Three Australian Plays. Mitcham,
     Victoria: Penguin, 1963, pp. 7-21.

772 ____ "Australian Drama since Summer of the Seventeenth Doll." Meanjin,
     23 (1967), 229-42.

773 ____ "Drama." In A. F. Davies and S. Encel, eds. Australia, a Sociological
     Introduction. Melbourne: Cheshire, 1965, pp. 190-204.

774 ____ "A Kiss for Our Own Cinderella." Sydney Morning Herald, 1 Oct.
     1967, p. 12.

775 Kirby-Smith, Virginia. "The Need for Research in Theatre History."
     Meanjin, 23 (1964), 315-19.

776 Kirsop, Wallace. Towards a History of the Australian Book Trade. Sydney:
     Wentworth, 1969.

777 Kramer, Leonie. "The Australian Heritage." EngA, 5 (1967), 43-55.

778 ____ "The Australian Short Story." Opinion, 9, no. 1 (1965), 17-21.

779 ____ "The Context of Australian Literature." Arts, 6 (1969), 18-29.
     [Revised as "'Not Quite What the Age Supposes': Australian Literature
     in a University." In Nancy Keesing, ed. Transition. Sydney: Angus &
     Robertson, 1970, pp. 210-15.]

780 ____ "Heroes, Villains and Sacred Cows." Bulletin (Sydney), 24 Oct.
     1964, p. 51.

781 ____ "Literary Criticism in Australia." Overland, 26 (1963), 25-27.

782 ____ "Modern Australian Literature." Hemisphere, 14, no. 12 (1970), 8-11.

783 Laird, J. T. "Australian Poetry of the First World War: A Survey." ALS, 4 (1970), 241-50.

784 Lane, Richard. "Australian Writers' Guild." AustA, 1, no. 2 (1969), 21-24.

785 Lansbury, Coral. Arcady in Australia: The Evocation of Australia in Nineteenth-Century English Literature. Carlton: Melbourne Univ. Press, 1970.

786 ____ "Charles Dickens and His Australia." JRAHS, 52 (1966), 115-28.

787 ____ "The Miner's Right to Mateship." Meanjin, 25 (1967), 435-43.

788 Larkin, Phillip. "Look, no Kangaroos." AustL, 2, no. 1 (1959), 31-33.

789 Lavater, Louis. The Sonnet in Australasia: A Survey and Selection. Sydney: Angus & Robertson, 1956.

790 Lee, S. E. "Taken to Task." Southerly, 18 (1957), 222-28.

791 Levien, Harold. "Voice: From Ideas to Practice." Quadrant, 7, no. 2 (1963), 13-20.

792 Levis, Ken. "The Role of the Bulletin in Indigenous Short Story Writing During the Eighties and Nineties." Southerly, 11 (1950), 220-28.

793 Liljegren, Sven B. Aspects of Australia in Contemporary Literature. Uppsala: Lundequistka Bokhandeln, 1962.

794 Lindsay, Jack. "The Alienated Australian Intellectual." Meanjin, 22 (1963), 48-59.

795 ____ "Autobiographical." Meanjin, 23 (1964), 442-45.

796 ____ "On Native Grounds." Meanjin, 27 (1968), 503-08.

797 ____ The Roaring Twenties: Literary Life in Sydney, New South Wales in the Years 1921-1926. London: Bodley Head, 1960.

798 Lindsay, Norman. Bohemians of the Bulletin. Sydney: Angus & Robertson, 1965.

799 ____ "Have We Reached Maturity?" Age, 16 July 1967, p. 25.

800 ____ "Looking Back in Anger." Age, 9 July 1967, p. 21.

801 Long, Lionel, and G. K. Jenkin, eds. Favourite Australian Bush Songs. Hartboro, Pa.: Folklore Associates, 1964; Adelaide: Rigby, 1964; London: Angus & Robertson, 1965

802 Lynraven, N. S. "Canberra's Literary Associations." AustLJ, 14 (1965), 76-78.

803 Macartney, F. T. Australian Literary Essays. Sydney: Angus & Robertson, 1957.

804 ____ An Historical Outline of Australian Literature. Sydney: Angus & Robertson, 1951.

805 ____ "The Matilda Muddle." Meanjin, 26 (1967), 211-15.

806 Macartney, Keith. "Louis Esson and Australian Drama." Meanjin, 6 (1947), 93-96.

807 MacAulay, Robie. "A Local Habitation and a Name." AustL, 6, no. 1 (1963), 35-45.

808 McAuley, James. "Literature and the Academics." LCrit, 6, no. 3 (1964), 107-12. [Repr. in item 866, pp. 107-12.]

809 ____ The Personal Element in Australian Poetry. Sydney: Angus & Robertson, 1970.

810 ____ Poetry and Australian Culture. Canberra: Univ. College, 1955.

811 MacColum, Joe. "Theatre in Australia." Bridge, 1, no. 2 (1964), 30-34.

812 McCrae, George Gordon. "'The Golden Age of Australian Literature': 1860-70." Southerly, 5, no. 4 (1944), 39-46.

813 McCuaig, Ronald. "Australian Poets of the 'Sixties.'" Hemisphere, 9, no. 9 (1965), 28-31.

814 ____ "Contemporary Australian Literature." LitR, 7 (1963), 165-71.

815 ____ "Ern Malley and His Consequences." Hemisphere, 9 [8], no. 9 (1964), 2-6.

816 ____ "An Introduction to Australian Poetry." Hemisphere, 7, no. 5 (1963), 22-35.

817 McGregor, Craig, ed. In the Making. Melbourne: Nelson, 1969.

818 ____ Profile of Australia. Sydney: Hodder & Stoughton, 1966.

819 McGuire, Paul, F. M. McGuire, and B. P. Arnott. The Australian Theatre. London: Oxford Univ. Press, 1948.

820 MacKaness, George. "Australian Private Presses." ABC, 10, no. 6 (1960), 18-32.

821 ____ Bibliomania: A Book Collector's Essays. Sydney: Angus & Robertson, 1965.

822 MacKerras, Catherine. "Adelaide Festival." TC (Melbourne), 16 (1962), 347-53.

823 McLachlan, Noel. "Australian Image; 4) The View from London Bridge." Meanjin, 21 (1962), 469-76.

824 McLaren, John. "The Depression--and Beyond." Overland, 30 (1964), 54-55.

825 ____ "The Image of Reality in Our Writing." Overland, 27-28 (1963), 43-47.

826 McLeod, A. L., ed. Australia Speaks: An Anthology of Speeches. Sydney: Wentworth, 1969.

827 ____, ed. The Pattern of Australian Culture. Melbourne: Oxford Univ. Press, 1963. [Incl. Cecil Hadgraft, "Literature," pp. 42-101; Sidney J. Baker, "Language," pp. 102-30.]

828 ____, ed. Walt Whitman in Australia and New Zealand: A Record of His Reception. Sydney: Wentworth, 1964.

829 Madler, Peter. "Australian Literature." BA, 40 (1966), 280-81.

830 Mahood, Marguerite. "Melbourne Punch and Its Early Artists." La TrobeLJ, 1 (1969), 65-80.

831 Maidment, W. M. "A. G. Stephens and the Gympie Miner." Southerly, 24 (1964), 190-205.

832 ____ "Australian Literary Criticism." Southerly, 24 (1964), 40-41.

833 Manifold, John. "The Australian Literary Balladists etc." In Who Wrote the Ballads? Sydney: Australasian Book Soc., 1964, pp. 101-28.

834 ____ The Violin, the Banjo and the Bones: An Essay on the Instruments of Bush Music. Ferntree Gully, Victoria: Rams Skull, 1957.

835 ____ "Who Wrote the Ballads." Realist Writer, 12 (1963), 3-4.

836 Martin, Arthur Patchett. The Beginnings of Australian Literature. London: Sotheran, 1899.

837 Martin, David. "Among the Bones: What Are Our Novelists Looking For?"
     Meanjin, 18 (1959), 52-58.

838 Massola, Aldo. Bunjil's Cave: Myths, Legends, and Superstitions of the
     Aborigines of South-East Australia. Melbourne: Lansdowne, 1968.

839 Mathew, Ray. "Writing and Criticism." Southerly, 20 (1959), 159-64.

840 Matthews, John Pengwerne. Tradition in Exile: A Comparative Study of
     Social Influences on the Development of Australian and Canadian
     Poetry in the Nineteenth Century. Melbourne: Cheshire, 1962.

841 May, Frederick. "Australia's Banned Books." BANQ, 1, no. 3 (1966), 5-14.

842 May, Sydney. The Story of Waltzing Mathilda. Brisbane: Smith & Paterson,
     1944.

843 Mendelsohn, Oscar. A Waltz with Matilda. Melbourne: Lansdowne, 1966.

844 Meredith, John. "Study in Black and White." Quadrant, 4, no. 1 (1959-60),
     59-62.

845 ____, and Hugh Anderson. Folk Songs of Australia and the Men and Women
     Who Sang Them. Sydney: Ure Smith, 1967.

846 Miller, E. Morris. Pressmen and Governors: Australian Editors and
     Writers in Early Tasmania. Sydney: Angus & Robertson, 1952.

847 Milliss, Roger. "Theatre in the Lucky Country." AustLR, 6 (1967), 41-48.

848 Mitchell, A. G. "The Australian Accent." Quadrant, 3, no. 1 (1959), 63-70.

849 ____ "Australian English." Southerly, 1, no. 3 (1940), 11-13.

850 ____ "The English Language in Australia." LCrit, 6, no. 3 (1964), 126-40.
     [Repr. in item 866, pp. 126-40.]

851 Mohay, Bela. "The Character of Contemporary Australian Literature."
     Helikon (Budapest), 4 (1964), 391-99.

852 Moore, T. Inglis. "Australian Letter." Landfall, 11 (1957), 317-21.

853 ____ "Introduction" to Poetry in Australia. Vol. I. Sydney: Angus &
     Robertson, 1964, pp. xxi-xliii.

854 ____ "The Meanings of Mateship." Meanjin, 24 (1965), 45-54.

855 ____ Six Australian Poets. Melbourne: Robertson & Mullens, 1942.

856 Moore, William. The Story of Australian Art. 2 vols. Sydney: Angus &
     Robertson, 1934.

857 Morgan, Patrick. "The Misuse of Australian Literature." Quadrant, 11,
     no. 3 (1967), 23-33. [Supported by a letter from Christopher Koch.
     Quadrant, 11, no. 5 (1967), 65-68.]

858 Muirden, Bruce. The Puzzled Patriots: The Story of the Australian First
     Movement. Melbourne: Melbourne Univ. Press, 1968.

859 Murphy, Arthur. Contemporary Australian Poets. Adelaide: Marinyah Press,
     1950.

860 Murphy, Frank. "Theatre in Melbourne, 1966-1967." TC (Melbourne), 21
     (1967), 354-61.

861 Murphy, Mary E. "The Digger and the Swagman Write: A Survey of Australian
     Literature." QQ, 66 (1959), 260-67.

862 Murray-Smith, Stephen, ed. An 'Overland' Muster: Selections from
     'Overland,' 1954-1964. Brisbane: Jacaranda, 1967.

863 Musgrove, S. "The Flowering of New Holland." Landfall, 4 (1950), 324-31.

864 Nadel, G. Australia's Colonial Culture. Cambridge, Mass.: Harvard Univ.
     Press, 1957.

865 Narasimhaiah, C. D. "Australia: A Visitor's Impressions of the Land, Life, and Literature." LCrit, 6, no. 3 (1964), 141-59. [Repr. in item 866, pp. 141-59.]

866 ____, ed. An Introduction to Australian Literature. Brisbane, Jacaranda, 1965.

867 Neild, J. M. Literary Pioneers. Melbourne: Meehan, 1939.

868 Nesbitt, Bruce. "Early Australian Poetry and Its Bibliographers." ALS, 4 (1969), 169-72.

869 ____ "Literary Nationalism and the 1890's." ALS, 5 (1971), 3-17.

870 O'Brien, Dennis. "Endlessly Asking 'Who are We?'" Bulletin (Sydney), 24 Aug. 1968, pp. 33-34.

871 O'Dowd, Bernard Patrick. Poetry Militant: An Australian Plea for Poetry of Purpose. Melbourne: Lothian, 1909.

872 Officer, Maryjean. "Discovering Australia's Songs." TC (Melbourne), 19 (1964), 101-06.

873 O'Grady, Desmond. "Carboni After Eureka." Southerly, 29 (1969), 59-62.

874 O'Grady, John. Aussie English. Sydney: Ure Smith, 1965.

875 O'Neill, Lloyd. "The Psycho-Pathology of Australian Publishing." Quadrant, 14 [13], no. 2 (1969), 62-66.

876 Oppenheim, Helen. "The Author of The Hibernian Father: An Early Colonial Playwright." ALS, 2 (1966), 278-88.

877 ____ "Coppin--How Great? Alec Bagot's Father of the Australian Theatre." ALS; 3 (1967), 126-37.

878 Osborne, W. A. Essays and Literary Sketches. Melbourne: Lothian, 1943.

879 O'Shaughnessy, Peter. "Development of Theatre in Australia: A Survey, 1956-57." Meanjin, 17 (1958), 60-66.

880 ____, Graeme Inson, and Peter Ward. The Restless Years, Being Some Impressions of the Origin of the Australian. Brisbane: Jacaranda, 1968.

881 Page, Roger. Australian Bookselling. Melbourne: Hill of Content, 1970.

882 Palmer, Nettie. Modern Australian Literature (1900-1923). Melbourne: Lothian, 1924.

883 ____ Talking it Over. Sydney: Angus & Robertson, 1932.

884 Palmer, Vance. "Australian Letter." Landfall, 5 (1951), 292-95; 6 (1952), 317-21; 7 (1953), 279-81; 8 (1954), 294-97; 9 (1955), 334-38; 10 (1956), 327-30; 12 (1958), 355-59.

885 ____ "An Australian National Art [1905]." In item 479, pp. 168-70.

886 ____ Intimate Portraits and Other Pieces. Introd. by H. P. Heseltine. Melbourne: Cheshire, 1969.

887 ____ The Legend of the Nineties. Melbourne: Melbourne Univ. Press, 1955.

888 ____ Louis Esson and the Australian Theatre. Melbourne: Meanjin, 1948.

889 ____ National Portraits. Melbourne: Melbourne Univ. Press, 1940; rev. ed. 1954.

890 Parsons, Phillip. "Drama and the Australian University." Quadrant, 9, no. 5 (1965), 62-65.

891 ____ "The New Fortune Theatre and Dramatic Style." Meanjin, 23 (1964), 294-98.

892 Patane, Leonardo R. "Scrittori Coloniali Australiani." Narrativa, 3 (1958), 113-23.

893 Phillips, A. A. "Australian Image: The Literary Heritage Reassessed."
     Meanjin, 21 (1962), 172-80.

894 _____ The Australian Tradition: Studies in a Colonial Culture. Melbourne:
     Cheshire-Lansdowne; rev. ed. 1966.

895 _____ "Being with It." Overland, 38 (1968), 27-29.

896 _____ "Provincialism and Australian Culture." Meanjin, 25 (1967), 265-74.

897 _____ "Short Story Chronicle." Meanjin, 21 (1962), 510-13.

898 Piper, H. W. "Academic Criticism in Australia." In item 962, pp. 81-88.

899 _____ "The Background of Romantic Thought." Quadrant, 2, no. 1 (1957-58),
     49-55.

900 Porteous, Alexander. "The Sentimental Bloke and His Critics." ALS, 1
     (1964), 260-73. [On C. J. Dennis.]

901 _____ "Some Recent Australian Plays and Problems of Their Criticism."
     ALS, 3 (1967), 83-97.

902 Porter, Hal. "Melbourne in the Thirties." LMag, 5, no. 6 (1965), 31-47.

903 Porter, Kenneth W. "'Johnny Troy': A 'Lost' Australian Bushranger
     Ballad in the United States." Meanjin, 24 (1965), 227-38.

904 Powell, Craig. "Sales of Poetry Books." Australian, 8 May 1967, p. 8.

905 Pratt, Noel. "The Little Magazines." Australian, 6 May 1967, p. 6.

906 Price, A. Grenfell. "Aid to National Literature." Meanjin, 14 (1957),
     289-94.

907 _____, ed. The Humanities in Australia. Sydney: Angus & Robertson, 1959.

908 Prichard, Katharine Susannah. "Some Perceptions and Aspirations."
     Southerly, 28 (1968), 235-44.

909 _____ "Some Thoughts on Australian Literature." Realist, 15 (1964), 10-11.

910 Pringle, John Douglas. "Poetry in Australia." Lines Review, 20 (1963),
     40-44.

911 _____, ed. Australian Accent. London: Chatto & Windus, 1958.

912 Radic, Leonard. "Alive but Not in Good Shape." Age, 31 Dec. 1967, p. 19.

913 Ramson, W. S. "Australian Aboriginal Words in the O. E. D." N&Q, 11
     (1966), 69-70.

914 _____ "Australian and New Zealand English: The Present State of Studies."
     Kivung, 2, no. 1 (1969), 42-56.

915 _____ Australian English: An Historical Study of the Vocabulary 1788-1898.
     Canberra: Australian National Univ. Press, 1966.

916 _____ "A Critical Review of Writings on the Vocabulary of Australian
     English." ALS, 1 (1963), 89-103.

917 _____ "Early Australian English: The Vocabulary of an Emigrant Mechanic."
     Southerly, 25 (1965), 116-30.

918 _____ "Primary Sources for the Study of the Vocabulary of Nineteenth-
     Century Australian English." ALS, 1 (1964), 251-59.

919 Rankin, Donald Hamilton. The Development and Philosophy of Australian
     Aestheticism. Melbourne: D. H. Rankin, 1949.

920 Read, Stanley Arnold. Australian Literary Criticism, 1939-1964. Austin:
     Univ. of Texas, 1965.

921 Reed, A. W., ed. Myths and Legends of Australia. Sydney: Reed, 1965.

922 Rees, Leslie. "Australian Drama: The Outlook in 1967." Overland, 37 (1967), 39-44.

923 ____ "Radio and Television Drama." Meanjin, 23 (1964), 259-65.

924 ____ "Theatre Australia: Drama Export." Masque 1, no. 3 (1968), 32-34.

925 ____ Towards an Australian Drama. Sydney: Angus & Robertson, 1953.

926 Reid, Ian. "The Australian City Novel." Quadrant, 14, no. 5 (1970), 26-31.

927 Rhodes, H. Winston. "Australian and New Zealand Literature." Meanjin, 27 (1969), 184-93.

928 Richardson, B. E. "The Aborigine in Fiction: A Survey of Attitudes since 1900." ADHSJP, 12 (1970), 1-13.

929 Rienits, Rex and Thea. Early Artists of Australia. Sydney: Angus & Robertson, 1963.

930 Rivett, Rohan. Writing About Australia. Sydney: Angus & Robertson, 1969.

931 Robinson, Roland, ed. Aboriginal Myths and Legends. Melbourne: Sun Books, 1966.

932 Rodd, L. C., ed. The Australian Essay. Introd. by Kylie Tennant. Melbourne: Cheshire, 1968.

933 Roderick, Colin. "Australian Literature; Some European Influences on Australian Literature." Expression, 3, no. 4 (1968), 3-9.

934 ____ The Australian Novel. Introd. by Miles Franklin. Sydney: Brooks, 1945.

935 ____ A Companion to Speaking Personally with an Appendix on the Essay in Australia. Sydney: Brooks, 1945.

936 ____ An Introduction to Australian Fiction. Sydney: Angus & Robertson, 1950.

937 ____ Suckled by a Wolf, or the Nature of Australian Literature. Sydney: Angus & Robertson, 1968.

938 ____ Twenty Australian Novelists. Sydney: Angus & Robertson, 1947.

939 Roe, Jill. "Historiography in Melbourne in the Eighteen Seventies and Eighties." ALS, 4 (1969), 130-38.

940 Roe, Michael. A History of the Theatre Royal, Hobart. Hobart: Law Soc. of Tasmania, 1965.

941 Rolls, Eric C. "What Are Poets For?" Poetry Magazine, 4 (1965), 3-8.

942 Ronan, Tom. Once There was a Bagman: A Memoir. Melbourne: Cassell, 1966.

943 ____ "The Other Bill Harney." Overland, 26 (1963), 29.

944 Rorabacher, Louis, ed. Aliens in Their Land: The Aborigine in the Australian Short Story. Melbourne: Cheshire, 1968.

945 Ross, E. "Literature and the Trade Unions." Realist, 14 (1964), 28-31.

946 Routh, S. J. "The Australian Career of John Lang, Novelist." ALS, 1 (1964), 206-07.

947 Rowbotham, David. "Poetry and Place--A Word for 'Nature' Poetry in 'Intellectual' Times." Makar, 20 (1964), 36-40.

948 Ruskin, Pamela. "Pages Turned by Children." Walkabout, 22, no. 12 (1967), 61-64.

949 Ryan, J. S. "The Evolution of Australian Fiction." LCrit, 6, no. 3 (1964), 38-46. [Repr. in item 866, pp. 38-46.]

950 ____ "Isolation and Generation Within a Conservative Framework: A Unique Dialectal Situation for English." Orbis, 15 (1966), 35-50.

951 ____ "Ned Kelly: The Flight of the Legend." ALS, 3 (1967), 98-115.

952 Saxby, H. M. A History of Australian Children's Literature, 1841-1941. Sydney: Wentworth, 1969.

953 ____, and Marjorie Cotton. A History of Australian Children's Literature, 1941-1970. Sydney: Wentworth, 1971.

954 Sayers, Stuart. "Writers and Readers." Age, 2 Nov. 1968, 10.

955 Schulz, Joachim. Geschichte der australischen Literatur. München: Huber, 1960.

956 Selby, Barbara. "Drama in Sydney." AustQ, 31, no. 3 (1959), 118-24.

957 Semmler, Clement. "Australian Poetry of the 1960's: Some Personal Impressions." Poetry Australia, 35 (1970), 44-52.

958 ____ "The Australian Short Story." Education Gazette, 62 (1968), 132-37.

959 ____ "The Australian Short Story." Hemisphere, 11, no. 8 (1967), 8-13.

960 ____ "Some Notes on the Literature of the Shearers' Strikes of 1891 and 1894." AustQ, 41, no. 4 (1969), 75-87.

961 ____, ed. Twentieth Century Australian Literary Criticism. Melbourne: Oxford Univ. Press, 1967.

962 ____, and Derek Whitelock, eds. Literary Australia. Melbourne: Cheshire, 1966.

963 Serle, Geoffrey. "The Digger Tradition and Australian Nationalism." Meanjin, 24 (1965), 149-58.

964 Seymour, Alan. "Who Has Disregarded Whom?" Masque, 1, no. 6 (1969), 26-27.

965 Shapcott, Thomas W. "Poetry in Queensland." Poetry Australia, 4 (1965), 5-6.

966 Sharwood, John, and Stanley Gerson. "The Vocabulary of Australian English." Moderna Språk, 57 (1963), 1-10.

967 ____, and Horton Ivor. "Phoneme Frequencies in Australian English: A Regional Study." AUMLA, 26 (1966), 272-302.

968 Simpson, R. A. "The Bulletin Poets." Bulletin (Sydney), 27 Feb. 1965, pp. 44-45.

969 Sinett, Frederick. The Fiction Fields of Australia. Ed. Cecil Hadgraft from the 1856 edition. St. Lucia: Univ. of Queensland Press, 1966. [Also repr. in item 479, pp. 8-32.]

970 Singer, Richard. "A Forgotten Poet--Or Two." Southerly, 21, no. 2 (1961), 2-10.

971 Slessor, Kenneth. "The Anatomy of Anecdote." Etruscan, 13 (June 1964), 16-18.

972 ____ "Australian Literature." Southerly, 6, no. 1 (1945), 31-35.

973 ____ "Poetry in Australia." Southerly, 26 (1966), 190-98.

974 Smith, B. J. "Early Western Australian Literature: A Guide to Colonial Life." USH, 4, no. 1 (1965), 24-100.

975 ____ "Western Australian Gold Fields Literature." USH, 4, no. 2 (1965), 81-155.

976   Smith, Bernard. European Vision and the South Pacific 1768-1850. London: Oxford Univ. Press, 1960.

977   Smith, Jeffrey. "Australia's Stampede of Animal Books." Airways, 34 (1968), 10-13.

978   Smith, Terry. "The 'Style of the Sixties.'" Quadrant, 14 [13], no. 2 (1969), 49-53.

979   Smith, Vivian. "Australian Poetry in the '60's: Some Mid-Century Notes." Balcony, 4 (1967), 46-51.

980   ____ "Poetic Richness." Bulletin (Sydney), 31 Dec. 1967, pp. 27-28.

981   Smithyman, Kendrick. "'The Ram of Albury.'" ALS, 4 (1969), 178-80.

982   Spencer, A. H. The Hill of Content: Books, Art, Music, People. Sydney: Angus & Robertson, 1959.

983   Sprott, S. E. "Amateur Poets in Australia." DR, 39 (1959), 393-405.

984   Stanley, Raymond. "Theatre Royal Hobart: Australia's Oldest Theatre." TN, 15 (1961), 89-92.

985   Steele, Peter, S. J. "Recent Poetry." Meanjin, 23 (1964), 439-41.

986   Stephens, A. G. Evenings with Australian Authors. Sydney: n. p., 1914.

987   ____ "Introduction to The Bulletin Story Book [1901]." In item 479, pp. 106-10.

988   ____ The Red Pagan. Sydney: Bulletin, 1904.

989   Stephensen, Percival Reginald. The Foundations of Culture in Australia: An Essay Towards National Self-Respect. Gordon, N. S. W.: Miles, 1936. [Repr. in item 479, pp. 204-44.]

990   Stern, Maida. "Drama in Adelaide." AustQ, 21, no. 3 (1959), 124-25.

991   Stewart, Douglas. "'Bellerive': Australia's Worst Poet." TQ, 5, no. 2 (1962), 104-09.

992   ____ The Flesh and the Spirit: An Outlook on Literature. Sydney: Angus & Robertson, 1948.

993   ____ "Introduction" to Poetry in Australia, Vol. II. Sydney: Angus & Robertson, 1964, pp. xxi-xxxv.

994   ____, and Nancy Keesing, eds. Bush Songs, Ballads, and Other Verse. Penrith, N. S. W.: Discovery Press, 1968.

995   Stivens, Dal. "Landscape in Australian Literature." Westerly, 3 (1964), 46-49.

996   ____ "Myth of the Songless Bird." Canberra Times, 16 April 1966, p. 9.

997   Store, R. "North Queensland's Literature, Part I." Islands Review, 1, no. 3 (1968), 9-13.

998   ____ "The Teacher in Australian Literature." QTJ, 73 (1969), 392-98.

999   Stow, Randolph. "Foreword." Poetry Australia, 12 (1967), 4-5.

1000 ____ "Our Children in Cole Land." AustL, 1, no. 3 (1958), 14-22.

1001 ____ "Wrap Me Up with My Portable Gramophone." AustL, 2, no. 1 (1959), 5-13.

1002 Strehlow, Theodor George Henry. An Australian Viewpoint. Sydney: Hawthorne, 1952.

1003 Strugnell, John. ". . . No Truth in Islands." AustL, 3, no. 1 (1960), 19-23

1004 Sutherland, A. Bruce. "An American Commentary." In item 962, pp. 161-64.

1005 Swan, Geoffrey. "Australian Literature in Education." QTJ, 71 (1967), 165-66.

1006 Taft, R. "The Pattern of Australian Culture." Westerly, 1 (1964), 71-73.

1007 Talbot, Norman, ed. XI Hunter Valley Poets + VII. Maitland: Maitland Mercury, 1966.

1008 Taylor, Andrew. "What's Stories For?" Dissent, 3, no. 3 (1963), 29-31.

1009 Taylor, George A. "Those Were the Days," Being Reminiscences of Australian Artists and Writers. Sydney: Tyrell, 1918.

1010 Tennant, Kylie. "Australian Literature Today." Opinion, 7 (1963), 32-39.

1011 ____ The Development of the Australian Novel. Canberra: Canberra Univ. College, 1959.

1012 ____ "Fiction Chronicle." Meanjin, 21 (1962), 505-09.

1013 ____ "[Letter to the Editor]." Bulletin (Sydney), 22 Jan. 1966, p. 25.

1014 Thiele, Colin. "Australian Verse Today." Opinion, 7 (1963), 6-10.

1015 Thompson, John. "Broadcasting and Australian Literature." In item 962, pp. 89-116.

1016 ____ "On Becoming Unprovincial." Southerly, 19 (1958), 42-44.

1017 Tolchard, Clifford. "D. H. Lawrence in Australia." Walkabout, 33, no. 11 (1967), 28-31.

1018 Tregenza, John. "Australian Literary Magazines of the Last Three Decades. . . ." AustL, 1, no. 1 (1957), 8-12; 2, no. 1 (1957), 28-30.

1019 Triebel, L. A. "Australia's Image in the Literature of the West." THRA, 17 (1969), 29-36. [Repr. in Australian Teacher, 45, no. 2 (1969), 26-32.]

1020 ____ "Some Factors of Australian Literature in the Making." TasE, 19, no. 1 (1968), 10-19.

1021 Turnbull, Clive. Australian Lives. Melbourne: Cheshire, 1965.

1022 Turner, G. W. The English Language in Australia and New Zealand. London: Longmans, 1966.

1023 ____ "The Urban Basis of Australian English." Opinion, 9, no. 3 (1965), 20-24.

1024 Turner, Henry Gyles, and Alexander Sutherland. The Development of Australian Literature. Melbourne: Robertson, 1898.

1025 Turner, Ian. "Ten Years of Australian Folklore." AustT, 3, no. 1 (1967), 7-8; 3, no. 2 (1967), 19-20.

1026 ____, ed. The Australian Dream. Melbourne: Sun Books, 1968.

1027 ____, ed. Cinderella Dressed in Yella. Melbourne: Heinemann Educational, 1969. ["The Play Rhymes of Australian Children," pp. 127-44.]

1028 ____ "Ten Years of Australian Folklore." AustT, 3, no. 1 (1967), 7-8; 3, no. 2 (1967), 19-20.

1029 Vallis, Val. "Artist and Environment: An Australian Study." BJA, 2 (1962), 328-36.

1030 ____ "The Literary Associations of Queensland." AustLJ, 16 (1967), 108-10.

1031 Wain, John. "The Outside View." AustL, 2, no. 1 (1957), 9-14.

1032 Walker, William. Australian Literature. Sydney: Reading & Wellbank, 1864.

1033 Wallace-Crabbe, Christopher. "Australian Poetry Chronicle, 1960." MCR, 4 (1961), 112-20.

1034 _____ "The Habit of Irony: Australian Poets of the 'Fifties." Meanjin, 20 (1961), 164-74.

1035 _____ "Intellectuals in Australian Literature." Dissent, 21 (1967), 9-13.

1036 Wannan, Bill, ed. The Heather in the South: Lore, Literature and Balladry of the Scots in Australia. Melbourne: Lansdowne, 1967.

1037 _____, ed. My Kind of Country, Yarns, Ballads, Legends and Traditions. Adelaide: Rigby, 1967.

1038 _____, ed. The Wearing of the Green: The Lore, Literature, Legend and Balladry of the Irish in Australia. Melbourne: Lansdowne, 1965.

1039 Ward, Peter. "Theatre in Adelaide, 1920-1960." AustL, 2, no. 4 (1960), 98-102.

1040 Ward, Robert. "Underground Poetry." AustBR, 8 (1969), 112-13.

1041 Ward, Russell. The Australian Legend. Melbourne: Oxford Univ. Press, 1966.

1042 _____ "Colonialism and Culture." LCrit, 6, no. 3 (1964), 21-27. [Repr. in item 866, pp. 21-27.]

1043 _____ "Folk Song and Ballad." AustT, 21 (1969), 20-25.

1044 Waten, Judah. "Australian Literature in 1962." Realist Writer, 12 (1963), 26-28.

1045 Waters, Edgar. "Song Notes." AustT, 3, no. 1 (1967), 9.

1046 _____ "Two Australian Folklore Journals." ALS, 1 (Dec. 1963), 137.

1047 Webby, Elizabeth. "Australian Literature and the Reading Public in the 1820's." Southerly, 29 (1969), 17-42.

1048 _____ "English Literature in Early Australia, 1820-29." Southerly, 27 (1967), 266-85.

1049 Weiner, Albert B. "The Hibernian Father: The Mystery Solved." Meanjin, 25 (1966), 456-64.

1050 Wighton, Rosemary. Early Australian Children's Literature. Melbourne: Lansdowne, 1963.

1051 Wilding, Michael. "Write Australian." JCL, 6, no. 1 (1971), 19-30.

1052 Wilkes, G. A. "Australian Literature." In G. A. Wilkes and J. C. Reid, The Literature of Australia and New Zealand. University Park and London: Penn. State Univ. Press, 1970, pp. 29-153.

1053 _____ Australian Literature: A Conspectus. Sydney: Angus & Robertson, 1969.

1054 _____ "The Development of Australian Literature." LCrit, 6, no. 3 (1964), 28-37. [Repr. in item 866, pp. 28-37.]

1055 _____ "The Emergence of the Australian Novel." Hemisphere, 9, no. 4 (1965), 22-24.

1056 _____ The University and Australian Literature. Sydney: Angus & Robertson, 1964.

1057 Wilson, Gwendoline. "Anna Maria Murray, Authoress of The Guardian." ALS, 3 (1967), 148-49.

1058 Wood, W. A. "Scholarly Publishing in Australia." SchP, 1 (1969), 99-106.

1059 Wright, David. "Commonwealth Poetry." Encounter, 39 (Dec. 1956), 78.

1060 Wright, Judith. "Australia's Double Aspect." LCrit, 6, no. 3 (1964),
    1-11. [Repr. in item 866, pp. 1-11.]

1061 ____ "Australian Letter." Landfall, 20 (1966), 367-81.

1062 ____ "Inheritance and Discovery in Australian Poetry." Poetry Magazine,
    5 (1965), 3-11. [Also in item 962, pp. 1-15.]

1063 ____ "Introduction" to A Book of Australian Verse. 2nd ed. Melbourne:
    Oxford Univ. Press, 1968, pp. 1-11.

1064 ____ "Poetry as a Bridge Between People." Hemisphere, 11, no. 3 (1967),
    14-19.

1065 ____ "Poets and Anthologies." Broadside, 3 (1967), 9-10.

1066 ____ Preoccupations in Australian Poetry. Melbourne: Oxford Univ.
    Press, 1965.

1067 ____ "The Role of Poetry in Education." EngA, (1966), 35-43. [See also
    pp. 61-64.]

1068 ____ "The Upside-Down Hut." AustL, 3, no. 4 (1961), 30-34. [Repr. in
    item 479, pp. 331-36.]

1069 ____, and John Thompson. "Poetry in Australia." Southerly, 27 (1967),
    35-44.

See Also: 53, 54, 3934, 6102-6127.

Individual Authors

ASTLEY, Thea

1070 Astley, Thea. "The Idiot Question." Southerly, 30 (1970), 3-8.

1071 Couper, J. M. "The Novels of Thea Astley." Meanjin, 26 (1967), 332-37.

1072 Drewe, Robert. "Profile of a Prize Novelist." Age, 28 May 1967, p. 22.

BAYNTON, Barbara

1073 Gullett, H. B. "Memoir of Barbara Baynton." In Barbara Baynton, Bush
    Studies. Sydney: Angus & Robertson, 1965, pp. 1-27.

1074 Lindsay, Jack. "Barbara Baynton, a Master of Naturalism." Meanjin, 25
    (1966), 345-48.

1075 Palmer, Vance. "[Barbara Baynton]." In item 886, pp. 83-87.

1076 Phillips, A. A. "Barbara Baynton and the Dissidence of the Nineties."
    In item 862, pp. 178-90. [Repr. from Overland, 22 (1961-62), 15-20.]

1077 ____ "Barbara Baynton's Stories." In Barbara Baynton, Bush Studies.
    Sydney: Angus & Robertson, 1965, pp. 27-45.

BEAVER, Bruce

1078 Fitzgerald, R. D. "Bruce Beaver's Poetry." Meanjin, 28 (1969),
    407-12.

1079 Powell, Craig. "The Gift-Bearing Hands: The Poetry of Bruce Beaver."
    Quadrant, 12, no. 5 (1968), 13-18.

1080   Tulip, James. "The Australia-American Connexion." Poetry Australia, 32 (1970), 48-49.

BECKE, Louis

1081   Day, A. Grove. "By Reef and Tide: Louis Becke's Literary Reputation." AustL, 6, no. 1 (1963), 17-26.

1082   _____ Louis Becke. New York: Twayne, 1966.

1083   _____ "Louis Becke's First Appearance in Print." BANQ, 1, no. 1 (1966), 19-20.

See also: 1086.

BOLDREWOOD, Rolf [T. A. Browne]

1084   Burke, Keast. Thomas Alexander Browne (Rolf Boldrewood): An Annotated Bibliography, Checklist and Chronology. (Studies in Australian Bibliography, 5.) Cremorne, N. S. W.: Stone Copying Co., 1956.

1085   Dowsley, G. "Robbery Under Arms: A Re-Assessment." TasE, 2 (1968), 73-77.

1086   Earnshaw, John. "South Seas Fact and Fiction." BANQ, 1, no. 2 (1967), 21-22.

1087   Hamer, Clive. "Rolf Boldrewood Reassessed." Southerly, 26 (1967), 263-78.

1088   Howarth, R. G. "Robbery Under Arms." Southerly, 6, no. 2 (1945), 21.

1089   Kettler, Ned. "My Colonial Oath." Realist, 31 (1968), 6-11.

1090   Middleton, D. E. J. "Villain or Hero? The Bushranger in Ralph Rashleigh, Robbery Under Arms, and The Hero of Too." ADHSJP, 12 (1970), 87-96.

1091   Moore, T. Inglis. Rolf Boldrewood. Melbourne: Melbourne Univ. Press, 1968.

1092   Ryan, J. S. "Rolf Boldrewood in Armidale." ADHSJP, 12 (1970), 27-36.

1093   Walker, R. B. "Another Look at the Lambing Flat Riots, 1860-1861." JRAHS, 56 (1970), 193-205.

1094   _____ "The Historical Basis of Robbery Under Arms." ALS, 2 (1965), 3-14.

1095   _____ "History and Fiction in Rolf Boldrewood's The Miner's Right." ALS, 3 (1967), 28-40.

1096   Wood, Thomas. "Introduction" to Rolf Boldrewood, Robbery Under Arms. London: Oxford Univ. Press, 1949, pp. v-xv.

BOYD, Martin [pseud. Martin Mills]

1097   Boyd, Martin. A Single Flame. London: Dent, 1939.

1098   _____ Day of My Delight. Melbourne: Lansdowne, 1965.

1099   _____ "Dubious Cartography." Meanjin, 23 (1964), 5-13.

1100   _____ "Preoccupations and Intentions." Southerly, 28 (1968), 83-90.

1101   _____ "Why I Am Expatriate." Bulletin (Sydney), 10 May 1961, 12-13.

1102   Bradley, Anthony. "The Structure of Ideas Underlying Martin Boyd's Fiction." Meanjin, 28 (1969), 177-83.

1103   Cantrell, Kerin. "Displaced Person." Southerly, 28 (1968), 141-44.

1104   Elliott, Brian. "Martin Boyd: An Appreciation." Meanjin, 16 (1957), 15-22.

1105 Fitzpatrick, Kathleen. "A Commentary." Meanjin, 23 (1964), 14-17.

1106 ____ Martin Boyd. Melbourne: Lansdowne, 1963.

1107 ____ Martin Boyd and the Complex Fate of the Australian Novelist. Canberra: Australian National Univ., 1953.

1108 French, A. L. "Martin Boyd: An Appraisal." Southerly, 26 (1966), 219-34.

1109 Green, Dorothy. "'The Fragrance of Souls': A Study of Lucinda Brayford." Southerly, 28 (1968), 110-26.

1110 Herring, Thelma. "Martin Boyd and the Critics: A Rejoinder to A. L. French." Southerly, 28 (1968), 127-40.

1111 Kramer, Leonie. "Martin Boyd." AustQ, 35, no. 2 (1963), 32-38.

1112 ____ "The Seriousness of Martin Boyd." Southerly, 28 (1968), 91-109.

1113 Marsh, Ida. "Martin Boyd." Realist, 20 (1965), 8-11.

1114 Neate, Anthony. "An Australian Novel in Form V." TEng, 9 (1967), 33-38.

1115 Niall, Brenda. "The Double Alienation of Martin Boyd." TC (Melbourne), 17 (1963), 197-206. [Reply by Boyd, vol. 18, pp. 73-74; reply by Niall, pp. 74-75.]

1116 O'Grady, Desmond. "Writer Between Two Worlds." Age, 20 Nov. 1965, p. 21.

1117 Phillip, Franz. Arthur Boyd. London: Thames & Hudson, 1967, pp. 19-26, 52-56.

1118 Ruskin, Pamela. "Those Brilliant Boyds." Walkabout, 35, no. 2 (1969), 20-23.

1119 Wallace, F. "The Craft of Martin Boyd." TC (Melbourne), 24 (1970), 336-42.

1120 Wallace-Crabbe, Christopher. "Martin Boyd and The Cardboard Crown." MCR, 3 (1960), 23-30.

1121 Wilkes, G. A. "The Achievement of Martin Boyd." Southerly, 19 (1958), 90-98.

See also: 6128.

BRENNAN, Christopher

1122 Andraud, Robert. "Christopher Brennan (1870-1932)." RAA, 12 (Dec. 1934), 117-23.

1123 Anon. "The Blank Verse of the 'Wanderer.'" Southerly, 5, no. 1 (1944), 16-17.

1124 Bavinton, Anne. "The Darkness of Brennan's 'Lilith.'" Meanjin, 23 (1964), 63-69.

1125 Braham, Noni. "Christopher Brennan's Prose." TC (Melbourne), 17, no. 3 (1963), 215-24.

1126 Chaplin, Harry F. A Brennan Collection: An Annotated Catalogue of First Editions, Inscribed Copies, Letters, Manuscripts and Association Items. (Studies in Australian Bibliography, 15.) Sydney: Wentworth, 1966.

1127 Chicoteau, Marcel. "Poems in French by Chris Brennan." Southerly, 19 (1958), 84-86.

1128 Chisholm, A. R. "Brennan and Mallarmé." Southerly, 21, no. 4 (1961), 2-11; 22, no. 1 (1962), 23-35.

1129 ____ "The Brennan I Remember." Quadrant, 1, no. 3 (1957), 79-82.

1130 _____ "Brennan, the Sea and the Seasons." Meanjin, 25 (1965), 192-95.

1131 _____ "Brennan's Poetry." Southerly, 10 (1949), 195-206.

1132 _____ "Christopher Brennan and the Idea of Eden." Meanjin, 26 (1967), 153-60.

1133 _____ Christopher Brennan: The Man and His Poetry. Sydney: Angus & Robertson, 1946.

1134 _____ "Christopher Brennan: Poet and Scholar." Meanjin, 29 (1970), 277-80.

1135 _____ "The Collected Edition of Brennan." Southerly, 18 (1957), 122-24.

1136 _____ "Introduction" to Christopher Brennan, Selected Poems. Sydney: Angus & Robertson; San Francisco: Tri-Ocean, 1966, pp. v-viii.

1137 _____ "Some Addenda for Brennan's Biography." Meanjin, 29 (1970), 511-15.

1138 _____ A Study of Christopher Brennan's "The Forest of Night." Carlton: Melbourne Univ. Press, 1970.

1139 _____, and J. J. Quinn, eds. The Prose of Christopher Brennan. Sydney: Angus & Robertson, 1962.

1140 Clarke, Margaret. "The Symbolism of Brennan and Mallarmé: A Comparison." Southerly, 4 (1949), 219-26.

1141 Coll, S. "C. B. in a Girls' School." BANQ, 1, no. 2 (1967), 13-15.

1142 Denat, A. "Christopher Brennan: Comparatiste Australien." RLC, 38 (1964), 431-39.

1143 Edmunds, Rosina. "Christopher Brennan, Poet." TC (Melbourne), 9 (1954), 44-52.

1144 French, A. L. "The Verse of C. J. Brennan." Southerly, 24 (1964), 6-19.

1145 Frost, Alan. "Brennan's 'Grand Oeuvre.'" Makar, 18 (1964), 18-23.

1146 Green, H. M. Christopher Brennan: Two Popular Lectures. Sydney: Angus & Robertson, 1939.

1147 Haley, Martin. "C. J. Brennan as Prose-Writer." Advocate, 31 Jan. 1963, p. 17.

1148 Heseltine, H. P. "The Australian Nineties: An Experiment in Critical Method." TEng, 6 (1965), 17-32.

1149 Howarth, R. G. "Chris Brennan." Southerly, 12 (1951), 228-31.

1150 _____ "Personalia." Southerly, 10 (1949), 209-18.

1151 _____ "Style and Form." Southerly, 10 (1949), 230-32.

1152 Hughes, Randolph W. C. J. Brennan: An Essay in Values. Sydney: P. R. Stephensen, 1934.

1153 _____ "C. J. Brennan: Unpublished Work and Further Discussion." AustQ, 19, no. 2 (1947), 27-39.

1154 _____ The Premier Poet of Australia: C. J. Brennan. London: Poetry Soc., 1939.

1155 Kermode, Frank, and M. Bryn Davies. "The European View of Christopher Brennan." AustL, 3, no. 3 (1961), 57-63.

1156 King, Alec. "Thoughts on the Poetry of Brennan." Westerly, 3 (1961), 3-6.

1157 Kirsop, Wallace. "Brennan, Critic and Scholar." Southerly, 23 (1963), 203-10.

1158 _____ "'The Greatest Renewal, the Greatest Revelation': Brennan's Commentary on Mallarmé." Meanjin, 29 (1970), 303-11.

1159 Letters, F. J. H. "Brennan's 'Unknown Ode.'" Southerly, 18 (1957), 143-44.

1160 Macainsh, Noel. "Brennan and Nietzsche." Southerly, 26 (1967), 259-61.

1161 _____ "Christopher Brennan and 'Die Romantick.'" Southerly, 23 (1963), 150-63.

1162 Macartney, F. T. "Ipsissima Verba: Brennan's Lectures on Comparative Literature." Southerly, 4 (1949), 183-92. [Transcribed by T. Inglis Moore.]

1163 _____ "Stephens on Brennan." Southerly, 10 (1949), 227-29.

1164 McAuley, James. Christopher Brennan. Melbourne: Lansdowne, 1963.

1165 _____ "The Erotic Theme in Brennan." Quadrant, 12, no. 6 (1968), 8-15.

1166 _____ "Homage to Chris Brennan." Southerly, 18 (1957), 135-42.

1167 Martin, David. "Neither So Great, Nor So Small." In item 862, pp. 156-61.

1168 Merewether, Mary. "The Burden of Tyre and Brennan's Poems (1913)." Southerly, 30 (1970), 267-84.

1169 Pennington, Richard. Christopher Brennan: Some Recollections. Sydney: Angus & Robertson, 1970.

1170 Philip, George Blackmore. Sixty Years Recollections and Impressions of a Bookseller: Christopher Brennan. Sydney: George B. Philip, 1939.

1171 Rhodes, H. Winston. "Christopher Brennan." Landfall, 18 (1964), 338-48.

1172 Roderick, Colin. "The Wanderer of the Ways of All the World: A Portrait of Christopher Brennan." AustQ, 23, no. 1 (1951), 67-80.

1173 Schulz, Joachim. "Christopher John Brennan." WuW, 16 (1961), 6-7.

1174 Scott, Robert Ian. "Christopher Brennan's 1913 Poems." Southerly, 18 (1957), 125-34.

1175 Smith, Sybille. "Brennan's Stature as a Critic." Quadrant, 7, no. 1 (1963), 65-70.

1176 Smith, Vivian. "Brennan for a New Generation." Quadrant, 5, no. 2 (1961), 9-15.

1177 _____ "Christopher Brennan and Arthur Symons." Southerly, 27 (1967), 219-22.

1178 Stephens, A. G. "Chris Brennan." In item 479, pp. 131-57.

1179 _____ Chris Brennan: A Monograph. Sydney: Bookfellow, 1933.

1180 Stewart, Annette. "Christopher Brennan: The Disunity of Poems 1913." Meanjin, 29 (1970), 281-302.

1181 Stone, Walter, and Hugh Anderson. Christopher John Brennan: A Comprehensive Bibliography with Annotations. Sydney: Stone Copying Co., 1959.

1182 Sturm, Terry L. "The Social Context of Brennan's Thought." Southerly, 28 (1968), 250-71.

1183 Wilkes, G. A. "The Art of Brennan's Towards the Source." Southerly, 21, no. 2 (1961), 28-40.

1184 _____ "Brennan and His Literary Affinities." AustQ, 31, no. 2 (1959), 72-84.

1185 _____ "Brennan's Collected Prose." Meanjin, 22 (1963), 80-84.

1186 _____ "Brennan's Collected Verse." Meanjin, 19 (1960), 367-79.

1187 _____ "Brennan's The Wanderer: A Progressive Romanticism?" Southerly, 30 (1970), 252-63.

1188 _____ "Christopher Brennan." In item 587, pp. 306-17.

1189 _____ "The Interpretation of The Burden of Tyre." Meanjin, 19 (1960), 71-77.

1190 _____ "New Perspectives on Brennan's Poetry." Southerly, 12 [13] (1952), 10-21, 86-96, 138-49, 203-14; 14 (1953), 160-71.

1191 _____ "The Uncollected Verse of C. J. Brennan." Southerly, 23 (1967), 164-202.

1192 _____ "The 'Wisdom' Sequence in Brennan's Poems." AUMLA, 14 (1960), 47-51.

1193 _____ "The Writings of C. J. Brennan: A Checklist." Meanjin, 15 (1956), 185-95.

1194 Wright, Judith. "Christopher Brennan." In item 1066, pp. 80-97.

1195 _____ "Christopher Brennan." Southerly, 30 (1970), 243-51.

1196 _____ "The Verse of Christopher Brennan." Geste, 6, no. 5 (1961), 38-41.

See also: 479, 1982, 6129-6131.

BUCKLEY, Vincent

1197 Buckley, Vincent. "Remembering What You Have To." Quadrant, 12, no. 5 (1968), 19-27.

1198 _____ "The Image of Man in Australian Poetry." In item 479, pp. 273-96.

1199 Curtis, Penelope. "Vincent Buckley as Poet." Quadrant, 6, no. 4 (1962), 55-66.

1200 Douglas, Dennis, et al. "Vincent Buckley's 'Stroke': A Discussion." ALS, 4 (1969), 139-47.

1201 Rosenbloom, Henry. "An Interview with Vincent Buckley." Meanjin, 28 (1969), 317-25.

1202 Steele, Peter, S. J. "Vincent Buckley as Critic." Meanjin, 28 (1969), 309-16.

1203 Thomson, A. K. "The Poetry of Vincent Buckley: An Essay in Interpretation." Meanjin, 28 (1969), 293-308.

CAMPBELL, David

1204 Dunlop, Ronald. "[Review of Selected Poems]." Poetry Australia, 26 (1969), 39-40.

1205 Kramer, Leonie. "David Campbell and the Natural Tongue." Quadrant, 13, no. 3 (1969), 13-17.

1206 Larkin, John. "David Campbell: Hands of a Farmer, Mind of a Poet." Age, 28 May 1970, p. 2.

1207 Lehmann, Geoffrey. "[Review of Selected Poems]." Bulletin (Sydney), 14 Dec. 1968, pp. 80-81.

1208 Smith, Vivian. "The Poetry of David Campbell." Southerly, 25 (1965), 193-98.

CASEY, Gavin

1209 Barnes, John. "Gavin Casey: The View from Kalgoorlie." _Meanjin_, 23
      (1964), 341-47.

1210 Drake-Brockman, Henrietta. "Gavin Casey." _Westerly_, 4 (1964), 7-10.

1211 Hewett, Dorothy. "A 'Literary Obituary.'" _Critic_ (Perth), 7 (1964),
      62-63.

1212 Kemeny, P. "Gavin Casey and the Australian Common Man." _AustQ_, 38,
      no. 3 (1967), 88-92.

1213 Mayman, Ted. "Gavin Casey." _Overland_, 23 (1962), 49-50.

1214 Vickers, F. B. "Gavin Casey--The Man I Knew." _Overland_, 30 (1964), 250.

CLARKE, Marcus

1215 Allen, L. H. "Introduction" to Marcus Clarke, _For the Term of His
      Natural Life_. London: Oxford Univ. Press, 1952, pp. v-xx.

1216 Barry, John Vincent. _The Life and Death of John Price_. Melbourne:
      Melbourne Univ. Press, 1964.

1217 Boehm, Harold J. "_His Natural Life_ and Its Sources." _ALS_, 5 (1971),
      42-64.

1218 Brazier, A. W. _Marcus Clarke, His Work and Genius_. Melbourne: Echo,
      1902.

1219 Denholm, Decie. "Port Arthur: The Men and the Myth." _HSANZ_, 14 (1970),
      406-23.

1220 ____ "The Sources of _His Natural Life_." _ALS_, 4 (1969), 174-78.

1221 Elliott, Brian. "Gerard Hopkins and Marcus Clarke." _Southerly_, 8
      (1947), 218-27.

1222 ____ _Marcus Clarke_. London: Oxford Univ. Press, 1958.

1223 Goodenough, Warwick. "_For the Term of His Natural Life_." _Opinion_, 10
      (1967), 31-40.

1224 Hamer, Clive. "Marcus Clarke: His Minor Novels and a Checklist." _BANQ_,
      1, no. 1 (1967), 4-11; 1, no. 2, 26; 1, no. 4, 29.

1225 Hergenhan, L. T. "The Corruption of Rufus Dawes." _Southerly_, 29 (1969),
      211-21.

1226 ____ "Marcus Clarke and the Australian Landscape." _Quadrant_, 13, no. 4
      (1969), 31-41.

1227 ____ "The Redemptive Theme in _His Natural Life_." _ALS_, 2 (1965), 32-49.

1228 Howarth, R. G. "Marcus Clarke's _For the Term of His Natural Life_."
      Southerly, 15 (1954), 268-76.

1229 Kingston, Claude. "1907 Film Epic Was Kind to Me." _Age_, 14 May 1967,
      p. 22.

1230 Murray-Smith, Stephen. "Introduction" to Marcus Clarke, _His Natural
      Life_. Harmondsworth: Penguin, 1970, pp. 7-23.

1231 Nesbitt, Bruce. "Marcus Clarke, 'Damned Scamp.'" _ALS_, 5 (1971), 93-98.

1232 Palmer, Vance. "Marcus Clarke and His Critics." _Meanjin_, 5 (1946),
      9-18.

1233 Patane, Leonardo R. "Letteratura dei 'Convicts' e l'opera di Marcus
      Clarke." _Narrativa_, 8 (1963), 78-91.

1234   Poole, Joan. "The Buncle Correspondence." BANQ, 3, no. 2 (1969), 21.

1235   ____ "Marcus Clarke and His Sources." Opinion, 10, no. 3 (1967), 38-42.

1236   ____ "Maurice Frere's Wife: Marcus Clarke's Revision of His Natural Life." ALS, 4 (1970), 383-94.

1237   Rees, Leslie. "His Natural Life, the Long and the Short of It." AustQ, 14, no. 2 (1942), 99-104.

1238   Robson, L. L. "The Historical Basis of For the Term of His Natural Life." ALS, 1 (1963), 104-21.

1239   Simmons, Samuel Rowe. A Problem and A Solution: Marcus Clarke and the Writing of "Long Odds," His First Novel. Melbourne: Simmons, 1946.

1240   Stephens, A. G. "The Making of a Masterpiece." Bulletin (Sydney), 27 Sept. 1906, red page.

1241   Wannan, Bill, ed. A Marcus Clarke Reader. London: Angus & Robertson. 1964.

See also: 587, 6132.

COUVREUR, Jessie [pseud. Tasma]

1242   Hadgraft, Cecil, and Ray Beilby. "Introduction to 'Tasma' (J. C. Couvreur)." In Uncle Piper of Piper's Hill. Melbourne: Nelson, 1969, pp. vii-xviii.

COWAN, Peter

1243   Barnes, John. "New Tracks to Travel: The Stories of White, Porter and Cowan." Meanjin, 25 (1967), 154-70.

1244   ____ "The Short Stories of Peter Cowan." Meanjin, 19 (1960), 136-46.

1245   Johnston, Grahame. "A Joyless World: The Fiction of Peter Cowan." Westerly, 1 (1967), 67-69.

1246   Jones, Evan. "The Anatomy of Frustration: Short Stories of Alan Davies and Peter Cowan." Bound with 2079, pp. 13-29.

1247   Lipscombe, Dan. "The Paradox of Peter Cowan." Bulletin (Sydney), 10 Sept. 1967, p. 36.

CUSACK, Dymphna

1248   Stirling, Monica. "Dymphna Cusack: A Profile." Meanjin. 24 (1964), 317-25.

DALEY, Victor

1249   Lindsay, Norman. "Victor Daley." In item 798, pp. 41-47.

1250   Oliver, Harold J. "Introduction" to Victor Daley. Sydney: Angus & Robertson, 1963, pp. v-xii.

1251   ____ "Victor Daley and Roderic Quinn." Meanjin, 10 (1951), 12-21.

1252   Stephens, A. G. Victor Daley: A Biographical and Critical Notice. Sydney: Bulletin, 1905.

DARK, Eleanor

1253   Anderson, Hugh. "Eleanor Dark: A Bulletin Checklist." BANQ, 3, no. 2 (1969), 20.

1254 Lowe, Eric. "The Novels of Eleanor Dark." Meanjin, 10 (1951), 341-49.

1255 McKellar, John. "The Black and the White." Southerly, 9 (1948), 92-98.

1256 Thomson, A. K. Understanding the Novel: The Timeless Land. Brisbane: Jacaranda, 1967.

1257 Wilkes, G. A. "Progress of Eleanor Dark." Southerly, 15 (1951), 139-48.

DAVISON, Frank Dalby

1258 Barnes, John. "Frank Dalby Davison." Westerly, 3 (1967), 16-20.

1259 ____ "Frank Dalby Davison's Last Book." Westerly, 1 (1971), 62-64.

1260 Davison, Frank D. "Testimony of a Veteran." Southerly, 29 (1969), 83-92.

1261 Heseltine, H. P. "The Fellowship of All Flesh: The Fiction of Frank Dalby Davison." Meanjin, 27 (1968), 275-90.

1262 Howarth, R. G. "Man Shy." Southerly, 6, no. 2 (1945), 11-12.

1263 Sayers, Stuart. "Four Hours with Farmer Frank." Age, 30 Aug. 1969, p. 10.

1264 ____ "Writers and Readers." Age, 9 Nov. 1968, p. 12.

1265 Waten, Judah. "Writer Returns to Fold with Mammoth Work." Sydney Morning Herald, 9 Nov. 1968, p. 23.

1266 Webster, Owen. "Frank Dalby Davison." Overland, 44 (1970), 35-37.

1267 ____ "Frank Davison's Magnum Opus Has a Soft Sell-Out." Bulletin (Sydney), 5 July 1969, pp. 43-44.

DAWE, Bruce

1268 Collins, Martin. "Here's a Poet with a Few Honest Thoughts on Sweat." Australian, 11 March 1967, p. 26.

1269 Curtis, Graeme. "Some Aspects of Bruce Dawe's Poetry." Makar, 6, no. 4 (1970), 4-10.

1270 Hetherington, John. "Bruce Dawe, Poet." Age, 11 March 1967, p. 24.

1271 McGregor, Craig, ed. In the Making. Melbourne: Nelson, 1969, pp. 30-37.

1272 Martin, Philip. "Public Yet Personal: Bruce Dawe's Poetry." Meanjin, 25 (1967), 290-94.

DOBSON, Rosemary

1273 Burrows, J. F. "Rosemary Dobson's Sense of the Past." Southerly, 30 (1970), 163-76.

1274 Dobson, Rosemary. "Introduction" to Australian Poets: Rosemary Dobson. Sydney: Angus & Robertson, 1963, pp. vii-ix.

1275 ____ Rosemary Dobson Reads from Her Own Work. St. Lucia: Univ. of Queensland Press, 1970.

1276 Excell, Patricia. "The Poetry of Rosemary Dobson." Meanjin, 10 (1951), 372-75.

1277 Kramer, Leonie. "The Poetry of Rosemary Dobson." Poetry Magazine, 2 (1968), 3-7.

1278 Lee, Stuart. "Rosemary Dobson." Quadrant, 9, no. 2 (1965), 56-62.

1279 Thompson, John. "Poetry in Australia: Rosemary Dobson." Southerly, 28 (1968), 203-14.

1280   Wescott, Pat. "An Angel Tips Her Halo: Rosemary Dobson's Place Among
        Our Poets." Bulletin (Sydney), 11 Jan. 1964, pp. 16-17.

DRAKE-BROCKMAN, Henrietta

1281   Barnes, John. "Henrietta Drake-Brockman." Westerly, 2 (1968), 71.

1282   Drake-Brockman, Geoffrey. "Some Memories." Westerly, 4 (1969), 77-79.

1283   Durack, Mary. "Henrietta as I Knew Her." Overland, 29 (1968), 46-47.

1284   Ewers, John K. "Henrietta and the Fellowship of Australian Writers."
        Westerly, 2 (1968), 75-78.

1285   Hasluck, Alexandra. "Henrietta as a Historian." Westerly, 2 (1968),
        72-74.

1286   _____ "Henrietta Drake-Brockman." Meanjin, 27 (1968), 233-37.

DUTTON, Geoffrey

1287   Hall, Sandra. "Why Write Novels?" Bulletin (Sydney), 26 Oct. 1968,
        pp. 52-54.

1288   Jones, M. "Can You Pick the Pornography?" Sydney Morning Herald, 1
        Nov. 1969, p. 16.

ELDERSHAW, Marjorie Barnard [Marjorie Barnard and Flora Eldershaw]

1289   Barnard, Marjorie. "How Tomorrow and Tomorrow Came to be Written."
        Meanjin, 29 (1970), 328-37.

1290   Burns, Robert. "Flux and Fixity: M. Barnard Eldershaw's Tomorrow and
        Tomorrow." Meanjin, 29 (1970), 320-27.

1291   Howarth, R. G. "The Glasshouse." Southerly, 6, no. 2 (1945), 19-21.

1292   Palmer, Vance, et al. "Tributes to Flora Eldershaw." Meanjin, 15 (1956),
        390-94.

FITZGERALD, R. D.

1293   Anderson, Hugh. "A Checklist of the Poems of Robert D. Fitzgerald,
        1917-1965." ALS, 4 (1970), 280-86.

1294   _____ "Robert Fitzgerald, Humanist." Southerly, 19 (1958), 2-10.

1295   Buckley, Vincent. "The Development of R. D. Fitzgerald." In item 509,
        pp. 122-41.

1296   Cantrell, Kerin. "Some Elusive Passages in Essay on Memory: A Reading
        Based on a Discussion with R. D. Fitzgerald." Southerly, 30 (1970),
        44-52.

1297   Day, A. Grove. "R. D. Fitzgerald and Fiji." Meanjin, 24 (1965), 277-86.

1298   Fitzgerald, R. D. "Introduction" to Australian Poets: R. D. Fitzgerald.
        Sydney: Angus & Robertson, 1963, pp. vii-x.

1299   _____ "Narrative Poetry." Southerly, 26 (1967), 11-24.

1300   _____ "A Pilgrimage in the Sud-Ouest." Meanjin, 25 (1966), 179-89.

1301   _____ "Places of Origin." Overland, 33 (1966), 19-23.

1302   Harris, Max. "Cheers for Men of Conscience." Australian, 25 Oct.
        1969, p. 21.

1303 Keesing, Nancy. "Robert D. Fitzgerald." Overland, 25 (1963), 31-32.

1304 Kramer, Leonie. "R. D. Fitzgerald: Philosopher or Poet." Overland, 33 (1965), 15-18.

1305 Lloyd, John. "R. D. Fitzgerald: Motif in Later Lyrical Development." Makar, 20 (1964), 26-35.

1306 McGregor, Craig. "A Kind of Life's Work." Sydney Morning Herald, 7 Aug. 1965, p. 14.

1307 Mares, F. H. "The Poetry of Robert Fitzgerald." Southerly, 26 (1966), 3-11.

1308 Oliver, Harold J. "The Achievement of R. D. Fitzgerald." Meanjin, 13 (1954), 39-48.

1309 Phillips, A. A. "The Poems of R. D. Fitzgerald." Meanjin, 24 (1965), 368-69.

1310 Seccombe, H. G. "A Contemporary Australian Poet." AustQ, 13, no. 1 (1941), 65-72.

1311 Stewart, Douglas. "Robert D. Fitzgerald, A Background to His Poetry." In item 587, pp. 332-41.

1312 Sturm, Terry L. "R. D. Fitzgerald's Poetry and A. N. Whitehead." Southerly, 29 (1969), 288-304.

1313 _____ "The Poetry of R. D. Fitzgerald." Landfall, 20 (1966), 162-67.

1314 Thompson, John, and R. D. Fitzgerald. "Poetry in Australia: R. D. Fitzgerald." Southerly, 27 (1967), 233-42.

1315 Todd, F. M. "The Poetry of R. D. Fitzgerald." TC (Melbourne), 9 (1954), 20-29.

1316 Van Wageningen, J., and Patricia O'Brien. R. D. Fitzgerald: A Bibliography. Adelaide: Libraries Board of South Australia, 1970.

1317 Wilkes, G. A. "The Poetry of R. D. Fitzgerald." Southerly, 27 (1967), 243-58.

1318 Wright, Judith. "R. D. Fitzgerald." In item 1066, pp. 154-69.

See also: 6150.

FRANKLIN, Miles [pseud. Brent of Bin Bin]

1319 Ashworth, Arthur. "Brent of Bin Bin." Southerly, 12 (1951), 196-202.

1320 _____ "Miles Franklin." Southerly, 9 (1948), 70-74.

1321 Barnard, Marjorie. "Miles Franklin." Meanjin, 4 (1955), 469-87.

1322 _____ Miles Franklin. Melbourne: Hill of Content, 1967.

1323 _____ Miles Franklin. New York: Twayne, 1967.

1324 Bright, Anne. "A Letter from Brent of Bin Bin." South Australiana, 4 (1965), 16-20.

1325 Franklin, Miles. Childhood at Brindabella. Sydney: Angus & Robertson, 1963.

1326 _____ My Brilliant Career. Sydney: Angus & Robertson, 1965.

1327 Hope, A. D. "Old Blastus of Bandicoot." Southerly, 6, no. 2 (1945), 14-15.

1328 Lindsay, Norman. "Miles Franklin." In item 798, pp. 143-45.

1329 Martin, David. "Miles Franklin." In item 862, pp. 13-15.

1330   Mathew, Ray. Miles Franklin. Melbourne: Lansdowne, 1963.

1331   Muir, Nigel. "Miles Franklin Confesses." Sydney Morning Herald, 16
        July 1967, p. 15.

1332   Stone, Walter. "Miles Franklin: Biography and Bibliography." In Miles
        Franklin's Manuscripts and Typescripts. (Berkelouw Catalogue no. 47.)
        Sydney: Berkelouw, 1962.

1333   Sutherland, A. Bruce. "Stella Miles Franklin's American Years."
        Meanjin, 24 (1965), 439-54.

1334   Tolchard, Clifford. "Miles Franklin--and All That Swagger." Walkabout,
        33 (Jan. 1967), 17-19.

See also: 701.

FURPHY, Joseph

1335   Antonini, Maria. "Il romanzo Australiano Such Is Life di Joseph Furphy."
        Convivium, 35 (1967), 746-55.

1336   Archer, A. L. Tom Collins, Joseph Furphy as I Knew Him. Melbourne:
        Bread & Cheese Club Addendum, 1941.

1337   Baker, Kate. "The True Furphy." Southerly, 6, no. 3 (1945), 60.

1338   Barnes, John. Joseph Furphy. Melbourne: Lansdowne, 1963.

1339   ____ Joseph Furphy. Melbourne: Oxford Univ. Press, 1967.

1340   ____ "Joseph Furphy's Such Is Life." Meanjin, 15 (1956), 374-89.

1341   Douglas, Dennis. "Tom Collins' Conscience." AustQ, 36, no. 4 (Dec.
        1964), 75-82.

1342   Drake-Brockman, Henrietta. "The House that Joseph Built." Southerly,
        11 (1950), 25-29.

1343   Ewers, John K. "No Ivied Walls." Westerly, 4 (1969), 60-68.

1344   ____ "Rigby's Romance: Its Social Significance for Today." Southerly,
        8 (1947), 40-43.

1345   ____ Tell the People. Sydney: Currawong, 1943.

1346   Franklin, Miles, and Kate Baker. Joseph Furphy: The Legend of a Man and
        His Book. Sydney: Angus & Robertson, 1944.

1347   Furphy, Joseph. "A Review of Such Is Life [1903]." In item 479, pp.
        128-30.

1348   ____, and A. G. Stephens. "On Publishing a Novel: A Correspondence."
        In item 479, pp. 117-27.

1349   Grattan, C. Hartley. "About Tom Collins." In Joseph Furphy, Such Is
        Life. Chicago: Univ. of Chicago Press, 1948, pp. 375-94.

1350   ____ "Tom Collins' Such Is Life." AustQ, 9, no. 3 (Sept. 1937), 67-76.

1351   Hamer, Clive. "The Christian Philosophy of Joseph Furphy." Meanjin,
        23 (1964), 142-53.

1352   ____ "The Hoax of Such Is Life." Southerly, 12, no. 2 (1951), 79-87.

1353   Hope, A. D. "[Review of Miles Franklin's Joseph Furphy]." Meanjin, 4
        (1945), 225-28.

1354   Howarth, R. G. "Joseph Furphy, the 'Tom Collins' Trilogy." Southerly,
        12 (1951), 72-78.

1355   Innes, Guy. "My Grandmother's Nephew." Southerly, 6, no. 3 (1945), 63-64.

1356   Johnson, Robert L. "The Road Out in Australian and American Fiction:
       A Study of Four Spokesmen." SoRA, 1, no. 3 (1965), 20-31.

1357   Kiernan, Brian. "The Comic Vision of Such Is Life." Meanjin, 23 (1964),
       132-41.

1358   _____ "The Form of Such Is Life." Quadrant, 6, no. 3 (1962), 19-27.

1359   _____ "Society and Nature in Such Is Life." ALS, 1 (1963), 75-88.

1360   Knight, Nina. "Furphy and Romance: Such Is Life Reconsidered."
       Southerly, 29 (1969), 243-55.

1361   Lebedewa, Nina. "Furphy Criticism since 1955: A Checklist." ALS, 3
       (1967), 149-50.

1362   Lee, S. E. "The Story of Mary O'Halloran." Drylight,(1967), 66-75.

1363   Lindsay, Norman. "Tom Collins." In item 798, pp. 146-47.

1364   McDougall, Robert L. Australia Felix: Joseph Furphy and Patrick White.
       Canberra: Australian National Univ. Press, 1966.

1365   McKenzie, K. A. "Joseph Furphy: Jacobean." ALS, 2 (1966), 266-77.

1366   Mares, F. H. "Such Is Life." AustQ, 34, no. 3 (1962), 62-71.

1367   Mitchell, A. G. "Such Is Life: The Title and Structure of the Book."
       Southerly, 6, no. 3 (1945), 43-59.

1368   Oliver, Harold J. "Joseph Furphy and 'Tom Collins.'" Southerly, 5, no. 3
       (1944), 14-18.

1369   _____ "Lawson and Furphy." In item 587, pp. 296-305.

1370   Phillips, A. A. "The Craftsmanship of Furphy." In item 894, pp. 18-34.

1371   Prescott, Edward Edgar. The Life Story of Joseph Furphy. Melbourne:
       Hawthorne, 1938.

1372   Pringle, John. "A Classic Novel of the Australian Wilds." TLS, 19 Sept.
       1958, p. 532.

1373   Stone, Walter. Joseph Furphy: An Annotated Bibliography. Sydney:
       Wentworth, 1955.

1374   Sutherland, A. Bruce. "Joseph Furphy, Australian." UTQ, 20 (1951), 169-82.

1375   Thomson, A. K. "The Greatness of Joseph Furphy." Meanjin, 2 (1943),
       20-23.

1376   Wallace, Gilbert. "How I Met Tom Collins." Southerly, 6, no. 3 (1945),
       61-62.

1377   Wallace-Crabbe, Christopher. "Furphy's 'Masculine Strength.'" LCrit,
       6, no. 3 (1964), 83-92. [Repr. in item 866, pp. 83-92.]

1378   _____ "Joseph Furphy, Realist." Quadrant, 5, no. 2 (1961), 49-56.
       [Repr. in item 751, pp. 139-47.]

1379   Wilkes, G. A. "The Australian Image in Literature: Such Is Life
       Reconsidered." TEng, 6 (1965), 5-16.

See also: 6133-6135.

GILMORE, Mary

1380   Anon. Mary Gilmore's Poetry." Bulletin (Sydney), 69 (Dec. 1948), 2.

1381   Bayley, William A. Dame Mary Gilmore and Silverton Public School.
       Silverton, N. S. W.: The Author, 1967.

1382   Cato, Nancy. "Woman and Poet." Overland, 26 (1963), 28.

1383 Cusack, Dymphna, T. Inglis Moore, and Barrie Ovenden. Mary Gilmore:
      A Tribute, with a Bibliography by Walter Stone. Sydney: Australasian
      Book Soc., 1965.

1384 Fitzgerald, R. D. "Introduction" to Australian Poets: Mary Gilmore.
      Sydney: Angus & Robertson, 1963, pp. v-vii.

1385 ____ "Mary Gilmore: Poet and Great Australian." Meanjin, 19 (1960),
      341-56.

1386 Green, Eleanor. "Mary Gilmore, an Impression." Makar, 19 (1964), 24-27.

1387 Lawson, Sylvia. Mary Gilmore. Melbourne: Oxford Univ. Press, 1967.

1388 McCrae, Hugh. "Mary Gilmore: Our Great National Poet." AustQ, 19, no. 3
      (1933), 94-96.

1389 Mackaness, George. "Dame Mary Gilmore and Henry Lawson." Southerly,
      24 (1964), 42-43.

1390 McLeod, A. L. "Mary Gilmore: A New Poem and Textual Autographs."
      Meanjin, 13 (1954), 570-72.

1391 Mares, F. H. "Dame Mary Gilmore." Southerly, 25 (1968), 234-45.

1392 Moore, T. Inglis. "Mary Gilmore." Southerly, 10 (1949), 122-30.

1393 Robertson, Constance. "Mary Gilmore." Southerly, 25 (1965), 247-50.

1394 Roderick, Colin. "The Teaching Life of Mary Gilmore." Education Gazette,
      57 (1963), 131-33.

1395 Souter, Gavin. "The New Australian Colony: The Graveyard at Las Ovejas."
      Meanjin, 25 (1966), 89-93.

1396 Stewart, Douglas. "The Paradoxes of Mary Gilmore." Sydney Morning
      Herald, 14 Aug. 1965, p. 15.

1397 Tennant, Kylie. "Vale--Mary Gilmore." Westerly, 3 (1963), 42-45.

1398 Tolchard, Clifford. "Mary Gilmore: Crusader and Poet." Walkabout, 34,
      no. 3 (1968), 12-15.

1399 Toms, Bruce. "Mary Gilmore's Life of Service." Realist, 19 (1965),
      6-7.

1400 Wilde, W. H. Three Radicals. Melbourne: Oxford Univ. Press, 1969.

1401 Wood, W. A. "The Best of Mary Gilmore." Realist Writer, 12 (1963), 8-12.

1402 ____ "Mary Gilmore's Heaven: A Letter to a Friend." Realist, 19 (1965),
      14-16.

1403 Wright, Judith. "A Tribute to Mary Gilmore." In item 862, pp. 19-20.

See also: 701, 1982.

GORDON, Adam Lindsay

1404 Adams, Francis. "Australian Criticism and the Reaction Against Gordon."
      CentM, 2 (1890), 547-52.

1405 ____ "The Poetry of Adam Lindsay Gordon." MelbR, 10 (1885), 196-210.

1406 Bernstein, D. L. First Tuesday in November: The Story of the Melbourne
      Cup. Melbourne: Heinemann, 1969.

1407 Clarke, Marcus. "Preface to Gordon's Poems [1876]." In item 479, pp. 33-37.

1408 Cleland, John B. "Margaret Kiddle's Men of Yesterday and Adam Lindsay
      Gordon." JRAHS, pt. 2 (1964), 156-58.

1409 Elliott, Brian. "The Friend of Charlie Walker: A Note on Adam Lindsay
      Gordon." AustL, 3, no. 3 (1961), 32-38.

1410 Gordon, Adam Lindsay. The Last Letters, 1868-1970 [to John Riddoch].
      Ed. with introd. by Hugh Anderson. Melbourne: Hawthorn, 1970.

1411 Humphris, Edith, and Douglas Sladen. Adam Lindsay Gordon and His
      Friends in England and Australia. London: Constable, 1912.

1411a Jamison, Greeba. "Adam Lindsay Gordon." Walkabout, 36, no. 6 (1970),
      48-51.

1412 Kramer, Leonie. "The Literary Reputation of Adam Lindsay Gordon."
      ALS, 1 (1963), 42-56.

1413 MacRae, C. F. Adam Lindsay Gordon. New York: Twayne, 1968.

1414 McCrae, George Gordon. "Adam Lindsay Gordon." Southerly, 5, no. 1
      (1944), 26-28.

1415 Stevens, J. Roy, ed. Adam Lindsay Gordon and Other Australian Writers.
      Melbourne: The Author, 1937.

1416 Wilding, Michael. "A. L. Gordon in England: The Legend of the
      Steeplechase." Southerly, 25 (1965), 99-107.

1417 Wright, Judith. "Adam Lindsay Gordon and Barcroft Boake." In item
      1066, pp. 57-67.

See Also: 1982.

HALL, Rodney

1418 Dalton, Warwick. "To Ask: To Dig: Perhaps to Find Meaning." Australian,
      27 July 1968, p. 11.

1419 Hall, Sandra. "The Other Poets." Bulletin (Sydney), 28 Sept. 1968,
      pp. 43-45.

1420 Shapcott, Thomas W. "The Early Volumes of Rodney Hall." Makar, 5, no. 1
      (1969), 21-24.

HARPUR, Charles

1421 Anon. "A Harpur Discovery." Southerly, 5, no. 1 (1944), 31.

1422 Aurousseau, Marcel. "Charles Harpur and His Biographer." Meanjin, 22
      (1963), 69-79.

1423 Clarke, Donovan. "Introduction" to Australian Poets: Charles Harpur.
      Sydney: Angus & Robertson, 1963, pp. v-x.

1424 Devlin, F. M. "The Problems of Charles Harpur: A Semi-Historical Note."
      Makar, 5, no. 2 (1969), 24-25.

1425 Normington-Rawling, J. "Charles Harpur." Bulletin (Sydney), 18 April
      1964, p. 42.

1426 _____ Charles Harpur, an Australian. Sydney: Angus & Robertson, 1962.

1427 _____ "A Currency Lad Poet: The Significance of Charles Harpur."
      Quadrant, 7, no. 25 (1963), 11-25.

1428 Salier, C. W. "Charles Harpur: A Pre-Centenary Note." AustQ, 15, no. 4
      (1943), 85-94.

1429 _____ "Charles Harpur's Translations from the Iliad." Southerly, 7
      (1946), 218-23.

1430 _____ "Harpur and His Editor." Southerly, 12 (1951), 47-53.

1431 _____ "Life and Writings of Charles Harpur." JRAHS, 32 (1946), 89-105.

1432 Wright, Judith. Charles Harpur. Melbourne: Lansdowne, 1963.

1433 _____ "Charles Harpur." In item 1066, pp. 1-18.

See also: 1982, 6136.

HARROWER, Elizabeth

1434 Anon. "The Novels of Elizabeth Harrower." AustL, 4, no. 2 (1961), 16-18.

1435 Geering, R. G. "Elizabeth Harrower's Novels: A Survey." Southerly, 30 (1970), 131-47.

HARWOOD, Gwen

1436 Douglas, Dennis. "Gwen Harwood--The Poet as Doppelganger." Quadrant, 58 (1969), 15-19.

1437 Moody, David. "The Poems of Gwen Harwood." Meanjin, 22 (1963), 418-21.

1438 Wallace-Crabbe, Christopher. "My Ghost, My Self: The Poetry of Gwen Harwood." Meanjin, 28 (1969), 264-67.

HAY, William Gosse

1439 Abbott, J. H. M. "William Hay: Extracts from a Memoir." Southerly, 12 [13] (1952), 22-32.

1440 Cato, Nancy. "William Hay's Old Homes." Southerly, 15 (1954), 292.

1441 Elliott, Brian. "The World of William Hay." In item 605, pp. 22-40.

1442 Gosse, Fayette. William Gosse Hay. Melbourne: Lansdowne, 1965.

1443 Hergenhan, L. T. "The Strange World of Sir William Heans and the Mystery of William Hay." Southerly, 27 (1967), 118-37.

1444 Herring, Thelma. "The Escape of Sir William Heans: Hay's Debt to Hawthorne and Melville." Southerly, 26 (1966), 75-92.

1445 Hooper, F. Earle. "The Background of Herridge of Reality Swamp." Southerly, 15 (1954), 290-91.

1446 _____ "Escape of Sir William Heans: The Technique." Southerly, 7 (1946), 158-62.

1447 _____ "A Memoir." Southerly, 7 (1946), 128-41.

1448 Howarth, R. G. "Escape of Sir William Heans: The Technique." Southerly, 7 (1946), 156-57.

1449 _____ "The Original Ending to William Hay's Herridge of Reality Swamp." Southerly, 11 (1950), 109-11.

1450 _____ "William Hay's Escape of Sir William Heans." AustQ, 26, no. 2 (1954), 73-84.

1451 M., K. "A Novel of Suspense." Athenaeum, 18 July 1919, p. 622. [Repr. in Southerly, 7 (1946), 163-64.]

1452 Macartney, F. T. "The Notorious Case of William Hay." Meanjin, 14 (1955), 244-48.

1453 _____ "Words and William Hay." In Item 803, pp. 47-57.

1454 Miller, E. Morris. "The Topography and Historical Background of William Hay's Novel, The Escape of the Notorious Sir William Heans." Southerly, 13 (1952), 160-71.

1455 Muecke, I. D. "'The Return of Robert Wasterton': A Commentary on an
      Unfinished Novel." South Australiana, 7 (1968), 84-105.

1456 ____ "William Hay and History: A Comment on Aims, Sources and Method."
      ALS, 2 (1965), 117-37.

See also: 6137.

HAZZARD, Shirley

1457 Colmer, John. "Patterns and Preoccupations of Love: The Novels of
      Shirley Hazzard." Meanjin, 29 (1970), 461-67.

1458 Harris, Max. "A Face to Remember." Australian, 14 May 1966, p. 10.

1459 Kramer, Leonie. "[Review of People in Glass Houses]." Bulletin (Sydney),
      10 Sept. 1966, pp. 44-45.

1460 MacAuley, R. "[Review of The Bay at Noon]." NYTBR, 5 April 1970, pp. 4-5.

1461 Raphael, F. "[Review of People in Glass Houses]." NYTBR, 15 Oct. 1967,
      p. 5.

1462 Wellein, L. "[Review of People in Glass Houses]." SSF, 5 (1968), 392-94.

HERBERT, Xavier

1463 Buckley, Vincent. "Capricornia." Meanjin, 19 (1960), 13-30.

1464 Herbert, Xavier. "I Sinned Against Syntax." Meanjin, 19 (1960), 31-35.

1465 ____ "The Writing of Capricornia." ALS, 4 (1970), 207-14.

1466 Kiernan, Brian. "Xavier Herbert: Capricornia." ALS, 4 (1970), 360-70.

1467 McLaren, John. "The Image of Reality in Our Writing." Overland, 27-28
      (1963), 43-47.

1468 Prideaux, H. "The Experimental Novel in Australia." Prospect, 2 (1960),
      13.

HIGHAM, Charles

1469 Hall, Sandra. "The Other Poets." Bulletin (Sydney), 28 Sept. 1968,
      pp. 43-45.

HOPE, A. D.

1470 Argyle, Barry. "The Poetry of A. D. Hope." JCL, 3 (1967), 87-96.

1471 Bewley, Marius. "Good Manners." NYRB, 18 May 1967, pp. 31-34.

1472 Brissenden, R. F. "A. D. Hope's New Poems." Southerly, 30 (1970), 83-96.

1473 Buckley, Vincent. "A. D. Hope: The Unknown Poet." In item 509, pp. 142-57.

1474 Cantrell, Leon. "Notes on A. D. Hope: A Bibliography (1968)." ALS, 5
      (1971), 87-91.

1475 Cross, Gustav. "The Poetry of A. D. Hope." In item 587, pp. 377-88.

1476 Davies, M. Bryn. "The Verse of A. D. Hope." AustL, 2, no. 1 (1959),
      42-45.

1477 Docker, John. "Sex and Nature in Modern Poetry." Arena, 22 (1970), 5-24.

1478 Dunlevy, Maurice. "Time to Write Poetry." Canberra Times, 29 Nov. 1969,
      p. 14.

1479   Goldberg, S. L. "The Poet as Hero: A. D. Hope's The Wandering Islands."
       Meanjin, 16 (1957), 127-39.

1480   Green, Dorothy. "The Chameleon Poet." Adult Education, 12, no. 2
       (1967), 6-12.

1481   ____ "A Mark for the Arrow: A. D. Hope's Dunciad Minor." Meanjin, 29
       (1970), 424-29.

1482   Gregory, Horace. "Speaking of Books: A. D. Hope." NYTBR, 5 Feb. 1967,
       p. 2.

1483   Heseltine, H. P. "Paradise Within: A. D. Hope's New Poems." Meanjin,
       29 (1970), 405-20.

1484   Hope, A. D. The Cave and the Spring: Essays on Poetry. Adelaide:
       Rigby, 1965.

1485   ____ "Introduction" to Australian Poets: A. D. Hope. Sydney: Angus &
       Robertson, 1963, pp. vii-x.

1486   McAuley, James. "Pyramid in the Waste: An Introduction to A. D. Hope's
       Poetry." Quadrant, 5, no. 4 (1961), 61-70.

1487   Mathew, Ray. "Noble Candid Speech?" AustL, 2, no. 2 (1959), 46-48.

1488   Millar, Daniel. "The Poetry of A. D. Hope." REL, 4 (1964), 29-38.

1489   Nagarajan, S. "Aspects of the Poetic Thought of A. D. Hope." JCL, 6,
       no. 1 (1971), 31-41.

1490   O'Brien, Patricia. A. D. Hope: A Bibliography. Adelaide: Libraries
       Board of South Australia, 1968.

1491   O'Hearn, D. J. "A Note on A. D. Hope." Prospect, 2, no. 4 (1959), 17-20.

1492   Rexroth, Kenneth. "What Is There to Alienate From?" Bulletin (Sydney),
       29 April 1967, p. 34.

1493   Somapala, Wijetunga. "Australia in Poetry." Hemisphere, 12, no. 2
       (1968), 8-10.

1494   Suchting, W. A. "The Poetry of A. D. Hope: A Frame of Reference."
       Meanjin, 21 (1962), 154-63.

1495   Thompson, John, and A. D. Hope. "Poetry in Australia: A. D. Hope."
       Southerly, 26 (1966), 237-46.

1496   Wallace-Crabbe, Christopher. "The Three Faces of Hope." Meanjin, 26
       (1967), 396-440.

1497   Wilkes, G. A. "The Poetry of A. D. Hope." AustQ, 36, no. 1 (1964),
       41-51.

1498   Wright, Judith. "A. D. Hope." In item 1066, pp. 181-92.

See also: 52, 817, 6138.

HORNE, Donald

1499   Horne, Donald. The Education of Young Donald. Sydney: Angus &
       Robertson, 1967.

1500   ____ "Writing The Education of Young Donald." Quadrant, 15, no. 2
       (1971), 42-46.

1501   Mander, John. "Death of a God." Quadrant, 14, no. 1 (1970), 13-19.

HUMPHRIES, Barry

1502   Deasey, Denison. "Barry Humphries." AustL, 2, no. 1 (1959), 24-25.

JOHNSTON, George

1503 Clift, Charmian. "My Husband George." Pol, 9 (1969), 83-85.

1504 ____ Peel Me a Lotus. Sydney: Collins, 1959.

1505 Hall, James. "And How Its Two for the Load." Australian, 23 Nov. 1968, p. 12.

1506 Hall, Sandra. "Why Write Novels." Bulletin (Sydney), 26 Oct. 1968, pp. 52-54.

1507 Johnston, George. "ANZAC . . . a Myth for all Mankind." Education Gazette, 40 (1966), 71-75.

1508 ____ "A Myths Fade--We Need an Identity." Walkabout, 36, no. 2 (1970), 5-8.

KENDALL, Henry

1509 Burke, Iris. "Four Extracts from a Chronology (in Preparation) of the Rev. T. H. Kendall and His Descendants." and "A Draft List of the Prose Writings of Henry Kendall," in Foreshadowings. Sydney: Australian Documentary Facsimile Society, 1963. [Appendix III and Appendix IV.]

1510 Clarke, Donovan. "Henry Kendall: A Study in Imagery." AustQ, 29, no. 4 (1957), 71-79; 30, no. 1 (1958), 89-98.

1511 ____ "Kendall's Views on Contemporary Writers: A Survey of His Correspondence." ALS, 1 (1964), 170-79.

1512 ____ "New Light on Henry Kendall." ALS, 2 (1966), 211-13.

1513 Hamilton-Grey, A. M. Facts and Fancies about Our Son of the Woods, Henry Clarence Kendall, and His Poetry. Sydney: Sands, 1920.

1514 MacKaness, George. "A Memory of Henry Kendall." Southerly, 24 (1964), 228-31.

1515 Mitchell, A. C. W. "The Radiant Dream: Notes on Henry Kendall." ALS, 4 (1969), 99-114.

1516 Moore, T. Inglis. "Introduction" to Australian Poets: Henry Kendall. Sydney: Angus & Robertson, 1963, pp. v-xii.

1517 Reed, Thomas Thornton. Henry Kendall, a Critical Appreciation. Adelaide: Rigby, 1960.

1518 ____ "Introduction" to The Poetical Works of Henry Kendall. Adelaide: Libraries Bd. of South Australia, 1966, pp. xxi-xxxv.

1519 Stephens, Samuel Rowe. Henry Kendall: A Critical Review for Use of Schools. Sydney: Bookfellow, 1928.

1520 Swancott, Charles. Gosford and the Henry Kendall Country (Koolewong to Lisarow). Woy Woy, N. S. W.: The Author, 1966.

1521 Tolchard, Clifford. "Thomas Kendall: Australia's Unhappy Pilgrim." Walkabout, 33, no. 5 (1967), 30.

1522 Wilkins, Una J. "Is it All 'Bell Birds'?" Drylight, (1966), 16-24.

1523 Williams, T. L. "Henry Kendall: A National Australian Poet." JRQHS, 8 (1967), 388-96.

1524 Wright, Judith. "Henry Kendall." In item 1066, pp. 19-44.

See also: 1982, 6139, 6140.

KENEALLY, Thomas

1525   Anon. "Tough Poetry on Stage." Australian, 21 Dec. 1967, p. 8.

1526   Anon. "'Trap' that Can Snare a Priest." Sydney Morning Herald, 14
       Feb. 1968, p. 6.

1527   Brady, Charles A. "Bring Larks and Heroes." Éire, 3, no. 3 (1968),
       169-73.

1528   Burns, Robert. "Out of Context: A Study of Thomas Keneally's Novels."
       ALS, 4 (1969), 31-48.

1529   Cameron, Richard. "The Art of Being a Writer." Bulletin (Sydney),
       6 July 1968, p. 34.

1530   Cantrell, Kerin. "Perspective on Thomas Keneally." Southerly, 28 (1968),
       54-67.

1531   Clancy, L. J. "Conscience and Corruption: Thomas Keneally's Three
       Novels." Meanjin, 27 (1968), 33-41.

1532   Hall, Sandra. "Writing for Dear Life." Bulletin (Sydney), 30 March
       1968, p. 7.

1533   Hutton, Geoffrey. "Keneally on Stage." Age, 2 March 1968, p. 7.

1534   Jillett, Neil. "Thomas Keneally." Age, 11 Nov. 1967, p. 24.

1535   Keneally, Thomas. "Keneally in Ireland." Bulletin (Sydney), 21 Nov.
       1970, pp. 47-49.

1536   ____ "Origin of a Novel." Hemisphere, 13, no. 10 (1969), 9-13.

1537   Kiernan, Brian. "Thomas Keneally and the Australian Novel: A Study of
       Bring Larks and Heroes." Southerly, 28 (1968), 189-99.

1538   Rolfe, Patricia. "The Flavour of Life." Bulletin (Sydney), 4 Sept.
       1965, p. 30.

1539   Souter, Gavin. "Refugee from Good Old Irish Theology." Sydney Morning
       Herald, 4 Nov. 1967, p. 18.

1540   Wilding, Michael. "Two Cheers for Keneally." Southerly, 29 (1969),
       131-38.

KINGSLEY, Henry

1541   Anderson, Hugh. "The Composition of Geoffrey Hamlyn: A Comment." ALS,
       4 (1969), 79-80.

1542   Baxter, Rosilyn. "Henry Kingsley and the Australian Landscape." ALS,
       4 (1970), 395-98.

1543   Elliott, Brian. "The Composition of Geoffrey Hamlyn: The Legend and
       the Facts." ALS, 3 (1968), 271-89.

1544   Hamer, Clive. "Henry Kingsley's Australian Novels." Southerly, 26
       (1966), 40-57.

1545   Hergenhan, L. T. "Geoffrey Hamlyn Through Contemporary Eyes." ALS,
       2 (1966), 289-95.

1546   Horner, J. C. "Geoffrey Hamlyn and Its Australian Setting." ALS, 1
       (1963), 3-15.

1547   Mares, F. H. "Henry Kingsley, Marcus Clarke and Rolf Boldrewood." In
       item 587, pp. 247-58.

1548   Scheuerle, William H. "Romantic Attitudes in Geoffry Hamlyn." ALS, 2
       (1965), 79-91.

1549 Wellings, N. G. "Henry Kingsley: Ravenshoe." ALS, 4 (1969), 115-29.
See also: 6141.

KOCH, Christopher

1550 Buckley, Vincent. "In the Shadow of Patrick White." Meanjin, 20 (1961),
       144-54.

1551 McPherson, Neil. "Writers for a 'No' Generation." Westerly, 1 (1966),
       59-62.

1552 Rolfe, Patricia. "The Novelist's Chances." Bulletin (Sydney), 19
       June 1965, p. 33.

LAWLER, Ray

1553 Cherry, Walter. "The Piccadilly Bushman and Prisoners' Country."
       Meanjin, 14 (1960), 92-95.

1554 Grant, Bruce. "English Critics and The Doll." Meanjin, 16 (1957),
       295-98.

1555 Hanger, Eunice. "Forebears of 'The Doll.'" Southerly, 18 (1957), 29-33.

LAWSON, Henry

1556 Adams, Philip. "Henry's Centenary." Bulletin (Sydney), 22 July 1967,
       p. 43.

1557 _____ "Lawson: Too Little with Us." Australian, 28 Sept. 1968, p. 11.

1558 Anon. "The Lawson Industry." Bulletin (Sydney), 8 July 1967, p. 13.

1559 Arnold, Rollo. "Henry Lawson: The New Zealand Visits." ALS, 3 (1968),
       163-89.

1560 _____ "Henry Lawson: 'The Sliprails and the Spur' at Pahiatua?" ALS, 4
       (1970), 286-92.

1561 _____ "A Reply to W. H. Pearson." ALS, 4 (1969), 73-79.

1562 Barnes, John. "Lawson and the Short Story in Australia." Westerly, 2
       (1968), 83-87.

1563 Barton, Hilton. "Bret Harte and Henry Lawson: Democratic Realists."
       Realist, 26 (1967), 7-10.

1564 _____ "Lawson's Editors." Overland, 10 (1957), 29-31.

1565 Bjørge, Odd. "Henry Lawson: En Norsk Australier." Vinduet, 15 (1961),
       313-15.

1566 Blair, Lyle, ed. Selected Works of Henry Lawson. East Lansing: Michigan
       State Univ. Press, 1957.

1567 Brereton, John Le Gay. Address on Henry Lawson. Sydney: Eagle Press,
       1927.

1568 Broomfield, F. J. Henry Lawson and His Critics. Sydney: Angus &
       Robertson, 1931.

1569 Browning, T. S., ed. Henry Lawson: Memories. Sydney: Worker,
       1931.

1570 Carswell, Doreen. "Kipling and Lawson, Contemporaries." Expression,
       8, no. 2 (1968), 50-52.

1571 Cleverly, J. F. "The School Days of Henry Lawson." Education (Sydney),
       44 (1963), 3-4.

1572 Douglas, Dennis. "The Text of Lawson's Prose." ALS, 2 (1966), 254-65.

1573 Dunlevy, Maurice. "The Price of a Decent Brassband." Canberra Times, 17 June 1967, p. 11.

1574 Dyson, L. "Centenary for Henry Lawson." Australian, 2 June 1967, p. 6.

1575 Evensen, Leif. "En norskaettet australsk dikter." Vinduet, 2 (1948), 705-12.

1576 Fox, Len. "Henry Lawson and Ragnar Redhead." Overland, 38 (1968), 31-37.

1577 ____ "Lawson: The Centenary Symposium Continues: Humanism and Mateship." Tribune, 21 June 1967, p. 14. [See also "100 Years of Henry Lawson." Tribune, 14 June 1967.]

1578 Garnett, Edward. "An Appreciation." Academy and Literature, 62 (1902), 250.

1579 Green, Dorothy. "Tent and Tree." Nation (Sydney), 4 Sept. 1965, pp. 21-22.

1580 Hardy, Frank. "The Genius of Henry Lawson: Time, Place, and Circumstance." Realist Writer, 13 (1963), 10-14; 14 (1964), 8-13.

1581 Harris, Max. "Our Most Successful Failure?" Australian, 17 June 1967, p. 6.

1582 Henry, W. E. Fitz. "A Lawson Bibliography." Bulletin (Sydney), 20 June 1951, p. 2.

1583 Heseltine, H. P. "St. Henry--Our Apostle of Mateship." Quadrant, 5, no. 1 (1960-1961), 5-12.

1584 Hewett, Dorothy. "The Journey of Henry Lawson." AustLR, 4 (1967), 56-62.

1585 Hodges, H. G. "Lawson Memories." BANQ, 2, no. 3 (1949), 25-26.

1586 Hope, A. D. "Steele Rudd and Henry Lawson." Meanjin, 15 (1956), 24-32.

1587 Johnston, Grahame. "His Yarns Endure." Canberra Times, 17 June 1967, p. 11.

1588 Kevans, Dennis. "Lawson: The Centenary Symposium Continues: Part of Our Heritage." Tribune, 21 June 1967, p. 14.

1589 Lawson, Bertha. My Henry Lawson. Sydney: Frank Johnson, 1943.

1590 ____ , and John Le Gay Brereton, eds. Henry Lawson by His Mates. Sydney: Angus & Robertson, 1931.

1591 Lawson, Henry. "'Pursuing Literature' in Australia [1899]." In item 479, pp. 71-79.

1592 Long, Gavin. "Young Paterson and Young Lawson." Meanjin, 23 (1964), 403-13.

1593 Mackaness, George. Annotated Bibliography of Henry Lawson. Sydney: Angus & Robertson, 1951.

1594 ____ "Henry Lawson's First Book." ABC, 8, no. 6 (1958), 20-22.

1595 Marshall, James Vance. "The Day Henry Lawson Talked to Me About His Father." AustL, 4, no. 3 (1962), 28-34.

1596 Matthews, Brian. "'The Drover's Wife' Writ Large: One Measure of Lawson's Achievement." Meanjin, 27 (1968), 54-66.

1597 ____ "'The Nurse and Tutor of Eccentric Minds': Some Developments in Lawson's Treatment of Madness." ALS, 4 (1970), 251-57.

1598 Milner, Ian. Henry Lawson: Zakladatel Australske Literatury. Prague: S. N. K. L. U., 1965.

1599 Moncrieff, R. A. "Back to the Lawson Country." Walkabout, 33, no. 9 (1967), 16-18.

1600 Moore, T. Inglis. "The Rise and Fall of Henry Lawson." Meanjin, 16
      (1958), 365-76.

1601 Murdoch, Walter. "Afterthoughts." Australian, 15 July 1967, p. 6.

1602 ____ "Lawson the Luckless." Australian, 24 June 1967, p. 8.

1603 Murray-Smith, Stephen. Henry Lawson. Melbourne: Lansdowne, 1962.

1604 Mutch, T. D. "The Early Life of Henry Lawson." JRAHS, 18, pt. 6 (1933),
      273-344.

1605 Neild, J. M. Lawson--and His Critics. Melbourne: Henry Lawson Memorial
      Soc., 1944.

1606 Nesbitt, Bruce. "Some Notes on Lawson's Contributions to the Bulletin,
      1887-1900." BANQ, 1 (1967), 17-20.

1607 Newton, Gloria. "Police Got Tired of Running Him In; Vivid Memories of
      Henry Lawson." AustWW, 2 March 1966, p. 9.

1608 O'Grady, Desmond. "Afterthoughts on Henry Lawson." Southerly, 18 (1957),
      62-73.

1609 O'Mallee, Myall. "Lawson: The Centenary Symposium Continues: Lawson
      and O'Dowd." Tribune, 21 June 1967, p. 14.

1610 Palmer, Vance. "The Writer, Henry Lawson." In item 873, pp. 159-66.

1611 Pearson, W. H. "Henry Lawson Among the Maoris." Meanjin, 27 (1968),
      67-73.

1612 ____ Henry Lawson Among Maoris. Canberra: Australian National Univ.
      Press, 1968.

1613 ____ "Henry Lawson's New Zealand Visits: A Comment." ALS, 4 (1969),
      68-73.

1614 ____ "Lawson Manuscripts in New Zealand and a Note on Lawson Autobi-
      ographies." BANQ, 2 (1967), 6-14.

1615 Perry, R. R. "Lawson--Bard of the Tribe." Sydney Morning Herald, 17
      June 1967, p. 14.

1616 Petrikovskaya, Alla. "Henry Lawson and the Soviet Reader." SovL, 7
      (1967), 171-73.

1617 ____ "Klasik australiis'koi noveli Genri Louson. Do 100-richchya z
      drya narod zhennya." RLz, 6 (1967), 57-67. [The Classic of the
      Australian Novel, Henry Lawson. To celebrate the Centenary of His
      birth.]

1618 Phillips, A. A. "The Craftsmanship of Lawson." In item 878, pp. 1-17.

1619 ____ Henry Lawson. New York: Twayne, 1970.

1620 ____ "Henry Lawson Revisited." Meanjin, 24 (1965), 5-17.

1621 Pizer, Marjorie, ed. The Men Who Made Australia. Melbourne: Australian
      Book Soc., 1957.

1622 Prout, Denton [pseud.]. Henry Lawson: The Grey Dreamer. Adelaide:
      Rigby, 1963.

1623 Rodd, L. C. His Father's Mate: The Story of Henry Lawson.
      Melbourne: Cheshire, 1966.

1624 Roderick, Colin. A Companion to Henry Lawson: Fifteen Stories. Sydney:
      Angus & Robertson, 1959.

1625 ____ "Henry Lawson and Hannah Thornburn." Meanjin, 27 (1968), 74-89.

1626 ____ "Henry Lawson: The Middle Years, 1893-1896." JRAHS, 53 (1967),
      101-21.

1627 ____ Henry Lawson: Poet and Short Story Writer. Sydney: Angus &
Robertson, 1966.

1628 ____ "Henry Lawson to W. W. Head (W. A. Woods)." Meanjin, 25 (1965),
81-85.

1629 ____, ed. Henry Lawson: Twenty Stories and Seven Poems with Observations
by His Friends and Critics. Sydney: Angus & Robertson, 1942

1630 ____ Henry Lawson's Formative Years, 1883-1893. Sydney: Wentworth,
1960. [Repr. from JRAHS, 45 (1959).]

1631 ____ "Henry Lawson's Norwegian Forebears." Southerly, 24 (1964), 150-57.

1632 ____ "Introduction" to Collected Verse of Henry Lawson, I: 1885-1900.
Sydney: Angus & Robertson, 1967, pp. xiii-xxxiv.

1633 ____ The Later Life of Henry Lawson (1910-1918). Sydney: Wentworth,
1961. [Repr. from JRAHS, 46 (1960).]

1634 ____ "Was Lawson Born in a Tent?" North, 5 (1966), 14-21.

1635 Saillens, Emile. "Le bush australien et son poète." Mercure de France,
87(1910), 428-50, 620-36. [Trans. by Colin Roderick as "Henry Lawson:
A Contemporary French View." Southerly, 30 (1970), 190-208.]

1636 Sargeson, Frank. "Henry Lawson: Some Notes After Rereading." Landfall,
20 (1966), 156-62.

1637 Smithyman, Kendrick. "A Few Remarks About Lawson." NZMR, 4, no. 38
(1963), 21-22.

1638 Stephens, A. G. "Henry Lawson: Collected Criticism 1896-1922." In item
479, pp. 80-105.

1639 Stokes, John. "Henry Lawson in Perth." WATJ, 54 (1964), 127-28.

1640 Stone, Walter. Henry Lawson: A Chronological Checklist of His
Contributions to the "Bulletin," 1887-1924. Sydney: Wentworth, 1964.

1641 Todd, F. M. "Henry Lawson." TC (Melbourne), 4 (1950), 5-15.

1642 Wallace-Crabbe, Christopher. "Lawson's 'Joe Wilson': A Skeleton Novel."
ALS, 1 (1964), 147-54.

1643 Waters, Edgar. "The Stories of Henry Lawson: Sydney or the Bush?"
Overland, 34 (1966), 41-42.

1644 Wilkes, G. A. "Henry Lawson Reconsidered." Southerly, 25 (1965), 264-75.

See also: 6142.

LINDSAY, Jack

1645 Burton, Herbert. "The Lives of Jack Lindsay." Meanjin, 20 (1961), 320-25.

1646 Hetherington, John. "Down at Bangslappers with Jack Lindsay." Age,
14 Sept. 1968, p. 11.

1647 Lindsay, Jack. Fanfrolico and After. London: Bodley Head, 1962.

1648 ____ Life Rarely Tells: An Autobiographical Account and Ending in the
Year 1921 and Situated Mostly in Brisbane, Queensland. London: Bodley
Head, 1959.

1649 Rivkis, Ja. "Postigaja Zakony Istorii (o tvorcestve Džeka Lindseja)."
VLit, 8 (1964), 174-88.

1650 Sitwell, Edith. "Letters to Jack Lindsay." Meanjin, 25 (1966), 76-80.

1651 Stewart, Douglas. "Aristophanes in Australia." Sydney Morning Herald,
23 April 1966, p. 18.

1652 Stone, Walter. "Beating the Salvage Bag." BANQ, 1, no. 4 (1966), 3-6.

1653 Waten, Judah. "Some Australians and Iris Murdoch." Age, 19 Feb. 1966, p. 22.

LINDSAY, Norman

1654 Allison, Jack. "'Futurity': Norman Lindsay's Creative Stimulus." Meanjin, 29 (1970), 346-55.

1655 Cavell, Norma. "A Poet Gone Where the Last Year's Leaves Go." Sydney Morning Herald, 22 July 1967, p. 18.

1656 Cawley, A. C. "Love's Fool Paradise." Meanjin, 23 (1964), 179-85.

1657 Chaplin, Harry F., ed. Norman Lindsay: His Books, Manuscripts and Autograph Letters in the Library of, and Annotated by, Harry F. Chaplin. Foreword by Norman Lindsay. Sydney: Wentworth, 1969.

1658 Hadgraft, Cecil. "Four Ages--Youth and Norman Lindsay." Southerly, 12 (1951), 62-68.

1659 Hetherington, D. J. Hope of the Bulletin. Sydney: Angus & Robertson, 1929.

1660 Hetherington, John. Norman Lindsay. Melbourne: Lansdowne, 1961.

1661 Hope, A. D. "The Pencil Drawings." Quadrant, 13, no. 6 (1969), 9-13.

1662 Jackson, N. "In Defence of Norman Lindsay." Quadrant, 13, no. 2 (1969), 20-28.

1663 James, Brian. "Norman Lindsay--Letter Writer." Southerly, 20 (1959), 19-21.

1664 Keesing, Nancy. "Norman Lindsay." Quadrant, 13, no. 6 (1969), 13-15.

1665 Lindsay, Jack. Life Rarely Tells. London: Bodley Head, 1958.

1666 _____ "Norman Lindsay: Problems of His Life and Work." Meanjin, 29 (1970), 39-48.

1667 Lindsay, Lionel. Comedy of Life: An Autobiography. Sydney: Angus & Robertson, 1967.

1668 Lindsay, Norman. My Mask: For What Little I Know of the Man Behind It: An Autobiography. Sydney: Angus & Robertson, 1970.

1669 _____ "On Life and Writing: Some Letters from Norman Lindsay." Bulletin (Sydney), 2 Feb. 1955, pp. 23-24, 26-32.

1670 _____ The Scribblings of an Idle Mind. Melbourne: Lansdowne, 1966.

1671 _____ "Unpublished Letters: Norman Lindsay to Lionel Lindsay." Southerly, 30 (1970), 289-300.

1672 Lindsay, Philip. I'd Live the Same Life Over. London: Hutchinson, 1941.

1673 Lindsay, Rose. Model Wife: My Life with Norman Lindsay. Sydney: Ure Smith, 1967.

1674 McCrae, Hugh. Story-Book Only. Sydney: Angus & Robertson, 1948.

1675 Mackaness, George. "Collecting Norman Lindsay, Part One of Three Parts." ABC, 7, no. 1 (1956), 15-20.

1676 _____ "Collecting Norman Lindsay." Southerly, 20 (1959), 24-28.

1677 Muirden, Bruce W. "The Great Australian Pagan." MUM, 43 (1950), 30-33.

1678 Slessor, Kenneth. "Australian Poetry and Norman Lindsay." Southerly, 16 (1955), 62-72.

1679 Stewart, Douglas. "Norman Lindsay's Novels." Southerly, 20 (1959),
      2-9.

MCAULEY, James

1681 Bradley, D. "James McAuley: The Landscape of the Heart." In item 587,
      pp. 389-406.

1682 Buckley, Vincent. "Classicism and Grace: James McAuley." In item 509,
      pp. 177-95.

1683 ____ "James McAuley, the Man and the Poet." Westerly, 3 (1960), 13-15.

1684 Dunlevy, Maurice. "Vis-a-vis McAuley." Canberra Times, 5 Aug. 1967,
      pp. 7-8.

1685 Hope, A. D. "Captain Quiros." TC (Melbourne), 19 (1964), 107-16.

1686 Hughes, Robert. "The Wrong End of Modernity." AustL, 2, no. 3 (1959),
      44-53.

1687 Kramer, Leonie. "James McAuley's Captain Quiros." Southerly, 25
      (1965), 147-61.

1688 ____, and T. Inglis Moore. James McCauley [sic]: Tradition in Australian
      Poetry. Canberra: Canberra Univ. College, 1958.

1689 McAuley, James. "Introduction" to Australian Poets: James McAuley.
      Sydney: Angus & Robertson, 1963, pp. vii-viii.

1690 ____ James McAuley Reads from His Own Work. St. Lucia: Univ. of
      Queensland Press, 1970.

1691 ____ "The McAuley Affair." Quadrant, 11, no. 5 (1967), 17-20.

1692 Reid, Owen. "James McAuley, the Academic Poet." TasE, 16 (1964), 79-83.

1693 Sister Mary Rosalie. "Culture Without Anarchy." AustL, 2, no. 3 (1959),
      54-57.

1694 Smith, Vivian. James McAuley. Melbourne: Lansdowne, 1965.

1695 ____ James McAuley's Recent Poetry. Canberra: Australian National Univ.
      Press, 1964.

1696 Talbot, Norman. "Reasonable, Decorous and Epic." Quadrant, 8, no. 4
      (1964), 69-75.

1697 Thompson, John. "Poetry in Australia." Southerly, 27 (1967), 96-106.

1698 Vassileff, Elizabeth. "The Temple and the People's Palace." Meanjin,
      12 (1953), 209-16.

MCCRAE, Hugh

1699 Chaplin, Harry F. A McCrae Miscellany. Sydney: Wentworth, 1967.

1700 Chisholm, A. R. "Hugh McCrae, O. B. E., 1876-1958." AustQ, 30, no. 2
      (1958), 39-41.

1701 Cowper, Norman. "McCrae the Man." Southerly, 19 (1958), 67-75.

1702 Fitzgerald, R. D. "Tributes to Hugh McCrae." Meanjin, 17 (1958), 73-82.

1703 Howarth, R. G. "'The Du Poissy Anecdoes.'" Southerly, 10 (1949), 17-27.

1704 ____ "Hugh McCrae as a Lyrist." Southerly, 17 (1956), 143-46.

1705 ____ "The Prose of Hugh McCrae." Southerly, 15 (1954), 209-13.

1706 ____ "The Ship of Heaven." Southerly, 18 (1957), 216-21.

1707 Lindsay, Norman. "Hugh McCrae." Bulletin (Sydney), 20 April 1949, p. 2.

1708 McCrae, Hugh. The Letters of Hugh McCrae, Ed. by R. D. Fitzgerald. Sydney: Angus & Robertson, 1970.

1709 ____ My Father, and My Father's Friends. Sydney: Angus & Robertson, 1935.

1710 Mackaness, George. "Collecting Hugh McCrae." ABC, 9, no. 4 (1958), 4-6.

1711 Slessor, Kenneth. "Australian Poetry and Hugh McCrae." Southerly, 17 (1956), 128-37.

1712 Stewart, Douglas. "An Introduction to McCrae: For a Proposed Selected Poems." Southerly, 22 (1962), 22-31.

1713 Thompson, John. Five to Remember. Sydney: Angus & Robertson, 1964.

MACKENZIE, Kenneth [pseud. Seaforth Mackenzie]

1714 Barnard, Marjorie. "The Novels of Seaforth Mackenzie." Meanjin, 13 (1954), 503-11.

1715 Clarke, Donovan. "Seaforth Mackenzie: Novelist of Alienation." Southerly, 25 (1965), 75-90.

1716 Cowan, Peter. "Seaforth Mackenzie's Novels." Meanjin, 24 (1965), 298-307.

1717 Davis, Diana. "A Checklist of Kenneth Mackenzie's Works." ALS, 4 (1970), 398-404.

1718 ____ "The Genesis of a Writer: The Early Years of Kenneth Mackenzie." ALS, 3 (1968), 254-70.

1719 ____ "Seaforth Mackenzie." Westerly, 3 (1966), 4-12.

1720 Geering, R. G. "Seaforth Mackenzie's Fiction: Another View." Southerly, 26 (1966), 25-39.

1721 Jones, Evan. "A Dead Man Rising: The Poetry of Kenneth Mackenzie." AustQ, 36, no. 2 (1964), 70-79.

1722 ____ Kenneth Mackenzie. Melbourne: Oxford Univ. Press, 1969.

1723 ____ "Kenneth Mackenzie's Hospital Poems." Westerly, 3 (1966), 13-14.

1724 Neggo, O. "Seaforth Mackenzie: An Introduction to an Australian Writer." WATJ, 56 (1966), 424-25.

1725 Stewart, Douglas. "Foreword" to The Young Desire It. Sydney: Angus & Robertson, 1963, pp. vii-xiii.

See also: 6143, 6144.

MANN, Leonard

1726 Burgess, O. N. "Flesh in Armour." Southerly, 6, no. 2 (1945), 10-11.

1727 Heseltine, H. P. "Review of Mann's Venus Half-Caste." Meanjin, 22 (1963), 422-26.

1728 Mann, Leonard. "A Double Life." Southerly, 29 (1969), 163-74.

1729 Vintner, Maurice. "Rediscovery--1. Leonard Mann's A Murder in Sydney." Overland, 44 (1970), 39-40.

MARTIN, David

1730 Anon. "Portrait of the Novel as a Play." Australian, 9 April 1966, p. 10.

1731 Buckley, Brian. "The Improbable Australian." Bulletin (Sydney),
      18 Sept. 1966, p. 32.

1732 Phillips, A. A. "The Writings of David Martin." Meanjin, 20 (1961),
      15-24.

See also: 1090.

MATHERS, Peter

1733 Burns, Robert. "The Underdog-Outsider: The Achievement of Mathers'
      Trap." Meanjin, 29 (1970), 95-105.

1734 Clancy, L. J. "Trap for Young Players: Peter Mathers' Novel." Meanjin,
      25 (1966), 485-88.

1735 Collinson, Lawrence. "Seeing Mathers Subjectively." Overland, 25 (1966),
      11-12.

1736 Mathers, Peter. "Pittsburgh Identity: 0000000621." Overland, 39 (1968),
      12-16.

MURDOCH, Walter

1737 Durack, Mary. "Walter Murdoch: The Man in the Mirror." Meanjin, 28
      (1969), 217-20.

1738 Murdoch, Walter. "Alfred Deakin on Australian Literature, with a
      Commentary by Walter Murdoch." Meanjin, 16 (1957), 427-30.

1739 Phillips, A. A. "Walter Murdoch: The Art of Good-Humoured Devastation."
      Meanjin, 28 (1969), 221-23.

1740 Triebel, L. A. "Walter Murdoch: Australia's Premier Essayist." SAQ,
      59 (1960), 556-67.

1741 ____ "Walter Murdoch: Essayist." Meanjin, 28 (1969), 209-16.

1742 ____ "Walter Murdoch, Essayist: Two Points of View, 1. 'Murdoch's
      Travels and Homecoming,' 2. 'Murdoch's Mask' by C. H. Hadgraft."
      Southerly, 8 (1947), 17-25.

NEILSON, Shaw

1743 Anderson, Hugh. "Green Singer." Southerly, 17 (1956), 9-16.

1744 ____ "A List of Uncollected Poems by Shaw Neilson." Southerly, 17
      (1956), 37-38.

1745 ____ Shaw Neilson: An Annotated Bibliography and Checklist, 1893-1964.
      Rev. ed. Sydney: Wentworth, 1964.

1746 Blake, Leslie J. Shaw Neilson and the Wimmera. Nhill, Victoria: Lowan
      Shore Hall, n.d.

1747 ____ "Talking to Ted." Overland, 35 (1966), 50-51.

1748 Chaplin, Harry F. A Neilson Collection: An Annotated Catalogue of First
      Editions, Inscribed Copies, Letters, Manuscripts and Association Items.
      Sydney: Wentworth, 1964.

1749 Chisholm, A. R. "The Celt in Shaw Neilson." Meanjin, 21 (1962), 438-43.

1750 ____, ed. Poems of Shaw Neilson, with an Introduction. Sydney: Angus &
      Robertson, 1965.

1751 ____ "Shaw Neilson's Metaphysic." Southerly, 17 (1956), 17-20.

1752 Devaney, James. "John Shaw Neilson's Poems." Meanjin, 24 (1965), 256-59.

1753 _____ "Neilson's Manuscripts." Southerly, 17 (1956), 34-36.

1754 _____ Shaw Neilson. Sydney: Angus & Robertson, 1944.

1755 Douglas, Dennis. "The Imagination of John Shaw Neilson." ALS, 5 (1971), 18-23.

1756 Harris, Max. "John Shaw Neilson." AustL, 6, nos. 3-4 (1964), 16-21.

1757 Harrison, Ruth. "Towards a Reassessment of the MSS of Shaw Neilson." ALS, 3 (1968), 305-12.

1758 Howarth, L. I. "Neilsonian Gleanings." Southerly, 17 (1956), 27-28.

1759 Howarth, R. G. "Shaw Neilson, 1872-1942." Southerly, 17 (1956), 2-8.

1760 John Shaw Neilson: A Memorial. Melbourne: Bread & Cheese Club, 1942.

1761 McAuley, James. "Shaw Neilson's Poetry." ALS, 2 (1966), 235-53.

1762 Meeking, Charles. "First-hand--Memories of Writers: Shaw Neilson." Southerly, 21, no. 3 (1961), 41-42.

1763 Oliver, Harold J. John Shaw Neilson. Melbourne: Oxford Univ. Press, 1968.

1764 _____ "A More Versatile Neilson: The Manuscript Evidence." Southerly, 17 (1956), 29-33.

1765 Reid, Owen. "John Shaw Neilson." TasE, 16 (1964), 13-17.

1766 Stewart, Annette. "A New Light on 'The Orange Tree'?" ALS, 5 (1971), 24-30.

1767 Wright, Judith. "John Shaw Neilson." In item 1066, pp. 111-30.

1768 _____ "Meanjin, Value and Poetry." Meanjin, 27 (1968), 244-49.

1769 _____ Shaw Neilson. Sydney: Angus & Robertson, 1965.

1770 _____ "The Unshielded Eye: The Paradox of Shaw Neilson." Quadrant, 3, no. 4 (1959), 61-75.

O'DOWD, Bernard

1771 Anderson, Hugh. Bernard O'Dowd. New York: Twayne, 1968.

1772 _____ Bernard O'Dowd (1866-1953): An Annotated Bibliography. Sydney: Wentworth, 1963.

1773 _____ "A List of Uncollected Poems [and] O'Dowd in Disguise." Southerly, 14 (1953), 125.

1774 _____ The Poet Militant: Bernard O'Dowd. Foreword by A. R. Chisholm. Melbourne: Hill of Content, 1968.

1775 Baker, Kate. "Bernard Patrick O'Dowd." Southerly, 14 (1953), 81-83. [See also F. T. Macartney, "A Footnote to Bernard O'Dowd." Meanjin, 14 (1955), 142-43.]

1776 Chisholm, A. R. "Bernard O'Dowd." Meanjin, 13 (1954), 136-37.

1777 _____ "The Bush: A Landmark." Southerly, 14 (1953), 90-93.

1777a Elliott, Brian. "The Poetry of Mr. Bernard O'Dowd." AustQ, 12, no. 4 (1940), 62-69.

1778 Foster, A. W. "Bernard O'Dowd, Rationalist." Meanjin, 14 (1955), 143.

1779 Kennedy, Victor, and Nettie Palmer. Bernard O'Dowd. Melbourne: Melbourne Univ. Press, 1954.

1780 Lee, S. E. "The Uncollected Poems of Bernard O'Dowd." Southerly,
      14 (1953), 110-24.

1781 Macartney, F. T. "The Poet Militant." Age, 9 April 1966, p. 15.

1782 ____ "The Poetry of Bernard O'Dowd." Meanjin, 8 (1949), 81-91.

1783 McQueen, Humphrey. A New Britannia. Harmondsworth: Penguin, 1970,
      pp. 101-03.

1784 Miller, E. Morris. "Bernard O'Dowd's Early Writings." Meanjin, 8 (1949),
      233-39.

1785 ____ "O'Dowd's The Bush: An Exposition." Diogenes (Hobart), 3 (1957),
      18-40.

1786 Murdoch, Walter. "Introduction" to The Poems of Bernard O'Dowd.
      Melbourne: Lothian, 1941, pp. v-xi.

1787 ____, et al. "Tributes to the Memory of Bernard O'Dowd." Meanjin,
      12 (1953), 407-19.

1788 Murray-Smith, Stephen, comp. "O'Dowd to Whitman, Whitman to O'Dowd."
      Overland, 23 (1962), 8-18.

1789 O'Dowd, Bernard. Poetry Militant: An Australian Plea for the Poetry
      of Purpose. Melbourne: Lothian, 1909.

1790 ____, et al. "Australian Writers and an English Critic." Bulletin
      (Sydney), 30 Nov. 1905, red page.

1791 O'Dowd, Rudel. "O'Dowd Paterfamilias." Overland, 39 (1968), 17-23.

1792 Phillips, A. A. "Introduction" to Bernard O'Dowd. Sydney: Angus &
      Robertson, 1963, pp. vi-xiii.

1793 Stewart, Douglas. "A Man With a Vision." Bulletin (Sydney), 28 Jan.
      1942, p. 2.

1794 Todd, F. M. "The Poetry of Bernard O'Dowd." Meanjin, 14 (1955), 91-97.

1795 Wilde, W. H. Three Radicals. Melbourne: Oxford Univ. Press, 1969.

1796 Wright, Judith. "The Reformist Poets." In item 1066, pp. 68-79.

See also: 605, 1609, 6364.

PALMER, Nettie

1797 Barrachi, Guido. "Nettie Palmer." Overland, 32 (1965), 37-38.

1798 Hope, A. D., et al. "The Prose of Nettie Palmer." Meanjin, 18 (1959),
      225-38.

1799 Levey, Esther. "Yours as Ever . . . NP." Meanjin, 24 (1965), 329-33.

1800 McLeod, Jessie. "Nettie Palmer: Some Personal Memories." Overland, 31
      (1965), 20-21.

See also: 1807, 1812.

PALMER, Vance

1801 Barnes, John. "The Man of Letters." Meanjin, 18 (1959), 193-205.

1802 Davison, Frank D. "Vance Palmer and His Writings." Meanjin, 7
      (1948), 10-27.

1803 Fitzpatrick, Brian. "The Palmer Pre-eminence." Meanjin, 18 (1959),
      211-17.

1804 Hadgraft, Cecil. "The Fiction of Vance Palmer." Southerly, 10 (1949),
        28-37.

1805 Heseltine, H. P. Vance Palmer. St. Lucia: Univ. of Queensland Press,
        1970.

1806 Hope, A. D. "Vance Palmer Reconsidered." Southerly, 16 (1955), 189-96.

1807 Hotimsky, C. M., and Walter Stone. "A Bibliographical Checklist."
        Meanjin, 17 (1958), 264-69.

1808 Lindsay, Jack. "The Novels." Meanjin, 18 (1959), 146-72.

1809 Macartney, K. "The Plays of Vance Palmer." Meanjin, 2 (1959), 182-92.

1810 McKellar, John. "Vance Palmer as a Novelist." Southerly, 15 (1954),
        16-25.

1811 Oliver, Harold J. "The Passage." Southerly, 6, no. 2 (1945), 18-19.

1812 Palmer, Nettie. "Remembrance of Things Past." Meanjin, 20 (1961), 297-
        301.

1813 Palmer, Vance. "Randolph Bedford." Overland, 26 (1963), 21-22.

1814 Phillips, A. A. "The Short Stories." Meanjin, 18 (1959), 173-81.

1814a Smith, Vivian. Vance Palmer. Melbourne: Lansdowne, 1965.

1815 "Vance Palmer." In item 862, p. 110.

1816 Ward, Russell, et al. "Vance Palmer: Homo Australiensis." Meanjin, 18
        (1959), 239-63.

1817 Waten, Judah. "Vance Palmer and His Literary Contribution." Realist
        Writer, 11 (1963), 22-24.

See also: 701, 6146.

PATERSON, A. B. [Banjo]

1818 Anon. "Whose Matilda?" Nation, 27 Nov. 1965, pp. 9-10.

1819 Edwards, Ron. "Josephine Peney and 'Waltzing Matilda.'" Northern Folk,
        4 (1966), 8-11.

1820 Elliott, Brian. "Australian Paterson." AustQ, 13, no. 2 (1941), 43-50.

1821 Forster, N. H. W. "Mirage and Matilda." Walkabout, 34, no. 1 (1968), 5.

1822 Green, H. M. "Banjo Paterson." In Fourteen Minutes. Sydney: Angus &
        Robertson, 1944, pp. 34-40.

1823 Heseltine, H. P. "Banjo Paterson: A Poet Nearly Anonymous." Meanjin,
        23 (1964), 386-402.

1824 Hooper, F. Earle. "A. B. Paterson: Some Adjustments." Southerly, 10
        (1949), 62-66.

1825 Macartney, F. T. "Jostling Matilda [with a reply by A. A. Phillips]."
        Meanjin, 24 (1965), 359-63.

1826 Manifold, John. "The Banjo." Overland, 1 (1954-55), 14-16.

1827 May, Sydney. The Story of Waltzing Matilda. Brisbane: Smith &
        Paterson, 1944.

1828 Palmer, Helen. A. B. 'Banjo' Paterson. Melbourne: Longmans, 1965.

1829 Semmler, Clement. A. B. Paterson. London and Melbourne: Oxford Univ.
        Press, 1967.

1830 ____ A. B. 'Banjo' Paterson. Melbourne: Lansdowne, 1965.

1831   ____ The Banjo of the Bush: The Work, Life, and Times of A. B. Paterson. Melbourne: Lansdowne, 1966.

1832   ____ "Banjo Paterson and the 1890's." Southerly, 24 (1964), 176-87,

1833   ____ "Kipling and A. B. Paterson: Men of Empire and Action." AustQ, 39, no. 2 (1967), 71-78.

1834   ____, ed. The World of 'Banjo' Paterson: His Stories, Travels, War Reports, and Advice to Racegoers. Sydney: Angus & Robertson, 1967.

1835   ____, ed. The World of 'Banjo' Paterson: Prose Writings of the Balladist. Sydney: Angus & Robertson, 1967.

See also: 1796.

PORTER, Hal

1836 Burns, Robert. "A Sort of Triumph Over Time: Hal Porter's Prose Narratives." Meanjin, 28 (1969), 19-28.

1837 Cantrell, Kerin. "Two Aspects of Hal Porter. 2. The Professor." Southerly, 27 (1967), 185-87. [See item 1842.]

1838 Duncan, R. A. "Hal Porter's Writing and the Impact of the Absurd." Meanjin, 29 (1970), 468-73.

1839 Ewers, John K. "[Review of Porter's The Watcher on the Cast-Iron Balcony]." Westerly, 4 (1963), 90-96.

1840 Finch, Janette. Bibliography of Hal Porter. Adelaide: Libraries Board of South Australia, 1966.

1841 Geering, R. G. "Hal Porter, the Watcher." Southerly, 24 (1964), 92-103.

1842 ____ "Two Aspects of Hal Porter. 1. The Paper Chase." Southerly, 27 (1967), 180-85. [See item 1837.]

1843 Harris, Max. "A Comeback from a Cast-Iron Balcony." Australian, 2 Jan. 1965, p. 9.

1844 Lord, Mary. "A Contribution to the Bibliography of Hal Porter." ALS, 4 (1970), 405-09.

1845 ____ "Hal Porter's Comic Mode." ALS, 4 (1970), 371-82.

1846 Porter, Hal. "Answers to the Funny, Kind Man." Southerly, 29 (1969), 3-14.

1847 ____ "Beyond Whipped Cream and Blood." Bulletin (Sydney), 28 April 1962, p. 66.

1848 ____ "Hal Porter's Australia." AustL, 6, no. 3-4 (1964), 22-50.

1849 ____ The Paper Chase. Sydney: Angus & Robertson, 1966.

1850 ____ The Watcher on the Cast-Iron Balcony. London: Faber & Faber, 1963.

1851 Rolfe, Patricia. "Hal Porter: The Middle Age of Innocence." Bulletin (Sydney), 14 Dec. 1963, pp. 35-37.

1852 Ward, Peter. "The Craft of Hal Porter." AustL, 5, no. 2 (1963), 40-44.

1853 Wilding, Michael. "Two Bibliographies: Hal Porter and Patrick White." ALS, 3 (1967), 142-48.

See also: 1243.

PORTER, Peter

1854   Douglas, Dennis. "Conversation with Peter Porter." Overland, 44 (1970),
       33-34.

1855   Horder, John. "Peter Porter: Expatriate Poet." Canberra Times, 28
       May 1966, p. 9.

1856   Porter, Peter. "A Land Fit for Conservatives." TLS, 30 Aug. 1971,
       pp. 891-93.

1857   Waten, Judah. "Some Australians and Iris Murdoch." Age, 19 Feb. 1966,
       p. 22.

PRICHARD, K. S.

1858   Beasley, Jack. The Rage for Life: The Work of Katharine Susannah
       Prichard. Sydney: Current Book Distributors, 1964.

1859   Cusack, Dymphna. "Katharine Susannah Prichard." Realist, 14 (1964),
       14-16.

1860   Drake-Brockman, Henrietta. Katharine Susannah Prichard.
       Melbourne: Oxford Univ. Press, 1967.

1861   ____   "Katharine Susannah Prichard: The Colour in Her Work." Southerly,
       14 (1953), 214-19.

1862   Eldershaw, M. Barnard. "Two Women Novelists: Henry Handel Richardson
       and Katharine Susannah Prichard." In item 587, pp. 1-41.

1863   Hewett, Dorothy. "Excess of Love." Overland, 42 (1969), 27-31. [See
       also "Katharine Susannah Prichard: 'excess of love'? Some comments."
       Overland, 44 (1970), 25-28.]

1864   ____   "Girl in a White Muslin Dress." Westerly, 4 (1963), 63-65.

1865   Holborn, Muir. "Katharine Susannah Prichard." Meanjin, 10 (1951),
       233-40.

1866   Lindsay, Jack. "The Novels of Katharine Susannah Prichard." Meanjin,
       20 (1961), 366-87.

1867   Lowery, E. S. "Haxby's Circus." Southerly, 6, no. 2 (1945), 6-7.

1868   Malos, Ellen. "Jack Lindsay's Essay on Katharine Susannah Prichard's
       Novels." Meanjin, 22 (1963), 413-17.

1869   ____   "Some Major Themes in the Novels of Katharine Susannah Prichard."
       ALS, 1 (1963), 32-41.

1870   Palmer, Aileen. "The Changing Face of Australia: Notes on the Creative
       Writing of K. S. Prichard." Overland, 12 (1958), 25-31; 13 (1958),
       29-33.

1871   Prichard, Katharine Susannah. Child of the Hurricane: An Autobiography.
       London: Angus & Robertson, 1964.

1872   ____   "Some Perceptions and Aspirations." Southerly, 28 (1968), 235-44.

1873   Roland, Betty. "Requiem for K. S. P." Overland, 44 (1970), 29-31.

1874   Sadleir, Richard. "The Writings of Katharine Susannah Prichard: A
       Critical Evaluation." Westerly, 3 (1961), 31-35.

1875   Wilkes, G. A. "The Novels of Katharine Susannah Prichard." Southerly,
       14 (1953), 220-31.

See also: 701, 6147.

RICHARDSON, Henry Handel [Ethel Florence Lindesay Robertson née Richardson]

1876 Andraud, Robert. "L'Australie dans les romans de Henry Handel Richardson." EA, 3 (1939), 132-41.

1877 Anon. "The Belated Recognition of an Australian Novelist of Genius." Current Opinion, 63 (Nov. 1917), 335-36.

1878 Anon. "The End of a Childhood." TLS, 6 Sept. 1934, p. 602.

1879 Anon. "Henry Handel Richardson." Overland, 1 (1954), 9-10.

1880 B., W. "Notes on Novels." New Republic, 62 (5 March 1930), 80-81.

1881 Baker, Sidney J. Australia Speaks. Sydney: Shakespeare Head, 1953.

1882 Barker, Uther. "Epitaph of a Novelist." Southerly, 10 (1949), 89-92.

1883 Barnes, John. "Henry Handel Richardson." BANQ, 3, no. 3 (1970), 23-25.

1884 Bartlett, Norman. "Pioneers of a New World Literature." SAQ, 49 (1950), 30-41.

1885 Beach, Joseph Warren. The Twentieth Century Novel: Studies in Technique. New York: Appleton-Century-Crofts, 1932, p. 224.

1886 Bentivoglio, Marie. "In the 'Land Down Under.'" Independent Woman, 15 (Sept. 1936), 284-86, 301-02.

1887 Bonnerot, Louis. "Henry Handel Richardson: The End of a Childhood and Other Stories." RAA, 12 (1935), 463.

1888 _____ "Henry Handel Richardson: The Young Cosima." EA, 3 (1939), 191.

1889 Buckley, Vincent. Henry Handel Richardson. Melbourne: Lansdowne, 1963.

1890 Clutton-Brock, M. H. "Mrs. Lins: Sister to Henry Handel Richardson." Southerly, 27 (1967), 46-59.

1891 _____ "The Melancholy Optimist." Meanjin, 29 (1970), 192-208.

1892 Connolly, G. K. "The Classic Australian Three Decker: A New Consideration of The Fortunes of Richard Mahony." Southerly, 19 (1958), 145-54.

1893 Dallimore, Jennifer. "The Malaise of Richard Mahony." Quadrant, 5, no. 4 (1961), 51-58.

1894 Elliott, William D. "French Influences in The Fortunes of Richard Mahony." Discourse, 11 (1968), 108-15.

1895 _____ "Richardson's Realism and The Getting of Wisdom." Discourse, 12 (1969), 12-16.

1896 _____ "Scandinavian Influences in the Novels of H. H. Richardson." Discourse, 12 (1969), 249-54.

1897 Foster, I. M. "Richard Mahony's Tragedy." ALS, 4 (1970), 279-80.

1898 Gibson [Kramer], Leonie J. Henry Handel Richardson and Some of Her Sources. Melbourne: Melbourne Univ. Press, 1954.

1899 Goldberg, Gerald Jay. "The Artist-Novel in Transition." EFT, 4, no. 3 (1961), 12-27.

1900 Gould, Gerald. The English Novel of Today. London: Castle, 1924, pp. 152-53.

1901 Grattan, C. Hartley. "Australian Literature." Bookman (New York), 57 (1928), 625-31.

1902 _____ "Ultima Thule." New Republic, 60 (1929), 278-79.

1903 Green, Dorothy. "The Pilgrim Soul: The Philosophical Structure of The Fortunes of Richard Mahony." Meanjin, 28 (1969), 328-37.

1904 ____ "Walter Lindesay Richardson: The Man, the Portrait, and the Artist." _Meanjin_, 29 (1970), 5-20.

1905 ____ "The Young Cosima." _ALS_, 4 (1970), 215-26.

1906 Hadgraft, Cecil. "Diagnosis of Mahony." _AustQ_, 27, no. 2 (1955), 87-95.

1907 ____ "The Novels of H. H. Richardson." _Southerly_, 9 (1948), 2-17.

1908 Heddle, Enid Moodie. _Australian Literature Now: A Reader's Survey_. Melbourne: Longmans Green, 1949, pp. 32-35.

1909 Henry, Alice. "Who Is Henry Handel Richardson?" _Bookman_ (New York), 70 (1929), 355-59.

1910 Hitchcock, George. "Maurice Guest." _CMis_, 5, no. 2 (1964), 124-27.

1911 Hope, A. D. "Henry Handel Richardson's _Maurice Guest_." _Meanjin_, 14 (1955), 186-99.

1912 Howarth, R. G. "H. H. Richardson's _Richard Mahony_ and The End of a Childhood." _AustQ_, 27, no. 1 (1955), 89-102.

1913 Howells, Gary. _Henry Handel Richardson, 1870-1946: A Bibliography to Honour the Centenary of Her Birth_. Canberra: National Library of Australia, 1970.

1914 Jeffares, A. Norman. "Maurice Guest." _Dubliner_, 1 (1961), 3-7.

1915 ____ "Preface" to _Maurice Guest_. Melbourne: Sun Books, 1965, pp. 3-14.

1916 ____ "Richard Mahony, Exile." _JCL_, 6 (1969), 106-19.

1917 K., B. M. "The Chronicles of The Fortunes of Richard Mahony." _CathW_, 131 (1930), 759-61.

1918 Kenton, Edna. "Maurice Guest and Richard Mahony." _Bookman_ (New York), 46 (1918), 580-82.

1919 Kiernan, Brian. "Romantic Conventions and _Maurice Guest_." _Southerly_, 28 (1968), 286-94.

1920 Kramer, Leonie. _A Companion to 'Australia Felix.'_ Melbourne: Heinemann Educational, 1962.

1921 ____ "Henry Handel Richardson." In item 587, pp. 318-31.

1922 ____ _Henry Handel Richardson_. Melbourne: Oxford Univ. Press, 1967.

1923 ____ "Henry Handel Richardson: The Limits of Realism." _MCR_, 3 (1960), 75-79.

1924 ____ _The Misfortunes of Henry Handel Richardson_. Canberra: Canberra Univ. College, 1958.

1925 ____ _Myself When Laura; Fact and Fiction in Henry Handel Richardson's School Career_. Melbourne: Heinemann, 1966.

1926 Liljegren, Sven B. _Ballarat and the Great Gold Rush According to the Richard Mahony Trilogy: A Study in the Literary Use of Sources_. Uppsala: Lundequistka Bokhandeln, 1964.

1927 Loder, Elizabeth. "The Fortunes of Richard Mahony: Dream and Nightmare." _Southerly_, 25 (1965), 251-63.

1928 ____ "_Maurice Guest_: An Innocent Abroad." _Balcony_, 4 (1966), 34-37.

1929 ____ "_Maurice Guest_: Some Nineteenth-Century Progenitors." _Southerly_, 26 (1966), 94-105.

1930 Mander, Jane. "Henry Handel Richardson." _Manuscripts_, 8 (Feb. 1934), 58-59.

1931 Mares, F. H. "The Fortunes of Richard Mahony: A Reconsideration." _Meanjin_, 21 (1962), 64-70.

1932 Miller, E. Morris. "The Fortunes of Richard Mahony: A Bibliographical
      Note." Meanjin, 3 (1948), 187-89.

1933 _____ "Richard Mahony's Euphoria." Meanjin, 11 (1952), 397-400.

1934 _____ "Richard Mahony's Grave." Meanjin, 8 (1949), 177-80.

1935 Millett, Fred B. Contemporary British Literature. New York: Harcourt &
      Brace, 1950, pp. 42-43, 433-34.

1936 New, William H. "Convention and Freedom: A Study of Maurice Guest."
      ES, Anglo-American supp. (1969), lxii-lxviii.

1937 Odeen, Elizabeth. Maurice Guest: A Study. Austin: Univ. of Texas, 1963.

1938 Palmer, Nettie. Henry Handel Richardson, A Study. Sydney: Angus &
      Robertson, 1950.

1939 _____ "Henry Handel Richardson: The Writer and Her Work." Meanjin, 7
      (1948), 154-63, 231-40.

1940 _____ "Notes for a Diary." Meanjin, 5 (1946), 109-13.

1941 _____ Purdie, Edna, and Olga M. Roncoroni, eds. Henry Handel Richardson,
      Some Personal Impressions. Sydney: Angus & Robertson, 1957.

1942 Richardson, Henry Handel. Myself when Young. London: Heinemann, 1948.

1943 _____ "Notes on Two Studies and The End of a Childhood." Southerly, 23
      (1963), 19-20.

1944 _____ "Some Notes on My Books." VQR, 16 (1940), 334-37. [Repr. in
      Southerly, 23 (1963), 8-19.]

1945 Robertson, J. G. "The Art of Henry Handel Richardson." In item 1942,
      pp. 153-210.

1946 Roderick, Colin. "The Personality of H. H. Richardson." AustQ, 20,
      no. 2 (1948), 44-55.

1947 Roncoroni, Olga M. "1895-1903." In item 1942, pp. 136-50.

1948 Sadleir, Richard. "The Fortunes of Richard Mahony." Westerly, 2-3
      (1962), 107.

1949 Scott-James, Marie. "A Portrait of Wagner." London Mercury, 39 (1939),
      455-56.

1950 Stewart, Kenneth. "The Prototype of Richard Mahony." ALS, 4 (1970),
      227-40.

1951 _____ "Their Road to Life: A Note on Richard Mahony and Walter Richardson."
      Meanjin, 29 (1970), 505-08.

1952 Stoller, Alan, and R. H. Emmerson. "The Fortunes of Walter Lindesay
      Richardson." Meanjin, 29 (1970), 21-33.

1953 Swinnerton, Frank Arthur. "Younger Novelists." In The Georgian Literary
      Scene. London: Hutchinson, 1954, pp. 279-316.

1954 Thomson, A. K. "Henry Handel Richardson's The Fortunes of Richard
      Mahony." Meanjin, 26 (1967), 423-34.

1955 Triebel, L. A. "Henry Handel Richardson's The Young Cosima." Southerly,
      9 (1948), 18-19.

1956 _____ "Source Books of The Young Cosima." Meanjin, 7 (1948), 56-47.

1957 _____ "Source Material for The Young Cosima." Meanjin, 14 (1955),
      200-02.

1958 _____ "The Young Cosima." AustL, 5, no. 1 (1963), 53-57.

1959 Van Kranendonk, A. G. "Een veronachtzaamd Meesterwerk." Stem, 7 (1927),
      218-31.

1960 Van Vechten, Carl. <u>Maurice Guest: Interpreters and Interpretations</u>.
New York: Knopf, 1917.

1961 Watkins, J. B. C. "Henry Handel Richardson." <u>CanF</u>, 11 (1931), 218-20.

1962 Wilkes, G. A. "Henry Handel Richardson: Some Uncollected Writings."
<u>Southerly</u>, 23 (1963), 6-7.

1963 Wittrock, Verna D. "Henry Handel Richardson: An Annotated Bibliography
of Writings About Her." <u>ELT</u>, 7 (1964), 146-87.

See also: 6148, 6149.

SHAPCOTT, Tom

1964 Clancy, L. J. "The Poetry of Thomas W. Shapcott." <u>Meanjin</u>, 26 (1967),
182-87.

SLESSOR, Kenneth

1965 Aldington, Richard. "Kenneth Slessor." <u>AustL</u>, 1, no. 3 (1958), 11-14.

1966 Buckley, Vincent. "Kenneth Slessor: Realist or Romantic." In item 509,
pp. 111-21.

1967 Croft, Julian. "Notes on Slessor's 'Five Visions.'" <u>ALS</u>, 4 (1969),
172-74.

1968 _____ "Slessor's 'Five Visions of Captain Cook.'" <u>ALS</u>, 4 (1969), 3-17.

1969 Frost, Alan. "Captain James Cook and the 'Passage into the Dark.'"
<u>ALS</u>, 4 (1970), 293-94.

1970 Harris, Max. <u>Kenneth Slessor</u>. Melbourne: Lansdowne, 1963.

1971 Higham, Charles. "City's Magic Inspired Slessor." <u>Sydney Morning Herald</u>,
14 Sept. 1957, p. 18.

1972 _____ "The Poetry of Kenneth Slessor." <u>Quadrant</u>, 4, no. 1 (1959-60),
65-74.

1973 Hope, A. D. "Slessor 20 Years After." <u>Bulletin</u> (Sydney), 1 Jan. 1963,
pp. 37-38.

1974 _____ "Slessor Twenty Years After: Why the Poems Survive." <u>Opinion</u>
(Burnside), 7 (1963), 43-45.

1975 Howarth, R. G. "Sound in Slessor's Poetry." <u>Southerly</u>, 16 (1955),
189-95.

1976 Mc, R. "More Slessor." <u>Bulletin</u> (Sydney), 9 Oct. 1957, p. 58.

1977 Macartney, F. T. "The Poetry of Kenneth Slessor." <u>Meanjin</u>, 16 (1957),
265-72.

1978 McGregor, Craig. "Conversation with Kenneth Slessor." <u>Sydney Morning
Herald</u>, 30 Oct. 1965, p. 18.

1979 Mitchell, A. C. W. "Kenneth Slessor and the Grotesque." <u>ALS</u>, 1 (1964),
242-50.

1980 Moore, T. Inglis. "Kenneth Slessor." <u>Southerly</u>, 8 (1947), 195-205.

1981 Semmler, Clement. <u>Kenneth Slessor</u>. London and New York: Longmans Green,
1966.

1982 Slessor, Kenneth. <u>Bread and Wine</u>. Sydney: Angus & Robertson, 1970.

1983 Stewart, Douglas. "Harbour and Ocean." In item 992, pp. 157-63.

1984 _____ "Kenneth Slessor's Poetry." <u>Meanjin</u>, 28 (1969), 149-68.

1985 Talbot, Norman. "Kenneth Slessor, His Elegies in Times." Stride, 1
      (1960), 1-7.

1986 Thomas, F. "Selected Poems of Kenneth Slessor." Poetry, 15 June 1945,
      pp. 42-46.

1987 Thompson, John. "Poetry in Australia: Kenneth Slessor." Southerly, 26
      (1966), 190-98.

1988 Thomson, A. K., ed. Critical Essays on Kenneth Slessor. Brisbane:
      Jacaranda, 1968.

1989 Wallace-Crabbe, Christopher. "Kenneth Slessor and the Powers of
      Language." In item 587, pp. 342-53.

1990 Wright, Judith. "Kenneth Slessor--Romantic and Modern." In item 1066,
      pp. 140-53.

See also: 6150.

STEAD, Christina

1991 Geering, R. G. "The Achievement of Christina Stead." Southerly, 22
      (1962), 193-212.

1992 _____ Christina Stead. New York: Twayne, 1969.

1993 _____ Christina Stead. Melbourne: Oxford Univ. Press, 1969.

1994 _____ "Christina Stead in the 1960's." Southerly, 28 (1968), 26-36.

1995 Green, Dorothy. "Chaos or a Dancing Star? Christina Stead's Seven
      Poor Men of Sydney." Meanjin, 27 (1968), 150-61.

1996 Hardwick, Elizabeth. "The Neglected Novels of Christina Stead." In A
      View of My Own: Essays in Literature and Society. London: Heinemann,
      1964, pp. 41-48.

1997 Jarrell, Randall. "'The Man Who Loved Children.'" Atlantic, 215 (1965),
      166-71.

1998 _____ "An Unread Book." Introd. to Christina Stead, The Man Who Loved
      Children. New York: Holt, Rinehart and Winston, 1965, pp. v-xli.

1999 Katz, Alfred H. "Some Psychological Themes in a Novel by Christina
      Stead." L&P, 15 (1965), 210-15.

2000 Miller, Anthony. "Seven Poor Men of Sydney." Westerly, 2 (1968), 61-66.

2001 Pybus, R. "The Light and the Dark: The Novels of Christina Stead."
      Stand, 10 (1969), 30-37.

2002 Raskin, Jonah. "Christina Stead in Washington Square." LMag, 11 (1970),
      70-77.

2003 Roderick, Colin. "Christina Stead." Southerly, 7 (1946), 87-92.

2004 Schofield, R. J. "The Man Who Loved Christina Stead." Bulletin (Sydney),
      22 May 1965, pp. 29-31.

2005 Stead, Christina. "A Writer's Friends: Piece on 'A Writer's Life.'"
      Southerly, 28 (1968), 163-68.

2006 Thomas, Tony. "Christina Stead." Westerly, 4 (1970), 46-53.

2007 Wilding, Michael. "Christina Stead's Australian Novels." Southerly, 27
      (1967), 20-33.

See also: 1884.

STEWART, Douglas

2008 Ashworth, Arthur. "From a Discussion of the Poetry of Douglas Stewart."
      Poetry Magazine, 5 (1966), 3-6.

2009 Bradley, David. "Second Thoughts About Douglas Stewart." Westerly, 3
      (1960), 23-27.

2010 Burrows, J. F. "An Approach to the Plays of Douglas Stewart."
      Southerly, 23 (1963), 94-108.

2011 Howarth, R. G. "Two Radio Plays." Southerly, 7 (1946), 38-41.

2012 Keesing, Nancy. Douglas Stewart. Melbourne: Lansdowne, 1965.

2013 Kreshner, H. A. Notes on 'The Fire on the Snow.' Sydney: Horwitz-
      Grahame, 1963.

2014 Lawson, Max. Companion to Douglas Stewart: The Fire on the Snow. Introd.
      by Douglas Stewart. Sydney: Angus & Robertson, 1965.

2015 _____ Companion to Douglas Stewart: Ned Kelly. Foreword by Douglas
      Stewart. Sydney: Angus & Robertson, 1965.

2016 Lindsay, Philip. "The Voice of Australia." Southerly, 9 (1948), 125-27.

2017 McAuley, James. "Douglas Stewart." In item 587, pp. 362-76.

2018 Oliver, Harold J. "Douglas Stewart and the Art of the Radio Play." TQ, 5,
      no. 2 (1963), 93-103.

2019 Phillips, A. A. "The Australian Romanticism and Stewart's Ned Kelly."
      In item 894, pp. 96-112.

2020 _____ "Douglas Stewart's Ned Kelly and Australian Romanticism." Meanjin,
      15 (1956), 260-71.

2021 _____ "The Poetry of Douglas Stewart." Meanjin, 28 (1969), 97-104.

2022 Rees, Leslie. "Douglas Stewart and Modern Australian Verse Drama."
      In item 925, pp. 129-48.

2023 Reid, Owen. "Douglas Stewart, Poet, Playwright, and Critic." TasE, 15
      (1963), 243-48.

2024 Smith, Vivian. "Douglas Stewart: Lyric Poet." Meanjin, 26 (1967), 41-50.

2025 Stewart, Douglas. "Introduction" to Australian Poets: Douglas Stewart.
      Sydney: Angus & Robertson, 1963, pp. v-ix.

2026 _____ "On Being a Verse Playwright." Meanjin, 22 (1964), 272-77.

2027 Thompson, John. "Poetry in Australia: Douglas Stewart." Southerly, 27
      (1967), 188-98.

2028 Tory, Alan. "The Shade of Ned Kelly." In Harbour in Heaven. Sydney:
      G. M. Dash, 1949 , pp. 21-25.

See also: 628.

STONE, Louis

2029 Green, Dorothy. "Louis Stone's Jonah: A Cinematic Novel." ALS, 2 (1965),
      15-31.

2030 Lindsay, Norman. "Louis Stone." In item 798, pp. 127-41.

2031 Oliver, Harold J. "Louis Stone." Meanjin, 12 (1954), 334-45.

2032 _____ Louis Stone. Melbourne: Oxford Univ. Press, 1968.

STOW, Randolph

2033 Bradley, J. "Randolph Stow: The Stamp of Greatness." Westerly, 1
       (1959), 8-10.

2034 Buckley, Vincent. "In the Shadow of Patrick White." Meanjin, 20 (1961),
       144-45.

2035 Burgess, O. N. "The Novels of Randolph Stow." AustQ, 37, no. 2 (1965),
       73-81.

2036 Clarke, Donovan. "'My Soul Is a Strange Country': On Randolph Stow."
       Bridge, 2, no. 1 (1965), 37-43.

2037 _____ "New Aspects of the Novel." AustH, 46, no. 3 (1966), 5-8.

2038 _____ "The Realities of Randolph Stow." Bridge, 2, no. 2 (1966), 37-42.

2039 Conron, Brandon. "Voyager from Eden." ArielE, 1, no. 4 (1970), 96-102.

2040 Dutton, Geoffrey. "The Search for Permanence: The Novels of Randolph
       Stow." JCL, 1 (1965), 135-48.

2041 Heseltine, H. P. "[Review of Tourmaline]." Meanjin, 22 (1963), 422-26.

2042 Johnston, G. K. W. "The Art of Randolph Stow." Meanjin, 20 (1961),
       139-43.

2043 Kramer, Leonie. "The Novels of Randolph Stow." Southerly, 24 (1964),
       78-91.

2044 Martin, David. "Among the Bones." Meanjin, 18 (1959), 52-58.

2045 Mitchell, A. C. W. "The Merry-go-round in the Sea." Opinion, 12, no. 3
       (1968), 7-16.

2046 Nelson, Penelope. "Randolph Stow, the Poet." Drylight, (1965), 37-38.

2047 New, William H. "Outsider Looking Out: The Novels of Randolph Stow."
       Critique (Minneapolis), 11, no. 1 (1967), 90-99.

2048 Newby, P. H. "The Novels of Randolph Stow." AustL, 1, no. 2 (1957),
       49-51.

2049 O'Brien, Patricia. Randolph Stow: A Bibliography. Adelaide: Libraries
       Board of South Australia, 1968.

2050 Oppen, Alice. "Myth and Reality in Randolph Stow." Southerly, 27
       (1967), 82-94.

2051 Tanner, Godfrey. "The Road to Jerusalem." Nimrod, 2, no. 1 (1964),
       33-39.

2052 Wightman, Jennifer. "Waste Places, Dry Souls: The Novels of Randolph
       Stow." Meanjin, 28 (1969), 239-52.

See also: 6267.

TENNANT, Kylie

2053 Auchterlonie, Dorothy. "The Novels of Kylie Tennant." Meanjin, 12
       (1953), 395-403.

2054 Dick, Margaret. The Novels of Kylie Tennant. Adelaide: Rigby; San
       Francisco: Tri-Ocean, 1966.

2055 Herring, Thelma. "Tiburon." Southerly, 6, no. 2 (1945), 8-9.

2056 Hersey, April. "Back to the Battling." Bulletin (Sydney), 29 April
       1967, p. 32.

2057   Kelly, Leo. "Kylie Tennant." Overland, 17 (1960), 41.

2058   Moore, T. Inglis. "The Tragi-Comedies of Kylie Tennant." Southerly,
        18 (1957), 2-8.

2059   Tennant, Kylie. "I'm Going to Jail . . . ." AustWW, 25 Oct. 1967, pp. 4-5.

TUCKER, James [pseud. Ralph Rashleigh]

2060   Argyle, Barry. "Ralph Rashleigh." ArielE, 2, no. 1 (1971), 5-25.

2061   Ellis, M. H. "Dr. Roderick's Latest." Bulletin (Sydney), 9 Feb. 1963,
        pp. 40-42.

2062   Healy, John J. "The Convict and the Aborigine: The Quest for Freedom
        in Ralph Rashleigh." ALS, 3 (1968), 243-53.

See also: 1090.

TURNER, George

2063   Burrows, J. F. "[Review of Turner's The Cupboard Under the Stairs]."
        Southerly, 23 (1963), 276-80.

2064   Kellaway, Frank. "The Novels of George Turner." Adult Education, 8
        (1963), 15-19.

2065   McLaren, John. "The Image of Reality in Our Writing." Overland, 27-28
        (1963), 43-47.

2066   Ward, Peter. "The Novels of George Turner." AustL, 5, no. 4 (1963),
        40-44.

WALLACE-CRABBE, Christopher

2067   Colman, E. A. "A Modest Radiance: The Poetry of Chris Wallace-Crabbe."
        Westerly, 1 (1969), 45-51.

2068   Steele, Peter. "To Move in Light: The Poetry of Chris Wallace-Crabbe."
        Meanjin, 29 (1970), 149-55.

2069   Wallace-Crabbe, Christopher. "Chris Wallace Crabbe Answers R. A. Simpson."
        Poetry Magazine, 3 (1966), 3-5.

WATEN, Judah

2070   Martin, David. "Three Realists in Search of Reality." Meanjin, 18
        (1959), 305-22.

2071   Waten, Judah. From Odessa to Odessa: The Journey of an Australian
        Writer. Melbourne: Cheshire, 1969.

2072   ____ "Going Back to Odessa." Communist Review, 288 (1966), 17-19.

WEBB, Francis

2073   Buckley, Vincent. "The Poetry of Francis Webb." Meanjin, 12 (1953),
        30-34.

2074   Feltham, Elizabeth. "Francis Webb and Robert Lowell." Quadrant, 6,
        no. 22 (1967), 19-28.

2075   Heseltine, H. P.   "The Very Gimbals of Unease: The Poetry of Francis
        Webb." Meanjin, 26 (1967), 255-74.

2076   Lawson, Sylvia.   "The World of Francis Webb." AustL, 4, no. 1 (1961),
        57-60.

2077   Read, Herbert.   "[Letter to the Editor on the Neglect of Francis Webb's
        Poetry]." LMag, 7, no. 9 (1967), 116.

2078   Tulip, James.   "The Poetry of Francis Webb." Southerly, 29 (1969), 184-91.

2079   Wallace-Crabbe, Christopher.   Order and Turbulence: The Poetry of Francis
        Webb. Carlton: Melbourne Univ. Press, 1961.

WEST, Morris

2080   Armstrong, Madeleine.   "Saints Alive." Bulletin (Sydney), 29 July 1967,
        p. 37.

2081   Brisbane, Katharine.   "Flamboyant Dancing--and the Worst of West."
        Australian, 15 July 1967, p. 8.

2082   Brown, Anthony.   "Who Killed the Cuckoo? Morris West's Saigon."
        Bulletin (Sydney), 15 May 1965, pp. 27-28.

2083   Cunningham, James.   "Morris West--An Interview." Sydney Morning Herald,
        17 July 1965, p. 13.

2084   Duprey, Richard A.   "Morris West: A Witness for Compassion." CathW,
        193 (1961), 360-66.

2085   Elliott, Brian, et al.   "A Morris West Symposium." AustBR, 2 (1963),
        142-43.

2086   Finkelstein, Sidney.   "Daughter of Silence." Mainstream, 15 (1962),
        57-58.

2087   Goldsmith, Arnold L.   "The Value of Contradiction in The Devil's
        Advocate." Renascence, 14 (1962), 199-205.

2088   H[astings], P[eter] D.   "Morris West at Home." Bulletin (Sydney), 10
        March 1962, p. 17.

2089   Johns, Brian.   "Second Calling: The Formative Years of Morris West."
        Nation,10 Aug. 1963, pp. 11-12.

2090   Kirvan, John J.   "The Shadow of Truth." Commonweal, 72 (1960), 421-24.

2091   Mondrone, Domenico.   "L'avvocato del Diavolo, di un meridionalista fuori
        serie." Civiltà Cattolica, 113 (1962), 443-55.

2092   Newquist, Roy.   "Morris West." In item 4644, pp. 635-43.

2093   Pearl, Cyril.   "Aye, Aye, Mr. West." Nation, 7 Aug. 1965, p. 7.

2094   Reid, John Howard.   "The Alien World of Morris West." AustL, 4, no. 2
        (1962), 52-57.

2095   Rolfe, Patricia.   "Profit Without Honour." Bulletin (Sydney) 24 Aug.
        1963, pp. 15-18.

2096   Thomas, Keith.   "Theatre: Wanted--A Devil's Advocate." Nation, 29 July
        1967, p. 18.

2097   West, Morris.   "The Struggle for Identity." Age, 3 Dec. 1966, p. 21.

WHITE, Patrick

2098   Anon.   "Attempting the Infinite." TLS, 15 Dec. 1961, pp. 889-91.

2099   "The Australian Novelists. 2. Patrick White." Bulletin (Sydney), 25 Jan. 1961, p. 17.

2100   "Patrick White and the Sino-Soviet Split." Bulletin (Sydney), 5 Oct. 1963, p. 8.

2101   "Our Trailer--on Homo Australiensis." Westerly, 2 (1961), 5-6.

2102 Argyle, Barry. Patrick White. Edinburgh and London: Oliver & Boyd, 1967.

2103 Aurousseau, Marcel. "The Identity of Voss." Meanjin, 17 (1958), 85-87.

2104   "Odi Profanum Vulgus: Patrick White's Riders in the Chariot." Meanjin, 21 (1962), 29-31

2105 Barden, Garrett. "Patrick White's The Tree of Man." Studies, 47 (1968), 78-85.

2106 Barnard, Marjorie. "The Four Novels of Patrick White." Meanjin, 15 (1956), 156-70.

2107   "Theodora Again." Southerly, 20 (1959), 51-55.

2108 Barnes, John. "A Note on Patrick White's Novels." LCrit, 6, no. 3 (1964), 93-101. [Repr. in item 866, pp. 93-101.]

2109 Beasley, Jack. "The Great Hatred." Realist Writer, 9 (1962), 11-14.

2110 Beatson, Peter. "The Three Stages: Mysticism in Patrick White's Voss." Southerly, 30 (1970), 111-21.

2111 Bradley, David. "Australia Through the Looking-Glass." Overland, 23 (1961), 41-45.

2112 Brand, M. "Another Look at Patrick White." Realist Writer, 12 (1963), 21-22.

2113 Bray, J. J. "The Ham Funeral." Meanjin, 21 (1962), 32-34.

2114 Bright-Holmes, J. "Australian Rebels." Time and Tide, 41 (1960), 733.

2115 Bríssenden, R. F. "Patrick White." Meanjin, 18 (1959), 410-25.

2116   Patrick White. London: Longmans Green, 1966.

2117   Patrick White. Canberra: Univ. College, 1958. [Repr. in Meanjin, 18 (1959), 410-25.]

2118   "The Plays of Patrick White." Meanjin, 23 (1964), 243-56.

2119 Buckley, Vincent. "The Novels of Patrick White." In item 587, pp. 413-26.

2120   "Patrick White and His Epic." In item 751, pp. 187-97.

2121 Burgess, O. N. "Patrick White, His Critics and Laura Trevelyan." AustQ, 33, no. 4 (1961), 49-57.

2122 Burrows, J. F. "Archetypes and Stereotypes: Riders in the Chariot." Southerly, 25 (1965), 46-68. [Repr. in item 2219, pp. 47-71.]

2123   "'Jardin Exotique': The Central Phase of The Aunt's Story." Southerly, 26 (1966), 152-73. [Repr. in item 2219, pp. 85-108.]

2124   "Patrick White's Four Plays." ALS, 2 (1966), 155-70.

2125   "The Short Stories of Patrick White." Southerly, 24 (1964), 116-25. [Repr. in item 2219, pp. 163-81.]

2126   "Stan Parker's Tree of Man." Southerly, 29 (1969), 257-79.

2127   "Voss and the Explorers." AUMLA, 26 (1966), 234-40.

2128 Christesen, C. B. "A Note on Patrick White." Meanjin, 16 (1956), 223-24.

2129 Clark, Manning. "Ludwig Leichhardt's Letters." Meanjin, 27 (1968), 405-08.

2130 Coe, R. N. "The Artist and the Grocer: Patrick White's The Vivisector."
      Meanjin, 29 (1970), 526-29.

2131 Covell, Roger. "Patrick White's Plays." Quadrant, 8, no. 1 (1964), 7-12.

2132 Cowburn, John. "The Metaphysics of Voss." TC (Melbourne), 18 (1964),
      352-61.

2133 Dillistone, F. W. "Meaning and Meaninglessness in Recent Literature."
      In E. W. Kemp, ed., Man, Fallen and Free: Oxford Essays on the
      Condition of Man. London: Hodder & Stoughton, 1969, pp. 59-77.

2134 ____ Patrick White's Riders in the Chariot. New York: Seabury Press,
      1969.

2135 Donaldson, I. "Return to Abyssinia." EIC, 14 (1964), 210-14.

2136 Dutton, Geoffrey. "The British and Us. II. Gentlemen vs. Lairs."
      Quadrant, 9, no. 1 (1965), 18-19.

2137 ____ "A Distinguished Australian Novelist." Hemisphere, 6, no. 7 (1962),
      12-14.

2138 ____ "The Novels of Patrick White." Critique (Minneapolis), 6, no. 3
      (1963), 7-28.

2139 ____ Patrick White. Melbourne: Lansdowne, 1961; rev. eds., 1963, 1971.

2140 Edwards, Allan. "Riders in the Chariot: A Note on the Title." Westerly,
      2-3 (1962), 108-10.

2141 Finch, Janette. Bibliography of Patrick White. Adelaide: Libraries
      Board of South Australia, 1966.

2142 Fitzpatrick, Kathleen. "Ludwig Leichhardt." VHM, 40 (1969), 190-203.

2143 Forrest, David. Patrick White. (Commonwealth Literary Fund Lectures, 5.)
      St. Lucia: Univ. of Queensland, 1962.

2144 Fry, Robert. "Voss." AustL, 1, no. 3 (1958), 40-42.

2145 Gzell, Sylvia. "Themes and Imagery in Voss and Riders in the Chariot."
      ALS, 1 (1964), 180-95.

2146 Hadgraft, Cecil. Patrick White. (Commonwealth Literary Fund Lectures.
      4.) St. Lucia: Univ. of Queensland, 1961.

2147 Hanger, Eunice. "Australian Drama Now." MD, 8 (1965), 79-81.

2148 ____ "Place in Australian Theatre." AustQ, 34, no. 2 (1962), 66-73.

2149 ____ "The Setting in Patrick White's Two Plays: Unlocalized in The Ham
      Funeral, Australian in Season at Sarsaparilla." In François Jost, ed.,
      Proceedings of the 4th Congress of the International Comparative
      Literature Association. 2 vols. The Hague: Mouton, 1966; I, 644-53.

2150 Hastings, Peter D. "The Writing Business: William Collins and Patrick
      White." Observer, 21 March 1959, pp. 175-76.

2151 Herring, Thelma. "Maenads and Goat-Song: The Plays of Patrick White."
      Southerly, 25 (1965), 219-33. [Repr. in item 2219, pp. 147-62.]

2152 ____ "Odyssey of a Spinster: A Study of The Aunt's Story." Southerly,
      25 (1965), 6-22. [Repr. in item 2219, pp. 3-20.]

2153 ____ "Self and Shadow: The Quest for Totality in The Solid Mandala."
      Southerly, 26 (1966), 180-89. [Repr. in item 2219, pp. 72-82.]

2154 ____ "The Solid Mandala: Two Notes." Southerly, 28 (1968), 216-22.

2155 Heseltine, H. P. "Patrick White's Style." Quadrant, 7, no. 3 (1963),
      61-74.

2156 ____ "Riders in the Chariot." Meanjin, 20 (1961), 474-77.

2157 _____ "Writer and Reader." Southerly, 25 (1965), 69-71.

2158 Hetherington, John. "Patrick White: Invulnerable to the Gibes of His Critics." Age, lit. supp., 16 July 1960, p. 17.

2159 Heuzenroeder, John. "Patrick White." Verve, 1 (1962), 2-7.

2160 Heydon, J. D. "Patrick White." Oxford Review, 1 (1966), 33-46.

2161 Hossain, Hameeda. "The Burnt Ones." AustQ, 37, no. 4 (1965), 120-23.

2162 Hughes, Ted. "Patrick White's Voss." Listener, 71 (1964), 229-30.

2163 Kantor, P. P. "Jews and Jewish Mysticism in Patrick White's Riders in the Chariot." BBBull, 11 (1963), 14-16, 20.

2164 Kershaw, A. "The Last Expatriate." AustL, 1, no. 3 (1958), 35-37.

2165 Kramer, Leonie. "Adventures of the Mind." Etruscan, 18, no. 3 (1969), 15-17.

2166 Laidlaw, R. P. "The Complexity of Voss." SoRA, 4 (1970), 3-14.

2167 Lindsay, Jack. "The Alienated Australian Intellectual." Meanjin, 22 (1963), 48-59.

2168 _____ "The Stories of Patrick White." Meanjin, 23 (1964), 372-76.

2169 Loder, Elizabeth. "The Ham Funeral and Its Place in the Development of Patrick White." Southerly, 23 (1963), 78-91.

2170 Macartney, Keith. "Patrick White's A Cheery Soul." Meanjin, 23 (1964), 93-95.

2171 McAuley, James. "The Gothic Splendours: Patrick White's Voss." Southerly, 25 (1965), 34-44. [Repr. in item 2219, pp. 34-46.]

2172 MacKenzie, Manfred. "Abyssinia Lost and Regained." EIC, 13 (1963), 293-300.

2173 _____ "Apocalypse in Patrick White's The Tree of Man." Meanjin, 25 (1966), 405-16.

2174 _____ "The Consciousness of 'twin consciousness': Patrick White's The Solid Mandala." Novel, 2 (1969), 241-54.

2175 _____ "Patrick White's Later Novels: A Generic Reading." SoRA, 1, no. 3 (1965), 5-17.

2176 _____ "The Tree of Man: A Generic Approach." In John Colmer, ed., Approaches to the Novel. Adelaide: Rigby, 1966, pp. 90-102.

2177 _____ "Yes, Let's Return to Abyssinia." EIC, 14 (1964), 433-35.

2178 McLaren, John. "The Image of Reality in Our Writing." Overland, 27-28 (1963), 43-47.

2179 _____ "Patrick White's Use of Imagery." ALS, 2 (1966), 217-20.

2180 Maes-Jelinek, Hena. "The Living and the Dead." RLV, 29 (1963), 521-28.

2181 Martin, David. "A Chariot Between Faith and Despair: On Patrick White's Riders in the Chariot." Bridge, 1, no. 1 (1964), 7-12.

2182 Mather, Rodney. "Patrick White and Lawrence: A Contrast." CR, 13 (1970), 34-50.

2183 _____ "Voss." MCR, 6 (1963), 93-101.

2184 O'Grady, Desmond. "Patrick White's Voss in Italy." Age, 10 Dec. 1966, p. 22.

2185 O'Grady, Helen. "Patrick White." Verve, 1 (1958), n. pag.

2186 Oliver, Harold J. "Patrick White's Significant Journey." Southerly, 19 (1958), 46-49.

2187   Osborne, Charles. "Patrick White's Plays." LMag, 5, no. 6 (1965), 95-100.

2188   Phillips, A. A. "The Dogs Have Their Day." Overland, 25 (1963), 33-34.

2189   ____ "Patrick White and the Algebraic Symbol." Meanjin, 24 (1966), 455-61.

2190   ____ "The Solid Mandala: Patrick White's New Novel." Meanjin, 25 (1966), 31-33.

2191   Porter, Peter. "Sydneyside." New Statesman, 69 (1965), 171.

2192   Potter, Nancy A. J. "Patrick White's Minor Saints." REL, 5 (1964), 9-19.

2193   Prideaux, H. "The Experimental Novel in Australia; Part Two: Patrick White." Prospect, 3, no. 3 (1960), 20-22.

2194   Rawlins, A. "Letter." Nation (Sydney), 27 Jan. 1962, p. 18.

2195   Richards, Jack. "Patrick White, Australian Novelist." SAP, 3 (1970), 113-19.

2196   Riemer, A. P. "Visions of the Mandala in The Tree of Man." Southerly, 27 (1967), 3-19. [Repr. in item 2219, pp. 109-26.]

2197   Roderick, Colin. "Riders in the Chariot: An Exposition." Southerly, 12 (1962), 62-77.

2198   Rolfe, Patricia. "Not a Common Office Boy." Bulletin (Sydney), 7 July 1962, p. 18.

2199   Rorke, John. "Patrick White and His Critics." Southerly, 20 (1959), 66-74.

2200   Scott, Margaret. "Riders in the Chariot." NZMR, 4, no. 35 (1963), 17-19.

2201   Semmler, Clement. "Sarsparilla in Solferino." AustBR, 1 (1962), 94-95.

2202   Shrubb, Peter. "Patrick White: Chaos Accepted." Quadrant, 53 (1968), 7-19.

2203   Small, J. "Patrick White's Opera: The Advent of Peter Sculthorpe." Bulletin (Sydney), 13 June 1964, p. 47.

2204   Stern, James. "Patrick White: The Country of the Mind." LMag, 5, no. 6 (1958), 49-56.

2205   Taft, R. "Mateship, Successship and Suburbia." Westerly, 2 (1961), 23-24.

2206   ____ "A Sociological Interpretation." Westerly, 3-4 (1965), 77-80.

2207   Tanner, Godfrey. "The Road to Jerusalem." Nimrod, 2, no. 1 (1964), 33-39.

2208   Tasker, John. "Notes on The Ham Funeral." Meanjin, 23 (1964), 299-302.

2209   Taylor, Andrew. "White's Short Stories." Overland, 31 (1965), 79-80.

2210   Thompson, John. "Australia's White Policy." AustL, 1, no. 3 (1958), 42-45.

2211   Thomson, A. K. "Patrick White's The Tree of Man." Meanjin, 25 (1966), 21-30.

2212   Turner, Ian. "The Parable of Voss." In item 862, pp. 71-75.

2213   Walters, Margaret. "Patrick White." NLR, 18 (1963), 37-50.

2214   Ward, Russell. "Colonialism and Culture." Overland, 31 (1965), 15-17.

2215   White, Patrick. "The Prodigal Son." AustL, 1, no. 3 (1958), 37-39.

2216   Wilkes, G. A. "An Approach to Patrick White's The Solid Mandala." Southerly, 29 (1969), 97-110.

2217 ____ "Patrick White's The Tree of Man." Southerly, 25 (1965), 23-33.
[Repr. in item 2219, pp. 21-33.]

2218 ____ "A Reading of Patrick White's Voss." Southerly, 28 (1967), 159-73.
[Repr. in item 2219, pp. 127-44.]

2219 ____, ed. Ten Essays on Patrick White, Selected from 'Southerly' (1964-
1967). Sydney: Angus & Robertson, 1970.

2220 Wood, Peter. "Moral Complexity in Patrick White's Novels." Meanjin,
21 (1962), 21-28.

See also: 52, 446, 1243, 1364, 1853, 2034, 6153-6163.

WRIGHT, Judith

2221 Anderson, Hugh. "A Bibliography of Judith Wright." ALS, 3 (1968),
312-13.

2222 Anon. "English as Highway or as Barrier." TLS, 16 Sept. 1965, p. 796.

2223 Beaver, Bruce. "Australian Letter." Landfall, 18 (1964), 352.

2224 Brissenden, R. F. "Five Senses." AustQ, 36, no. 1 (1964), 85-91.

2225 ____ "Poetry of Judith Wright." Meanjin, 12 (1953), 255-67.

2226 Buckley, Vincent. "[Judith Wright]." In item 509, pp. 158-76.

2227 Ewers, John K. "The Genius of Judith Wright." Westerly, 1 (1968), 42-51.

2228 Fleming, William. "Keeping the Home Fires Burning . . . Australian
Poetry, Judith Wright." Shenandoah, 9, no. 3 (1958), 33-39.

2229 Foley, Larry. "All Eyes on the Reef." Sydney Morning Herald, 31 Aug.
1968, p. 20.

2230 G., C. C. "The Time Theme in Judith Wright's Poetry." Drylight, (1959),
28-33.

2231 Green, Dorothy. "Judith Wright." Walkabout, 18, no. 7 (1952), 8-9.

2232 Harris, Max. "Judith Wright." In item 587, pp. 353-61.

2233 Hay, R. G. "Judith Wright's Achievements." AustL, 3, no. 1 (1960),
30-33.

2234 Higham, Charles. "Judith Wright's Vision." Quadrant, 5 (1961), 33-41.

2235 Hope, A. D. Representative Australian Poets. (Commonwealth Literary
Fund Lectures, 4.) St. Lucia: Univ. of Queensland, 1954.

2236 Irvin, Margaret. "Judith Wright's 'Dark Gift.'" TC (Melbourne), 23
(1968), 131-34.

2237 King, Alec. "Australian Poet and Settler--Tough or Sentimental."
Westerly, 2-3 (1962), 93-96.

2238 Kohli, Devindra. "The Crystal Glance of Love: Judith Wright as a Love
Poet." JCL, 6, no. 1 (1971), 42-52.

2239 Lindsay, Philip. "Poetry in Australasia . . . Judith Wright." PoetryR,
41 (1950), 207-11.

2240 McAuley, James. "Some Poems of Judith Wright." ALS, 3 (1968), 201-13.

2241 Mares, F. H. "Judith Wright and Australian Poetry." DUJ, 19 (1958),
76-84.

2242 ____ "The Poetry of Judith Wright." AustL, 3 (1960), 24-29.

2243 Moore, T. Inglis. "The Quest of Judith Wright." Meanjin, 3 (1968),
237-50.

2244   O'Brien, Patricia, and E. Robinson. Judith Wright: A Bibliography. Adelaide: Libraries Board of South Australia, 1968.

2245   Rexroth, Kenneth. "What Is There to Alienate From?" Bulletin (Sydney), 29 April 1967, p. 34.

2246   Rowbotham, David. "The Poetry of Judith Wright." Galmahra, 26 (1947), 6-8.

2247   Scott, Robert Ian. "Judith Wright's World View." Southerly, 4 (1956), 189-95

2248   Scott, W. N. Focus on Judith Wright. St. Lucia: Univ. of Queensland Press, 1967.

2249   Shapcott, Thomas W. "Judith Wright--Her Year." Bulletin (Sydney), 14 Nov. 1964, p. 34.

2250   Stewart, Douglas. "Judith Wright's Poetry." In item 992, pp. 268-73.

2251   Thompson, John. "Interview with Judith Wright." Opinion, 9, no. 8 (1965), 40-46.

2252   _____ "Poetry in Australia: Judith Wright." Southerly, 27 (1967), 35-44.

2253   Thomson, A. K., ed. Critical Essays on Judith Wright. Brisbane: Jacaranda, 1968.

2254   _____ "Judith Wright: An Introductory Essay in Interpretation." In item 2253, pp. 1-33.

2255   _____ "Judith Wright and Her Poetry." Opinion, 7 (1963), 5-14.

2256   Wallace-Crabbe, Christopher. "Australian Poetry Chronicle, 1960." MCR, 4 (1961), 117.

2257   Wesson, Alfred. "The Poetry of Judith Wright." Adult Education, 8 (1963), 20-24.

2258   Wilkes, G. A. "The Later Poetry of Judith Wright." Southerly, 25 (1965), 163-71.

2259   Wilson, Richard. "The Short Stories of Judith Wright." ALS, 1 (1963), 58-61.

2260   Wright, Judith. "Judith Wright and Baylebridge." Quadrant, 20 (1961), 85-86.

2261   _____, ed. "Introduction" to Australian Poets: Judith Wright. Sydney: Angus & Robertson, 1963, pp. v-viii.

See also: 6164.

Canada

Research Aids

2262 Avis, W. S. A Bibliography of Writings on Canadian English (1857-1965). Scarborough, Ont.: Gage, 1965.

2263 Ball, J. L. "Theatre in Canada: A Bibliography." CanL, 14 (1962), 85-100.

2264 Bell, Inglis, and Susan Port. Canadian Literature/Littérature Canadienne 1959-1963. Vancouver: Univ. of British Columbia Pub. Centre, 1966.

2265 Berton, Pierre. "Gold Rush Writing: The Literature of the Klondike." CanL, 4 (1960), 59-67.

2266 Brown, George W., ed. Dictionary of Canadian Biography. Vol. 1 (1000-1700). Toronto: Univ. of Toronto Press, 1965.

2267 Brown, Mary Markham. An Index to 'The Literary Garland' (Montreal, 1838-1851). Toronto: Bibliog. Soc. of Canada, 1962.

2268 Canadiana. Ottawa: National Library of Canada. 1951-d., monthly, with annual cumulations.

2269 Canadian History and Literature. Cambridge, Mass.: Harvard Univ. Press, 1968. [Widener Library shelflist no. 20.]

2270 Canadian Index to Periodicals and Documentary Films. Ottawa: National Library of Canada, 1948-1959 (cumulated). 1960-d., monthly, with annual cumulations.

2271 Hamilton, Robert M. Canadian Quotations and Phrases, Literary and Historical. Toronto: McClelland & Stewart, 1952.

2272 Hayne, David M., and André Vachon, eds. Dictionary of Canadian Biography, Vol. II: 1701-1740. Toronto: Univ. of Toronto Press, 1969.

2273 Hilton-Smith, R. D. Northwestern Approaches: The First Century of Books. Victoria: Adelphi Bookshop, 1969. [Also a special issue of BCLQ, 32, no. 3 (1969).]

2274 "Letters in Canada." UTQ; a survey and checklist of the year's publications, annually since 1936 by various editors.

2275 Long, Robert James. Nova Scotia Authors and Their Work. East Orange, N. J.: The Author, 1918.

2276 Matthews, William. Canadian Diaries and Autobiographies. Berkeley: Univ. of California Press, 1950.

2277 Morgan, Henry J. Bibliotheca Canadensis; or, a Manual of Canadian Literature. Ottawa: Desbarats, 1867. [Repr. Detroit: Gale, 1969.]

2278 Naaman, Antoine. Guide bibliographique des thèses littéraires canadiennes de 1921 à 1969. Sherbrooke: Editions Cosmos, 1970.

2279 Peel, Bruce. _Bibliography of the Prairie Provinces to 1953_.
      Toronto: Univ. of Toronto Press, 1956; supp. 1963.

2280 Story, Norah. _The Oxford Companion to Canadian History and Literature_.
      Toronto: Oxford, 1967; supp. 1973.

2281 Sylvestre, Guy, Brandon Conron, and Carl F. Klinck, eds. _Canadian
      Writers/ecrivains canadiens: A Biographical Dictionary_. Toronto:
      Ryerson, 1964.

2282 Tanghe, Raymond. _Bibliography of Canadian Bibliographies_. Toronto:
      Univ. of Toronto Press, 1960. [2nd. rev. ed., comp. by Douglas
      Lochhead, 1972.]

2283 Thomas, Clara. _Canadian Novelists, 1920-1945_. Toronto: Longman's, 1946.

2284 Tod, Dorothea D., and Audrey Cordingley. "A Bibliography of Canadian
      Literary Periodicals, 1789-1900: Part I--English-Canadian." _PTRSC_,
      ser. 3, 26, sect. 2 (1932), 87-96.

2285 _____ _A Check-List of Canadian Imprints, 1900-1925_. Ottawa: King's
      Printer, 1950.

2286 Tremaine, Marie. _A Bibliography of Canadian Imprints, 1751-1800_.
      Toronto: Univ. of Toronto Press, 1952.

2288 Wallace, W. Stewart. _The Macmillan Dictionary of Canadian Biography_.
      Toronto: Macmillan, 1963.

2289 Watters, Reginald Eyre. _A Check List of Canadian Literature and
      Background Materials 1628-1950_. Toronto: Univ. of Toronto Press,
      1959; rev. ed. 1972.

2290 _____, and Inglis Bell. _On Canadian Literature 1806-1960_. Toronto:
      Univ. of Toronto Press, 1966.

See also: 6220, 6227, 6260.

General

2291 Anon. "The Arts in Canada." _FfT_, 10 (1950), 1-60.

2292 Avison, Margaret. "Poets in Canada." _Poetry_ (Chicago), 94 (1959),
      182-85.

2293 Bailey, Alfred G. "The Fredericton Poets." _NR_, 3, no. 3 (1950), 11.

2294 _____ "Literature and Nationalism After Confederation." _UTQ_, 25 (1956),
      409-24.

2295 Baker, Ray Palmer. _A History of English-Canadian Literature to the
      Confederation: Its Relation to the Literature of Great Britain and
      the United States_. Cambridge, Mass.: Harvard Univ. Press, 1920.

2296 Barbour, Douglas. "The Young Poets and the Little Presses, 1969." _DR_,
      50 (1970), 112-25.

2297 Beattie, Alexander Munro. "Poetry Chronicle." _QQ_, 65 (1958), 313-20.

2298 Berger, Carl. "The True North Strong and Free." In _Nationalism in
      Canada_, ed. Peter Russell. Toronto: McGraw-Hill, 1966, pp. 3-26.

2299 Bessette, Gerard. "French Canadian Society as Seen by Contemporary
      Novelists." _QQ_, 69 (1962), 165-76.

2300 Bevington, Stan, and Dave Godfrey. "Small Presses: An Interview."
      CanF, 47 (1967), 107-08.

2301   Birney, Earle. "Advice to Anthologists: Some Rude Reflections on Canadian Verse." CanF, 21 (1942), 338-40.

2302   ____   The Creative Writer. Toronto: CBC Publications, 1966.

2303   ____   "Has Poetry a Future in Canada?" ManAR, 5, no. 1 (1946), 7-15.

2304   ____   "On Being a Canadian Author." CanLAB, 9 (1952), 77-79.

2305   ____   "On the Pressing of Maple Leaves." CanL, 6 (1960), 53-56.

2306   ____   "To Arms with Canadian Poetry." CanF, 19 (1940), 322-24.

2307   Bissell, Claude T. "A Common Ancestry: Literature in Australia and Canada." UTQ, 25 (1956), 131-42.

2308   ____   "Edmund Wilson's O Canada Revisited." JCanS, 3, no. 3 (1968), 11-16.

2309   ____   "Literary Taste in Central Canada during the Late Nineteenth Century." CanHR, 31 (1950), 237-51.

2310   ____, ed. Our Living Tradition. Toronto: Univ. of Toronto Press, 1957.

2311   Bonenfant, Jean-Charles. "L'influence de la littérature canadienne-anglaise au Canada français." Culture, 17 (1956), 251-60. [Repr. in item 2371, pp. 256-64.]

2312   Booth, Michael R. "Gold Rush Theatres of the Klondike." Beaver, 292 (Spring 1962), 32-37.

2313   ____   "Pioneer Entertainment: Theatrical Taste in the Early Canadian West." CanL, 4 (1960), 52-58.

2314   Bourinot, John G. The Intellectual Development of the Canadian People. Toronto: Hunter Rose, 1881.

2315   ____   "Literature and Art in Canada." AngloAmR, 3 (1900), 99-110.

2316   ____   Our Intellectual Strength and Weakness: A Short Historical and Critical Review of Literature, Art, and Education in Canada. Montreal: Brown, 1893.

2317   Bowering, George. "Poets in Their Twenties." CanL, 20 (1964), 54-64. [See item 2642.]

2318   Brodersen, George L. "Towards a Canadian Theatre." ManAR, 5, no. 3 (1947), 18-23.

2319   Brodie, A. D. "Canadian Short Story Writers." CanM, 4 (1895), 334-44.

2320   Brown, E. K. "L'age d'or de notre poésie." GdC, 11 (1946), 7-17.

2321   ____   "The Development of Poetry in Canada, 1880-1940." Poetry (Chicago), 58 (1941), 34-47.

2322   ____   "The Immediate Present in Canadian Literature." SR, 41 (1933), 430-42.

2323   ____   On Canadian Poetry. Toronto: Ryerson, 1943; rev. ed. 1944.

2324   ____, et al. Canadian Literature Today. Toronto: Univ. of Toronto Press, 1938.

2325   Brown, Lloyd W. "Beneath the North Star: The Canadian Image in Black Literature." DR, 50 (1970), 317-29.

2326   Burpee, Lawrence J. "Canadian Novels and Novelists." SR, 11 (1903), 385-411.

2327   ____   Canadian Novels and Novelists. N.p.: n. pub., 1901.

2328   Bush, Douglas. "Is There a Canadian Literature?" Commonweal, 11 (1929), 12-14.

2329   Callaghan, Morley. "The Plight of Canadian Fiction." UTQ, 7 (1938), 152-61. [See item 2416.]

2330   _____ "Writers and Critics: A Minor League." SatN, 70 (6 Nov. 1954), 7-8.

2331   Cameron, Donald. "Letter from London." CanL, 27 (1966), 53-58.

2332   Campbell, William. "Scottish-Canadian Poetry." CanM, 28 (1907), 585-92; 29 (1907), 169-79.

2333   Ciardi, John. "Sounds of the Poetic Voice." SatR, 42 (24 Oct. 1959), 18-21.

2334   Clark, J. Wilson. "The Line of National Subjugation in Canadian Literature." L&I, 7 (1970), 81-88.

2335   Cogswell, Fred. "Eros or Narcissus? The Male Canadian Poet." Mosaic, 1, no. 2 (1968), 103-11.

2336   Cohen, Nathan. "Television and the Canadian Theatre--Another Treadmill to Futility?" QQ, 64 (1957), 1-11.

2337   _____ "Theatre Today: English Canada." TamR, 13 (1959), 24-37.

2338   Collet, Pauline. L'hiver dans le roman Canadien français. Québec: Presses de l'université Laval, 1965.

2339   Collin, W. E. The White Savannahs. Toronto: Macmillan, 1936.

2340   Daniells, Roy. "Canadian Prose Style." ManAR, 5, no. 3 (1947), 3-11.

2341   _____ "High Colonialism in Canada." CanL, 40 (1969), 5-16.

2342   _____ "The Long-Enduring Spring." CanL, 12 (1962), 6-14.

2343   Davey, Frank. "Anything But Reluctant: Canada's Little Magazines." CanL, 13 (1962), 39-44. [Repr. in item 2371, pp. 222-27.]

2344   _____ "Black Days on Black Mountain." TamR, 35 (1965), 62-71.

2345   Davies, Robertson. "The Northern Muse." Holiday, 35, no. 4 (1964), 10-21.

2346   _____ A Voice from the Attic. Toronto: McClelland & Stewart, 1960.

2347   Deacon, William Arthur. "Canada's Literary Revolution." CanAB, 23, no. 3 (1947), 21-25.

2348   _____ "Critic Speaks: Significance of Canadian Literature." CanA, 15 no. 1 (1937), 13-16.

2349   _____ Poteen, a Pot-Pourri of Canadian Essays. Ottawa: Graphic, 1926.

2350   DeMille, A. B. "Canadian Poetry: A Word in Vindication." CanM, 8 (1897), 433-38.

2351   Denison, Merrill. "Hart House Theatre." CanB, 5 (1923), 61-63.

2352   _____ "Nationalism and Drama." In Bertram Brooker, ed., Yearbook of the Arts in Canada 1928/29. Toronto: Macmillan, 1929, pp. 51-55.

2353   Dewart, Edward Hartley. "Introductory Essay" to Selections from Canadian Poets. Montreal: Lovell, 1864, pp. ix-xix.

2354   Djwa, Sandra. "Canadian Poetry and the Computer." CanL, 46 (1970), 43-54.

2355   Dobbs, Bryan G. "A Case for Canadian Literature." WCSMLL, 1 (1969), 44-50.

2356   Dobbs, Kildare. Reading the Time. Toronto: Macmillan, 1968.

2357   Dooley, D. J. "The Satiric Novel in Canada Today." QQ, 64 (1958), 576-90.

2358 Dorsinville, Max. "La negritude et la littérature québecoise." <u>CanL</u>, 42 (1969), 26-36.

2359 Doyle, Mike. "Notes on Concrete Poetry." <u>CanL</u>, 46 (1970), 91-95.

2360 Dudek, Louis. "Academic Literature." <u>First Statement</u>, 2, no. 8 (1944), 17-20. [Repr. in item 2371, pp. 104-06.]

2361 ____ "Geography, Politics and Poetry." <u>First Statement</u>, 1, no. 16 (n.d.), 2-3.

2362 ____ "The Mirror of Art: Relations Between French and English Literature in Canada." <u>Culture</u>, 31 (1970), 225-31.

2363 ____ "The Montreal Poets." <u>Culture</u>, 18 (1957), 149-54. [Repr. in item 3783, pp. 6-11.]

2364 ____ "Nationalism in Candian Poetry." <u>QQ</u>, 75 (1968), 557-67.

2365 ____ "Patterns of Recent Canadian Poetry." <u>Culture</u>, 19 (1968), 399-415.

2366 ____ "Poets of Revolt . . . or Reaction." <u>First Statement</u>, 1, no. 20 (n.d.), 3-5.

2367 ____ "The State of Canadian Poetry: 1954." <u>CanF</u>, 34 (1954), 153-55.

2368 ____ "Transition in Candian Poetry." <u>Culture</u>, 20 (1959), 282-95.

2369 ____ "The Two Traditions: Literature and the Ferment in Quebec." <u>CanL</u>, 12 (1962), 44-51.

2370 ____ "The Writing of the Decade: 2. Poetry in English." <u>CanL</u>, 41 (1969), 111-20.

2371 ____, and Michael Gnarowski, eds. <u>The Making of Modern Poetry in Canada</u>. Toronto: Ryerson, 1967.

2372 Duncan, Sara Jeannette. "American Influences on Canadian Thought." <u>Week</u>, 4 (1887), 518.

2373 ____ "Outworn Literary Methods." <u>Week</u>, 4 (1887), 450-51.

2374 ____ "Saunterings." <u>Week</u>, 3 (1886), 771-72.

2375 Edgar, Pelham. <u>Across My Path</u>, ed. Northrop Frye. Toronto: Ryerson, 1952.

2376 ____ "Canadian Poetry." <u>ActaV</u>, 46 (1922), 198-200.

2377 ____ "Canadian Poetry." <u>Bookman</u> (New York), 49 (1919), 623-28.

2378 ____ "Literary Criticism in Canada." <u>UTQ</u>, 8 (1939), 420-30.

2379 ____ "Recent Canadian Poets." <u>OntLR</u>, 5 (1920), 3-9.

2380 Eggleston, Wilfred. "Canadian Geography and National Culture." <u>CanGJ</u>, 43 (1951), 254-73.

2381 ____ "Canadians and Canadian Books." <u>QQ</u>, 52 (1945), 208-13.

2382 ____ <u>The Frontier and Canadian Letters</u>. Toronto: Ryerson, 1957.

2383 Egoff, Sheila. <u>The Republic of Childhood: A Critical Guide to Canadian Children's Literature in English</u>. Toronto: Oxford Univ. Press, 1967.

2384 Fergusson, C. Bruce. "The Rise of the Theatre at Halifax." <u>DR</u>, 29 (1950), 419-27.

2385 Foster, W. G. "The Sonnet in Canadian Literature." <u>BritAL</u>, 1 (1928), 64-69.

2386 Francis, Wynne. "Literary Underground: Little Magazines in Canada." <u>CanL</u>, 34 (1967), 63-70.

2387 ____ "The Little Presses." CanL, 33 (1967), 56-62.

2388 ____ "Montreal Poets of the Forties." CanL, 14 (1962), 21-34. [Repr. in item 2707, pp. 36-52.]

2389 Fraser, A. Ermatinger. "Influences and Tendencies in Modern Canadian Poetry." CanA, 6, no. 1 (1928), 46-52.

2390 Frye, Northrop. The Bush Garden: Essays on the Canadian Imagination. Toronto: House of Anansi, 1971.

2391 ____ "Canada and Its Poetry." CanF, 23 (1943), 207-10. [Repr. in item 2371, pp. 86-97; also in item 2390, pp. 129-43.]

2392 ____ The Educated Imagination. Toronto: CBC Publications, 1963.

2393 ____ "English Canadian Literature, 1929-1954." BA, 29 (1955), 270-74.

2394 ____ "Preface to an Uncollected Anthology." In E. G. D. Murray, ed., Studia Varia. Toronto: Univ. of Toronto Press, 1957, pp. 21-36. [Repr. in item 2390, pp. 163-79.]

2395 ____ "La tradition narrative dans la poésie canadienne-anglaise." GdC, 11 (1946), 19-30. [Trans. as "The Narrative Tradition in English-Canadian poetry." In Carl F. Klinck and Reginald Eyre Watters, eds., Canadian Anthology. Toronto: Gage, rev. ed., 1966, pp. 523-28. Repr. in item 2390, pp. 145-55.]

2396 Fulford, Robert. Crisis at the Victory Burlesk: Culture, Politics and Other diversions. Toronto: Oxford Univ. Press, 1968.

2397 ____ "The Yearning for Professionalism." TamR, 13 (1959), 80-85.

2398 Galloway, Myron. "The Canadian Play and Playwright." NR, 3, no. 2 (1949-50), 38-40.

2399 ____ "Robert Speaight on Canadian Theatre: An Interview." NR, 3, no. 3 (1950), 48-50.

2400 Gélinas, Gratien. "Credo of the Comedie-Canadienne." QQ, 66 (1959), 18-25.

2401 Gibbon, John Murray. "The Canadian Lyric and Music." PTRSC, ser. 3, 28, sect. 2 (1934), 95-102.

2402 ____ "The Coming Canadian Novel." CanB, 1, no. 3 (1919), 13-15.

2403 ____ "Where Is Canadian Literature?" CanM, 50 (1918), 333-40.

2404 Glassco, John, ed. English Poetry in Quebec. Montreal: McGill, 1965.

2405 Gnarowski, Michael. "Anti-intellectualism in Canadian Poetry." CanAB, 40, no. 3 (1965), 3-5.

2406 ____ "Canadian Poetry Today, 1964-1966." Culture, 27 (1966), 74-80.

2407 ____ "Contact Press: A Note on Its Origins." Culture, 29 (1968), 356-66.

2408 ____ "The Role of 'Little Magazines' in the Development of Poetry in English in Montreal." Culture, 24 (1963), 274-86. [Repr. in item 2371, pp. 212-22.]

2409 Gordon, Alfred. "Comments on Canadian Poetry." CanM, 49 (1917), 132-40.

2410 Grant, Douglas. "Notes and Comments." CanHR, 41 (1960), 183-84.

2411 Granville-Barker, Harley. "The Canadian Theatre." QQ, 43 (1936), 256-67.

2412 Green, Paul. "The Relevance of Surrealism with Some Canadian Perspectives." Mosaic, 2, no. 4 (1969), 59-70.

2413 Greene, Donald. "Western Canadian Literature." WAL, 2 (1968), 257-80.

2414 Greening, W. E. "Wanted: Reciprocity in Canadian Literature." DR, 29 (1949), 271-74.

2415 Grosskurth, Phyllis. "The Canadian Critic." CanL, 46 (1970), 55-61.

2416 Grove, Frederick Philip. "The Plight of Canadian Fiction? A Reply."
UTQ, 7 (1938), 451-67. [See item 2329.]

2417 Guillet, Edwin Clarence. Early Canadian Literature: Literary Pioneers
of the Old Newcastle District. 2 vols. Toronto: privately printed,
1942.

2418 Gustafson, Ralph. "Anthology and Revaluation." UTQ, 13 (1944), 229-35.

2419 _____ "Introduction" and "Foreword" to The Penguin Book of Canadian
Verse. Rev. ed. Harmondsworth: Penguin, 1967, pp. 21-34.

2420 _____ "New Wave in Canadian Poetry." CanL, 32 (1967), 6-14.

2421 _____ "New York Letter." NR, 1, no. 1 (1945-46), 18-21.

2422 _____ "Writing and Canada." NR, 3, no. 3 (1950), 17-22.

2423 Haig-Brown, Roderick. "The Writer in Isolation." CanL, 1 (1959), 5-12.

2424 Hamelin, Jean. "Theatre Today: French Canada." TamR, 13 (1959), 38-47.

2425 Hamilton, L. "Some Aspects of Anglo-Canadian Literature." NMon, 3
(1932), 227-37.

2426 Harlow, Robert. "Bastard Bohemia: Creative Writing in the Universities."
CanL, 27 (1966), 32-43.

2427 Harris, Cole. "The Myth of the Land in Canadian Nationalism." In
item 2298, pp. 27-43.

2428 Harrison, Richard T. "The American Adam and the Canadian Christ."
TCL, 16 (1970), 161-68.

2429 Harte, W. B. "Some Canadian Writers of Today." NEM, N.S. 3 (1890),
21-40.

2430 Hathaway, E. J. "The Province of Ontario in Fiction." CanM, 64 (1925),
234, 251-53, 262, 279-80, 283-87.

2431 _____ "The Trail of the Romanticist in Canada." CanM, 24 (1910), 529-37.

2432 Hicks, Granville. "Novelists in the Fifties." SatN, 74 (24 Oct. 1959),
18-20.

2433 Hirano, Keiichi. "The Aborigene [sic] in Canadian Literature: Notes
by a Japanese." CanL, 14 (1962), 43-52.

2434 Hodgson, Maurice. "Initiation and Quest: Early Canadian Journals."
CanL, 38 (1968), 29-40.

2435 Hope, A. D. "Australian and Canadian Poetry." DR, 43 (1963), 99-102.

2436 Hopkins, J. Castell. "Canadian Literature." AAPSS, 45 (1913), 189-215.

2437 Hornyansky, Michael. "Countries of the Mind, I and II." TamR, 26 (1963),
56-68; 27 (1963), 80-89.

2438 Innis, Harold Adams. The Strategy of Culture, with Special Reference
to Canadian Literature--A Footnote to the Massey Report. Toronto:
Univ. of Toronto Press, 1952.

2439 Innis, Mary Quayle, ed. The Clear Spirit. Toronto: Univ. of Toronto
Press, 1966.

2440 Jackel, Susan. "The House on the Prairies." CanL, 42 (1969), 46-55.

2441 Jacob, Fred. "Waiting for a Dramatist." CanM, 43 (1914), 142-46.

2442 Jewitt, A. R. "Early Halifax Theatres." DR, 5 (1926), 444-59.

2443 Jones, D. G. Butterfly on Rock: A Study of Themes and Images in
Canadian Literature. Toronto: Univ. of Toronto Press, 1970.

2444 _____ "The Sleeping Giant." CanL, 26 (1965), 3-21. [Repr. in item 2707, pp. 3-24.]

2445 Jones, Emrys Maldwyn. "The University's Duty Towards Canadian Drama." Culture, 7 (1946), 311-24.

2446 Jones, Joseph and Johanna. Authors and Areas of Canada. Austin: Steck-Vaughn, 1970.

2447 Kattan, Naim. "Montreal and French-Canadian Culture: What They Mean to English-Canadian Novelists." TamR, 40 (1966), 40-43.

2448 _____ "Le roman canadien anglais." LetN, (Dec. 1966-Jan. 1967), 21-30.

2449 Kennedy, Leo. "Direction for Canadian Poets." New Frontier, 1, no. 3 (1936), 21-24. [Repr. in item 3783, pp. 11-19.]

2450 _____ "The Future of Canadian Literature." CanMer, 1 (1929), 99-100. [Repr. in item 2371, pp. 34-37.]

2451 Kenner, Hugh. "The Case of the Missing Face." Here and Now, 1, no. 2 (1948), 73-78. [Repr. in item 2591, pp. 203-08.]

2452 _____ "Regional Muses." Poetry (Chicago), 86 (1955), 111-16.

2453 Kesterton, Wilfred H. A History of Journalism in Canada. Foreword by Wilfrid Eggleston. Toronto: McClelland & Stewart, 1967.

2454 Kirkconnell, Watson. "New-Canadian Poetry." CPM, 5, no. 4 (1941), 5-8.

2455 Klinck, Carl F. "Early Creative Literature of Western Ontario." Ontario History, 44 (1953), 155-63.

2456 _____ "Salvaging Our Literary Past." OntLR, 27 (1943), 339-41.

2457 _____ "Some Anonymous Literature of the War of 1812." Ontario History, 49 (1957), 49-60.

2458 _____, et al., eds. Literary History of Canada. Toronto: Univ. of Toronto Press, 1965.

2459 Kline, Marcia B. Beyond the Land Itself: Views of Nature in Canada and the United States. Cambridge, Mass.: Harvard Univ. Press, 1970.

2460 Knister, Raymond. "The Canadian Short Story." Introduction to Canadian Short Stories. Toronto: Macmillan, 1928, pp. xi-xix.

2461 Kreisel, Henry. "The Prairie: A State of Mind." PTRSC, ser. 4, 6 (1968), 171-80. [Repr. in item 2501, pp. 254-66.]

2462 Legris, Maurice. "The Modern French-Canadian Novel." TCL, 16 (1970), 169-74.

2463 Lighthall, W. D. "Canadian Poets of the Great War." CanB, 1, no. 2 (1919), 14-22.

2464 _____ "Introduction" to Songs of the Great Dominion. London: Scott, 1889, pp. xxi-xxxii.

2465 Liljegren, Sven B. Canadian Studies in Sweden. Uppsala: A-B. Lundequistka Bokhandeln, 1961.

2466 Livesay, Dorothy. "This Canadian Poetry." CanF, 24 (1944), 20-21. [Reply by Patrick Anderson, 24 (1944), 44; rejoinder, 24 (1944), 89.]

2467 Livesay, Florence Randal. "Canadian Poetry Today." Poetry (Chicago), 27 (1925), 36-40.

2468 Locke, George H. "The Influence of Canadian Literature on American Literature." BCM, 26 (1926), 13-15.

2469 Logan, J. D. Aesthetic Criticism in Canada: Its Aims, Methods and Status. Toronto: McClelland & Stewart, 1917.

2470 _____ "Canadian Poetry of the Great War." CanM, 48 (1917), 412-17.

2471 _____ "Re-Views of the Literary History of Canada: Canadian Fictionists and Other Creative Prose Writers." CanM, 48 (1916), 125-32.

2472 _____, and Donald G. French. Highways of Canadian Literature. Toronto: McClelland & Stewart, 1924.

2473 Lower, Arthur R. M. "Canadian Values and Canadian Writing." Mosaic, 1, no. 1 (1967), 79-93.

2474 Luchkovich, Michael. "Racial Integration and Canadian Literature." CanAB, 36, no. 2 (1960), 14-16.

2475 Ludwig, Jack. "Clothes in Search of an Emperor." CanL, 5 (1960), 63-66.

2476 Lyndon, Patrick. "Literature and Mass Media." CanL, 46 (1970), 6-10.

2477 McCormack, Robert. "Unspeakable Verse." CanL, 12 (1962), 28-36.

2478 McCourt, E. A. "The Canadian Historical Novel." DR, 26 (1946), 30-36.

2479 _____ The Canadian West in Fiction. Toronto: Ryerson, 1949.

2480 MacDonald, E. R. "The Genius Loci in Canadian Verse." CanM, 53 (1919), 236-40.

2481 _____ "The Sonnet in Canadian Poetry." CanM, 53 (1919), 101-04.

2482 MacDonald, W. L. "Nationality in Canadian Poetry." CanM, 62 (1924), 299-306.

2483 McDougall, Robert L. "The Dodo and the Cruising Auk: Class in Canadian Literature." CanL, 18 (1963), 6-20.

2484 _____, ed. Our Living Tradition. (2nd & 3rd series.) Toronto: Univ. of Toronto Press, 1959.

2485 _____, ed. Our Living Tradition. (4th series.) Toronto: Univ. of Toronto Press, 1962.

2486 McKenzie, Ruth. "Life in a New Land: Notes on the Immigrant Theme in Canadian Fiction." CanL, 7 (1961), 24-33.

2487 _____ "Proletarian Literature in Canada." DR, 19 (1939), 49-64.

2488 MacLennan, Hugh. Scotchman's Return and Other Essays. Toronto: Macmillan, 1960.

2489 MacMechan, Archibald. Head-Waters of Canadian Literature. Toronto: McClelland & Stewart, 1924.

2490 McMullin, Stanley E. "Walt Whitman's Influence in Canada." DR, 49 (1969), 361-68.

2491 MacMurchy, Archibald. Handbook of Canadian Literature (English). Toronto: Briggs, 1906.

2492 MacPhail, Andrew. "Canadian Writers and American Politics." UnivM, 9 (1910), 3-17.

2493 McPherson, Hugo. "Canadian Writing, Present Declarative." English, 15 (1965), 212-16.

2494 MaGee, William H. "Local Colour in Canadian Fiction." UTQ, 28 (1959), 176-89.

2495 _____ "Trends in the Recent English-Canadian Novel." Culture, 10 (1949), 29-42.

2496 Mainer, R. Henry. "Canadian War Fiction." Culture, 6 (1945), 10-14.

2497 Mandel, Eli. "A Lack of Ghosts: Canadian Poets and Poetry." HAB, 16 (1965), 59-67.

2498 ____ "Modern Canadian Poetry." TCL, 16 (1970), 175-84.

2499 ____ "Poetry Chronicle: Giants, Beasts, and Men in Recent Canadian Poetry." QQ, 67 (1960), 285-93.

2500 ____ "Turning New Leaves (1)." CanF, 42 (1963), 278-80.

2501 ____, ed. Contexts of Canadian Criticism. Chicago and London: Univ. of Chicago Press; Toronto: Univ. of Toronto Press, 1971.

2502 Marquis, T. G. "A History of English Canadian Literature." In Adam Shortt, ed. Canada and Its Provinces. Toronto: Glasgow Brook, 1914, pp. 493-589.

2503 Massey, Vincent. On Being Canadian. Toronto: Dent, 1948.

2504 ____ "The Prospects of a Canadian Drama." QQ, 30 (1922), 194-212.

2505 ____ Speaking of Canada. Toronto: Macmillan, 1959.

2506 Mathews, Robin. "Parochialism and the Past." JCL, 6 (1969), 100-05.

2507 Matthews, John. "The Inner Logic of a People: Canadian Writing and Canadian Values." Mosaic, 1, no. 3 (1968), 40-50.

2508 Michener, Wendy. "Towards a Popular Theatre." TamR, 13 (1959), 63-79.

2509 Moisan, Clement. L'âge de la littérature canadienne. Montréal: Editions HMH, 1969.

2510 Moore, Jocelyn. "Theatre for Canada." UTQ, 26 (1956), 1-16.

2511 Moore, Mavor. "The Canadian Theatre." CanF, 30 (1950), 108-10.

2512 Morgan-Powell, Samuel. This Canadian Literature. Toronto: Macmillan, 1940.

2513 Morton, W. L. "Seeing an Unliterary Landscape." Mosaic, 3, no. 3 (1970), 1-10.

2514 Mowat, Farley. "How to be a Canadian Writer--and Survive." SatN, 68 (16 May 1953), 22-23.

2515 Muddiman, Bernard. "The Immigrant Element in Canadian Literature." QQ, 20 (1913), 404-15.

2516 Muise, D. A. "Some Nova Scotia Poets of Confederation." DR, 50 (1970), 71-82.

2517 Mullins, Stanley G. "The Didactic Novel in Post-War Canadian Fiction." Culture, 23 (1962), 137-53.

2518 Needler, G. H. The Lone Shieling: Origin and Authorship of the Blackwood 'Canadian Boat-Song.' Toronto: Univ. of Toronto Press, 1941.

2519 ____ Moore and His Canadian Boat Song. Toronto: Ryerson, 1950.

2520 Nesbitt, Bruce. "Matthew Arnold in Canada: A dialogue begun?" Culture, 28 (1967), 53-54.

2521 New, William H. "Africanadiana: The African Setting in Canadian Literature." JCanS, 6, no. 1 (1971), 33-38.

2522 ____ "In Defence of Private Worlds: An Approach to Irony in Canadian Fiction." JCL, 10 (1970), 132-44.

2523 ____ "Six Canadian Poets." Poetry Australia, 27 (1969), 47-52.

2524 ____ "A Wellspring of Magma: Modern Canadian Writing." TCL, 14 (1968), 123-32.

2525 ____ "The Writing of the Decade: 3. The Novel in English." CanL, 41 (1969), 121-25.

2526 Newton, Norman. "The Old Age of the New." CanL, 38 (1968), 72-74.
      [Comment: CanL, 40 (1969), 95-99.]

2527 Nims, John Frederick. "Five Young Canadian Poets." Poetry (Chicago),
      66 (1954), 334-40.

2528 Novek, Ralph. "Radio Drama in Canada." NR, 2, no. 2 (1948), 29-33.

2529 Ó Broin, Padraig. "Canadian Poetry in English, 1965." BA, 40 (1966),
      150-52.

2530 ____ "Fire-Drake: Report of a Talk by Irving Layton on Jewish Writers
      in Canadian Literature." Teangadóir, 1, ser. 2 (1961), 73-80.

2531 ____ "Poetry--Ante 1962." Teangadóir, 1, ser. 2 (1962), 81-91.

2532 O'Hagan, Thomas. Canadian Essays, Critical and Historical. Toronto:
      Briggs, 1901.

2533 ____ Intimacies in Canadian Life and Letters. Ottawa, Graphic, 1927.

2534 Oryol, Lia. "Canadian Authors in Russian Translations." SovL, 3 (1965),
      189-91.

2535 Ower, John. "Portrait of the Landscape as Poet: Canadian Nature as
      Aesthetic Symbol of Three Confederation Writers." JCanS, 6, no. 1
      (1971), 27-32.

2536 Pacey, Desmond. "Areas of Research in Canadian Literature." UTQ, 23
      (1953), 58-63.

2537 ____ "The Canadian Imagination." LitR, 8 (1965), 437-44.

2538 ____ "Canadian Literature, 1966: A Good-to-Middling Year." Commentator,
      11 (1967), 22-25.

2539 ____ Creative Writing in Canada. Toronto: Ryerson, 1952; rev. ed. 1961.

2540 ____ "English-Canadian Poetry, 1944-1954." Culture, 15 (1954), 255-65.

2541 ____ Essays in Canadian Criticism 1938-1968. Toronto: Ryerson, 1969.

2542 ____ "Introduction" to A Book of Canadian Stories. Toronto: Ryerson,
      1947, pp. xi-xxxvii.

2543 ____ "Literary Criticism in Canada." UTQ, 19 (1950), 113-19.

2544 ____ "The Novel in Canada." QQ, 52 (1945), 322-31.

2545 ____ "The Outlook for Canadian Fiction." ActaV, 70 (1946), 9-11.

2546 ____ "The Outlook for Canadian Literature." CanL, 36 (1968), 14-25.

2547 ____ Ten Canadian Poets. Toronto: Ryerson, 1966.

2548 ____ "The Young Writer and the Canadian Milieu." QQ, 69 (1962), 378-90.

2549 Page, Malcolm. "Three New Canadian Plays." TCL, 16 (1970), 203-06.

2550 Park, Julian, ed. The Culture of Contemporary Canada. Ithaca, N.Y.:
      Cornell Univ. Press, 1957.

2551 Park, M. G. "Canadian Poetry." Meanjin, 78 (1959), 350-52.

2552 Parker, Gilbert. "Fiction--Its Place in the National Life." NAR, 186
      (1907), 495-509.

2553 Paterson, Isabel. "The Absentee Novelists of Canada." Bookman (New
      York), 55 (1922), 133-38.

2554 Peel, Bruce. "English Writers in the Early West." AHR, 16, no. 2 (1968),
      1-4.

2555 Penfield, Wilder. "The Liberal Arts in Canada." DR, 38 (1959), 497-507.

2556   Percival, Walter Pilling, ed. Leading Canadian Poets. Toronto:
       Ryerson, 1948.

2557   Phelps, Arthur L. "Canadian Drama." UTQ, 9 (1939), 82-94.

2558   ____ "Canadian Literature and Canadian Society." NR, 3, no. 4 (1950),
       23-35.

2559   ____ Leading Canadian Writers. Toronto: McClelland & Stewart, 1951.

2560   Pierce, Lorne. "English Canadian Literature 1882-1932." In Royal Society
       of Canada Fifty Years' Retrospect. Ottawa: The Society, 1932, pp. 55-62.

2561   ____ An Outline of Canadian Literature. Toronto: Ryerson, 1927.

2562   ____ Three Fredericton Poets. Toronto: Ryerson, 1933.

2563   ____ Unexplored Fields of Canadian Literature. Toronto: Ryerson, 1932.

2564   Poirier, Michel. "The Animal Story in Canadian Literature." QQ, 34
       (1927), 298-312, 398-419.

2565   Povey, John F. "Poor Waifs upon Creation's Skirts." DR, 47 (1967),
       213-21.

2566   Pratt, E. J. "Canadian Poetry Past and Present." UTQ, 8 (1938), 1-10.

2567   Pritchard, Allan. "From These Uncouth Shores: Seventeenth-Century
       Literature of Newfoundland." CanL, 14 (1962), 5-20.

2568   Purdy, A. W. "Canadian Poetry in English since 1867." JCL, 3 (1967),
       19-33.

2569   Reaney, James. "The Canadian Imagination." Poetry (Chicago), 94 (1959),
       186-89.

2570   ____ "The Canadian Poet's Predicament." UTQ, 26 (1957), 284-95. [Repr.
       in item 2632, pp. 110-22.]

2571   ____ "A Hut in the Global Village." PTRSC, ser. 4, 5 (1967), 51-56.

2572   ____ "Poetry Worth Shouting About." Quill and Quire, 33, no. 2 (1967),
       14-15.

2573   Reeves, John. "The Various Voices: Poems of the Unofficial Culture."
       CanL, 42 (1969), 37-45.

2574   Reid, J. A. "The Canadian Novel." CanF, 2 (1922), 658-60.

2575   Rhodenizer, V. B. "Background of English-Canadian Poetry." DR, 33
       (1953), 187-95.

2576   ____ "Contemporary Scene in Canadian Poetry." CanAB, 24, no. 1 (1958),
       10, 12.

2577   ____ A Handbook of Canadian Literature. Ottawa: Graphic, 1930.

2578   ____ "Introduction" to Canadian Poetry in English, ed. with Bliss
       Carman and Lorne Pierce. Toronto: Ryerson, 1922; rev. ed. 1954,
       pp. xxiii-xxvi. [Repr. in item 2371, pp. 124-37.]

2579   Richler, Mordecai. "Canadian Outlook." New Statesman, 60 (1960), 346-47.

2580   Rimanelli, Giose. "Canadian Literature: An Italian View." CanL, 21
       (1964), 13-20.

2581   Robertson, George. "Alan Crawley and Contemporary Verse." CanL, 41
       (1969), 87-96.

2582   ____ "Drama on the Air." CanL, 2 (1959), 59-65.

2583   Robins, J. D. "Backgrounds of Future Canadian Poetry." ActaV, 39 (1915),
       309-17.

2584   Robson, Frederic. "The Drama in Canada." CanM, 31 (1908), 58-61.

2585   Roland, P. H. "Criticism and Canada's Tomorrow." CanAB, 39, no. 2 (1963), 8-10, 14.

2586   Roper, Gordon. "Turning New Leaves (1)." CanF, 39 (1959), 134-36.

2587   Rosenberger, Coleman. "On Canadian Poetry." Poetry (Chicago), 64 (1944), 281-87.

2588   Roskolenko, Harry. "Post-War Poetry in Canada." Here and Now, 2, no. 4 (1949), 23-31.

2589   Ross, Malcolm. "Introduction" to Poets of the Confederation. Toronto: McClelland & Stewart, 1960, pp. ix-xiv.

2590   ____, ed. The Arts in Canada. Toronto: Macmillan, 1958.

2591   ____, ed. Our Sense of Identity: A Book of Canadian Essays. Toronto: Ryerson, 1954.

2592   Ross, Philip Dansken. Canadian Poets and the Short Word. Ottawa: The Author, 1938.

2593   Ross, W. W. E. "On National Poetry." CanF, 24 (1944), 88.

2594   ____   "Poetry and Frogs." NR, 5, no. 5 (1952), 30-33.

2595   Roy, George Ross. Le sentiment de la nature dans la poésie canadienne anglaise, 1867-1918. Paris: A. G. Nizet, 1961.

2596   Roz, F., and E. Préclin. "L'influence de la France sur la vie intellectuelle des canadiens-anglais et des États-Unis." France-Amerique, Jan. 1935, pp. 7-11; May-June 1935, pp. 111-12.

2597   Rubinger, Catherine. "Two Related Solitudes: Canadian Novels in French and English." JCL, 3 (1967), 49-57.

2598   Sabboth, Lawrence. Interview with Gratien Gélinas: Gratien Gélinas Speaks out on Canadian Playwrights." Performing Arts, 2, no. 3 (1963), 27.

2599   Saeki, Shoichi. "Canada Bungaku Kaigan." EigoS, 114 (1968), 720-21; 115 (1969), 14-16.

2600   Saint-Denis, J. M. "Drama in Canada." CanC, 5, no. 6 (1961), 23-26.

2601   Sandwell, B. K. "Imaginative Literature in the United States and Canada." In R. G. Trotter, ed., Conference of Canadian-American Affairs. Boston: Ginn, 1937, pp. 148-68.

2602   ____   "Sandwell on Humour." CanAB, 28, no. 3 (1952), 30-34.

2603   ____   "The Social Function of Fiction." QQ, 49 (1942), 322-32.

2604   Sargent, Winthrop. The Loyalist Poetry of the Revolution. Philadelphia: Collins, 1857.

2605   Scott, Duncan Campbell. "A Decade of Canadian Poetry." CanM, 17 (1901), 153-58.

2606   ____   "Poetry and Progress." PTRSC, ser. 3, 16 (1922), xlvii-lxvii. [Repr. in Duncan Campbell Scott. The Circle of Affection. Toronto: McClelland & Stewart, 1947, pp. 123-47.]

2607   Scott, F. R. "Canadian Writers' Conference [1955]." UTQ, 25 (1955), 96-103.

2608   Seamon, Roger. "Open City: Poetry Vancouver 1968." FPt, 1 (1968), 48-59.

2609   Selby, Joan. "The Transmutation of History: Landmarks in Canadian Historical Fiction for Children." CanL, 6 (1960), 32-40.

2610   Shapiro, L. S. B. "The Myth that's Muffling Canada's Voice." Maclean's 68 (29 Oct. 1955), 12-13, 43-45.

2611   Shoolman, R. "Is There a Canadian Literature?" Story, 6 (1931), 2-7,
       119.

2612   Sime, Jessie Georgina. Orpheus in Quebec. London: Allen & Unwin, 1942.

2613   Sinclair, Lister. "The Canadian Idiom." Here and Now, 2, no. 4 (1949),
       16-18. [Repr. in item 2591, pp. 234-40.]

2614   Sirois, Antoine. "Deux littératures." CanL, 43 (1970), 36-41.

2615   _____ Montréal dans le roman canadien. Montréal: Didier, 1970.

2616   Skelton, Robin. "Canadian Poetry?" TamR, 29 (1963), 71-82.

2617   Skinner, M. H. "Arthurian Legend and Canadian Poets." ActaV, 21 (1897),
       130-37.

2618   Smethurst, S. E. "Towards a National Literature." QQ, 59 (1952-53),
       455-63.

2619   Smith, A. J. M. "Canadian Anthologies, New and Old." UTQ, 11 (1942),
       457-74.

2620   _____ "Canadian Literature: The First 10 Years." CanL, 41 (1969), 97-103.

2621   _____ "The Canadian Poet [Parts I & II: Before and After Confederation]."
       CanL, 37 (1968), 6-14; 38 (1968), 41-59.

2622   _____ "Canadian Poetry--A Minority Report." UTQ, 8 (1939), 125-38.

2623   _____ "Colonialism and Nationalism in Canadian Poetry Before Confederation."
       In Canadian Historical Association Report, ed. R. M. Saunders. Toronto:
       Univ. of Toronto Press, 1944, pp. 74-85.

2624   _____ "Eclectic Detachment: Aspects of Identity in Candian Poetry."
       CanL, 9 (1961), 6-14. [Repr. in item 2707, pp. 25-35.]

2625   _____ "Introduction" to The Book of Canadian Poetry. Toronto: Gage,
       1957, pp. 1-36.

2626   _____ "Introduction" to The Book of Canadian Prose: I. Early Beginnings
       to Confederation. Toronto: Gage, 1965, pp. xiii-xxii.

2627   _____ "Nationalism and Canadian Poetry." NR, 1, no. 1 (1945-46), 33-42.
       [Also pub. as "Le nationalisme et les poètes canadiens anglais." GdC,
       8 (1945), 87-99.]

2628   _____ "'Our Poets': A Sketch of Canadian Poetry to the Nineteenth
       Century." UTQ, 12 (1942), 75-94.

2629   _____ "A Rejected Preface." CanL, 24 (1965), 6-9. [Repr. in item 2371,
       pp. 38-41.]

2630   _____ "Wanted--Canadian Criticism." CanF, 8 (1928), 600-01. [Repr. in
       item 2371, pp. 31-33.]

2631   _____, ed. Masks of Fiction: Canadian Critics on Candian Prose. Toronto:
       McClelland & Stewart, 1961.

2632   _____, ed. Masks of Poetry: Canadian Critics on Canadian Verse. Toronto:
       McClelland & Stewart, 1962.

2633   Smith, Marion B. "What Is the Role of the DDF?" SatN, 75 (25 June 1960),
       33. [Dominion Drama Festival.]

2634   Stainsby, Mari. "A Paraphrase of the Vision, French-Canadian Writing
       in Translation." BCLQ, 26, no. 3 (1963), 3-10.

2635   Stanley, Arthur. "Our Canadian Poets." London Mercury, 26 (1932),
       537-47.

2636   Stephen, A. M. "Canadian Poets and Critics." New Frontier, 1, no. 5
       (1936), 20-23.

2637 ____ "The Major Note in Canadian Poetry." DR, 9 (1929), 54-67.

2638 ____ "Views on Canadian Literature." IntFR, 1, no. 1 (1926), 25-30.

2639 ____ "The Western Movement in Canadian Poetry." DR, 5 (1925), 210-17.

2640 Stephens, Donald. "Lilacs Out of the Mosaic Land: Aspects of the Sacrificial Theme in Canadian Fiction." DR, 48 (1968-69), 500-09.

2641 ____ "The Writing of the Decade: 4. The Short Story in English." CanL, 41 (1969), 126-30.

2642 Stevens, Peter. "A Counterblast to Mr. Bowering." CanL, 22 (1964), 78-80. [See item 2317.]

2643 ____ "The Writing of the Decade: 5. Criticism." CanL, 41 (1969), 131-38.

2644 Stevenson, Lionel. Appraisals of Canadian Literature. Toronto: Macmillan, 1926.

2645 ____ "Canadian Fiction Then and Now." CanAB, 39, no. 1 (1963), 11-13, 23-24.

2646 ____ "The Human Touch in Canadian Poetry." CanB, 10 (1928), 69-75.

2647 ____ "Is Canadian Poetry Modern?" CanB, 9 (1927), 195-201.

2648 ____ "Literature in an Emerging Nation." SAQ, 64 (1965), 394-400.

2649 ____ "Overseas Literature from a Canadian Point of View." EngR, 39 (1924), 876-86.

2650 Stewart, Alexander Charles. The Poetical Review: A Brief Notice of Canadian Poets and Poetry. Toronto: Anderson, 1896.

2651 Sutherland, John. "Critics on the Defensive." NR, 2, no. 1 (1947), 18-23.

2652 ____ "New Canadian Poetry: Reply with Rejoinder." CanF, 27 (1947), 17-18.

2653 ____ "The Past Decade in Canadian Poetry." NR, 4, no. 2 (1950-51), 42-47. [Repr. in item 2371, pp. 116-22.]

2654 ____, ed. Other Canadians. Montreal: First Statement Press, 1947.

2655 Sutherland, Ronald. "The Body-Odour of Race." CanL, 37 (1968), 46-67. [Repr. in item 2657, pp. 28-59.]

2656 ____ "The Calvinist-Jansenist Pantomine: An Essay in Comparative Canadian Literature." JCanS, 5, no. 2 (1970), 10-21. [Repr. in item 2657, pp. 60-87.]

2657 ____ Second Image: Comparative Studies in Quebec/Canadian Literature. Toronto: New Press, 1971.

2658 ____ "Twin Solitudes." CanL, 31 (1967), 5-24.

2659 Symons, Julian. "A National Style?" CanL, 36 (1968), 58-61.

2660 Tait, Michael. "Playwrights in a Vacuum: English-Canadian Drama in the Nineteenth Century." CanL, 16 (1963), 3-18.

2661 Tallman, Warren. "Wolf in the Snow." CanL, 5 (1960), 7-20; 6 (1960), 41-48. [Repr. in item 2707, pp. 53-76.]

2662 Thomas, Clara. "Happily Ever After: Canadian Women in Fiction and Fact." CanL, 34 (1967), 43-53.

2663 Thompson, Eileen B. "Rus in Urbe." DR, 8 (1928), 87-91.

2664 Tompkinson, Grace. "Colonialism and Art." DR, 11 (1931), 147-54.

2665 ____ "The Watched Pot of Canadian Poetry." DR, 14 (1935), 459-70.

2666   Tougas, Gérard. Histoire de la littérature canadienne-française.
       Paris: Presses Universitaires de France, 1964. [Trans. Alta Lind
       Cook, History of French-Canadian Literature. Toronto: Ryerson, 1966.]

2667   Tovell, Vincent, and George McCowan. "A Conversation." TamR, 13 (1959),
       5-23.

2668   Trotter, R. G. "Has Canada a National Culture?" QQ, 44 (1937), 215-27.

2669   Tweedie, R. A., et al. The Arts in New Brunswick. Fredericton:
       Brunswick Press, 1967.

2670   Vandry, F. "French Culture and Canadian Civilization." DR, 31 (1951),
       73-81.

2671   Waldron, Gordon. "Canadian Poetry, a Criticism." CanM, 8 (1896), 101-08.

2672   Warwick, Jack. The Long Journey: Literary Themes of French Canada.
       Toronto: Univ. of Toronto Press, 1968.

2673   Waterston, Elizabeth. "The Politics of Conquest in Candian Historical
       Fiction." Mosaic, 3, no. 1 (1969), 116-24.

2674   Watson, Wilfred. "Education in the Tribal/Global Village." TCL, 16
       (1970), 207-16.

2675   Watt, Frank W. "Climate of Unrest: Periodicals in the Twenties and
       Thirties." CanL, 12 (1962), 15-27.

2676   _____ "The Growth of Proletarian Literature in Canada, 1872-1920." DR,
       40 (1960), 157-73.

2677   _____ "Nationalism in Canadian Literature." In item 2298, pp. 235-51.

2678   _____ "The Theme of 'Canada's Century,' 1896-1920." DR, 38 (1958), 154-66.

2679   Watters, Reginald Eyre. "[Canada's] Unknown Literature." SatN, 70
       (17 Sept. 1955), 31-33, 35-36.

2680   Weaver, Robert. "The Economics of Our Literature." QQ, 60 (1954), 476-85.

2681   _____ "Literature: Some Promise." SatN, 74 (29 Aug. 1959), 34.

2682   _____ "Notes on Canadian Literature." Nation (New York), 162 (1946),
       198-200.

2683   _____ "A Sociological Approach to Canadian Fiction." Here and Now, 2,
       no. 4 (1949), 12-15.

2684   Wells, H. W. "The Awakening of Canadian Poetry." NEQ, 18 (1945), 3-24.

2685   Wendell, W. L. "The Modern School of Canadian Literature." Bookman
       (New York), 11 (1900), 515-26.

2686   West, Paul. "Canadian Attitudes: Pastoral with Ostriches and Mocking-
       Birds." CanL, 16 (1963), 19-27.

2687   _____ "Canadian Fiction and Its Critics." CanF, 41 (1962), 265-66.

2688   _____ "Ethos and Epic: Aspects of Contemporary Canadian Poetry." CanL,
       4 (1960), 7-17.

2689   _____ "The Unwitting Elegiac: Newfoundland Folk Song." CanL, 7 (1961),
       34-44.

2690   Whalley, George. "The Great Canadian Novel." QQ, 55 (1948), 318-26.

2691   _____, ed. Writing in Canada: Proceedings of the Canadian Writers'
       Conference, Queen's University, 28-31 July, 1955. Introd. by
       F. R. Scott. Toronto: Macmillan, 1956.

2692   Whiteside, Ernestine R. "Canadian Poetry and Poets." McMaster University
       Monthly, 8 (1898-99), 21-28, 68-74, 114-18, 167-72, 209-12.

2693 Whittaker, Herbert. "Canada on Stage." QQ, 60 (1953-54), 495-500.

2694 Wilgar, W. P. "Poetry and the Divided Mind in Canada." DR, 24 (1944), 266-71. [Repr. in item 2632, pp. 65-71.]

2695 Williams, N. "Prospects for the Canadian Dramatist." UTQ, 26 (1958), 273-83.

2696 Wilson, Edmund. O Canada: An American's Notes on Canadian Culture. New York: Farrar, Straus & Giroux, 1965.

2697 Wilson, Ethel. "Of Alan Crawley." CanL, 19 (1964), 33-42.

2698 Wilson, Milton. "Klein's Drowned Poet: Canadian Variations on an Old Theme." CanL, 6 (1960), 5-17. [Repr. in item 3119, pp. 92-98.]

2699 ____ "Other Canadians and After." TamR, 9 (1958), 77-92. [Repr. in item 2632, pp. 123-38.]

2700 ____ "Recent Canadian Verse." QQ, 66 (1959), 268-74.

2701 Wiseman, Adele. "English Writing in Canada: The Future." PTRSC, ser. 4, 5 (1967), 45-51.

2702 Woodcock, George. "An Absence of Utopias." CanL, 42 (1969), 3-5.

2703 ____ "Away from Lost Worlds." In Richard Kostelanetz, ed. On Contemporary Literature. New York: Avon, 1964, pp. 97-109. [Repr. in item 2704, pp. 1-11.]

2704 ____ Odysseus Ever Returning. Introd. by William H. New. Toronto: McClelland & Stewart, 1970.

2705 ____ "Recent Canadian Poetry." QQ, 62 (1955), 111-15.

2706 ____ "View of Canadian Criticism." DR, 35 (1955), 216-23. [Repr. in item 2704, pp. 130-37.]

2707 ____, ed. A Choice of Critics. Toronto: Oxford Univ. Press, 1966.

2708 ____, ed. The Sixties: Canadian Writers and Writing of the Decade. Vancouver: Univ. of British Columbia Press, 1969. [Repr. from CanL, 41 (1969).]

2709 ____, ed. Wyndham Lewis in Canada. Vancouver: Univ. of British Columbia Press, 1970.

2710 Young, George Renny. On Colonial Literature, Science and Education. Halifax: Crosskill, 1842.

See also: 53, 54, 720, 840, 3893, 6113, 6115, 6165-6287.

Individual Authors

ACORN, Milton

2711 Bowering, George. "Acorn Blood." CanL, 42 (1969), 84-86.

2712 Cogswell, Fred. "Three Arc-Light Gaps." Fiddlehead, 56 (1963), 57-58.

2713 Gnarowski, Michael. "Milton Acorn: A Review in Retrospect." Culture, 25 (1964), 119-29.

2714 Livesay, Dorothy. "Search for a Style: The Poetry of Milton Acorn." CanL, 40 (1969), 33-42.

See also: 2371.

ANDERSON, Patrick

2715 Anderson, Patrick. The Character Ball: Chapters of Autobiography.
      London: Chatto & Windus, 1963.

2716 ____ Search Me: An Autobiography. London: Chatto & Windus, 1957.

2717 ____ Snake Wine: A Singapore Episode. London: Chatto & Windus, 1955.

2718 Anon. "Biographical Note." CanAB, 34, no. 1 (1958), 5.

2719 Frye, Northrop. "[Review of The Color as Naked]." UTQ, 23 (1954), 254-56.

2720 North, Jessica Nelson. "Mercurial." Poetry (Chicago), 69 (1947), 284-86.

2721 Ringrose, Christopher Xerxes. "Patrick Anderson and the Critics."
      CanL, 43 (1970), 10-23. [See also comments by P. K. Page and Wynne
      Francis, CanL, 45 (1970), 103-04.]

2722 Smith, A. J. M. "New Canadian Poetry." CanF, 26 (1947), 252.

2723 Sutherland, John. "The Poetry of Patrick Anderson." NR, 2, no. 5 (1949),
      8-20, 25-34.

2724 ____ "The Writing of Patrick Anderson." First Statement, 1, no. 19
      (1943), 3-6.

2725 Wreford, James [Wreford Watson.] "Canadian Background." Index, 1 (1946),
      6-10.

ATWOOD, Margaret

2726 Woodcock, George. "The Symbolic Cannibals." CanL, 42 (1969), 98-100.
See also: 2523, 6287.

AVISON, Margaret

2727 Ghiselin, Brewster. "The Architecture of Vision." Poetry (Chicago), 70
      (1947), 324-28.

2728 Jones, Lawrence M. "A Core of Brilliance: Margaret Avison's Achievement."
      CanL, 38 (1969), 50-57.

2729 Manning, Gerald. "Margaret Avison's 'Perspective': An Interpretation."
      Quarry, 18, no. 2 (1969), 21-24.

2730 New, William H. "The Mind's Eyes (I's) (Ice): The Poetry of Margaret
      Avison." TCL, 16 (1970), 185-202.

2731 Redekop, Ernest. Margaret Avison. Toronto: Copp Clark, 1970.

2732 Smith, A. J. M. "Critical Improvisations on Margaret Avison's Winter
      Sun." TamR, 18 (1961), 81-86.

2733 ____ "Margaret Avison's New Book." CanF, 46 (1966), 132-34.

2734 Wilson, Milton. "The Poetry of Margaret Avison." CanL, 2 (1959),
      47-58. [Repr. in item 2707, pp. 221-32.]
See also: 6288, 6289.

BIRNEY, Earle

2735 Anon. "Two Canadian Poets." TLS, 12 June 1948, p. 332.

2736 Bailey, Alfred G. "[Review of The Straight of Anian]." DR, 30 (1950),
      205-08.

2737 Birney, Earle. "_Turvey_ and the Critics." _CanL_, 30 (1966), 21-25.

2738 Brown, E. K. "To the North: A Wall Against Canadian Poetry." _SatRL_,
       27 (29 April 1944), 9-11.

2739 Carruth, Hayden. "Up, Over, and Out: The Poetry of Distraction."
       TamR, 42 (1967), 61-69.

2740 Clay, Charles. "Earle Birney, Canadian Spokesman." _EdR_, 61 (1945),
       83-87. [Repr. in item 2556, pp. 23-29.]

2741 Colombo, John Robert. "Poetic Ambassador." _CanL_, 24 (1965), 55-59.

2742 Daniells, Roy. "Earle Birney et Robert Finch." _GdC_, 11 (1946), 83-96.

2743 _____ "Lorne Pierce Medal." _PTRSC_, ser. 3, 47 (1953), 37-38.

2744 Elliott, Brian. "Earle Birney: Canadian Poet." _Meanjin_, 18 (1959),
       338-47.

2745 Fredeman, William E. "Earle Birney: Poet." _BCLQ_, 23, no. 3 (1960),
       8-15.

2746 Frye, Northrop. "[Review of _David_]." _CanF_, 22 (1942), 278-79.

2747 Livesay, Dorothy. "Earle Birney--Author, Poet." _UBCAC_, 4, no. 1 (1950),
       9, 28.

2748 Noel-Bentley, Peter C., and Earle Birney. "Earle Birney: A Bibliography
       in Progress, 1923-1969." _WCR_, 5 (1970), 45-53.

2749 Pratt, E. J. "[Review of _David_]." _CPM_, 6, no. 4 (1943), 34-35.

2750 Smith, A. J. M. "A Unified Personality: Birney's Poems." _CanL_, 30
       (1966), 4-13.

2751 Sutherland, John. "Earle Birney's _David_." _First Statement_, 1, no. 9
       (n. d.), 6-8.

2752 West, Paul. "Earle Birney and the Compound Ghost." _CanL_, 13 (1962),
       5-14. [Repr. in item 2707, pp. 131-41.]

2753 Wilson, Milton. "Poet Without a Muse." _CanL_, 30 (1966), 14-20.

See _also_: 2704, 2547, 6165, 6371.

BROOKE, Frances

2754 Baker, Ernest A. "Mrs. Frances Brooke." In _The History of the English
       Novel_. London: Witherby, 1934, Vol. 5, pp. 144-46.

2755 Blue, Charles S. "Canada's First Novelist." _CanM_, 58 (1921), 3-12.

2756 Burpee, Lawrence J. "Introduction" to Frances Brooke, _The History of
       Emily Montague_. Appendix by Frederick Philip Grove. Ottawa: Graphic,
       1931, pp. iii-vi, 327-33.

2757 Burwash, Ida. "An Old Time Novel." _CanM_, 28 (1907), 252-56.

2758 Chateauclair, Wilfrid. "The First Canadian Novel," _DomI_, 4 (11 Jan.
       1890), 31.

2759 Humphreys, J. "Mrs. Frances Brooke." _Dictionary of National Biography_.
       London: Oxford, 1921, Vol. 2, pp. 1328-329.

2760 Klinck, Carl F. "Introduction" to Frances Brooke, _The History of Emily
       Montague_. Toronto: McClelland & Stewart, 1961, pp. v-xiv.

2761 Mayo, Robert D. _The English Novel in the Magazines 1740-1815_. Evanston,
       Ill.: Northwestern Univ. Press, 1962.

2762 Morgan, H. R. "Frances Brooke: A Canadian Pioneer." _McGill News_,
       supp. (June 1930), 1-5.

2763 Needham, Gwendolyn B. "Mrs. Frances Brooke: Dramatic Critic." TN, 15, no. 2 (1960-61), 47-52.

2764 Pacey, Desmond. "The First Canadian Novel." DR, 26 (1946), 143-50.

2765 Poole, E. Phillips. "Introduction" to Frances Brooke, Lady Julia Mandeville. London: Eric Partridge, Scholartis Press, 1930, pp. 11-37.

2766 Tompkins, J. M. S. The Popular Novel in England 1770-1800. London: Constable, 1932; repr. London: Methuen, 1969.

2767 Woodley, E. C. "The First Canadian Novel and Its Author." EdR, 57 (1941), 31-36.

BUCKLER, Ernest

2768 Anon. "Biographical Note." Maclean's, 62 (1 Jan. 1949), 2-3.

2769 Bissell, Claude T. "Introduction to Ernest Buckler, The Mountain and the Valley. Toronto: McClelland & Stewart, 1961, pp. vii-xii.

2770 Buckler, Ernest. Ox Bells and Fireflies: A Memoir. Toronto: McClelland & Stewart, 1968.

2771 Spettigue, Douglas. "The Way It Was: Ernest Buckler." CanL, 32 (1967), 40-56.

See also: 2661, 6294-6297.

CALLAGHAN, Morley

2772 Anon. "Prodigal Who Stayed Home." SatN, 70 (12 May 1956), 1, 21-22.

2773 Avison, Margaret. "Callaghan Revisited." CanF, 39 (1960), 276-77.

2774 Brown, E. K. "The Immediate Present in Canadian Literature." SR, 41 (1933), 430-42.

2775 Callaghan, Morley. "The Imaginative Writer." TamR, 41 (1966), 5-11.

2776 ____ "An Ocean Away." TLS, 4 June 1964, p. 493.

2777 ____ That Summer in Paris. Toronto: Macmillan, 1963.

2778 ____ "Those Summers in Toronto." Maclean's, 76 (5 Jan. 1963), 25-27, 37-40.

2779 Conron, Brandon. Morley Callaghan. New York: Twayne, 1966.

2780 ____ "Morley Callaghan as a Short Story Writer." JCL, 3 (1967), 58-75.

2781 Davis, H. J. "Morley Callaghan." CanF, 15 (1935), 398-99.

2782 Glassco, John. Memoirs of Montparnasse. Introd. by Leon Edel. Toronto: Oxford Univ. Press, 1970.

2783 Hoar, Victor. Morley Callaghan. Toronto: Copp Clark, 1969.

2784 Koch, E. A. "Callaghan: Lend-Lease from the Bohemians." SatN, 60 (21 Oct. 1944), 16-17.

2785 Lewis, Wyndham. "What Books for Total War." SatN, 58 (10 Oct. 1942), 16.

2786 McPherson, Hugo. "Introduction" to Morley Callaghan, More Joy in Heaven. Toronto: McClelland & Stewart, 1960, pp. v-x.

2787 ____ "A Tale Retold." CanL, 7 (1961), 59-61.

2788 ____ "The Two Worlds of Morley Callaghan." QQ, 64 (1957), 350-65.

2789 Moon, Barbara. "The Second Coming of Morley Callaghan." Maclean's, 73 (3 Dec. 1960), 19, 62-64.

2790 Preston, Bernard. "Toronto's Callaghan." SatN, 51 (18 Jan. 1936), 12.

2791 Ross, Malcolm. "Introduction" to Such Is My Beloved. Toronto: McClelland & Stewart, 1957, pp. v-xiii.

2792 Sandwell, B. K. "Hurt without Help." SatN, 66 (27 March 1951), 7.

2793 Steinhauer, H. "Canadian Writers of Today." CanF, 12 (1932), 177-78.

2794 Walsh, William. "Streets of Life." ArielE, 1 (1970), 31-42.

2795 Watt, Frank W. "Morley Callaghan as Thinker." DR, 39 (1959), 305-13. [Repr. in item 2631, pp. 116-27.]

2796 Weaver, Robert. "Introduction" to Morley Callaghan, Strange Fugitive. Rev. ed., Edmonton: Hurtig, 1970, pp. vii-xii.

2797 ____ "Stories by Callaghan." CanL, 2 (1959), 67-70.

2798 ____ "A Talk with Morley Callaghan." TamR, 7 (1958), 3-29.

2799 Wilson, Edmund. "Morley Callaghan of Toronto." NY, 36 (1960), 224-36.

2800 Wilson, Milton. "Callaghan's Caviare." TamR, 22 (1962), 88-92.

2801 Woodcock, George. "The Callaghan Case." CanL, 12 (1962), 60-64.

2802 ____ "Lost Eurydice." CanL, 21 (1964), 21-35. [Repr. in item 2707, pp. 185-202. Also in item 2704, pp. 24-39.]

See also: 52, 2696, 6299-6306.

CAMERON, George Frederick

2803 Bourinot, Arthur S. Five Canadian Poets. Montreal: Quality Press, 1956, pp. 22-26.

2804 ____ "George Frederick Cameron." CanAB, 29, no. 4 (1954), 3-5.

2805 Dyde, S. W. "The Two Camerons." Queen's Review, 3 (1929), 196-98.

2806 Kyte, E. C. "George Frederick Cameron." EdR, 63 (1947), 117-22.

2807 Lampman, Archibald. "Two Canadian Poets." UTQ, 13 (1944), 406-23. [Pref. by E. K. Brown. Repr. in item 2632, pp. 26-44.]

2808 M., J. "Who's Who in Canadian Literature: George Frederick Cameron." CanB, 13 (1931), 179-80.

2809 Vivien, Geoffrey. "A Forgotten Canadian Poet." CanAB, 23, no. 3 (1947), 57.

See also: 3721, 6307.

CAMPBELL, William Wilfred

2810 Allison, W. T. "William Wilfred Campbell." CanB, 1, no. 2 (1919), 65-66.

2811 Barnett, E. S. "The Poetry of William Wilfred Campbell." CanB, 17 (1935), 93-94.

2812 Burpee, Lawrence J. "Canadian Poet: W. W. Campbell." SR, 8 (1900), 425-36.

2813 Charlesworth, Hector. "Poets and Women Writers of the Past." In Candid Chronicles. Toronto: Macmillan, 1925, pp. 87-104.

2814 Graham, Jean. "Canadian Celebrities: 66. Mr. Wilfred Campbell." CanM, 26 (1905), 109-11.

2815   Klinck, Carl F. Wilfred Campbell: A Study in Late Provincial
       Victorianism. Toronto: Ryerson, 1942.

2816   ____   "William Wilfred Campbell: Poet of Lakes." CanB, 21, no. 3 (1939),
       34-37.

2817   Knister, Raymond. "The Poetical Works of Wilfred Campbell." QQ, 31
       (1924), 435-49.

2818   MacKay, L. A. "W. W. Campbell." CanF, 14 (1933), 66-67.

2819   Muddiman, Bernard. "William Wilfred Campbell." QQ, 27 (1919), 201-10.

2820   Scott, Colin A. "William Wilfred Campbell." CanM, 2 (1894), 270-74.

2821   Stevenson, O. J. "Who's Who in Canadian Literature: William Wilfred
       Campbell." CanB, 9 (1927), 69-71.

2822   Sutherland, M. H. "William Wilfred Campbell." ActaV, 17 (1894), 181-85.

2823   Sykes, W. J. "Wilfred Campbell." EdR, 62 (1946), 93-97. [Repr. in
       item 2556, pp. 37-44.]

2824   Tucker, J. A. "The Poems of William Wilfred Campbell." UTQ, 1 (1895),
       140-45.

2825   Yeigh, Frank. "William Wilfred Campbell, a Scotch-Canadian Poet."
       Book News, 29 (1910), 897-900.

See also: 6249, 6308.

CARMAN, Bliss

2826   Anon. "Poems to Remember: Vagabond Song, with Biographical Note."
       Scholastic, 41 (5 Oct. 1942), 20.

2827   Archer, William. "Bliss Carman." In Poets of the Younger Generation.
       London: Lane, 1902, pp. 66-82.

2828   Blanck, Jacob. Bibliography of American Literature, Vol. 2. New Haven:
       Yale Univ. Press, 1957, pp. 42-76.

2829   Brown, Harry W. "Bliss Carman's Latest Book of Poems." CanM, 6 (1896),
       477-81.

2830   Cappon, James. "Bliss Carman's Beginnings." QQ, 36 (1929), 637-65.

2831   ____   Bliss Carman and the Literary Currents and Influences of His Time.
       Toronto: Ryerson, 1930.

2832   Carman, Bliss. "[A Letter About Himself]." Critic (London), 26 (1896),
       164-65.

2833   Colum, P. "Bliss Carman's Sanctuary." Commonweal, 11 (1929), 225.

2834   De La Mare, Walter. "The Poetry of Life." Bookman (London), 30 (1906),
       72.

2835   Douglas, R. W. "Canada's Poet Laureate--Bliss Carman." BCM, 19, no. 7
       (1922), 5-6, 12; 19, no. 8 (1922), 3-4, 14-16.

2836   Edgar, Pelham. "Bliss Carman." In item 2556, pp. 45-50.

2837   Garvin, J. W. "Bliss Carman." CanB, 14 (1932), 34-35.

2838   Gundy, H. P. "The Bliss Carman Centenary." Douglas Library Notes, 10
       (1961), 1-16.

2839   Hathaway, R. H. "Bliss Carman: An Appreciation." CanM, 56 (1921),
       521-36.

2840   ____   "Bliss Carman's First Editions." CanB, 6 (1924), 8-9.

2841 ____ "Bliss Carman's Rare Editions." CanB, 1, no. 4 (1919), 16-17.

2842 ____ "Carman's Books: A Bibliographical Essay." Acadie, 1 (15 April 1930), 4-6.

2843 ____ "The Poetry of Bliss Carman." SR, 33 (1925), 467-83.

2844 ____ "Vale! Bliss Carman." CanB, 11 (1929), 155-59.

2845 ____ "Who's Who in Canadian Literature: Bliss Carman." CanB, 8 (1926), 299-302.

2846 Hawthorne, Julian. Bliss Carman, 1861-1929. Palo Alto, Calif.: The Author, 1929.

2847 Hind, C. Lewis. "Bliss Carman." In More Authors and I. New York: Dodd, Mead, 1922, pp. 65-70.

2848 Lee, H. D. C. Bliss Carman: A Study in Canadian Poetry. Buxton, England: 'Herald' Print Co., 1912.

2849 Livesay, F. H. R. "Bliss Carman at Nassau." SatN, 59 (20 Nov. 1943), 27.

2850 MacDonald, Allan H. Richard Hovey: Man and Craftsman. Durham, N. C.: Duke Univ. Press, 1957, passim.

2851 MacFarland, Kenneth. "The Poetry of Bliss Carman." Literary Miscellany, 2 (1909), 35-39.

2852 MacKay, L. A. "Bliss Carman." CanF, 13 (1933), 182-83.

2853 Marshall, J. "Pipes of Pan." QQ, 11 (1903), 203-08.

2854 Miller, Muriel. Bliss Carman, a Portrait. Toronto: Ryerson, 1933.

2855 Morse, William Inglis. Bliss Carman: Bibliography, Letters, Fugitive Verses, and Other Data. Windham, Conn.: Hawthorne House, 1941.

2856 Muddiman, Bernard. "A Vignette in Canadian Literature." CanM, 40 (1913), 451-58.

2857 Pacey, Desmond. "Bliss Carman: A Reappraisal." NR, 3, no. 3 (1950), 2-10.

2858 ____ "Garland for Bliss Carman." AtlanticA, 51, no. 8 (1961), 17-24.

2859 Pierce, Lorne. "Introduction" to The Selected Poems of Bliss Carman. Toronto: McClelland & Stewart, 1954, pp. 17-30.

2860 ____, ed., and postscript. Bliss Carman's Scrap Book. Toronto: Ryerson, 1931.

2861 Pollock, F. L. "Canadian Writers in New York." ActaV, 22 (1899), 434-39.

2862 Rittenhouse, Jessie B. "Bliss Carman." In Younger American Poets. Boston: Little, Brown, 1904, pp. 46-74.

2863 Roberts, C. G. D. "Bliss Carman." DR, 9 (1930), 409-17.

2864 ____ "Carman and His Own Country." Acadie, 1 (15 April 1930), 2-4.

2865 ____ "Mr. Bliss Carman's Poems." Chap-Book, 1 (1894), 53-57.

2866 ____ "More Reminiscences of Bliss Carman." DR, 10 (1930), 1-9.

2867 Roberts, Lloyd. "Bliss Carman: A Memory." CanB, 21, no. 1 (1939), 42-46.

2868 Ross, M. M. "Carman by the Sea." DR, 27 (1947), 294-98.

2869 ____ "A Symbolic Approach to Carman." CanB, 14 (1932), 140-44.

2870 Shepard, Odell. Bliss Carman. Toronto: McClelland & Stewart, 1923.

2871 Sherman, F. F. A Check List of First Editions of Bliss Carman. New York: The Author, 1915.

2872 Stephens, Donald. Bliss Carman. New York: Twayne, 1966.

2873 _____ "Maritime Myth." CanL, 9 (1961), 38-48.

2874 Stringer, Arthur. "Canadians in New York, America's Foremost Lyrist: Bliss Carman." NatR, 4 (1904), 3-5.

2875 _____ "Wild Poets I've Known: Bliss Carman." SatN, 56 (1 March 1941), 29, 36.

2876 Van Patten, Nathan. "Bliss Carman and the Bibliophile." QQ, 33 (1925), 202-05.

2877 Waldron, Gordon. "Canadian Poetry--a Criticism." CanM, 8 (1896), 101-08.

2878 White, Gleeson. "Carman Saeculare." Bookman (London), 5 (1894), 155-56.

See also: 2547, 6309-6311.

CARR, Emily

2879 Burns, F. H. "Emily Carr." In item 2439, pp. 221-41.

2880 Carr, Emily. The Book of Small. Toronto: Oxford Univ. Press, 1942.

2881 _____ Growing Pains. Toronto: Oxford Univ. Press, 1946.

2882 _____ The House of All Sorts. Toronto: Oxford Univ. Press, 1944.

2883 _____ Hundreds and Thousands: The Journals. Toronto: Clarke Irwin, 1966.

2884 _____ Pause: A Sketch Book. Toronto: Clarke Irwin, 1953.

2885 Colman, M. E. "Emily and Her Sisters." DalR, 27 (1947), 29-32.

2886 Daniells, Roy. "Emily Carr." In item 2485, pp. 119-34.

2887 Dilworth, Ira. "Emily Carr--Canadian Artist-Author [and] Canadian Painter and Poet in Prose." SatN, 57 (1 Nov. 1941), 26; (8 Nov. 1941), 26.

2888 _____ "Foreword" to Emily Carr, Klee Wyck. Toronto: Oxford Univ. Press, 1951, pp. v-xvi.

2889 _____ "Preface" to Emily Carr, The Heart of a Peacock. Toronto: Oxford Univ. Press, 1953, pp. xi-xv.

2890 Harris, Lawren. "Emily Carr and Her Work." CanF, 21 (1941), 277-78.

2891 Hembraff-Schleigher, Edythe. M. E.: A Portrayal of Emily Carr. Toronto: Clarke Irwin, 1969.

2892 Humphrey, Ruth. "Emily Carr--An Appreciation." QQ, 65 (1958), 270-76.

2893 McDonald, J. A. "Emily Carr: Painter as Writer." BCLQ, 22, no. 4 (1959), 17-23.

2894 Nesbitt, J. K. "The Genius We Laughed At." Maclean's, 64 (7 Jan. 1951), 12-13, 29-30.

2895 Pearson, Carol. Emily Carr as I Knew Her. Toronto: Clarke Irwin, 1954.

2896 Sanders, Byrne Hope. "Emily Carr." In Canadian Portraits--Famous Women. Toronto: Clarke Irwin, 1954, pp. 3-43.

2897 Stacton, David D. "The Art of Emily Carr." QQ, 57 (1950), 499-509.

2898 Turpin, M. The Life and Work of Emily Carr (1871-1945): A Selected Bibliography. Vancouver: Univ. of British Columbia School of Librarianship, 1965.

See also: 6312.

COHEN, Leonard

2899 Batten, Jack. "Leonard Cohen: The Poet as Hero (1) His Songs and His
       Followers." SatN, 84, no. 6 (1969), 23-26.

2900 Djwa, Sandra. "Leonard Cohen: Black Romantic." CanL, 34 (1967), 32-42.

2901 Gose, E. B. "Of Beauty and Unmeaning." CanL, 29 (1966), 61-63.

2902 Harris, Michael. "Leonard Cohen: The Poet as Hero (2) Cohen by Himself."
       SatN, 84, no. 6 (1969), 26-31.

2903 Ondaatje, Michael. Leonard Cohen. Toronto: McClelland & Stewart, 1970.

2904 Owen, Don. "Leonard Cohen. The Poet as Hero (3) Cohen Remembered."
       SatN, 84, no. 6 (1969), 31-32.

2905 Pacey, Desmond. "The Phenomenon of Leonard Cohen." CanL, 34 (1967),
       5-23.

2906 Purdy, A. W. "Leonard Cohen: A Personal Look." CanL, 23 (1965), 7-16.

2907 Scobie, Stephen. "Magic, Not Magicians: Beautiful Losers and Story of O."
       CanL, 45 (1970), 56-60.

See also: 2370, 2523, 2704, 6314, 6315, 6355.

CONNOR, Ralph [Charles William Gordon]

2908 Adams, Harris L. "The Career of 'Ralph Connor.'" Maclean's, 25 (April
       1913), 109-13.

2909 Beharriell, Ross. "Introduction" to Ralph Connor The Man from Glengarry.
       Toronto: McClelland & Stewart, 1960, pp. vii-xii.

2910 Daniells, Roy. "Glengarry Revisited." CanL, 31 (1967), 45-53.

2911 Doran, George H. "A Modern Apostle." In Chronicles of Barabbas 1884-
       1934. Toronto: McLeod, 1935, pp. 200-06.

2912 French, Donald G. "Who's Who in Canadian Literature: Ralph Connor." CanB,12
       (1930), 77-79.

2913 Gordon, Charles William. Postscript to Adventure: The Autobiography of
       Ralph Connor. New York: Farrar, 1938.

2914 ____ "Ralph Connor and the New Generation." Mosaic, 3, no. 3 (1970),
       11-18.

2915 Paterson, Beth. "Ralph Connor and His Million-Dollar Sermons."
       Maclean's, 66 (15 Nov. 1953), 26, 56-60.

2916 Watt, Frank W. "Western Myth, the World of Ralph Connor." CanL, 1
       (1959), 26-36.

See also: 6316.

CRAWFORD, Isabella Valancy

2917 Bessai, Frank. "The Ambivalence of Love in the Poetry of Isabella
       Valancy Crawford." QQ, 77 (1970), 404-18.

2918 Burpee, Lawrence J. "Isabella Valancy Crawford, a Canadian Poet."
       Poet Lore, 13 (1901), 575-86.

2919 Garvin, J. W. "Who's Who in Canadian Literature: Isabella Valancy
       Crawford." CanB, 9 (1927), 131-33.

2920 Hale, Katherine. Isabella Valancy Crawford. Toronto: Ryerson, 1923.

2921 ____ "Isabella Valancy Crawford." In item 2556, pp. 63-70.

2922 Hathaway, E. J. "Isabella Valancy Crawford." CanM, 5 (1895), 569-72.

2923 Ower, John. "Isabella Valancy Crawford: The Canoe." CanL, 34 (1967), 54-62.

2924 Pomeroy, Elsie. "Isabella Valancy Crawford." CPM, 7, no. 4 (1944), 36-38.

2925 Reaney, James. "Isabella Valancy Crawford." In item 2484, pp. 268-88.

2926 Seranus [Mrs. J. W. F. Harrison]. "Isabella Valancy Crawford." Week, 4 (1887), 202-03.

2927 Wetherald, Ethelwyn. "Introduction" to J. W. Garvin, ed., The Collected Poems of Isabella Valancy Crawford. Toronto: Briggs, 1905, pp. 15-29.

See also: 6317.

DAVIES, Robertson

2928 Callwood, June. "The Beard." Maclean's, 65 (15 March 1952), 16-17, 30-33.

2929 Kirkwood, Hilda. "Robertson Davies." CanF, 30 (1950), 59-60.

2930 Lawrence, Robert G. "A Survey of the Three Novels of Robertson Davies." BCLQ, 32, no. 4 (1969), 3-9.

2931 McPherson, Hugo. "The Mask of Satire: Character and Symbolic Pattern in Robertson Davies' Fiction." CanL, 4 (1960), 18-30. [Repr. in item 2707, pp. 233-47; also in item 2631, pp. 162-75.]

2932 Marchbanks, Samuel [Robertson Davies]. "The Double Life of Robertson Davies." Liberty (April 1954), 18-19, 53-58. [Rev. version in Carl F. Klinck and Reginald Eyre Watters, eds., Canadian Anthology. Rev. ed., Toronto: Gage, 1966, pp. 393-400.]

2933 Owen, Ivon. "The Salterton Novels." TamR, 9 (1958), 56-63.

2934 Read, S. E. "A Call to the Clerisy." CanL, 7 (1961), 65-68.

2935 Steinberg, M. W. "Don Quixote and the Puppets: Theme and Structure in Robertson Davies' Drama." CanL, 7 (1961), 45-53.

See also: 6318-6322, 6409.

DE LA ROCHE, Mazo

2936 Brown, E. K. "The Whiteoaks Saga." CanF, 12 (1931), 23.

2937 de la Roche, Mazo. "My First Book." CanAB, 28, no. 1 (1952), 3-4.

2938 ____ Ringing the Changes: An Autobiography. Toronto: Macmillan, 1957.

2939 Eayrs, Hugh. "Mazo de la Roche." CanB, 20, no. 4 (1938), 17-22.

2940 Edgar, Pelham. "The Cult of Primitivism." In Bertram Brooker, ed., Yearbook of the Arts in Canada 1928/29. Toronto: Macmillan, 1929, pp. 39-42.

2941 Hambleton, Ronald. Mazo de la Roche of Jalna. Toronto: General, 1966.

2942 Livesay, Dorothy. "The Making of Jalna: A Reminiscence." CanL, 23 (1965), 25-30.

2943 ____ "Mazo de la Roche." In item 2439, pp. 242-59.

2944 Macklem, John. "Who's Who in Canadian Literature: Mazo de la Roche." CanB, 9 (1927), 259-60.

2945   Moore, Jocelyn. "Mazo de la Roche." CanF, 12 (1932), 380-81.

2946   Overton, Grant. The Women Who Make Our Novels. 1928; repr. Freeport,
       N.Y.: Books for Libraries, 1967, pp. 108-12.

2947   Pringle, Gertrude. "World Fame to Canadian Author, Mazo de la Roche."
       CanM, 67 (1927), 19, 31-32.

2948   Sandwell, B. K. "The Work of Mazo de la Roche." SatN, 68 (8 Nov. 1952), 7.

2949   Weeks, Edward. "Mazo de la Roche." In In Friendly Candor. Boston:
       Little, Brown, 1959, pp. 86-97.

2950   Wuorio, Eva-Lis. "Mazo of Jalna." Maclean's, 62 (1 Feb. 1949), 19,
       39-41.

See also: 18, 6323, 6324.

DE MILLE, James

2951   Bevan, A. R. "James De Mille and Archibald MacMechan." DR, 36 (1955),
       201-15.

2952   Burpee, Lawrence J. "James De Mille." CanM, 8 (1926), 203-06.

2953   Douglas, R. W. "James De Mille." CanB, 4 (1922), 39-44.

2954   MacMechan, Archibald. "Concerning James De Mille." CanB, 4 (1922),
       125-26.

2955   ____ "De Mille, The Man and the Writer." CanM, 27 (1906), 404-16.

2956   Stewart, George. Professor James de Mille. N.p., n. d.

2957   Watters, Reginald Eyre. "Introduction" to James de Mille, A Strange
       Manuscript Found in a Copper Cylinder. Toronto: McClelland & Stewart,
       1969, pp. vii-xviii.

See also: 6325.

DRUMMOND, William Henry

2958   Anon. "Two Canadian Poets: Fréchette and Drummond." Edinburgh Review,
       209 (1909), 474-99.

2959   Burpee, Lawrence J. "William Henry Drummond." Nation (New York), 84
       (1907), 334-36.

2960   ____ "William Henry Drummond." In item 2556, pp. 71-78.

2961   Craig, Robert H. "Reminiscences of W. H. Drummond." DR, 5 (1925), 161-69.

2962   Drummond, Mary Harvey. "Preface" [and] "William Henry Drummond." In
       The Great Fight: Poems and Sketches. New York: Putnam's, 1908, pp.
       vii-xviii, 3-48.

2963   Fréchette, Louis. "Introduction" to The Poetical Works of William
       Henry Drummond. New York: Putnam's, 1912, pp. xxi-xxv.

2964   Gibbon, John Murray. "William Henry Drummond." EdR, 60 (1944), 93-96.

2965   MacDonald, John Ford. William Henry Drummond. Toronto: Ryerson, 1923.

2966   Mahon, A. W. "The Poet of the Habitant." CanM, 29 (1907), 56-60.

2967   Munro, Neil. "William Henry Drummond." In The Poetical Works of William
       Henry Drummond. New York: Putnam's, 1912, pp. v-xx.

2968   Phelps, Arthur L. "Introduction" to W. H. Drummond, Habitant Poems.
       Toronto: McClelland & Stewart, 1959, pp. 7-16.

2969   Rashley, R. E.   "W. H. Drummond and the Dilemma of Style." DR, 28
       (1949), 387-96.

2970   Rhodenizer, V. B.   "Who's Who in Canadian Literature: William Henry
       Drummond." CanB, 9 (1927), 35-36.

2971   Stringer, Arthur.   "Wild Poets I've Known: W. H. Drummond." SatN, 56
       (26 April 1941), 33.

2972   V., E. Q.   "Canadian Celebrities: III, Dr. W. H. Drummond." CanM, 13
       (1899), 62-64.

See also: 6326, 6354.

DUDEK, Louis

2973   Anon.   "Biographical Note." CanAB, 34, no. 1 (1958), 7.

2974   Francis, Wynne.   "A Critic of Life: Dudek as Man of Letters." CanL, 22
       (1964), 5-23.

2975   Gnarowski, Michael.   "Louis Dudek, A Note." Yes, 14 (1965), 4-6.

2976   Layton, Irving.   "An Open Letter to Louis Dudek." Cataract, 1, no. 2
       (1962), n. pag.

2977   Livesay, Dorothy.   "The Sculpture of Poetry." CanL, 30 (1966), 26-35.

2978   Smith, A. J. M.   "Turning New Leaves." CanF, 27 (1947), 42-43.

See also: 2371.

DUNCAN, Norman

2979   Cogswell, Fred.   "Way of the Sea, a Symbolic Epic." DR, 35 (1956),
       374-81.

2980   Hathaway, E. J.   "Who's Who in Canadian Literature: Norman Duncan."
       CanB, 8 (1926), 171-74.

2981   Niven, Frederick.   "To Remember Norman Duncan." SatN, 57 (20 June 1942),
       29.

DUNCAN, Sara Jeannette [Mrs. Everard Cotes]

2982   Bissell, Claude T.   "Introduction" to S. J. Duncan, The Imperialist.
       Toronto: McClelland & Stewart, 1961, pp. v-ix.

2983   Burness, Jean F.   "Sara Jeannette Duncan--a Neglected Canadian Author."
       OntLR, 45 (1961), 205-06.

2984   Donaldson, F.   "Mrs. Everard Cotes." Bookman (London), 14 (1898), 65-67.

2985   MacMurchy, M.   "Mrs. Everard Cotes." Bookman (London), 48 (1915), 39-40.

2986   R[oss], M. E.   "Sara Jeannette Duncan, Personal Glimpses." CanL, 27
       (1966), 15-19.

See also: 6327.

FRYE, Northrop

2987   Dudek, Louis.   "Northrop Frye's Untenable Position." Delta (Montreal),
       22 (1963), 23-27.

2988   Edgar, Pelham. "Northrop Frye." In item 2375, pp. 83-89.

2989   Krieger, Murray, ed. Northrop Frye in Modern Criticism. New York:
       Columbia Univ. Press, 1966.

2990   Mandel, Eli. "The Language of Humanity." TamR, 29 (1963), 82-89.

2991   Reaney, James. "Frye's Magnet." TamR, 30 (1964), 72-78.

2992   Smith, A. J. M. "The Critic's Task: Frye's Latest Work." CanL, 20
       (1964), 6-14.

2993   Watt, Frank W. "The Critic's Critic." CanL, 19 (1964), 51-54.

GARNER, Hugh

2994   Anderson, Allan. "An Interview with Hugh Garner." TamR, 52 (1969),
       19-34.

2995   Hall, W. F. "New Interest in Reality." CanL, 40 (1969), 66-68.

See also: 6299.

GODFREY, David

2996   Laurence, Margaret. "Des voix ancestrales prophetisant . . . ."
       Ellipse, 4 (1970), 71-80; trans. in Mysterious East, Dec. book supp.
       (1970), 6-10.

GOLDSMITH, Oliver

2997   Gnarowski, Michael, ed. The Rising Village of Oliver Goldsmith.
       Montreal: Delta, 1968. [A variorum text.]

2998   Goldsmith, Oliver. The Autobiography of Oliver Goldsmith. Toronto:
       Ryerson, 1943.

2999   Kyte, E. C., ed. The Manuscript Book of Oliver Goldsmith, Author of
       'The Rising Village.' Toronto: Bibliog. Soc. of Canada, 1950.

3000   Lande, Lawrence M. "Oliver Goldsmith." In Old Lamps Aglow. Montreal:
       The Author, 1957, pp. 67-74.

3001   Pacey, Desmond. "The Goldsmiths and Their Villages." UTQ, 21 (1951),
       27-38.

See also: 6204.

GROVE, Frederick Philip

3002   Ayre, Robert. "Canadian Writers of Today--Frederick Philip Grove."
       CanF, 12 (1932), 255-57. [Repr. as "A Solitary Giant" in item 3017,
       pp. 17-24.]

3003   Birbalsingh, Frank M. "Grove and Existentialism." CanL, 43 (1970), 67-76.

3004   Clarke, G. H. "A Canadian Novelist and His Critic." QQ, 53 (1946),
       362-68.

3005   Collin, W. E. "La tragique ironie de Frederick Philip Grove." GdC,
       4 (1946), 15-40.

3006   Eggleston, Wilfrid. "Frederick Philip Grove." In item 2310, pp. 105-27.

3007   Grove, Frederick Philip. "Apologia pro Vita et Opere Sua." CanF, 11
       (1931), 420-22.

3008   ____   "In Search of Myself." UTQ, 10 (1940), 60-67. [Repr. in item 2631, pp. 14-22.]

3009   ____   In Search of Myself. Toronto: Macmillan, 1946.

3010   ____   "A Postscript to A Search for America." QQ, 49 (1942), 197-213.

3011   Holliday, W. B.   "Frederick Philip Grove: An Impression." CanL, 3 (1960), 17-22.

3012   McMullin, Stanley E.   "Grove and the Promised Land." CanL, 49 (1971), 10-19.

3013   Nesbitt, Bruce.   "The Seasons: Grove's Unfinished Novel." CanL, 18 (1963), 47-51.

3014   Pacey, Desmond.   "Frederick Philip Grove." ManAR, 3, no. 3 (1943), 28-41.

3015   ____   Frederick Philip Grove. Toronto: Ryerson, 1945.

3016   ____   "Frederick Philip Grove: A Group of Letters." CanL, 11 (1962), 28-38.

3017   ____, ed.   Frederick Philip Grove. Toronto: Ryerson, 1970.

3018   Parks, M. G.   "Introduction" to Frederick Philip Grove, Fruits of the Earth. Toronto: McClelland & Stewart, 1965, pp. vii-xiii.

3019   Pierce, Lorne.   "Frederick Philip Grove (1871-1948)." PTRSC, ser. 3, 41, sect. 2 (1949), 113-19.

3020   Ranna, H. O.   "Notable Canadian Author." Bookman (London), 80 (1939), 9.

3021   Ross, Malcolm.   "Introduction" to Frederick Philip Grove, Over Prairie Trails. Toronto: McClelland & Stewart, 1957, pp. v-x.

3022   Sandwell, B. K.   "Frederick Philip Grove and the Culture of Canada." SatN, 61 (24 Nov. 1945), 18. [Repr. in item 3017, pp. 56-59.]

3023   Saunders, Doris B.   "The Grove Collection in the University of Manitoba: A Tentative Evaluation." BSCP, 2 (1963), 7-20.

3024   Saunders, Thomas.   "The Grove Papers." QQ, 70 (1963), 22-29.

3025   ____   "Introduction" to Frederick Philip Grove, Settlers of the Marsh. Toronto: McClelland & Stewart, 1966, pp. vii-xiii.

3026   ____   "A Novelist as Poet: Frederick Philip Grove." DR, 43 (1963), 235-41. [Repr. in item 3017, pp. 88-96.]

3027   Sirois, Antoine.   "Grove et Ringuet." CanL, 49 (1971), 20-27.

3028   Skelton, Isobel.   "Frederick Philip Grove." DR, 19 (1939), 147-63. [Repr. as "One Speaking into a Void" in item 3017, pp. 24-44.]

3029   Spettigue, Douglas.   Frederick Philip Grove. Toronto: Copp Clark, 1969.

3030   ____   "Frederick Philip Grove in Manitoba." Mosaic, 3, no. 3 (1970), 19-33.

3031   Stanley, C.   "Frederick Philip Grove." DR, 25 (1946), 433-41.

3032   ____   "Voices in the Wilderness." DR, 25 (1945), 173-81.

3033   Sutherland, Ronald.   Frederick Philip Grove. Toronto: McClelland & Stewart, 1969.

See also: 6330-6341.

HALIBURTON, Thomas Chandler

3034 Baker, Ernest A. "Introduction" to Thomas Chandler Haliburton, Sam Slick
       the Clockmaker. London: Routledge, 1904, pp. xi-xvi.

3035 Baker, Ray Palmer. "Introduction" to Thomas Chandler Haliburton,
       Sam Slick. Toronto: McClelland & Stewart, 1941, pp. 13-28.

3036 Bengtsson, Elna. The Language and Vocabulary of Sam Slick. Uppsala:
       A-B Lundequistka Bokhandeln, 1956.

3037 Bissell, Claude T. "Haliburton, Leacock and the American Humourous [sic]
       Tradition." CanL, 39 (1969), 5-19.

3038 Bond, William H., ed. "The Correspondence of Thomas Chandler Haliburton
       and Richard Bentley." In William Inglis Morse, ed., The Canadian
       Collection at Harvard University. Cambridge: Harvard Univ. Printing
       Office, 1947, pp. 48-105.

3039 Calnek, W. A., and A. W. Savary. "Thomas Chandler Haliburton." In
       History of the County of Annapolis. Toronto: Briggs, 1897, pp. 418-26.

3040 Chasles, Philarète. "Samuel Slick." In Etudes sur la littérature et
       les moeurs des Anglo-Americains au XIXe siècle. Paris: Amyot, 1851,
       pp. 389-419.

3041 Chisholm, M. P. F. "Sam Slick and Catholic Disabilities in Nova Scotia."
       CathW, 64 (1897), 459-65.

3042 Chittick, V. L. O. "Books and Music in Haliburton." DR, 38 (1958),
       207-21.

3043 ____ "Haliburton as Member of Parliament." UTQ, 33 (1963), 78-88.

3044 ____ "Haliburton on Men and Things." DR, 38 (1958), 55-64.

3045 ____ "Haliburton Postscript I: Ring-Tailed Yankee." DR, 37 (1957), 19-36.

3046 ____ "Haliburton's 'Wise Saws' and Homely Imagery." DR, 38 (1958), 348-63.

3047 ____ "The Hybrid Comic: Origins of Sam Slick." CanL, 14 (1962), 35-42.

3048 ____ "Many-Sided Haliburton." DR, 61 (1961), 194-207.

3049 ____ "The Persuasiveness of Sam Slick." DR, 33 (1953), 88-101.

3050 ____ Thomas Chandler Haliburton ('Sam Slick'). New York: Columbia Univ.
       Press, 1924.

3051 Crofton, F. Blake. Haliburton, the Man and the Writer. Winslow, N. S.:
       Anslow, 1889.

3052 ____ "Thomas Chandler Haliburton." Atlantic, 69 (1892), 355-63.

3053 Eaton, A. W. H. "Haliburton Genealogy." NEHGR, 71 (1917), 57-74.

3054 Fenety, G. E. Life and Times of the Hon. Joseph Howe. Saint John,
       N. B.: Carter, 1896, pp. 39-46.

3055 Frye, Northrop. "Haliburton: Mask and Ego." Alphabet, 5 (1962), 58-63.

3056 Haliburton Club, King's College, Windsor, N. S. Haliburton. Toronto:
       Briggs, 1897.

3057 Harding, L. A. A. "Compassionate Humour in Haliburton." DR, 49 (1969),
       224-28.

3058 ____ "Folk Language in Haliburton's Humour." CanL, 24 (1965), 47-51.

3059 ____ "Yankee at the Court of Judge Haliburton." CanL, 39 (1969), 62-73.

3060 Harvey, D. C. "The Centenary of Sam Slick." DR, 16 (1937), 429-40.

3061 Howells, W. D. "Editor's Easy Chair." Harper's, 134 (1917), 442-45.

3062 Jefferys, Charles W. Sam Slick in Pictures. Ed. and introd. by Lorne Pierce. Toronto: Ryerson, 1956.

3063 Liljegren, Sven B. Canadian History and Thomas Chandler Haliburton: Some Notes on Sam Slick. Uppsala: A-B Lundequistska Bokhandeln, 1969.

3064 Logan, J. D. Scott and Haliburton. Halifax: Allen, 1921.

3065 _____ Thomas Chandler Haliburton. Toronto: Ryerson, 1923.

3066 _____ "Why Haliburton Has No Successor." CanM, 57 (1921), 362-68.

3067 McDougall, Robert L. "Introduction" to Thomas Chandler Haliburton, The Clockmaker. Toronto: McClelland & Stewart, 1958, pp. ix-xvi.

3068 _____ "Thomas Chandler Haliburton." In item 2484, pp. 3-30.

3069 MacMechan, Archibald. "Who's Who in Canadian Literature: Thomas Chandler Haliburton." CanB, 8 (1926), 8-9.

3070 Mahon, A. Wylie. "Sam Slick Letters." CanM, 44 (1914), 75-79.

3071 Marquis, T. G. "Biographical Sketch." In Thomas Chandler Haliburton, Sam Slick the Clockmaker. Centenary ed. Toronto: Musson, n. d., pp. ix-xxii.

3072 Montégut, Emile. "Un humoriste anglo-americaine." RDM, 5 (1850), 731-48.

3073 Murray, Florence B., ed. Muskoka and Haliburton, 1615-1875, a Collection of Documents. Toronto: Univ. of Toronto Press, 1963.

3074 O'Brien, Arthur Henry. Haliburton ('Sam Slick'). Montreal: Gazette, 1909.

3075 _____ "Thomas Chandler Haliburton, 1796-1865: A Sketch and a Bibliography." PTRSC, ser. 3, 3, sect. 2 (1909), pp. 43-66.

3076 Rimmington, Gerald T. "The Geography of Haliburton's Nova Scotia." DR, 48 (1968-69), 488-99.

3077 Ross, Effie May. "Thomas Chandler Haliburton: Sam Slick, the Founder of American Humor." Americana, 16 (1922), 62-70.

3078 Stuart-Stubbs, Basil. "On the Authorship of 'A General description of Nova Scota, 1823.'" BSCP, 4 (1965), 14-18.

3079 Trent, William P. "A Retrospect of American Humor." Century, 41 (1921), 45-64.

3080 Watters, Reginald Eyre, ed. and introd. Thomas Chandler Haliburton. The Old Judge, or Life in a Colony: a Selection of Sketches. Toronto: Clarke Irwin, 1968.

3081 _____ , and W. S. Avis, eds. The Sam Slick Anthology. Toronto: Clarke Irwin, 1969.

3082 Wood, Ruth K. "The Creator of the First Yankee in Literature." Bookman (New York), 41 (1915), 152-60.

See also: 6342-6346, 6371.

HOOD, Hugh

3083 Duffy, Dennis. "Grace: The Novels of Hugh Hood." CanL, 47 (1971), 10-25.

3084 Godfrey, Dave. "Turning New Leaves (2)." CanF, 42 (1963), 229-30.

3085 Hood, Hugh. "The Ingenue I Should Have Kissed But Didn't." TamR, 25 (1962), 60-68.

3086 ____ "Sober Colouring." CanL, 49 (1971), 28-34.

JOHNSON, Pauline

3087 Charlesworth, Hector. "Miss Pauline Johnson's Poems." CanM, 5 (1895), 478-80.

3088 Foster, W. G. "The Lyric Beauty of Pauline Johnson's Poetry." CanB, 16 (1934), 37, 43.

3089 ____ The Mohawk Princess. Vancouver: Lion's Gate, 1931.

3090 Hammond, M. O. "Who's Who in Canadian Literature: E. Pauline Johnson." CanB, 8 (1926), 41-43.

3091 Loosely, E. "Pauline Johnson." In item 2439, pp. 74-90.

3092 MacKay, Isabel Ecclestone. "Pauline Johnson: A Reminiscence." CanM, 41 (1913), 273-78.

3093 McRaye, Walter. "East and West with Pauline Johnson." CanM, 60 (1923), 381-89, 494-502.

3094 ____ "Pauline Johnson." In item 2556, pp. 88-97.

3095 Mair, Charles. "Pauline Johnson: An Appreciation." CanM, 41 (1913), 281-83.

3096 Scott, Jack. "The Passionate Princess." Maclean's, 65 (1 April 1952), 12-13, 54, 57.

3097 Shrive, F. Norman. "What Happened to Pauline?" CanL, 13 (1962), 25-38.

3098 Van Steen, Marcus. Pauline Johnson, Her Life and Work. Toronto: Musson, 1965.

3099 Waldie, Jean H. "The Iroquois Poetess, Pauline Johnson." OntHSP, 40 (1948), 65-75.

3100 Yeigh, Frank. "Memories of Pauline Johnson." CanB, 11 (1929), 227-29.

KIRBY, William

3101 Anon. "William Kirby." DomI, 2 (11 May 1889), 298.

3102 Carnochan, Janet. "Reminiscences of William Kirby, F. R. S. C." TUELA, 6 (1914), 49-56.

3103 Crawley, Derek. "Introduction" to William Kirby, The Golden Dog. Toronto: McClelland & Stewart, 1969, pp. vii-xi.

3104 De Guttenberg, A. C. "William Kirby." RevL, 9 (1954), 337-45.

3105 Pierce, Lorne, ed. Alfred, Lord Tennyson and William Kirby: Unpublished Correspondence, to Which Are Added Some Letters from Hallam, Lord Tennyson. Toronto: Macmillan, 1929.

3106 ____ "Who's Who in Canadian Literature: William Kirby." CanB, 11 (1929), 35-39.

3107 ____ William Kirby: The Portrait of a Tory Loyalist. Toronto: Macmillan, 1929.

3108 Riddell, William R. William Kirby. Toronto: Ryerson, 1923.

3109 Sandwell, B. K. "Debunking The Golden Dog." SatN, 45 (4 Oct. 1930), 2.

See also: 6352, 6353.

KLEIN, A. M.

3110 Crawley, Alan. "Notes on A. M. Klein." ContV, 28 (1949), 20.

3111 Dudek, Louis. "A. M. Klein." CanF, 30 (1950), 10-12. [Repr. in item 3119, pp. 66-74.]

3112 Edel, Leon. "Abraham M. Klein." CanF, 12 (1932), 300-02.

3113 ____ "Poetry and the Jewish Tradition." Poetry (Chicago), 58 (1941), 51-53. [Repr. in item 3119, pp. 15-17.]

3114 Fischer, G. K. "A. M. Klein's Forgotten Play." CanL, 43 (1970), 42-53.

3115 Gotlieb, Phyllis. "Klein's Sources." CanL, 26 (1965), 82.

3116 Lewisohn, Ludwig. "Foreword" to A. M. Klein, Hath Not a Jew. New York: Behrman's, 1940, pp. v-viii. [Repr. in item 3119, pp. 12-14.]

3117 Livesay, Dorothy. "The Polished Lens: Poetic Techniques of Pratt and Klein." CanL, 25 (1965), 33-42. [Repr. in item 3119, pp. 119-31.]

3118 Marshall, Thomas. "Theorems Made Flesh: Klein's Poetic Universe." CanL, 25 (1965), 43-52. [Repr. in item 3119, pp. 151-62.]

3119 ____, ed. A. M. Klein. Toronto: Ryerson, 1970.

3120 Matthews, John. "Abraham Klein and the Problem of Synthesis." JCL, 1 (1965), 149-63. [Repr. in item 3119, pp. 132-50.]

3121 Mendelbaum, Allen. "Everyman on Babylon's Shore." Commentary, 12 (1951), 602-04.

3122 Régimbal, A. "Artistes israélites au Canada français." Rélations, 8 (1948), 184-85.

3123 Samuel, Maurice. "The Book of the Miracle." Jewish Frontier, 18 (1951), 11-15. [Repr. in item 3119, pp. 79-81.]

3124 Smith, A. J. M. "Abraham Moses Klein." GdC, 11 (1946), 67-81. [Repr. in item 3119, pp. 26-40.]

3125 Steinberg, M. W. "Poet of a Living Past: Tradition in Klein's Poetry." CanL, 25 (1965), 5-20. [Repr. in item 3119, pp. 99-118; also in item 2707, pp. 203-20.]

3126 ____ "A Twentieth Century Pentateuch: A. M. Klein's The Second Scroll." CanL, 2 (1959), 37-46. [Repr. in item 2631, pp. 151-61.]

3127 Sutherland, John. "Canadian Comment." NR, 2, no. 6 (1949), 30-34. [Repr. in item 3119, pp. 59-65.]

3128 ____ "The Poetry of A. M. Klein." Index, 1 (1946), 8-12. [Repr. in item 3119, pp. 41-54.]

3129 Waddington, Miriam. "The Cloudless Day: The Radical Poems of A. M. Klein." TamR, 45 (1967), 65-90, 92.

3130 ____ A. M. Klein. Toronto: Copp Clark, 1970.

3131 ____ "Signs on a White Field: Klein's Second Scroll." CanL, 25 (1965), 21-32. [Repr. in item 2707, pp. 142-55.]

3132 Wilson, Milton. "Biographical Note." CanAB, 34, no. 1 (1958), 13.

See also: 2339, 2547, 2698, 6354-6359.

KNISTER, Raymond

3133 Child, Philip. "Introduction" to Raymond Knister, White Narcissus. Toronto: McClelland & Stewart, 1962, pp. 7-16.

3134 Kennedy, Leo. "Raymond Knister." CanF, 12 (1932), 459-61.

3135 Livesay, Dorothy. "Memoir." In Collected Poems of Raymond Knister.
      Toronto: Ryerson, 1949, pp. xi-xli. [Margaret Ray, comp. "Raymond
      Knister: A Bibliography of His Works," pp. 39-45.]

3136 Stevens, Peter. "The Old Futility of Art: Knister's Poetry." CanL,
      23 (1965), 45-52.

See also: 6360.

KREISEL, Henry

3137 Anon. "Handling the English Language." CanAB, 24, no. 4 (1948), 40.

3138 Stedmond, John. "Introduction" to Henry Kreisel, The Rich Man. Toronto:
      McClelland & Stewart, 1961, pp. v-vii.

LAMPMAN, Archibald

3139 Barry, Lilly E. F. "Prominent Canadians: Archibald Lampman." Week, 8
      (1891), 298-300. [Repr. in item 3152, pp. 6-19.]

3140 Beattie, Alexander Munro. "Archibald Lampman." In item 2310, pp. 63-88.

3141 Begley, Lucille. "Harmonies canadiennes: Pamphile le May, Archibald
      Lampman." Lectures, 6 (1960), 296-97.

3142 Bourinot, Arthur S., ed. Archibald Lampman's Letters to Edward William
      Thomson (1890-1898). Ottawa: The Author, 1956.

3143 ____, ed. Some Letters of Duncan Campbell Scott, Archibald Lampman and
      Others. Ottawa: The Author, 1959.

3144 Brown, E. K. "Foreword" to Archibald Lampman, At the Long Sault
      and Other New Poems. Toronto: Ryerson, 1943, pp. vii-xxix.

3145 Burton, Jean. "Archibald Lampman's Poetry of Release." Will, 3 (1928),
      425-27.

3146 Colgate, William. "Archibald Lampman: A Dedication and a Note." CanF,
      36 (1957), 279-80.

3147 Collin, W. E. "Archibald Lampman." UTQ, 4 (1934), 104-20. [Repr. in
      item 3152, pp. 125-42.]

3148 Connor, Carl Y. Archibald Lampman, Canadian Poet of Nature. New York:
      Carrier, 1929.

3149 Crawford, A. W. "Archibald Lampman." ActaV, 17 (1895), 77-81. [Repr.
      in item 3152, pp. 27-32.]

3150 Dudek, Louis. "The Significance of Lampman." Culture, 18 (1957), 277-90.
      [Repr. in item 3152, pp. 85-201.]

3151 Fidelis. [Agnes Maule Machar.] "Among the Millet." Week, 6 (1889),
      251-52. [Repr. in item 3152, pp. 1-5.]

3152 Gnarowski, Michael, ed. Archibald Lampman. Toronto: Ryerson, 1970.

3153 Gustafson, Ralph. "Among the Millet." NR, 1, no. 5 (1947), 26-34.
      [Repr. in item 3152, pp. 142-53.]

3154 Guthrie, Norman G. The Poetry of Archibald Lampman. Toronto: Musson, 1927.

3155 Howells, W. D. "Editor's Study." Harper's, 78 (1889), 821-23.

3156 Kennedy, Leo. "Archibald Lampman." CanF, 13 (1933), 301-03. [Repr. in
      item 3152, pp. 110-25.]

3157   Knister, Raymond. "The Poetry of Archibald Lampman." DR, 7 (1927),
        348-61. [Repr. in item 3152, pp. 100-18.]

3158   Logan, J. D. "Literary Group of '61." CanM, 37 (1911), 555-63.

3159   MacDonald, E. R. "A Little Talk About Lampman." CanM, 52 (1919), 1012-
        016.

3160   Marshall, John. "Archibald Lampman." QQ, 9 (1901), 63-79. [Repr. in
        item 3152, pp. 33-54.]

3161   Muddiman, Bernard. "Archibald Lampman." QQ, 22 (1915), 233-43. [Repr.
        in item 3152, pp. 68-80.]

3162   Munday, Don. "Soul-Standards of Archibald Lampman." WestH, 4 (1914),
        15-17.

3163   Pacey, Desmond. "A Reading of Lampman's 'Heat.'" Culture, 14 (1953),
        292-97. [Repr. in item 3152, pp. 178-84.]

3164   Scott, Duncan Campbell. "Archibald Lampman." In item 2556, pp. 98-106.

3165   ____ "Decade of Canadian Poetry." CanM, 17 (1901), 153-58.

3166   ____ "Introduction" to Archibald Lampman, Lyrics of Earth. Toronto:
        Musson, 1925, pp. 3-47.

3167   ____ "Letter to Ralph Gustafson [17 July 1945]." Fiddlehead, 41 (1959),
        12-14. [Repr. in item 3152, pp. 154-58.]

3168   ____ "Memoir." In Selected Poems of Archibald Lampman. Toronto:
        Ryerson, 1947, pp. xiii-xxvii.

3169   ____ "Memoir." In The Poems of Archibald Lampman. Toronto: Morang,
        1900, pp. xi-xxv.

3170   ____ "Who's Who in Canadian Literature: Archibald Lampman." CanB, 8
        (1926), 107-09.

3171   Stringer, Arthur. "A Glance at Lampman." CanM, 2 (1894), 545-48. [Repr.
        in item 3152, pp. 20-27.]

3172   Sutherland, John. "Edgar Allan Poe in Canada." NR, 4, no. 3 (1951),
        22-37. [Repr. in item 3152, pp. 159-78.]

3173   Swift, S. C. "Lampman and le Comte de Lisle." CanB, 9 (1927), 261-64.

3174   Untermeyer, L. "Archibald Lampman and the Sonnet." Poet Lore, 20
        (1909), 432-37. [Repr. in item 3152, pp. 54-67.]

3175   Unwin, G. H. "The Poetry of Lampman." UnivM, 16 (1917), 55-73. [Repr.
        in item 3152, pp. 80-100.]

3176   Voorhis, Ernest. "The Ancestry of Archibald Lampman, Poet." PTRSC,
        ser. 3, 15, sect. 2 (1921), pp. 103-21.

3177   Watt, Frank W. "The Masks of Archibald Lampman." UTQ, 27 (1958), 169-
        84. [Repr. in item 3152, pp. 202-22.]

3178   Wendell, W. L. "Modern School of Canadian Writers." Bookman (New York),
        11 (1900), 515-26.

See also: 2323, 2339, 2547, 3721, 6249, 6361-6367.

LAURENCE, Margaret

3179   Anon. "Laurence of Manitoba." CanAB, 41, no. 2 (1966), 4-6.

3180   Callaghan, Barry. "The Writings of Margaret Laurence." TamR, 36 (1965),
        45-51.

3181   Gotlieb, Phyllis. "On Margaret Laurence." TamR, 52 (1969), 76-80.

3182 Kreisel, Henry. "The African Stories of Margaret Laurence." CanF, 41
      (1961), 8-10.

3183 Laurence, Margaret. The Prophet's Camel Bell. Toronto: McClelland &
      Stewart, 1963. [Also pub. as New Wind in a Dry Land. New York: Knopf,
      1964.]

3184 ____ "Sources." Mosaic, 3, no. 3 (1970), 80-84.

3185 ____ "Ten Years' Sentences." CanL, 41 (1969), 10-16.

3186 New, William H. "Introduction" to Margaret Laurence, The Stone Angel.
      Toronto: McClelland & Stewart, 1968, pp. iii-x.

3187 Read, S. E. "The Maze of Life: The Work of Margaret Laurence." CanL,
      27 (1966), 5-14.

3188 Robertson, George. "An Artist's Progress." CanL, 21 (1964), 53-55.

3189 Swayze, Walter. "The Odyssey of Margaret Laurence." EngQ, 3, no. 3
      (1970), 7-17.

3190 Thomas, Clara. "Introduction" to Margaret Laurence, The Tomorrow-Tamer.
      Toronto: McClelland & Stewart, 1970, pp. xi-xvii.

3191 ____ Margaret Laurence. Toronto: McClelland & Stewart, 1969.

See also: 6368.

LAYTON, Irving

3192 Anon. "Biographical Note." CanAB, 34, no. 1 (1958), 11.

3193 ____ "Three New Poets." First Statement, 1, no. 12 (n. d.), 1-4.

3194 Carruth, Hayden. "That Heaven-Sent Lively Rope-Walker Irving Layton."
      TamR, 39 (1966), 68-73.

3195 Dudek, Louis. "Layton Now and Then." QQ, 63 (1956), 291-93.

3196 ____ "Layton on the Carpet." Delta (Montreal), 9 (1959), 17-19.

3197 Ellenbogen, George. "An Open Letter to Irving Layton." Cataract, 1,
      no. 3 (1962), n. pag.

3198 Francis, Wynne. "Irving Layton." JCL, 3 (1967), 34-48.

3199 Junkins, Donald. "Irving Layton, Selected Poems." FPt, 3 (1969), 61-69.

3200 Layton, Irving. "Correspondence." CanF, 41 (1962), 281-82; 42 (1962),
      41-42.

3201 ____ "Foreword " to A Red Carpet for the Sun. Toronto: McClelland &
      Stewart, 1959, pp. v-viii. [Repr. in item 2632, pp. 139-43.]

3202 Lund, K. A. "Satyric Layton." CanAB, 42, no. 3 (1967), 8.

3203 Mandel, Eli. Irving Layton. Toronto: Forum House, 1969.

3204 Marcotte, Gilles. "Le poète Irving Layton, vu d'ici." Devoir, 17 Oct.
      1959, p. 11.

3205 Mathews, Robin. "Correspondence." CanF, 42 (1962), 58.

3206 Smith, A. J. M. "The Recent Poetry of Irving Layton." QQ, 62 (1956),
      587-91. [Reply by Louis Dudek, 63 (1956), 291-93.]

3207 Smith, Patricia Keeney. "Irving Layton and the Theme of Death." CanL,
      48 (1971), 6-15.

3208 Taaffe, Gerald. "Diary of a Montreal Newspaper Reader." TamR, 27
      (1963), 49-62.

3209 Waterston, Elizabeth. "Irving Layton: Apocalypse in Montreal." CanL,
      48 (1971), 16-24.

3210 Williams, William Carlos. "A Note on Layton." In Irving Layton, The
      Improved Binoculars. Highlands, N. C.: Williams, 1956, pp. 9-10.
      [Repr. in item 2371, pp. 233-34.]

3211 Woodcock, George. "A Grab at Proteus: Notes on Irving Layton." CanL,
      28 (1966), 5-21. [Repr. in item 2704, pp. 75-92.]

See also: 2371, 2530, 6355, 6369, 6370.

LEACOCK, Stephen

3212 Allen, C. K. Oh, Mr. Leacock. London: Lane, 1925.

3213 Braybrooke, Patrick. Peeps at the Mighty. London: Drane, 1927, pp. 130-
      46.

3214 Caldwell, William. "A Visit to a Canadian Author." CanM, 59 (1922),
      55-60.

3215 Cameron, Donald. "The Enchanted Houses: Leacock's Irony." CanL, 23
      (1965), 31-44.

3216 _____ Faces of Leacock: An Appreciation. Toronto: Ryerson, 1967.

3217 _____ "Introduction" to Stephen Leacock, Behind the Beyond. Toronto:
      McClelland & Stewart, 1969, pp. v-viii.

3218 _____ "Stephen Leacock: The Boy Behind the Arras." JCL, 3 (1967), 3-18.

3219 _____ "Stephen Leacock: The Novelist Who Never Was." DR, 46 (1966),
      15-28.

3220 Clements, C. "An Evening with Stephen Leacock." CathW, 159 (1944),
      236-41.

3221 Collins, J. P. "Professor Leacock, Ph.D.: Savant and Humorist."
      Bookman (London), 51 (1916), 39-44.

3222 Crooks, Grace. "A Taste for Humour." CanLJ, 26 (1969), 222-28.

3223 Curry, Ralph L. "Introduction" to Stephen Leacock, Acadian Adventures
      with the Idle Rich. Toronto: McClelland & Stewart, 1959, pp. vii-xi.

3224 _____ "Stephen Butler Leacock, A Check-List." BB, 22 (1958), 106-09.

3225 _____ Stephen Leacock: Humorist and Humanist. Garden City, N. Y.:
      Doubleday, 1959.

3226 _____ "Unknown Years of Stephen Leacock." Maclean's, 72 (4 July 1959),
      20-21, 45-47; 72 (18 July 1959), 26-27, 34.

3227 Davies, Robertson. "Introduction" to Stephen Leacock, Literary Lapses.
      Toronto: McClelland & Stewart, 1957, pp. vii-ix.

3228 _____ "Stephen Leacock." In item 2310, pp. 128-49. [Repr. in item 2631,
      pp. 93-114.]

3229 _____ Stephen Leacock. Toronto: McClelland & Stewart, 1970.

3230 Day, J. P. "Professor Leacock at McGill." CanJEPS, 10 (1944), 226-28.

3231 Edgar, Pelham. "Stephen Leacock." QQ, 53 (1946), 173-84.

3232 Feibleman, James Kerr. "Criticism of Modern Theories of Comedy." In
      In Praise of Comedy: A Study of Its Theory and Practice. London:
      Allen & Unwin, 1939, pp. 123-67.

3233 Hind, C. Lewis. "Stephen Leacock." In More Authors and I. New York:
      Dodd Mead, 1922, pp. 180-85.

3234 Innis, Harold Adams. "Stephen Butler Leacock (1869-1944)." CanJEPS,
      10 (1944), 216-26.

3235 Kimball, Elizabeth. The Man in the Panama Hat. Toronto: McClelland &
      Stewart, 1970.

3236 Larned, William T. "Professor Leacock and Other Professors." New
      Republic, 9 (1917), 299.

3237 Leacock, Stephen. The Boy I Left Behind Me. New York: Doubleday, 1946.

3238 ____ "Humor as I See It and Something About Humor in Canada." Maclean's,
      29 (May 1916), 11-13, 111-13.

3239 ____ My Memories and Miseries as a Schoolmaster. Toronto: Upper Canada
      College, n. d.

3240 Legate, David. Stephen Leacock. Toronto: Doubleday, 1970.

3241 Lomer, Gerhard R. Stephen Leacock: A Check-list and Index of His
      Writings. Ottawa: National Library, 1954.

3242 Lower, Arthur R. M. "The Mariposa Belle." QQ, 58 (1951), 220-26.

3243 McArthur, Peter. Stephen Leacock. Toronto: Ryerson, 1923.

3244 MacPhail, Andrew. "Stephen Leacock." In The Yearbook of Canadian Art,
      1913. Toronto: Dent, 1914, pp. 1-7.

3245 Masson, T. L. "Stephen Leacock." In Our American Humorists. New York:
      Dodd Mead, 1931, pp. 209-29.

3246 Mikes, George. "Stephen Leacock." In Eight Humorists. London: Wingate,
      1954, pp. 41-65.

3247 Miller, Margaret J. Seven Men of Wit. London: Hutchinson, 1960.

3248 Murphy, Bruce. "Stephen Leacock--The Greatest Living Humorist." OntLR,
      12 (1928), 67-69.

3249 Nimmo, Barbara. "Preface" to Stephen Leacock, Last Leaves. New York:
      Dodd Mead, 1945, pp. vii-xx.

3250 O'Hagan, Howard. "Stephie." QQ, 68 (1961), 135-46.

3251 Pacey, Desmond. "Leacock as a Satirist." QQ, 68 (1951), 208-19.

3252 Priestley, J. B. "Introduction" to The Bodley Head Leacock. London:
      Bodley Head, 1957, pp. 9-13.

3253 Robinson, J. M. "Introduction" to Stephen Leacock, Last Leaves. Toronto:
      McClelland & Stewart, 1970, pp. vi-xii.

3254 Ross, Malcolm. "Preface" to Stephen Leacock, Sunshine Sketches of a
      Little Town. Toronto: McClelland & Stewart, 1960, pp. ix-xvi.

3255 Sandwell, B. K. "Leacock Recalled: How the 'Sketches' Started." SatN,
      67 (23 Aug. 1952), 7.

3256 Sedgewick, G. G. "Stephen Leacock as a Man of Letters." UTQ, 15 (1945),
      17-26.

3257 Stevens, John. "Introduction" to Stephen Leacock, My Remarkable Uncle.
      Toronto: McClelland & Stewart, 1965, pp. vii-xii.

3258 Watt, Frank W. "Critic or Entertainer?" CanL, 5 (1960), 33-42.

3259 Watters, Reginald Eyre. "Leacock in Limbo." CanL, 3 (1960), 68-70.

3260 ____ "A Special Tang: Stephen Leacock's Canadian Humour." CanL, 5
      (1960), 21-32.

3261 Wheelwright, J. "Poet as Funny Man." Poetry (Chicago), 50 (1937),
      210-15.

See also: 3037, 6371-6376.

LEMELIN, Roger

3262 Collin, W. E. "Roger Lemelin: The Pursuit of Grandeur." QQ, 41 (1954), 195-212.

3263 Keate, Stuart. "The Boy from the Town Below." Maclean's, 63 (1 Feb. 1950), 17, 26, 28.

3264 Lemelin, Roger. "My First Novel." QQ, 61 (1954), 189-94.

3265 _____ "The 'Not-so-Innocent' Abroad." SatN, 55 (7 Nov. 1950), 12-13, 37.

LE PAN, Douglas

3266 Brown, E. K. "[Review of The Wounded Prince]." UTQ, 18 (1949), 257-58.

3267 Davies, Marilyn. "The Bird of Heavenly Airs: Thematic Strains in Douglas Le Pan's Poetry." CanL, 15 (1963), 27-39.

3268 Frye, Northrop. "[Review of The Net and the Sword]." UTQ, 23 (1954), 256-58.

3269 Hamilton, S. C. "European Emblem and Canadian Image: A Study of Douglas Le Pan's Poetry." Mosaic, 3, no. 2 (1970), 62-73.

LIVESAY, Dorothy

3270 Crawley, Alan. "Dorothy Livesay." In item 2556, pp. 117-24.

3271 Gibbs, Jean. "Dorothy Livesay and the Transcendentalist Tradition." HAB, 21, no. 2 (1970), 24-39.

3272 Livesay, Dorothy. "A Prairie Sampler." Mosaic, 3, no. 3 (1970), 85-92.

3273 _____ "Song and Dance." CanL, 41 (1969), 40-48.

3274 Pacey, Desmond. "Introduction" to Selected Poems of Dorothy Livesay 1926-1956. Toronto: Ryerson, 1957, pp. xi-xix.

3275 Pratt, E. J. "Dorothy Livesay." GdC, 11 (1946), 61-65.

3276 Steinberg, M. W. "Dorothy Livesay: Poet of Affirmation." BCLQ, 24, no. 2 (1960), 9-13.

3277 Stephan, Ruth. "A Canadian Poet." Poetry (Chicago), 65 (1945), 220-22.

3278 Stevens, Peter. "Dorothy Livesay: The Love Poetry." CanL, 47 (1971), 26-43.

3279 Weaver, Robert. "The Poetry of Dorothy Livesay." ContV, 26 (1948), 18-22.

See also: 2339, 6359, 6378, 6379.

LOWRY, Malcolm

3280 Aiken, Conrad. "Malcolm Lowry: A Note." CanL, 8 (1961), 29-30. [Repr. in item 3369, pp. 101-02.]

3281 _____ Ushant. New York: Duell, Sloan, 1952.

3282 Albérès, R. M. [René Marill.] "Le lyrisme et le mythe: de Joyce à Malcolm Lowry." In Métamorphoses du Roman. Paris: Editions Albin Michel, 1966, pp. 119-31.

3283   Barnes, Jim. "The Myth of Sisyphus in Under the Volcano." PrS, 42
       (1968-69), 341-48.

3284   Benham, David. "Lowry's Purgatory: Versions of Lunar Caustic." CanL,
       44 (1970), 28-37. [Repr. in item 3369, pp. 56-65.]

3285   Birney, Earle. "Five Signallings in Darkness: Malcolm Lowry."
       Evidence, 4 (1962), 76-78.

3286   ____   "Foreword [to poems by Lowry]." Northwest Review, 5 (1962),
       57-59.

3287   ____   "Glimpses into the Life of Malcolm Lowry." TamR, 19 (1961), 35-41.

3288   ____   "Preface [to a group of poems]." CanL, 8 (1961), 17-19. [Repr. in
       item 3369, pp. 91-93.]

3289   ____   "Malcolm Lowry's Poetry: A Note." Contact, 7 (1961), 81-82.

3290   ____   "The Unknown Poetry of Malcolm Lowry." BCLQ, 24, no. 1 (1961),
       33-40.

3291   ____, and Margerie Lowry. "Bibliography of Malcolm Lowry: Part I,
       Works by Malcolm Lowry." CanL, 8 (1961), 81-88. "Part II: Works About
       Malcolm Lowry." 9 (1961), 80-84. [First supp., 11 (1962), 90-93;
       second supp., 19 (1964), 83-89.]

3292   Bonnefoi, Geneviève. "Souvenir de Quauhnahuac." LetN, 5 (1960), 94-108.

3293   Breit, Harvey. "Malcolm Lowry." Paris Review, 23 (1960), 84-85.

3294   Calder-Marshall, Arthur. "A Portrait of Malcolm Lowry." Listener, 78
       (1967), 461-63.

3295   Carey, Maurice J. "Life with Malcolm Lowry." In item 3369, pp. 163-70.

3296   Carroy, Jean-Roger. "Malcolm et les ambiguités." In Malcolm Lowry,
       Ultramarine. Trans. by Clarisse Fancillon and Jean-Roger Carroy.
       Paris: Denoël, 1965, pp. 235-65.

3297   ____   "Obscur présent, le feu . . . ." LetN, 5 (1960), 83-88.

3298   Castelnau, Marie-Pierre. "Malcolm Lowry: un écrivain 'inclassable.'"
       Gazette, 53 (1961), 13, 17.

3299   Chittick, V. L. O. "Ushant's Malcolm Lowry." QQ, 71 (1964), 67-75.

3299   Christella Marie, Sister. "Under the Volcano: A Consideration of the
       Novel by Malcolm Lowry." XUS, 4 (1965), 13-27.

3301   Corrigan, Matthew. "The Writer as Consciousness: A View of October
       Ferry to Gabriola." In item 3369, pp. 71-77.

3302   Costa, Richard Hauer. "The Lowry Aiken Symbiosis." Nation (New York),
       26 June 1967, pp. 823-25.

3303   ____   "Lowry's Overture as Elegy." In A Malcolm Lowry Catalogue.
       New York: J. Howard Woolmer, 1968, pp. 26-44.

3304   ____   "Malcolm Lowry and the Addictions of an Era." UWR, 5 (1970), 1-10.

3305   ____   "'Ulysses,' Lowry's 'Volcano' and the 'Voyage' Between: A Study
       of an Unacknowledged Literary Kinship." UTQ, 36 (1967), 335-52.

3306   Davenport, John. "Malcolm Lowry." Spectator, 207 (1961), 287, 290-91.

3307   Day, Douglas. "Malcolm Lowry: Letters to an Editor." Shenandoah, 15,
       no. 3 (1964), 3-15.

3308   ____   "Of Tragic Joy." PrS, 37 (1963-64), 354-62.

3309   ____   "Preface" to Malcolm Lowry, Dark as the Grave Wherein My Friend
       Is Laid. Toronto: General, 1968, pp. ix-xxiii.

3310 Dodson, Daniel B. Malcolm Lowry. New York and London: Columbia Univ. Press, 1970.

3311 Doyen, Victor. "Elements Towards a Spatial Reading of Malcolm Lowry's Under the Volcano." ES, 50, no. 1 (1969), 65-74.

3312 Durrant, Geoffrey. "Death in Life: Neo-Platonic Elements in 'Through the Panama.'" CanL, 44 (1970), 13-27. [Repr. in item 3369, pp. 42-55.]

3313 Editorial. TLS, 28 Oct. 1960, p. 693.

3314 Edmonds, Dale. "The Short Fiction of Malcolm Lowry." TSE, 15 (1967), 59-80.

3315 _____ "Under the Volcano: A Reading of the 'Immediate Level.'" TSE, 16 (1968), 63-105.

3316 Epstein, Perle. "Malcolm Lowry: In Search of Equilibrium." In A Malcolm Lowry Catalogue. New York: J. Howard Woolmer, 1968, pp. 15-25.

3317 _____ The Private Labyrinth of Malcolm Lowry: Under the Volcano and the Cabbala. New York: Holt, Rinehart and Winston, 1969.

3318 _____ "Swinging the Maelstrom: Malcolm Lowry and Jazz." CanL, 44 (1970), 57-66. [Repr. in item 3369, pp. 144-53.]

3319 Fernandez, Diane. "Malcolm Lowry et le feu infernal." Preuves, 215-216 (1969), 129-34.

3320 Fouchet, Max-Pol. "Le feu central." Chapter IX of Les Appels. Paris: Mercure de France, 1967, pp. 95-105. [Inc. material pub. in LetN, (1960), 5 and CanL, 8 (1961), under the title "No se Puede . . . ."]

3321 Francillon, Clarisse. "Malcolm, mon ami." LetN, 5 (1960), 8-19.

3322 _____ "Souvenirs sur Malcolm Lowry." LetN, 5 (1957), 588-603.

3323 Gass, William H. Fiction and the Figures of Life. New York: Knopf, 1971.

3324 Heilman, Robert B. "The Possessed Artist and the Ailing Soul." CanL, 8 (1961), 7-16. [Repr. in item 3369, pp. 16-25.]

3325 _____ "[Review of Under the Volcano]." SR, 55 (1947), 483-92.

3326 Hirschman, Jack. "Kabbala/Lowry, etc." PrS, 37 (1963-64), 347-53.

3327 Kilgallin, Anthony R. "Eliot, Joyce and Lowry." CanAB, 40, no. 2 (1964), 3-4, 6.

3328 _____ "Faust and Under the Volcano." CanL, 26 (1965), 43-54.

3329 _____ "The Long Voyage Home: October Ferry to Gabriola." In item 3369, pp. 78-87.

3330 _____ "'Why Has God Given This to Us?'" Vancouver Life, 3, no. 4 (1968), 28-31, 48.

3331 Kim, Suzanne. "Les lettres de Malcolm Lowry." EA, 22 (1969), 58-61.

3332 _____ "Les oeuvres de jeunesse de Malcolm Lowry." EA, 18 (1965), 383-94.

3333 _____ "Par l'eau et feu: deux oeuvres de Malcolm Lowry." EA, 18 (1965), 395-97.

3334 Kirk, Downie. "More than Music: Glimpses of Malcolm Lowry." CanL, 8 (1961), 31-38. [Repr. in item 3369, pp. 117-24.]

3335 Knickerbocker, Conrad. "Lowry à vingt ans." LetN (1967), 68-94.

3336 _____ "Swinging the Paradise Street Blues: Malcolm lowry in England." Paris Review, 38 (1966), 13-38.

3337 _____ "The Voyages of Malcolm Lowry." PrS, 37 (1963-64), 301-14.

3338   Leech, Clifford. "The Shaping of Time: Nostromo and Under the Volcano."
       In Maynard Mack and Ian Gregor, eds., Imagined Worlds. London:
       Methuen, 1968, pp. 323-41.

3339   Lowry, Malcolm. "Preface to a Novel." CanL, 9 (1961), 23-29. [Repr.
       in item 3369, pp. 9-15.]

3340   _____ Selected Letters. ed. Harvey Breit and Margerie Lowry.
       Philadelphia and New York: Lippincott, 1965.

3341   Lowry, Margerie. "Introductory Note" to Malcolm Lowry, Ultramarine.
       London: Cape, 1963, pp. 5-8.

3342   McConnell, William. "Recollections of Malcolm Lowry." CanL, 6 (1960),
       24-31. [Repr. in item 3369, pp. 154-62; also in item 2631, pp. 141-50.]

3343   McCormick, John. Catastrophe and Imagination. New York and Toronto:
       Longmans, 1957, pp. 65-66, 85-89.

3344   Magee, A. Peter. "The Quest for Love." Emeritus, 1 (1965), 24-29.

3345   "Malcolm Lowry." TLS, 26 Jan. 1967, pp. 57-59.

3346   Markson, David. "Malcolm Lowry: A Reminiscence." NatR, 7 Feb. 1966,
       pp. 164-67.

3347   _____ "Myth in Under the Volcano." PrS, 37 (1963-64), 339-46.

3348   Moore, Brian. "The Albatross of Self." Spectator, 208 (1962), 589.

3349   Myrer, Anton. "Le monde au-dessous le volcan." LetN, 5 (1960), 59-66.

3350   Nadeau, Maurice. "Lowry." LetN, 5 (1960), 3-7.

3351   New, William H. "Lowry, the Cabbala and Charles Jones." CanL, 43 (1970),
       83-87.

3352   _____ "Lowry's Reading: An Introductory Essay." CanL, 44 (1970), 5-12.
       [Repr. in item 3369, pp. 125-32.]

3353   Nimmo, D. C. "Lowry's Hell." N&Q, 16 (1969), 265.

3354   Noxon, Gerald. "Malcolm Lowry: 1930." PrS, 37 (1963-64), 315-20.

3355   Parsons, Ian. "Malcolm Lowry." TLS, 13 April 1967, p. 317.

3356   Ponce, Juan García. "Malcolm Lowry en su obra." RevUM, 19, no. 3
       (1964), 10-11.

3357   Purdy, A. W. "Dormez-vous? A Memoir of Malcolm Lowry." Canada Month
       (Sept. 1962), 24-26.

3358   Romijn Meijer, Henk. "Malcolm Lowry." Tirade, 7 (1963), 918-22.

3359   Spender, Stephen. "Introduction" to Malcolm Lowry, Under the Volcano.
       Philadelphia and New York: Lippincott, 1965.

3360   Spriel, Stephen. "Le Cryptogramme Lowry." LetN, 5 (1960), 67-81.

3361   Stern, James. "Malcolm Lowry: A First Impression." Encounter, 29
       (1967), 58-68.

3362   Tiessen, Paul G. "Malcolm Lowry and the Cinema." CanL, 44 (1970), 38-
       47. [Repr. in item 3369, pp. 133-43.]

3363   Tuohy, Frank. "Day of a Dead Man." Spectator, 25 (1961), 262.

3364   Widmer, Eleanor. "The Drunken Wheel: Malcolm Lowry and Under the
       Volcano." In Warren French, ed., The Forties. Deland, Fla.: Everett/
       Edwards, 1969, pp. 217-26.

3365   Wild, Bernadette. "Malcolm Lowry: A Study of the Sea Metaphor in
       Under the Volcano." UWR, 4 (1968), 46-60.

3366   Woodcock, George. "Art as the Writer's Mirror: Literary Solipsism in
       Dark as the Grave." In item 3369, pp. 66-70.

3367   _____ "French Thoughts on Lowry." CanL, 6 (1960), 79-80.

3368   _____ "Malcolm Lowry as Novelist." BCLQ, 24, no. 1 (1961), 25-32.
       [Repr. in item 2704, pp. 62-67.]

3369   _____, ed. Malcolm Lowry: The Man and His Work. Vancouver: Univ. of
       British Columbia Press, 1971.

3370   _____ "Malcolm Lowry's Under the Volcano." MFS, 4 (1948), 151-56.
       [Repr. in item 2704, pp. 56-62.]

3371   _____ "On the Day of the Dead." NR, 6, no. 5 (1953-54), 15-21.

3372   _____ "Under Seymour Mountain." CanL, 8 (1961), 3-6. [Repr. in item
       3369, pp. 38-41; also in item 2704, pp. 67-70.]

3373   Wright, Terence. "Under the Volcano--The Static Art of Malcolm Lowry."
       ArielE, 1, no. 4 (1970), 67-76.

3374   Zimmer, Dieter E. "Die Verwüstung des Gartens." Zcit, 41 (11 Oct.
       1963), 20.

See also: 6380-6397.

MCCULLOCH, Thomas

3375   Frye, Northrop. "Introduction" to Thomas McCulloch The Stepsure Letters.
       Toronto: McClelland & Stewart, 1960, pp. iii-ix.

3376   Harvey, D. C. "Thomas McCulloch." In R. G. Riddell, ed., Canadian
       Portraits. Toronto: Oxford Univ. Press, 1940, pp. 22-28.

3377   Irving, John A. "The Achievement of Thomas McCulloch." In The Stepsure
       Letters. Toronto: McClelland & Stewart, 1960, pp. 150-56.

3378   Lochhead, Douglas. "A Bibliographical Note." In The Stepsure Letters.
       Toronto: McClelland & Stewart, 1960, pp. 156-59.

3379   McCulloch, William. The Life of Thomas McCulloch. Truro, N. S.: The
       Albion, 1920.

3380   MacIntosh, F. C. "Some Nova Scotia Scientists." DR, 10 (1930), 199-213.

MACEWEN, Gwendolyn

3381   Atwood, Margaret. "MacEwen's Muse." CanL, 45 (1970), 23-32.

3382   Gose, E. B. "They Shall Have Arcana." CanL, 21 (1964), 36-45.

3383   MacEwen, Gwendolyn. "Genesis." Teangadóir, ser. 2, 1 (1961), 57-63.

MACLENNAN, Hugh

3384   Ballantyne, M. G. "Theology and the Man on the Street: A Catholic
       Commentary on Cross Country." Culture, 10 (1949), 392-96.

3385   Bissell, Claude T. "Introduction" to Hugh MacLennan, Two Solitudes.
       School ed., Toronto: Macmillan, 1951, pp. vii-xxiii.

3386   Boeschenstein, Hermann. "Hugh MacLennan, ein kanadischer Romancier."
       ZAA, 8, no. 2 (1960), 117-35.

3387   Buitenhuis, Peter. Hugh MacLennan. Toronto: Forum House, 1969.

3388   Chambers, Robert D. "The Novels of Hugh MacLennan." JCanS, 2, no. 3
       (1967), 3-11.

3389   Cockburn, Robert H.   The Novels of Hugh MacLennan. Montreal: Harvest
       House, 1970.

3390   Davies, Robertson.   "MacLennan's Rising Sun." SatN, 74 (28 March 1959),
       29-31.

3391   Duncan, Dorothy.   "My Author Husband." Maclean's, 58 (15 Aug. 1945), 7,
       36, 38, 40.

3392   Farmiloe, Dorothy.   "Hugh MacLennan and the Canadian Myth." Mosaic, 2,
       no. 3 (1969), 1-9.

3393   Goetsch, Paul.   Das Romanwerk Hugh MacLennans; Eine Studie zum
       literarischen Nationalismus in Kanada. Hamburg: Cram, de Gruyter,
       1961.

3394   ____   "Too Long to the Courtly Muses: Hugh MacLennan as a Contemporary
       Writer." CanL, 10 (1961), 19-31.

3395   Hirano, Keiichi.   "Jerome Martell and Norman Bethune: A Note on Hugh
       MacLennan's The Watch that Ends the Night." SELit, Eng. no. (1968),
       37-59.

3396   Lucas, Alec.   Hugh MacLennan. Toronto: McClelland & Stewart, 1970.

3397   Lynn, S.   "A Canadian Writer and the Modern World." MarxQ, 1 (1962),
       36-43.

3398   MacLennan, Hugh.   "The Challenge to Prose." PTRSC, ser. 3, 49, sect. 2
       (1955), 45-55.

3399   ____   "My First Book." CanAB, 28, no. 2 (1952), 3-4.

3400   ____   "Reflections on Two Decades." CanL, 41 (1969), 28-39.

3401   ____   "The Story of a Novel." CanL, 3 (1960), 35-39. [Repr. in item
       2631, pp. 33-38.]

3402   McPherson, Hugo.   "Introduction" to Hugh MacLennan, Barometer Rising.
       Toronto: McClelland & Stewart, 1958, pp. ix-xv.

3403   ____   "The Novels of Hugh MacLennan." QQ, 60 (1953-54), 186-98.

3404   Marshall, Thomas.   "Some Working Notes on The Watch that Ends the Night."
       Quarry, 17 (1968), 13-16.

3405   New, William H.   "The Apprenticeship of Discovery." CanL, 29 (1966),
       18-33.

3406   ____   "The Storm and After: Imagery and Symbolism in Hugh MacLennan's
       Barometer Rising." QQ, 74 (1967), 302-13.

3407   ____   "Winter and the Night-people." CanL, 36 (1968), 26-33.

3408   O'Donnell, Kathleen.   "The Wanderer in Barometer Rising." UWR, 3 (1968),
       12-18.

3409   Roberts, Ann.   "The Dilemma of Hugh MacLennan." MarxQ, 3 (1962), 58-66.

3410   Vallerand, Jean.   "Hugh MacLennan ou la tendresse dans la littérature
       canadienne." Devoir, 28 Nov. 1959, p. 11.

3411   Watters, Reginald Eyre.   "Hugh MacLennan and the Canadian Character."
       In Edmund Morrison and William Robbins, eds., As a Man Thinks. . . .
       Toronto: Gage, 1953, pp. 228-43.

3412   Woodcock, George.   "A Nation's Odyssey: The Novels of Hugh MacLennan."
       CanL, 10 (1961), 7-18. [Repr. in item 2707, pp. 79-92; also in item
       2631, pp. 128-40; also in item 2704, pp. 12-23.]

3413   ____   "Hugh MacLennan." NR, 3, no. 4 (1950), 2-10.

3414   ____   Hugh MacLennan. Toronto: Copp Clark, 1969.

See also: 2657, 2696, 6403-6409.

MCLUHAN, Marshall

3415   Carey, James W.   "Harold Adams Innis and Marshall McLuhan." AR, 27
        (1967), 5-39.

3416   Duffy, Dennis. Marshall McLuhan. Toronto: McClelland & Stewart, 1969.

3417   Edwards, Thomas R. "The Soft Machine." PR, 35 (1968), 433-43.

3418   Jones, Edward T. "Marshall McLuhan: Media Analyst." UES, 2 (1968),
        3-12.

3419   Kostelanetz, Richard. "Il pensiero di Marshall McLuhan." Nuova presenza,
        11 (1968), 13-33.

3420   McCormack, Thelma. "Innocent Eye on Mass Society." CanL, 22 (1964),
        55-60.

3421   Miller, Jonathan. McLuhan. London: Fontana/Collins, 1971.

3422   Newton-De Molina, David. "McLuhan: Ice-Cold." CritQ, 12 (1970), 78-88.

3423   Petillon, Pierre-Yves. "Avant et après McLuhan." Critique (Paris),
        25 (1969), 504-11.

3424   Rabil, Albert, Jr. "The Future as History and History as the End: An
        Interpretation of Marshall McLuhan." Soundings, 51 (1968), 80-100.

3425   Richardson, Robert D., Jr. "McLuhan, Emerson, and Henry Adams." WHR,
        22 (1968), 235-42.

3426   Stearn, Gerald E., ed. McLuhan, Hot & Cool. New York: New American
        Library, 1969.

3427   Wagner, Geoffrey. "This Understanding Media: Obscurity as Authority."
        KR, 29 (1967), 246-55.

3428   Williams, Barbara. "Dichter on McLuhan." TC, 1037 (1968), 10-16.

MACPHERSON, Jay

3429   Reaney, James. "The Third Eye: Jay MacPherson's The Boatman." CanL,
        3 (1960), 23-24. [Repr. in item 2707, pp. 156-68.]

MAIR, Charles

3430   Charlesworth, Hector. "Patriots and the Poets of the West." In More
        Candid Chronicles. Toronto: Macmillan, 1928, pp. 18-36.

3431   Denison, George Taylor. The Struggle for Imperial Unity: Recollections
        and Experiences. London: Macmillan, 1909.

3432   Dooley, D. J., and F. Norman Shrive. "Voice of the Burdash." CanF,
        37 (1957), 80-82.

3433   Fraser, A. Ermatinger. "A Poet Pioneer of Canada." QQ, 35 (1928), 440-50

3434   Garvin, J. W. "Who's Who in Canadian Literature: Charles Mair." CanB,
        8 (1926), 335-37.

3435   Macbeth, R. G. "A Tribute to Charles Mair." CanB, 7 (1925), 45.

3436   MacKay, Isabel Ecclestone. "Charles Mair, Poet and Patriot." CanM, 59
        (1922), 162-65.

3437   Morgan, H. R. "Dr. Charles Mair." Will, 2 (1926), 110-11.

3438 Norwood, Robert. "Charles Mair." In item 2556, pp. 152-57.

3439 Shrive, F. Norman. Charles Mair: Literary Nationalist. Toronto: Univ. of Toronto Press, 1965.

3440 _____ "Poets and Patriotism: Charles Mair and Tecumseh." CanL, 20 (1964), 15-26.

3441 _____ "Poet and Politics: Charles Mair at Red River." CanL, 17 (1963), 6-21.

3442 Tait, Michael. "Playwrights in a Vacuum: English-Canadian Drama in the Nineteenth Century." CanL, 16 (1963), 3-18.

3443 Wheeler, Christine Gordon. "The Bard of Bathurst." CanB, 18, no. 1 (1936), 10-11.

See also: 6410.

MANDEL, Eli

3444 Dudek, Louis. "Two Canadian Poets: Ralph Gustafson and Eli Mandel." Culture, 22 (1961), 145-51.

3445 McMaster, R. D. "The Unexplained Interior: A Study of E. W. Mandel's Fuseli Poems." DR, 40 (1960), 392-96.

3446 Ower, John. "Black and Secret Poet: Notes on Eli Mandel." CanL, 42 (1969), 14-25.

MITCHELL, W. O.

3447 Anon. "Biographical Note." Maclean's, 61 (15 July 1948), 2.

3448 Barclay, Patricia. "Regionalism and the Writer: A Talk with W. O. Mitchell." CanL, 14 (1962), 53-56.

3449 New, William H. "A Feeling of Completion: Aspects of W. O. Mitchell." CanL, 17 (1963), 22-33.

3450 Sutherland, Ronald. "Children of the Changing Wind." JCanS, 5, no. 4 (1970), 3-11. [Repr. in item 2657, pp. 88-107.]

See also: 2437, 2479, 2657, 2661, 6371, 6436.

MOODIE, Susanna

3451 Hume, Blanche. "Grandmothers of Canadian Literature." Will, 3 (1928), 474-77.

3452 _____ The Strickland Sisters. Toronto: Ryerson, 1928.

3453 Klinck, Carl F. A Gentlewoman of Upper Canada." CanL, 1 (1959), 75-77.

3454 _____ "Introduction" to Susanna Moodie, Roughing It in the Bush. Toronto: McClelland & Stewart, 1962, pp. ix-xiv.

3455 McCourt, E. A. "Roughing It with the Moodies." QQ, 52 (1945), 77-89. [Repr. in item 2631, pp. 81-92.]

3456 McDougall, Robert L. "Introduction" to his ed. of Susanna Moodie, Life in the Clearings. . . . Toronto: Macmillan, 1959, pp. vii-xxiii.

3457 Needler, G. H. Otonabee Pioneers: The Story of the Stewarts, the Stricklands, the Traills and the Moodies. Toronto: Burns & MacEachern, 1953.

3458 _____ "The Otonabee Trio of Women Naturalists--Mrs. Stewart, Mrs. Traill, Mrs. Moodie." CanFN, 60 (1946), 97-101.

3459 New, William H. "Introduction" to Susanna and J. W. Moodie, The Victoria Magazine 1847-1848. Vancouver: Univ. of British Columbia Pub. Centre, 1968, pp. vii-x. [Repr.]

3460 Partridge, F. G. "The Stewarts and the Stricklands, the Moodies and the Traills." OntLR, 40 (1956), 179-81.

3461 Scott, Lloyd M. "The English Gentlefolk in the Backwoods of Canada." DR, 39 (1959), 56-69.

3462 Strickland, Jane Margaret. Life of Agnes Strickland. Edinburgh: Blackwood, 1887.

3463 Thomas, Clara. "The Strickland Sisters." In item 2439, pp. 42-73.

3464 Weaver, Emily. "Mrs. Traill and Mrs. Moodie, Pioneers in Literature." CanM, 48 (1917), 473-76.

See also: 6231, 6247, 6412, 6413.

MOORE, Brian

3465 Brady, Charles A. "I Am Mary Dunne, by Brian Moore." Éire, 3, no. 4 (1968), 136-40.

3466 Cronin, John. "Ulster's Alarming Novels." Éire, 4, no. 4 (1969), 27-34.

3467 Dahlie, Hallvard. Brian Moore. Toronto: Copp Clark, 1969.

3468 _____ "Brian Moore's Broader Vision: The Emperor of Ice Cream." Critique (Minneapolis), 9, no. 1 (1967), 43-55.

3469 _____ "Moore's New Perspective." CanL, 38 (1968), 81-84.

3470 Foster, John W. "Crisis and Ritual in Brian Moore's Belfast Novels." Éire, 3, no. 3 (1968), 66-74.

3471 Fulford, Robert. "Robert Fulford Interviews Brian Moore." TamR, 23 (1962), 5-18.

3472 Ludwig, Jack. "A Mirror of Moore." CanL, 7 (1961), 18-23.

3473 Moore, Brian. "An Interview." TamR, 46 (1968), 7-29.

3474 Sale, Richard B. "An Interview in London with Brian Moore." StN, 1, no. 1 (1969), 67-80.

3475 Stedmond, John. "Introduction" to Brian Moore, Judith Hearne. Toronto: McClelland & Stewart, 1964, pp. 5-8.

See also: 2704, 6414.

NEWLOVE, John

3476 Ferns, John. "A Desolate Country: John Newlove's Black Night Window." FPt, 2 (1969), 68-75.

See also: 2523.

NIVEN, Frederick John

3477 Adcock, A. St. John. The Glory that Was Grub Street. London: Low, Marston, 1928, pp. 247-57.

3478 Burpee, Lawrence J. "Frederick Niven." DR, 24 (1944), 74-76.

3479 George, Walter Lionel. "Who Is the Man?" In A Novelist on Novels.
London, Collins, 1918, pp. 65-66.

3480 Gibson, Gretchen. "Frederick Niven Had Novelist's Memory and Loved
His West." SatN, 59 (1 April 1944), 24.

3481 McCourt, E. A. "The Transplanted." In item 2479, pp. 39-54.

3482 Mansfield, Katherine. Novels and Novelists, ed. John Middleton Murry.
London: Constable, 1930; repr. Boston: Beacon, 1959, pp. 263-65.

3483 Morley, Christopher. "The Bowling Green." SatRL, 6 (26 Dec. 1929), 603.

3484 New, William H. "A Life and Four Landscapes: Frederick John Niven."
CanL, 32 (1967), 15-28.

3485 Niven, Frederick. Coloured Spectacles. London: Collins, 1938.

3486 Reid, Alexander. "A Scottish Chekhov?" Scotland's Magazine, 58 (1962),
45-56.

3487 Stevenson, Y. H. "Frederick Niven, 'Kootenay Scribe.'" CanAB, 17,
no. 1 (1940), 7-8.

3488 Walpole, Hugh, and Christopher Morley. "[Two Prefaces]" to Frederick
John Niven, Justice of the Peace. New York: Boni & Liveright, 1923,
pp. ix-xviii.

3489 West, Rebecca. "Notes on Novels." New Statesman, 16 (1920), 22.

See also: 6415.

NOWLAN, Alden

3490 Bly, Robert. "For Alden Nowlan with Admiration." TamR, 54 (1970), 32-38.

3491 Buckler, Ernest. "Alden Nowlan: An Appreciation." Fiddlehead, 81
(1969), 46-47.

3492 Cameron, Donald. "[Review of Alden Nowlan]." DR, 48 (1969), 591-93.

3493 Cook, G. M. "New Wine, New Vessel, and New Bibber." Fiddlehead, 81 (1969),
75-81.

3494 Dudek, Louis. "A Reading of Two Poems by Alden Nowlan." Fiddlehead,
81 (1969), 51-59.

3495 Ford, J. H. "Local Color--The Myth and the Cult." Fiddlehead, 81
(1969), 41-45.

3496 Fraser, Keath. "Notes on Alden Nowlan." CanL, 45 (1970), 41-51.

3497 Greer, Anne. "Confessions of a Thesis Writer OR the Hope of the World
Is Alive and Well and Living in Fredericton." Fiddlehead, 81 (1969),
20-23.

3498 Ives, E. S. "Alden Nowlan's Poetry: A Personal Chronicle." Fiddlehead,
81 (1969), 61-66.

3499 Nowlan, Alden. "An Interview with Alden Nowlan." Fiddlehead, 81 (1969), 5-13.

3500 Rosengarten, Herbert. "Enjoyable Pessimism." CanL, 40 (1969), 82-83.

See also: 2523.

OSTENSO, Martha

3501 Colman, Morris. "Martha Ostenso, Prize Novelist." Maclean's, 38 (1
Jan. 1925), 56-58.

3502 King, Carlyle A. "Introduction" to Martha Ostenso, Wild Geese. Toronto: McClelland & Stewart, 1961, pp. v-vii.

3503 MacLellan, W. E. "Real 'Canadian Literature.'" DR, 6 (1926), 18-23.

3504 Mullins, Stanley G. "Some Remarks on Theme in Martha Ostenso's Wild Geese." Culture, 23 (1962), 359-62.

3505 Overton, Grant. "Martha Ostenso." In item 2946, pp. 245-52.

See also: 6417, 6418.

ONDAATJE, Michael

3506 Kahn, Sy. "Michael Ondaatje, The Dainty Monsters." FPt, 1 (1968), 70-76.

3507 Lane, M. Travis. "Dream as History." Fiddlehead, 86 (1970), 158-62.

PAGE, P. K.

3508 Anon. "Biographical Notes." CanAB, 34, no. 1 (1958), 9.

3509 Meredith, William. "A Good Modern Poet and a Modern Tradition." Poetry (Chicago), 70 (1947), 208-11.

3510 Page, P. K. "Questions and Images." CanL, 41 (1969), 17-22.

3511 ____ "Traveller, Conjurer, Countryman." CanL, 46 (1970), 35-42.

3512 Shaw, Neufville. "The Poetry of P. K. Page." EdR, 64 (1948), 152-56.

3513 Smith, A. J. M. "New Canadian Poetry." CanF, 26 (1947), 252.

3514 Sutherland, John. "The Poetry of P. K. Page." NR, 1, no. 4 (1946-47), 13-23.

See also: 2527.

PARKER, Gilbert

3515 Adams, John Coldwell. "Sir Gilbert Parker as a Dramatist." CanAB, 40, no. 2 (1964), 5-6.

3516 Carman, Bliss. "Gilbert Parker." Chap-Book, 1 (1894), 338-43.

3517 Comer, Cornelia A. P. "The Novels of Gilbert Parker." Critic (London), 33 (1898), 271-74.

3518 Cooper, J. A. "Canadian Celebrities: Sir Gilbert Parker." CanM, 25 (1905), 494-96.

3519 Friden, Georg. The Canadian Novels of Sir Gilbert Parker: Historical Elements and Literary Technique. Uppsala: A-B Lundenquistka Bokhandeln, 1953.

3520 Garvin, J. W. "Sir Gilbert Parker and Canadian Literature." CanB, 14 (1932), 92.

3521 Horning, L. E. "Gilbert Parker." ActaV, 11 (1896), 252-54.

3522 Hume, Blanche. "Who's Who in Canadian Literature: Sir Gilbert Parker." CanB, 10 (1928), 131-34.

3523 Ingraham, Mary Kinley. "Letters from Sir Gilbert Parker." CanB, 15 (1933), 3-4.

3524 Logan, J. D. "Sir Gilbert Parker as a Poet." CanM, 62 (1924), 179-82.

3525 McArthur, James, et al. "Sir Gilbert Parker--The Man and the Novelist."
      Book News, 27 (1908), 325-34.

3526 MacPhail, Andrew. "Sir Gilbert Parker: An Appraisal." PTRSC, ser. 3,
      33, sect. 2 (1939), 123-36.

3527 Parker, Gilbert. "Fiction--Its Place in the National Life." NAR, 186
      (1907), 495-509.

3528 Rutledge, J. L. "Gilbert Parker the Novelist." ActaV, 27 (1904), 404-08.

3529 Thorold, W. J. "Gilbert Parker." Massey's, 3 (1897), 117-23.

PICKTHALL, Marjorie

3530 Adcock, A. St. John. "Marjorie Pickthall." Bookman (London), 52 (1922),
      127-29.

3531 Collin, W. E. "Marjorie Pickthall 1883-1922." UTQ, 1 (1932), 352-80.

3532 Dunlop, W. R. "The Poems of Marjory [sic] Pickthall." BCM, 20 (1923), 6.

3533 Gordon, Alfred. "Marjorie Pickthall as an Artist." CanB, 4, no. 6
      (1922), 157-59.

3534 Gordon, B. K. "Marjorie Pickthall's Poetry." CanB, 4, no. 11 (1922),
      52, 54.

3535 Hassard, Albert R. "The Dawn of Marjorie Pickthall's Genius." CanB,
      4, no. 6 (1922), 159-61.

3536 Logan, J. D. "The Genius of Marjorie Pickthall: An Analysis of Aesthetic
      Paradox." CanM, 59 (1922), 154-61.

3537 ____ Marjorie Pickthall, Her Poetic Genius and Art. Halifax: Allen, 1922.

3538 Pierce, Lorne. "Marjorie Pickthall." ActaV, 67 (1943), 21-30.

3539 ____ "Marjorie Pickthall." In item 2556, pp. 168-76.

3540 ____ Marjorie Pickthall: A Book of Remembrance. Toronto: Ryerson, 1925.

3541 ____ Marjorie Pickthall: A Memorial Address. Toronto: Ryerson, 1943.

3542 Pratt, E. J. "Marjorie Pickthall." CanF, 13 (1933), 334-35.

3543 Toye, D. E. "The Poetry of Marjorie Pickthall." ActaV, 47 (1923), 15-18.

3544 Whitney, V. L. "Marjorie Pickthall." ActaV, 39 (1915), 332-41.

3545 Wilson, Anne Elizabeth. "Magnificent Prose of Marjorie Pickthall."
      CanB, 4, no. 7 (1922), 185.

See also: 2339, 6419, 6420.

PRATT, E. J.

3546 Anon. "Biographical Note." CanAB, 34, no. 1 (1958), 16.

3547 Bénet, William Rose. "Introduction" to E. J. Pratt, Collected Poems.
      New York: Knopf, 1945, pp. ix-xiv.

3548 Benson, Nathaniel. "Who's Who in Canadian Literature: Edwin J. Pratt."
      CanB, 9 (1927), 323-26.

3549 Birney, Earle. "Canadian Poem of the Year: Brébeuf and His Brethren."
      CanF, 20 (1940), 180-81.

3550 ____ "E. J. Pratt and His Critics." In item 2484, pp. 123-47. [Repr.
      in item 2632, pp. 72-95.]

3551   Brockington, L. W.   "Tribute to a Poet." AtlanticA, 52, no. 9 (1962),
       22-23.

3552   Brown, E. K.   "The Originality of E. J. Pratt." In Ralph Gustafson,
       ed., Canadian Accent. London: Penguin, 1944, pp. 32-44.

3553   _____   "Pratt's Collected Work." UTQ, 14 (1945), 211-13.

3554   Cogswell, Fred.   "E. J. Pratt's Literary Reputation." CanL, 19 (1964),
       6-12.

3555   Davey, Frank.   "E. J. Pratt, Apostle of Corporate Man." CanL, 43 (1970),
       54-66.

3557   Deacon, William Arthur.   "Laureate Uncrowned: A Personal Study of E. J.
       Pratt." CanAB, 38, no. 3 (1963), 2, 20.

3558   Dudek, Louis.   "A Garland for E. J. Pratt: Poet of the Machine Age."
       TamR, 6 (1958), 74-80. [Repr. in item 3572, pp. 88-94.]

3559   Edgar, Pelham.   "Edwin John Pratt." In item 2375, pp. 109-17.

3560   _____   "E. J. Pratt." In item 2556, pp. 177-83.

3561   Frye, Northrop.   "Introduction" to The Collected Poems of E. J. Pratt,
       2nd ed.   Toronto: Macmillan, 1958, xiii-xxviii. [Repr. as "Silence
       in the Sea" in item 2390, pp. 181-97.]

3562   _____   "Silence Upon the Earth." CPM, 27, no. 4 (1964), 71-73.

3563   _____, and Roy Daniells.   "Ned Pratt: Two Recollections." CanL, 21 (1964),
       6-12.

3564   Gibbs, R. J.   "The Living Contour: The Whale Symbol in Melville and
       Pratt." CanL, 40 (1969), 17-25.

3565   Gustafson, Ralph.   "Portrait of Ned." QQ, 74 (1967), 437-51.

3566   Horwood, Harold.   "E. J. Pratt and William Blake: An Analysis." DR, 39
       (1959), 197-207. [Repr. in item 3572, pp. 95-108.]

3567   King, Carlyle.   "The Mind of E. J. Pratt." CanF, 36 (1956), 9-10.
       [Repr. in item 3572, pp. 83-87.]

3568   Leslie, Arthur K.   "E. J. Pratt, One of Canada's Leading Poets."
       AtlanticA, 54, no. 10 (1964), 40-41.

3569   McCrath, M. Helen.   "Bard from Newfoundland: The Story of Dr. E. J.
       Pratt." AtlanticA, 49, no. 3 (1958), 13-15, 17-21.

3570   MacKay, L. A.   "The Poetry of E. J. Pratt." CanF, 24 (1944), 208-09.
       [Repr. in item 3572, pp. 39-42.]

3571   MacKinnon, Murdo.   "A Garland for E. J. Pratt: The Man and the Teacher."
       TamR, 6 (1958), 71-74.

3572   Pitt, David G., ed.   E. J. Pratt. Toronto: Ryerson, 1969.

3573   Pratt, E. J.   "My First Book." CanAB, 28, no. 4 (1952-53), 5-6.

3574   Pratt, Mildred Claire.   The Silent Ancestors: The Forebears of E. J.
       Pratt. Toronto: McClelland & Stewart, 1971.

3575   Reaney, James.   "Towards the Last Spike: The Treatment of a Western
       Subject." NR, 7, no. 3 (1955), 18-25. [Repr. in item 3572, pp. 73-82.]

3576   Ross, Mary Lowrey.   "Dr. E. J. Pratt: A Poet's Quarter-Century." SatN,
       73 (1 Feb. 1958), 14-15, 35.

3577   Scott, Winfield Townley.   "Poetry and Event." Poetry (Chicago), 56
       (1945), 329-34. [Repr. in item 3572, pp. 50-53.]

3578   Sharman, Vincent.   "E. J. Pratt and Christianity." CanL, 19 (1964),
       21-32. [Repr. in item 3572, pp. 109-23.]

3579 Smith, A. J. M. "A Garland for E. J. Pratt: The Poet." TamR, 6 (1958), 66-71.

3580 _____ Some Poems of E. J. Pratt: Aspects of Imagery and Theme. St. John's, Nfld.: Memorial Univ., 1969.

3581 Sutherland, John. "E. J. Pratt: A Major Contemporary Poet." NR, 5, no. 3-4 (1952), 36-64. [Repr. in item 3572, pp. 54-72.]

3582 _____ "Foremost Poet of Canada." Poetry (Chicago), 82 (1953), 350-54.

3583 _____ "The Poetry of E. J. Pratt." First Statement, 2, no. 11 (1945), 27-30. [Repr. in item 3572, pp. 42-46.]

3584 _____ The Poetry of E. J. Pratt: A New Interpretation. Toronto: Ryerson, 1956.

3585 Sylvestre, Guy. "Un grande poète canadien anglais." Devoir, 12 May 1945, p. 8.

3586 Watt, Frank W. "Edwin John Pratt." UTQ, 29 (1959), 77-84.

3587 Wells, H. W. "Canada's Best-Known Poet: E. J. Pratt." CE, 7 (1946), 452-56.

3588 _____, and Carl F. Klinck. Edwin John Pratt: The Man and His Poetry. Toronto: Ryerson, 1947.

3589 West, Paul. "E. J. Pratt's Four-ton Gulliver." CanL, 19 (1964), 13-20. [Repr. in item 2707, pp. 101-09.]

3590 Wilson, Milton. E. J. Pratt. Toronto: McClelland & Stewart, 1969.

3591 _____ "Pratt's Comedy." JCanS, 3, no. 2 (1968), 21-30.

See also: 2339, 2395, 2547, 3117, 6421-6425.

PURDY, A. W.

3592 Bowering, George. Al Purdy. Toronto: Copp Clark, 1970.

3593 _____ "Purdy: Man and Poet." CanL, 43 (1970), 10-35.

3594 Geddes, Gary. "A. W. Purdy: An Interview." CanL, 41 (1969), 66-72.

3595 Helwig, David. "The Winemaker." QQ, 76 (1969), 340-44.

3596 Stevens, Peter. "In the Raw: The Poetry of A. W. Purdy." CanL, 28 (1966), 22-30.

See also: 2371, 6426.

RADDALL, Thomas

3597 Bevan, Allan. "Introduction" to Thomas Raddall, At the Tide's Turn and Other Stories. Toronto: McClelland & Stewart, 1959, pp. v-ix.

3598 Hawkins, W. J. "Thomas H. Raddall: The Man and His Work." QQ, 75 (1968), 137-46.

3599 Raddall, T. H. "Literary Art." DR, 34 (1954), 138-46.

3600 _____ "My First Book." CanAB, 28, no. 3 (1952), 5-8.

3601 _____ "Sword and Pen in Kent." DR, 32 (1952), 145-52.

3602 Walbridge, E. F. "Biographical Sketch." WLB, 25 (1951), 576.

3603 Wright, Ethel Clark. "A Conflict of Loyalties." DR, 23 (1943), 83-86.

See also: 6427.

REANEY, James

3604   Anon. "Biographical Note." CanAB, 34, no. 1 (1958), 11.

3605   Atwood, Margaret. "Eleven Years of Alphabet." CanL, 49 (1971), 60-64.

3606   Bowering, George. "Why James Reaney Is a Better Poet, 1) Than Any Northrop Frye Poet, 2) Than He Used to Be." CanL, 36 (1968), 40-49.

3607   James, Esther. "Crime and No Punishment." CanL, 49 (1971), 56-59.

3608   Lee, Alvin. James Reaney. New York: Twayne, 1969.

3609   ____ "A Turn to the Stage: Reaney's Dramatic Verse." CanL, 15 (1963), 40-51; 16 (1963), 43-51.

3610   Reaney, James. "An Evening with Babble and Doodle." CanL, 12 (1962), 37-43.

3611   ____ "Manitoba as a Writer's Environment." Mosaic, 3, no. 3 (1970), 95-97.

3612   ____ "Ten Years at Play." CanL, 41 (1969), 53-61.

3613   Sutherland, John. "Canadian Comment." NR, 3, no. 4 (1950), 36-42.

3614   Tait, Michael. "The Limits of Innocence: James Reaney's Theatre." CanL, 19 (1964), 43-48.

3615   Watson, Wilfred. "An Indigenous World." CanL, 15 (1963), 64-66.

3516   Wilson, Milton. "On Reviewing Reaney." TamR, 26 (1963), 71-78.

RICHARDSON, John

3617   Beasley, David. "Tempestuous Major: The Canadian Don Quixote." BNYPL, 74 (1970), 3-26, 95-106.

3618   Burwash, Ida. "John Richardson, 1796-1852, Young Volunteer of 1812." CanM, 39 (1912), 218-25.

3619   Carstairs, John Stewart. "Richardson's War of 1812." CanM, 29 (1901), 72-74.

3620   Casselman, A. C. "[Biography of John Richardson]." In John Richardson, War of 1812. Toronto: Historical Publishing Company, 1902, pp. xi-lvii.

3621   Klinck, Carl F. "Introduction" to Major Richardson's 'Kensington Gardens in 1830.' Toronto: Bibliographical Society of Canada, 1957, pp. vii-xiii.

3622   ____ "Introduction" to John Richardson, Wacousta, or the Prophecy. Toronto: McClelland & Stewart, 1967, pp. v-xiii.

3623   Lande, Lawrence M. "Major John Richardson." In Old Lamps Aglow. Montreal: The Author, 1957, pp. 228-40.

3624   Morley, W. F. E. "A Bibliographical Study of John Richardson." BSCP, 4 (1965), 21-89.

3625   Pacey, Desmond. "A Colonial Romantic: Major John Richardson, Soldier and Novelist." CanL, 2 (1959), 20-31; 3 (1960), 47-56.

3626   ____ "A Note on Major John Richardson." CanL, 39 (1969), 103-04.

3627   Riddell, William R. John Richardson. Toronto: Ryerson, 1923.

RICHLER, Mordecai

3628   Bevan, Allan. "Introduction" to Mordecai Richler, The Apprenticeship of Duddy Kravitz. Toronto: McClelland & Stewart, 1969, pp. 5-8.

3629 Bowering, George. "And the Sun Goes Down." CanL, 29 (1966), 7-17.

3630 Carroll, John. "On Richler and Ludwig." TamR, 29 (1963), 98-102.

3631 Cohen, Nathan. "A Conversation with Mordecai Richler." TamR, 2 (1957), 6-23.

3632 ____ "Heroes of the Richler View." TamR, 6 (1958), 47-49; 51-60.

3633 Kattan, Naim. "Mordecai Richler." CanL, 21 (1964), 46-52.

3634 New, William H. "Cock and Bull Stories." CanL, 39 (1969), 83-86.

3635 Richler, Mordecai. "The Apprenticeship of Mordecai Richler." Maclean's, 74 (20 May 1961), 21, 44-48.

3636 ____ "How I Became an Unknown with My First Novel." Maclean's, 71 (1 Feb. 1958), 18-19, 40-42.

3637 ____ "The Uncertain World." CanL, 41 (1969), 23-27.

3638 Scott, P. D. "A Choice of Certainties." TamR, 8 (1958), 73-82.

3639 Tallman, Warren. "Beyond Camelot." CanL, 42 (1969), 77-81.

3640 ____ "Richler and the Faithless City." CanL, 3 (1960), 62-64.

3641 Woodcock, George. "Introduction" to Mordecai Richler, Son of a Smaller Hero. Toronto: McClelland & Stewart, 1966, pp. vii-xii.

3642 ____ Mordecai Richler Toronto: McClelland & Stewart, 1970.

See also: 2661, 3405.

ROBERTS, Charles G. D.

3643 Benson, Nathaniel. "Sir Charles G. D. Roberts." In item 2556, pp. 184-92.

3644 Cappon, James. Charles G. D. Roberts. Toronto: Ryerson, 1925.

3645 ____ "Roberts and the Influence of His Times." CanM, 24 (1905), 224-31, 321-28, 419-24, 514-20.

3646 ____ Roberts and the Influences of His Time. Toronto: Briggs, 1905.

3647 Carman, Bliss. "Contemporaries: 5. Charles G. D. Roberts." Chap-Book, 2 (1895), 163-71.

3648 Deacon, William Arthur. "Sir Charles G. D. Roberts: An Appreciation." CanAB, 19, no. 4 (1934), 4.

3649 De Mille, A. B. "Canadian Celebrities: The Roberts Family." CanM, 15 (1900), 426-30.

3650 Edgar, Pelham. "Charles G. D. Roberts." ActaV, 52 (1928), 33-34.

3651 ____ "Sir Charles G. D. Roberts and His Times." UTQ, 13 (1943), 117-26.

3652 ____ "Sir Charles G. D. Roberts, 1860-1943." PTRSC, ser. 3, 38 (1944), 111-14.

3653 Gold, Joseph. "The Precious Speck of Life." CanL, 26 (1965), 22-32.

3654 Harkins, Edward F. "The Literary Career of Roberts." In Little Pilgrimages among the Men Who Have Written Famous Books. Boston: Page, 1902, pp. 299-315.

3655 Henry, Lorne J. "Sir Charles G. D. Roberts (1860-1943)." In Canadians: A Book of Biographies. Toronto: Longman's, 1950, pp. 69-75.

3656 Horning, L. E. "Animal Stories." ActaV, 25 (1902), 277-79.

3657 Keith, W. J. Charles G. D. Roberts. Toronto: Copp Clark, 1969.

3658   Kirkconnell, Watson. "Sir Charles Roberts: A Tribute." CanAB, 19, no. 4 (1943), 3.

3659   Lesperance, John. "The Poets of Canada." PTRSC, ser. 1, 2 (1884), 31-44.

3660   Livesay, Dorothy. "Open Letter to Sir Charles G. D. Roberts." CanB, 21, no. 1 (1939), 34-35.

3661   Lock, D. R. "Charles G. D. Roberts." World Wide, 31 (1931), 1187.

3662   Lucas, Alec. "Introduction" to Sir Charles G. D. Roberts, The Last Barrier and Other Stories. Toronto: McClelland & Stewart, 1958, pp. v-x.

3663   Magee, William H. "The Animal Story: A Challenge in Technique." DR, 44 (1964), 156-64.

3664   Marquis, T. G. "Professor Charles G. D. Roberts, M. A." Week, 5 (1888), 558-59.

5665   ____ "Roberts." CanM, 1 (1893), 572-75.

3666   ____ "Songs of the Common Day." Week, 10 (1893), 1023.

3667   Massey, Vincent. "Roberts, Carman, Sherman: Canadian Poets." CanAB, 23, no. 2 (1947), 29-32.

3668   Middleton, J. E. "Dean of Canadian Letters." SatN, 58 (1943), 20-21.

3669   Muddiman, Bernard. "Vignette in Canadian Literature." CanM, 40 (1913), 451-58.

3670   Pacey, Desmond. "Sir Charles G. D. Roberts." In item 2485, pp. 31-56.

3672   Pollock, F. L. "Canadian Writers in New York." ActaV, 22 (1899), 434-39.

3673   Pomeroy, Elsie. Sir Charles G. D. Roberts: A Biography. Toronto: Ryerson, 1943.

3674   ____ Tributes Through the Years: The Centenary of the Birth of Sir Charles G. D. Roberts, January 10, 1960. Toronto: Priv. Printed, 1959.

3675   Rhodenizer, V. B. "Who's Who in Canadian Literature: Charles G. D. Roberts." CanB, 8 (1926), 267-69.

3676   Rittenhouse, Jessie B. "Charles G. D. Roberts." In The Younger American Poets. Boston: Little, Brown, 1904, pp. 132-50.

3677   Roberts, Lloyd. The Book of Roberts. Toronto: Ryerson, 1923.

3678   Stephen, A. M. "The Poetry of C. G. D. Roberts." QQ, 36 (1929), 48-64.

3679   Stringer, Arthur. "Eminent Canadians in New York: II, The Father of Canadian Poetry." NatM, 4 (1904), 61-64.

3680   Sykes, W. J. "Charles G. D. Roberts." ActaV, 17 (1894), 112-15.

3681   Whiteside, Ernestine R. "Canadian Poetry and Poets." McMaster University Monthly, 8 (1898), 21-28.

See also: 2547, 2564, 2807, 6204, 6431-6434.

ROSS, Sinclair

3682   Anon. "Canadian Writer." Country Guide, 61 (1942), 38.

3683   Daniells, Roy. "Introduction" to Sinclair Ross, As for Me and My House. Toronto: McClelland & Stewart, 1957, pp. v-x.

3684   Fraser, Keath. "Futility at the Pump: The Short Stories of Sinclair
       Ross." QQ, 77 (1970), 72-80.

3685   Laurence, Margaret. "Introduction" to Sinclair Ross, The Lamp at Noon
       and Other Stories. Toronto: McClelland & Stewart, 1968, pp. 7-12.

3686   New, William H. "Sinclair Ross's Ambivalent World." CanL, 40 (1969),
       26-32.

3687   Ross, Sinclair. "On Looking Back." Mosaic, 3, no. 3 (1970), 93-94.

3688   Stephens, Donald. "Wind, Sun and Dust." CanL, 23 (1965), 17-24.

3689   Stubbs, R. S. "Presenting Sinclair Ross." SatN, 56 (9 Aug. 1941), 17.

See also: 2479, 6409, 6436.

ROSS, W. W. E.

3690   Callaghan, Barry. "Memoir." In W. W. E. Ross, Shapes and Sounds, ed.
       Raymond Souster and John Robert Colombo. Toronto: Longmans, 1968,
       pp. 1-7.

3691   Moore, M. "Experienced Simplicity." Poetry (Chicago), 38 (1931), 280-81.

3692   Stevens, Peter. "On W. W. E. Ross." CanL, 39 (1969), 43-61.

ROY, Gabrielle

3693   Bessette, Gérard. "Alexandre Chenevert, de Gabrielle Roy." ELit, 2
       (1969), 177-202.

3694   Blais, Jacques. "L'Unité organique de Bonheur d'occasion." EF, 6, no. 1
       (1970), 25-50.

3695   Brochu, André. "Themes et structures de Bonheur d'occasion." Ecrits
       du Canada français, 22 (1966), 163-208.

3696   Brown, Alan. "Gabrielle Roy and the Temporary Provincial." TamR, 1
       (1956), 61-70.

3697   Charland, Roland-M., and Jean-Noel Samson. Gabrielle Roy. Montréal:
       Fides, 1967.

3698   Duncan, Dorothy. "Le triomphe de Gabrielle." Maclean's, 60 (14 April
       1947), 23, 51, 54.

3699   Genuist, Monique. Le création romanesque chez Gabrielle Roy. Montréal:
       Cercle du Livre de France, 1966.

3700   Grosskurth, Phyllis. Gabrielle Roy. Toronto: Forum House, 1969.

3701   ____ "Gabrielle Roy and the Silken Noose." CanL, 42 (1969), 6-13.

3702   Hayne, David M. "Gabrielle Roy." CMLR, 21, no. 1 (1964), 20-26.

3703   Jones, R., and F. G. Howlett. "Rue Deschambault: une analyse." CMLR,
       24, no. 3 (1968), 58-63.

3704   Le Grand, Albert. "Gabrielle Roy ou l'être partagé." EF, 1, no. 2
       (1965), 39-65.

3705   Le Mire, Maurice. "Bonheur d'occasion, ou le salut par la guerre."
       Recherches Sociographiques, 10 (1969), 23-35.

3706   McPherson, Hugo. "The Garden and the Cage." CanL, 1 (1959), 46-57.
       [Repr. in item 2707, pp. 110-22.]

3707   ____ "Introduction" to Gabrielle Roy, The Tin Flute. Toronto: McClelland
       & Stewart, 1958, pp. v-xi.

3708   Murphy, John J.   "Alexandre Chenevert: Gabrielle Roy's Crucified
        Canadian." QQ, 72 (1965), 334-46.

3709   Roy, Paul-Emile.   "Gabrielle Roy, ou la difficulté de s'ajuster à la
        realité." Lectures, 11 (1964), 55-61.

3710   Thério, Adrien.   "Le portrait du père dans Rue Deschambault de Gabrielle
        Roy." In Livres et auteurs québécois 1969. Montréal: Jumonville, 1970,
        pp. 237-43.

3711   Thorne, W. B.   "Poverty and Wrath: A Study of The Tin Flute." JCanS,
        3, no. 3 (1968), 3-10.

See also: 2437, 2657.

RYGA, George

3712   Carson, Neil.   "George Ryga and the Lost Country." CanL, 45 (1970),
        33-40.

SALVERSON, Laura Goodman

3713   Fuller, Muriel.   "Laura Goodman Salverson." CanAB, 35, no. 1 [34, no. 4]
        (1958-59), 12.

3714   McDonald, W. S.   "A Great Canadian Novel." CanA, 16, no. 1 (1938), 13.

3715   Salverson, Laura Goodman.   "An Autobiographical Sketch." OntLR, 14
        (1930), 69-73.

See also: 2479.

SANGSTER, Charles

3716   Bourinot, Arthur S.   "Charles Sangster." In item 2556, pp. 202-12.

3717   Dewart, Edward Hartley.   "Charles Sangster." CanM, 7 (1896), 28-34.

3718   ____   "Charles Sangster, a Canadian Poet of the Last Generation." In
        Essays for the Times. Toronto: Briggs, 1898, pp. 38-51.

3719   Macklem, John.   "Who's Who in Canadian Literature: Charles Sangster."
        CanB, 10 (1928), 195-96.

3720   Morgan, Henry J.   Sketches of Celebrated Canadians. Quebec: Hunter Rose,
        1862, pp. 684-93.

See also: 2547, 2556, 3721, 6204, 6439.

SCOTT, Duncan Campbell

3721   Bourinot, Arthur S.   Five Canadian Poets. Ottawa: The Author, 1954.

3722   ____, ed.   More Letters of Duncan Campbell Scott. Ottawa: Bourinot,
        1960.

3723   Brodie, A. D.   "Canadian Short Story Writers." CanM, 4 (1895), 334-44.

3724   Brown, E. K.   "Duncan Campbell Scott, an Individual Poet." ManAR, 2,
        no. 3 (1941), 51-54.

3725   ____   "Memoir." In Selected Poems of Duncan Campbell Scott. Toronto:
        Ryerson, 1951, pp. xi-xliii.

3726   Burrell, Martin.   "Canadian Poet." In Betwixt Heaven and Charing Cross.
        New York: Macmillan, 1928, pp. 253-61.

3727   Clarke, G. H.   "Duncan Campbell Scott, 1862-1948."   PTRSC,
          ser. 3, 42 (1948), 115-19.

3728   Edgar, Pelham.   "Duncan Campbell Scott."   DR, 7 (1927), 38-46.

3729   ____   "Duncan C. Scott."   Week, 12 (1895), 370-71.

3730   ____   "Travelling with a Poet."   In item 2375, pp. 58-74.

3731   Garvin, J. W.   "The Poems of Duncan Campbell Scott."   CanB, 8 (1926),
          364-65.

3732   Geddes, Gary.   "Piper of Many Tunes, Duncan Campbell Scott."   CanL, 37
          (1968), 15-27.

3733   Knister, Raymond.   "Duncan Campbell Scott."   Will, 2 (1927), 295-96.

3734   Muddiman, Bernard.   "Duncan Campbell Scott."   CanM, 43 (1914), 63-72.

3735   Pacey, Desmond.   "The Poetry of Duncan Campbell Scott."   CanF, 28
          (1948), 107-09.

3736   Percival, Walter Pilling.   "Duncan Campbell Scott."   In item 2556,
          pp. 213-19.

3737   Scott, Duncan Campbell.   Letter to Ralph Gustafson.   Fiddlehead, 41
          (1959), 12-14.

3738   Smith, A. J. M.   "Duncan Campbell Scott."   In item 2484, pp. 73-94.

3739   ____   "Duncan Campbell Scott, a Reconsideration."   CanL, 1 (1959), 13-25.

3740   ____   "The Poetry of Duncan Campbell Scott."   DR, 28 (1948), 12-21.

3741   Stevenson, Lionel.   "Who's Who in Canadian Literature: Duncan Campbell
          Scott."   CanB, 11 (1929), 59-62.

3742   Sykes, W. J.   "The Poetry of Duncan Campbell Scott."   QQ, 46 (1939), 51-64.

3743   Wilton, Margaret Harvey.   "Duncan Campbell Scott, Man and Artist."
          CanAB, 38, no. 1 (1962), 3-5, 20.

3744   Wright, Percy H.   "Who Is Our Poet Laureate?"   SatN, 53 (4 Dec. 1937), 20.

See also: 2547, 3143, 6440-6443.

SCOTT, F. R.

3745   Anon.   "Biographical Note."   CanAB, 34, no. 1 (1958), 9.

3746   Bell, W.   "Profs and Propaganda."   SatN, 54 (19 Aug. 1939), 10.

3747   Bourinot, Arthur S.   "Satiric Scott."   CanAB, 42, no. 3 (1967), 9.

3748   Dudek, Louis.   "F. R. Scott and the Modern Poets."   NR, 4, no. 2 (1950-
          51), 14-15. [Repr. in item 3783, pp. 57-71.]

3749   Lefolii, Ken.   "Poet Who Outfought Duplessis."   Maclean's, 72 (11 April
          1959), 16-17, 70-72, 74-76.

3750   Skelton, Robin.   "A Poet of the Middle Slopes."   CanL, 31 (1967), 40-44.
          [Repr. in item 3783, pp. 77-81.]

3751   Smith, A. J. M.   "F. R. Scott and Some of His Poems."   CanL, 31 (1967),
          25-35. [Repr. in item 3783, pp. 82-94.]

See also: 2339, 2547, 3783, 6165, 6359, 6444.

SERVICE, Robert

3752   Anon.   "Biographical Note."   CanAB, 34, no. 1 (1958), 11.

3753   Bucco, Martin. "Folk Poetry of Robert W. Service." Alaska Review, 2 (1965), 16-26.

3754   Finnie, R. "When the Ice-Worms Nest Again." Maclean's, 58 (1 Nov. 1945), 10, 62.

3755   Hamer-Jackson, Celesta. "Robert W. Service." In item 2556, pp. 227-33.

3756   Hellman, G. T. "Whopping It Up." NY, 22 (30 March 1946), 34-38; (6 April 1946), 32-36.

3757   Horning, L. E. "Robert W. Service." ActaV, 41 (1917), 295-301.

3758   Pacey, Desmond. "Service and MacInnes." NR, 4, no. 3 (1951), 12-17.

3759   Service, Robert W. Harper of Heaven. New York: Dodd Mead, 1948.

3760   ____ The Ploughman of the Moon: An Adventure into Memory. New York: Dodd Mead, 1945.

3761   ____ "So I Have a Mild Face." Maclean's, 54 (15 Jan. 1941), 9, 28, 30.

3762   Stouffer, R. P. "Robert W. Service." ActaV, 39 (1914), 55-63.

See also: 2559, 6445, 6446.

SETON, Ernest Thompson

3763   Bodsworth, C. F. "Backwoods Genius with the Magic Pen." Maclean's, 72 (6 June 1959), 22, 32, 34, 38-40.

3764   Chapman, F. M. "Champion of E. T. Seton." SatRL, 16 (2 Oct. 1937), 9.

3765   ____ "Naturalist, Artist, Author, Educator." Bird Lore, 37 (1935), 245-47.

3766   Garst, Shannon and Warren. Ernest Thompson Seton, Naturalist. New York: Messner, 1959.

3768   Read, S. E. "Flight to the Primitive: Ernest Thompson Seton." CanL, 13 (1962), 45-57.

3769   Seton, Ernest Thompson. Trail of an Artist-Naturalist. New York: Scribner's, 1940.

3770   Wiley, Farida A., ed. and introd. Ernest Thompson Seton's America. Biography by Julia Seton. New York: Devin-Adair, 1954.

3771   Zahniser, H. "Nature in Print." Nature, 46 (1953), 450-51.

See also: 2564.

SINCLAIR, Lister

3772   Franklin, Bert. "Patriarch at 27." Maclean's, 61 (1 Nov. 1948), 8, 50-52.

SMITH, A. J. M.

3773   Birney, Earle. "A. J. M. S." CanL, 15 (1963), 4-6.

3774   Brown, E. K. "A. J. M. Smith and the Poetry of Pride." ManAR, 3, no. 5 [4, no. 1] (1944), 30-32. [Repr. in item 3783, pp. 95-98.]

3775   Collin, W. E. "Arthur Smith." GdC, 11 (1946), 47-60. [Repr. in item 3783, pp. 99-111.]

3776   Fuller, Roy. "Poet of the Century." CanL, 15 (1963), 7-10.

3777 Klein, A. M. "The Poetry of A. J. M. Smith." CanF, 23 (1944), 257-58.

3778 Ó Broin, Padraig. "After Strange Gods (A. J. M. Smith and the Concept of Nationalism)." CanAB, 39, no. 4 (1964), 6-8. [Repr. in item 3783, pp. 111-20.]

3779 S., J. "Literary Colonialism." First Statement, 2, no. 4 (1944), 3.

3780 Scott, F. R. "A. J. M. Smith." EdR, 64 (1948), 24-29. [Repr. in item 2556, pp. 234-44.]

3781 Smith, A. J. M. "The Poetic Process: On the Making of Poems." CentR, 8 (1964), 353-70.

3782 ____ "A Self-Review." CanL, 15 (1963), 20-26. [Repr. in item 3783, pp. 136-43.]

3783 Stevens, Peter, ed. The McGill Movement. Toronto: Ryerson, 1969.

3784 Sutherland, John. "Mr. Smith and 'The Tradition.'" In item 2654, pp. 5-12.

3785 Wilson, Milton. "Second and Third Thoughts About Smith." CanL, 15 (1963), 11-17. [Repr. in item 3783, pp. 127-35; also in item 2707, pp. 93-100.]

3786 Woodcock, George. "Turning New Leaves." CanF, 42 (1963), 257-58. [Repr. in item 3783, pp. 120-25.]

See also: 2339, 2547, 2556, 2559, 2704, 6165, 6359, 6448.

SOUSTER, Raymond

3787 Acorn, Milton. "The Art of Raymond Souster." Progressive Worker, 2, no. 9 (1966), 13-16.

3788 Carruth, Hayden. "To Souster from Vermont." TamR, 34 (1965), 81-95.

3789 Dudek, Louis. "Groundhog Among the Stars: The Poetry of Raymond Souster." CanL, 22 (1964), 34-49. [Repr. in item 2707, pp. 169-84.]

3790 Fulford, Robert. "On Raymond Souster: A Good Toronto Poet Toronto Never Discovered." Maclean's, 77 (18 April 1964), 59.

3791 Gnarowski, Michael. "Raymond Souster: 'Au-dessus de la mêlée.'" Culture, 25 (1965), 58-63.

3792 Mandel, Eli. "Internal Resonances." CanL, 17 (1963), 62-65.

3793 Weeks, R. L. "Picked Clean and Unpurple." FPt, 1 (1968), 76-79.

See also: 2371, 2527, 6449, 6450.

WADDINGTON, Miriam

3794 Anon. "Portrait." CanAB, 34, no. 1 (1958), 4.

3795 Sowton, Ian. "The Lyric Craft of Miriam Waddington." DR, 39 (1959), 237-42.

WATSON, Sheila

3796 Child, Philip. "Canadian Prose-Poem." DR, 39 (1959), 233-36.

3797 Grube, John. "Introduction" to Sheila Watson, The Double Hook. Toronto: McClelland & Stewart, 1966, pp. 5-14.

3798   Morriss, Margaret. "The Elements Transcended." CanL, 42 (1969), 56-71.

3799   Theall, D. F. "A Canadian Novella." CanF, 39 (1959), 78-80.

WEBB, Phyliss

3800   Anon. "Biographical Note." CanAB, 34, no. 1 (1958), 13.

3801   Hulcoop, John. "Introduction" to Phyllis Webb, Collected Poems 1954-1965. Vancouver: Talonbooks, 1971, n. pag.

3802   _____   "Phyllis Webb and the Priestess of Motion." CanL, 32 (1967), 29-39.

3803   Sonthoff, Helen W. "Structure of Loss: The Poetry of Phyllis Webb." CanL, 9 (1961), 15-22.

3804   Webb, Phyllis. "Poet and Publisher." QQ, 61 (1955), 498-512.

WIEBE, Rudy

3805   Wiebe, Rudy. "An Author Speaks About His Novel." CanMenn, 11 April 1963, p. 8.

3806   _____   "Passage by Land." CanL, 48 (1971), 25-27.

WILKINSON, Anne

3807   Smith, A. J. M. "Introduction" to The Collected Poems of Anne Wilkinson. Toronto: Macmillan, 1968, pp. 13-21.

3808   _____   "A Reading of Anne Wilkinson." CanL, 10 (1961), 32-39. [Repr. in item 2707, pp. 123-30.]

3809   Wilkinson, Anne. Lions in the Way. Toronto: Macmillan, 1969.

WILSON, Ethel

3810   Birbalsingh, Frank M. "Ethel Wilson." CanL, 49 (1971), 35-46.

3811   Livesay, Dorothy. "Ethel Wilson: West Coast Novelist." SatN, 67 (26 July 1952), 20, 36.

3812   New, William H. "The 'Genius' of Place and Time: The Fiction of Ethel Wilson." JCanS, 3, no. 4 (1968), 39-48.

3813   _____   "The Irony of Order: Ethel Wilson's The Innocent Traveller." Critique (Minneapolis), 10, no. 3 (1968), 22-30.

3814   Pacey, Desmond. Ethel Wilson. New York: Twayne, 1967.

3815   _____   "Ethel Wilson's First Novel." CanL, 29 (1966), 43-55.

3816   _____   "The Innocent Eye: The Art of Ethel Wilson." QQ, 61 (1954), 42-52.

3817   Sonthoff, Helen W. "The Novels of Ethel Wilson." CanL, 26 (1965), 33-42.

3818   Watters, Reginald Eyre. "Ethel Wilson, The Experienced Traveller." BCLQ, 21, no. 4 (1958), 21-27.

3819   Wilson, Ethel. "The Bridge or the Stokehold? Views of the Novelist's Art." CanL, 5 (1960), 43-47.

3820   _____   "A Cat Among the Falcons." CanL, 2 (1959), 10-19. [Repr. in item 2631, pp. 23-32.]

See also: 6453-6457.

WISEMAN, Adele

3821 Mullins, Stanley G. "Traditional Symbolism in Adele Wiseman's The
      Sacrifice." Culture, 19 (1958), 287-97.

3822 Wiseman, Adele. "A Brief Anatomy of an Honest Attempt at a Pithy
      Statement about the Impact of the Manitoba Environment on My
      Development as an Artist." Mosaic, 3, no. 3 (1970), 98-106.

New Zealand

Research Aids

3823 Alcock, Peter. "An Invisible Literature?" Landfall, 22 (1968), 397-405.

3824 Andersen, Johannes. The Lure of New Zealand Book Collecting. Auckland: Whitcombe & Tombs, 1936.

3825 Collier, James. The Literature Relating to New Zealand. Wellington: Didsbury, 1889.

3826 Hocken, T. M. A Bibliography of the Literature Relating to New Zealand. Wellington: Mackay, 1909; rpt. Wellington: Newrick, 1973.

3827 Index to New Zealand Periodicals. Wellington: N. Z. Library Assoc., later National Library Service. 1941-1962 (6 cumulations); 1963-d., ann.

3828 Park, Iris M. New Zealand Periodicals of Literary Interest. Wellington: Library School, National Library Service, 1962.

See also: 429, 437.

General

3829 Alcock, Peter. "Eros Marooned: Ambivalence in Eden." In Marriage and the Family in New Zealand, ed. S. Houston. Wellington: Sweet & Maxwell, 1970, pp. 242-75.

3830 _____ "Informing the Void: Initial Cultural Displacement in New Zealand Writing." JCL, 6, no. 1 (1971), 84-102.

3831 _____ "New Zealand Poetic Realities." JCL, 3 (1967), 107-10.

3832 _____ "Sexual Inadequacy in the New Zealand Novel." Quadrant, 11, no. 1 (1967), 22-32.

3833 "All Our Own Work." NZL, 43 (23 Sept. 1960), 8.

3834 Anon. "New Zealand in the New World." TLS, 16 Aug. 1957, pp. xxxviii-xxxix.

3835 Ashton, Beatrice. "Theatre in Wellington." Landfall, 2 (1948), 140-43.

3836 Ashworth, Arthur. "Contemporary New Zealand Poetry." Southerly, 10 (1949), 2-16.

3837   Baxter, James K.   Aspects of Poetry in New Zealand. Christchurch:
       Caxton, 1967.

3838   ____   The Fire and the Anvil: Notes on Modern Poetry. Wellington: New
       Zealand Univ. Press, 1960.

3839   ____   The Man on the Horse. Denedin: Univ. of Otago, 1967.

3840   ____   Recent Trends in New Zealand Poetry. Christchurch: Caxton, 1951.

3841   "Beneath Another Sun." NZL, 50 (29 May 1964), 4.

3842   Bertram, James.   "New Zealand Landfall." New Statesman, 60 (1960),
       352-53.

3843   ____   "Note on a War Generation." Landfall, 19 (1965), 138-40.

3844   ____   "Tom Arnold's New Zealand." Landfall, 20 (1966), 260-67.

3845   Brasch, Charles, ed.   Landfall Country. Christchurch: Caxton, 1962.

3846   Brooke, R.   "A Look at the Myth or the Bourgeois Crock at the End of
       the Rainbow." Frontiers, 2, no. 1 (1969), 5-10.

3847   Broughton, W. S.   "Problems and Responses of Three New Zealand Poets in
       the 1920's." In Proceedings of the 10th Congress of the A. U. L. L. A.
       Auckland: Univ. of Auckland, 1966.

3848   Burgess, Bevan.   "A Necessary Crusade." Landfall, 21 (1967), 96-100.

3849   Burns, James A. S.   A Century of New Zealand Novels, 1861-1960.
       Wellington: Whitcombe & Tombs, 1962.

3850   ____   "New Zealand Literary Scene." BA, 41 (1967), 288-91.

3851   ____   "New Zealand Writing in 1964." BA, 39 (1965), 152-55.

3852   ____   "New Zealand Writing 1965." BA, 40 (1966), 152-55.

3853   ____   "Poetry and Drama in New Zealand." BA, 40 (1966), 36-38.

3854   Burton, Ormond.   Spring Fires: A Study in New Zealand Writing. Auckland:
       Book Centre, 1956.

3855   Bystander [pseud.].   "New Zealand Books, 1962." NZMR, 31 (1963), 21-
       22.

3856   Chapman, Robert.   "Fiction and the Social Pattern: Some Implications of
       Recent New Zealand Writing." Landfall, 7 (1953), 26-58.

3857   ____   "Introduction" to An Anthology of New Zealand Verse. London:
       Oxford Univ. Press, 1956, pp. xix-xxxii.

3858   Commons, Jerry.   "New Zealand Opera." Landfall, 16 (1962), 68-72.

3859   Copland, R. A.   "New Zealand: The Contemporary Scene." English, 15
       (1965), 225-28.

3860   Curnow, Allen.   "Introduction" to The Penguin Book of New Zealand Verse.
       Harmondsworth: Penguin, 1960, pp. 17-67.

3861   ____   "New Zealand Literature: The Case for a Working Definition."
       In M. F. Lloyd Prichard, ed., The Future of New Zealand. Christchurch:
       Whitcombe & Tombs for the Univ. of Auckland, 1964, pp. 84-107.

3862   Dalziel, Margaret.   "Comics in New Zealand." Landfall, 9 (1955), 41-69.

3863   ____   Popular Fiction a 100 Years Ago. New Zealand: Cohen & West,
       1958.

3864   Davin, D. M.   "New Zealand Novel." PPSB, 10, no. 1 (1956), 1-31; 10,
       no. 2 (1956), 33-64.

3865 Dobbie, James M. "The Relation Between Readers and Writers." Arena,
      18 (1948), 21-23.

3866 Doyle, Charles. "Making It with the Muse." In Conspectus 1964: Auckland:
      Auckland Univ. Lit. Soc., 1965, pp. 1-13.

3867 ____, ed. Recent Poetry in New Zealand. Auckland: Collins, 1965.
      [Includes notes by Fleur Adcock, J. K. Baxter, Peter Bland, Alistair
      Campbell, Gordon Challis, Charles Doyle, Louis Johnson, M. K. Joseph,
      Owen Leeming, W. H. Oliver, Keith Sinclair, Kendrick Smithyman, and
      C. K. Stead on their own poetry.]

3868 "Drama at Home." NZL, 54 (14 Oct. 1966), 7.

3869 Dunmor, John. "A Plea for the Playwright." Landfall, 11 (1957), 314-17.

3870 "Even Writers Must Eat." NZL, 54 (4 March 1966), 4.

3871 Fairburn, A. R. D. "Some Reflections on New Zealand Painting." Landfall,
      1 (1947), 49-56.

3872 ____ The Woman Problem and Other Prose. Auckland: Blackwood & Janet
      Paul, 1967.

3873 Folio [pseud.]. "New Zealand Book Notes." NZM, 28, no. 2 (1949), 30-31;
      28, no. 3 (1949), 24.

3874 Franklin, H. "Time, Place and People: 'A Geographical Projection of
      the New Zealand Novel.'" NZL, 38 (7 March 1958), 6.

3875 G., J. W. "In Search of New Zealand." NatEd, 45 (1963), 183-85.

3876 Gabites, G. L. "Centennial Survey: A Note on Canterbury Writing."
      NZL, 23 (8 Feb. 1950), 10-11.

3877 Glue, W. A. History of the Government Printing Office. Wellington: Owen,1966.

3878 Gordon, Ian. "Chair of New Zealand Literature." NZL, 48 (8 March 1963), 4.

3878a ____ "Writers' Dilemma in New Zealand." JOLW, 63 (1954), 453-54.

3879 ____ "Writing in New Zealand's Early Journals and Records." PPSB,
      9, no. 4 (1955), 1-32.

3880 ____ "Writing in New Zealand: Pioneers and Professionals." PPSB, 9,
      no. 5 (1955), 1-32. [Repr. separately. Wellington: Govt. Printer,
      n. d.]

3881 Grammaticus [pseud.]. "Literature of the Pioneers." Week News, 27
      March 1963, p. 26.

3882 Gurr, A. J. "The Two Realities of New Zealand Poetry." JCL, 1 (1965),
      122-34.

3883 Hall, D. "Writers of Otago." HBg, 22, no. 10 (1960), 21-25.

3884 Hall, Leslie M. "Women and Men in New Zealand." Landfall, 12 (1958),
      47-56.

3885 Hart-Smith, William. "Poetry in New Zealand." ANZY, 3 (1947), 145-47.

3886 Healey, R. "Literature and the Welfare State." Education, 4, no. 8
      (1965), 25-29.

3887 Holcroft, M. H. Creative Problems in New Zealand. Christchurch: Caxton,
      1948.

3888 ____ Discovered Isles. Christchurch: Caxton, 1950.

3889 ____ Islands of Innocence: The Childhood Theme in New Zealand Fiction.
      Wellington: Reed, 1964.

3890 ____ Reluctant Editor: The 'Listener' Years, 1949-1967. Wellington:
      Reed, 1967.

3891   Hooker, J. "Last Outpost?" AustBR, 4 (1965), 100.

3892   Jackson, MacD. P. "Drama in Auckland." Landfall, 20 (1966), 385-91.

3893   Jackson, R. L. P. "Canadian and New Zealand Short Stories." JCL, 6 (1969), 143-47.

3894   Johnson, Louis. "1960: Another Vintage Year for New Zealand Books." NZPC, 8, no. 6 (1960), 14-16.

3895   ____ "Poetry Yearbook and the New Zealand Literary Fund." Comment, 5, no. 2 (1964), 30-33.

3896   ____ "The Year the Drought Broke." NZPY, 11 (1964), 9-30.

3897   Jones, Joseph. The Cradle of "Erewhon": Samuel Butler in New Zealand. Melbourne: Melbourne Univ. Press, 1960.

3898   ____ "Frontier to Metropolis." NZL, 30 (19 March 1954), 18-19.

3899   Joseph, M. K. "Writing in New Zealand: The New Zealand Short Story." PPSB, 10, no. 7 (1956), 1-35; 10, no. 8 (1956), 1-35.

3900   Kenner, Hugh. "Regional Muses." Poetry (Chicago), 86 (May 1955), 111-16.

3901   Koanui [pseud.]. "Approach to New Zealand Poetry." Northland, 9, no. 1 (1966), 23-26.

3902   Lowry, R. "Who'd be a Writer in New Zealand? A Rotten Row to Hoe." Here and Now, 2, no. 4 (1952), 35-36.

3903   M., J. F. "Character in Search of an Author." NZL, 53 (10 Dec. 1965), 4.

3904   Macaskill, P. "Comments on the Year's Fiction." ANZY, 6 (1950), 145-48.

3905   McCormick, E. H. Letters and Art in New Zealand. Wellington: Dept. of Internal Affairs, 1940.

3906   ____ New Zealand Literature, a Survey. Oxford: Oxford Univ. Press, 1959.

3907   ____ "Voice of a Silent Land: New Zealand Writing." BA, 29 (1955), 285-88.

3908   McEldowney, Dennis. "Scholarly Publishing in New Zealand." SchP, 1 (1969), 107-11.

3909   ____ "Ultima Thule to Little Bethel: Notes on Religion in New Zealand Writing." Landfall, 20 (1966), 50-59.

3910   McKay, Frank. New Zealand Poetry. Wellington: New Zealand Univ. Press, 1970.

3911   McLeod, A. L., ed. The Pattern of New Zealand Culture. Ithaca, N. Y.: Cornell Univ. Press, 1969. [J. C. Reid, "Literature," pp. 17-48.]

3912   Marsh, Ngaio. "Theatre: A Note on the Status Quo." Landfall, 1 (1947), 37-43.

3913   Mason, Bruce. "Et in Arcadia Ego: A Chapter of Reminiscence." Landfall, 9 (1955), 294-99.

3914   ____ "The New Zealand Players' Second Season." Landfall, 7 (1953), 285-88.

3915   ____ "Towards a Professional Theatre." Landfall, 17 (1963), 70-77.

3916   ____ "Wellington's Unity Theatre." Landfall, 9 (1955), 153-60.

3917   Middleton, P. "New Zealand Survey." Bulletin (Sydney), 5 Feb. 1958, pp. 58-59.

3918   Miller, H. "Writing in New Zealand: Some Early Historians." PPSB, 4, no. 2 (1950), 1-10.

3919 Mitcalfe, B. "Of Writers." NatEd, 33 (1951), 430-31.

3920 Mountjoy, W. J. "The Theatre in 1951." Landfall, 6 (1952), 60-66.

3921 Mountjoy, Z. "Modern New Zealand Poetry." NatEd, 29 (1947), 372-73.

3922 Mulgan, Alan. Great Days in New Zealand Writing. Wellington: Reed, 1962.

3923 _____ Literature and Authorship in New Zealand. London: Allen & Unwin, 1943.

3924 _____ Literature and Landscape in New Zealand. Dunedin: n. p.; repr. from NZG, 2, no. 1 (1946), 1-18.

3925 Murray-Smith, Stephen. "Australian Look at the New Zealand Book." AustBR, 4 (1965), 53-54.

3926 Musgrove, S. "Flowering of New Holland." Landfall, 4 (1950), 324-31.

3927 Nelson, Erle. "Towards a New Zealand Drama." Landfall, 17 (1963), 122-34.

3928 "New Zealand Books Today." NZL, 33 (1955), 6-7.

3929 Noonan, Michael A. "New Zealand Theatre in the 'Seventies?" Landfall, 22 (1968), 364-67.

3930 Oliver, W. H. "Poetry in New Zealand." PPSB, 13, no. 6 (1960).

3931 Olssen, E. A. "The Conditions of Culture." In item 3845, pp. 395-411.

3932 O'Neill, Joseph B. "Community Arts Service Drama." Landfall, 7 (1953), 133-37.

3933 O'Sullivan, Vincent. "Poetry Censorship." Comment, 5, no. 2 (1964), 2-3.

3934 Palmer, Nettie. "New Zealand and Australia." Meanjin, 3 (1944), 165-68.

3935 Parsonage, J. S. "Introduction to New Zealand Fiction." LibW, 45 (1963), 9-16.

3936 Pearson, W. H. "Attitudes to the Maori in Some Pakeha Fiction." JPS, 67 (1958), 211-38.

3937 _____ "Fretful Sleepers: A Sketch of New Zealand Behaviour and Its Implications for the Artist." Landfall, 6 (1952), 201-30. [Repr. in item 3845, pp. 330-72.]

3938 _____ "The Maori and Literature, 1938-1965." In The Maori People in the Nineteen-Sixties. Auckland: Paul, 1969, pp. 217-56.

3939 _____ "The Recognition of Reality." In item 36, pp. 32-47.

3940 Penguin [pseud.]. "When New Zealand Books First Made Impact." Week News, 27 Nov. 1963, pp. 1-4.

3941 Plomer, William. "Some Books from New Zealand." In Penguin New Writing 17, ed. John Lehmann. Harmondsworth: Penguin, 1943, pp. 149-54.

3942 Pocock, J. G. A. "On Two New Zealand Plays." Landfall, 8 (1954), 26-35.

3943 _____ "Theatre--Southern View." Landfall, 7 (1953), 199-202.

3944 Q. E. D. [pseud.]. "If Winter Comes . . . A Literary Argument for Several Voices." NZL, 25 (7 Sept. 1951), 7.

3945 Reid, J. C. Creative Writing in New Zealand. Wellington: Pub. for the Author by Whitcombe & Tombs, 1946.

3946 _____ "New Zealand Literature." In item 1052, pp. 155-233.

3947 _____ "New Zealand Writing Today." Books, 12 (1953), 145-50.

3948 _____ "Note on New Zealand Poetry." AmPM, 36, no. 4 (1955), 1-3.

3949 _____ "Regional Writing." Northland, 5, no. 11 (1958), 4-5.

3950 _____ "Vom Werden eigenen Schrifttums." InstAM, 6 (1956), 1-35.

3951 _____ "Year's Work in Writing." ANZY, 7 (1951), 136-44.

3952 Rhodes, H. Winston. New Zealand Fiction since 1945. Dunedin: John McIndoe, 1968.

3953 _____ New Zealand Novels. Wellington: New Zealand Univ. Press, 1969.

3954 _____ "Writers and Writing in New Zealand: A Series of Studies." NZL, 10 (1947), 123-28, 147-51, 166-70, 179-83, 206-10, 230-35.

3955 Robinson, Margaret. "Writing in New Zealand." Arena, 33 (1953), 21-22.

3956 Ruthven, K. K. "Ezra Pound, Alice Kenny, and the Triad." Landfall, 23 (1969), 73-84.

3957 Sargeson, Frank. "What Is the Literary Situation?" Numbers, 3 (1955), 3-4.

3958 Smith, E. M. A History of New Zealand Fiction from 1862 to the Present Time, with Some Account of Its Relation to the National Life and Character. Wellington: Reed, 1939.

3959 Smithyman, Kendrick. "Post-War New Zealand Poetry 4. True Voice of Feeling." Mate, 11 (1963), 31-48.

3960 _____ "Reflections of Social Attitudes in 'Epic' Poetry of the Drawing Room in Pre-1900 New Zealand." UAHSA, (1967), 28-41.

3961 _____ A Way of Saying: A Study of New Zealand Poetry. Auckland: Collins, 1965.

3962 Stead, C. K. "'For the hulk of the world's between': New Zealand Writing." In Distance Looks Our Way, ed. Keith Sinclair. Auckland: Paul's Book Arcade, 1961, pp. 79-96.

3963 Stevens, Joan. The New Zealand Novel, 1860-1960. Wellington: Reed, 1961.

3964 _____ New Zealand Short Stories. Wellington: New Zealand Univ. Press, 1968.

3965 Sturm, Terry L. "New Zealand Poetry and the Depression." JCL, 2 (1967), 124-37.

3966 _____, and H. Winston Rhodes. "Two Views: The Short Story in New Zealand." Landfall, 21 (1967), 76-89.

3967 Swan, George, et al. "A National Theatre." Landfall, 3 (1949), 63-72.

3968 Thomas, K. "Books About Our Own Land." HBg, 22, no. 12 (1960), 35.

3969 _____ "Little About New Zealand Literature." HBg, 21, no. 1 (1958), 13-16.

3970 Tombs, H. H., ed. Year Book of the Arts in New Zealand, 5. Wellington: H. H. Tombs, 1950.

3971 Wadman, Howard, ed. Year Book of the Arts in New Zealand, 3. Wellington: H. H. Tombs, 1947.

3972 _____, ed. Year Book of the Arts in New Zealand, 4. Wellington: H. H. Tombs, 1949.

3973 Walker, D. C., and James Bertram. "A New Anthology: Two Views." Landfall, 24 (1970), 356-73.

3974 Waller, C. F. "New Zealand Culture." JCL, 8 (1969), 152-53.

3975 Whalley, George. "Celebration and Elegy in New Zealand Verse." QQ, 74 (1967), 738-53.

3976 "Writers in New Zealand: A Questionnaire." Landfall, 14 (1960), 36-70.
See also: 1022, 6117, 6119, 6124, 6499-6508.

Individual Authors

ASHTON-WARNER, Sylvia

3977 McEldowney, Dennis. "Sylvia Ashton Warner: A Problem of Grounding."
      Landfall, 23 (1969), 230-45.

BAUGHAN, Blanche E.

3978 Mulgan, Alan. "B. E. Baughan: Some Memories." Landfall, 12 (1958),
      333-35.

BAXTER, James

3979 Baxter, James K. "Beginnings." Landfall, 19 (1965), 237-42.

3980 ____ "James K. Baxter: Worksheets." MalR, 5 (1968), 114-17.

3981 Bertram, James. "Two New Zealand Poets." Education, 2, no. 3 (1949),
      56-59; 2, no. 4 (1949), 59-61.

3982 Hart-Smith, William. "The Poetry of James K. Baxter." Meanjin, 11
      (1952), 383-90.

3983 Keesing, Nancy. "New Zealand Voice." Southerly, 20 (1959), 104-06.

3984 Leeming, Owen. "And the Clay Man? Reflections on 'The Rock Woman,'
      Selected Poems by James K. Baxter." Landfall, 25 (1971), 9-19.

3985 Smith, Harold W. "James K. Baxter: The Poet as Playwright." Landfall,
      22 (1968), 56-62.

3986 Walker, D. C. "Baxter's Notebook." Landfall, 25 (1971), 20-24.

3987 Weir, J. E. "The Green Inn--Some Reflections on the Poetry of James
      K. Baxter." Comment, 10, no. 4 (1970), 22-28.

3988 ____ The Poetry of James K. Baxter. Wellington: Oxford Univ. Press, 1970.
See also: 6509.

BETHELL, Mary Ursula

3989 Baigent, Lawrence. "The Poetry of Ursula Bethell." Landfall, 5 (1951),
      23-30.

3990 Grave, S. A. "The Image of New Zealand in the Poetry of Ursula Bethell."
      Meanjin, 13 (1954), 381-88.

3991 Somerset, H. C. D., et al. "Ursula Bethell: Some Personal Memories."
      Landfall, 2 (1948), 275-95.
See also: 6510.

BOLITHO, Hector

3992 Bolitho, Hector. "My Friendship with Denton Welch." $\underline{TQ}$, 10, no. 4
      (1967), 235-40.

BRASCH, Charles

3993 O'Sullivan, Vincent. "Brief Permitted Morning--Notes on the Poetry of
      Charles Brasch." Landfall, 23 (1969), 338-52.

See also: 3981.

COURAGE, James

3994 Copland, R. A. "The New Zealand Novels of James Courage." Landfall,
      18 (1964), 235-49.

3995 Wilson, Phillip. "James Courage: A Recollection." Landfall, 18 (1964),
      234-35.

CRESSWELL, D'Arcy

3996 Carrington, C. E., Oliver Duff, et al. "D'Arcy Cresswell, by His
      Friends." Landfall, 14 (1960), 341-61.

3997 Finlayson, R. "Meeting with D'Arcy Cresswell." Mate, 5 (1960), 38-40.

3998 Shaw, Helen. "Lady Ottoline Morrell and D'Arcy Cresswell: An Exchange
      of Letters." Landfall, 22 (1969), 280-309.

CURNOW, Alan

3999 Stead, C. K. "Allen Curnow's Poetry: Notes Towards a Criticism."
      Landfall, 17 (1963), 26-45.

See also: 3892.

DALLAS, Ruth

4000 Dallas, Ruth. "Beginnings." Landfall, 19 (1965), 348-57.

DOMETT, Alfred

4001 Domett, Alfred. Canadian Journal, ed. E. A. Horsman and Lilian Rea
      Benson. London (Canada): Univ. of Western Ontario, 1956.

4002 Horsman, E. A. The Diary of Alfred Domett, 1872-1885. Oxford: Univ.
      of Durham Publications, 1954.

4003 McEldowney, Dennis. "The Unbridled Bridal Pair: 'Ranolf and Amohia.'"
      Landfall, 22 (1968), 374-83.

DUGGAN, Maurice

4004 Duggan, Maurice. "Beginnings." Landfall, 20 (1966), 324-33.

4005 Sturm, Terry L. "The Short Stories of Maurice Duggan." Landfall, 25
      (1971), 50-71.

FAIRBURN, A. R. D.

4006   Broughton, W. S.   A. R. D. Fairburn. Wellington: Reed, 1968.

4007   ____   "Lyricism and Belief in A. R. D. Fairburn." Dispute, 2, no. 4
       (1967), 12-17.

4008   Hamilton, Ian. "Fairburn and Dr Stead." Comment, 8, no. 4 (1967),
       36-41.

4009   Jackson, MacD. P. "The Visionary Moment--An Essay on the Poetry of
       A. R. D. Fairburn." Kiwi, (1961), 22-31.

4010   Johnson, Louis, and Erik Schwimmer. "A. R. D. Fairburn--An Assessment."
       Numbers, 7 (1957), 15-24.

4011   Johnson, Olive. A. R. Fairburn, 1904-1957: A Bibliography of His
       Published Work. Auckland: Univ. Publications, 1958.

4012   Mason, R. A. K. Rex Fairburn. Dunedin: Univ. of Otago Press, 1962.

4013   O'Sullivan, Vincent. "A. R. D. Fairburn--Definitions of Emptiness."
       Comment, 7, no. 4 (1966), 29-35.

4014   Stead, C. K. "Fairburn." Landfall, 20 (1966), 367-81.

4015   Wynne, Christine. "A. R. D. Fairburn: An Impression." Arena, 15 (1947),
       14-15.

See also: 6511.

FRAME, Janet

4016   Frame, Janet. "Beginnings." Landfall, 19 (1965), 40-47.

4017   Jones, Lawrence. "No Cowslip's Bell in Waimaru: The Personal Vision of
       Owls do Cry." Landfall, 24 (1970), 280-96.

4018   Middleton, O. E. "A State of Siege at the Globe." Landfall, 25 (1971),
       81-83.

GLOVER, Denis

4019   Campbell, Alistair. "Glover and Georgianism." Comment, 6, no. 1 (1964),
       23-33.

4020   Curnow, Wystan. "Two New Zealand Poets: The 'Man Alone' Theme in the
       Poetry of Denis Glover and Kendrick Smithyman." QQ, 74 (1967), 726-37.

4021   Roddick, Alan. "A Reading of Denis Glover." Landfall, 19 (1965), 48-58.

4022   Thomson, J. E. "Time and Youth in the Poetry of Denis Glover." Landfall,
       21 (1967), 192-97.

HYDE, Robin [Iris Wilkinson]

4023   Bertram, James. "Robin Hyde: A Reassessment." Landfall, 7 (1953), 181-91.

4024   Hyde, Robin. Journalese. Auckland: National Printing, 1934.

4025   ____   "The Singers of Loneliness." THM, 6 (1938), 9-23.

4026   Partridge, Colin J. "Wheel of Words: The Poetic Development of Robin
       Hyde." JCL, 5 (1969), 92-104.

4027   Rawlinson, Gloria. "Introduction" to Robin Hyde, The Godwits Fly.
       Auckland: Auckland Univ. Press, 1970, pp. ix-xviii.

4028 Stevens, Joan. "Introduction" to Robin Hyde, Check to Your King. Wellington: Reed, 1960, pp. v-x.

MANSFIELD, Katherine [Kathleen Beauchamp]

4029 Aiken, Conrad. "Katherine Mansfield." Freeman, 5 (1922), 357-58.

4030 ____ "The Short Story as Confession." New Statesman and Nation, 33 (1923), 490.

4031 ____ "The Short Story as Poetry." Freeman, 3 (1921), 210.

4032 Allbright, Rachel. "Katherine Mansfield and Wingley." Folio, 24, no. 3 (1959), 23-29.

4033 Alpers, Anthony. Katherine Mansfield. London: Jonathan Cape, 1954.

4034 Anon. "A Fashion in the Forest of Fontainebleau." Graphic, 107 (1923), 335.

4035 ____ "Katherine Mansfield." TLS, 1 Nov. 1928, p. 801.

4036 ____ "Katherine Mansfield." TLS, 25 April 1958, p. 225.

4037 ____ "Katherine Mansfield's Hold on Literary Immortality." CO, 74 (1923), 436-37.

4038 ____ "Katherine Mansfield's Stories." TLS, 2 March 1946, p. 102.

4039 ____ "Miss Mansfield's Last Stories." TLS, 28 June 1923, p. 437.

4040 ____ "Miss Mansfield's New Stories." TLS, 2 March 1922, p. 137.

4041 ____ "Miss Mansfield's Stories." TLS, 16 Dec. 1920, p. 855.

4042 ____ "The New Cult of Gurdjieff." CO, 76 (1924), 467-68.

4043 ____ "Real Life and Dream Life." New Statesman and Nation, 28 (1921-22), 639-40.

4044 ____ "[Review of The Garden Party]." EngR, 34 (June 1922), 602.

4045 Armstrong, Martin. "The Art of Katherine Mansfield." FortR, 29 (1923), 484-90.

4046 ____ "Katherine Mansfield." Spectator, 130 (1923), 211.

4047 Assad, Thomas J. "Mansfield's 'The Fly.'" Expl, 14 (1955), Item 10.

4048 Aubrion, M. K. "Mansfield ou le rêve fracassé." RGB, 6 (1967), 45-55.

4049 Audiat, Pierre. "Le journal de Katherine Mansfield." Européen, 164 (3 June 1932), 4.

4050 Baker, Ernest A. The History of the English Novel. New York: Barnes & Noble, 1960, Vol. 10, pp. 226-43.

4051 [Baker, Ida Constance]. Katherine Mansfield: The Memories of LM. London: Michael Joseph, 1971.

4052 Baldeshwiler, Eileen. "Katherine Mansfield's Theory of Fiction." SSF, 7 (1970), 421-32.

4053 Barreta, Rose Worms. "Les petites servantes méridionales vues par Katherine Mansfield." RevH, 15 Sept. 1934, pp. 358-62.

4054 Bates, H. E. The Modern Short Story. London: Nelson, 1941.

4055 Bateson, F. W., and B. Schahevitch. "Katherine Mansfield's 'The Fly': A Critical Exercise." EIC, 12 (1962), 39-53.

4056 Bay, Andre. L'oeuvre romanesque de Katherine Mansfield. Paris: Stock, 1955.

4057   Beach, Joseph Warren. "Katherine Mansfield and Her Russian Master." VQR, 27 (1951), 604-08.

4058   Beachcroft, T. O. "Katherine Mansfield." In The Modest Art: A Survey of the Short Story in English. London: Oxford Univ. Press, 1968, pp. 162-75.

4059   Beauchamp, Sir Harold. "Katherine Mansfield's Career." SatRL, 10 (1933), 144.

4060   Bechhofer, C. E. "The Forest Philosophers." Century, 86 (1924), 66-78.

4061   Bell, Margaret. "In Memory of Katherine Mansfield." Bookman (London), 74 (1933), 36-46.

4062   Bell, Pauline P. "Mansfield's 'The Fly'." Expl, 19 (1960), Item 20.

4063   Berkman, Sylvia. Katherine Mansfield. New Haven: Yale Univ. Press, 1951.

4064   Bertram, James. "Le tombeau de Katherine Mansfield." Landfall, 6 (1952), 193-201.

4065   Bertrand, C. P. "L'Attitude spirituelle de Katherine Mansfield." Cahiers du sud, 18 (1931), 646-65.

4066   Blanchet, André. "Le secret de Katherine Mansfield." Etudes, 241 (1939), 410-27, 510-29.

4067   Bompard, Jacques. "Sur une jeune femme morte: Katherine Mansfield." GrR, 140 (1933), 540-56.

4068   Bordeaux, Henri. "Katherine Mansfield toujours vivante." NL, 27 May 1939, pp. 1-2.

4069   _____ "Le souvenir de Katherine Mansfield." RevH, 17 June 1939, pp. 265-79.

4070   Bosanquet, Theodora. "Katherine Mansfield." YR, 18 (1929), 801-03.

4071   Bowen, Elizabeth. "A Living Writer." Cornhill, 140 (1956-57), 120-34.

4072   Boyer, P. "Katherine Mansfield's l'oeuvre romanesque?" Esprit, 10 (1966), 558-61.

4073   Boyle, Elizabeth. "Katherine Mansfield: A Reconsideration." New Republic, 82 (1937), 309.

4074   Boyle, Ted E. "The Death of the Boss: Another Look at Katherine Mansfield's 'The Fly.'" MFS, 11 (1965), 183-85.

4075   Brewster, Dorothy, and Angus Burrell. Modern Fiction. New York: Columbia Univ. Press, 1934.

4076   Brophy, Brigid. "Katherine Mansfield's Self-Deception." MQR, 5 (1966), 93-98.

4077   Brown, Grace Z. "Katherine Mansfield's Quest." Bookman (London), 61 (1925), 687-91.

4078   Carco, Francis. Souvenirs sur Katherine Mansfield. Paris: Le Divan, 1934.

4079   Cather, Willa. Not Under Forty. New York: Knopf, 1936.

4080   Cazamian, Louis. "D. H. Lawrence and Katherine Mansfield as Letter-Writers." UTQ, 3 (1934), 286-307.

4081   Chimes, Omana [pseud.]. "Katherine Mansfield at School." NZEA, 10 Oct. 1929, n. pag.

4082   Christen, Marcel. Katherine Mansfield. De la Nouvelle-Zélande à Fontainebleau. Niort: Chiron, 1951.

4083 Church, Richard. "Sensibility." Spectator, 141 (1928), 597.

4084 Citron, Pierre. "Katherine Mansfield et la France." RLC, 20 (1940), 173-93.

4085 Clarke, Isabel C. Katherine Mansfield. Wellington: Beltane Book Bureau, 1944.

4086 Collins, Joseph. "The Greatest Short Story Writer." LitD, 76 (1923), 32-33.

4087 _____ "The Rare Craftsmanship of Katherine Mansfield." NYTBR, 18 Feb. 1923, p. 7.

4088 Corin, Fernand. "Creation of Atmosphere in Katherine Mansfield's Stories." RLV, 22 (1956), 65-78.

4089 Cowley, Joy, et al. "Mansfield: How She Stands Today." NZL, 59 (11 Oct. 1968), 8-9.

4090 Cowley, Malcolm. "The Author of 'Bliss.'" Dial, 73 (1922), 230-32.

4091 _____ "Page Dr. Blum!" Dial, 71 (1921), 365-67.

4092 Cox, Sidney. "The Fastidiousness of Katherine Mansfield." SR, 39 (1931), 158-61.

4093 Crawford, J. W. "Katherine Mansfield Reconsidered." NYTBR, 31 Jan. 1926, p. 2.

4094 Curnow, Heather. Katherine Mansfield. Wellington: Reed, 1968.

4095 Daiches, David. The Novel and the Modern World. Chicago: Univ. of Chicago Press, 1940.

4096 Daly, Saralyn R. Katherine Mansfield. New York: Twayne, 1965.

4097 Davin, D. M. Katherine Mansfield in Her Letters. Wellington: Govt. Printer, 1959.

4098 Davis, Robert Murray. "The Unity of 'The Garden Party.'" SSF, 2 (1964), 61-65.

4099 Deffrennes, Pierre. "La correspondance de Katherine Mansfield." Etudes, 209 (1931), 314-24.

4100 D'Escola, Marguerite. "Katherine Mansfield." RevBl, 1 Sept. 1934, pp. 643-49.

4101 Dinkins, Paul. "Blythe Sybil." SatR, 36 (1953), 34-35.

4102 _____ "Katherine Mansfield: The Ending." SWR, 28 (1953), 203-10.

4103 Distel, M. "Katherine Mansfield's Erzahlung 'Je ne parle pas français' Ein Beitrag zur Interpretation anhand der Originalfassung." NS (1959), 249-63.

4104 Dominique, Jean. "Katherine Mansfield." Thyrse (April 1952), 156-68; (May 1952), 197-205; (June 1952), 252-62.

4105 Eisinger, Chester. "Mansfield's 'Bliss.'" Expl, 7 (1949), Item 48.

4106 Eustace, Cecil John. An Infinity of Questions: A Study of the Religion of Art, and of the Art of Religion in the Lives of Five Women. Freeport, N. Y.: Books for Libraries, 1969.

4107 Foot, John. The Edwardianism of Katherine Mansfield. Wellington: Brentwoods Press, 1969.

4108 Fort, J. B. "Katherine Mansfield et lui." EA, 5 (1952), 59-65.

4109 Freeman, Kathleen. "The Art of Katherine Mansfield." CanF, 7 (1927), 302-07.

4110   Friis, Anne. _Katherine Mansfield, Life and Stories_. Copenhagen: Einar
       Munksgaard, 1946.

4111   Gargano, James W. "Mansfield's 'Miss Brill.'" _Expl_, 19 (1959), Item 10.

4112   Garlington, J. "Katherine Mansfield: The Critical Trend." _TCL_, 2
       (1956), 49-61.

4113   ____   "Unattributed Story by Katherine Mansfield?" _MLN_, 71 (1956), 91-93.

4114   Gateau, Andrée-Marie. "Katherine Mansfield impressioniste: Ou, quand
       et comment se déroulent les nouvelles de Katherine Mansfield."
       Caliban, 6 (1969), 33-48.

4115   ____   "Poétesse, musicienne et peintre d'un moment éphémère, ou
       Katherine Mansfield impressioniste." _Caliban_, 5 (1968), 93-102.

4116   Gérard, Albert. "Katherine Mansfield, ou le duo de l'innocence et de
       l'experience." _Revue Nouvelle_, 7 (1951), 413-20.

4117   ____   "The Triumph of Beauty: Katherine Mansfield's Progress." _RLV_, 18
       (1952), 325-34.

4118   Gillet, Louis. "'Kass' ou la jeunesse de Katherine Mansfield." _RDM_,
       19, ser. 8 (1934), 456-58.

4119   ____   "Katherine Mansfield." _RDM_, 24, ser. 7 (1924), 929-42.

4120   ____   "Les lettres de Katherine Mansfield." _RDM_, 51, ser. 7 (1929),
       213-27.

4121   Gordon, Ian. "The Editing of Katherine Mansfield's _Journal_ and
       Scrapbook." _Landfall_, 13 (1959), 62-69.

4122   ____   "Katherine Mansfield, New Zealander." _NZNW_, 3 (1944), 58-63.

4123   ____   _Katherine Mansfield_. Rev. ed. London: Longmans, Green, 1963.

4124   Greenfield, Stanley B. "Mansfield's 'The Fly.'" _Expl_, 17 (1958), Item 2.

4125   Gregory, Alyse. "Artist or Nun." _Dial_, 75 (1923), 484-86.

4126   H., R. "'Bliss.'" _New Republic_, 26 (1921), 114-15.

4127   Haferkamp, Berta. "Zur Bildersprache Katherine Mansfields." _NS_, 18
       (1969), 221-39.

4128   Hagopian, John T. "Capturing Mansfield's 'Fly.'" _MFS_, 9 (1963-64),
       385-90.

4129   Hale, Nancy. "Through the Looking-Glass to Reality." _SatR_, 42 (1959),
       10-12.

4130   Harper, G. M. "Katherine Mansfield." _Quarterly Review_, 252 (1929),
       377-87.

4131   Harwood, H. C. "Katherine Mansfield." _Outlook_, 51 (1923), 519.

4132   Henriot, Emile. "Le souvenir de Katherine Mansfield." _Temps_, 12 March
       1935, p. 3.

4133   Hoare, Dorothy. _Some Studies in the Modern Novel_. London: Chatto &
       Windus, 1938.

4134   Hormasji, Nariman. _Katherine Mansfield: An Appraisal_. London: Collins,
       1967.

4135   Houghton, Elizabeth. "Life at Close Range." _LitR_, 3 (1922), 737.

4136   Hubbell, George Shelton. "Katherine Mansfield and Kezia." _SR_, 25
       (1927), 325-35.

4137   Hudson, Stephen. "First Meeting with Katherine Mansfield." _Cornhill_,
       170 (1958), 202-12.

4138 Hull, Robert L. "Alienation in 'Miss Brill.'" SSF, 5 (1967), 74-76.

4139 Huxley, Aldous. "The Traveller's-Eye View." Nation and Athenaeum, 37 (1925), 202-04.

4140 Hynes, Sam. "The Defeat of the Personal." SAQ, 52 (1953), 555-60.

4141 Iverson, Anders. "A Reading of Katherine Mansfield's 'The Garden Party.'" OL, 23 (1968), 5-34.

4142 Jacobs, Willis D. "Mansfield's 'The Fly.'" Expl, 5 (1947), Item 32.

4143 Jacoubet, E. "Katherine Mansfield et Tchekov." EA, 3 (1939), 251-52.

4144 Kafian, Adele. "The Last Days of Katherine Mansfield." Adelphi, 23 (1946), 36-38.

4145 Kleine, Don W. "The Chekhovian Source of 'Marriage a la Mode.'" PQ, 42 (1963), 284-88.

4146 ____ "An Eden for Insiders: Katherine Mansfield's New Zealand." CE, 27 (1965), 201-09.

4147 ____ "'The Garden Party': A Portrait of the Artist." Criticism, 5 (1963), 360-71.

4148 ____ "Katherine Mansfield and the Prisoner of Love." Critique (Minneapolis), 3, no. 2 (1960), 20-33.

4149 Krutch, J. W. "Imponderable Values." Nation, 117 (1929), 210-11.

4150 ____ "The Unfortunate Mendoza." Nation, 115 (1922), 100.

4151 Lang, W. Sprach und Stil in Katherine Mansfields Kurz-geschichten. Leipzig: Noske, 1937.

4152 Lawlor, P. A. The Loneliness of Katherine Mansfield. Wellington: Beltane Book Bureau, 1950.

4153 ____ The Mystery of Maata. Wellington: Beltane Book Bureau, 1946.

4154 Lea, F. A. "Murry and Marriage." DHLR, 2 (1969), 1-23.

4155 Leeming, Owen. "Katherine Mansfield and Her Family." NZL, 48 (29 March 1963), 4.

4156 ____ "Katherine Mansfield in Europe." NZL, 48 (11 April 1963), 6.

4157 ____ "Katherine Mansfield's Rebellion." NZL, 48 (5 April 1963), 6.

4158 ____ "Katherine Mansfield's Sisters." NZL, 48 (1 March 1963), 4.

4159 Le Mée, Jean-Pierre. "Des vers inédits de Katherine Mansfield." Temps, 4 Aug. 1942, p. 3.

4160 Lenoel, Odette. La vocation de Katherine Mansfield. Paris: Editions Albin Michel, 1946.

4161 Littell, Robert. "Katherine Mansfield." New Republic, 34 (1923), 22.

4162 ____ "Katherine Mansfield." New Republic, 31 (1922), 166.

4163 Lynd, Sylvia. "Answer to Conrad Aiken." New Statesman and Nation [and Athenaeum], 33 (1923), 519.

4164 ____ "Katherine Mansfield." WWG, 1 (20 Jan. 1923), 12.

4165 M., D. L. "Short Stories of Life Among the English Middle Class." Boston Transcript, 22 July 1922, p. 4.

4166 Madden, David. "Katherine Mansfield's 'Miss Brill.'" UR, 31 (1964), 89-92.

4167 Magalaner, Marvin. The Fiction of Katherine Mansfield. Carbondale: Southern Illinois Univ. Press, 1971.

4168 Mairet, Philip. John Middleton Murry. London: Longmans, Green, 1958.

4169 Mantz, Ruth Elvish, and John Middleton Murry. The Life of Katherine Mansfield. London: Constable, 1933.

4170 Marcel, Gabriel. "Katherine Mansfield." RevH, 11 July 1931, pp. 172-81.

4171 ____ "Katherine Mansfield." NRF, 32 (1929), 268.

4172 ____ "Lectures." NRF, 32 (1929), 268-73.

4173 Marion, Bernard. A la rencontre de Katherine Mansfield. Brussels: La Sixaine, 1946.

4174 Mathews, T. S. "Creation of a Writer." New Republic, 58 (1929), 147-48.

4175 Maurois, André. "Katherine Mansfield." RevH, 20 April 1935, pp. 307-33.

4176 ____ Poets and Prophets. Trans. by Hamish Miles. London: Cassell, 1936. [Pub. as Prophets and Poets, New York: Harper, 1936.]

4177 Merlin, Roland. Le drame secret de Katherine Mansfield. Paris: Editions du Seuil, 1950.

4178 Mills, Tom L. "Katherine Mansfield." NZRM, 8 (1933), 6-7.

4179 Morris, G. N. "Katherine Mansfield Additions." TLS, 13 July 1940, p. 344.

4180 Morris, M. E. "Katherine Mansfield's 'At the Bay.'" TLR, n.s. 1, no. 4 (1968), 19-24.

4181 Mortellier, C. "The Genesis and Development of the Katherine Mansfield Legend in France." AUMLA, 34 (1970), 252-63.

4182 Moult, T. "Katherine Mansfield." Bookman (London), 63 (1923), 227-28.

4183 Murry, John Middleton. Between Two Worlds. New York: J. Messner, 1936.

4184 ____ "In Memory of Katherine Mansfield." Adelphi, n.s. 1 (1924), 663-65.

4185 ____ "Katherine Mansfield." TLS, 20 March 1948, p. 163.

4186 ____ "Katherine Mansfield." Literary Review, 3 (1923), 461-62.

4187 ____ Katherine Mansfield and Other Literary Portraits. London: P. Nevill, 1949; repr. London: Constable, 1959.

4188 ____ "Katherine Mansfield, Stendhal, and Style." Adelphi, n.s. 1 (1923), 342-43.

4189 ____ "Katherine Mansfield in France." Atlantic, 184 (1949), 72-75.

4190 ____ "A Month After." Adelphi, n.s. 1 (1923), 94-95.

4191 ____ "The Short Story." Nation and Athenaeum, 31 (1922), 712-13.

4192 ____ "Tchekov Revisited." Adelphi, 14 (1937), 19-23.

4193 ____ "The Weariness of Ivan Bunin." Dial, 76 (1924), 194-97.

4194 ____, ed. The Journal of Katherine Mansfield. London: Constable, 1927; rev. ed. 1954.

4195 Murry, Mary Middleton. "Katherine Mansfield and John Middleton Murry." LMag, 6, no. 4 (1959), 69-71.

4196 Nathan, Nell. "Katherine Mansfield: Biographical Data Wanted." N&Q, 175 (1938), 29. [See also: Otto F. Babler, N&Q, 175 (1938), 70, and W. F. Benns, N&Q, 175 (1938), 124.]

4197 Norman, Sylva. "A Word on Katherine Mansfield." FortR, 163 (1948), 278-84.

4198 O'Brien, Edward J. "The Fifteen Finest Short Stories." Forum (New York), 79 (1928), 908.

4199 O'Connor, Frank. "An Author in Search of a Voice." In The Lonely Voice: A Study of the Short Story. London: Macmillan, 1963, pp. 128-42.

4200 Odle, E. V. "['The Dove's Nest']." Bookman (London), 64 (1923), 236-37.

4201 Olgivanna [Mrs. Frank Lloyd Wright]. "The Last Days of Katherine Mansfield." Bookman (New York), 73 (1931), 6-13.

4202 Orage, A. R. "Talks with Katherine Mansfield." Century, 109 (1924-25), 36-40.

4203 Orton, William. The Last Romantic. New York and Toronto: Farrar & Rinehart, 1937.

4204 Orvis, Mary Buchard. The Art of Writing Fiction. New York: Prentice-Hall, 1948.

4205 Palmer, Vance. "Katherine Mansfield." Meanjin, 14 (1955), 177-85.

4206 Peltzie, Bernard E. "Teaching Meaning Through Structure in the Short Story." EJ, 55 (1966), 703-09, 713.

4207 Porter, Katherine Anne. "The Art of Katherine Mansfield." Nation, 145 (1923), 435-36.

4208 Praz, Mario. Studi e Svaghi Inglesi. Firenze: Sansoni, 1937.

4209 Priestley, J. B. "The Dove's Nest." London Mercury, 8 (1923), 438-39.

4210 Pritchett, V. S. "Katherine Mansfield." New Statesman and Nation, 31 (1946), 87.

4211 Rea, J. "Mansfield's 'The Fly.'" Expl, 23 (1965), Item 68.

4212 Renault, Michel. "Katherine Mansfield." GrR, 43 (1939), 362-71.

4213 Rice, A. E. "Memories of Katherine Mansfield." Adam, 300 (1966), 76-85.

4214 Robinson, Fred C. "Mansfield's 'The Garden Party.'" Expl, 24 (1966), Item 66.

4215 Rodriguez Aleman, Maria A. Perfil y contorno de Katherine Mansfield. La Habana: Cooperacion, 1947.

4216 Salomon, Odette. "Souffrances et beauté dans la vie et la personnalité de Katherine Mansfield." FGB, 130 (1933), 531-42; 132 (1934), 1-9.

4217 Saurat, D. "Visit to Gourdyev." Living Age, 145 (1934), 428-29.

4218 Schahevitch, B. "From Simile to Short Story: On Katherine Mansfield's 'The Fly.'" Hasifrut, 1 (1966), 368-77.

4219 Schneider, Elisabeth. "Katherine Mansfield and Chekhov." MLN, 50 (1935), 394-97.

4220 Scholefield, G. H. "[On Katherine Mansfield]." In Sir Harold Beauchamp, Reminiscences and Recollections. New Plymouth, N. Z.: Thomas Avery & Son, 1937, pp. 190-217.

4221 Schwinn, Liesel. "Katherine Mansfield." Hochland, 53 (1961), 333-42.

4222 Scott, M. A. "Unpublished Manuscripts of Katherine Mansfield." TLR, n.s. 3 (1970), 4-28, 128-36; 4 (1971), 4-20.

4223 Sellon, Hugh. "Le souvenir de Katherine Mansfield." RevH, 48 (1939), 96-100.

4224 Sewell, Arthur. Katherine Mansfield. Auckland: Unicorn Press, 1936.

4225 Shanks, Edward. "Katherine Mansfield." London Mercury, 17 (1928), 286-93.

4226 Shaw, Helen. "Katherine Mansfield." Meanjin, 10 (1951), 376-82.

4227 Sinclair, Keith. "Men, Woman, and Mansfield." Landfall, 4 (1950),
      128-38.

4228 Sliwowski, Rene. "Czechow i Katarzyna Mansfield." Twórczość, 3 (1959),
      179-83.

4229 Stallman, Robert Wooster. "Mansfield's 'The Fly.'" Expl, 3 (1945),
      Item 49.

4230 Stanley, C. W. "The Art of Katherine Mansfield." DR, 10 (1931), 26-41.

4231 Street, G. S. "Nos et Mutamur." London Mercury, 5 (1921), 54-56.

4232 Sullivan, J. W. N. "The Story-Writing Genius." Athenaeum, 96 (1920),
      447.

4233 Sutherland, Ronald. "Katherine Mansfield: Plagiarist, Disciple or
      Ardent Admirer?" Critique (Minneapolis), 5, no. 2 (1962), 58-76.

4234 T., H. M. "Katherine Mansfield." Nation and Athenaeum, 31 (1923), 609.

4235 Tasset-Nissolle, E. "Katherine Mansfield." Correspondent, 25 Sept.
      1933, pp. 900-08.

4236 Taylor, Donald S., and Daniel A. Weiss. "Crashing the Garden Party."
      MFS, 4 (1958), 361-64.

4237 Thiebaut, Marcel. "Katherine Mansfield." RevP, Nov. 1933, pp. 462-75.

4238 Thomas, J. D. "Symbolism and Parallelism in 'The Fly.'" CE, 23 (1961),
      256-62. [Reply by Clinton W. Oleson, pp. 585-86; by Thomas, p. 586.]

4239 Thorp, W. "Unburned Letters of Katherine Mansfield." New Republic,
      126 (1952), 18.

4240 Thorpe, Peter. "Teaching 'Miss Brill.'" CE, 23 (1962), 661-63.

4241 Van Kranendonk, A. G. "Katherine Mansfield." ES, 12 (1930), 49-57.

4242 Van Weddingen, Marthe. "Lumière de Katherine Mansfield." RGB, 45 (1949),
      48-57.

4243 Villard, Leonie. "Katherine Mansfield." LanM, 43 (1949), 304-13.

4244 Vittorini, Elio. "Caterina Mansfield." Pegaso, Nov. 1932, pp. 553-73.

4245 Von Heiseler, B. "Katherine Mansfield." Literatur, 40 (1937), 16-21.

4246 Vowinckel, E. "Katherine Mansfield." ZFEU, 30 (1931), 588-61.

4247 Wagenknecht, Edward. "Dickens and Katherine Mansfield." Dickensian,
      26 (1929), 15-23.

4248 _____ "Katherine Mansfield." EJ, 17 (1928), 272-84.

4249 Wagner, G. Damon. "A Race Against Time." Personalist, 11 (1930), 120-25.

4250 Walker, Warren S. "The Unresolved Conflict in 'The Garden Party.'" MFS,
      3 (1957), 354-58.

4251 Weiss, Daniel A. "The Garden Party of Proserpine." MFS, 4 (1958), 363-64.

4252 Welty, Eudora. "The Reading and Writing of Short Stories." Atlantic,
      183 (1949), 54-58.

4253 Whitridge, Arnold. "Katherine Mansfield." SR, 48 (1940), 256-72.

4254 Williams, Orlo. "Katherine Mansfield." New Criterion, 8 (1929), 508.

4255 Willy, Margaret. Three Women Diarists. London and New York: Longmans
      Green, 1964. [Celia Fiennes, Dorothy Wordsworth, and Katherine
      Mansfield.]

4256 Woolf, Virginia. "Katherine Mansfield." In Granite and Rainbow, ed.
      Leonard Woolf. New York: Harcourt, Brace, 1958, pp. 70-75.

4257 Wright, Celeste Turner. "Darkness as a Symbol in Katherine Mansfield."
        MP, 51 (1954), 204-07.

4258 ____ "Genesis of a Short Story." PQ, 34 (1955), 91-96.

4259 ____ "Katherine Mansfield and the 'Secret Smile.'" L&P, 5 (1955), 44-48.

4260 ____ "Katherine Mansfield's Boat Image." TCL, 1 (1955), 128-31.

4261 ____ "Katherine Mansfield's Dog Image." L&P, 10 (1960), 80-81.

4262 ____ "Katherine Mansfield's Father Image." In B. H. Lehman, et al.,
        eds., The Image of the Work. Berkeley and Los Angeles: Univ. of
        California Press, 1955, pp. 137-55.

4263 ____ "Mansfield's 'The Fly.'" Expl, 12 (1954), Item 27.

4264 Yanson, M. M. Problemy stilya zrelykh rasskazov Ketria Mensfild i ee
        vzglyady na literaturnoe masterstvo. Riga: i Latviiskii Gosudarst
        vennyi Universitet, 1967.

See also: 18, 52, 3922, 6512-6534.

MASON, R. A. K.

4265 Broughton, W. S. "Sponges Steeped in Vinegar: A Note on the Collected
        Poems of R. A. K. Mason." Education, 12 (1963), 16-18.

4266 Curnow, Allen, et al. "R. A. K. Mason: Some Tributes." Landfall, 25
        (1971), 222-42.

4267 Stead, C. K. "R. A. K. Mason's Poetry: Some Random Observations."
        Comment, 4, no. 4 (1963), 34-39.

MULGAN, Alan

4268 McEldowney, Dennis. "Alan Mulgan." Landfall, 18 (1964), 226-33.

4269 Mulgan, Alan. "Auckland Days: Another Chapter of Autobiography."
        Landfall, 9 (1955), 127-38.

4270 ____ "Two Worlds: A Chapter of Autobiography." Landfall, 2 (1948),
        181-89.

MULGAN, John

4271 Davin, D. M. "[John Mulgan]." Landfall, 2 (1948), 50-55. [Repr. in
        item 3845, pp. 373-78.]

4272 Day, Paul W. John Mulgan. New York: Twayne, 1968.

4273 ____ "Mulgan's Man Alone." Comment, 6, no. 4 (1965), 15-22.

PEARSON, William

4274 Sargeson, Frank. "Conversation in a Train, or What Happened to Michael's
        Boots." Landfall, 21 (1967), 352-61.

REEVES, William Pember

4275 Sinclair, Keith. William Pember Reeves: New Zealand Fabian. Oxford:
        Clarendon, 1965.

SARGESON, Frank

4276   Anon. "A Sad and Savage World." TLS, 17 June 1965, p. 494.

4277   Beveridge, Michael. "Conversation with Frank Sargeson." Landfall, 24 (1970), 4-27, 142-60.

4278   Broughton, W. S. "Frank Sargeson's Play." Landfall, 15 (1961), 256-59.

4279   Copland, R. A. "The Goodly Roof: Some Comments on the Fiction of Frank Sargeson." Landfall, 22 (1968), 310-23.

4280   Horsman, E. A. "The Art of Frank Sargeson." Landfall, 19 (1965), 129-34.

4281   McNaughton, Howard. "In the Sargeson World." Landfall, 24 (1970), 39-43.

4282   Mason, Bruce. "Professor Mackenzie and Frank Sargeson." Landfall, 20 (1966), 88-89.

4283   Rhodes, H. Winston. Frank Sargeson. New York: Twayne, 1969.

4284   ____ "The Moral Climate of Sargeson's Stories." Landfall, 9 (1955), 25-40. [Repr. in item 3845, pp. 412-29.]

4285   Sargeson, Frank. "Beginnings." Landfall, 19 (1965), 122-28.

4286   ____ "Up On to the Roof and Down Again." Landfall, 4 (1950), 282-88; 5(1951), 8-20, 104-14, 245-50. [Pt. 2 repr. in item 3845, pp. 379-94.]

4287   Shaw, Helen, ed. The Puritan and the Waif. Auckland: n. p., 1954.

4288   Sturm, Terry L. "Frank Sargeson's Joy of the Worm." Landfall, 24 (1970), 33-38.

See also: 6535, 6536.

SATCHELL, William

4289   Wilson, Phillip. The Maorilander. Christchurch: Whitcombe & Tombs, 1961.

4290   ____ William Satchell. New York: Twayne, 1969.

SHADBOLT, Maurice

4291   Pearson, W. H. "In the Shadbolt Country." Comment, 1, no. 3 (1960), 26-28.

4292   Shadbolt, Maurice. "Writer Out of Hiding." NZL, 57 (21 July 1967), 19-20.

SMITHYMAN, Kendrick

4293   Savage, Roger. "Curiousness in Smithyman." Comment, 5, no. 1 (1963), 30-32.

See also: 4020.

TUWHARE, Hone

4294   "Maori Writers Establish Landmarks in New Zealand Literature." Week News, 14 Oct. 1964, p. 10.

South Africa and Rhodesia

Research Aids

4295 Astrinsky, A. A Bibliography of South African English Novels, 1930-1960. Cape Town: Cape Town Univ. School of Librarianship, 1965.

4296 Index to South African Periodicals. Johannesburg: Public Library. 1940-1949 (cumulated 1953); 1950-1959 (cumulated 1962); 1960-d, ann.

4297 Mendelsohnn, Sidney. A South African Bibliography. 2 vols. London: Kegan Paul, 1910.

4298 Musiker, R. "South African Bibliography: A Review." CRL, 24 (1963), 496-500.

4299 ____ "South African English Literature: Bibliographical and Biographical Resources and Problems." ESA, 13 (1970), 265-74.

See also: 57, 5793, 6549.

General

4300 Alexander, Muriel. "Two Colonial Novelists." Trek, 10, no. 21 (1946), 14.

4301 Anon. "Literature and Resistance in South Africa." AAW, 1, no. 2-3 (1968), 88-95.

4302 ____ "A Literature of Empire." SAfQ, 4, no. 3 (1922), 7-9.

4303 ____ "Nation to Nation." TLS, 15 March 1963, p. 177.

4304 ____ "On Some Recent South African Verse." SAfM, 1 (1906), 123-47, 200-25.

4305 ____ "South African Literature." Times (London), 5 Nov. 1910, p. 46.

4306 ____ "South African Short Story Writers." Trek, 12, no. 10 (1948), 24-25.

4307 ____ "[Survey of South African Literature]." TLS, supp., 5 Aug. 1955, p. xiv. [See also pp. i-xlviii.]

4308 Antonissen, R. "Facets of Contemporary Afrikaans Literature." ESA, 13 (1970), 191-206.

4309 ____ "Styl is alles: Bekroonde Afrikaanse dramatiese werk uit die jare, 1948-1952." Standpunte, 7, no. 1 (1952), 75-84.

4310 Bacon, Margaret H. "Writing in a Troubled Land." AR, 25 (1965), 446-52.

4311 Beeton, D. R. "Achievement of South African English Literature." New Nation, Oct. 1968, pp. 4-5.

4312 _____ "Concern and Evocation: Some Aspects of South African English Poetry since the War." ESA, 13 (1970), 125-38.

4313 _____ "New Voices: Some Contemporary South African Poets and Their Work." UES, 2 (1968), 23-39.

4314 _____, and W. D. Maxwell-Mahon, eds. South African Poetry: A Critical Anthology. Pretoria: Univ. of South Africa, 1966.

4315 Berlyn, Phillipa. "The Modern Trend in African Poetry." Nada, 9, no. 5 (1968), 39-41.

4316 Blishen, Edward. "A Report on the Ife Conference on African Writing in English, December, 1968." CulEA, 48 (1968), 4-6.

4317 Borland, C. H. "The Oral and Written Culture of the Shona." Limi, 8 (1969), 1-16.

4318 Bosman, H. C. "Aspects of South African Literature." Trek, 12, no. 9 (1948), 24-25.

4319 Brutus, Dennis. "Protest Against Apartheid: Alan Paton, Nadine Gordimer, Athol Fugard, Alfred Hutchinson and Arthur Nortje." In item 249, pp. 93-100.

4320 Bulano, M. "Then and Now: The Praise Poem in Southern Sotho." NewA, 7, no. 1 (1969), 40-43.

4321 Butler, Guy. "The English Poet in South Africa." Listener, 55 (1956), 680-81.

4322 _____ "The Future of English in Africa." Optima, 14 (1964), 88-97.

4323 _____ "Introduction" to A Book of South African Verse. Cape Town: Oxford Univ. Press, 1959, pp. xvii-xli.

4324 Carew, Jan. "The Role of the Novel in Developing Countries." Afro-Caribbean Heritage, 1, no. 1 (1965), 9-15.

4325 Cartey, Wilfred. "Recent South African Novels." AForum, 1, no. 3 (1966), 115-21.

4326 Cassity, Turner. "Report from Goli." Poetry, 95 (1960), 242-43.

4327 Cope, Jack. "A Quick Look at South African Literature." Quest, 30 (1961), 64-69.

4328 _____ "South African Letter." Landfall, 15 (1961), 240-44; 16(1962), 277-83; 17(1963), 266-71; 18(1964), 258-63.

4329 _____, and Uys Krige. "Introduction" to The Penguin Book of South African Verse. Harmondsworth: Penguin, 1968, pp. 15-22.

4330 Dathorne, O. R. "The African Novel--Document to Experiment." BAALE, 3 (1965), 18-39.

4331 Dau, R. Sh. "The Short Story in Venda." Limi, 6 (1968), 82-84.

4332 Delius, Anthony. "Danger from the Digit." Standpunte, 7, no. 3 (1953), 80-92.

4333 _____ "Exile and the Aboriginal." Standpunte, 7, no. 4 (1953), 77-93.

4334 _____ "In Search of Ourselves." Standpunte, 7, no. 2 (1952), 95-105.

4335 _____ "Struggle of the Tongues: The South African Literary Scene." BA, 29 (1955), 261-69.

4336 _____ "Study in Black and White." Standpunte, 5, no. 3 (1951), 1-16.

4337 Desmond, N. Candlelights: Poets of the Cape. Cape Town: Timmins, 1967.

4338 Dett, V. S. "New South African Literature, 1967: A Critical Chronicle." ESA, 11 (1968), 61-69.

4339 Durham, M. K. "Creative Writing." ESA, 13 (1970), 155-74.

4340 Dyer, B. L. "Literature at the Cape, Seventy Years Ago." LibAR, 4
      (1902), 366-70.

4341 Eglington, Charles. "South African English Culture." Trek, 15, no. 10
      (1951), 6-7.

4342 Feuilleton [pseud.]. "'Twak Road.'" Contrast, 15 (1967), 90-94.

4343 Feuser, W. "Beyond British Cultural Assumptions: The Ife Conference
      on African Writing in English, 16th-19th, December, 1968." L'Afrique
      Actuelle, 25-26 (1969), 47-51.

4344 Gérard, Albert. "African Literature in Rhodesia." AfricaR, 13, no. 5
      (1968), 41-42.

4345 Girling, H. K. "Provincial and Continental: Writers in South Africa."
      ESA, 3 (1960), 113-18.

4346 ____ "South African Novelists and Story Writers." ESA, 4 (1961), 80-86.

4347 ____ "Writers in South Africa: Provincial and Continental." QQ, 69
      (1962), 237-43.

4348 Gordimer, Nadine. "How Not to Know the African." Contrast, 15 (1967),
      44-49.

4349 ____ "Modern African Writing." MQR, 9 (1970), 221-29.

4350 ____ "The Novel and the Nation in South Africa." TLS, 11 Aug. 1961,
      pp. 520-23.

4351 ____ "Politics: A Dirtier Word Than Sex!" Solidarity, 2, no. 11 (1968),
      69-71.

4352 ____ "South Africa: Towards a Desk Drawer Literature." Classic, 2, no. 4
      (1968), 64-74.

4353 ____ "Writing Belongs to Us All." Forum (Johannesburg), 3, no. 6 (1954),
      9-10.

4354 Gordon, Suzanne, and F. E. de Villiers. Poetry: Now and Then.
      Johannesburg: Macmillan, 1968.

4355 Guma, S. M. The Form, Content and Technique of Traditional Literature
      in South Africa. Pretoria: Univ. of South Africa, 1967.

4356 Haarhoff, T. J. "The European Background of South African Literature."
      SAPEN, (1954), 16-17.

4357 Hall, A. D. "Pringle, Somerset and Press Freedom." ESA, 3 (1960), 160-78.

4358 Haresnape, Geoffrey. "The Literary Picture in South Africa." BA, 39
      (1965), 32-34.

4359 Harnett, R. "New Voices." ESA, 13 (1970), 139-54.

4360 Harris, P. "Are South African English Writers Derivative?" Trek, 16,
      no. 1-2 (1952), 16-17.

4361 Harvey, C. J. D. "Local Colour in South African Poetry." Theoria, 7
      (1955), 93-100.

4362 Horn, P. "Poet at Every Street Corner, or Grow Onions Instead of
      Laurels." Wurm, 9 (1968), 121-23.

4363 Howarth, R. G. "An Australian's View of South African Literature."
      SAPEN, (1955), 75-77.

4364 Hugo, L. "Search for Identity: Some Observations on South African
      English Poetry." UNISA, 22 (1968), 47-50.

4365 Jacobson, Dan, and Lewis Nkosi. "The Colonial and the Metropolitan."
      NewA, 7 (1965), 172-73.

4366 Jahn, Janheinz, trans. W. Feuser. "Bantu Literature: The Tragedy of Southern Bantu Literature." BO, 21 (1967), 44-52.

4367 Jeffreys, M. K. "Stryd van die Engelse Boervriendin." Huis, 39, no. 1722 (1955), 61-63.

4368 Jurgens, Heather L. "Children's Theatre: Cheep Like Birds?" TeaterSA, 1, no. 1 (1968), 12-13.

4369 _____ "Playwriting in South Africa." TeaterSA, 1, no. 3 (1969), 5-7.

4370 K., N. "Syndicated Literature." Trek, 10, no. 4 (1946), 14.

4371 Kartuzov, S. P. "Some Problems of Modern Prose in S. A. R." In item 181, pp. 138-54.

4372 Kidd, A. S. "English Language and Literature in South Africa." SAJS, 6 (1910), 152-62.

4373 Krog, E. W. African Literature in Rhodesia. Salisbury: Mambo Press, 1966.

4374 Kunene, Daniel P. "Deculturation--The African Writer's Response." AT, 15, no. 4 (1968), 19-24.

4375 _____, and Randal A. Kirsch. The Beginnings of South African Vernacular Literature. Foreword by John F. Povey. Los Angeles: Lit. Comm. of the African Studies Assoc. 1967. [Daniel P. Kunene, "Background to the South African Vernacular Author and His Writings," 1-13; Randal A. Kirsch, "Brief Biographies of South Africa Bantu Language Authors," i-ix, 1-55.]

4376 Langham-Carter, R. R. "Literary Contribution of the 'Indians' at the Cape." QBSAL, 22 (1968), 88-91.

4377 Lindfors, Bernth. "Postwar Literature in English by African Writers from South Africa: A Study of the Effects of Environment on Literature." In Corinne P. Armstrong, et al., eds., Proceedings of the Third Graduate Academy of the University of California. Los Angeles: Univ. of California, 1966, pp. 149-62. [Also in Phylon, 27 (1966), 50-62.]

4378 _____ "Robin Hood Realism in South African English Fiction." AT, 15, no. 4 (1968), 16-18.

4379 McDowell, Robert E. "African Drama, West and South." AT, 15, no. 4 (1968), 25-28.

4380 _____ "The Brief Search for an African Hero: The Chaka-Mzilikazi Story in South African Novels." Discourse, 11 (1968), 276-83.

4381 MacLennan, D. "The South African Short Story." ESA, 13 (1970), 105-24.

4382 MacNab, R. "Let Us 'tell the world' about South African Writers." Outspan, 50, no. 1302 (1952), 27.

4383 Margarey, Kevin. "The South African Novel and Race." SoRA, 1 (1963), 27-45.

4384 _____ "The South African Novel in English." AUMLA, 2 (1964), 49-50.

4385 Marquard, Leo. The Peoples and Policies of South Africa. New York: Oxford Univ. Press, 1960.

4386 Marsh, Ina. "South African Letter." Landfall, 19 (1965), 256-61.

4387 Maxwell-Mahon, W. D. "Voices in the Wilderness; A Comment on South African Verse." UES, 2 (1969), 75-79.

4388 Meiring, Jane. Thomas Pringle His Life and Times. Cape Town: Balkema, 1968.

4389 Mendelsohnn, Sidney. "South African Literature." [Paper read to members of the Kimberley Athenaeum, 7 Aug. 1903; in the Mendelsohnn Collection, Cape Town.]

4390 Miller, G. M., and Howard Sergeant. A Critical Survey of South African Poetry in English. Cape Town: Balkema, 1957.

4391 Mohr, Robert. "Theatres: Have We Got What We Need?" TeaterSA, 1, no. 1 (1968), 5-7.

4392 Morice, Mr. Justice. "South African Literature." CapeIM, 4, no. 3 (1893), 65-72.

4393 Mphahlele, Ezekiel. The African Image. London: Faber & Faber, 1962.

4394 _____ "African Literature for Beginners." AT, 14, no. 1 (1966), 25-31.

4395 _____ "Black and White." New Statesman, 60 (1960), 342-43.

4396 Nathan, Manfred. South African Literature. Cape Town: Juta, 1925.

4397 New South African Writing and a Survey of Fifty Years of Creative Achievement. Johannesburg: South African P. E. N. Centre, 1960.

4398 Nienaber-Luitingh, W. Digters en Disgoorte. Johannesburg: Afrikaanse persbockhandel, 1967.

4399 Nkosi, Lewis. "Die afrikanische literatur in Sudafrika." Afrika Heute, 1 (1964), 168-70.

4400 _____ "Fiction by Black South Africans." BO, 19 (1966), 48-54. [Repr. in item 91, pp. 211-17.]

4401 _____ Home and Exile. London: Longmans, 1965.

4402 Partridge, A. C. "Condition of South African English Literature." Standpunte, 4, no. 4 (1950), 46-51, 89-90.

4403 _____ "English Literature in South Africa." In E. Rosenthal, ed., Encyclopaedia of Southern Africa. London: Warne, 1961, pp. 159-61.

4405 _____ "The Novel of Social Purpose in South Africa." SAPEN, (1956-57), 59-64.

4406 _____ "Poets and Humanitarians in the Wilderness: The Beginnings of English Literature in South Africa." ESA, 2 (1959), 203-17.

4407 _____ "Recent Trends in South African English Writing." English, 15 (1965), 235-37.

4408 Paton, Alan. "Last Journey." NRJ, 4, no. 1 (1959), 97-99.

4409 _____ "Some Thoughts on the Contemporary Novel in Afrikaans." ESA, 2 (1959), 159-66.

4410 Peck, Anthony. "South African English Literature." Trek, 11, no. 23 (1947), 32-33.

4411 Pinchuck, I. "South African Image." PRen, 5 (1963), 72-84.

4412 Plomer, William. "Notes from South Africa." Encounter, 7, no. 6 (1956), 43-45.

4413 _____ "South African Writing." LMag, 4, no. 2 (1957), 52-56.

4414 Povey, John F. "Memory and Its Wound: A Comment on South African Poetry." ESA, 9 (1966), 61-71.

4415 _____ "The Myrrh of Parting: A Study of the Theme of Exile in South African Poetry." UTQ, 35 (1966), 158-75.

4416 _____ "Styles and Themes in the African Novel in English." ESA, 13 (1970), 207-20.

4417 _____ "The Threatened Language: English Loses Ground in South Africa." NewA, 4, no. 10 (1966), 242-43.

4418 Purves, John. "Our Poets, 1902-1908." Bulletin (Pretoria), n. s. 1 (1909), 51-55.

4419 _____ "Our Poets, 1909." Bulletin (Pretoria), 4 (1910), 250-53.

4420   Rive, Richard.   "African Poets in Berlin." Contrast, 3 (1965), 66-69.

4421   _____   "Brave Minority." Contrast, 21 (1969), 93-95.

4422   _____   "Race and Poetry." Contrast, 16 (1967), 49-61.

4423   Rose, Brian.   "Some Thoughts on Modern Poetry and Its Criticism."
       SAPEN (1955), 31-33.

4424   Sampson, Anthony.   "The Discovery of Africa." Nation (New York), 188
       (1959), 279-80.

4425   Sands, R.   "The South African Novel: Some Observations." ESA, 13 (1970),
       89-104.

4426   Sinclair, F. D.   "On the Spirit of South Africa." Trek, 13, no. 5 (1949),
       26-27.

4427   Skaife, Sydney Harold.   "Censorship of Books in South Africa." SAPEN,
       (1955), 88-91.

4428   Snyman, J. P. L.   "Aard van die Engelse romans uit Suid Afrika." Huis,
       40 (1956), 26-27.

4429   Sowden, Lewis.   "On Writing About South Africa." SAPEN, (1955), 13-17.

4430   _____   "South African Writers Abroad." Trek, 14, no. 9 (1950), 4-6.

4431   Speight, W. L.   "South African Poetry." ERM, 57 (1933), 39-44.

4432   Staniland, Martin.   "Apartheid and the Novel." NewA, 4, no. 1 (1965),
       15-17.

4433   Thompson, W. R.   "South African Poetry." CapeMM, 4 (1858), 342-55.

4434   Thomson, E. M.   A South African Literary Reader. Cape Town: Juta, 1926.

4435   Titlestad, R. M.   "Engelse Poezie in Z. Afrika." Nederlandse Post, 6,
       no. 7 (1952), 9.

4436   _____   "Engelse Proza in Z. Afrika." Nederlandse Post, 6, no. 8 (1952),
       9-10.

4437   Tucker, Martin.   "Color and Guilt." AT, 12, no. 2 (1965), 13-14.

4438   Van Zyl, T. A.   "Drama in South Africa." BAALE, 2 (1965), 25.

4439   W.   "Recent South African Verse." SAfB, 4 (1911), 207-14.

4440   Wale, Laurie.   "War Has Revealed Several South African Soldier Poets."
       Outspan, 37, no. 961 (1945), 13-15.

4441   Walker, Oliver.   "Post-War Boom in South African Literature." SAPEN,
       (1954), 5-10.

4442   Wallis, J. P. R.   "A Literature in the Making." Times, 31 May 1935,
       p. 25.

4443   Webster, Mary Morison.   "Trends in South African Literature." Forum
       (Johannesburg), 3, no. 6 (1954), 18-19.

4444   Woodrow, M.   "South African Drama in English." ESA, 13 (1970), 391-410.

4445   Worsfold, W. B.   "South African Literature." In South Africa: A Study
       in Colonial Administration and Development. London: Methuen, 1895,
       186-202.

4446   Wright, David.   "South African Poetry." Poetry, 95 (1960), 244-47.

4447   Ziervogel, D.   "Bantu Literature, Writers and Poets." Bantu, 13 (1966),
       384-86.

See also: 91, 249, 295, 306, 6537-6550.

Individual Authors

ABRAHAMS, Peter

4448 Abrahams, Peter. "Letter to My Mother: Author of Wild Conquest Explains His Motives." AfrD, 1 (1951), 24.

4449 _____ Return to Goli. London: Faber, 1953.

4450 _____ Tell Freedom. London: Faber, 1954.

4451 Cartey, Wilfred. "Introduction" to Peter Abrahams, Tell Freedom. New York: Collier-Macmillan, 1970, pp. vii-xiv.

4452 Echeruo, M. J. C. "Peter Abrahams and the Novel of Politics: An Aspect of A Wreath for Udomo." AfrWr, 1 (1962), 16-18.

4453 Gecau, James. "The Various Levels of Betrayal in A Wreath for Udomo." Busara, 2, no. 1 (1969), 4-10.

4454 Gérard, Albert. "Peter Abrahams et la littérature sud-africaine." RevN, 45 (1967), 651-54.

4455 _____ "Le roman neo-africaine: Peter Abrahams." RevN, 28 (1963), 374-81.

4456 Gray, Alan. "The Work of Peter Abrahams." AfrW, 17 (1952), 17.

4457 Holm, Ivar. "Peter Abrahams: Om motiver og modeller i hans författerskap." Vinduet, 15 (1961), 298-306.

4458 Lewis, Primila. "Politics and the Novel: An Appreciation of A Wreath for Udomo and This Island Now by Peter Abrahams." Zuka, 2 (1968), 41-47.

4459 Maes-Jelinek, Hena. "Race Relationship and Identity in Peter Abrahams' 'Pluralia.'" ES, 50 (1969), 106-12.

4460 McDowell, Robert E. "Plus ça change, plus c'est la même chose: The Shifting Geography of Peter Abrahams." New Campus Review, 1, no. 4 (1968), 41-47.

4461 Taylor, Dora. "Peter Abrahams: A Study of a Dark Testament." Trek, 7, no. 18 (1943), 144.

4462 Wade, Michael. "The Novels of Peter Abrahams." Critique (Minneapolis), 11, no. 1 (1969), 82-95.

4463 Wästberg, Per. "Segrarens Krans: Bakgrunden til en roman av Peter Abrahams." BLM, 32 (1963), 311-17.

See also: 333, 6099.

ADAMS, Perseus

4464 Anon. "[Perseus Adams]." Contrast, 1, no. 3 (1961), 96.

4465 _____ "[Perseus Adams]." New Nation, June 1968, p. 13.

4466 Eglington, Charles. "South African Poets." JAf, 21, no. 2 (1966), 33-34.

BECKER, Jillian

4467 Abrahams, Lionel. "The Keep." Classic, 2, no. 2 (1970), 72-73.

BLOOM, Harry

4468 Hendricks, D. "Riot and Reality." PRen, 2 (1957), 34-38.

4469 Valensin, Charlyne. "Transvaal Episode." PA, 49 (1964), 271-72.

BOSMAN, Herman Charles

4470 Abrahams, Lionel, ed. Bosman at His Best: A Selection. Cape Town:
      Human & Rousseau, 1965.

4471 ____ "A Note on the Poetry of Herman Charles Bosman." Standpunte, 12,
      no. 3 (1958), 74-76.

4472 Sachs, B. "Profiles." Trek, 15, no. 11 (1951), 5-7.

4473 Sachs, J. "Short Stories of Gordimer, Lessing and Bosman." Trek, 15,
      no. 11 (1951), 15-16.

4474 Snyman, J. P. L. "South African Writers: 7. Herman Charles Bosman."
      Femina, 29 Aug. 1963, p. 51.

4475 Stopforth, L. M. D. "Herman Charles Bosman: An Evaluation." UCWCA, 1
      (1964), 1-37.

4476 Wright, David. "A South African Zoschenko." LMag, n. s. 3, no. 4 (1963),
      78-82.

BRUTUS, Dennis

4477 Abasiekong, Daniel. "Poetry Pure and Applied: Rabearivelo and Brutus."
      Transition, 23 (1965), 45-48.

4478 Pieterse, Cosmo. "Interview: Dennis Brutus Talks About His Poetry."
      CulEA, 26, supp. (1967), i-iii.

4479 Povey, John F. "Simply to Stand." JNALA, 3 (1967), 95-100.

BUTLER, Guy

4480 Anon. "[Guy Butler]." Contrast, 1, no. 4 (1961), 96.

4481 Snyman, J. P. L. "South African Writers: 22. Guy Butler." Femina,
      26 March 1964, p. 51.

CAMPBELL, Roy

4482 Abrahams, Lionel. "Roy Campbell: Conquistador-Refugee." Theoria, 8
      (1956), 46-65.

4483 Anon. Hommage à Roy Campbell. Montpellier: 'La Licorne,' 1958.

4484 ____ "The Poetry of Statement." TLS, 24 March 1950, p. 184.

4485 Bergonzi, Bernard. "Roy Campbell--Outsider on the Right." JCH, 2
      (1967), 133-47.

4486 Bonnerot, Louis. "Roy Campbell; un poète pecheur d'images." RAA, 10
      (1933), 43-48.

4487 Campbell, Roy. Broken Record. London: Bodley Head, 1934.

4488 ____ Light on a Dark Horse. London: Hollis & Carter, 1951.

4489 Collins, Harold R. "Roy Campbell: The Talking Bronco." BUSE, 4 (1960),
      49-63.

4490 Davis, E. The "Spoilt Boy in Roy Campbell." Trek, 15, no. 3 (1951),
      12-14.

4491 Delius, Anthony. "Slater and Campbell." Standpunte, 9, no. 3 (1954), 64-70.

4492 Durrant, Geoffrey. "Poems of Roy Campbell." Standpunte, 14, no. 1 (1960),
      65-70.

4493 Eglington, Charles. "Roy Campbell's Manuscripts." Outspan, 59, no. 1576
      (1957), 25.

4494 Eyre, C. J. "Roy Campbell Exhibition." SALi, 22 (1954), 35-36.

4495 Gardner, W. H. "Poetry and Actuality." Theoria, 3 (1950), 19-31.

4496 ____ "Voltage of Delight: An Appraisal of Roy Campbell." Month, 19
      (1958), 5-17, 133-47.

4497 Gillett, Eric. "Two Poets: Campbell and Auden." NatER, 135 (1950),
      136-40.

4498 Girling, H. K. "Roy Campbell." Forum (Johannesburg), 6, no. 2 (1957),
      45-46.

4499 Gray, Alan. "Genius of Roy Campbell." AfrW, March 1952, p. 14.

4500 Grobler, P. du P. "Campbell en Van Wyk Louw." Standpunte, 9, no. 5
      (1955), 73-76.

4501 Guibert, Armand. "Roy Campbell, poète solaire." JdP, 5 (1957), 4.

4502 ____ "Roy Campbell (1901-1957)." Preuves, 98 (1959), 28-31.

4503 Hamm, Victor M. "Roy Campbell: Satirist." Thought (New York), 37 (1962),
      194-210.

4504 Harvey, C. J. D. "The Poetry of Roy Campbell." Standpunte, 5, no. 1
      (1950), 53-59.

4505 ____ "Roy Campbell and 'Les Fleurs du Mal.'" Ons Eie Boek, 20 (1954),
      117-18.

4506 Holt, B. "Roy Campbell's Early Years." AfrN, 17 (1967), 268-77.

4507 John, Augustus. "Candid Impressions - 3. The Flaming Terrapin: Roy
      Campbell, Poet from South Africa." Times, 12 Oct. 1958, p. 23.

4508 Joost, Nicholas. "From Authentic Artists." Renascence, 10 (1958), 137-43.

4509 ____ "The Poetry of Roy Campbell." Renascence, 8 (1956), 115-20.

4510 Jurgens, Heather L. "Behind the Poetry of Roy Campbell." Lantern, 14,
      no. 4 (1965), 26-35.

4511 Kirk, Russell. "The Last of the Scalds." SR, 114 (1956), 164-70.

4512 Krige, Uys. "Eerste outmoeting met Roy Campbell." Die Nieuwe Stem, 16
      (1960), 606-13. [Eng. version, "First Meeting with Roy Campbell."
      Theoria, 12 (1959), 24-28.]

4513 ____ "The Poetry of Roy Campbell: A Few Aspects." In Poems of Roy
      Campbell. Cape Town: Miller, 1960, pp. 1-32.

4514 ____ "Profiles." Trek, 15, no. 10 (1951), 3-5.

4515 ____ "Roy Campbell as Lyrical Poet: Some Quieter Aspects." ESA, 1
      (1958), 81-94.

4516 Lucas, F. L. Authors Dead and Living. London: Chatto & Windus, 1926,
       pp. 217-21.

4517 Monro, H. "[Review of Adamastor]." New Criterion, 10 (1931), 349-53.

4518 Newbolt, Sir Henry. New Paths on Helicon. London: Nelson, 1928,
       pp. 410-41.

4519 Opperman, D. J. "Roy Campbell en die South African Poesie." Standpunte,
       8, no. 2 (1954), 4-15.

4520 Paton, Alan. "Roy Campbell: Poet and Man." Theoria, 9 (1957), 19-31.

4521 Povey, John F. "A Lyre of Savage Thunder: A Study of the Poetry of
       Roy Campbell." WSCL, 7 (1966), 85-102.

4522 Pujals, Esteban. España y la guerra de 1936 en la poesía de Roy Campbell.
       Madrid: Ateneo, 1959.

4523 Rose, Brian. "Roy Campbell: A Tribute." SAPEN, (1956-57), 26-29.

4524 Russell, Peter. "The Poetry of Roy Campbell." Nine, 3 (1950), 81-86.

4525 Scott, Tom. "Impressions of Roy Campbell's Poetry." WR, 14 (1950),
       214-22.

4526 Sergeant, Howard. "Restive Steer: A Study of the Poetry of Roy Campbell."
       E&S, 10 (1957), 105-22.

4527 Seymour-Smith, Martin. "Zero and the Impossible." Encounter, 9, no. 5
       (1957), 3-51.

4528 Sitwell, Edith. "Roy Campbell." Poetry, 92 (1958), 42-48.

4529 Snyman, J. P. L. "South African Writers: 10. Roy Campbell." Femina,
       10 Oct. 1963, p. 117.

4530 Stone, Geoffrey. "Roy Campbell: Romantic Paradox." American Review,
       8 (1936), 164-76.

4531 Van Den Bergh, Tony. "Roy Campbell: Flaming Toreador." PoetryR, 48
       (1957), 135-38.

4532 Walker, Oliver. "Footnote to Voorslag." Trek, 7, no. 13-14 (1942-43), 8.

4533 Watkin-Jones, A. "South African Bard and English Reviewers." Critic (Cape
       Town), 1, no. 3 (1933), 133-45.

4534 Wright, David. Roy Campbell. London and New York: Longmans, Green, 1961.

See also: 4715, 6551.

CLOETE, Stuart

4535 Anon. "Krisis van ons naaste buurman: [S. Rhodesie]." Huis, 42, no. 2168
       (1963), 14-15.

4536 Brewster, Paul G. "An Unacknowledged Borrowing in Stuart Cloete's
       The Mask." RLMC, 12 (1959), 206-10.

4537 Hartman, W. "Stuart Cloete--sy Hart sit tog Reg." Huis, 42, no. 2157
       (1963), 14-17.

4538 Sherman, Adele. "Profiles 3. Stuart Cloete." Trek, 11, no. 14 (1947), 15.

4539 Shilton, M. "Wheels Turn Again . . . Stuart Cloete." Spotlight, June
       1958, pp. 17-18.

4540 Snyman, J. P. L. "South African Writers: 6. Stuart Cloete." Femina,
       15 Aug. 1963, p. 50.

4541 Trichardt, C. "My volgende boek sal weer verban word." Brandwag, 26
       (1955), 25-26.

CLOUTS, Sydney

4542 Anon. "[Sydney Clouts]." Contrast, 1, no. 2 (1961), 94.

4543 Davis, E. "The Poetry of Sydney Clouts." JAf, 22, no. 1 (1967), 38-39.

4544 Delius, Anthony. "The Secret of the Man in Klapmuts." Contrast, 4, no. 2 (1966), 89-95.

COPE, Jack

4545 Anon. "[Jack Cope]." Contrast, 1, no. 2 (1961), 94.

4546 Paton, Alan. "A Growth of the Soil." Contrast, 5, no. 1 (1970), 89-90.

4547 Snyman, J. P. L. "South African Writers: 23. Jack Cope." Femina, 9 April 1964, p. 49.

CURREY, R. N.

4548 Anon. "[R. N. Currey]." Contrast, 1, no. 1 (1960), 97.

DELIUS, Anthony

4549 Anon. "[Anthony Delius]." Contrast, 1, no. 1 (1960), 96.

4550 Durrant, Geoffrey. "Delius as a Poet." Standpunte, 9, no. 5 (1955), 66-69.

4551 Harvey, C. J. D. "Corner of the World [by] Anthony Delius." Standpunte, 16, no. 4 (1963), 35-37.

4552 K., N. "Twee Dramas van Blywende betekenis: The Fall [deur Anthony Delius] en Nie vir Geleerdes [deur N. P. Van Wyk Louw]." Taalgenoot, 29, no. 10 (1960), 16-17.

4553 Ryling, R. F. ". . . Fall from Grace." JAf, 15, no. 9 (1960), 35-37.

4554 Snyman, J. P. L. "South African Writers: 21. Anthony Delius." Femina, 12 March 1964, p. 61.

4555 Van Rensburg, F. I. J. "Twee Feesstukke: Nie vir Geleerdes [deur Van Wyk Louw] en The Fall [deur Anthony Delius]." Standpunte, 13, no. 5 (1960), 52-66.

DREYER, Peter

4556 Anon. "[Peter Dreyer]." SAO, 94 (1964), 191.

EGLINGTON, Charles

4557 Anon. "[Charles Eglington]." Contrast, 1, no. 4 (1961), 96.

4558 ____ "Charles Eglington." Personality, 5 April 1962, p. 43.

FAIRBRIDGE, Kingsley

4559 Fairbridge, Kingsley. The Autobiography of Kingsley Fairbridge. Oxford: Oxford Univ. Press, 1928.

4560 Lorimer, E. K. "Kingsley Ogilivie Fairbridge." Looking Back, 3, no. 2 (1963), 8-10.

FUGARD, Athol

4561 Green, Robert J. "Athol Fugard's Hello and Goodbye." MD, 13 (1970),
      139-55.

4562 Nkosi, Lewis. "Athol Fugard: His Work and Us." SAIA, 63 (1968), 1-8.

4563 Woodward, A. G. "South African Writing [and] a New Play." Contrast,
      2, no. 1 (1962), 45-50.

See also: 4319.

GORDIMER, Nadine

4564 Abrahams, Lionel. "Nadine Gordimer: The Transparent Ego." ESA, 3 (1960),
      146-51.

4565 Abramowitz, A. "Nadine Gordimer and the Impertinent Reader." PRen, 1
      (1956), 13-17.

4566 Anon. "[Nadine Gordimer]." Femina, 23 Nov. 1961, pp. 19-21.

4567 _____ "[Nadine Gordimer]." Contrast, 1, no. 1 (1960), 96.

4568 Burrows, Edwin G. "An Interview with Nadine Gordimer." MQR, 9 (1970),
      231-34.

4569 Callan, Edward. "The Art of Nadine Gordimer and Alan Paton." ESA, 13
      (1970), 291-92.

4570 De Beer, Mona. "Nadine Writes from a Position of Involvement." Times,
      9 April 1969, p. 7.

4571 Delius, Anthony. "Next Installment." Standpunte, 8, no. 3 (1954), 66-74.

4572 Gardner, W. H. "Moral Somnambulism: A Study in the Art of the Short
      Story." Month, 30 (1957), 160-69.

4573 Gordimer, Nadine. "Leaving School--II." LMag, n. s. 3, no. 2 (1963),
      58-65.

4574 _____ "Nadine Gordimer Talks to Andrew Salkey." Listener, 82 (1969),
      184-85.

4575 Gullason, Thomas H. "The Short Story: An Underrated Art." SSF, 2, no. 1
      (1964), 13-31.

4576 MacDonald, T. "Miss Gordimer . . . ." Spotlight, Jan. 1954, pp. 24-25.

4577 McGuiness, Frank. "The Novels of Nadine Gordimer." LMag, 5, no. 3
      (1965), 97-102.

4578 Nell, Racilia Jilian. Nadine Gordimer: Novelist and Short Story Writer:
      A Bibliography of Her Works and Selected Literary Criticism.
      Johannesburg: Univ. of the Witwatersrand, 1964.

4579 Nkosi, Lewis. "Les grandes dames." NewA, 7 (1965), 163.

4580 Rabkin, L. "The Art of Nadine Gordimer." Forum (Johannesburg), 2, no. 8
      (1953), 40-42.

4581 Ross, Alan. "A Writer in South Africa: Nadine Gordimer." LMag, 5, no. 2
      (1965), 21-28. [Interview.]

4582 Sachs, J. "Short Stories of Gordimer, Bosman and Lessing." Trek, 15,
      no. 11 (1951), 15-16.

4583 Scott, Catherine. "Nadine Gordimer." Guardian (Manchester), 30 May
      1969, p. 9.

4584 Snyman, J. P. L. "South African Writers: 3. Nadine Gordimer." Femina,
      4 July 1963, p. 61.

4585 Woodward, A. G. "Nadine Gordimer." Theoria, 16 (1961), 1-12.

See also: 249, 4319, 6552, 6557.

JACOBSON, Dan

4586 Abrahams, Lionel. "The Beginners." Classic, 2, no. 2 (1970), 77-80.

4587 Anon. "[Dan Jacobson]." Contrast, 1, no. 2 (1961), 96.

4588 ____ "Dan Jacobson's New Novel." JAf, 21, no. 8 (1966), 113-17.

4589 Decter, Midge. "Novelist of South Africa." Commentary, 25 (1958),
       539-44. [Repr. in The Liberated Woman and Other Essays. New York:
       Coward McCann, 1971.]

4590 Gard, Roger. "Dan Jacobson." Delta (Cambridge), 30 (1963), 29-33.

4591 Girling, H. K. "Compassion and Detachment in the Novels of Dan Jacobson."
       PRen, 2 (1957), 16-23.

4592 Jacobson, Dan. "Boyhood in Kimberley." In item 306, pp. 85-91.

4593 ____ "The Secret of the English." TLS, 30 Aug. 1971, p. 884.

4594 Lightfoot, Martin. "Dan Jacobson." Delta (Cambridge), 36 (1965), 31.

4595 Mindlin, Meir. "Talk with Dan Jacobson." JAf, 14, no. 8 (1959), 22-24.

4596 Ricks, Christopher. "One Little Liberal: The Beginners by Dan Jacobson."
       New Statesman, 71 (1966), 812.

4597 Snyman, J. P. L. "South African Writers: 15. Dan Jacobson." Femina,
       19 Dec. 1963, p. 41.

4598 Winegarten, Renee. "The Novels of Dan Jacobson." Midstream, 12 (1966),
       69-73.

4599 Yudelman, Myra. Dan Jacobson: A Bibliography. Johannesburg: Univ. of
       the Witwatersrand, Dept. of Bibliography, Librarianship & Typography,
       1967.

See also: 6557.

JONKER, Ingrid

4600 Anon. "[Ingrid Jonker]." SAO, 95 (1965), 147.

4601 ____ "[Ingrid Jonker]." Drum, 146 (1963), 49-51.

4602 Bouwer, S. "Ingrid Jonker." Wurm, 2 (1966), 12-15.

4603 Fugard, Athol. "Letter." Classic, 2, no. 1 (1966), 78-80.

4604 Naudé, Adele. "Ingrid Jonker in Translation." Contrast, 5, no. 3
       (1969), 93-94.

KRIGE, Uys

4605 Anon. "Uys Krige: die eensame skeppende . . . ." Brandwag, 24 (1960),
       10-13.

4606 ____ "[Uys Krige]." Brandwag, 26 (1961), 53.

4607 ____ "[Uys Krige]." Contrast, 1, no. 1 (1960), 97.

4608 Antonissen, R. "Klein bout Patroon van verse 1961." Standpunte, 15,
       no. 2-3 (1961-62), 56-67.

4609 ____ "Last-oes van Vyftig." Standpunte, 14, no. 2 (1960), 61-71.

4610 ____ "Nuwe dramas van Uys Krige." Helikon, 2, no. 7 (1952), 55-61.

4611 ____ "Uiterstles." Standpunte, 16, no. 5 (1963), 16-22.

4612 ____ "Wit muur en ander eenbedrywe [deur] Uys Krige." Ons Eie Boek, 19, no. 3 (1953), 154-55.

4613 Aucamp, H. "Voorgeskrewe werk: Sout van die aarde deur Uys Krige." Kriterium, 3, no. 2 (1965), 45-48.

4614 Burgers, M. P. O. "Goue Kring [deur] Uys Krige." Huis, 40, no. 1821 (1957), 11.

4615 De Villiers, M. "Akademie prys vir vertaalde werke: ofdeling poesie, 1951." T. Wetenskap Kuns, 12, no. 1 (1952), 5-9.

4616 Eglington, Charles. "Uys Krige." JAf, 14, no. 7 (1959), 32-34.

4617 Jurgens, M. L. "Voorgeskrewe boeke: sol y sombra Uys Krige." Huis, 41, no. 1855 (1957), 18-19.

4618 Kannemeyer, J. C. "Goue Kring: van legende tot drama." Kriterium, 3, no. 3 (1965), 1-9.

4619 Nienaber, C. J. M. "Bespreking van 'Woord en masker.' Alle paaie gaan na Rome." Klasgids, 2, no. 4 (1967), 13-15.

4620 O., F. M. P. "Uys Krige als Vertaler." Nederlandse Post, 5, no. 1 (1951), 15-16.

4621 Prins, M. J. "Sout va die aarde." Klasgids, 3, no. 3 (1968), 18-22.

4622 Snyman, J. P. L. "South African Writers: 9. Uys Krige." Femina, 26 Sept. 1963, p. 97.

4623 Swart, J. K. "Sol Y Sombra deur Uys Krige." Ons Eie Boek, 18, no. 1 (1952), 40-42.

4624 Van Bruggen, J. R. L. "Romantikus onder ons digters Uys Krige." Helikon (Johannesburg), 2, no. 10-11 (1953), n. pag.

4625 Van Heyningen, Christina, and Jacques Bertoud. Uys Krige. New York: Twayne, 1966.

4626 Verhage, J. A. "Los Gebruik van die woord 'ironie.'" Standpunte, 9, no. 6 (1955), 63-66.

LA GUMA, Alex

4627 July, Robert. "The African Personality in the African Novel." In item 91, pp. 218-33.

4628 Lindfors, Bernth. "Form and Technique in the Novels of Richard Rive and Alex La Guma." JNALA, 2 (1966), 10-15.

4629 Nkosi, Lewis. "Alex La Guma: The Man and His Work." SAIA, 59 (1968), 1-8.

LESSING, Doris

4630 Anon. "The Fog of War." TLS, 27 April 1962, p. 280.

4631 Barker, Paul. "Doris Lessing: The Uses of Repetition." New Society, 5 (1965), 27-28.

4632 Brewer, Joseph E. "The Anti-Hero in Contemporary Literature." IEY, 12 (1967), 55-60.

4633   Brewster, Dorothy. Doris Lessing. New York: Twayne, 1965.

4634   Burkom, Selma R. "A Doris Lessing Checklist." Critique (Minneapolis),
       11, no. 1 (1969), 69-81.

4635   ____   "Only Connect: Form and Content in the Works of Doris Lessing."
       Critique (Minneapolis), 11, no. 1 (1969), 51-68.

4636   Gindin, James B. Postwar British Fiction. London: Cambridge Univ.
       Press, 1963, pp. 65-86.

4637   Graustein, Gottfried. "Entwicklungs tendenzen im Schaffen Doris
       Lessings." WZUL, 12 (1963), 529-33.

4638   Hartwig, Dorothea. "Die Widerspiegelung afrikanischer Probleme in Werk
       Doris Lessings." WZUR, 12 (1963), 87-104.

4639   Ipp, C. Doris Lessing: A Bibliography. Johannesburg: Univ. of the
       Witwatersrand, 1967.

4640   Klein, Marcus. "[Review of The Habit of Loving]." HudR, 11 (1958-59),
       620-23.

4641   Kramer, Stanley. "Doris Lessing's Black Notebook." New Leader, 25 Oct.
       1965, pp. 21-22.

4642   McDowell, Frederick P. W. "The Fiction of Doris Lessing: An Interim
       View." ArQ, 21 (1965), 315-45.

4643   Millar, Gavin. "End as a Seer--Doris Lessing's New Novel." Listener,
       82 (1969), 21-22.

4644   Newquist, Roy. "Interview with Doris Lessing." In Counterpoint. New
       York, Chicago, and San Francisco: Rand McNally, 1964, pp. 413-24.

4645   Raban, Jonathan. "Mrs. Lessing's Diary." LMag, 9, no. 6 (1969), 111-15.

4646   Taubman, Robert. "Free Women." New Statesman, 63 (1962), 569.

4647   ____   "Near Zero." New Statesman, 66 (1963), 653-54.

4648   Thorpe, Michael. "Real and Ideal Cities." JCL, 9 (1970), 119-22.

4649   White, Ellington. "[Review of The Golden Notebook]." KR, 24 (1962),
       750-52.

4650   Wiseman, Thomas. "Mrs. Lessing's Kind of Life." Time and Tide, 43
       (1962), 26.

4651   Worsley, T. S. "The Do-Gooders." New Statesman, 55 (1958), 405.

See also: 4582, 6553-6556.

MATSHIKIZA, Todd

4652   Cassirer, Reinhardt, et al. "Todd Matshikiza." Classic, 3, no. 1 (1968),
       5-11.

MILLIN, Sarah Gertrude   .

4653   Bernstein, Edgar. "Sarah Gertrude Millin; the Writer and the Jewess."
       JAf, 23, no. 7 (1968), 14-18.

4654   ____   "Sarah Gertrude Millin: Trail-Blazer of South African Realism."
       SAPEN, (1955), 101-05.

4655   Buchanan-Gould, Vera. "Sarah Gertrude Millin; South Africa's Most
       Prolific Author." Outspan, 50, no. 1306 (1952), 47-49.

4656   Cipolla, E. "Last Years--A Personal Impression and a Valedictory."
       Lantern, 18, no. 2 (1968), 49-55.

4657   Sachs, B. South African Personalities and Places. Johannesburg: Kayor,
       1959.

4658   Snyman, J. P. L. "South African Writers: 1. Sarah Gertrude Millin."
       Femina, 6 June 1963, p. 46.

4659   ____ The Works of Sarah Gertrude Millin. Johannesburg: Central New
       Agency, 1955.

4660   Taylor, Dora. "Sarah Gertrude Millin, South African Realist." Trek,
       7, no. 23 (1943), 14; 7, no. 24 (1943), 12; 7, no. 25 (1943), 12.

4661   Wren, R. M. "A Talk with Sarah Gertrude Millin." Contrast, 5 (1969),
       65-67.

MILLER, Ruth

4662   Anon. "[Ruth Miller]." Contrast, 1 (1960), 96.

4663   Abrahams, Lionel. "Terrible to the Cage: A Tribute to Ruth Miller."
       JAf, 24, no. 6 (1969), 14-16.

4664   Eglington, Charles. "Homage to Ruth Miller." Contrast, 6, no. 2 (1969),
       39-53.

4665   ____ "Ruth Miller: A South African Poet." JAf, 15, no. 11 (1960), 27-31.

4666   ____ "Ruth Miller: A South African Poet." JAf, 20, no. 12 (1965), 32-35.

MPHAHLELE, Ezekiel

4667   Cartey, Wilfred. "The Realities of Four Negro Writers." CUF, 9, no. 3
       (1966), 34-42.

4668   Moore, Gerald. "Ezekiel Mphahlele: The Urban Outcast." In item 217,
       pp. 92-102.

4669   Mphahlele, Ezekiel. A Guide to Creative Writing: A Short Guide to Short
       Story and Novel Writing. Nairobi: East African Literary Bureau, 1966.

4670   Pieterse, Cosmo. "Ezekiel Mphahlele Interviewed." CulEA, 45 (1968),
       i-iv.

4671   Themba, D. C. "'Zeke': Past Bachelor of Arts." Drum, 79 (1957), 31-33.

4672   Wake, Clive H. "The Political and Cultural Revolution: . . . Ezekiel
       Mphahlele and Others." In item 249, pp. 43-55.

See also: 4723.

NAUDE, Adele

4673   Anon. "[Adele Naudé]." Contrast, 1, no. 1 (1960), 96.

4674   Eglington, Charles. "South African Poets." JAf, 21, no. 2 (1966), 33-34.

PATON, Alan

4675   Anon. "[Alan Paton]." Contrast, 1, no. 4 (1961), 96.

4676   ____ "Alan Paton Now Works on the 'Beloved Land.'" Spotlight, Aug.
       1953, pp. 36-37.

4677 ____ "First a Civil Servant--Now a Well-known Author." Public Servant, 29, no. 3 (1949), 9.

4678 Baker, Sheridan, ed. Paton's 'Cry The Beloved Country': The Novel, the Critics, the Setting. New York: Scribner's, 1968.

4679 ____ "Paton's Beloved Country and the Morality of Geography." CE, 19 (1957), 56-61.

4680 ____ "Paton's Late Phalarope." ESA, 2 (1960), 152-59.

4681 Barkham, Margot. "South Africa's First Novel Is a Best-Seller." Outspan, 43 no. 1103 (1948), 31.

4682 Brett, Harvey. The Writer Observed. New York: World, 1956.

4683 Brownsword, W. 'Cry the Beloved Country': Study Guide. New York: Scribner's, 1968.

4684 Bruell, Edwin. "Keen Scalpel on Racial Ills." EJ, 53 (1964), 658-61.

4685 Callan, Edward. Alan Paton. New York: Twayne, 1968.

4686 ____ "Alan Paton and the Liberal Party." In Alan Paton, The Long View. New York: Frederick A. Praeger, 1968, pp. 3-44.

4687 Davies, Horton. "Alan Paton: Literary Artist and Anglican." HibJ, 1 (1952), 262-68.

4688 ____ A Mirror for the Ministry in Modern Novels. New York: Oxford Univ. Press, 1959.

4689 ____ "Paton of 'the Beloved Country.'" Outspan, 50, no. 1285 (1951), 43-45.

4690 Delius, Anthony. "Next Installment." Standpunte, 8, no. 3 (1954), 66-74.

4691 Driver, Jonty. "Alan Paton's Hofmeyr." Race, 4 (1965), 269-80.

4692 Fuller, Edmund. "Alan Paton: Tragedy and Beyond." In Books with the Man Behind Them. New York: Random House, 1962, pp. 83-101.

4693 Gailey, Harry A. "Sheridan Baker's 'Paton's Beloved Country.'" CE, 20 (1958), 143-44.

4694 Gardiner, Harold. In All Conscience: Reflections on Books and Culture. New York: Hanover House, 1959.

4695 Gassner, John. Theatre at the Crossroads. New York: Holt, 1960, pp. 177-80. [Discusses R. L. Libbott's dramatisation of Cry the Beloved Country.]

4696 Howard, Helen. "Paton the Person." Personality, 18 Jan. 1968, pp. 85-87.

4697 Huddleston, Trevor. Naught for Your Comfort. New York: Doubleday, 1956.

4698 Huxley, Elspeth. "A Human Document: Review of Cry the Beloved Country by Alan Paton." NatR, 132 (1949), 449-553.

4699 Marcus, Fred H. "Cry the Beloved Country and Strange Fruit: Exploring Man's Inhumanity to Man." EJ, 51 (1962), 609-16.

4700 Nienaber, C. J. M. "Literere oorskatting van Cry the Beloved Country, [vergelyking met Swart Pilgrim deur F. A. Venter]." Standpunte, 10, no. 2 (1955), 14-17.

4701 Paton, Alan. "Hofmeyr Biography." Contrast, 3, no. 2 (1964), 32-36.

4702 ____ "Story of Cry the Beloved Country." SAfP, 1, no. 5 (1951), 2-3.

4703 Prescott, Orville. In My Opinion: An Inquiry Into the Contemporary Novel. New York: Bobbs-Merrill, 1952, pp. 240-43.

4704 Rooney, F. Charles. "The 'Message' of Alan Paton." CathW, 194 (1961), 92-98.

4705 Snyman, J. P. L. "South African Writers: 14. Alan Paton." _Femina_, 5
      Dec. 1963, p. 87.

4706 Woodward, A. G. "Biographie engagée." _Contrast_, 3, no. 3 (1967), 91-94.

4707 Worsley, T. C. "A Modern Morality." _New Statesman and Nation_, 47
      (1964), 159.

See also: 249, 4319, 4569, 6557-6560.

PLOMER, William

4708 Anon. "Life in Two Parts." _TLS_, 5 Oct. 1951, p. 628.

4709 Campbell, Roy. "The Significance of _Turbott Wolfe_." _Voorslag_, 1 (1926),
      39-45.

4710 Doyle, John R. "The Poetry of William Plomer." _SR_, 75 (1967), 634-61.

4711 ____ _William Plomer_. New York: Twayne, 1969.

4712 Eccles, A. F. "William Plomer." _UNISA_, 21 (1967), 35-37.

4713 Gordimer, Nadine. "A Wilder Fowl: _Turbott Wolfe_ by William Plomer."
      LMag, 5, no. 3 (1965), 268-78.

4714 Plomer, William. _Double Lives: An Autobiography_. London: Cape, 1943.

4715 ____ "_Voorslag_ Days." _LMag_, 6, no. 7 (1959), 46-52.

4716 Snyman, J. P. L. "South African Writers: 25. William Plomer." _Femina_,
      21 May 1964, p. 50.

4717 Taylor, Dora. "Prelude to Plomer." _Trek_, 8, no. 1 (1943), 12; no. 2,
      12; no. 3, 8.

4718 Van Der Post, Laurens. "The _Turbott Wolfe_ Affair." _Cornhill_, 1043
      (1965), 297-321. [Also in _Turbott Wolfe_. London: Hogarth, 1965, pp.
      9-55.]

See also: 249.

PRINCE, F. T.

4719 Inglis, Fred. "F. T. Prince and the Prospects for Poetry." _UDQ_, 1,
      no. 3 (1966), 23-44.

4720 Strickland, Geoffrey. "The Poetry of F. T. Prince." _Delta_ (Cambridge),
      39 (1964), 36-39.

RIVE, Richard

4721 Anon. "[Richard Rive]." _Contrast_, 1, no. 1 (1960), 96.

4722 ____ "South African Writer Opens 1965-66 Lecture Series." _ASACN_, 8,
      no. 1 (1966), 5-6.

4723 Nkosi, Lewis. "Fiction by Black South Africans." In item 91, pp. 211-17.

SCHREINER, Olive

4724 Anon. "Hulle het Olive Schreiner geken." _Sarie Marais_, 6, no. 35 (1955),
      33.

4725 ____ "In the Footsteps of Olive Schreiner." _Veldtrust_, 11 (1961), n. pag.

4726 Ballinger, Margaret. "Olive Schreiner and the Causes for which She Stood." SAPEN, (1955), 119-21.

4727 Beeton, D. R. "'African Farm.'" Lantern, 16, no. 4 (1967), 81-85.

4728 ____ "Olive Schreiner and Realism." Trek, 12, no. 8 (1948), 28-29.

4729 ____ "Short Life of Olive Schreiner." Lantern, 16, no. 4 (1967), 74-80.

4730 Bouwer, A. "Vir vrede en die vrou het Olive Schreiner geveg." Sarie Marais, 6, no. 35 (1955), 32.

4731 Bradlow, E. "Olive Schreiner." JAf, 22, no. 10 (1967), 45-47.

4732 Buchanan-Gould, Vera. "Few People in South Africa Realize the True Greatness of Olive Schreiner." Outspan, 44, no. 1136 (1948), 21-23.

4733 Campbell, D. C. "Daughter of the Karoo." Femina, 9 May 1963, pp. 93-94.

4734 Colby, Vineta. "The Imperative Impulse: Olive Schreiner." In The Singular Anomaly. New York: New York Univ. Press, 1970, pp. 47-109.

4735 Cronwight-Schreiner, S. C. The Life of Olive Schreiner. London: T. Fisher Unwin, 1924.

4736 Delarey, N. "Is dit S. Afr. se grootste liefdestragedie [die van Olive Schreiner en Havelock Ellis]." Rooi Rose, 21, no. 7 (1964), 9.

4737 Dyer, M. "Olive Schreiner's Liberalism." Reality, 2, no. 5 (1970), 18-22.

4738 Evans, Bergen. "Introduction" to Olive Schreiner, The Story of An African Farm. Greenwich, Conn.: Fawcett, 1960, pp. vii-x.

4739 Findlay, George. "Family Reminiscences of Olive Schreiner." SAPEN, (1955), 116-18.

4740 Friedlander, Zelda. "Olive Schreiner at De Aar." LMag, 7, no. 1 (1967), 75-76.

4741 ____, ed. Until the Heart Changes: A Garland for Olive Schreiner. Cape Town: Tofelberg Uitgewers, 1967.

4742 Friedman, Marion. "Citizen of the World." Forum (Johannesburg), 3, no. 12 (1955), 17-18.

4743 Friedmann, M. V. Olive Schreiner: A Study in Latent Meanings. Cape Town: Witwatersrand Univ. Press, 1955.

4744 Gray, Alan. "The Troubled Mirror: Notes on Olive Schreiner." AfrAff, 54, no. 207 (1955), 300-05.

4745 Gregg, Lyndall. "Memories of Olive Schreiner." Chamber's Journal, 123 (1946), 537-39.

4746 ____ Memories of Olive Schreiner: Life on the Karoo." Chamber's Journal, 125 (1948), 16-18.

4747 ____ Memories of Olive Schreiner. London: W. & R. Chambers, 1957.

4748 ____ "More Memories of Olive Schreiner." Chamber's Journal, 124 (1947), 225-28.

4749 Gregory, R. M. "Olive Schreiner." Bluestocking, 23, no. 1 (1955), 34-38.

4750 Harmel, Michael. Olive Schreiner, 1855-1955. Cape Town: Real Print & Pub. Co., 1955.

4751 Harris, Frank. Contemporary Portraits. London: Richards, 1924.

4752 Heard, Raymond. "Olive Schreiner and Death." ESA, 2 (1959), 110-17.

4753 Herrman, L. "Olive Schreiner, 1855-1920." QBSAL, 9 (1955), 69-72.

4754 ____ "Olive Schreiner." Suid-Afrika, 15, no. 7 (1955), 16-18.

4755   Hobman, D. L. Olive Schreiner, Her Friends and Times. London: Watts, [1955].

4756   ____ [On The Story of a South African Farm]." ContR, 171 (1947), 230-36.

4757   Jeffreys, M. K. "Olive Schreiner: An Assessment." Lantern, 5 (1956), 240-41.

4758   Krige, Uys, ed. Olive Schreiner: A Selection. Cape Town: Oxford Univ. Press, 1968.

4759   Laredo, Ursula. "Olive Schreiner." JCL, 8 (1969), 107-24.

4760   Lessing, Doris. "Afterword" to Olive Schreiner, The Story of an African Farm. Greenwich, Conn.: Fawcett, 1968, pp. 273-90.

4761   Lewin, Julius. "Olive Schreiner--The Cassandra of South Africa." Forum (Johannesburg), 3, no. 12 (1955), 11-13.

4762   Meintjes, Johannes. Olive Schreiner: Portrait of a South African Woman. Johannesburg: Hugh Keartland, 1965.

4763   Nevinson, W. H. The Fire of Life. London: J. Nisbet, 1935.

4764   Partridge, A. C. "Olive Schreiner: The Literary Aspect." SAPEN, (1955), 109-15.

4765   Paton, Alan. "Olive Schreiner, the Forerunner." Forum (Johannesburg), 4, no. 1 (1955), 25-29.

4766   Plomer, William. "Olive Schreiner: Her Life and Ideals." Listener, 53 (1955), 521-22.

4767   Renier, Olive. "A South African Rebel." Listener, 53 (1955), 613-14.

4768   Rochlin, S. A. "Olive Schreiner." AfrN, 11 (1955), 345-52.

4769   Snyman, J. P. L. "South African Writers: 5. Olive Schreiner." Femina, 1 Aug. 1963, p. 79.

4770   Van Rensburg, P. J. J. "Cradock en Olive Schreiner." SAfRHM, (March 1964), 259.

4771   Van Zyl, John. "Rhodes and Olive Schreiner." Contrast, 6, no. 1 (1969), 86-90.

4772   Verster, E. Olive Emilie Albertina Schreiner (1855-1920): Bibliography. Cape Town: Univ. of Cape Town, 1946.

4773   Webster, Mary Morison. "Strange Genius." Forum (Johannesburg), 3, no. 12 (1955), 13-17.

4774   Young, Francis Brett. "South African Literature." London Mercury, 19 (1928), 507-16.

See also: 18, 52, 6561, 6562.

SLATER, F. C.

4775   Anon. "Honour for South African Poet: Dr. Francis Carey Slater." SAO, 78 (1948), 93-95.

4776   Campbell, Roy. "Preface" to The Collected Poems of Francis Carey Slater. London: Blackwood, 1957.

4777   Clark, J. "The Poetry of F. C. Slater." SAfQ, 6, no. 4 (1924), 21-25.

4778   Snyman, J. P. L. "South African Writers: 32. Francis Carey Slater." Femina, 27 Aug. 1964, p. 49.

4779   W., R. "Poetic Banker." JIBSA, 46 (1949), 215-16.

4780   Walker, Oliver. "Literature Honours Banker-Poet." <u>JIBSA</u>, 47 (1950), 297-99.

4781   Webster, Mary Morison. "Francis Carey Slater, A Critical Comment." <u>SAPEN</u>,(1960), 27-29.

See also: 4361.

SMITH, Pauline

4782   Eglington, Charles. "'Quaintness' in Pauline Smith." <u>ESA</u>, 3 (1960), 48-56.

4783   Haresnape, Geoffrey. "A Note about Pauline Smith's Unpublished Essay 'How and Why I Became an Author.'" <u>ESA</u>, 6 (1963), 149-50.

4784   _____ "A Note on Pauline Smith's Presentation of Country Life." <u>ESA</u>, 9 (1966), 83-86.

4785   _____ <u>Pauline Smith</u>. New York: Twayne, 1969.

4786   _____ "Pauline Smith and Arnold Bennett." <u>ESA</u>, 6 (1963), 144-48.

4787   _____ "Pauline Smith and the Place of Her Inspiration." <u>ESA</u>, 6 (1963), 70-76.

4788   Ravenscroft, Arthur. "Pauline Smith." <u>REL</u>, 4, no. 2 (1963), 55-67.

4789   Smith, Pauline. "Why and How I Became an Author." <u>ESA</u>, 6 (1963), 149-53.

4790   Stopforth, L. M. D. "Short Stories of Pauline Smith: A Critical Survey." <u>UCWCA</u>, 4 (1967), 1-37.

See also: 6563.

VAN DER POST, Laurens

4791   Anon. "Nation to Nation." <u>TLS</u>, 15 March 1963, 177-78.

4792   Baker, I. L. <u>Laurens Van Der Post: Venture to the Interior</u>. Bath, England: James Brodie,[1963].

4793   Carpenter, Frederick I. <u>Laurens Van Der Post</u>. New York: Twayne, 1969.

4794   Debenham, Frank. <u>Kalahari Sand</u>. London: Bell, 1953.

4795   Michelmore, Cliff. "Laurens Van Der Post in Conversation with Cliff Michelmore." <u>Listener</u>, 80 (1968), 815-16.

4796   Newquist, Roy. "Laurens Van Der Post." In item 4644, pp. 603-12.

4797   Rabkin, L. "Laurens Van Der Post." <u>Forum</u> (Johannesburg), 1, no. 2, (1952), 53-54.

4798   Snyman, J. P. L. "South African Writers: 12. Laurens Van Der Post." <u>Femina</u>, 7 Nov. 1963, p. 65.

4799   Spender, Stephen. <u>The Destructive Element</u>. London: Jonathan Cape, 1935, pp. 236-50.

4800   Young, Desmond. <u>All the Best Years</u>. New York: Harper & Row, 1961.

VILAKAZI, Benedict

4801   Dhlomo, H. I. E. "Dr. Vilakazi." <u>AfrD</u>, 2, no. 7 (1952), 30-31.

4802   Partridge, A. C. "The Poems of B. W. Vilakazi." <u>BAALE</u>, 2 (1964), 26.

WRIGHT, David

4803   Durrant, Geoffrey.   "Promising Young Men."   <u>Standpunte</u>, 11, no. 3 (1956-57), 63-69.

4804   Wright, David.   "Leaving School-VI."   <u>LMag</u>, 5, no. 1 (1968), 55-61.

South Asia (India and Pakistan, Ceylon)

Research Aids

4805 Alphonso-Karkala, John B. "Indo-English Criticism." <u>WLWE Newsletter</u>, 18 (1970), 7-26.

4806 <u>Guide to Indian Periodical Literature</u>. Gurgaon: Prabhu Book Service, 1964-d., quarterly.

4807 Hartley, Lois. "Checklist on the Indian Novel." <u>LE&W</u>, 7 (1963), 86-90.

4808 <u>Index India</u>. Jaipur: Rajesthan Univ. Library, 1967-d., quarterly.

4809 Jain, Sushil Kumar. "Indian Literature in English: A Select Reading List." <u>BACLALS</u>, 5 (1968), 1-39.

4810 Kanwar, H. I. S. "Selected Bibliography on Ceylon Arranged Chronologically." <u>UA</u>, 15 (1963), 205-07.

4811 Kesavan, B. S., and V. Y. Kulkarni, eds. <u>The National Bibliography of Indian Literature 1901-1953</u>. Vol. 1. New Delhi: Sahitya Akademi, 1962.

4812 McDowell, Robert E. "A Bibliography of Twentieth-Century Indo-English Fiction." <u>WLWE Newsletter</u>, 17, supp. (1970), 1-22.

4813 Perkins, Susan. "A Selected Bibliography Useful for a Study of Indo-Anglian Literature." In <u>Introducing India</u>. Calcutta: Asiatic Society, 1957, pp. 267-79.

4814 Spencer, Dorothy M. <u>Indian Fiction in English: An Annotated Bibliography</u>. Philadelphia: Univ. of Pennsylvania, 1960. ["Introductory Essay on Indian Society, Culture, and Fiction," pp. 9-38.]

4815 <u>Who's Who of Indian Writers</u>. New Delhi: Sahitya Akademi, 1961.

General: India and Pakistan

4816 Abbas, K. A. "All That Two Hands Can Carry." <u>NOB</u>, 7 (1968), 133-35.

4817 ____ "Bread, Beauty and Revolution." <u>CIL</u>, 8, no. 3 (1968), 6-8, 29.

4818 ____ "A New Literature for the New Literates." <u>CIL</u>, 2, no. 3 (1962), 8-9.

4819 Ageya. "Words, Silence, Existence: A Writer's Credo." <u>IndL</u>, 9, no. 1 (1966), 86-91.

4820 Aldan, Daisy. "Indian Poetry Today." <u>BA</u>, 40 (1966), 397-402.

4821 Ali, S. Amjad. "The Book World of Pakistan." <u>PakQ</u>, 12, no. 3 (1964), 56-65, 74-77.

4822   Alphonso-Karkala, John B. "Indo-English Fiction." LE&W, 8 (1964), 6-14.

4823   Amin, Razia Khan. "Modern Poetry in East Pakistan: A Survey." Mahfil,
       3, no. 4 (1967), 62-84.

4824   Amir, S. Javed. "Theatre in Lahore." PakR, 15 (1967), 4-9.

4825   Anand, Mulk Raj. "At What Price, My Brothers." IndL, 10, no. 1 (1967),
       52-60.

4826   _____ "Folk Tradition as an Aid to Modern Expression." IAC, 17, no. 3
       (1968), 3-6.

4827   _____ The Indian Theatre. New York: Roy, 1951.

4828   _____ Is There a Contemporary Indian Civilisation? New York: Asia House,
       1963.

4829   _____ "Is Universal Criticism Possible?" LCrit, 7, no. 1 (1965), 68-75.

4830   _____ The King-Emperor's English, or the Role of the English Language
       in Free India. Bombay: Hind Kitabs, 1947.

4831   _____ "Modernism in Indian and Soviet Literature." Amity, 4, no. 1 (1966),
       44-47.

4832   _____ "New Bearings in Indian Literature." LitR, 4 (1961), 453-57.

4833   _____ "A Note on Modern Indian Fiction." IndL, 8, no. 1 (1965), 44-57.

4834   _____ "Old Myths and New Myths: Recital Versus Novel." BP, 13 (1969),
       27-36.

4835   _____ "The Role of Creative Writers and Artists in the Developing
       Countries of Afro-Asia." AAWA, 3, no. 1 (1966), 18-21.

4836   _____ "Survivals of Folk Tradition in the Indian Theatre: An Essay."
       ArtL, 24, no. 1 (1950), 25-32.

4837   _____ "Task Before the Writers." CIL, 2, no. 9 (1962), 16-17.

4838   Anderson, David D. "Contemporary Pakistani Literature." PakQ, 12,
       no. 2 (1964), 13-18.

4839   _____ "English Writing in Pakistan." Scintilla, 5 (1964), 46-51.

4840   _____ "Modern Asian Writing." AsSt, 2 Nov. 1968, 8.

4841   _____ "New Insight in the Pakistani Short Story." UCQ, 12, no. 3 (1967),
       31-40.

4842   _____ "Pakistani Literature Today." LE&W, 10 (1966), 235-44.

4843   Anjaneyulu, D. "Across All Barriers." Statesman, 9 May 1968, p. 6.

4844   _____ "Fifty Years of Indian Writing in English." Swarajya, 12 (1968),
       223-28.

4845   _____ "Indian Writing in English." WrW, 11 (1962), 43-45.

4846   _____ "Indian Writing in English, from K. S. Venkataramani to Kamala
       Markandaya." Triveni, 32 (1963), 19-28.

4847   Anon. "All India Poet's Conference." Indian P.E.N., 34 (1968), 215-18.

4848   _____ "Asian Poetry: India." EWR, 2 (1966), 201-20.

4849   _____ "Creative Writing in the Present Crisis." IndL, 6, no. 1 (1963),
       66-69.

4850   _____ "English Poetry in Pakistan." Vision, 16, no. 2 (1967), 19-24.

4851   _____ Indian Drama. Calcutta and New Delhi: Pub. Div. of the Ministry
       of Information and Broadcasting, 1956.

4852 _____ "Indian English." Economic Times, 20 Dec. 1969, p. 5.

4853 _____ "Indian English." Indian Express, 21 June 1967, p. 6.

4854 _____ "Indian Writers and the West." Statesman, 23 Oct. 1967, pp. 649-64.

4855 _____ "Indian Writing in English." IWT, 4, no. 1 (1970), 3-5.

4856 _____ "Indo-Anglian Writers." Statesman, 22 May 1968, p. 6.

4857 _____ "Indo-English Literature." BP, 13 (1969), 131-33.

4858 _____ "Literary Landscape." Statesman, 6 Oct. 1968, p. 8.

4859 _____ "Literary Sense and Sensibility." Hindustan Times, 14 Sept. 1969, p. 7.

4860 _____ "Modern Indian Poetry." Indian P.E.N., 27 (1961), 1-7, 75-77, 113-18, 149-54, 187-90.

4861 _____ Modernity and Contemporary Literature. Simla: Indian Inst. of Advanced Study, 1969.

4862 _____ "New Situation and the Writer." CIL, 7, no. 5 (1967), 16-18, 25.

4863 _____ "Notes on Indian Literature." OrientR, 3 (1957), 25-41.

4864 _____ "The Theatre in Transition: A Symposium." UA, 10 (1958), 99-129.

4865 _____ "Why Write in English? India's Search for Self-Expression." TLS, 10 Aug. 1962, pp. 584-85.

4866 Anwar, Saquib. "Impact of Western Fiction on Indian Students." CIL, 7, no. 5 (1967), 16-25.

4867 Ashraf, Syed Ali. "Foreword." Venture, 6, no. 1 (1969), 1-7.

4868 _____ "Our Culture and Its Relation to Literature." PakR, 13 (1965), 3-5.

4869 Azam, Ikram. "The Role of Writers and Poets in the War." PakR, 14 (1966), 32-33, 38.

4870 Azhicode, Sukumar. "Neo-Criticism and Creative Writing in Kerala." CIL, 5, no. 9 (1965), 10-11.

4871 Azraf, Dewan Mohammed. "Literature in East Pakistan." PakQ, 12, no. 1 (1964), 24-31.

4872 Bakshi, C. K. "Modernity in Contemporary Literature." IWT, 3, no. 2 (1969), 21-24.

4873 Balin, V. I. "Jawaharlal Nehru and Indian Literature." Amity, 3, no. 4 (1966), 34-38.

4874 Banerjee, N. N. "Recent Indian Writing in English." CIL, 4, no. 1 (1964), 12-13; no. 2 (1964), 24-26; no. 3 (1964), 11-12; no. 4 (1964), 12-13.

4875 Banerjee, Ranjan. "Indo-Anglian Writers." Statesman, 14 May 1968, p. 6.

4875a Barua, Bhaben. "An Indian Novel." AssamQ, 4 (1967), 203-27.

4876 Barua, D. K. "Poetry and Revolution." AssamQ, 4 (1967), 109-20.

4877 Baso, Manoje. "The Truth He Couldn't Tell." IndL, 9, no. 2 (1966), 67-74.

4878 Basu, Lotika. Indian Writers of English Verse. Preface by Rabindranath Tagore. Calcutta: The University, 1933.

4879 Bedekar, D. K. "Indian Literature." MahP, 1, no. 5 (1969), 19-20, 27.

4880 Belliappa, N. Meena. "East-West Encounter: Indian Women Writers of Fiction in English." LCrit, 7, no. 3 (1966), 18-27.

4881   Bey, Hamdi. "A Look at Indo-Anglian Fiction." Thought, 21 (1969), 18-19.

4882   _____ "Novels of a Ruling Caste." Thought, 21 (1969), 13-16.

4883   Bhagat, O. P. "Sword and Shield." Quest, 51 (1966), 82-87.

4884   Bhalla, Mada Mohan. "In Search of Indian Theatre." Diogenes (New York),
       45 (1964), 37-48.

4885   Bhaskaran, M. P. "Indianness of Indo-Anglian Writers and Their Critics."
       Statesman, 4 May 1968, p. 8.

4886   Bhattacharya, Amitrasudan. "English Works by Bengali Literrateurs."
       CIL, 6, no. 2 (1966), 10-11, 22-23; no. 3 (1966), 14-15, 20.

4887   Bhattacharya, Bhabani. "Baseless Prejudice Against Indians Writing
       English." Statesman, 20 April 1968, p. 8.

4888   Bhattacharya, Deben. "Two Themes in Indian Poetry." Encounter, 2, no. 3
       (1954), 42-47.

4889   Bhattacharya, Lokenath. "Modern Indian Literature: Myth or Reality?"
       IndL, 9, no. 1 (1966), 78-86.

4890   Bhave, S. S. "The New Poetic Idiom in Indian Poetry." IWT, 2, no. 4
       (1967), 62-64. [Comment by Yashwant Chittal, "Poetic Idiom, Sensibility,"
       pp. 65-67.]

4891   Bhushan, V. N. The Moving Finger: Anthology of Essays in Literary and
       Aesthetic Criticism by Indian Writers. Bombay: Padma, 1945.

4892   Bose, Amalendu. "The Impact of the West on Bengali Literature." LHY,
       1, no. 2 (1960), 61-68.

4893   Bose, Buddhavdeva. "Indian Poetry in English." Miscellany, 33 (1969),
       3-5; 35 (1969), iii-v; 36 (1969), iii-v.

4894   Bowers, Faubion. Theatre in the East. New York: Grove, 1956.

4895   Brandon, James R. "The Social Role of Popular Theatre of South East
       Asia." MD, 9 (1967), 398-403.

4896   Cerna, Z., et al. "On the Paths of the Asian Literatures to Modernity."
       NOB, 6 (1967), 1-6, 33-37, 65-71, 114-20.

4897   Chaitanya, Krishna. "Modern Indian Drama." MD, 2 (1960), 403-09.

4898   Chari, V. Krishna. "Decorum as a Critical Concept in Indian and Western
       Poetics." JAAC, 26 (1967), 53-63.

4899   _____ "Whitman and Indian Thought." WHR, 13 (1959), 291-302.

4900   Chatterjee, P. C. "Poetry and Belief." Conspectus, 2 (1966), 62-70.

4901   Chatterjee, Suyamal. "Literature for the People: A Controversy of the
       Forties." Quest, 49 (1966), 39-46.

4902   Chatterji, S. K. Languages and Literatures of Modern India. Calcutta:
       Bengal Publishers, 1963.

4903   Chattopadhyay, Kamaladevi. "The Indian Theatre." ArtL, 32 (1958), 53-56.

4904   Chattopadhyay, Sisir. The Novel as the Modern Epic. Calcutta: Firma
       K. L. Mukhopadhyay, 1966.

4905   Chowdhury, Kabir. "East Pakistani Literature and the Western World."
       YCGL, 40 (1962), 191-97.

4906   Contemporary Indian Literature: A Symposium. New Delhi: Sahitya Akademi,
       1957.

4907   Corlett, J. E. "Contemporary South Indian Poetry." LHY, 5, no. 2 (1964),
       30-36.

4908 Damodaran, K. "The Role of Writer in Modern Society." CIL, 7, no. 2 (1967), 33-36.

4909 Das, Deb Kumar. "On the Technique of Indo-Anglicism." WrW, 7 (1961), 27-32.

4910 ____ "The Multiple Theme: A Study in Technique." WrW, 8 (1961), 101-09.

4911 Das, Manoj. "Good Gray Poet and the Last Great Rishi." IndL, 12, no. 3 (1969), 87-91.

4912 Dasgupta, R. K. English Poets on India and Other Essays. Calcutta: Book House, 1945.

4913 ____ "Indian Response to Paradise Lost." IndL, 12, no. 1 (1969), 62-70.

4914 ____ "Western Response to Indian Literature." IndL, 10, no. 1 (1967), 5-15.

4915 Daswami, Tilottama. "The English Language and Its Contribution to Modern Indian Languages." Indian P.E.N., 29 (1963), 317-19, 345-49.

4916 Datta, Jyotirmoy. "On Caged Chaffinches and Polyglot Parrots." Quest, 28 (1961), 26-32. [Comment by K. Raghavendra Rao. "Indo-Anglian Writing." Quest, 29 (1961), 116.]

4917 Davies, M. Bryn. "British and Indian Images of India." ArielE, 1, no. 4 (1970), 48-55.

4918 De Bary, William Theodore, et al., eds. Sources of Indian Tradition. 2 vols. New York and London: Columbia Univ. Press, 1958.

4919 Derrett, M. E. The Modern Indian Novel in English: A Comparative Approach. Brussels: Université Libre de Bruxelles, 1966.

4920 Desai, Anita. "Aspects of the Indian Novel: Women Writers." Quest, 65 (1970), 39-43.

4921 Desai, M. P. The Problem of English. Ahmedabad: n.p., 1964.

4922 Devahuti, D. "Literary and Dramatic Traditions in Contemporary India." AustJPH, 12 (1966), 202-12.

4923 Dhringra, Baldoon. "Aspects du théâtre contemporain de l'Inde." RevT, 37 (1958), 71-75.

4924 ____ "La litérrature indienne contemporaine." Synthèses, 18 (1963), 386-96.

4925 ____ "Littérature indienne." In Pierre Gioan, ed., Histoires générales des litérratures. Paris: Libraire Aristide Quillet, 1961. Vol. 1, pp. 62-67, 311-20, 455-70, 789-96; Vol. 3, pp. 635-56, 821-27.

4926 ____ A National Theatre for India. Bombay: Padma, 1944.

4927 Dunn, Theodore O. Douglas. Bengali Writers of English Verse. Calcutta: Thacker, Spink, 1918.

4928 Ekambaram, E. J. "Some Aspects of Indian Response to Fiction in English." LCrit, 7, no. 3 (1966), 8-17.

4929 Enayetullah, Anwar. "Theatre in Pakistan." PakQ, 12, no. 4 (1964), 54-59.

4930 Enright, D. J. "The Daffodil Transplanted." Phoenix, 11 (1967), 1-9.

4931 Esnoul, Anne Marie. "Les traites de dramaturgie indienne." In Jean Jacquot, ed., Les théâtres d'Asie. Paris: Centre nationale de la recherche scientifique, 1961, pp. 19-27.

4932 Evans, Hubert. "Recent Soviet Writing on Pakistan." CAR, 15 (1967), 148-59.

4933 Ezekiel, Nissim. "The Thoreau-Ghandi Syndrome: An Ambiguous Influence." Quest, 58 (1968), 21-26.

4934 _____ Writing in India. Bombay: P.E.N. All India Centre, n.d.

4935 _____, et al. "A Discussion: Modern Indian Writing." WrW, 28 (1968), 61-74.

4936 Fiske, Adele M. "Karma in Five Indian Novels." LE&W, 10 (1966), 98-111.

4937 Gabriel, M. C., and Gwen Gabriel. "Indian Short Story: Struggle for a Genre." Thought, 19 (1968), 15-17.

4938 Gadgil, Gangadhar. "Some Parallels in the Development of American and Indian Literatures." WHR, 17 (1963), 107-16.

4939 Gangoly, Orhendra Coomar. Landscape in Indian Literature and Art. Lucknow: Univ. of Lucknow, 1963.

4940 _____ "New Light on Indian Dramas." ModR, 110 (1961), 462-63.

4941 Gargi, Balwant. Folk Theatre of India. Seattle: Univ. of Washington Press, 1967.

4942 _____ Theatre in India. New York: Theatre Arts Books, 1960.

4943 Ghosh, S. K., and E. C. Chaudhuri. "Indian Writing in English: Two Views." WrW, 3 (1960), 37-39.

4944 Gilder, Rosamond. "The New Theatre in India: An Impression." ETJ, 11 (1957), 200-04.

4945 Gokak, V. K. English in India. New York: Asia House, 1964.

4946 _____ "Introduction" to The Golden Treasury of Indo-Anglian Poetry. New Delhi: Sahitya Akademi, 1970, pp. xix-xlvi.

4947 _____, ed. Literature in Modern Indian Languages. Delhi: Ministry of Information & Broadcasting, 1957.

4948 Gonda, Jan. "De indische Roman." FdL, 1 (1960), 98-107.

4949 Gopalakrishnan, Adiga M. "Literature and State Patronage in India." Quest, 39 (1963), 43-49.

4950 Gowda, H. H. Anniah. "Contemporary Creative Writers in English in India." LHY, 10, no. 1 (1969), 17-39.

4951 _____ "A Defence of Indian Verse in English." LHY, 9, no. 2 (1968), 23-36.

4952 _____ "Humour: Indo-Anglian Literature." In Nissim Ezekiel, ed., Indian Writers in Conference: Sixth P.E.N. All India Writers' Conference. Bombay: P.E.N. All India Centre, 1964.

4953 _____ "Indian Writing in English." Indian P.E.N., 28 (1962), 278-80.

4954 Gowen, Herbert. A History of Indian Literature. New York: Appleton, 1931.

4955 Greenberger, Allen J. The British Image of India: A Study in the Literature of Imperialism 1880-1960. London: Oxford Univ. Press, 1969.

4956 Gupta, P. C. Kabir. "Modern Indian Literature as a Factor in Moulding Social Life." NOB, 4 (1965), 114-19.

4957 Habib, Kamal Mohammed. "The Place of English in the Pakistani Society." Vision, 17, no. 5 (1968), 9-12, 17-19.

4958 Hess, Linda. "Post-Independence Indian Poetry in English." Quest, 49 (1966), 28-38.

4959 Hookens, William. "Creative Writing in India." Triveni, 37 (1968), 62-67.

4960 Husain, S. Sajjad. "The Literature of Pakistan." In item 28, pp. 142-66.

4961 Ikramullah, Begum Shaista Suhrawardy. "The Role of Women in the Literature of Pakistan." AsR, 55 (1959), 14-26.

4962 Isenburg, Artur. "Modern Indian Literature." IndL, 6, no. 1 (1963), 51-65.

4963 Iyengar, K. R. Srinivasa. The Indian Contribution to English Literature. Bombay: Karnatak, 1945.

4964 _____ Indian Writing in English. Bombay: Asia House, 1962.

4965 _____ Indo-Anglian Literature. Bombay: International Book House, 1943.

4966 _____ "Indo-Anglian Literature." In Writers in Free India. Proceedings of the Second All-India Writers' Conference, Benares, 1947. Bombay: P.E.N. All India Centre, 1950, pp. 181-89.

4967 _____ Literature and Authorship in India. London: Allen & Unwin, 1943.

4968 _____ "The Literature of India." In item 28, pp. 115-41.

4969 _____ "Modern Indian Poetry: Indo-Anglian." Indian P.E.N., 36 (1960), 317-21.

4970 _____ "Shakespeare in India." IndL, 7, no. 1 (1964), 1-11.

4971 _____ The Study of Indian Writing in English. Bombay: Popular Book Depot, 1959.

4972 _____, ed. Drama in Modern India and the Writer's Responsibility in a Rapidly Changing World: 1957 P.E.N. Conference. Bombay: P.E.N. All India Centre, 1961.

4973 _____, et al. "The Impact of Ghandian Thought on Our Writers." Indian P.E.N., 25 (1959), 65-69, 101-05.

4974 Jain, J. C. "Indian Translations of Anglo-Indian Literature." CIL, 7, no. 8 (1967), 33-34.

4975 _____ "The Influence of Ghandian Thought on Indian Literature." UA, 20 (1968), 272-75.

4976 Jain, Sushil Kumar. "Trends in Modern Indian Literature and Bibliography." ModR, 124 (1969), 489-92.

4977 Jamil, M. "Indian and Pakistan Writers of English Fiction." UnivS, 1, no. 1 (1965), 61-68.

4978 _____ "A Study in Literary Influences." PakQ, 7, no. 3 (1957), 8-13.

4979 Jasimuddin. "The Drama of the People: East Pakistan's Soul in Action." PakQ, 9, no. 3 (1959), 36-39.

4980 Joshi, Umashankar. "Modernism and Indian Literature." IndL, 1, no. 2 (1958), 19-30.

4981 _____ "The Novelist's Quest for India." IndL, 8, no. 1 (1965), 58-81.

4982 Jussawalla, Adil. "The New Poetry." JCL, 5 (1968), 65-78.

4983 Kabir, Humayun, ed. Modern Indian Literature. London: Chapman & Hall, 1959.

4984 _____ "Western Influence on Indian Fiction." OrientR, 5 (1959), 33-36.

4985 Kachru, Braj B. "The Indianness in Indian English." BACLALS, 7 (1970), 18-23.

4986 Kahn, Saifur Islam. "Contemporary Poetry in East Pakistan." Scintilla, 3 (1963), 27-30.

4987 Karanth, K. S. "How Deep Is Western Influence on Indian Writers of Fiction?" LCrit, 7, no. 2 (1960), 33-40.

4988 Karnani, Chetan. "Renaissance in Indo-Anglian Literature." BP, 13
      (1969), 110-12.

4989 Kaul, J. L. "Contemporary Trends in Indian Writing." Indian P.E.N.,
      26 (1960), 197-201.

4990 Kohli, Suresh. "Indian Poetry in English." Times of India, 16 March
      1969, p. iii.

4991 _____ "Indian Writing in English." WeekR, 22 April 1967, pp. 31-32.

4992 Kripalani, Krishna. Modern Indian Literature: A Panoramic Glimpse.
      Bombay: Nirmala Sadanand, 1968.

4993 Krishna Warrior, N. V. "Creative Writing at a Cross-Road." Mainstream,
      6, no. 18 (1967), 11-12.

4994 Krishnamoorty, K. "The Nature of Meaning in Poetry: An Indian Approach."
      Aryan Path, 34, no. 4-5 (1963), 148-54.

4995 Krishnamurthi, M. G. "Problems of the Indian Writer in English." BP,
      13 (1969), 113-14.

4996 Krishnamurti, S. R. "Future of the Amateur Stage." BITC, pt. 2 (1962),
      215-24.

4997 Kularesthra, Mahendra. "Letters from India [and] Indian Letter."
      Landfall, 17 (1963), 55-60; 18 (1964), 62-67; 19 (1965), 58-62; 20
      (1966), 83-88.

4998 Kumarappa, Bharatan, ed. The Indian Literatures of Today: A Symposium.
      Bombay: P.E.N. All India Centre, 1947.

4999 Kunder, L. K. "English Language in an Indian Setting." Mirror, 8, no. 10
      (1969), 26-27.

5000 Lahiri, K. "The Equipment and Recognition of Bengali Writers of English
      Verse and the Range of Their Poetry." CalR, 162 (1962), 109-30.

5001 _____ "The Flora and Fauna in the English Verse Written by Bengalees."
      CalR, 166 (1963), 117-34.

5002 _____ "Imagery in the Poetry of Bengalee Writers of English Verse."
      CalR, 170 (1964), 119-26.

5003 _____ "Some Aspects of Form and Technique in English Verse Written by
      Bengalees." JDLUC, n.s. 3 (1960), 199-224.

5004 Lal, P. The Concept of an Indian Literature: Six Essays. Calcutta:
      Writers Workshop, 1968.

5005 _____ "Indian Writing in English." Quest, 29 (1961), 83-86.

5006 _____ "Indian Writing in English." HER, 34 (1964), 316-21.

5007 _____ "Indian Writing in English." Language and Learning, 9 (1965),
      316-19.

5008 _____ "Indian Writing in English Since Independence." IWI, 29 Jan. 1967,
      pp. 32-34.

5009 _____ "Indo-Anglian Verse." WrW, 11 (1962), 46-47.

5010 _____ "Introduction" to Modern Indian Poetry in English. Calcutta:
      Writers Workshop, 1969, pp. i-xliv.

5011 Lewis, Dearing. "Past and Present in Modern Indian and Pakistani
      Poetry." LE&W, 10, no. 1-2 (1966), 69-85; Part II, 11 (1968), 301-12.

5012 McArthur, Herbert. "In Search of the Indian Novel." MR, 2 (1961), 600-13.

5013 McCutchion, David. "The Indianness of Indian Criticism." WrW, 29 (1968),
      59-63.

5014 ____ "Indian Poetry in English." WrW, 29 (1968), 40-58.

5015 ____ "Indian Writing in English." Quadrant, 6, no. 4 (1962), 48-54;
7, no. 26 (1963), 27-36.

5016 ____ "Indian Writing in English." WrW, 29 (1968), 19-38.

5017 ____ Indian Writing in English. Calcutta: Writers Workshop, 1968.

5018 ____ "Indo-Anglian Nostalgia." WrW, 29 (1968), 64-66.

5019 ____ "The New Poetry." WrW, 29 (1968), 67-70.

5020 ____ "Western and Indian Approaches to Literature." Mahfil, 4, no. 1
(1967), 21-33.

5021 Machwe, P. "1857 and Indian Literature." IndL, 1, no. 4 (1957), 53-59.

5022 ____ "Sterility in Indian Literature after Independence." Conspectus,
1, no. 1 (1965), 81-86.

5023 ____ "Writers within the Walls of Language." AsR, 2, no. 1 (1968), 61-68.

5024 Majeed, M. A. "The Role of Our Poets in the War." PakR, 14 (1966),
3-6, 20.

5025 Malabari, Behramji. The Indian Muse in English Garb. Bombay: Merwanjee
Nowrojee Daboo, 1877.

5026 Malik, Aslam. "Contemporary Literature of Pakistan." AsH, 1, no. 4 (1949),
58-66.

5027 Malik, Hafeez. "The Marxist Literary Movement in India and Pakistan."
JASt, 26 (1967), 649-64.

5028 Malu, Bharati. "Degeneration of Literature." Economic Times, 21 Oct.
1967, p. 5.

5029 Marshall, R. "Sophistication in the Indian Dramatists and the Later
Shakespeare." In Critical Essays on English Literature Presented to
Professor M. S. Duraiswami. Calcutta: Orient Longmans, 1966, pp. 105-22.

5030 Mathur, J. C. Drama in Rural India. New York: Asia House, 1964.

5031 Mathur, P. N., et al. "Indo-English Literature: Some Views." BP, 12
(1969), 4-9.

5032 Meghani, Jhaverchand. "A Lamp of Humanity." IndL, 9, no. 3 (1966),
56-70.

5033 Melwani, Murli Das. "Failing of Indo-Anglian Novelists and Their
Critics." Statesman, 28 Dec. 1968, p. 8.

5034 ____ "The Paucity of Indo-Anglian Drama." Quest, 64 (1970), 71-76.

5035 Menezes, A. "A Symposium on the Writer and the Public: I) The
Responsibilities of the Writer." LCrit, 5, no. 4 (1963), 42-54.

5036 Menon, K. P. S. "Dignity of Men of Letters." CIL, 6, no. 6-7 (1966),
6-8.

5037 Mishra, A. L. "Problems Indo-Anglian Literature Is Faced With." URSE,
4 (1969), 63-66.

5038 Misra, Kripa Narain. "The Nature and Function of Poetic Power (A
Critical Evaluation of the Indian and Western Theories)." Prajna, 11,
no. 1 (1965), 261-78.

5039 Mitchell, John D. "The Theatre of India and Southeast Asia." AsHum,
2 (1959), 146-55.

5040 Mitra, Sid M. Anglo-Indian Studies. London: Longmans Green, 1913.

5041   Mugali, R. S. "Nationalism and Cosmopolitanism in Literature: An
       Indian Outlook." In François Jost, ed., Proceedings of the IVth
       Congress of the Comparative Literature Association. 2 vols. The
       Hague: Mouton, 1966. I, pp. 680-86.

5042   Mukherjee, Meenakshi. "Awareness of Audience in Indo-Anglian Fiction."
       Quest, 52 (1967), 37-40.

5043   ____ "Style in Indo-Anglian Fiction." IWT, 4, no. 1 (1970), 6-13.

5044   Mukherjee, Sujit. "Aspects of the Indo-Anglian Novel: The Best Seller."
       Quest, 65 (1970), 34-48.

5045   ____ "India's Entry in English Fiction." Quest, 47 (1965), 51-55.

5046   Mukherji, Ramaranjan. "Imagery in Poetry: An Indian Approach." BORIA,
       48-49 (1968), 395-401.

5047   Murti, Mukkavalli Suryanarayana. "A Survey of Indian Literary Criticism."
       Triveni, 33 (1964), 37-42.

5048   Nagarajan, K. "The Development of the Novel in India." ArtL, 23 (1949),
       39-44.

5048a Nagendra, D. "The Essential Unity of the Indian Literature." JNAA, 8
       (1963), 26-31.

5049   ____, ed. Indian Literature: A Symposium. Agra: Lakshmi Narain Agarwal,
       1959.

5050   Naik, M. K. "Echo and Voice in Indian Poetry in English." IWT, 4, no. 1
       (1970), 32-41.

5051   ____, S. K. Desai, and G. S. Amur, eds. Critical Essays on Indian
       Writing in English. Dharwar: Karnatak Univ. Press, 1968.

5052   Naipaul, V. S. "Commonwealth Literature: Indian Autobiographies."
       New Statesman, 69 (1965), 156-58.

5053   Nalapat, Madhar. "Indo-Anglian." CenturyM, 17 Feb. 1968, p. 12.

5054   Nandakumar, Prema. "The Achievement of the Indo-Anglian Novelist."
       LCrit, 5, no. 1 (1961), 152-65.

5055   ____ "English Literary Journals in India." Indian P.E.N., 29 (1963),
       195-202.

5056   ____ "English Writing by Indians: Another Rich Year." IndL, 11, no. 4
       (1968), 19-32.

5057   ____ "Indian Writing in English: A Growingly Significant Literature."
       IndL, 12, no. 4 (1969), 141-52.

5058   ____ "Lyricists Lead: A Review of Indian Writing in English in 1966."
       IndL, 10, no. 4 (1967), 9-19.

5059   ____ "Modern Indian Poetry." Indian P.E.N., 25 (1959), 109-11.

5060   Narasimhaiah, C. D. "How Major Is Our Literature of the Past 50 Years?"
       LCrit, 7, no. 4 (1967), 80-89.

5061   ____ "Indian Writing in English." LCrit, 5, no. 2 (1962), 80-90.

5062   ____ "Indian Writing in English: An Introduction." JCL, 5 (1968), 3-15.

5063   ____ "Literary Criticism: European and Indian Traditions." LCrit, 7,
       no. 1 (1966), 1-8.

5064   ____ The Swan and the Eagle. Simla: Indian Inst. of Advanced Study,
       1969. ["Towards an Understanding of the Species Called 'Indian
       Writing in English,'" pp. 1-18.]

5065   ____, ed. Fiction and the Reading Public in India. Mysore: Univ. of
       Mysore Press, 1967.

5066 Narasimhan, Raji. "Indian Writing in English." IndL, 6, no. 2 (1963), 81-86.

5067 Narayan, R. K. "English in India." In item 36, pp. 102-04.

5068 Neog, Maheshwar, et al. "Annual Review of Indian Writing in 1964." IndL, 7, no. 2 (1965), 38-143.

5069 Oaten, Richard Farley. Sketch of Anglo-Indian Literature. London: Kegan Paul, 1908.

5070 Ould, Hermon. "Some Impressions of the Indian Literary Scene." IAL, 20, no. 1 (1946), 15-22.

5071 Padhye Prabhakar, and Sadanand Bhatkal. "Indo-Anglian Writing in English." IWT, 4, no. 1 (1970), 3-5.

5072 Pandia, M. N. "Gandhiji and Indo-Anglian Novels." Indian Express, 2 Oct. 1969, p. 7.

5073 Patel, Gieve. "The National School of Drama." Quest, 54 (1967), 63-66.

5074 Prakrit [pseud.]. "Contemporary Indian Literature." EH, 4, no. 10 (1965), 20-27.

5075 Prasad, H. Y. Sharada. "Translation of Indian Fiction into English." LCrit, 7, no. 1 (1965), 63-67.

5076 Rafat, Taufiq. "Towards a Pakistani Idiom." Venture, 6, no. 1 (1969), 60-73.

5077 Raghavacharyulu, D. V. K. "Search for Literary Identity." In Unpunctual Pen. Hyderabad: Maruthi Book Depot, 1968, pp. 7-19. [See also pp. 97-104.]

5078 Raha, Kiranmoy. "The Minority Theatre in India." Quest, 22 (1959), 72-76.

5079 Rahman, K. "An Anglo-Indian Novelist of the Thirties: A Study in Race Relations." UnivS, 1 (1964), 63-80.

5080 Rai, Amrit. "Situation in Our Country and the Progressive Writers." CIL, 7, no. 8 (1967), 12-13, 28.

5081 Rajan, B. "Identity and Nationality." In item 36, pp. 106-09.

5082 ____ "The Indian Virtue." JCL, 1 (1969), 79-85.

5083 Rajiva, Stanley F. "Contemporary Indian Writing in English." Quest, 60 (1969), 72-75.

5084 Ramamurthy, K. S. "The Puranic Tradition and Indo-Anglian Fiction." IWT, 4, no. 1 (1970), 42-46.

5085 Ramasubramaniam, V., et al. "Theatre Indian and Western: Their Mutual Impacts--A Seminar." BITC, pt. 1 (1962), 41-105.

5086 Rao, A. V. Krishna. "Feminine Sensibility in Indo-Anglian Fiction." Triveni, 35 (1967), 51-58.

5087 ____ "The Ghandi Legend in Indo-Anglian Fiction." Triveni, 31 (1963), 59-64.

5088 Rao, G. Subba. Indian Words in English. Oxford: Clarendon, 1954.

5089 Ray, Lila. "A Meeting of Writers and Translators." Indian P.E.N., 29 (1963), 261-63.

5090 Ray, Robert J. "A Look at Recent Indian Novels in English." BA, 37 (1963), 286-88.

5091 Reid, John T. "A Note on Modern Indian Literature in America." LHY, 1, no. 1 (1960), 5-8.

5092 Renou, Louis. Indian Literature. Trans. by Patrick Evans. New York: Walker, 1964. [Orig. pub. 1951.]

5093 Saha, Subhas Chandra. "Indo-Anglian." CenturyM, 20 Jan. 1968, pp. 11-12.

5094 ____ "Indo-Anglian Verse: A Comic Attitude." Thought, 21 (1969), 15-16.

5095 Said, Y. "English Poetry in Pakistan." Perspective, 3, no. 2 (1969), 29-33.

5096 Sajjad, Zeheer. "National Life and Literature Today." Mainstream, 6, no. 6 (1967), 22-24.

5097 Seal, Anita. "English Writing in India." WrW, 19 (1966), 41-45.

5098 Seal, Brajendranath. New Essays in Criticism. Calcutta: Som Bros., 1903.

5099 Seshadri, P. Anglo-Indian Poetry. Madras: Srinivasa Varadachari, 1915.

5100 Shah, A. B. "Indian Tradition and Modernity." Quest, 46 (1966), 9-19.

5101 Shahani, Ranjee G. "Literary India 5. The Indian Branch of English Literature." AsRev, 38 (1942), 436-39.

5102 Sharpe, Patricia L. "The Plight of the Indian Writer Today." Quest, 59 (1968), 31-39.

5103 Shivpuri, Jagdish. "A Forest of Convex Mirrors." IWT, 1, no. 3 (1967), 33-43.

5104 Singh, Bhupal. A Survey of Anglo-Indian Fiction. London: Oxford Univ. Press, 1954.

5105 Singh, Hukum. Literary Essays. Kampur: Kitab Ghar, [1963?].

5106 Singh, Khushwant. "India: The Literary Scene." IntLA, 3 (1961), 167-75.

5107 ____ "Indian Literature in the Doldrums." WeekR, 7 Jan. 1967, pp. 29-30.

5108 ____ "State of Indian Writing in English." WeekR, 25 March 1967, pp. 30-31.

5109 Speight, E. E., ed. Indian Masters of English. London: Longmans, 1934.

5110 Square [pseud.]. "Indo-English Literature." Hindustan Times, 9 Nov. 1969, p. 7.

5111 Srinath, C. N. "Contemporary Indian Poetry in English." LCrit, 8, no. 2 (1968), 55-66.

5112 Subramanyam, Ka Naa. "Causes for Our Own Stagnation in Creative Arts." Hindustan Times, 28 May 1967, p. 8.

5113 ____ "Criticism and the Writer." Quest, 34 (1962), 28-30.

5114 ____ "How Indian Is the Indian Novel?" CitWR, 25 Oct. 1969, pp. 28-29.

5115 ____ "Humour in Indian Literature." IWI, 17 Dec. 1967, pp. 14-15.

5116 ____ "The Lot of Non-Conformist Writers in India." Statesman, 11 May 1968, p. 6.

5117 ____ "Modern Indian Poetry as the Search for an Identity." Cosmic Society, 7, no. 9 (1969), 14-17.

5118 ____ "Search for the Indian Writer." Cosmic Society, 7, no. 11 (1969), 18-20.

5119 Sudhir, P. "Indo-Anglian Poetry." Times of India, 5 Oct. 1969, p. 8.

5120 Swann, Darius L. "Indian and Greek Drama: Two Definitions." CompD, 3 (1969), 110-19.

5121 Travers-Ball, Ian. "The Writer in India Today." Month, 27 (1962), 333-40.

5122 Tripathi, S. "Changing Horizons: Indian Poetry." IFR, 5, no. 5 (1967), 11, 18.

5123 ____ "Comments on Contemporary Indian Poetry." IndL, 10, no. 1 (1967), 22-31.

5124 ____ "Indian Fiction: A Survey." IFR, 5, no. 14 (1968), 11, 17-18.

5125 Vaid, Krishna B. "Contemporary Short Story: Quest for Quality." BA, 43 (1969), 503-08.

5126 Vatsyayan, Sachchidananda. "Conflict as a Bridge: Some Aspects of the Fiction of Modern India." Diogenes (New York), 45 (1964), 49-65.

5127 ____ "Tradition and Contemporary Reality: Some Aspects of Indian Literature." Solidarity, 2, no. 6 (1967), 81-89.

5128 ____, et al. "Writer at Bay: A Symposium on the Problems of the Writer in Our Country." Seminar, 21 (1961), 10-43.

5129 Venugopal, C. V. "Indian Short Story in English: A Survey." BP, 12 (1969), 98-104.

5130 Verghese, C. Paul. "Problems of the Indian Novelist in English." BP, 12 (1969), 83-97.

5131 Villauri, Mario, ed. Teatro Indiano. Milano: Nuova Academia Editrice, 1960.

5132 Vimala, Rao C. "Four Indian Women Novelists and Their Concern with the Indian Element." JMU, 28 (1968), 8-16.

5133 Vora, Batuk. "Current Trends in Our Literature." New Age, 7 July 1968, p. 11.

5134 Wadia, A. R. The Future of English in India. Bombay: Asia House, 1955.

5135 Walsh, William. "Nataraja and the Packet of Saffron: The Indian Novel in English." Encounter, 23, no. 4 (1964), 78-83.

5136 Wasi, Muriel. "Theatre at Delhi Today." IndL, 1 (1958), 145-50.

5137 Wells, H. W. "Indian Drama and the West." JCL, 1 (1965), 86-94.

5138 ____ "Poetic Drama in England and India." LHY, 2, no. 2 (1961), 27-39.

5139 ____ "Poetic Imagination in Ireland and India." LHY, 9, no. 2 (1968), 37-48.

5140 ____ "Varieties of Conflict in Asian Drama." JOIB, 11 (1963) 269-76.

5141 Wendt, Allan. "Babu to Sahib: Contemporary Indian Literature." SAQ, 64 (1965), 166-80.

5142 ____ "Indian Fiction for Indians: A Study of the Short Fiction in The Illustrated Weekly of India." LE&W, 10, no. 1-2 (1966), 42-50.

5143 White, Robin. "Fiction in India." Reporter, 28, no. 4 (1963), 54-60.

5144 Williams, H. Moore. "English Writing in Free India, (1947-1967)." TCL, 16 (1970), 3-15.

5145 Winternitz, Moriz. A History of Indian Literature. 2 vols. Trans. by S. Ketkar and H. Kohn. Calcutta: Univ. of Calcutta, 1927-1933. [Orig. pub. 1920.]

5146 Zaheer, Sajjad. "Indian Drama and Stage Today." IndL, 1, no. 2 (1958), 75-144.

5147 ____ "Thirty Years of the Progressive Writer's Movement." CIL, 6, no. 1 (1966), 16-18; 6, no. 6-7 (1966), 13-15.

See also: 22, 622, 4814, 6458-6479.

General: Ceylon

5148   Bandaranaike, Y. D. "The Literature of Ceylon." In item 28, pp. 100-14.

5149   Fernando, Chitra. "Contemporary Drama in Ceylon." Hemisphere, 8, no. 4 (1964), 35-36.

5150   Godakumbura, Charles Edmund. The Literature of Ceylon. Ceylon: Dept. of Cultural Affairs, 1963.

5151   ____ Sinhalese Literature. Colombo: Colombo Apothecaries, 1955.

5152   Gooneratne, Yasmine. "In Search of a Tradition: The Creative Writer in Ceylon." English, 16 (1967), 133-38.

5153   ____ "Towards Fiction: Ceylon Writing in English in the Nineteenth Century." In item 5157, pp. 33-67.

5154   Goonewardene, James. "The Writers in Ceylon Must Hang Together or Perish Separately." BACLALS, 7 (1970), 7-13.

5155   Gunawardena, A. J. "Martin Wickramasinghe and Modern Sinhalese Writing." UA, 15 (1963), 184-88.

5156   ____ "The New Novelists." In item 5157, pp. 93-104.

5157   Hensman, C. R., ed. Ceylonese Writing: Some Perspectives. 2 parts. Colombo: Community Inst., 1963-64. [See also Community, 4 (1966), 5-6.]

5158   Jayawardhene, Bandula. "Sinhalese Poetry: The Tradition and Contemporary Trends." UA, 12 (1960), 143-50.

5159   Kandiah, Thiru. "Directions in the Sinhalese Theatre." In item 5157, pp. 116-35.

5160   Ludowyck, E. F. C. "The East-West Problem in Sinhalese Literature." YCGL, 6 (1957), 31-35.

5161   Reynolds, C. H. B. "British Writers on Ceylon in the 19th and Early 20th centuries." ABOB, n.s. 1, no. 2 (1963), 7-12.

5162   Sarachandra, Ediriweera R. The Folk Drama of Ceylon. Colombo: Dept. of Cultural Affairs, 1966.

5163   Seneviratne, Gamini. "Ceylonese Poetry Today." UA, 15 (1963), 189-92.

5164   Siriwardena, R. "Twentieth Century Writing in Ceylon." Ceylon Observer, (1950), 77-80, 91.

5165   Somapala, Wijetunga. "Modern Sinhala Poetry." Hemisphere, 11, no. 7 (1967), 31-35.

5166   ____ "New Drama in Sinhalese." Hemisphere, 12, no. 3 (1968), 33-36.

5167   ____ "The Rapid Growth of Modern Sinhalese Fiction." Hemisphere, 11, no. 9 (1967), 24-27.

Individual Authors

ALI, Ahmed

5168   Brander, Lawrence.   "Two Novels by Ahmed Ali." JCL, 3 (1967), 76-87.

ANAND, Mulk Raj

5169   Anand, Mulk Raj.   Apology for Heroism. London: Drummond, 1946.

5170   ____   "How I Became a Writer." CIL, 5, no. 11-12 (1965), 13-15.

5171   ____   Seven Summers. London: Hutchinson, 1951.

5172   ____   "Story of My Experiment with a White Lie." IndL, 10, no. 3 (1967), 28-43.

5173   Anon.   "Mulk Raj Anand: Chronology." CIL, 5, no. 11-12 (1965), 42-47.

5174   Balaramagupta, G. S.   "Anand's Big Heart: A Study." BP, 13 (1969), 37-43.

5175   ____   "Coolie--A Prose Epic of Modern India." JKU, 12 (1968), 92-99.

5176   ____   "The Humanism of Dr. Mulk Raj Anand." CIL, 7, no. 8 (1967), 6-8.

5177   ____   "Untouchable: A Study." CIL, 7, no. 11 (1967), 12-13.

5178   Berry, Margaret.   "'Purpose' in Mulk Raj Anand's Fiction." Mahfil, 5, no. 1-2 (1969), 85-90.

5179   Cowasjee, Saros.   "Introduction" to Mulk Raj Anand, Private Life of an Indian Prince. Toronto: Copp Clark, 1970, pp. 11-22.

5180   ____   "Mulk Raj Anand and His Critics." BP, 12 (1969), 57-63.

5181   ____   "Mulk Raj Anand's Princes and Proletarians." JCL, 5 (1968), 52-64.

5182   ____   "Princes and Politics." LCrit, 8, no. 4 (1969), 10-18.

5183   Dutt, Prabhat Kumar.   "Mulk Raj Anand in Relation to Tagore, Prem Chand and Sarat Chatterji." CIL, 5, no. 11-12 (1965), 19-20.

5184   Gowda, H. H. Anniah.   "Mulk Raj Anand." LHY, 6, no. 1 (1965), 51-60.

5185   Kurmanadham, K.   "The Novels of Dr. Mulk Raj Anand." Triveni, 36 (1967), 50-57.

5186   ____   "Women Characters in Dr. Mulk Raj Anand's Novels." CIL, 6, no. 6-7 (1966), 11-12, 26-27.

5187   Lindsay, Jack.   "Mulk Raj Anand--A Study." CIL, 5, no. 11-12 (1965), 21-33.

5188   Mareth, S. Menon.   "Three Indian Novelists." L&L, 59 (1948), 187-92.

5189   Murthi, K. V. Suryanarayana.   "The 'Motif' of Virtue in Dr. Mulk Raj Anand's Novels." CIL, 6, no. 1 (1966), 12-13, 26.

5190   ____   "The Theme of Salvation: Treatment by Mulk Raj Anand and R. K. Narayan." Triveni, 34 (1965), 50-59.

5191   Narasimhaiah, C. D.   "Mulk Raj Anand--The Novel of Human Centrality." In item 5064, pp. 106-34.

5192 Pant, M. C. "Mulk Raj Anand--The Man." CIL, 5, no. 11-12 (1965), 16-18.

5193 Riemenschneider, D. "An Ideal of Man in Mulk Raj Anand's Novels." IndL, 10, no. 1 (1967), 29-51.

5194 Sahiar, D. H. "Mulk Raj Anand's First Novel." JCL, 7 (1969), 1-16.

5195 Tarinayya, M. "Mulk Raj Anand's Untouchable: An Analysis." JMU, 26 (1969), 22-45.

5196 Zaheer, Sajjad. "Mulk Raj Anand." CIL, 5, no. 11-12 (1965), 11-12.

See also: 4936, 5051, 5387, 6474, 6480.

BHATTACHARYA, Bhabani

5197 Anon. "Bhabani Bhattacharya." Mahfil, 5 (1969), 43-48. [Interview.]

5198 ____ "Rural World of Bhabani." Enlite, 3 (1968), 27-30.

5199 Iyengar, K. R. Srinivasa. "Ideal and Real." Swarajya, 13 (1968), 13-14.

5200 Joshi, Sudhakar. "Evening with Bhabani." Indian Express, 27 April 1969, p. vii.

5201 Kalinnikova, E. I. "Ob ideinoi napravlenosit romana Bkhabani Bkhattachariia 'Boginiazoloto.'" ANSSSR, 80 (1965), 150-56.

5202 Ray, Lila. "Bhabani Bhattacharya: A Profile." IndL, 11, no. 2 (1968), 73-76.

5203 Shappe, Patricia L. "Bhabani Bhattacharya, Shadow from Ladakh." Mahfil, 5, no. 1-2 (1968-69), 31-39.

5204 Singh, Ram Sewak. "Bhabani Bhattacharya: A Novelist of Dreamy Wisdom." BP, 13 (1969), 60-75.

5205 Stock, A. G. "Kinds of Dedication." JCL, 5 (1968), 124-25.

CHAUDHURI, Nirad C.

5206 Bertocci, Peter J. "The Intellectuality of N. C. Chaudhuri." Mahfil, 5, no. 1-2 (1968-69), 91-98.

5207 Chitre, Dilip. "Nirad's Nightmare." Quest, 62 (1969), 43-52.

5208 Deva, Rajiva. "On Nirad C. Chaudhuri." Quest, 57 (1968), 69-75.

5209 Karnani, Chetan. "Nirad Chaudhuri and The Continent of Circe." Quest, 57 (1968), 76-81.

5210 Murthi, V. Rama. "Nirad C. Chaudhuri and the Indian Psyche." BP, 13 (1969), 102-09.

5211 Naipaul, V. S. "The Last of the Aryans." Encounter, 26, no. 1 (1966), 61-66.

5212 Siddiqui, M. N. "Nirad Chaudhuri: A Study in Alienation." OJES, 7, no. 1 (1969), 11-36.

See also: 52, 5051.

DAS, Kamala

5213 Barnard, J. "The Poet's Audience." JCL, 5 (1968), 116-18.

5214 Kohli, Devindra. "The Poetry of Kamala Das." WrW, 27 (1968), 58-75.

5215 _____ "Virgin Whiteness: An Interpretation of the Poetry of Kamala Das."
      LCrit, 7, no. 4 (1967), 64-80.

5216 Kohli, Suresh. "Poetic Craft of Kamala Das." Thought, 20 (1968), 17-78.

DEROZIO, Henry

5217 Verghese, C. Paul. "The First Indian Poet in English." Thought, 21
      (1969), 13-19.

DESAI, Anita

5218 Dunn, T. A. "Intensity and Crispness." JCL, 5 (1968), 126-27.

5219 Iyengar, K. R. Srinivasa. "A Note on Anita Desai's Novels." BP, 12
      (1969), 64-69.

DUTT, Michael Madhusudan

5220 Das, Sisir Kumar. "Michael Madhusudan Datta and the Sonnet in Bengal."
      Mahfil, 3, no. 4 (1967), 102-05.

5221 Dasgupta, Harendra Mohan. Studies in Western Influence on Nineteenth
      Century Bengali Poetry, 1857-87. Calcutta: Chuckervertty, Chatterjee,
      1935; 2nd. ed. Calcutta: Semushi, 1969.

5222 Dasgupta, R. K. "France Honours Michael Madhusudan Datta." SAMNB, 44
      (1967), 1-2.

5223 Dey, Bishnu. "A Note on Michael Madhusudan Datta." Quest, 17 (1958),
      13-18.

5224 Ray, Sibnarayan. "Michael Madhusudan Datta: The First Modern Poet of
      India." Humanist Review, 2 (1969), 135-47.

DUTT, Romesh Chunder

5225 Gupta, Jogendranath. Life and Work of Romesh Chunder Dutt, C.I.E.
      London: Dent, 1911.

DUTT, Toru

5226 Das, Harihar. Life and Letters of Toru Dutt. London: Humphrey Milford,
      Oxford Univ. Press, 1921.

5227 Dasgupta, Alokeranjan. "'This Fragile Exotic Blossom of Songs.'" IndL,
      9, no. 2 (1966), 6-14.

5228 Dutt, Toru. "Toru Dutt's Letters." IndL, 9, no. 2 (1966), 33-38.

5229 Gowda, H. H. Anniah. "Toru Dutt and Sarojini Naidu as Poets." LHY, 9,
      no. 1 (1968), 19-30.

5230 Mitra, Dipendranath. "The Writings of Toru Dutt." IndL, 9, no. 2 (1966),
      33-38.

5231 Rele, Subhash J. "Indian Among English Poets (Toru Dutt)." Hindustan
      Times, 2 March 1969, p. iii.

5232 Sengupta, Padmini. Toru Dutt. New Delhi: Sahitya Akademi, 1968.

EZEKIEL, Nissim

5233   McCutchion, David. "Examen de midi." WrW, 29 (1968), 71-72.

5234   Singh, Satyanarain. "Ramanujan and Ezekiel." OJES, 7, no. 1 (1969),
       67-75.

5235   Taranath, Rajeev. "Nissim Ezekiel's Poetry." WrW, 19 (1966), 47-64.

See also: 5051.

GHOSE, Aurobindo

5236   Chandrasekharam, V. Sri Aurobindo's 'The Life Divine.' Pondicherry:
       Sri Aurobindo Ashram, 1941.

5237   Chaudhuri, Haridas, and Frederic Spiegelberg, eds. The Integral
       Philosophy of Sri Aurobindo: A Commemorative Symposium. London:
       Allen & Unwin, 1960.

5238   _____ Sri Aurobindo: The Prophet of Life Divine. Pondicherry: Sri
       Aurobindo Ashram, 1960.

5239   Diwakar, R. R. Mahayogi: Life, Sadhana and Teachings of Aurobindo.
       Bombay: Bharatiya Vidya Bhavan, 1954.

5240   Ghose, Sisirkumar. "The Future Poetry of Sri Aurobindo." YCGL, 11
       (1962), 149-53.

5241   _____ "Looking back on Sri Aurobindo's Poetry." IndL, 10, no. 3 (1967),
       77-92.

5242   _____ The Poetry of Sri Aurobindo: A Short Survey. Calcutta: Chatuskone,
       1969.

5243   Gupta, Nolini Kanta. Poets and Mystics. Madras: Sri Aurobino Library,
       1951.

5244   Gupta, Rameshwar. "Opening Lines of Sri Aurobindo's Savitri: A Study."
       LCrit, 7, no. 4 (1967), 42-50.

5245   Iyengar, K. R. Srinivasa. On the Mother. Pondicherry: Sri Aurobindo
       Ashram, 1952.

5246   _____ Sri Aurobindo. Calcutta: Aryan Pub. House, 1945; rev. ed. 1950.

5247   _____ Sri Aurobindo: An Introduction. Mysore: Rao & Raghavan, 1961.

5248   Lal, P., and K. D. Sethna. "Controversy on Sri Aurobindo's Poetry:
       Correspondence." Mother India, 20 (1968), 707-11.

5249   Lalitha, K. S. "Some Poets of Sri Aurobindo." JMU, 26 (1969), 61-70.

5250   Langley, G. H. Sri Aurobindo: Poet, Philosopher and Mystic. London:
       Royal India & Pakistan Soc., 1949.

5251   La Violette, Wesley. "Aurobindo's Savitri." UA, 12 (1960), 516-18.

5252   Maitra, Sisirkumar. An Introduction to the Philosophy of Sri Aurobindo.
       Calcutta: Culture Publishers, 1941.

5253   _____ The Meeting of East and West in Sri Aurobindo's Philosophy.
       Pondicherry: Sri Aurobindo Ashram, 1956.

5254   _____ Studies in Sri Aurobindo's Philosophy. Banaras: Hindu Univ., 1945.

5255   Mitra, Sisirkumar. The Dawn Eternal: The Secret of India's Evolution.
       Pondicherry: Sri Aurobindo Ashram, 1954.

5256   _____ The Liberator: Sri Aurobindo, India and the World. Delhi, 1954;
       2nd ed. Bombay: Jaico, 1970.

5257 Mukherjee, Haridas, and Uma Mukherjee. Sri Aurobindo's Political Thought, 1893-1908. Calcutta: K. L. Mukhopadhyay, 1958.

5258 Nandakumar, Prema. A Study of Savitri. Pondicherry: Sri Aurobindo Ashram, 1962.

5259 Niel, André. "Shri Aurobindo, prophète d'une surhumanité cosmique." Synthèses, 227-228 (1965), 369-87.

5260 Pandit, M. P. Sadhana in Sri Aurobindo's Yoga. Pondicherry: Sri Aurobindo Ashram, 1962.

5261 ____ Sri Aurobindo in England. Pondicherry: Sri Aurobindo Ashram, 1956.

5262 ____ Sri Aurobindo: Studies in the Light of His Thought. Pondicherry: Sri Aurobindo Ashram, 1961.

5263 Purani, A. B. The Life of Sri Aurobindo. Pondicherry: Sri Aurobindo Ashram, 1958.

5264 ____ Sri Aurobindo's 'Savitri': An Approach and a Study. 2nd ed. Pondicherry: Sri Aurobindo Ashram, 1956.

5265 Romen. "Studies in Aurobindo's Poetry: 2. Fundamental Concepts in Sri Aurobindo's Poetry." Srinvantu, 16 (1968), 41-45.

5266 ____ "Studies in Sri Aurobindo's Poetry." Srinvantu, 15 (1967), 569-73.

5267 ____ "Studies in Sri Aurobindo's Poetry: 3. Rishi." Srinvantu, 16 (1968), 89-92.

5268 Roy, Anilbaran. Sri Aurobindo and the New Age. London: Allen & Unwin, 1940.

5269 Roy, Dilip Kumar. Sri Aurobindo Came to Me. Bombay: Jaico, 1952.

5270 Sastri, T. V. Kapali. Sri Aurobindo: Lights on His Teachings. Pondicherry: Sri Aurobindo Ashram, 1948.

5271 Sastry, L. S. R. Krishna. "Two Poems of Sri Aurobindo." BP, 13 (1969), 18-26.

5272 Seetarman, M. V. "'Because Thou Art All-Beauty and All-Bliss.'" Advent, 18, no. 4 (1961), 33-43.

5273 ____ "'The Divine Worker,' a Sonnet by Sri Aurobindo: A Commentary." Advent, 17, no. 2 (1960), 22-36.

5274 ____ "'The Dual Being,' a Sonnet by Sri Aurobindo: A Commentary." Advent, 16, no. 4 (1959), 21-29.

5275 ____ "'Krishna,' a Sonnet by Aurobindo: A Commentary." Advent, 17, no. 4 (1960), 31-43.

5276 ____ "'Lila,' a Sonnet by Sri Aurobindo: A Commentary." Advent, 17, no. 3 (1960), 22-33.

5277 ____ "Rodogune as a Tragedy." Sri Aurobindo Circle, 15 (1959), 67-81.

5278 ____ "The Self's Infinity." Advent, 18, no. 3 (1961), 25-35.

5279 ____ "Shiva." Advent, 18, no. 1 (1961), 23-33.

5280 ____ "Sri Aurobindo's Perseus the Deliverer: A Commentary." Mother India, 11 (1959), 40-62.

5281 ____ "Sri Aurobindo's Vasavadutta: A Commentary." Mother India, 11 (1959), 101-10.

5282 ____ "'Surrender,' a Sonnet by Sri Aurobindo: A Commentary." Advent, 17, no. 1 (1960), 18-25.

5283 ____ "The Viziers of Bassora as a Romantic Comedy." Sri Aurobindo Circle, 16 (1960), 76-92.

5284 _____ "The World of the Silence." Advent, 18, no. 2 (1961), 74-84.

5285 Sethna, K. D. "Aurobindo and the Longest Sentences in English."
Mother India, 20 (1968), 410-11.

5286 _____ The Poetic Genius of Sri Aurobindo. Bombay: Sri Aurobindo Circle,
1947.

5287 _____ "The Poetry of Sri Aurobindo." Mother India, 7 (1955), 28-34.

5288 _____ The Vision and Work of Sri Aurobindo. Pondicherry: Sri Aurobindo
Ashram, 1969.

5289 Shree, Krishna Prasad. "The Importance of the Future Poetry and
Letters of Sri Aurobindo." Advent, 26, no. 4 (1969), 34-40.

5290 Srivastava, Rama Shankar. Sri Aurobindo and the Theories of Evolution.
Varanasi: Chowkamba Sanskrit Series Office, 1970.

5291 Tan Yun-Shan, and Sisirkumar Mitra. Sri Aurobindo: A Homage. Madras:
Sri Aurobindo Library, 1941.

See also: 22, 5499, 6481.

GHOSE, Manmohan

5292 B., C. "Centenary of a Poet (Manmohan Ghose)." Thought, 21 (1969),
18-19.

5293 Bairagi, Mahendranath. "Manmohan Ghose's Centenary." ModR, 124 (1969),
293.

5294 Lahiri, K. C. "Manmohan Ghose: Here and There." CalR, 1, no. 1 (1969),
71-97.

5295 Lal, P. "The Poetry of Manmohan Ghose." ModR, 124 (1969), 175-76.

GHOSE, Zulfikar

5296 Wignesan, T. "Pakistani Novelists." JCL, 5 (1968), 119-20.

HOSAIN, Shahid

5297 Ireland, K. "English Verse on Asian Soil." JCL, 5 (1968), 113-15.

JHABVALA, Ruth Prawer

5298 Hartley, Lois. "R. Prawer Jhabvala, Novelist of Urban India." LE&W, 9
(1965), 265-73.

5299 Kapoor, S. D. "A Study in Contrasts." CalR, 178 (1968), 165-70.

5300 Williams, H. Moore. "Strangers in a Backward Place: Modern India in
the Fiction of Ruth Prawer Jhabvala." JCL, 6, no. 1 (1971), 53-64.

5301 _____ "The Yogi and the Babitt: Themes and Characters of the New India
in the Novels of R. Prawer Jhabvala." TCL, 15 (1969), 81-90.

LAL, P.

5302 Barnard, J. "The Poet's Audience." JCL, 5 (1968), 116-18.

5303 Mokashi, Punekar S. "P. Lal: An Appreciation." WrW, 26 (1968), 29-71.
[Also pub. separately. Calcutta: Writers Workshop, 1968.]

5304   Saha, Subhas Chandra. "P. Lal: A Major Indo-English Poet." BP, 12
       (1969), 153-61.

MALGONKAR, Manohar

5305   Mukherjee, M. "Review of A Bend in the Ganges." LHY, 6, no. 2 (1965),
       79-82.

5306   Powers, Janet M. "Three by Manohar Malgonkar." Mahfil, 3, no. 2-3
       (1966), 76-84.

See also: 5182.

MARKANDAYA, Kamala

5307   Harrex, S. C. "A Sense of Identity: The Novels of Kamala Markandaya."
       JCL, 6, no. 1 (1971), 65-78.

5308   Kumar, Shiv K. "Tradition and Change in the Novels of Kamala
       Markandaya." BA, 43 (1969), 508-13. [Repr. in OJES, 7, no. 1 (1969),
       1-9.]

5309   Parameswaran, Uma. "India for the Western Reader: A Study of Kamala
       Markandaya's Novels." TQ, 11, no. 2 (1958), 231-47.

5310   Rao, K. S. N. "Kamala Markandaya: Nectar in a Sieve: A Footnote to the
       Title." Indian P.E.N., 35 (1969), 315-17.

5311   _____ "Kamala Markandaya: The Novelist as Craftsman." IWT, 3, no. 2
       (1969), 32-40.

See also: 4936, 5051, 6474, 6482.

MORAES, Dom

5312   Bains, Y. S. "A Reading of Dom Moraes." LE&W, 10 (1966), 124-37.

5313   Doherty, Francis. "Poetic Parable: A Note on the Poetry of Dom Moraes."
       Studies, 52 (1963), 205-11.

5314   Verghese, C. Paul "A Reading of Dom Moraes." Thought, 21 (1969), 13-16.

See also: 5051.

NAGARAJAN, K.

5315   Krishnamurthi, M. E. "The Chronicles of Kedaram." IWT, 4, no. 1 (1970),
       27-31.

NAIDU, Sarojini

5316   Bhatnagar, R. Sarojini Naidu: The Poet of a Nation. Allahabad: Kitab
       Mahal, n.d.

5317   Cousins, James H. "The Poetry of Sarojini Naidu." In The Renaissance
       in India. Madras: Ganesh, 1918, pp. 249-77.

5318   Dustoor, P. E. Sarojini Naidu. Mysore: Rao & Raghavan, 1961.

5319   Gowda, H. H. Anniah. "Toru Dutt and Sarojini Naidu as Poets." LHY, 9,
       no. 1 (1968), 19-30.

5320   Lingwood, Dennis Edward. "Krishna's Flute." PoetryR, 36, no. 5-6
       (1945), 29-38.

5321   Mukherjea, S. V. "The Art of Sarojini Naidu." In Disjecta Membra: Studies in Literature and Life. Bangalore: Indian Inst. of World Culture, 1959.

5322   Munro, John M. "The Poet and the Nightingale: Some Unpublished Letters from Sarojini Naidu to Arthur Symons." CalR, n.s. 1, no. 1 (1969), 135-46.

5323   Narasimhaiah, C. D. "Tradition and Experiment--The Poets: Sarojini Naidu, Toru Dutt, Aurobindo and After." In item 5064, pp. 19-41.

5324   Natesan, G. A. Mrs. Sarojini Naidu: A Sketch of Her Life and an Appreciation of Her Works. Madras: G. A. Natesan, 1914.

5325   Rao, K. Raghavendra. "A Forgotten Nightingale: Some Reflections on Sarojini Naidu." EH, 2, no. 11 (1963), 32-35.

5326   Sarangpani, M. P. "Mrs. Sarojini Naidu." ModR, 39 (1926), 98-107.

5327   Sengupta, Padmini. Sarojini Naidu: A Biography. Bombay: Asia House, 1966.

5328   Thomas, E. M. "East Indian Alabaster Box." Critic (London), 33 (July 1898), 50-53.

See also: 5051, 5229, 5402.

NARAYAN, R. K.

5329   Alphonso-Karkala, John B. "Symbolism in The Financial Expert." IWT, 4, no. 1 (1970), 14-18.

5330   Anon. "R. K. Narayan Honoured." Swarajya, 12 (1967), 10.

5331   ____ "Well Met in Malgudi." TLS, 9 May 1958, p. 254.

5332   Beerman, Hans. "R. K. Narayan." Fulbright News Letter, 15, no. 2 (1967), 7-10.

5333   ____ "Two Indian Interviews." BA, 39 (1965), 290-94.

5334   Dale, James. "The Rootless Intellectual in the Novels of R. K. Narayan." UWR, 1 (1965), 128-37.

5335   Gerow, Edwin. "The Quintessential Narayan." LE&W, 10 (1966), 1-18.

5336   Gowda, H. H. Anniah. "R. K. Narayan." LHY, 6, no. 1 (1965), 25-39.

5337   Harrex, S. C. "R. K. Narayan's Grateful to Life and Death." LCrit, 8, no. 3 (1968), 52-65.

5338   Hartley, Lois. "In 'Malgudi' with R. K. Narayan." LE&W, 9 (1965), 87-90.

5339   Malhotra, Tara. "Old Places, Old Tunes: A Critical Study of R. K. Narayan's Latest Fiction." BP, 13 (1969), 53-59.

5340   Mehta, Ved. "The Train Had Just Arrived at Malgudi Station." NY, 38 (15 Sept. 1962), 51-90.

5341   Mukerji, Nirmal. "Some Aspects of the Literary Development of R. K. Narayan." BP, 13 (1969), 114-15.

5342   ____ "Some Aspects of the Technique of R. K. Narayan's The Guide." WHR, 15 (1961), 372-73.

5343   Narasimhaiah, C. D. "R. K. Narayan--The Comic as a Mode of Study in Maturity." In item 5064, pp. 135-58.

5344   Nazareth, Peter. "R. K. Narayan: Novelist." ESA, 8 (1965), 121-34.

5345   Onlooker [pseud.]. "City People Have Forgotten How to Live Laments Author." Hindustan Times, 2 Dec. 1968, p. 9.

5346 Raizada, Harish. R. K. Narayan: A Critical Study of His Works. New
      Delhi: Young Asia Publications, 1969.

5347 Rao, A. V. Krishna. "Significant National Symbols in the Novels of R. K.
      Narayan." LHY, 8, no. 1-2 (1967), 80-84.

5348 Rao, K. Subba. "The Guide: A Glimpse of Narayan's Attitude and
      Achievement." Triveni, 36 (1967), 65-67.

5349 ____ "R. K. Narayan's Art and The Vendor of Sweets." Triveni, 37 (1969),
      37-42.

5350 Rao, M. Rama. "A Play by R. K. Narayan." JMU, 28 (1968), 25-30.

5351 Rao, V. Panduranga. "The Art of R. K. Narayan." JCL, 5 (1968), 29-40.

5352 ____ "Tea with R. K. Narayan." JCL, 6, no. 1 (1971), 79-83.

5353 Rosenthal, A. M. "Talk with Rasipuram Krishnaswami Narayan of Malgudi,
      India." NYTBR, 23 March 1958, pp. 5, 44.

5354 Singh, Ram Sewak. "R. K. Narayan's The Vendor of Sweets: An Explication."
      KURJ, 2, no. 2 (1968), 360-65.

5355 Sio, Kewlian. "Meeting R. K. Narayan." WrW, 5 (1961), 21-22.

5356 Syal, Harshbala. "Narayan and the Emerging Indian Fiction." Busara,
      2, no. 1 (1969), 52-54.

5357 Venkatachari, K. "R. K. Narayan's Novels: Acceptance of Life." OJES,
      7, no. 1 (1969), 51-65.

5358 Walsh, William. "The Intricate Alliance: The Novels of R. K. Narayan."
      REL, 2, no. 4 (1961), 91-99.

5359 ____ "The Spiritual and the Practical." JCL, 5 (1968), 121-23.

5360 ____ "Sweet Mangoes and Malt Vinegar." Listener, 67 (1962), 380-81.

5361 ____ "Sweet Mangoes and Malt Vinegar: The Novels of R. K. Narayan."
      In A Human Idiom. London: Chatto & Windus, 1964, pp. 128-48.

5362 Westbrook, P. D. "The Short Stories of R. K. Narayan." JCL, 5 (1968),
      41-51.

See also: 52, 5051, 5067, 5188, 5190, 5387, 6474, 6483-6485.

RAJAN, Balachandra

5363 Gowda, H. H. Anniah. "Rajan: The Serious and the Comic." LHY, 5, no. 1
      (1964), 45-56.

5364 McCutchion, David. "Le style c'est l'homme." WrW, 6 (1961), 21-24.

RAMANUJAN, A. K.

5365 Nakulan. "Meeting with A. K. Ramanujan." Thought, 21 (1969), 11-13.

See also: 5234.

RAO, Raja

5366 Ali, Ahmed. "Illusion and Reality: The Art and Philosophy of Raja Rao."
      JCL, 5 (1968), 16-28.

5367 Amur, G. S. "Raja Rao: The Kannada Phase." JKU, 10 (1966), 40-52.

5368 Bhattacharaya, Sujit K. "Meeting Raja Rao." CitWR, 11 Oct. 1969, p. 37.

5369   Iyengar, K. R. Srinivasa. "Literature as Sadhana: A Note on Raja Rao's
       The Cat and Shakespeare." Aryan Path, 40 (1969), 301-05.

5370   Kohli, Suresh. "Ambivalence and Individuality: An Interview with Raja
       Rao." IFR, 6, no. 17 (1969), 11-13.

5371   Krishnasastri, L. S. R. "Raja Rao." Triveni, 36, no. 4 (1968), 16-30.

5372   Mukherjee, Meenahsi. "Raja Rao's Shorter Fiction." IndL, 10, no. 3
       (1967), 66-76.

5373   Nagarjan, S. "An Indian Novel." SR, 72 (1964), 512-17.

5374   Naik, M. K. "The Achievement of Raja Rao." BP, 12 (1969), 44-56.

5375   ____   "The Cow of the Barricades and Other Stories: Raja Rao as a Short
       Story Writer." BA, 40 (1966), 392-96.

5376   ____   "Kanthapura: The Indo-Anglian Novel as Legendary History." JKU,
       10 (1966), 26-39.

5377   ____   "The Kingdom of God Is Within a 'Mew': A Study of The Cat and
       Shakespeare." JKU, 12 (1968), 123-50.

5378   Narasimhaiah, C. D. "The Cat and Shakespeare." LCrit, 8, no. 3 (1968),
       65-95.

5379   ____   "Raja Rao--The Metaphysical Novel (The Serpent and The Rope) and
       Its Significance for Our Age." In item 5064, pp. 159-202.

5380   ____   "Raja Rao: The Serpent and the Rope." LCrit, 5, no. 4 (1963), 62-89.

5381   ____   "Raja Rao's Kanthapura: An Analysis." LCrit, 7, no. 2 (1966),
       54-78.

5382   O'Brien, A. P. "Meeting Raja Rao." Prajna, 11, no. 2 (1966), clxxx-clxxxiv.

5383   Parameswaran, Uma. "Karma at Work: The Allegory in Raja Rao's The Cat
       and Shakespeare." JCL, 7 (1969), 107-15.

5384   Ranchan, P. S. "A Meeting with Raja Rao." Thought, 20 (1968), 14-16.

5385   Ray, Robert J. "The Novels of Raja Rao." BA, 60 (1966), 411-14.

5386   Subramanyam, Ka Naa. "Raja Rao and Current Literature." Hindustan Times,
       6 June 1969, p. iv.

5387   Verghese, C. Paul. "Raja Rao, Mulk Raj, Narayan and Others." IWT, 3,
       no. 1 (1969), 31-38.

See also: 4936, 5051, 5188, 6474.

ROY, Dilip Kumar

5388   Ruben, Walter. "Dilip Kumar Roy The Upward Spiral (1949) und F. M.
       Dostojewski Die Bruder Karamasoff (1879/80)." In Beiträge zur
       Sprachwissenschaft Volkskunde und Literaturforschung: Wolfgang Steinitz
       zum 60. Geburtstag am 28. Februar dargebracht, ed. A. V. Isačenko et
       al. Berlin: Akademie, 1965, pp. 324-33.

See also: 5506.

SAHGAL, Nayantara

5389   Sahgal, Nayantara. "Storm Within." Hindustan Times, 9 Nov. 1969, p. iv.
       [Interview by Suresh Kohli.]

SINGH, Khushwant

5390 Anon. "Khushwant Singh." Mahfil, 5 (1969), 27-42. [Interview.]

5391 ____ "Of Sorrow and Anger." Statesman, 31 May 1968, p. 3.

5392 Dulai, Surjit Singh. "The Legacy of Paternalism: The Socio-Political
       Syndrome in Khushwant Singh's Fiction." Mahfil, 5, no. 1-2 (1968-69),
       1-8.

5393 Kulshrestha, Chirantan. "Khushwant Singh's Fiction." IWT, 4, no. 1
       (1970), 19-26.

5394 Shahane, V. A. "Theme and Symbol in Khushwant Singh's I Shall Not Hear
       the Nightingale." OJES, 7, no. 1 (1969), 11-36.

5395 Singh, Khushwant. "Khushwant Singh on Language and Literature." WLWE
       Newsletter, 18 (1970), 27-32.

TAGORE, Rabindranath

5396 Aikat, Amulya Chandra. On the Poetry of Matthew Arnold, Robert Browning
       and Rabindranath Tagore. Calcutta: Univ. of Calcutta, 1921.

5397 Aiyanger, M. Vencatesa. Rabindranath Tagore. Bangalore: B. B. D. Power,
       1946.

5398 Alanker, S. N. Gurudeva in My Vision: Rabindranath Tagore. Foreword by
       Sarojini Naidu. Hyderabad: S. N. Alanker, 1953.

5399 Ali, A. Yusuf. "The Religion of Rabindranath Tagore." In Essays by
       Divers Hands, vol. 9, ed. John Bailey. London: Humphrey Milford,
       1930, pp. 79-102.

5400 Amirthanayagam, Guy. "The Poetry of Tagore." OrientR, 5 (1959), 49-58.

5401 Anand, Mulk Raj. The Golden Breath: Studies in the Fine Poets of the
       New India. London: John Murray, 1933.

5402 ____ Homage to Tagore. Lahore: Sangam, 1946.

5403 ____ "Rabindranath Tagore: A Bridge Between East and West." EH, 1,
       no. 11 (1961), 13-21.

5404 Anon. "Bharati on Tagore." IndL, 12, no. 1 (1969), 28-30.

5405 ____ "Jehad Against Tagore." Now, 9 Aug. 1968, p. 5.

5406 ____ "Letters from Bhanusina." VQ, 19 (1953), 173-83.

5407 ____ "Rabindranath: Our National Poet." Prabuddha Bharata, 66 (1961),
       204-09.

5408 ____ "Rabindranath Tagore." Unitas, 35 (1962), 411-34.

5409 ____ "Rabindranath Tagore." ModR, 124 (1969), 328.

5410 ____ Rabindranath Tagore, 1861-1961: A Centenary Volume. New Delhi:
       Sahitya Akademi, [1961].

5411 ____ "Tagore and Einstein." Contemporary, 13, no. 5 (1969), 37-38.

5412 ____ "Tagore and Lohia on Language." Mankind, 12, no. 1 (1968), 49-57.

5413 ____ "Tagore and Rolland." Contemporary, 13, no. 5 (1969), 35.

5414 ____ "Tagore and Wells." Contemporary, 13, no. 5 (1969), 36, 54.

5415 ____ "Tagore Centenary Celebrations: Unveiling of Memorial Plaque at
       Hampstead." AsR, 58 (1962), 14-18.

5416 ____ "Tagore for Today: Some Passages from Tagore's Writings."
Mainstream, 6, no. 36 (1968), 17-18.

5417 Aronson, A. "Rabindranath Through Western Eyes." VQ, 7 (1942), 169-88.

5418 ____ Rabindranath Through Western Eyes. Allahabad: Kitabistan, 1943.

5419 ____ "Rabindranath's Literary Criticism." VQ, 7 (1941-42), 57-72.

5420 Assagioli, Roberto. "Rabindranath, Poeta, Mistico, Educatore." Rassegna
Italiana (Oct. 1926), 684-94.

5421 Bagghi, Krishna. "Tagore's English Gitanjali." BP, 12 (1969), 121-26.

5422 Balasundaram, S. N. "Gandhi-Tagore Controversy of 1921: A Retrospect."
Now, 14 Feb. 1969, pp. 9-12.

5423 Bandyopadhyaya, Deviprasad. "Tagore, the Modern Exponent of Rain."
Folklore, 4 (1963), 221-36.

5424 Banerjee, Hiran May. How Thou Singest, My Master! Calcutta: Orient
Longmans, 1961.

5425 ____ Humanism of Tagore. Mysore: Univ. of Mysore, 1968.

5426 Banerjee, Sri Kumar. "The Short Stories of Rabindranath." IAC, 10
(1961), 9-18.

5427 Banerjee, Subrata. "Rabindranath, the Prophet of Universal Man." Indian
P.E.N., 27 (1961), 254-60.

5428 Banja, Nilendra Nath. Das religiöse Weltbild bei Rabindranath Tagore.
Gelnhausen: H. Schwab, [1964].

5429 Basak, Radhagovinda. "The Kusā-jātaka of the Mahāvastu Avadāna and
Tagore's Rajā and SapMocan." IAC, 10 (1961), 19-29.

5430 Basu, Abinash Chandra. "Rabindranath Tagore." Commonwealth Journal,
4 (1961), 190-93.

5431 ____ Three Mystic Poets: A Study of W. B. Yeats, A. E. and Rabindranath
Tagore. Kolhapur: Moghe, 1945.

5432 Baumer, Sybil. An Introduction to Rabindranath Tagore's Mysticism.
London: Allenson, 1925.

5433 Bhagwat, Durga. "Tagore on Folk Literature." UA, 13 (1961), 90-94.

5434 Bharat, Gauranamaya. Lives of Guru Nanak and Tagore. Delhi: Rashtra
Bhaga Prkashan, 1965.

5435 Bhaskar, Babu R. P. "Tagore the Novelist." DilR, 7 (1959), 333-34.

5436 Bhatnagar, R. K. "Rabindranath Tagore: The Great Sentinel." CenturyM,
25 May 1968, pp. 17-18.

5437 ____ "Rabindranath Tagore: The Great Sentinel." Women on the March,
12, no. 8 (1968), 8-9.

5438 Bhattacharya, Batukuath. "Brahma Rada in Rabindranath." CalR, 168
(1963), 56-62.

5439 Bhattacharya, Bhabani. "Gandhiji and Gurudev Tagore." Indian Railways,
14 (1969), 272-74.

5440 Bhattacharya, Birendra. "Rabindranath: The Poet." UA, 13 (1961), 95-98.

5441 Bhattacharya, Debiprasad. "Rolland and Tagore: Disenchantment Came
Soon." Statesman, 25 May 1969, p. 8.

5442 Bhattacherje, M. M. Rabindranath Tagore, Poet and Thinker. Allahabad:
Kitab Mahal, [1961].

5443 Bhavan, Max Muller. Rabindranath in Germany: A Cross-Section of Contemporary Reports. Ed. Heimo Rau. New Delhi: German Culture Inst., 1961.

5444 Bhave, S. S. "'Tagore in German.'" JMSUB, 11, no. 1 (1962), 123-29.

5445 Bhushan, V. N. "Tagore and Telugu Literature." VQ, 7 (1941-42), 33-40.

5446 Bose, Buddhadeva. "Tagore in Translation." YCGL, 12 (1963), 15-26.

5447 Bose, D. M. "Rabindranath Tagore, 1861-1961." Science and Culture, 27 (1961), 265-71.

5448 Bose, Dakshina Ranjan. "Tagore Song." Cosmic Society, 7, no. 9 (1969), 51.

5449 Bose, Joges C. "Rift in the Lute: Tagore's Drama." ModR, 111 (1962), 216-19.

5450 ____ "Tagore at a Glance." ModR, 109 (1961), 447-551.

5451 ____ "Tagore, the Poet of Human Value." ModR, 102 (1957), 127-30, 312-15.

5452 Bose, Nandalal. "On Gurudev's Art." VQ, 7 (1943), 201-09.

5453 ____ "The Paintings of Rabindranath." VQ, 1 (1936), 29-34.

5454 Brosalina, E. K. "Osnovnye napravlenija v dramaturgii R. Tagora." VLU, 22, no. 1 (1967), 54-57.

5455 Callis, Helmut G. "Rabindranath Tagore: India's Message to the Modern World." WHR, 14 (1960), 311-22.

5456 Carter, Albert Howard. "Rabindranath Tagore." BA, 41 (1967), 36.

5457 Catlin, George E. Gordon. "Rabindranath Tagore." JRSA, 109 (1961), 613-27. [Abridged as "Rabindranath Tagore." Quest, 32 (1962), 9-13.]

5458 ____ Rabindranath Tagore. Bombay and New York: Allied Publishers, [1964].

5459 Chakravarti, Amiya. "A Note on Last Writings." VQ, 7 (1941-42), 89-92.

5460 ____ "Tagore and China." VQ, 7 (1942), 189-92.

5461 ____ "Tagore as an Educationist." Swarajya, ann. supp. (1964), 209-12.

5462 ____, ed. A Tagore Reader. New York: Macmillan, 1961.

5463 ____, et al. Rabindranath. Calcutta: Calcutta Book Exchange, 1938.

5464 Chakravarty, Basudha. "Post-Tagore Literary Trends in Bengal." Triveni, 37 (1969), 16-19.

5465 ____ "Rabindranath as a Dramatist." AgraUJ, 9 (1961), 23-41.

5466 Chander, Jagdish. "Sartor Resartus and Gitanjali: Studies in Mystic Experience." CalR, 170 (1964), 251-56.

5467 Chandhury, Provosjivan. "Tagore and the Problem of God." VQ, 19 (1953), 184-95.

5468 Chandrasekharan, K. "Tagore and Modern Tamil Literature." CIL, 2, no. 4 (1962), 10-11, 30-31.

5469 ____ "Tagore's Influence on Tamil-Nad." ModR, 108 (1960), 59-61.

5471 Chatterjee, D. N. "Tagore and French Literature." CalR, 166 (1963), 257-69.

5472 Chatterjee, Ramananda, ed. The Golden Book of Tagore. Calcutta: Golden Book Committee, 1931.

5473 ____ "Rabindranath Tagore." OrientR, 2 (1956), 67-75.

5474 _____ "Rabindranath Tagore." ModR, 109 (1961), 353-62.

5475 Chatterjee, Sisir. "Stray Thoughts on the Novels of Rabindranath Tagore." BIASLIC, 6 (1961), 74-75.

5476 Chatterji, S. C. "Rabindranath Tagore on Education." EH, 2, no. 2 (1962), 26-32.

5477 Chattopadhyaya, Sudhakar. "Tagore's Vision of Indian History." IFR, 4, no. 8 (1967), 10-11, 17.

5478 Chaudhuri, Pramatha. "My First Impressions of Rabindranath." Visvabharati News, 27, no. 2 (1968), 37.

5479 Chaudhuri, Satyabrata. "Tagore's Genius." IWI, 9 June 1968, p. 4.

5480 Chaudhury, P. C. Roy. "Gandhiji and His Contemporaries: The Poet and the Politician, a Unique Friendship." Indian Express, 10 Nov. 1968, p. 1.

5481 Chaudhury, Prabas Jiban. Tagore on Literature and Aesthetics. Calcutta: Rabindra Bharati, 1965.

5482 Chaudhury, Provosjivan. "Tagore and the Problem of God." VQ, 19 (1953), 184-95.

5483 Chelysev, E. P. "O Khudozhestvennom Metode Rabindranat Tagore." ANSSSR, 80 (1965), 62-79.

5484 Chi Hsien-Lin. "How Tagore Lives in My Heart." ChinL, 7 (1961), 126-29.

5485 Chidambarantha, Chettiar. "Rabindranath Tagore and Modern Tamil Literature." JMU, 33 (1962), 131-36.

5486 Chisholm, A. R. "Rabindranath Tagore." Meanjin, 20 (1961), 312-14.

5487 Choudhary, K. P. S. "The Destiny of Man in Tagore's Philosophy." VQ, 32 (1966-67), 267-76.

5488 Choudhuri, A. D. "Tagore and the West." VQ, 30 (1965), 253-61.

5489 Coles, Mervyn D. "The Plays of Tagore." ContR, 183 (1953), 293-95.

5490 Das, Jahar. "Tagore and Nehru: A Study of Comparative Greatness." Mirror, 6, no. 10 (1967), 16-20.

5491 Das, Jibanananda. "Rabindranath and Modern Bengali Poetry." Mahfil, 3, no. 4 (1967), 5-10.

5492 Das, P. K. "Līlā as the Creation of Love, with Gleanings from Rabindranath." VQ, 29 (1963-64), 62-75.

5493 Das, S. R. "Tagore as a Teacher and a Pioneer." AsR, 60 (1964), 44-50.

5494 Das, Taraknath. Rabindranath Tagore: His Religious, Social, and Political Ideals. Calcutta: Sarasvati Library, 1932.

5495 _____ "Rabindranath Tagore, Poet and Patriot." Thought, 17 (1942), 105-18.

5496 Dasgupta, Alokeranjan. "Bengali Poetry: Tagore and After." CIL, 5, no. 4 (1965), 11-12, 47.

5497 Dasgupta, Debendra Chandra. "Psychological Interpretations of Tagore's Gitanjali." CalR, 164 (1962), 37-48; 166 (1963), 173-88; 168 (1963), 237-49; 176 (1965), 9-34; 179 (1966), 145-71.

5498 Dasgupta, H. "Tagore as a Humanist." CalR, 157 (1960), 142-46.

5499 Dasgupta, N. K. "Brief Review of the Structure of Personality as Conceived by the West and the East with Reference to Tagore and Sri Aurobindo." Educational Miscellany, 3, no. 1-2 (1966), 60-67.

5500 Das Gupta, Nilima. Lodestar: Or a Guide to English Translations of Tagore's Poems. New Delhi: Sudha, 1968.

5501 Dasgupta, P. R. "Lord Buddha and Buddhism in the Eyes of Poet Tagore." Guardian (Bangalore), 9 (1962), 34-35.

5502 Dasgupta, Surendranath. Rabindranath, the Poet and Philosopher. Calcutta: Mitra & Ghosh, 1948.

5503 Dasgupta, Tamonash Chandra. "Some Aspects of Rabindranath's Literature." CalR, 171 (1964), 33-40.

5504 Datta, Bhabatosh. "Western Influence in Tagore's Thought." BRMIC, 20 (1969), 353-61.

5505 Deshpande, Kusumavati. "Tagore and the Marathi Literature." CIL, 2 no. 12 (1962), 6-7, 11.

5506 Dhar, Niranjan. "Roy and Tagore." Radical Humanist, 31 (1967), 375-76.

5507 Dhar, Somnath. "Tagore in Singapore and Malaya in 1927." IAC, 10 (1961), 49-61.

5508 Dimock, Edward C., Jr. "Foreword." Mahfil, 3, no. 1 (1966), 1-3.

5509 ____ "Rabindranath Tagore--'The Greatest of the Bauls of Bengal.'" JASt, 19 (1959), 33-51.

5510 Drummond, W. H. "Tagore, (1861-1941)." HibJ, 60 (1941), 34-37.

5511 D'Souza, J., and P. Doncoeur. "La vie et l'œuvre de Rabindranath Tagore." Etudes (1934), 513-28, 673-94.

5512 Durrany, K. S. "The Humanist Tradition and Tagore." Darshana International, 7, no. 3 (1967), 42-48.

5513 Dutt, Ihwar. "Rabindranath Tagore--Der indische Dichter und Nobelpreisträger." Universitas, 15 (1960), 939-46.

5514 Dwivedi, Pandit Hazariprasad. "Rabindranath as an Inspirer of Modern Hindi Literature." VQ, 7 (1941-42), 19-26.

5515 Elenjimittam, Anthony. The Poet of Hindustan. Calcutta: Orient, 1948.

5516 Elmhirst, Leonard. "Rabindranath Tagore and Sriniketan." VQ, 24 (1958), 124-44.

5517 ____ "Tagore on Detachment." VQ, 31 (1965-66), 111-14.

5518 Engelhardt, Emil. Rabindranath Tagore als Mensch, Dichter und Philosoph. Berlin: Furche, 1921.

5519 Enright, D. J. "Tagore's Social Poetry and Social Thought." LCrit, 5, no. 1 (1961), 108-15.

5520 Faurot, Albert. "Tagore as an English Poet." SJ, 8 (1961), 301-04.

5521 Franci, Giorgio Renato. "Prima Notizia della lirica bengali dopo Tagore." Ouderni, 6 (1961 [1962]), 33-44.

5522 Gadgil, Gangadhar. "Short Stories of Tagore." UA, 13 (1961), 86-89.

5523 Garnier, Ch.-M. "L'occidentalisme de Tagore." RAA, 7 (1930), 231-46.

5524 ____ "Tagore et George Russell ('A.E.')." RAA, 7 (1930), 97-112.

5525 Ghandi, M. K. "Great Sentinel." Bhavan's Journal, 5 Oct. 1969, pp. 40-49. [Reply to Tagore; see item 5736.]

5526 Ghose, Sisirkumar. "An Introduction to the Poetry of Tagore." Vidya, 1, no. 1 (1961), 15-26.

5527 ____ The Later Poems of Tagore. New York: Asia House, 1961.

5528 _____ "Rabindranath and Modernism." IndL, 2, no. 3 (1968), 12-20.

5529 Ghose, Sudhin N. "Paintings and Drawings of Tagore." AsR, 57 (1961), 246-50.

5530 Ghosh, D. N. Rabindranath Tagore: His Early Life and Works. Calcutta: Modern Book Agency, 1947.

5531 Ghosh, Gouriprasad. "The Songs of Rabindranath Tagore." VQ, 26 (1960), 150-61.

5532 Ghosh, Sachindra Lal. "Rabindranath: An Artist in Life." IAC, 18, no. 2 (1969), 46-56.

5533 Ghosh, Sati. Rabindranath. Calcutta: S. Gupta, 1945.

5534 Ghoshal, Satyendranath. "Rabindranath Tagore and His Dramatic Genius." JPU, 22, no. 1 (1967), 42-51.

5535 Gilkey, Robert. "Tagore and Whitman." Quest, 34 (1962), 21-27.

5536 Gillet, Louis. "Le théâtre de Rabindranath Tagore." RDM, 12 (1922), 672-84.

5537 G., N. M. "Tagore Centenary Celebrations." Indian P.E.N., 27 (1961), 45-48.

5538 Gokak, V. K. "Tagore and Kannada Literature." CIL, 2, no. 5 (1962), 16-17.

5539 Gommes, Marou. "Tagore Chez Lui." JdD, (Nov. 1941), 15-16.

5540 Gopala, Reddi B. "Tagore and Modern Telugu Literature." CIL, 3, no. 1 (1963), 6-7.

5541 Gopalam, Vajjhala. "Gitanjali (the English Version): A Study." ModR, 116 (1964), 339-49.

5542 _____ "Tagore's Karna and Kunti: A Study." ModR, 92 (1962), 36-39.

5543 Guehenno, Jean. "Tagore m'a réappris l'esperance. . . ." FL, 11 (1961), 1, 6.

5544 Guha, Naresh. "Discovery of a Modern Indian Poet." Mahfil, 3, no. 1 (1966), 58-73.

5545 _____ "Yeats and Rabindranath Tagore." Quest, 36 (1963), 9-19.

5546 Gupta, Subodh Bhushan. "Gitanjali: A Political Interpretation." Political Science Review, 1 (1962), 92-98.

5547 Haldar, Aruna. "Tagore's Internationalism, Its Roots and Character." JPU, 22, no. 3 (1967), 65-78.

5548 Haldor, Gopal. "[Tagore]." In Saroj Acharya, ed., Great Rebels: Studies in Life and Letters. Calcutta: Book Forum, 1944, 1.

5549 Hay, Stephen N. "Rabindranath Tagore in America." AQ, 14 (1962), 439-63.

5550 Hazaressingh, K. "Tagore and His Message." ArtL, 21 (1957), 1-6.

5551 Herbert, Jean. "Tagore, prophéte de l'amour et porte-parole de l'Inde." Cahiers du Sud, 19 (1942), 83-97.

5552 Holmes, John Haynes. "The Religion of Tagore." Unity, 86 (1921), 343.

5553 Hurwitz, Harold M. "Ezra Pound and Rabindranath Tagore." AL, 36 (1964), 53-63.

5554 _____ "Tagore's English Reputation." WHR, 16 (1962), 77-83.

5555 _____ "Tagore's English Gitanjali: Reasons for Its Success." ArtL, 25 (1962), 32-37.

5556 ____ "Whitman, Tagore and A Passage to India." WWR, 13 (1967), 51-54.

5557 ____ "Yeats and Tagore." ConL, 16 (1964), 55-64.

5558 Huxley, Aldous. "Aldous Huxley on Tagore." IndL, 11, no. 3 (1968), 5-11.

5559 Iyengar, K. R. Srinivasa. Rabindranath Tagore. Bombay: Popular Prakasan.

5560 ____ "Tagore's Ministry of Culture." Swarajya, 13 (28 June 1969), 28-29.

5561 Iyengar, Masti Venkatesa. Rabindranath Tagore. Bangalore: The Author, 1946.

5562 J., S. "[Tagore's Birthday Celebrations]." Now, 28 May 1968, pp. 6-7.

5563 Jacinto, Jose S., Jr. "Tagore and the Indian Scene." SJ, 8 (1961), 287-95.

5564 Jagadisan, S. "Influence on Tagore." ModR, 125 (1969), 933.

5565 Jain, Sushil Kumar. "Indian Elements in the Poetry of Yeats: On Chatterji and Tagore." CLS, 7, no. 1 (1970), 82-96.

5566 Jaloux, Edmond. "Rabindranath Tagore." Temps, 20 Aug. 1941, p. 3.

5567 Jimmy. "Tagore and Einstein." CenturyM, 16 Dec. 1967, pp. 11-13.

5568 Joag, R. S. "Tagore and Marathi Literature." VQ, 7 (1941-42), 27-32.

5569 Johnson, Robert. "Juan Ramon Jimenez, Rabindranath Tagore and 'La Poesia Desnuda.'" MLR, 60 (1965), 534-46.

5570 Joshi, R. B. "A Note on Professor P. V. Kopnin's View of Tagore's Humanism." Publisher's Monthly 11, no. 11 (1969), 21-22.

5571 Kabir, Humayun. "The Poetry of Rabindranath Tagore." IAC, 9 (1960), 11-25.

5572 ____ "Rabindranath Tagore." In The Bengali Novel: Rabindranath Tagore. Calcutta: Firma K. L. Mukhopadhyay, 1968, pp. 94-121.

5573 ____ Rabindranath Tagore. London: School of Oriental & African Studies, Univ. of London, 1962.

5574 ____ "Tagore's Poetry." IndL, 2, no. 1 (1959), 5-20.

5575 Kalelkar, Kakasaheb. "The Literary Legacy of Tagore." UA, 13 (1961), 102-04.

5576 Kantak, V. Y. "Tagore's Views on Poetry and Art." JMSUB, 11, no. 1 (1962), 107-21.

5577 ____ "Tagore's Views on Poetry and Art." BP, 13 (1969), 1-17.

5578 Kent, Muriel. "Rabindranath Tagore and His Origins." Quarterly Review, 143 (1929), 545-56.

5579 Khanolkar, G. D. The Lute and the Plough: A Life of Rabindranath Tagore. Trans. (from Marathi) by Thomas Gray. Bombay: Book Centre, 1963.

5580 Kitch, Ethel May. "Rabindranath Tagore (Rāvindra Nātha Thākura): A Bibliography." BB, 11 (1921), 5.

5581 Klein, Nikolaus. "Rabindranath Tagore: Das Leben des Dichters." Indo Asia, 3 (1961), 45-51.

5582 Kocięcka, Mirostawa. "Rabindranath Tagore w Polsce." PHum, 5, no. 4 (1961), 125-34.

5583 Kopnin, P. V. "Humanism of Rabindranath Tagore." Publisher's Monthly, 11, no. 9 (1969), 15-19.

5584 Kowalska, Agrieszka. "Z dziejów recepcji Rabindranath a Tagore w Polsche." PrzO, 39 (1961), 265-81.

5585 Kripalani, Krishna. Rabindranath Tagore: A Biography. London: Oxford
      Univ. Press, 1962; New York: Grove, 1962.

5586 Krishnamurthy, Vidya. "The Humour of Tagore." Public Affairs, 8 (1964),
      55-60A.

5587 Kruger, Horst. Rabindranath Tagore und die Revolutionare
      Befreiungsbewegung in Indien 1905 bis 1918. Berlin: Akademie Verlag,
      1964.

5588 Kshitis, Roy. "Gandhi and Tagore: A Study in Contrast and Convergence."
      Times of India, 2 Oct. 1969, p. 1.

5589 _____ "A Prologue to the Gandhiji-Tagore Drama." Link (New Delhi), 12,
      no. 8 (1969), 33-34.

5590 Kumara, Pillai G. "Tagore the Poet." KUY, 12 (1967), 14-16.

5591 Lago, Mary M. "Modes of Questioning in Tagore's Short Stories." SSF,
      5 (1967), 24-36.

5592 _____ "The Parting of the Ways: A Comparative Study of Tagore and
      Yeats." Mahfil, 3, no. 1 (1966), 32-57.

5593 _____ "Tagore's Temporal Encounters." LE&W, 10 (1966), 19-41.

5594 Leela, Manilal. "Rabindranath Tagore." Hindustan Times, 4 May 1969,
      pp. 71-79.

5595 Lesný, Vincene. Rabindranath Tagore: His Personality and Work. Trans.
      by Guy McKeever Phillips. London: Allen & Unwin, 1939.

5596 Levi, D. Sylvain. "Rabindranath Tagore à Santiniketan." Europe, 1
      (15 Dec. 1923).

5597 Litman, A. D. "Homage to Tagore in the U.S.S.R." Statesman, 9 May 1967,
      p. 6.

5598 Loewenbach, Josef. "Rabindranath Tagore and Leŏs Janáček." NOB, 2
      (1961), 68-70.

5599 McHugh, Roger. "The Poetry of Tagore." Threshold, 5, no. 1 (1961),
      16-24.

5600 MacKenzie, Kathleen C. "Rabindranath Tagore." DR, 25 (1945), 68-78.

5601 MacNicol, M. "Sir Rabindranath Tagore." Bookman (London), 52 (1917),
      112-14.

5602 Madaule, Jacques. "Autour d'un centenaire: Rabindranath Tagore (1861-
      1941)." TableR, 162 (1961), 92-101.

5603 Mahalanobis, P. C. "Humanist Element in Modern Indian Culture: The
      Role of Rabindranath Tagore." In Towards a Sociology of Culture in
      India, ed. T. K. N. Unnithan. New Delhi: Prentice-Hall, 1965,
      pp. 237-41.

5604 _____ "Tagore and Japan." JapQ, 6 (1959), 157-65.

5605 Maheshwari, R. C. "He Gave Us Gintanjali." ModR, 118 (1965), 129-33.

5606 Mahmoud, Zaki Naguib. "Tagore and the Arab World." CIL, 6, no. 8 (1966),
      16-20.

5607 Maitra, Sisirkumar. "Rabindranath and Bergson." CalR, 19 (1926), 189-205.

5608 Majumdaar, Bimanbehari. Heroines of Tagore; A Study in the Transformation
      of Indian Society, 1875-1941. Calcutta: Firma K. L. Mukhopadhyay,
      1968.

5609 Malkani, M. U. "Tagore the Playwright." IndL, 1, no. 2 (1958), 62-66.

5610 Masani, R. "Celebration of Tagore Centenary in Bombay." AsR, 57 (1961),
      183.

5611 Meireles, Cecilia. "A imortalidade de Rabindranath Tagore." Comentário, 2 (1961), 219-30.

5612 Mitra, S. N. "Rolland and Tagore." Statesman, 11 May 1969, p. 8.

5613 Mitter, Sushil Chandra. La pensée de Rabindranath Tagore. Paris: Adrien-Maisonneuve, 1930.

5614 Mookherjee, Girija K. "Rabindranath Tagore and Romain Rolland." Aussenpolitic, 12 (1961), 852-58.

5615 ____ "Tagore's View of Asia." UA, 13 (1961), 79-81.

5616 More, Paul Elmer. "Rabindranath Tagore." WrW, 4, Tagore supp. (1961), i-ii.

5617 Mukherjea, Sunil Kumar. "Rabindranath's Punascha: A Study of Prose Poems." VQ, 28 (1962), 48-67.

5618 Mukherjee, Bhupen N. "Tagore's Influence on the Music of Hindustan." IAL, 18, no. 1 (1943), 1-7.

3619 Mukherjee Hiren. Himself a True Poem: A Study of Rabindranath Tagore. New Delhi: People's Pub. House, 1961.

3620 ____ "Rabindranath Tagore: Nationalism, Internationalism and Socialism." Contemporary, 13 (1969), 83-86.

5621 Mukherjee, Kalipada. "Tagore's 'Char Adhyaya.'" OrientR, 4 (1958), 41-50.

5622 Mukherjee, Sujit. "Tagore's Literary Work in America." EWR, 2 (1966), 140-47.

5623 Mukherji, Dhurjati Prasad. Tagore: A Study. Bombay: Padma, 1943.

5624 Mukherji, Prafulla C. "Rabindranath Tagore in America." ModR, 110 (1961), 383-92.

5625 Mukherji, S. Passage to America. Calcutta: Bookland, 1965.

5626 Murthi, K. V. Suryanarayana. "Love in Tagore's Works." CIL, 6, no. 3 (1966), 10-12; 6, no. 4 (1966), 12-13, 18.

5627 ____ "Tagore's Chitra: A Grammatical Clue to Character." Aryan Path, 37 (1966), 311-16.

5628 Murthi, R. K. "Mahatma and His Mentors, 5: Tagore and Gandhiji." Mirror, 8, no. 12 (1969), 37-38, 43.

5629 Murty, D. V. S. R. "Nature in Chitra." ModR, 120 (1966), 13-16.

5630 Mustafi, Dilip. "The Gitanjali: A Study in 'thou' and 'his.'" CalR, 157 (1960), 265-66.

5631 Nag, Jamuna. "Tagore and Japan." Indian Express, 8 May 1969, p. 6.

5632 ____ "Tagore and Secularism: A Birthday Tribute." Indian Express, 8 May 1968, p. 6.

5633 Nair, Thankappan. "A Visit to the House of the Tagores." Indian Express, 12 May 1968, p. iii.

5634 Nandakumar, Prema. "Tagore and Bharati." IndL, 12, no. 1 (1969), 31-39.

5635 Nandi, S. K. "Acharya Brojendranath on Kaviguru Rabindranath." VQ, 30 (1964), 17-23.

5636 ____ "Avindranath Tagore's Concept of Aesthetic Universality." JAAC, 18 (1959), 255-57.

5637 Naravane, V. S. "Eternal Traveller: Glimpses from the Life of Rabindranath Tagore." In Elephant and Lotus: Essays in Philosophy and Culture. Bombay: Asia House, 1965, pp. 83-98. ["Ethics of Rabindra Nath," pp. 125-34.]

5638 _____ "Tagore and Nehru on South East Asia." Cultural Forum, 8, no. 4
        (1966), 22-28.

5639 Nehru, Jawaharlal. "Nehru on Rabindranath Tagore." Contemporary,
        5 May 1969, p. 10.

5640 Nemes, Graciela P. "Of Tagore and Jiménez." BA, 35 (1961), 319-23.

5641 Noel-Paton, N. H. "A Personal Recollection." PoetryR, 35, no. 4 (1944),
        213-14.

5642 Novikova, V. A. "Bankimchandra and Rabindranath." Bengali Literature,
        3, no. 1 (1969), 1-9.

5643 Ocampo, Victoria. "West Meets East: Tagore on the Banks of the River
        Plate." IndL, 2, no. 2 (1959), 13-22.

5644 Ohdedar, A. K. "Tagore in Translation." BIASLIC, 6 (1961), 87-91.

5645 Pai, M. S. "Some Reflections on Gitanjali." UA, 13 (1961), 99-101.

5646 Pandit, S. L. "Rabindranath Tagore as a Playwright." JUJK, (1953), 6-16.

5647 _____ "Three Novels of Rabindranath Tagore." JKUR, 4, no. 1 (1961), 32-41.

5648 Parandowski, Jan. "Rabindranath Tagore." PolP, 4 (1961), 54-58.

5649 Patabhi Ram Reddy, M. "Tagore: Poet of Peace." CIL, 7, no. 11 (1967),
        14-15.

5650 Patel, C. N. "Gitanjali as Religious Poetry." Aryan Path, 34 (1963),
        392-97.

5651 Paz, Octavio. "Los Manuscritos de Tagore." CA, 149 (1966), 207-10.

5652 Perse, Saint-John. "Hommage de la mémoire de Rabindranath Tagore."
        NRF, 18 (1961), 868-71.

5653 Piper, Raymond F. "Report of an Interview with Rabindranath Tagore, on
        the Porch of His Cottage at Santiniketan in February, 1933." Folklore,
        3 (1962), 91-94.

5654 Pobozniak, Tadeusz. "Rabindranath Tagore: 6. V. 1861-1867; VIII. 1941."
        PrzO, 39 (1961), 259-64.

5655 Pochammer, Wilhelm Von. "Begegnung mit Tagore." Indo Asia, 3 (1961),
        32-38.

5658 Popa, George. "Sensul Cosmic Poeziei lui Rabindranath Tagore." ILit,
        19, no. 9 (1968), 43-46.

5659 Pound, Ezra. "Rabindranath Tagore." WrW, 4, Tagore supp. (1961),
        xxix-xxxiv.

5660 Pushp, P. N. "Tagore as Lyric Incarnate." JKUR, 4, no. 1 (1961), 23-31.

5661 Radhakrishnan, S. East and West in Religion. London: Allen & Unwin,
        1933.

5662 _____ "'Most Dear to All the Muses.'" HibJ, 59 (1961), 303-10.

5663 _____ The Philosophy of Rabindranath Tagore. London: Macmillan, 1918.

5664 _____ "Teachings of Tagore." CIL, 2, no. 1 (1962), 17-19; 2, no. 2
        (1962), 12-13.

5665 Raghavacharyulu, D. V. K. "Plays of Rabindranath Tagore." In Unpunctual
        Pen. Hyderabad: Maruthi Book Depot, 1968, pp. 105-19. ["Form and Idea
        in Tagore's Later Drama," pp. 120-28.]

5666 _____ "The Plays of Rabindranath Tagore." Aryan Path, 32 (1961), 148-51,
        197-202, 252-55.

5667 Raghavan, N. Y. "A Tribute to Tagore." AsR, 57 (1961), 180-82.

5668 Rajasingam, S. Durai, ed. Tagore--100 Years; A Malayan Homage. Kuala Lumpur: Printcraft, 1961.

5669 Ramachandran, G. "A Student's Memories of Gurudev." VQ, 7 (1941-42), 5-13.

5670 Ramachandrudu, P. "Geetanjali." Unilit, 7, no. 1 (1967), 23-26.

5671 Ranade, D. B. "Pathway to God in Tagore's Poetry: A Study in Indian Mysticism." JUP, 17 (1963), 85-103.

5672 Rao, A. V. Krishna. "The Novels of Rabindranath Tagore." Triveni, 33 (1964), 61-69.

5673 Rao, M. Rama. "Tagore's Gitanjali--An Interpretation." JMU, 16 (1957), 26-40.

5674 Rao, P. Nagaraja. "Devotion in the Religious Philosophy of Tagore." Prabuddha Bharata, 67 (1962), 234-36.

5675 Rao, Raja. "Tagore, homme de la renaissance." Preuves, 128 (1961), 35-38.

5676 Rau, Heimo. "Tagore in Germany." UA, 13 (1961), 115-17.

5677 Ray, Ashim. "Tagore's Impact on Writers of East Pakistan." Statesman, 30 March 1969, p. 7.

5678 Ray, Lila. "The Plays of Tagore." IAC, 6 (1954), 79-90.

5679 Ray, Niharranjan. An Artist in Life. Trivandrum: Univ. of Kerala, 1968.

5680 Recto, Deanna. "The Humanism of Rabindranath Tagore." DilR, 11 (1963), 276-87.

5681 Rehfield, Werner. "Tagore als Sprachschöpfer; Vergleich mit der neuen deutschen Literatur." Indo Asia, 3 (1961), 63-69.

5682 Rhys, Ernest. Rabindranath Tagore: A Biographical Study. London: Macmillan, 1915.

5683 Rice, Stanley. "Appreciation of Rabindranath Tagore." AsRev, 38 (1942), 74-81.

5684 Richards, Phillip Ernest. "The Personality of Tagore." Thought, 21 (1969), 19.

5685 Rolland, Romain, et al. "Hommage à Rabindranath Tagore." France-Asie, 17 (1961), 2647-780. [Avec les collaborations de Romain Rolland, Sarvepalli Radhakrishnan, Jean Filliozat, Nolini Kanta Gupta, Bhabani Bhattacharya, Andrée Karpelès, Suzanne Siauve, Pratima Tagore, Sandi Koffler, Sisirkumar Mitra, Srimayi Pitoeff, Jun Ohrui, Suzanne Karpelès, Nishikant, Jean Rousselot, Nirmal C. Sinha, Hem Day, Tatsuo Morimoto. "Le centenaire de Rabindranath Tagore dans le monde." Repr. as Hommage de la France à Rabindranath Tagore; pour le centenaire de sa naissance, 1961. Paris: Inst. de civilisation indienne, 1963.]

5686 Romanov, V., and Stephen N. Hay. "Tagore's Message to the World." Quest, 30 (1961), 91-93.

5687 Roos, Jacques. "Romain Rolland et Rabindranath Tagore." In Etudes de littérature étrangère et comparée. Connaisance de l'étranger. Mélanges offerts à la mémoire de Jean-Marie Carré. Paris: Didier, 1964, pp. 452-64.

5688 Roy, Basanta Koomar. Rabindranath Tagore: The Man and His Poetry. New York: Dodd, Mead, 1916.

5689 Roy, Dilip Kumar. Among the Great. Bombay: Nalanda Publications, 1945.

5690 Roy, U. C. Poetry and Religion and Rabindranath Tagore. Calcutta: Standard Press, 1961.

5691   Ruben, Walter. Indische Romane. Eine ideologische Untersuchung. Bd. 1:
        Einige Romane Bankim Chatterjees und Rabindranath Tagores. Berlin:
        Akademie-Verlag, 1964.

5692   ____ Rabindranath Tagores Weltdeutung. Berlin: Akademie-Verlag, 1962.

5693   ____ "Der Terrorist Sandip in Rabindranath Tagore's 'Das Heim un Die
        Welt' das Porträt eines indischen Materialisten (Carvaka)." In
        Eduard Erkes in memoriam 1891-1958. Leipzig: n.p., n.d., pp. 178-89.
        [Repr. from WZUL, 9 (1959-60), 291-302.]

5694   Rudra, Ashok. "Friendship in Tagore Songs." Conspectus, 3, no. 1 (1967),
        66-75.

5695   Sankara, Kurup G. "Tagore's Influence in Malayalam." CIL, 2, no. 3
        (1962), 12-13.

5696   Sanyal, Bhabani Gopal. "Rabindranath and India." CalR, 161 (1961),
        245-54.

5697   Sarkar, Amal. "Symbolism and Rabindranath." BIASLIC, 6 (1961), 76-86.

5698   Sarkar, Sunil Chandra. "The Educational Philosophy of Tagore." IAC,
        5 (1967), 265-74.

5699   Sastri, K. S. Ramaswami. Rabindranath Tagore: Poet, Patriot, Philosopher.
        Sriranagam: Sri Vani Vilas Press, 1924.

5700   ____ Sir Rabindranath Tagore: His Life, Personality and Genius. Madras:
        Ganesh, 1917.

5701   Sastry, C. N. "Walt Whitman and Rabindranath Tagore: A Study in
        Comparison and Contrast." Triveni, 38 (1969), 22-31.

5702   Satiraju, K. "The Cosmic Relevance of Tagore's Symbolic Plays." Triveni,
        34 (1965), 47-56.

5703   Schneps, Maurice. "Rabindranath Tagore: A Dialogue." UA, 13 (1961),
        105-09.

5704   Schurig, Arthur. Tagore. Seine Personlichkeit, seine Werk, seine
        Weltanschauung. Dresden: C. Reissmer, 1921.

5705   Sehanavis, Chinmohan. Tagore and the World. Calcutta: Mukand, [1961].

5706   Sen, Jiten. "Tagore in Persia." Now, 10 Jan. 1969, pp. 6-7.

5707   Sen, Nabaneeta. "An Aspect of Tagore-Criticism in the West: The Cloud
        of Mysticism." Mahfil, 3, no. 1 (1966), 9-23.

5708   ____ "The Foreign Incarnation of Rabindranath Tagore." JASt, 26 (1966),
        275-86.

5709   Sen, Pulinbihari, and Sobhanlal Ganguli, comps. "Works of Rabindranath
        Tagore in English: Bibliography." JJCL, 8 (1968), 85-95.

5710   Sen, Satya Bhooshan. "Tagore on Death." ContR, 180 (1951), 239-42.

5711   Sen, Sukumar. "Some Early Influences in Tagore's Life." IAC, 10 (1961),
        147-52.

5712   Sengupta, Benoyendra. "U.S.A.'s Interest in Rabindranath." ModR, 102
        (1957), 148-54, 316-19.

5713   Sengupta, Subodh Chandra. The Great Sentinel: A Study of Rabindranath
        Tagore. Calcutta: A. Mukherjee, 1949.

5714   Sen Gupta, S. P. "Swami Vivekananda and Rabindranath." Prabuddha
        Bharata, 72 (1967), 179-84.

5715   Shahane, V. A. "Rabindranath Tagore: A Study in Romanticism." SIR, 3
        (1963), 53-64.

5716 Shamsuddin. "The Influence of Folk Music on Tagore's Songs." Indian
P.E.N., 2 (1961), 230-32.

5717 _____ "Poetic Heart of Tagore." Sikh Review, 18, no. 197 (1969), 30-32.

5718 Sham Suzzoha. "Ban on Tagore." Now, 11 Aug. 1967, p. 22.

5719 Shome, Arun. "Tagore the Seer." Statesman, 11 May 1969, p. 1.

5720 Shridharani, Krishnalal. "Rabindranath Tagore, 1861-1941." SatRL, 34,
no. 17 (1941), 3-4, 14-15.

5721 Shrivastava, S. N. L. "The Philosophy of Rabindranath Tagore." Aryan
Path, 38 (1967), 349-52, 403-08.

5722 _____ "Tagore on Detachment." VQ, 31 (1965-66), 111-14.

5723 Singh, Baldev. Tagore and the Romantic Ideology. Bombay: Orient
Longmans, 1963.

5724 Singh, Iqbal. "Tagore: A Determination." Life and Letters Today, 32
(1942), 178-90.

5725 Singh, Mohan. "Tagore, Puran Singh, and Iqbal." Sikh Review, 18,
no. 190 (1969), 36-37.

5726 Sinha, Sasadhar. Social Thinking of Rabindranath Tagore. London: Asia
House, 1962.

5727 Sinhar Dinkar, A. D. "Musings on Tagore." In Reflections on Men and
Things. Ajmer: Krishna Bros., 1968, pp. 22-29.

5728 Smith, Harriet. "Walt Whitman and Rabindranath Tagore: Precursors of
Universal Man." VQ, 29 (1963-64), 4-14.

5729 Streiker, Lowell D. "The Religious Thought of Rabindranath Tagore."
CraneR, 9 (1967), 159-76.

5730 Subramanyam, G. V. "Vaishnavism in the Writings of Tagore." TTDJ, 18,
no. 7 (1967), 25-26.

5731 Subramanyam, Ka Naa. "What Tagore Means to Me." UA, 13 (1961), 82-85.

5732 Subroto. "[Rabindranath Tagore]." IWI, 5 May 1968, p. 17.

5733 Suhrawardy, Shaheed. "Tagore at Oxford." OrientR, 2 (1956), 111-19.

5734 Sykes, Marjorie. Rabindranath Tagore. London: Longmans, 1943.

5735 "Tagore and His Land." Quest (Special Issue, May 1961), 9-78. [S. Datta,
"Tagore as a Lyric Poet"; A. S. Ayyub, "The Aesthetic Philosophy of
Rabindranath Tagore"; Sudhin N. Ghose, "Paintings and Drawings of Tagore";
Stephen N. Hay, "The Origins of Tagore's Message to the World"; S. Ray,
"Rabindranath Tagore and Modern Bengal."]

5736 Tagore, Rabindranath. "Call of Truth." Bhavan's Journal, 5 Oct. 1969, pp.
40-45. [Repr. from ModR, 30, no. 4 (1921), 423-33; see also item
5525.]

5737 _____ "Childhood Days." VQ, 18 (1952), 148-63.

5738 _____ "Father as I Knew Him." VQ, 18 (1953), 336-53.

5739 _____ "Letters to His Wife." VQ, 19 (1953), 2-19.

5740 Tennyson, Hallam. "Rabindranath Tagore." Listener, 65 (1961), 825-26.

5741 Thompson, E. T. Rabindranath Tagore; His Life and Work. London: Milford,
1921.

5742 _____ Rabindranath Tagore: Poet and Mystic. London: Milford, 1926.

5743 Tiempo, Edith L. "The Short Stories of Rabindranath Tagore." SJ, 8
(1961), 296-300.

5744   Titman, Lily. "Eminent Sussex Visitor of 1881." Sussex County Magazine,
       17 (1943), 246-48.

5745   Tögel, Fritz. Rabindranath Tagore und seine Sendung. Leipzig: Tietz,
       1922.

5746   Urmeneta, Fermín de. "Tagore, o la estética de un humanismo a lo
       divino." RIE, 19 (1961), 239-41.

5747   Vaillat, Leandre. Le poète hindou Rabindranath Tagore. Paris: Bossard,
       1922.

5748   Van Bunsen, Marie. "Von und uber Rabindranath Tagore." LitEcho, 24
       (1922), 1363-366.

5749   Van Der Plas, C. O. "What Rabindranath Tagore Means to Me." UA, 14
       (1962), 340-43.

5750   Varma, Rajendra. Tagore, Prophet Against Totalitarianism. Bombay:
       Asia House, 1965.

5751   Watson, Francis. "Rabindranath Tagore: Poet and Prophet." Listener,
       65 (1961), 924-26.

5752   Wickramasinghe, Martin. "Tagore and Ceylon." UA, 15 (1963), 163-67.

5753   Wilkinson, Marguerite. "Tagore on Indian Poetry." WrW, 4, Tagore supp.
       (1961), xvii-xviii.

5754   Woolf, S. J. "India's Poet Who Waits for the Dawn." WrW, 4, Tagore
       supp. (1961), xxv-xxviii.

5755   Younghusband, Sir Francis, et al. "Memorial Meeting." IAL, 15, no. 2
       (1942), 57-72.

5756   Zbavitel, Dušan. "The Poet's Responsibility." NOB, 2 (1961), 65-66.

5758   ____   "Rabindranath and the Folk-Literature of Bengal." Folklore, 2
       (1961), 9-14.

5759   ____   "Rabindranath Tagore and Czechoslovakia." VQ, 22 (1956-57), 274-82.

5760   ____   "Rabindranath Tagore in 1887-1891." ArO, 24 (1956), 581-90.

5761   ____   "Rabindranath Tagore in 1891-1905." ArO, 24 (1956), 599-609.

5762   ____   "Rabindranath Tagore in 1905-1913." ArO, 26 (1958), 101-13.

5763   ____   "Rabindranath Tagore in 1913-1930." ArO, 26 (1958), 366-84.

5764   ____   "Rabindranath Tagore in 1930-1937." ArO, 27 (1959), 60-75.

5765   ____   "Rabindranath Tagore, 1937-1941." ArO, 27 (1959), 251-71.

5766   ____   "Winternitz and Tagore." VQ, 24 (1958), 1-21.

5767   Zils, Paul. "Rabindranath Tagore in Indian Films." Indo-Asia, 3 (1961),
       80-82.

See also: 5051, 6486-6491.

VENKATARAMANI, K. S.

5768   Subramanyam, Ka Naa. "'Kandan the Patriot,' Murugan the Tiller."
       Times of India, 12 Jan. 1969, p. iii.

Southeast Asia
(Malaysia, Singapore, Philippines)

General

5769 Bernad, Miguel A. Bamboo and the Greenwood Tree. Manila: Bookmark, 1961.

5770 ____ "Philippine Literature: A Twofold Renaissance." Thought (New York), 37 (1962), 427-48.

5771 Brandon, James R. Theatre in South East Asia. Cambridge, Mass.: Harvard Univ. Press, 1967.

5772 Casper, Leonard. New Writing From the Philippines: A Critique and Anthology. Syracuse, N. Y.: Syracuse Univ. Press, 1966.

5773 Castrence, Pura S. "Philippine Literature." DilR, 13 (1965), 359-65.

5774 Del Castillo y Tuazon, Teofilo. Brief History of Philippine Literature. Manila: Progressive Schoolbooks, 1937.

5775 Fernando, Lloyd. "Introduction" to Twenty-two Malaysian Stories. Singapore: Heinemann Educational, 1968, pp. 1-7.

5776 Lim Chor Pee. "Drama and the University." Tumasek, 2 (1964), 49-51.

5777 ____ "Is Drama Non-Existent in Singapore?" Tumasek, 1 (1964), 42-44.

5778 Lopez, Salvador P. Literature and Society. Manila: Philipine Book Guild, 1940.

5779 Osman, Mohammed Taib Bin. "Trends in Modern Malay Literature." In Malaysia: A Survey, ed. Wang Gungwu. New York, Washington, and London: Frederick A. Praeger, 1965, pp. 210-24.

5780 Singaravelu, S. "A Comparative Study of the Sanskrit, Tamil, Thai and Malay Versions of the Story of Rama with Special Reference to the Process of Acculturation in the Southeast Asia Versions." JSSB, 56, no. 2 (1968), 137-185.

5781 Song Ong Siang. One Hundred Years History of the Chinese in Singapore. Kuala Lumpur: Univ. of Malaya Press, 1968.

5782 Viray, Manuel A. "Certain Influences in Filipino Writing." Pacific Spectator, 6 (1952), 292-99.

5783 ____ "Philippine Writing Today." LitR, 3 (1960), 465-77.

5784 Wignesan, T. "A Brief Survey of Contemporary Malay Literature." In Bunga Emas. Kuala Lumpur: Rayirath [Raybooks] Publications, 1965, pp. 243-48.

5785 ____ "Literature in Malaysia." JCL, 2 (1966), 113-23.

5786 ____ "The Malayan Short Story in English." In Bunga Emas, pp. 234-39. [See item 5784.]

5787   Zieseniss, Alexander. <u>The Rama Saga in Malaysia: Its Origin and</u>
       <u>Development</u>. Trans. P. N. Burch. Singapore: Malaysian Sociological
       Res. Inst., 1963. [Orig. pub. 1928.]

<u>See also</u>: 5039, 6492-6498.

Individual Authors

GOH Poh Seng

5788   Doggett, V. "[Review of First Production of <u>The Moon is Less Bright</u>]."
       <u>Sunday Mail</u>, 6 Dec. 1964.

HAN Suyin [Elizabeth Comber, née Chou]

5789   Fernando, Lloyd. "Picture of the Artist as a Eurasian." <u>Tenggara</u>, 2,
       no. 1 (1968), 92-95.

WONG, Phui Nam

5790   Mottram, E. N. W. "Wong Phui Nam." In <u>Bunga Emas</u>, pp. 229-33. [See
       item 5784.]

West Indies

Research Aids

5791 Boxill, Anthony. "A Bibliography of West Indian Fiction 1900-1970."
      WLWE, 19 (1971), 23-44.

5792 Harris, L. J., and David Ormerod. "A Preliminary Check-List of West
      Indian Fiction in English, 1949-1964." TCL, 11 (1965), 146-49.

5793 Index to Periodical Articles by and about Negroes. 1960-1970 (cumulated).
      Boston: G. K. Hall, 1971. Cont. of Index to Selected Periodicals.
      Wilberforce, Ohio: Central State College, 1950-1959 (cumulated).

5794 Walkley, Jane. "A Decade of Caribbean Literary Criticism: A Select
      Annotated Bibliography." LHY, 11, no. 2 (1970), 187-95.

See also: 57, 61, 62.

General

5795 Abrahams, Peter. Jamaica: An Island Mosaic. London: H. M. Stationery
      Office, 1957.

5796 Anon. "Africa in West Indian Poetry." CarQ, 4, no. 1 (1955), 5-13.

5797 _____ "The Caribbean Mixture: Variations and Fusions in Race and Style."
      TLS, 10 Aug. 1962, p. 578.

5798 Baugh, Edward. "Towards a West Indian Criticism." CarQ, 14, no. 1-2
      (1968), 140-44.

5799 _____ "West Indian Prose Fiction in the Sixties: A Survey." Bim, 47
      (1968), 157-65.

5800 Bennett, Wycliffe. "The Jamaican Poets." L&L, 57 (1948), 58-61.

5801 _____ "West Indian Poetry." CarV, 24 Aug. 1958, pp. 1-7.

5802 Blackman, Peter. "Is There a West Indian Literature?" L&L, 57 (1948),
      96-102.

5803 Blundell, Margaret. "Caribbean Readers and Writers." Bim, 43 (1966),
      163-67.

5804 Brathwaite, L. Edward. "The Caribbean Artists' Movement." CarQ, 14,
      no. 1-2 (1968), 57-59.

5805 _____ "Caribbean Critics." NWQ, 5, no. 1-2 (1969), 5-12.

5806 _____ "Creative Literature of the British West Indies During the Period
      of Slavery." Savacou, 1 (1970), 46-73.

5807 ____ "Jazz and the West Indian Novel." Bim, 44 (1967), 275-84; 45 (1967), 39-50; 46 (1968), 115-26.

5808 ____ "Kyk-over-al and the Radicals." NWQ, 2, no. 3-4 (1966), 55-57.

5809 ____ "The New West Indian Novelists." Bim, 31 (1960), 199-209; 32 (1961), 271-77.

5810 ____ "Rehabilitations." Bim, 51 (1970), 174-84.

5811 ____ "Sir Galahad and the Islands." Bim, 25 (1957), 8-16.

5812 ____ "Themes from the Caribbean." TES, 6 Sept. 1968, p. 396.

5813 ____ "West Indian Prose Fiction in the Sixties: A Survey." Bim, 47 (1968), 157-65.

5814 Brown, Lloyd W. "The Crisis of Black Identity in the West Indian Novel." Critique (Minneapolis), 2, no. 3 (1969), 97-112.

5815 Calder-Marshall, Arthur, et al. "A West Indian Symposium." CarV, 9 July 1950, pp. 1-8.

5816 Cameron, Norman E. Thoughts on Life and Literature. Georgetown: F. A. Persick, 1950.

5817 Carew, Jan. "An Artist in Exile--From the West Indies." NWF, 27-28 (1966), 23-30.

5818 ____ "Literature and Language in Developing Countries." NWF, 22 (1965), 25-29; 23 (1965), 23-27.

5819 Carr, W. I. "Literature and Society." CarQ, 8, no. 2 (1962), 76-93.

5820 ____ "Reflections on the Novel in the British Caribbean." QQ, 70 (1963), 585-97.

5821 ____ "The West Indian Novelist: Prelude and Context." CarQ, 11, no. 1-2 (1965), 71-84.

5822 Collymore, Frank A. "Writing in the West Indies: A Survey." TamR, 14 (1960), 111-24.

5823 Coulthard, G. R. "The Coloured Woman in Caribbean Poetry (1800-1960)." Race, 2 (1961), 53-61.

5824 ____ "La literatura de las Antillas britanicas." RIB, 19 (1969), 39-55.

5825 ____ La literatura de las Antillas inglesas. Santiago de Cuba: Universidad de Oriente, 1954.

5826 ____ "Literature of Latin America and the Caribbean." CarQ, 10, no. 4 (1964), 46-54.

5827 ____ Race and Colour in Caribbean Literature. London: Oxford Univ. Press, 1962.

5828 ____ "Recent Marxist Interpretations of Latin American Literature." CarQ, 9, no. 3 (1963), 10-15.

5829 ____ "Rejection of European Culture as a theme in Caribbean Literature." CarQ, 5, no. 4 (1959), 231-44.

5830 ____ "The West Indian Novel of Immigration." Phylon, 20 (1959), 32-41.

5831 Crozier, Jimmy. "The Beginnings of Bim." Bim, 48 (1969), 245-48.

5832 Currey, R. N. "Recent West Indian Anthologies." CarV, 20 March 1949, pp. 1-4.

5833 Daly, Patrick O. H. West Indian Freedom and West Indian Literature. Georgetown: Daily Chronicle, 1951.

5834 Dathorne, O. R. "Africa in the Literature of the West Indies." JCL, 1 (1965), 95-116.

5835 ____ "Introduction" to Caribbean Narrative. London: Heinemann Educational, 1966, pp. 1-16.

5836 ____ "Introduction" to Caribbean Verse. London: Heinemann Educational, 1967, pp. 1-15.

5837 ____ "The Theme of Africa in West Indian Literature." Phylon, 26 (1965), 255-76.

5838 Dawes, Neville. "The Need for a Critical Tradition." CarV, 8 June 1952, pp. 5-8.

5839 D'Costa, J. "Language and Dialect in Jamaica." JJ, 2, no. 1 (1968), 71-74.

5840 Derrick, A. C. "An Introduction to Caribbean Literature." CarQ, 15, no. 2-3 (1969), 65-78.

5841 Dillard, J. "English in the West Indies." HER, 34 (1964), 312-16.

5842 Drayton, Arthur D. "West Indian Consciousness in West Indian Verse; A Historical Perspective." JCL, 9 (1970), 66-88.

5843 ____ "West Indian Fiction and West Indian Society." KR, 25 (1963), 129-41.

5844 Drummett, Joan, ed. "A Guyanese National Theatre." NWF, 24 (1966), 12-26; 25 (1966), 15-27; 26 (1966), 13-24.

5845 Eliet, Edouard. Panorama littérature negro-africaine, (1921-1962). Paris: Présence Africaine, 1965.

5846 Ellis, Keith. "The Poetry of the Spanish American Countries: A Historical Perspective." NWQ, 5, no. 1-2 (1969), 22-31.

5847 Figueroa, John. "Dreams and Visions: A Critical Introduction" to Caribbean Voices. Vol. 2. The Blue Horizons. London: Evans, 1970, pp. 1-21.

5848 ____ "Some Provisional Comments on West Indian Novels." In item 36, pp. 90-97.

5849 Fuller, Roy. "Criticism of Recent West Indian Poetry." CarV, 16 May 1948, pp. 5-7.

5850 Garvey, Amy Jacques. Garvey and Garveyism. London: Collier-Macmillan, 1970.

5851 Gospard, David. "Calypso as Literature." Link (Castries), 2, no. 1 (1970), n. pag.

5852 Gray, C. "Folk Themes in West Indian Drama: An Analysis." CarQ, 14, no. 1-2 (1969), 102-09.

5853 Harris, Wilson. History, Fable and Myth in the Caribbean and Guianas. Georgetown: Ministry of Information and Culture, 1970.

5854 ____ Tradition and the West Indian Novel. London: London West Indian Students Union, 1966.

5855 ____ Tradition the Writer and Society. London: New Beacon, 1967.

5856 ____ "The Unresolved Constitution." CarQ, 14, no. 1-2 (1968), 43-47.

5857 Herring, Robert. "What I Look for in West Indian Literature--Jamaica." CarV, 18 April 1948, pp. 1-4.

5858 Hill, Errol, ed. The Artist in West Indian Society: A Symposium. Port of Spain: Univ. of the West Indies, n.d. [Errol Hill, "West Indian Drama," pp. 7-24.]

5859 ____ "Calypso Drama." CarQ, 15, no. 2-3 (1969), 81-98.

5860 Irish, James. "Magical Realism: A Search for Caribbean and Latin
      American Roots." LHY, 11, no. 2 (1970), 127-40.

5861 Ismond, Patricia. "Problems of the Artist in the West Indies." Link
      (Castries), 2, no. 1 (1970), n. pag.

5862 James, C. L. R. The Black Jacobins. New York: Vintage, 1963, pp. 413-18.

5863 James, Louis. "Caribbean Poetry in English--Some Problems." Savacou,
      2 (1970), 78-86.

5864 _____ "Islands of Man: Reflection on the Emergence of a West Indian
      Literature." SoRA, 2 (1966), 150-63.

5865 _____, ed. The Islands in Between. London: Oxford Univ. Press, 1968.

5866 Jekyll, Walter, ed. Jamaican Song and Story. Introds. by Philip Sherlock,
      Louise Bennett, and Rex Nettleford. New York: Dover, 1966.

5867 Jones, Joseph and Johanna. Authors and Areas of the West Indies. Austin:
      Steck-Vaughn, 1970.

5868 Lamming, George. "Caribbean Literature: The Black Rock of Africa."
      AForum, 1, no. 4 (1966), 32-52.

5869 Le Page, R. B. "Dialect in West Indian Literature." JCL, 8 (1969), 1-7.

5870 Lucie-Smith, E. "[Review of The Islands In Between]." LMag, 8, no. 4
      (1968), 68, 96-102.

5871 Maes-Jelinek, Hena. "The Myth of El Dorado in the Caribbean Novel."
      JCL, 6, no. 1 (1971), 113-27.

5872 Manley, Edna, et al. "Focus, 1-3." UWIRST, n.d.

5873 McDonald, I. "The Unsteady Flame: A Short Account of Guianese Poetry."
      NWF, 17 (1965), 19-22; 18 (1965), 24-25; 19 (1965), 19-20.

5874 McDowell, Robert E. "Mothers and Sons." PrS, 43 (1969-70), 356-68.

5875 McFarlane, Basil. "On Jamaican Poetry." Kyk-over-al, 13 (1951), 207-09.

5876 McFarlane, J. E. Clare. "The Prospect of West Indian Poetry." Kyk-over-al,
      16 (1953), 125-27.

5877 McGuiness, F. "West Indian Windfall." LMag, 7, no. 1 (1967), 117-20.

5878 Moore, Gerald. The Chosen Tongue: English Writing in the Tropical World.
      London: Longmans, 1969.

5879 Morris, Mervyn. "Some West Indian Problems of Audience." English, 16
      (1967), 127-31.

5880 Naipaul, V. S. "Comments on West Indian Literature." CarV, 31 Aug.
      1958, pp. 0-3.

5881 _____ "The Past Year." CarV, 16 Sept. 1956, pp. 2-5.

5882 _____ "Speaking of Writing." London Times, 2 Jan. 1964, p. 11.

5883 _____ "Survey of West Indian Literature, 1955." CarV, 22 Jan. 1956, pp. 1-6.

5884 Nettleford, Rex. "African Connexion: 1. Parallels, 2. Historical
      Continuity, 3. Panafricanism, 4. African in the World." UWIRST, n. d.

5885 _____ Mirror Mirror. Kingston: Sangster & William Collins, 1970.

5886 New World Group. "The Intellectual Tradition and Social Change in the
      Caribbean: An Appraisal of New World." NWF, 17 (1966), 9-17.

5887 Owens, R. J. "West Indian Poetry." CarQ, 7, no. 3 (1961), 120-27.

5888 Page, Malcolm. "West Indian Writers." Novel, 3 (1970), 167-72.

5889 Pearse, Andrew C. "West Indian Themes." CarQ, 2, no. 2 (1951), 12-23.

5890 Porter, Dorothy. "African and Caribbean Creative Writings: A
      Bibliographic Survey." AForum, 1, no. 4 (1966), 107-11.

5891 Ramchand, Kenneth. "Concern for Criticism." CarQ, 16, no. 2 (1970),
      51-60.

5892 ____ "Concern for Criticism." LHY, 11, no. 2 (1970), 151-62.

5893 ____ "Decolonization in West Indian Literature." Transition, 22 (1966),
      48-49.

5894 ____ "Dialect in West Indian Fiction." CarQ, 14, no. 1-2 (1968), 27-42.

5895 ____ "Terrified Consciousness." JCL, 7 (1969), 8-9.

5896 ____ West Indian Narrative: An Introductory Anthology. London: Nelson,
      1966.

5897 ____ The West Indian Novel and Its Background. London: Faber & Faber,
      1970.

5898 Ramsaran, J. A. "The Social Groundwork of Politics in Some West Indian
      Novels." NegroD, 18, no. 10 (1969), 71-77.

5899 ____ "Some West Indian Novelists." Ibadan, 4 (1958), 19-22.

5900 ____ "Sun, Sea and Sonnets: The Afro-Carib Literary Scene." NegroD,
      11, no. 1 (1962), 52-57.

5901 Rawlins, R. "Migrants with Manuscripts: Social Background of the West
      Indian Novel." BO, 4 (1958), 46-50.

5902 Seymour, A. J. "Guianese Poetry." Kyk-over-al, 2 (1946), 13-16.

5903 ____ "Nature Poetry in the West Indies." Kyk-over-al, 11 (1950), 39-47.

5904 ____ "The Novel in the British Caribbean." Bim, 43 (1965), 83-85; 44
      (1966), 176-80, 238-42; 46 (1968), 75-80.

5905 ____ "The Novel in the West Indies." Kyk-over-al, 17 (1953), 221-27.

5906 ____ "Open Letter to West Indian Writers." Kyk-over-al, 9 (1949), 23-27.

5907 ____, et al. "Is There a West Indian Way of Life?" Kyk-over-al, 20
      (1955), 188-203.

5908 Sherlock, Philip. West Indies. London: Thames & Hudson, 1966, pp. 136-68.

5909 Soons, Alan. "Patterns of Imagery in Two Novels of Curacao." CarQ, 13,
      no. 2 (1967), 33-35.

5910 Sparer, Joyce L. "Attitudes Towards Race in Guyanese Literature."
      CarSt, 8, no. 2 (1968), 23-62.

5911 Swanzy, H. L. V. "Caribbean Voices: Prolegomena to a West Indian Culture."
      CarQ, 1, no. 2 (1949), 21-28.

5112 ____ "Literary Situation in the Contemporary Caribbean." BA, 30 (1956),
      266-74.

5913 ____ "Prolegomena to a West Indian Culture." CarQ, 8, no. 2 (1962),
      121-28.

5914 Turpin, Waters E. "Four Short Fiction Writers of the Harlem Renaissance--
      Their Legacy of Achievement." CLAJ, 11 (1967), 59-72.

5915 Vancura, Zdenek. "The New English Writing in the West Indies." WZUG,
      16 (1967), 167-72.

5916 Van Sertima, Ivan. Caribbean Writers: Critical Essays. London: New
      Beacon, 1968.

5917 Waites, J. Arthur. "Is There a West Indian Culture?" Kyk-over-al, 9
      (1949), 5-8.

5918 Wickham, John. "West Indian Writing." Bim, 49 (1970), 68-79.

5919 Williams, Aubrey. "The Predicament of the Artist in the Caribbean." CarQ, 14, no. 1-2 (1968), 60-62.

5920 Williams, Denis. "Guiana Today." Kyk-over-al, 9 (1949), 9-10.

5921 _____ Image and Idea in the Arts of Guyana. Georgetown: Ministry of Information, 1969.

5922 Williams, Eric. "Four Poets of the Greater Antilles." CarQ, 2, no. 4 (1952), 8-15.

5923 _____ "Four Poets of the Greater Antilles." CarQ, 8, no. 1 (1962), 4-12.

5924 Wynter, Sylvia. "Reflections on West Indian Writing and Criticism." JJ, 2, no. 4 (1968), 22-32; 3, no. 1 (1969), 27-42.

See also: 158, 261, 262, 4324, 6071, 6564-6571.

Individual Authors

ANTHONY, Michael

5925 James, C. L. R., and Michael Anthony. "Discovering Literature in Trinidad: Two Experiences." JCL, 7 (1969), 79-87.

5926 MacMillan, M. "Language and Change." JCL, 1 (1965), 174-75.

5927 Ramchand, Kenneth, and Paul Edwards. "The Art of Memory: Michael Anthony's The Year in San Fernando." JCL, 7 (1969), 59-72.

BENNETT, Louise

5928 Bennett, Louise. "Me and Annancy." In item 5866, pp. ix-xi.

5929 _____ "Notes and Commentary, V--Bennett on Bennett." CarQ, 14, no. 1-2 (1968), 97-101.

5930 Morris, Mervyn. "On Reading Louise Bennett Seriously." JJ, 1, no. 1 (1967), 67-74.

BRATHWAITE, L. Edward

5931 Aidoo, Ama Ata. "Review of Masks." WA, 21 Dec. 1968, p. 1099.

5932 Baugh, Edward. "Review of Masks." Bim, 47 (1968), 209-11.

5933 Birbalsingh, Frank M. "To John Bull, with Hate." CarQ, 14, no. 4 (1968), 74-81.

5934 D'Costa, J. "The Poetry of Edward Brathwaite." JJ, 2, no. 3 (1968), 24-28.

5935 Grant, Damian. "Emerging Image: The Poetry of Edward Brathwaite." CritQ, 12 (1970), 186-92.

5936 Morris, Mervyn. "Niggers Everywhere." NWQ, 3, no. 4 (1967), 61-65.

5937 Rohlehr, Gordon. "The Historian as Poet." LHY, 11, no. 2 (1970), 171-78.

5938 Walmsley, Ann. "Dimensions of Song." Bim, 51 (1970), 152-67.

See also: 233.

CARTER, Martin

5939 Seymour, A. J. "A Guyanese Poet in Cardiff." Kaie, 2 (1966), 18-21.
See also: 5956.

CLARKE, Austin C.

5940 Boxill, Anthony. "The Novels of Austin Clarke." Fiddlehead, 75 (1968),
      69-72.

5941 Brown, Lloyd W. "The West Indian Novel in North America: A Study of
      Austin Clarke." JCL, 9 (1970), 89-103.

5942 Waddington, Miriam. "No Meeting Points." CanL, 35 (1968), 74-78.

COLLYMORE, Frank A.

5943 Baugh, Edward. "Frank Collymore and the Miracle of Bim." NWQ, 3, no.
      1-2 (1966-67), 129-33.

HARRIS, Wilson

5944 Adler, Joyce [Sparer]. "Tumatumari and the Imagination of Wilson
      Harris." JCL, 7 (1969), 20-31.

5945 Brathwaite, L. Edward. "The Controversial Tree of Time." Bim, 30 (1960),
      104-14.

5946 Gool, Reshard. "To Harris with Love." NWQ, 3, no. 4 (1967), 73-75.

5947 Gowda, H. H. Anniah. "Wilson Harris's Tumatumari." LHY, 11, no. 1
      (1970), 31-38.

5948 Harris, Wilson. "Form and Realism in the West Indian Artist." Kyk-over-al,
      15 (1952), 23-27.

5949 _____ "Impressions after Seven Years." NWF, 44 (1966), 17-20.

5950 _____ "Personal Statement on Eternity to Season." CarV, 17 Oct. 1954,
      pp. 1-4.

5951 _____ "The Phenomenal Legacy." LHY, 11, no. 2 (1970), 1-6.

5952 Hearne, John. "The Fugitive in the Forest: A Study of Four Novels by
      Wilson Harris." JCL, 4 (1967), 99-112.

5953 Howard, W. J. "Wilson Harris and the 'Alchemical Imagination.'" LHY,
      11, no. 2 (1970), 17-26.

5954 _____ "Wilson Harris's 'Guiana Quartet': From Personal Myth to National
      Identity." ArielE, 1, no. 1 (1970), 46-60.

5955 James, C. L. R. Wilson Harris--A Philosophical Approach. St. Augustine,
      Trinidad: Univ. of the West Indies, n.d.

5956 James, Louis. "The Necessity of Poetry." NWQ, 2, no. 3-4 (1966), 111-15.

5957 Ramchand, Kenneth. "The Dislocated Image." NWQ, 2, no. 3-4 (1966),
      107-10.

5958 _____ "The Significance of the Aborigine in Wilson Harris' Fiction."
      LHY, 11, no. 2 (1970), 7-16.

5959 Seymour, A. J. "The Novels of Wilson Harris." Bim, 38 (1964), 139-41.

5960 Sparer, Joyce L. "The Art of Wilson Harris." In John La Rose, ed.,
      New Beacon Reviews, I. London: New Beacon, 1968, pp. 22-30.

See also: 5865.

HEARNE, John

5961 Birbalsingh, Frank M. "'Escapism' in the Novels of John Hearne." CarQ,
        16, no. 1 (1970), 28-38.
5962 Cartey, Wilfred. "The Novels of John Hearne." JCL, 7 (1969), 45-58.
5063 Salkey, Andrew. "Review of Voices Under the Window." CarV, 22 Sept.
        1955, pp. 1-4.
5964 Seymour, A. J. "A Letter to John Hearne." Kyk-over-al, 24 (1958), 78-81.
See also: 5865.

LAMMING, George

5965 Calder-Marshall, Arthur. "A Review of In the Castle of My Skin." CarV,
        22 March 1953, pp. 1-15.
5966 Carr, W. I. "The Pleasures of Exile." UWIRS, n.d.
5967 Cartey, Wilfred. "Lamming and the Search for Freedom." NWQ, 2, no. 1-2
        (1966-67), 121-38.
5968 ____ "The Realities of Four Negro Writers." CUF, 9, no. 3 (1966), 34-42.
5969 Gunther, Helmut. "George Lamming." In item 91, pp. 205-10.
5970 Lamming, George. The Pleasures of Exile. London: Michael Joseph, 1960.
5971 Munro, Ian, et al. "Writing and Publishing in the West Indies: An
        Interview with George Lamming." WLWE, 19 (1971), 17-22.
5972 Naipaul, V. S. "Review of The Emigrants." CarV, 2 Jan. 1955, pp. 1-3.
5973 Ramchand, Kenneth. "The Artist in the Balm-Yard: Season of Adventure."
        NWQ, 5, no. 1-2 (1969), 13-21.
5974 Yarde, Gloria. "George Lamming: The Historical Imagination." LHY, 11,
        no. 2 (1970), 35-46.
See also: 5865.

LUCIE-SMITH, Edward

5975 Ferguson, R. I. "A Short Note on Edward Lucie-Smith's The Lime Tree."
        UES, 1 (1968), 24-26.

MCKAY, Claude

5976 Bone, R. The Negro Novel in America. New Haven: Yale Univ. Press,
        1958, pp. 67-75.
5977 Cooper, Wayne, and Robert C. Reinders. "Claude McKay in England, 1920."
        In John La Rose, ed. New Beacon Reviews, I. London: New Beacon, 1968,
        pp. 3-21.
5978 Drayton, Arthur D. "McKay's Human Pity: A Note on His Protest Poetry."
        BO, 17 (1965), 39-48. [Repr. in item 91, pp. 76-88.]
5979 Kent, George E. "The Soulful Way of Claude McKay." BlackW, 20, no. 1
        (1970), 37-51.
5980 McFarlane, J. E. Clare. "An Appreciation of Claude McKay." CarV, 5
        Sept. 1948, pp. 1-4.

5981 Mendes, Alfred, interviewed by Clifford Sealy. "Talking About the
      Thirties." Voices, 1, no. 5 (1965), 3-7.

5982 Ramchand, Kenneth. "Claude McKay and Banana Bottom." SoR, 4, no. 1
      (1970), 53-66.

See also: 5914, 6572.

MAIS, Roger

5983 Akanji, S. "Roger Mais." BO, 5 (1959), 33-37.

5984 Allsopp, Joy. "Thinking About Roger Mais." Kyk-over-al, 24 (1958), 75-77.

5985 Carr, W. I. "Roger Mais--Design from a Legend." CarQ, 13, no. 1 (1967),
      3-29.

5986 Lacovia, R. M. "Roger Mais and the Problem of Freedom." BARev, 1, no. 3
      (1970), 45-54.

5987 Ramchand, Kenneth. "Literature and Society: The Case of Roger Mais."
      CarQ, 15, no. 4 (1969), 23-30.

5988 Seymour, A. J., et al. "A Green Blade in Triumph: Memorial to Roger
      Mais." Kyk-over-al, 20 (1955), 147-70.

5989 Williamson, Karina. "Roger Mais: West Indian Novelist." JCL, 2 (1967),
      138-47.

See also: 5865.

MITTELHOLZER, Edgar

5990 Birbalsingh, Frank M. "Edgar Mittelholzer: Moralist or Pornographer?"
      JCL, 7 (1969), 88-103.

5991 Cartey, Wilfred. "The Rhythm of Society and Landscape." NWQ, 2, no. 3-4
      (1966), 97-104.

5992 Collymore, Frank A. "Edgar Mittelholzer." Bim, 41 (1965), 23-26.

5993 Guckian, Patrick A. "Mittelholzer Re-Assessment." JJ, 4, no. 1 (1970),
      38-45.

5994 Lamming, George. "But Alas Edgar." NWQ, 2, no. 3-4 (1966), 18-19.

5995 Mittelholzer, Edgar. "Literary Criticism and the Creative Writer."
      Kyk-over-al, 15 (1952), 19-22.

5996 _____ A Swarthy Boy. London: Putnam, 1963.

5997 Rickards, Colin. "A Tribute to Edgar Mittelholzer." Bim, 42 (1965),
      98-105.

5998 Seymour, A. J. "Edgar Mittelholzer." Kyk-over-al, 15 (1952), 15-17.

5999 _____ Edgar Mittelholzer: The Man and His Work. Georgetown: Nat. History
      & Arts Council, 1968.

6000 _____ "Edgar Mittleholzer [sic] the Preacher." Kaie, 1 (1965), 31-33.

6001 _____ "An Introduction to the Novels of Edgar Mittelholzer." Kyk-over-al,
      24 (1958), 60-74.

6002 Wagner, Geoffrey. "Edgar Mittelholzer: Symptoms and Shadows." Bim,
      33 (1961), 29-34.

NAIPAUL, Vidia S.

6004 Broberg, Jan. "En Västindier: London: Mote med författaren V. S. Naipaul." Studiekamraten, 47 (1965), 36-37.

6005 Bryden, Ronald. "New Map of Hell: The Middle Passage by V. S. Naipaul." Spectator, 209 (1962), 161.

6006 Carr, W. I. "A House for Mr. Biswas." UWIRST, n.d.

6007 _____ "The Middle Passage." UWIRST, n.d.

6008 Cartey, Wilfred. "The Knight's Companion--Ganesh, Biswas, and Stone: Novels by Vidia Naipaul." NWQ, 2, no. 1 (1965), 93-98.

6009 Derrick, A. C. "Naipaul's Technique as a Novelist." JCL, 7 (1969), 32-44.

6010 Enright, D. J. "Who Is India? On V. S. Naipaul's Journey into 'Darkness.'" Encounter, 23, no. 6 (1964), 59-64.

6011 Gowda, H. H. Anniah. "Naipaul in India." LHY, 11, no. 2 (1970), 163-70.

6012 Krikler, Bernard. "V. S. Naipaul's A House for Mr. Biswas." Listener, 71 (1964), 270-71.

6013 Lee, R. H. "The Novels of V. S. Naipaul." Theoria, 27 (1966), 31-46.

6014 Maes-Jelinek, Hena. "V. S. Naipaul: A Commonwealth Writer?" RLV, 33 (1967), 499-513.

6015 Miller, Karl. "Naipaul's Emergent Country." Listener, 78 (1967), 402-03.

6016 _____ "V. S. Naipaul and the New Order." KR, 29 (1967), 685-98.

6017 Moore, Gerald. "East Indians and West: The Novels of V. S. Naipaul." BO, 7 (1960), 11-15.

6018 Naipaul, V. S., and Ian Hamilton. "Without a Place." TLS, 30 Aug. 1971, pp. 897-98.

6019 Nandakumar, Prema. "V. S. Naipaul." In The Glory and the Good: Essays in Literature. New Delhi: Asia House, 1966, pp. 267-77.

6020 Narasimhaiah, C. D. "'Somewhere Something Has Snapped': A Close Look at V. S. Naipaul's An Area of Darkness." LCrit, 6, no. 4 (1968), 83-96.

6021 Nazareth, Peter. "The Mimic Men as a Study of Corruption." EAJ, 7, no. 7 (1970), 18-22.

6022 Ormerod, David. "In a Derelict Land: The Novels of V. S. Naipaul." WSCL, 9 (1968), 74-90.

6023 _____ "Theme and Image in V. S. Naipaul's A House for Mr. Biswas." TSLL, 8 (1967), 589-602.

6024 Pritchett, V. S. "Climacteric." New Statesman, 65 (1963), 831-32.

6025 Ramchand, Kenneth. "A House for Mr. Biswas." CarQ, 15, no. 1 (1969), 60-72.

6026 Rohlehr, Gordon. "Character and Rebellion in A House for Mr. Biswas." NWQ, 4, no. 4 (1968), 66-72.

6027 _____ "Predestination, Frustration and Symbolic Darkness in Naipaul's A House for Mr. Biswas." CarQ, 10, no. 1 (1964), 3-11.

6028 Singh, H. B. "V. S. Naipaul: A Spokesman for Neo-Colonialism." L&I, 2 (1969), 71-85.

6029 Thorpe, Marjorie. "The Mimic Men: A Study in Isolation." NWQ, 4, no. 4 (1968), 55-59.

6030 Wade, C. Alan. "The Novelist as Historian." LHY, 11, no. 2 (1970), 187-96.

6031 Walsh, William. "Meeting Extremes." JCL, 1 (1965), 169-72.

6032 _____ "Necessary and Accommodated: The Work of V. S. Naipaul." LuganoR, 1, no. 3-4 (1965), 169-81.

6033 _____ "V. S. Naipaul." In item 52, pp. 62-85.

See also: 5865, 6573-6576.

PATTERSON, H. Orlando

6034 Brathwaite, L. Edward. "Jamaican Slave Society." Race, 9 (1968), 331-42.

REID, Victor

6035 Carter, Martin. "A Note on Vic Reid's New Day." Kyk-over-al, 24 (1958), 81-82.

6036 Dewar, Lilian. "Jamaica in the Novel." Kyk-over-al, 12 (1951), 108-13.

6037 Laski, Margarita. "Review of V. S. Reid's The Leopard." CarV, 4 May 1958, pp. 1-4.

See also: 5865.

RHYS, Jean

6038 Athill, Diana. "Jean Rhys and the Writing of Wide Sargasso Sea." Bookseller, 20 Aug. 1966, pp. 1378-79.

6039 Bernstein, Marcelle. "The Inscrutable Miss Jean Rhys." Observer, 1 June 1969, p. 40.

6040 Braybrooke, Neville. "Between Dog and Wolf." Spectator, 218 (1967), 77-78.

6041 Froshaug, Judy. "The Book-Makers." Nova, 3 (1967), 4-5.

6042 Lai, Wally Look. "The Road to Thornfield Hall." In John La Rose, ed., New Beacon Reviews, I. London: New Beacon, 1968, pp. 38-52. [Also in NWQ, 4, no. 2 (1968), 17-27.]

6043 Webb, W. L. "Lately Prized." Guardian, 14 Dec. 1967, p. 7.

6044 Wyndham, Francis. "Introduction to Jean Rhys." LMag, 7, no. 1 (1960), 15-18.

SALKEY, Andrew

6045 Gray, Cecil. "Mr. Salkey's Truth and Illusion." JJ, 2, no. 2 (1968), 46-54.

See also: 5865.

SELVON, Samuel

6046 Naipaul, V. S. "Review of An Island Is a World." CarV, 1 May 1955, pp. 1-3.

SEMOUR, Arthur J.

6047 Dolphin, C. "The Poetry of A. J. Seymour." NWF, 13 (1966), 31-39.

6048 Harris, Wilson. "The Guiana Book by A. J. Seymour." <u>Kyk-over-al</u>, 7
(1948), 37-40.

See <u>also</u>: 5956.

SIMPSON, Louis

6049 Rizzardi, Alfredo. "Poesia di Louis Simpson." <u>Presenza</u>, 1 (1958), 45-52.

6050 Simpson, Louis. "Confessions of an American Poet." <u>NYTM</u>, 2 May 1965,
pp. 108-10; 21 May 1965, pp. 121-34.

WALCOTT, Derek

6051 Anon. "[Photographs and Review of Derek Walcott's <u>Ti Jean and His
Brothers</u>]." <u>Link</u> (Castries), 2, no. 2-3 (1970), n. pag.

6052 Baugh, Edward. "Metaphor and Plainness in the Poetry of Derek Walcott."
<u>LHY</u>, 11, no. 2 (1970), 47-58.

6053 Carr, W. I. "<u>In a Green Night</u>." <u>UWIRST</u>, n.d.

6054 Fuller, Roy. "The Poetry of D. A. Walcott." <u>CarV</u>, 22 May 1949, pp. 1-4.

6055 King, C. G. O. "The Poems of Derek Walcott." <u>CarQ</u>, 10, no. 3 (1964),
3-30.

6056 Morris, Mervyn. "Walcott and the Audience for Poetry." <u>CarQ</u>, 14, no. 1-2
(1968), 7-24.

6057 St. Omer, Garth. "Dream, But Not, Please, on Monkey Mountain." <u>Voice
of St. Lucia</u>, 2 Nov. 1968.

6058 Scott, Dennis. "Walcott on Walcott." <u>CarQ</u>, 14, no. 1-2 (1968), 77-82.

6059 Sharp, Stanley. "The Verse of Derek Walcott." <u>CarV</u>, 1 Feb. 1953, pp. 1-8.

6060 Walcott, Derek. "Leaving School." <u>LMag</u>, 5, no. 6 (1965), 4-14.

6061 ____ "What the Twilight Says: An Overture." In <u>Dream on Monkey Mountain
and Other Plays</u>. New York: Farrar, Straus & Giroux, 1970, pp. 3-40.

See <u>also</u>: 5865, 5938.

WILLIAMS, Denis

6062 Harris, Wilson. "Two Periods in the Work of a West Indian Artist."
<u>Kyk-over-al</u>, 20 (1955), 183-87.

6063 Williams, Denis, and A. J. Seymour. "An Exchange of Letters." <u>Kyk-over-al</u>,
24 (1958), 93-99.

See <u>also</u>: 5991.

Theses and Dissertations

General

6064 Elliott, A. G. Rudyard Kipling and the Philosophy of Imperialism. M.A.: Western Australia, 1939.

6065 Espey, D. B. The Imperial Protagonist: Hero and Anti-Hero in Fiction of the Late British Empire. Ph.D.: Michigan, 1971.

6066 Meyers, Jeffrey. The Hero in British Colonial Fiction. Ph.D.: Berkeley, 1967.

6067 New, William H. The Problems of "Growing Up" Treated in Selected English, American and Commonwealth Novels, 1908-1959. Ph.D.: Leeds, 1966.

6068 Raskin, Jonah. The Mythology of Imperialism: A Study of Joseph Conrad and Rudyard Kipling. Ph.D.: Manchester, 1967.

6069 Sandison, A. G. The Imperial Idea in English Fiction: A Study of the Literary Expression of the Ideas, with Special Reference to the Works of Kipling, Conrad, and Buchan. Ph.D.: Cambridge (Peterhouse), 1964.

6070 Shah, S. A. The Empire in the Writings of Kipling, Forster, and Orwell. Ph.D.: Edinburgh, 1968.

6071 Sullivan, Harry Richards. The Eyre Trial and the Literary World: British Empire Policy at the Crossroads. M.A.: Stanford, 1950. [See also item 6571.]

6072 Vincent, Theophilus. Changing Concepts of the Negro in English Literature with Special Reference to the Period 1700-1807. Ph.D.: Ibadan, 1969.

Africa: General

6073 Astley, Sir F. J. D. The Black Races of Africa in the Classics. Ph.D.: London (Univ. College), 1954.

6074 Dabo, S. K. A Comparative Study of the Treatment of Human Relationships in Fiction by Modern African Writers in French and English. B.Litt.: Oxford, 1967.

6075 Fonlon, B. La poésie et le réveil de l'homme noir. Ph.D.: National Univ. of Ireland, 1961.

6076 Gleason, Judith S. I. African Novels. Ph.D.: Columbia, 1964.

6077 Graham-White, A. West African Drama: Folk, Popular and Literary. Ph.D.: Stanford, 1969.

6078 Hammond, Dorothy. The Image of Africa in British Literature of the Twentieth Century. Ph.D.: Columbia, 1963.

6079 Izevbaye, D. S. The Relevance of Modern Literary Theory in English to Poetry and Fiction in English-Speaking West Africa. Ph.D.: Ibadan, 1968.

6080 Killam, G. D. The Presentation of Africa Between the Sahara and the Union of South Africa in Novels Written in English, 1860-1939. Ph.D.: London (Univ. College), 1965.

6081 McDowell, Robert E. The African-English Novel. Ph.D.: Denver, 1966.

6082 Makward, E. Negro-African Novelists: A Comparative Study of Themes and Influences in Novels by Africans in French and English. Ph.D.: Ibadan, 1968.

6083 Moody, P. R. Joyce Cary and Africa: An Account of Cary's Nigerian Experience and a Critical Analysis of His African Writings. Ph.D.: Cambridge (St. Catharine's), 1963.

6084 Moore, Jane Ann. Social Strain and Culture Conflict in West African Novels. Ph.D.: Boston, 1966.

6085 Morin, John Charles. Africa as Seen in the Modern English Novel. M.A.: Laval, 1960.

6086 Niven, Alastair. Literary Criticism and the West African Novel Written in English 1962-1968. M.A.: Ghana, 1968.

6087 Nwoga, Donatus. West African Literature in English. Ph.D.: London, 1965.

6088 Obiechina, Emmanuel N. Cultural Change and the Novel in West Africa. Ph.D.: Cambridge, 1967.

6089 Rigsby, G. U. Négritude: A Critical Analysis. Ph.D.: Howard, 1969.

6090 Roscoe, Adrian Alan. Nigerian Literature in English: An Introductory Survey. M.A.: McMaster, 1965.

6091 _____ Nigerian Literature in English: Problems and Progress. Ph.D.: Queen's (Kingston, Ont.), 1968.

6092 Sey, K. A. The Characteristics of Educated Ghanaian English--An Exploratory Survey. M.A.: Manchester, 1970.

6093 Stanislaus, J. The Growth of African Literature: A Survey of the Works Published by African Writers in English and French. Ph.D.: Montréal, 1952.

6094 Thumboo, Edwin. A Study of African Poetry in English. M.A.: Singapore, 1969.

6095 Young, P. The Language of West African Writing in English, with Special Reference to Nigerian Prose Fictions. Ph.D.: Durham, 1970.

Africa: Individual Authors

ACHEBE, Chinua

6096 Melone, Thomas. Chinua Achebe et la tragédie de l'histoire. D.Lett.: Grenoble, 1969.

6097 Murphy, Thomas. The Novels of Chinua Achebe, with Special Reference to the Theme of Conflict of European and Southern Nigerian Cultures, from the Late Nineteenth Century Onwards. M.Litt.: Newcastle-upon-Tyne, 1967.

6098 Uhiara, Albert O. Two Dispensations: A Study of the Impact of Western Culture on Modern Nigeria As Revealed in the Novels of Chinua Achebe. M.A.: Queen's (Kingston, Ont.), 1964.

6099 Ward, M. R. An Analysis of the Ways in which Colonialism, Tribalism and Associated Political Themes are Handled in Novels by the African Authors Peter Abrahams, Chinua Achebe and James Ngugi. M.Phil.: Leeds, 1969.

SOYINKA, Wole

6100 Horton, Joel. Background Guide for the Study and Production of Soyinka's "The Swamp Dwellers" and Other Dramas. M.A.: Iowa, 1965.

6101 Rosenior, F. B. The Indigenous and Foreign Elements in the Drama of Wole Soyinka. M.A.: Sierra Leone, 1970.

Australia: General

6102 Argyle, Barry. The First Century, 1830 to 1930: A Study of Selected Novels in the First Hundred Years of Australian Literature. Ph.D.: Leeds, 1968.

6103 Bielenstien, G. M. Aim and Object in the Novel: Valuations of Character in Society in the Works of Three Australian Novelists. M.A.: Melbourne, 1958.

6104 Bladen, Peter Louis. The Attitude of Australian Poets to Nature: A Selective Examination of Australian Poetry from the Earliest Days Settlement to the Present. . . M.A.: Melbourne, 1961.

6105 Haas, Charles Eugene. Convictism and the Australian Novel. M.A.: Iowa, 1956.

6105a Harrington, Charles David. Landscape in Australian Fiction: The Rendering of a Human Environment. Ph.D.: Indiana, 1970.

6106 Healy, John J. The Treatment of the Aborigine in Australian Literature from the Beginning to the Present Day. Ph.D.: Texas (Austin), 1969.

6107 Heuzenroeder, John. The Image of Australia in the European Eye: A Study of Interpretation of a Group of Novelists from Charles Reade to Nevil Shute. M.A.: Adelaide, 1968.

6108 Horner, J. C. The Modern Australian Novel: A Study of Theme, Characterisation and Background. M.A.: Tasmania, 1953.

6109 Jones, Dorothy L. M. The Treatment of the Aborigine in Australian Fiction. M.A.: Adelaide, 1960.

6110 Kirby-Smith, Virginia. The Development of Australian Theatre and Drama: 1788-1964. Ph.D.: Duke, 1970.

6111 Kirk, Pauline. Some Aspects of the Development of the Australian Novel Before 1900. M.A.: Monash, 1969.

6112 Macainsh, Noel Leslie. Nietzsche in Australia. Ph.D.: Melbourne, 1967.

6113 Matthews, John Pengwerne. A Comparative Study of the Development of Australian and Canadian Poetry in the Nineteenth Century. Ph.D.: Toronto, 1957.

6114 Melendres, Patricia. Social Criticism in the Australian Novel: The Aboriginal Theme. M.A.: Australian National Univ., 1968.

6115 Mitchell, A. C. W. Towards the Source: A Comparison of Two Fundamental Images in Australian and Canadian Literature. M.A.: Queen's (Kingston, Ont.), 1965.

6116 Naughtin, P. C. The Literary Importance of Sydney "Bulletin." M.A.: Adelaide, 1956.

6117 Nesbitt, Bruce. Literary Nationalism in Australia and New Zealand 1880-1900. Ph.D.: Australian National Univ., 1968.

6118 Patterson, Frank Morgan. Australian Literature from 1890-1900. M.A.: Iowa, 1957.

6119 Reid, Ian. The Influence of the Depression on Australian and New Zealand Fiction 1930-1950. Ph.D.: Adelaide, 1970.

6120 Rosenberg, J. H. A World Apart: Comparative Studies in American and Australian Literary Development of the Nineteenth Century. Ph.D.: Texas (Austin), 1971.

6121 Rye, L. H. South Australian Verse, Verse Connected with South Australia: A Survey and Appreciation Together with a Bibliography and Biographical Data, Complete to December 31st 1934. M.A.: Queensland, 1936.

6122 Smith, B. Early Western Australian Literature: A Guide to Colonial and Goldfields Life. M.A.: Western Australia, 1962.

6123 South, R. J. Australian Short Story of the Eighteen Nineties. M.A.: Melbourne, 1955.

6124 Sturm, Terence L. Problems of Cultural Dependences in New Zealand and Australian Poetry. Ph.D.: Leeds, 1967.

6125 Tierney, J. L. Australian Literature. M.A.: Sydney, 1922.

6126 Tregenza, John. Australian Little Magazines, 1923-1954. M.A.: Adelaide, 1956.

6127 Wittman, Richard Eugene. Australian Love Poetry in the Forties. M.A.: Melbourne, 1968.

Australia: Individual Authors

BOYD, Martin

6128 Nase, Pamela. Martin Boyd's Langton Novels: An Interpretive Essay. M.A.: Australian National Univ., 1969.

BRENNAN, Christopher

6129 Hildyard, Annette. The Symbolism of C. J. Brennan. M.A.: Tasmania, 1966.

6130 Macainsh, Noel Leslie. Christopher Brennan: Über die Beziehung zur deutschen Romantik in "Towards the Source": Unter besonderer Berücksichtigung Friedrich von Hardenbergs. M.A.: Melbourne, 1964.

6131 Wilkes, G. A. The Poetry of Chris Brennan: An Exegetical Study. M.A.: Sydney, 1952.

CLARKE, Marcus

6132 Elliott, Brian. Marcus Clarke: A Study of Literary Life and Character in Colonial Australia. D.Litt.: Adelaide, 1955.

FURPHY, Joseph

6133 Barnes, Richard John. Joseph Furphy's "Such Is Life": An Introduction. M.A.: Melbourne, 1960.

6134 Gilding, Kevin Rex. The Political, Social and Literary Significance of Joseph Furphy's Novels. M.A.: Adelaide, 1967.

6135 Kiernan, Brian F. "Such Is Life": An Interpretation. M.A.: Melbourne, 1963.

HARPER, Charles

6136 Gray, A. The Collected Poems of Charles Harper. M.A.: Sydney, 1965.

HAY, William

6137 Muecke, Ian Donald. The Life and Novels of William Hay. M.A.: Adelaide, 1965.

HOPE, A. D.

6138 Peachey, Joyce. The Vision of A. D. Hope. M.A.: Melbourne, 1967.

KENDALL, Henry

6139 Clarke, D. C. A Critical Edition of the Letters of Henry Kendall. M.A.: Sydney, 1959.

6140 Reed, T. H. Life and Poetical Works of Henry Kendall. D.Litt.: Adelaide, 1953.

KINGSLEY, Henry

6141 Scheuerle, William Howard. Henry Kingsley, a Study. Ph.D.: Syracuse, 1964.

LAWSON, Henry

6142 Matthews, Brian. The Prose Work of Henry Lawson: A Critical Study. M.A.: Melbourne, 1968.

MACKENZIE, Kenneth

6143   Davis, Diana.   Kenneth Mackenzie. M.A.: Melbourne, 1967.

6144   Hamilton, James Stuart.   An Anatomy of Failure: The Novels and Poems of
       Kenneth Mackenzie. M.A.: Melbourne, 1965.

O'REILLY, J. B.

6145   Carroll, Martin Clement.   Behind the Lighthouse: The Australian Sojourn
       of John Boyle O'Reilly (1844-1890). Ph.D.: Iowa, 1955.

PALMER, Vance

6146   Botsman, Peter B.   The Novels of Vance Palmer: A Study in the Development
       of Australian Fiction. M.A.: Monash, 1969.

PRICHARD, K. S.

6147   Malos, Ellen May.   Some Major Themes and Problems in the Novels of
       Katharine Susannah Prichard. M.A.: Melbourne, 1962.

RICHARDSON, H. H.

6148   Elliott, William D.   "The Fortunes of Richard Mahoney": A Critical
       Appraisal. Ed.D.: Michigan,1967.

6149   Faust, Beatrice.   Richardson's Novel. M.A.: Melbourne, 1965.

SLESSOR, Kenneth

6150   Croft, Julian C. B.   The Concept of Time, History and Memory in the
       Poetry of Kenneth Slessor and R. D. Fitzgerald. M.A.: Newcastle
       (Australia), 1968.

WARUNG, Price

6151   Andrews, B. G.   Price Warung: The Later Years. M.A.: New South Wales,
       1969.

WENZ, Paul

6152   Wolff, E. G.   A French-Australian Writer: Paul Wenz. Ph.D.: Melbourne,
       1948.

WHITE, Patrick

6153   Bellette, Anthony Frank.   Four Novels of Patrick White. M.A.: British
       Columbia, 1963.

6154   Bernard, Ruth.   The Development of the Themes of Suffering and Redemption
       in the Novels of Patrick White. M.A.: Tasmania, 1965.

6155   Brady, Mother Veronica.   "The Hard Enquiring Wind": A Study of Patrick
       White as an Australian Novelist. Ph.D.: Toronto, 1968.

6156 _____ Patrick White's Discovery and Exploration of Australia. M.A.: Toronto, 1966.

6157 Burrows, J. F. The Novels and Stories of Patrick White: A Critical Study. M.A.: Sydney, 1965.

6158 Duncan, R. Existentialist Sensibility in the Novels of Patrick White. M.A.: Monash, 1969.

6159 Hayward, C. J. The Vision and Form of Patrick White's Fiction: A Study of the First Four Novels. M.A.: Toronto, 1967.

6160 Norton, Sister P. A. The Novels of Patrick White. M.A.: Australian National Univ., 1964.

6161 Roberts, Ernest Albert Kevin. Patrick White's Four Plays in the Light of His Novels. M.A.: Simon Fraser, 1968.

6162 Schermbrucker, W. G. The Vision of Alienation: Patrick White. M.A.: British Columbia, 1966.

6163 Sutherland, John. The Women of Patrick White: A Mandalic Vision. M.A.: Simon Fraser, 1970.

WRIGHT, Judith

6164 Gaut, C. C. The Poetry of Judith Wright. M.A.: New South Wales, 1960.

Canada: General

6165 Adelman, Seymour. Elements of Social Criticism in Canadian Poetry: With Emphasis on the Poetry of F. R. Scott and A. J. M. Smith. M.A.: Montréal, 1961.

6166 Alexander, P. V. French Canada in Fiction. M.A.: Toronto, 1951.

6167 Ashcroft, Edith. The Sonnet in Canadian Poetry. M.A.: Queen's (Kingston, Ont.), 1932.

6168 Asher, Stanley. Playwriting in Canada: An Historical Survey. M.A.: Montréal, 1962.

6169 Atherton, Stanley Scott. Five Writers of the Canadian North 1850-1910. M.A.: Western Ontario, 1964.

6170 Balcuinas, Ina. The Small Town as a Fictional Element, 1895-1914. M.A.: Toronto, 1968.

6171 Ballstadt, Carl P. The Quest for Canadian Identity in Pre-Confederation English-Canadian Literary Criticism. M.A.: Western Ontario, 1959.

6172 Barnett, Elizabeth S. The Memoirs of Pioneer Women Writers in Ontario. M.A.: McGill, 1934.

6173 Beattie, Alexander Munro. The Advent of Modernism in Canadian Poetry in English, 1912-1940. Ph.D.: Columbia, 1957.

6174 Bell, Lily May. English-Canadian Literature before 1867 and Its Authors. M.A.: Western Ontario, 1916.

6175 Berger, Carl Clinton. The Vision of Grandeur: Studies in the Ideas of Canadian Imperialism, 1867-1914. Ph.D.: Toronto, 1967.

6176 Beyea, George P. The Canadian Novel before Confederation. M.A.: New Brunswick, 1950.

6177 Brierley, James Gossage. A Study of Literature Produced in the Province of Quebec Prior to Confederation with Its Historical Background. M.A.: McGill, 1929.

6178 Brown, Lillian Rogers. The Evolution of Canadian Poetry. M.A.: Manitoba, 1914.

6179 Blanar, Michael. Early British Travellers in French Canada. Ph.D.: Montréal, 1960.

6180 Brown, Allison. Anglo-French Literary Relations in Canada from 1820-1950. M.A.: New Brunswick, 1954.

6181 Brown, Yvonne. The Origin of French-Canadian Journalism. M.A.: Queen's (Kingston, Ont.), 1955.

6182 Burns, Dean Keer. Canadian Orators and Oratory. M.A.: McGill, 1925.

6183 Cameron, Doris Margaret. Puritanism in Canadian Prairie Fiction. M.A.: British Columbia, 1966.

6184 Clark, Margaret L. American Influences on the Canadian Novel. M.A.: New Brunswick, 1940.

6185 Codère, Annette. The Evolving Role of Women in Canadian Fiction in English and French. M.A.: Sherbrooke, 1968.

6186 Cogswell, Frederick William. The Canadian Novel Between Confederation and World War I. M.A.: New Brunswick, 1950.

6187 Cole, Yolanda. Journey to Water Motif in Canadian Prairie Novel. M.A.: Alberta, 1970.

6188 Condell, Angus Tyndall. A Consideration of Canadian Verse. M.A.: Manitoba, 1903.

6189 Conroy, Patricia. A History of the Theatre in Montreal Prior to Confederation. M.A.: McGill, 1936.

6190 Copp, E. A. Canada First Party (Charles Mair). M.A.: Queen's (Kingston, Ont.), 1926.

6191 Corbett, Nancy Jean. "Sexual Provinciality" and Characterization: A Study of Some Recent Canadian Fiction. M.A.: British Columbia, 1970.

6192 Cowperthwaite, Avonne Elizabeth. Harmony and Discord: A Study of the Transition from the Old to the Modern Ways of Life as Handled by a Group of Prairie Novelists. M.A.: Manitoba, 1965.

6193 Cruikshank, Marion Gertrude. The Influence of the University on the Development of the Drama in the United States and Canada. M.A.: McGill, 1931.

6194 Culham, T. A. The Royal Canadian Mounted Police in Literature. D.Ph.: Ottawa, 1947.

6195 Dalton, Sister Mary Katherine. Canadian Confederation Poetry 1855-1880. M.A.: British Columbia, 1964.

6196 Djwa, Sandra Ann. Metaphor, World View and the Continuity of Canadian Poetry: A Study of the Major English Canadian Poets with a Computer Concordance to Metaphor. Ph.D.: British Columbia, 1968.

6197 Dorsinville, Max. A Comparative Analysis of the Protest Novel in American Negro and French-Canadian Literature. M.A.: Sherbrooke, 1968.

6198 Drolet, Gilbert. War in French and English Canadian Fiction 1935-1965. Ph.D.: Montréal, 1968.

6199   Edwards, Margaret Christian.   Canadian Drama, Dramatists and Players.
       M.A.: McGill, 1926.

6200   Edwards, Mary Jane.   Fiction and Montreal, 1769-1885.   Ph.D.: Toronto,
       1969.

6201   _____   The Search for Unity: Modern Canadian Poetry and the Critics.
       M.A.: Queen's (Kingston, Ont.), 1962.

6202   Farley, Thomas Ernest Hilary.   Love and Death in Canadian Poetry.   M.A.:
       Carleton, 1963.

6203   Francis, Wynne.   Urban Images in Canadian Poetry.   M.A.: McGill, 1963.

6204   Gammon, Donald B.   The Concept of Nature in Nineteenth Century Canadian
       Poetry, with Special Reference to Goldsmith, Sangster and Roberts.
       M.A.: New Brunswick, 1948.

6205   Garvey, Margaret.   The Loyalist Prose Writers of the American Revolution.
       Ph.D.: Columbia, 1945.

6206   Glover, Thomas.   Nature in Early Canadian Poetry.   Ph.D.: Montréal, 1951.

6207   Gnarowski, Michael.   A Reference and Bibliographical Guide to the Study
       of English Canadian Literature.   Ph.D.: Ottawa, 1967.

6208   Graham, Robert S.   Bilingualism and the Creative Writer of French Canada.
       Ph.D.: Colorado, 1955.

6209   Greer, Reginald Thomas.   Influence of Canadian Literature upon the Growth
       of Canadian Nationality to Confederation.   M.A.: Ottawa, 1937.

6210   Grever, Ronald.   A Study of the Poets of the Canadian Confederation.
       B.Phil.: St. Andrews, 1970.

6211   Hagerman, Verna B.   The Literature of the Maritime Provinces--Its
       Tendencies and Its Influence.   M.A.: McGill, 1934.

6212   Hall, Chipman.   A Survey of the Indians' Role in English-Canadian
       Literature to 1900.   M.A.: Dalhousie, 1969.

6213   Harder, Helga Irene.   English-Canadian Poetry, 1935-1955: A Thematic
       Study.   M.A.: British Columbia, 1965.

6214   Hodgins, Samuel Raymond Norris.   The Status of the Familiar Essay in
       Canadian Literature.   M.A.: McGill, 1929.

6215   Hodgson, John Maurice D.   Initiation and Quest in Some Early Canadian
       Journals.   M.A.: British Columbia, 1966.

6216   Jackel, Susan.   The Role of Women in Prairie Fiction.   M.A.: Toronto,
       1966.

6217   Jackson, Elva Ethel.   Canadian Regional Novels.   M.A.: Acadia, 1938.

6218   Johnston, Helen.   Literary and Cultural Soundings: Regional Study of
       "South Shore" (Nova Scotia) Literature.   M.A.: Acadia, 1968.

6219   Johnston, Norma Elizabeth.   The Governor General's Non-Fiction Awards,
       1936-1956.   M.L.S.: McGill, 1961.

6220   Jones, Kim (Ondaatje).   A Content Guide and Index to "The University
       Magazine" Vols. IX-XIX, 1910-1920.   M.A.: Queen's (Kingston, Ont.),
       1954.

6221   Keller, Ella Lorraine.   The Development of the Canadian Short Story.
       M.A.: Saskatchewan (Saskatoon), 1950.

6222   Kidd, Gordon.   Les éléments politiques dans les romans canadiens
       d'expression française et anglaise.   D.U.: Laval, 1967.

6223   Kilgallin, Anthony R.   Toronto in Prose and Poetry.   Phil.M.: Toronto, 1966.

6224 King, Joanne. Canadian Woman Poets. Ph.D.: Montréal, 1950.

6225 Klinck, Carl F. Formative Influences upon the "1860 Group" of Canadian Poets. Ph.D.: Columbia, 1929.

6226 Lawler, James. Wordsworth's Influence on Major Early Canadian Poets. M.A.: Montréal, 1963.

6227 Lawrence, Robert Gilford. A Descriptive Bibliography of the Manuscript Material in the Rufus Hathaway Collection of Canadian Literature, University of New Brunswick Library. M.A.: New Brunswick, 1947.

6228 Lee, A. H. Some Themes of Community and Exile in Six Canadian Novels. M.A.: Toronto, 1966.

6229 Leechman, Douglas. The Popular Concept of the "Red Indian" as Revealed in Literature. M.A.: Ottawa, 1940.

6230 ____ The "Red Indian" of Literature: A Study in the Perpetuation of Error. Ph.D.: Ottawa, 1941.

6231 Loggie, Leon James. The "Literary Garland": A Critical and Historical Study. M.A.: New Brunswick, 1948.

6232 Loughlin, Dorothy Aileen. The Development of Social and Intellectual Attitudes as Revealed in the Literature of New Brunswick. M.A.: New Brunswick, 1948.

6233 McBrine, Ronald William. The Development of the Familiar Essay in English Canadian Literature from 1900-1920. M.A.: New Brunswick, 1967.

6234 McCaffrey, Helen Katherine. L'image du canadien-français dans le roman canadien-anglais. Ph.D.: Montréal, 1964.

6235 McDougall, Robert L. Drama Designed for Listening: Radio Drama in Canada. M.A.: Toronto, 1948.

6236 ____ A Study of Canadian Periodical Literature of the 19th Century. Ph.D.: Toronto, 1957.

6237 McDowell, Marjorie. A History of Canadian Children's Literature to 1900, Together with a Checklist. M.A.: New Brunswick, 1957.

6238 Mackie, Richard G. A. Three Seventeenth Century Newfoundland Propagandists. M.A.: New Brunswick, 1968.

6239 McLaren, Lydia B. Application of Criteria for Poetry to the Selection of Seventy Canadian Poems for Early Childhood. Ed.D.: Columbia, 1967.

6240 MacLeod, Alistair. The Canadian Short Story in the 1930's with Special Reference to Stories of Social Protest. M.A.: New Brunswick, 1961.

6241 MacLure, Evelyn. The Short Story in Canada: Development from 1935-1955 with Attached Bibliography. M.A.: British Columbia, 1969.

6242 McMullen, Grace. Les canadiens français d'après les romans anglo-canadiens contemporains (1925-1945). M.A.: Laval, 1951.

6243 McNair, Dorothy Livesay. Rhythm and Sound in Contemporary Canadian Poetry. M.Ed.: British Columbia, 1966.

6244 MacOdrum, Murdoch Maxwell. Survival of the English and Scottish Popular Ballads in Nova Scotia: A Study of Folk-song in Canada. M.A.: McGill, 1924.

6245 McPherson, Hugh Archibald. A Study in the Development of Canadian Taste in Poetry. M.A.: Western Ontario, 1950.

6246 McRae, C. F. The Victorian Age and Canadian Poetry. Ph.D.: Toronto, 1953.

6247 Markham, Mary Matilda Sparks. An Index to the "Literary Garland,"
      1838-1851, with Three Essays on Colonial Fiction. M.A.: Western
      Ontario, 1949.

6248 Maybee, Janet. A Calendar of Theatre Performances in Halifax 1850-1880.
      M.A.: Dalhousie, 1965.

6249 Miller, Judith. Towards a Canadian Aesthetic: Descriptive Colour in the
      Landscape Poetry of Duncan Campbell Scott, Archibald Lampman, and
      William Wilfred Campbell. M.A.: Waterloo, 1970.

6250 Morriss, Margaret. The Image of the Family: Its Nature and Function in
      Three Canadian Novels. M.A.: Toronto, 1968.

6251 Munro, Patricia Jane. Seas, Evolution and Images of Continuing Creation
      in English-Canadian Poetry. M.A.: Simon Fraser, 1970.

6252 Nelson, Eda Maude. The Literature of the Maritime Provinces of Canada
      and Its Bearing on the Struggle for Educational and Political Freedom.
      M.A.: McGill, 1928.

6253 O'Brien, Kevin H. F. Oscar Wilde and the Maritimes. M.A.: New Brunswick,
      1967.

6254 O'Connell, Mary Sheila. Images of Canadians in Children's Realist
      Fiction. Ed.D.: Columbia, 1966.

6255 Oland, Sidney C. M. Material for a History of the Theatre in Early
      Halifax. M.A.: Dalhousie, 1967.

6256 Opala, Beatrice. Matthew Arnold in Canada. M.A.: McGill, 1968.

6258 Parker, George, L. A History of a Canadian Publishing House [McClelland
      and Stewart] 1890-1940. Ph.D.: Toronto, 1969.

6259 Paustian, Shirley Irene. Farm Life on the Great Plains as Represented
      in the Literature of Western America. M.A.: Saskatchewan (Saskatoon),
      1948.

6260 Pearson, Willis Barry. A Bibliographical Study of Canadian Radio and
      Television Drama Produced on the Canadian Broadcasting Corporation's
      National Network, 1944 to 1967. M.A.: Saskatchewan (Saskatoon), 1968.

6261 Procunier, Edwin R. Attitudes to French Canada: A Study of "Canadien"
      Culture as It Appears in English-Canadian Novels. M.A.: Queen's
      (Kingston, Ont.), 1953.

6262 Rashley, R. E. Canadian Literature: A Survey and Evaluation. M.A.:
      Saskatchewan (Saskatoon), 1936.

6363 Read, Stanley Merrit Ellery. An Account of English Journalism in
      Canada from the Middle of the Eighteenth Century to the Beginning of
      the Twentieth Century, with Special Emphasis Being Given to the
      Periods Prior to Confederation. M.A.: McGill, 1925.

6264 Ricou, Laurence R. Canadian Prairie Fiction: A Significance of the
      Landscape. Ph.D.: Toronto, 1970.

6265 Ringrose, Christopher Xerxes. "Preview": Anatomy of a Group. M.A.:
      Alberta, 1969.

6266 Rogers, Amos Robert. American Recognition of Canadian Authors Writing
      in English 1890-1960. Ph.D.: Michigan, 1964.

6267 Rogers, Linda. Environment and the Quest Motif in Selected Works of
      Canadian Prairie Fiction. M.A.: British Columbia, 1969.

6268 Roman, Patricia (Robinson). The English-Canadian Urban and Industrial
      Novel and Periodical Fiction. M.A.: Western Ontario, 1960.

6269 Roy, George Ross. Symbolism in English Canadian Poetry, 1880-1939. Ph.D.: Montréal, 1959.

6270 Samson, Wilma Louise. Some Aspects of the Development of Drama in New Brunswick. M.A.: New Brunswick, 1953.

6271 Schoch, Margaret Mahajahla (Aitken). The Evolution of Canadian Nature Poetry. M.A.: Bishop's, 1945.

6272 Scott, Robert Barry. A Study of Amateur Theatre in Toronto: 1900-1930. M.A.: New Brunswick, 1966.

6273 Sharman, Vincent D. The Satiric Tradition in the Works of Seven English-Canadian Satirists. Ph.D.: Alberta, 1968.

6274 Sigworth, Donald Francis. Some Inquiries into Literary Criticism. M.A.: Montréal, 1955.

6275 Sinclair, Nora R. Social Criticism in the Canadian Novel, 1920-1945. M.A.: Alberta, 1959.

6276 Spettigue, Douglas O. The English Canadian Novel: Some Attitudes and Themes in Relation to Form. Ph.D.: Toronto, 1966.

6277 Stevens, Peter. The Development of Canadian Poetry Between the Wars and Its Reflection of Social Awareness. Ph.D.: Saskatchewan (Saskatoon), 1969.

6278 Stevenson, Laura Alice. The Image of Canada in Canadian Children's Literature. M.A. Western Ontario, 1967.

6279 Stock, Marie L. Les histoires d'animaux dans la littérature canadienne-anglaise. M.A.: McGill, 1937.

6280 Stocks, William. Images of Outrage: The English-Canadian Prose Documentary. M.A.: Alberta, 1970.

6281 Tait, Michael S. Studies in the Theatre and Drama of English Canada. M.A.: Toronto, 1963.

6282 Thibodeau, Colleen. Recent Canadian Poetry. M.A.: Toronto, 1950.

6283 Thomas, Clara. Canadian Novelists, 1920-1944. M.A.: Western Ontario, 1944.

6284 Tisdall, D. M. Continuity in Canadian Poetry: Some Recurrent Themes and Subjects. M.A.: Toronto, 1961.

6285 Ward, William Clark. Historical Aspects of Canadian Fiction. M.A.: Acadia, 1943.

6286 Watt, F. W. Radicalism in English-Canadian Literature Since Confederation. Ph.D.: Toronto, 1957.

6287 Yeo, Margaret Elizabeth. The Living Landscape: Nature Imagery in the Poetry of Margaret Atwood and Other Modern Canadian Lyric Poets. M.A.: Carleton, 1969.

Canada: Individual Authors

AVISON, Margaret

6288 Ade, Janet. The Poetry of Margaret Avison. M.A.: Toronto, 1966.

6289 Williamson, Hendrika. Man and Mandala: The Poetry of Margaret Avison. M.A.: Simon Fraser, 1970.

BAILEY, Jacob

6290 Harvey, Evelyn B. The Indefatigable Inditer: The Reverend Jacob Bailey, 1731-1808. M.A.: Carleton, 1966.

BIRD, W. R.

6291 Heyworth, Mann Vida. The Regional Novels and Travel Books of Will R. Bird. M.A.: Montréal, 1960.

BIRNEY, Earle

6292 Noel-Bentley, Peter C. A Chronological Study of the Poetry of Earle Birney. M.A.: Toronto, 1966.

BRUCE, Charles

6293 Haughton, Kathryn M. Parker. John Frederic Herbin and Charles Tory Bruce: Two Generations of Regional Literature. M.A.: New Brunswick, 1970.

BUCKLER, Ernest

6294 Atkinson, I. A. "The Mountain and the Valley": New Horizons in Canadian Fiction. M.A.: Guelph, 1969.
6295 Cook, G. M. Ernest Buckler: His Creed and His Craft. M.A.: Acadia, 1967.
6296 Harris, Bernita Helena. "The Waste Land's Cruelest Month": The Influence of T. S. Eliot on Ernest Buckler's "The Cruelest Month." M.A.: New Brunswick, 1969.
6297 Orange, John. Ernest Buckler: The Masks of the Artist. Phil.M.: Toronto, 1969.

BUCHAN, John

6298 Dawson, Jeremy Orme. The Search Theme in the Early Novels of John Buchan. M.A.: Manitoba, 1969.

CALLAGHAN, Morley

6299 Arthur, Constance Joyce. A Comparative Study of the Short Stories of Morley Callaghan and Hugh Garner. M.A.: New Brunswick, 1967.
6300 Dupuis, Louis George. The Spirituality of the Priest in Morley Edward Callaghan. M.A.: Ottawa, 1963.

6301   Fajardo, Salvador.   Morley Callaghan's Novels and Short Stories. M.A.:
       Montréal, 1962.

6302   McCarvell, Joan.   Morley Callaghan as a Short Story Writer. M.A.:
       Laval, 1957.

6303   McGregory, Robert Grant.   A Comparative Study of the Short Stories of
       Morley Callaghan and Ernest Hemingway. M.A.: New Brunswick, 1967.

6304   McKellar, Iain Howell.   The Innocents of Morley Callaghan. M.A.:
       Carleton, 1968.

6305   Martineau, François.   Morley Callaghan as a Novelist. Ph.D.: Montréal, 1961.

6305a Orange, John.   Morley Callaghan's Catholic Conscience. M.A.: Toronto, 1966.

6306   Ripley, John Daniel.   A Critical Study of the Novels and Short Stories
       of Morley Callaghan. M.A.: New Brunswick, 1959.

CAMERON, G. F.

6307   Labonté, Biron Coates.   George Frederick Cameron: World Poet. M.A.:
       Montréal, 1956.

CAMPBELL, W. W.

6308   Coulby, Margaret Evelyn.   Poet of the Mist: Critical Estimation of the
       Position of William Wilfred Campbell in Canadian Literature. M.A.:
       Ottawa, 1950.

CARMAN, Bliss

6309   McCracken, M. S.   Bliss Carman: His Status in the Annals of Canadian
       Literature. M.A.: Ottawa, 1936.

6310   Miller, Muriel M.   A Mental Biography of Bliss Carman in a Creative
       Interpretation of His Poetry. M.A.: Toronto, 1933.

6311   Stephens, Donald.   The Influence of English Poets Upon the Poetry of
       Bliss Carman. M.A.: New Brunswick, 1955.

CARR, Emily

6312   O'Hara, Martin.   Emily Carr: A Study of Her Development as Writer and
       Painter. M.A.: Montréal, 1953.

CHILD, Philip

6313   Kupsh, Linzey.   An Introduction to the Novels of Philip Child. M.A.:
       Laval, 1958.

COHEN, Leonard

6314   Allen, Roy.   The World of Leonard Cohen: A Study of His Poetry. M.A.:
       Simon Fraser, 1970.

6315   Knelsen, Richard J.   Flesh and Spirit in the Writings of Leonard Cohen.
       M.A.: Manitoba (Univ. of Winnipeg), 1969.

CONNOR, Ralph

6316   Leclerc, Cyprian.   Ralph Connor, Canadian Novelist. M.A.: Montréal,
         1962.

CRAWFORD, I. V.

6317   MacGillivray, S. F.   Isabella Valancy Crawford. M.A.: New Brunswick,
         1963.

DAVIES, Robertson

6318   Fisher, Elspeth.   Robertson Davies, Canadian Novelist. M.A.: New
         Brunswick, 1965.

6319   Murphy, Sharon M.   Self-Discovery: The Search for Values in the Work of
         Robertson Davies. M.A.: Carleton, 1968.

6320   Theobald, Alice.   Regionalism in the Imaginative Writings of Robertson
         Davies. M.A.: Montréal, 1964.

6321   Turner, James Ogdem Freeman.   Robertson Davies: Critic and Author.
         M.A.: Manitoba, 1958.

6322   Ursell, Geoffrey Barry.   A Triple Mirror: The Plays of Merrill Denison,
         Gwen Pharis Ringwood, and Robertson Davies. M.A.: Manitoba, 1966.

DE LA ROCHE, Mazo

6323   Neely, Mary Ann.   Sources of Energy in the Jalna Novels of Mazo de la
         Roche. M.A.: Western Ontario, 1970.

6324   Ogulnik, Maurice Arnold.   "The Books of Jalna": A Social History. M.A.:
         Montréal, 1951.

DE MILLE, James

6325   MacLeod, Douglas E.   A Critical Biography of James DeMille. M.A.:
         Dalhousie, 1968.

DRUMMOND, W. H.

6326   Dustan, William Gordon.   The Interpretation of the Habitant, William
         Henry Drummond. M.A.: Dalhousie, 1928.

DUNCAN, Sara Jeannette

6327   Goodwin, R. E.   The Early Journalism of Sara Jeanette Duncan. M.A.:
         Toronto, 1964.

GALT, John

6328   Avery, G. M. K.   John Galt's "Canadian" Writings 1779-1839. M.Litt.:
         Strathclyde, 1970.

GIBBON, J. M.

6329   Dwyer, Mary.   Social Satire in the Novels of Murray Gibbon. M.A.:
       Montréal, 1953.

GROVE, F. P.

6330   Dunphy, John W.   The Technique of Fiction in the Novels of F. P. Grove.
       M.A.: Dalhousie, 1969.

6331   Eaton, Charles Ernest.   The Life and Works of Frederick Philip Grove.
       M.A.: Acadia, 1940.

6332   Grant, Gwendolyn Margaret.   Frederick Philip Grove: Birth of the
       Canadian Novel. M.A.: Dalhousie, 1946.

6333   Lorens, Alfons.   Les emancipées de Prus et Grove et le rôle de la
       femme dans la société. M.A.: Montréal, 1952.

6334   McLeod, Gordon Duncan.   The Primeval Element in the Prairie Novels of
       Frederick Philip Grove. M.A.: Manitoba, 1966.

6335   McMullin, Stanley E.   The Promised Land Motif in the Works of Frederick
       Philip Grove. M.A.: Carleton, 1968.

6336   Myles, E.   The Self as Theme in Grove's Novels. M.A.: Alberta, 1965.

6337   Plamondon, Louis.   Nature in Frederick Philip Grove. M.A.: Montréal,
       1956.

6338   Rideout, E. Christopher.   The Woman in the Novels of Frederick Philip
       Grove. M.A.: Alberta, 1969.

6339   Taylor, James R.   Grove, the Novelist. M.A.: Mount Allison, 1950.

6340   Thompson, Joyce Lesley.   Structural Technique in the Fiction of
       Frederick Philip Grove. M.A.: Manitoba (Univ. of Winnipeg), 1969.

6341   Wilson, Jennie May.   A Comparative Study of the Novels of Frederick
       Philip Grove and Theodore Dreiser. M.A.: New Brunswick, 1962.

HALIBURTON, Thomas

6342   Avis, Walter S.   The Speech of Sam Slick. M.A.: Queen's (Kingston, Ont.),
       1950.

6343   Fredericks, Carrie MacMillan.   The Development of Sam Slick: Twenty
       Years of Change in a Character, 1835-1855. M.A.: Dalhousie, 1970.

6344   Harding, L. A. A.   The Humour of Haliburton. Ph.D.: Montréal, 1964.

6345   Thompson, David Glen.   Thomas Chandler Haliburton and the Failure of
       Canadian Humour. M.A.: Manitoba, 1965.

6346   Van Tongerloo, R. R.   Thomas Chandler Haliburton, Political Satirist.
       M.A.: Manitoba, 1967.

HEAVYSEGE, Charles

6347   Dale, Thomas Randall.   The Life and Work of Charles Heavysege, 1816-1876.
       Ph.D.: Chicago, 1951.

HOWE, Joseph

6348   Beaton, Margaret.   Joseph Howe, a Literary Figure. Ph.D.: Montréal, 1958.

6349 Lumsden, Susan. Joseph Howe: Editor of the "Novascotian." M.A.:
      Carleton, 1966.

HUNTER DUVAR, J.

6350 Campbell, Stephen. John Hunter-Duvar. A Biographical Introduction,
      Check-list of His Works, and Selected Bibliography. M.A.: New
      Brunswick, 1966.

JAMESON, Anna

6351 Thomas, Clara. Anna Jameson: The Making of a Reputation. Ph.D.:
      Toronto, 1962.

KIRBY, William

6352 Deguire, Armand. The United Empire Loyalist William Kirby. M.A.:
      Montréal, 1959.

6353 Richard, Raymond G. Historical Accuracy and Inaccuracy Found in "The
      Golden Dog." M.A.: Laval, 1963.

KLEIN, A. M.

6354 Bell, Merirose. The Image of French Canada in the Poetry of William
      Henry Drummond, Emile Coderre and A. M. Klein. M.A.: McGill, 1967.

6355 Lyons, Roberta. Jewish Poets from Montreal: Concepts of History in
      Poetry of A. M. Klein, Irving Layton, and Leonard Cohen. M.A.:
      Carleton, 1966.

6356 Marshall, Thomas. The Poetry of A. M. Klein. M.A.: Queen's (Kingston,
      Ont.), 1964.

6357 Palnick, E. E. A. M. Klein: A Biographical Study. M.A.: Hebrew Union
      College (Cincinnati), 1959.

6358 Schultz, Gregory Peter. The Periodical Poetry of A. J. M. Smith, F. R.
      Scott, Leo Kennedy, A. M. Klein and Dorothy Livesay (1925-1950).
      M.A.: Western Ontario, 1957.

6359 Scullion, John. Abraham Moses Klein: Poet and Novelist. M.A.: Montréal,
      1953.

KNISTER, Raymond

6360 Ross, G. Arthur. Three Minor Canadian Poets: Louis Alexander Mackay,
      Leo Kennedy, and Raymond Knister. M.A.: Alberta, 1969.

LAMPMAN, Archibald

6361 Anderson, Elmer Lloyd. Polarities and Neutrality in Archibald Lampman.
      M.A.: Montréal, 1966.

6362 Brennan, Ursula. The Prosody of Archibald Lampman. M.A.: Queen's
      (Kingston, Ont.), 1931.

6363 Davies, Barrie. The Alien Mind: A Study of the Poetry of Archibald
      Lampman. Ph.D.: New Brunswick, 1970.

6364 Nesbitt, Bruce. Lampman and O'Dowd: A Comparative Study of Poetic
      Attitudes in Canada and Australia in the Late Nineteenth Century.
      M.A.: Queen's (Kingston, Ont.), 1965.

6365 Purcell, Mary Aillen. The Nature Poetry of Lampman. M.A.: Montréal,
      1953.

6367 Robinson, Maud Celestine. Archibald Lampman Lyrist. M.A.: Montréal,
      1955.

LAURENCE, Margaret

6368 Boyd, Bonita Jane. The Maze of Life: The Art of Margaret Laurence.
      M.A.: Acadia, 1968.

LAYTON, Irving

6369 Edelstein, George. Irving Layton: A Study of the Poet in Revolt.
      M.A.: Montréal, 1962.

6370 Reif, Eric Anthony. Irving Layton: The Role of the Poet. M.A.:
      Toronto, 1967.

LEACOCK, Stephen

6371 Bélanger, Reynald. Canadian Humourists: Leacock, Haliburton, Earle
      Birney, W. O. Mitchell. M.A.: Laval, 1968.

6372 Gilliss, Kenneth Edmund. Stephen Leacock as a Satirist. M.A.: New
      Brunswick, 1957.

6373 Ross, David W. Stephen Leacock, Scholar and Humorist. Ph.D.: Columbia,
      1947.

6374 Spilker, Albert. Stephen Leacock, the Humorist. M.A.: Montréal, 1958.

6375 Stewart, Patrick Douglas McLean. Stephen Leacock: His Role as a Critic.
      M.A.: New Brunswick, 1969.

6376 Walsh, Joan A. Stephen Leacock as an American Humorist. M.A.: Toronto,
      1962.

LEPROHON, Rosanna

6377 Deneau, Henri. Life and Works of Mrs. Leprohon. M.A.: Montréal, 1949.

LIVESAY, Dorothy

6378 Boylan, Charles Robert. The Social and Lyric Voices of Dorothy Livesay.
      M.A.: British Columbia, 1969.

6379 O'Donnell, Kathleen. Dorothy Livesay. Ph.D.: Montréal, 1959.

LOWRY, Malcolm

6380 Albaum, E. Myth and Madness in the Novels of Malcolm Lowry. Ph.D.:
      SUNY (Stony Brook), 1971.

6381 Atkins, Elizabeth. Aspects of the Absurd in Modern Fiction, with Special
      Reference to "Under the Volcano" and "Catch 22." M.A.: British
      Columbia, 1969.

6382 Benham, David S. A Liverpool of Self: A Study of Lowry's Fiction Other than "Under the Volcano." M.A.: British Columbia, 1969.

6383 Butson, Barry. Structural Organization in "Under the Volcano." M.A.: Western Ontario, 1967.

6384 Casari, Laura E. R. Malcolm Lowry's Drunken Divine Comedy in "Under the Volcano" and Shorter Fiction. Ph.D.: Nebraska, 1967.

6385 Costa, Richard Hauer. Quest for Eridanus: Malcolm Lowry's Evolving Art in "Under the Volcano." Ph.D.: Purdue, 1968.

6386 Jewison, D. J. P. Grand Circle Sailing: A Study of the Imagery of Malcolm Lowry. M.A.: Manitoba, 1966.

6387 Johnson, Carrell. The Making of "Under the Volcano": An Examination of Lyrical Structure, with Reference to Textual Revisions. M.A.: British Columbia, 1969.

6388 Kilgallin, Anthony R. The Use of Literary Sources for Theme and Style in Lowry's "Under the Volcano." M.A.: Toronto, 1965.

6389 Lloyd, Rodney Osten. Mexico and "Under the Volcano." M.A.: Western Ontario, 1967.

6390 Milici, D. Malcolm Lowry's Mysticism in "Under the Volcano" and "The Forest Path to the Spring." M.A.: Toronto, 1968.

6391 Moore, Dennis. The Transformations of "Billy Budd." Ph.D.: Northwestern, 1970.

6392 Nyland, Agnes Cecilia [Sister Mary Rosalinda]. The Luminous Wheel: A Study of Malcolm Lowry. Ph.D.: Ottawa, 1967.

6393 Ramsey, Robin. The Impact of Time and Memory in Malcolm Lowry's Fiction. M.A.: British Columbia, 1969.

6394 Robertson, Anthony. Aspects of the Quest in the Minor Fiction of Malcolm Lowry. M.A.: British Columbia, 1966.

6395 Thomas, Hilda L. Malcolm Lowry's "Under the Volcano": An Interpretation. M.A.: British Columbia, 1965.

6396 Tiessen, Paul G. "Under the Volcano": Lowry and the Cinema. M.A.: Alberta, 1968.

6397 Wild, Bernadette. Malcolm Lowry: A Study of the Sea Metaphor in "Ultramarine" and "Under the Volcano." M.A.: Windsor, 1967.

MCCOURT, E. A.

6398 Graham, Neil. Theme and Form in the Novels of Edward A. McCourt. M.A.: Windsor, 1968.

MACDONALD, Wilson

6399 Quinlan, Anna. A Survey of Wilson MacDonald. M.A.: Ottawa, 1936.

MCGEE, T. D.

6400 Belding, Patricia [Sister Mary Louise]. Thomas D'Arcy McGee as a Man of Letters. M.A.: New Brunswick, 1960.

6401 O'Donnell, Kathleen. Thomas Darcy McGee's Irish and Canadian Ballads. M.A.: Western Ontario, 1956.

MACINNES, Tom

6402 Prouty, William. Tom MacInnes. M.A.: New Brunswick, 1956.

MACLENNAN, Hugh

6403 Cockburn, Robert H. Hugh MacLennan as Novelist. M.A.: New Brunswick, 1966.

6404 George, Gerald. Theme and Symbol in the Novels of Hugh MacLennan. M.A.: Laval, 1966.

6405 Gilley, R. Keith. Myth and Meaning in Three Novels of Hugh MacLennan. M.A.: British Columbia, 1967.

6406 Goetsch, Paul. Hugh MacLennan's Novels. M.A.: Marburg, 1960.

6407 Morley, Patricia A. Puritanism in the Novels of Hugh MacLennan. M.A.: Carleton, 1967.

6408 Ogulnik, Léa (Lutherman). The Realistic Novels of Hugh MacLennan. M.A.: Montréal, 1957.

6409 Wing, Ted. Puritan Ethic and Social Response in the Novels of Sinclair Ross, Robertson Davies, and Hugh MacLennan. M.A.: Alberta, 1969.

MAIR, Charles

6410 Shrive, Frank Norman. Charles Mair: A Study in Canadian Literary Nationalism. Ph.D.: Queen's (Kingston, Ont.), 1961.

MONTGOMERY, L. M.

6411 McLaughlin, Gertrude [Sister Joanne of Christ]. The Literary Art of L. M. Montgomery. M.A.: Montréal, 1961.

MOODIE, Susanna

6412 Ballstadt, Carl P. The Literary History of the Strickland Family. Ph.D.: London, 1965.

6413 Park, Sheila S. Susanna Moodie and the "Literary Garland." M.A.: Carleton, 1966.

MOORE, Brian

6414 Harrison, Richard T. The Fictional World in Four Novels by Brian Moore. M.A.: British Columbia, 1965.

NIVEN, F. J.

6415 New, William H. Individual and Group Isolation in the Fiction of Frederick John Niven: Setting as a Basis for a Study of Conflict and Resolution. M.A.: British Columbia, 1963.

ODELL, Jonathan

6416 Anderson, Joan (Johnston). A Collection of the Poems of Jonathan Odell with a Biographical and Critical Introduction. M.A.: British Columbia, 1961.

OSTENSO, Martha

6417 Jones, Alexander Henry. Martha Ostenso's Novels--A Study of Three Dominant Themes. M.A.: British Columbia, 1970.

6418 Stanko, Stanley Carl. Image, Theme and Pattern in the Works of Martha Ostenso. M.A.: Alberta, 1968.

PICKTHALL, Marjorie

6419 MacDonald, John Harry. Marjorie Pickthall. M.A.: Dalhousie, 1927.

6420 St. Cecilia, Sister. Marjorie Pickthall, the Ethereal Minstrel of Canada. M.A.: Ottawa, 1941.

PRATT, E. J.

6421 Conrad, Brother. The Dialectic of Love and Ferocity in the Shorter Poems of E. J. Pratt. Ph.D.?: Atenio de Manila, 1964.

6422 Gibbs, Robert. Aspects of Irony in the Poetry of E. J. Pratt. Ph.D.: New Brunswick, 1970.

6423 Paisley, Alice Catherine. Epic Features of "Brebeuf and His Brethren" by E. J. Pratt. M.A.: Windsor (Assumption College), 1960.

6424 St. Dorothy Marie, Sister. The Epic Note in the Poetry of Edwin John Pratt. M.A.: Ottawa, 1956.

6425 Sharman, Vincent. Patterns of Imagery and Symbolism in the Poetry of E. J. Pratt. M.A.: British Columbia, 1963.

PURDY, A. W.

6426 Wilson, Jean L. The Sense of Place and History in the Poetry of A. W. Purdy. M.A.: Saskatchewan, 1968.

RADDALL, T. H.

6427 Hawkins, W. J. The Life and Fiction of Thomas H. Raddall. M.A.: New Brunswick, 1965.

RICHARDSON, Evelyn

6428 Johnston, Helen Pauline. Evelyn Richardson: Fact and Fiction. M.A.: Acadia, 1968.

6429 Rowse, Winnifred Hovey Barkhouse. Evelyn Richardson, Essayist and Novelist. M.A.: Montréal, 1960.

RINGUET

6430 Bond, William Ross. A Changing Way of Life as Seen in the Principal Novels of Ringuet. M.A.: McMaster, 1968.

ROBERTS, Charles G. D.

6431   Boucher, Bro. Laurent, C. S. C.   Sources of Inspiration in Charles G. D.
       Roberts' Poetry of Nature. M.A.: Laval, 1966.

6432   Campbell, John Hugh.   The Prose Works of Sir Charles G. D. Roberts.
       M.A.: New Brunswick, 1963.

6433   Forbes, Elisabeth Alexis.   The Development of Style and Thought in
       Charles G. D. Roberts' Poetry to 1897. M.A.: New Brunswick, 1953.

6434   Roy, George Ross.   Charles G. D. Roberts, Canadian Poet of Nature.
       M.A.: Montréal, 1951.

ROBERTS, Theodore G.

6435   Heaney, Frances Gale.   Theodore Goodridge Roberts. M.A.: New Brunswick,
       1960.

ROSS, Sinclair

6436   A'Court, Mary.   The Faiths of Four Men: Emerson, W. O. Mitchell,
       Melville, Sinclair Ross. M.A.: Toronto, 1966.

RYERSON, Egerton

6437   McDonald, F. J.   Egerton Ryerson: A Pedagogical and Historical Essay.
       Ph.D.: Ottawa, 1937.

6438   Stubbs, Gordon Thomas.   The Role of Egerton Ryerson in the Development
       of Public Library Service in Ontario. M.A.: British Columbia, 1965.

SANGSTER, Charles

6439   Hamilton, Willis David.   An Edition of the Hitherto Uncollected Poems
       of Charles Sangster, with a Biographical and Critical Introduction.
       M.A.: New Brunswick, 1958.

SCOTT, D. C.

6440   Crozier, Daniel F.   The Use of the Indian in the Poetry of Duncan
       Campbell Scott. M.A.: New Brunswick, 1963.

6441   Denham, William Paul.   Music and Painting in the Poetry of Duncan
       Campbell Scott. M.A.: Western Ontario, 1964.

6442   Dragland, Stanley L.   Duncan Campbell Scott. Ph.D.: Queen's (Kingston,
       Ont.), 1970.

6443   Wilcox, W. J.   The Poetry of Duncan Campbell Scott. M.A.: Toronto, 1958.

SCOTT, F. R.

6444   Martin, Jane.   F. R. Scott. M.A.: Carleton, 1967.

SERVICE, Robert

6445 Bolla, Raymond Peter. The Northern Ballads of Robert Service. M.A.:
      Montréal, 1952.

6446 Migone, Pietro. Robert Service, Poet of the Canadian North. M.A.:
      Ottawa, 1949.

SHERMAN, Francis

6447 Wilson, Laurence R. The Life and Poetry of Francis Sherman. M.A.:
      New Brunswick, 1957.

SMITH, A. J. M.

6448 McCallum, Maureen Fay. A. J. M. Smith. M.A.: Queen's (Kingston, Ont.),
      1970.

SOUSTER, Raymond

6449 Campbell, Robert. A Study of the History and Development of Raymond
      Souster's "Direction," "Contact," and "Combustion." M.A.: New
      Brunswick, 1969.

6450 Cook, Harry Hugh. The Poetry of Raymond Souster. M.A.: Simon Fraser,
      1968.

STEAD, R. J. C.

6451 Thompson, Eric Callum. A Critical Study of the Poetry and Prose of
      Robert J. C. Stead: Prairie Poet and Novelist. M.A.: New Brunswick,
      1965.

TRAILL, C. P.

4652 McNeil, J. L. Mrs. Traill in Canada. M.A.: Queen's (Kingston, Ont.),
      1948.

See also: 6412.

WILSON, Ethel

6453 Campbell, Barbara. The Fiction of Ethel Wilson: A Study of Theme and
      Technique. M.A.: Toronto, 1967.

6454 Campbell, Robert. Imagery and Symbolism in the Fiction of Ethel Wilson.
      M.A.: New Brunswick, 1967.

6455 Clarke, Helen Marguerite. Appearance and Reality in the Fiction of
      Ethel Wilson. M.A.: British Columbia, 1964.

6456 Robinson, S. The Novels and Short Stories of Ethel Wilson. M.A.:
      Saskatchewan (Saskatoon), 1969.

6457 Walker, Dorothy Frances. A World in Grain of Sand: An Appreciation of
      Ethel Wilson, a Canadian Writer with Identity. M.A.: Mount Allison,
      1967.

India and Pakistan

6458 Alphonso-Karkala, John B. Indo-English Literature in the Nineteenth Century. Ph.D.: Columbia, 1964.

6459 Bhardwaj, V. S. Kipling's India. M.A.: Univ. of East Africa (Nairobi), 1967.

6460 Bokhari, Z. A. A Study of Anglo-India in Fiction. Ph.D.: Cambridge (Girton), 1965.

6461 Bostrom, Irene. India in English Fiction, 1770-1860. Ph.D.: Wisconsin, 1955.

6462 Das, G. K. E. M. Forster as an Interpreter of India. Ph.D.: Cambridge, 1970.

6463 Derrett, M. E. The Novel About India Since Independence, Written by Indians in English. M.A.: London (Kings), 1964.

6464 Hale, Frances. Indo-British Writing During the Raj. Ph.D.: Nottingham, 1970.

6465 Hawkes, Carol A. Anglo-Indian Fiction: A Conflict of Cultures as Seen by the Novelist. Ph.D.: Columbia, 1953.

6466 Husain, S. Sajjad. Rudyard Kipling and India. Ph.D.: Nottingham, 1952.

6467 Khera, Sunit Bala. E. M. Forster and India, with Special Reference to "A Passage to India." M.A.: New Brunswick, 1966.

6468 Lego, Mary M. English Literature and Modern Bengali Short Fiction: A Study in Influences. Ph.D.: Columbia, 1970.

6469 Livingston, Ray Frederic. Ananda K. Coomaraswamy's Theory of Literature. Ph.D.: Minnesota, 1956.

6470 Lloyd, S. J. A Study of Anglo-Indian Fiction in the Period 1857-99. B.Litt.: Oxford, 1969.

6471 Mukerjee, Meenakshi. Indo-Anglian Fiction, 1930-1964: Themes and Techniques. Ph.D.: Poona, 1969.

6472 Musa, K. The Linguistic World of Anglo-India. M.Phil.: Leeds, 1968.

6473 Parry, B. The Image of India: Some Literary Expressions of the British Experience in India. M.A.: Birmingham, 1967.

6474 Rao, A. V. Krishna. The Indo-Anglian Novel and the Changing Tradition (A Study of the Novels of Mulk Raj Anand, Kamala Markandaya, R. K. Narayan and Rajarao). Ph.D.: Andhra, 1965.

6475 Ray, S. N. Anglo-Indian Poetry. London, 1929.

6476 Singh, K. K. Kipling's India. Ph.D.: London (Royal Holloway), 1966.

6477 Sud, Radha Krishna. A Survey of Indian Writers in English Verse. Punjab, 1942.

6478 Talookdar, Byram K. A Survey of Anglo-Indian Poetry from the Beginning to the Present Time. Dublin, 1935.

6479 Verghese, C. Paul. Problems of the Indian Writer in English. Ph.D.: Poona, 1968.

ANAND, Mulk Raj

6480 Kaushik, Raj Kumar. Mulkraj Anand--A Committed Artist. Ph.D.: Delhi,
      1968.

GHOSE, Aurobindo

6481 Nandakumar, Prema. Aurobindo's "Savitri." Ph.D.: Andhra, 1961.

MARKANDAYA, Kamala

6482 Rao, Kolar Surya Narayan. The New Harvest: The Indian Novel in English
      in the Post-Independence Era: Women at Work: Kamala Markandaya.
      Ph.D.: Pennsylvania State Univ., 1968.

NARAYAN, R. K.

6483 Holmstrom, L. Indian Writing in English: R. K. Narayan. B.Litt.:
      Oxford, 1969.

6484 Mukherji, Nirmal. The World of Malgudi: A Study of the Novels of
      R. K. Narayan. Ph.D.: Louisiana, 1961.

6485 Rao, V. Panduranga. The Art of R. K. Narayan. Ph.D.: Andhra, 1965.

TAGORE, Rabindranath

6486 Dasgupta, Pranabendu. The "Subjective" Tradition: A Comparative Analysis
      of the Dramatic Motives in the Plays of W. B. Yeats and Rabindranath
      Tagore. Ph.D.: Minnesota, 1963.

6487 Fretin. Hindu Elements in Rabindranath Tagore's Works. Diplome
      d'études supérieures: Paris (Sorbonne), 1922.

6488 Haque, A. S. M. Zahurul. Folklore in the Nationalist Thought and
      Literary Expression of Rabindranath Tagore. Ph.D.: Indiana, 1968.

6489 Hurwitz, Harold Murvin. Rabindranath Tagore and England. Ph.D.:
      Illinois, 1960.

6490 Mukherjee, Sujit Kumar. Passage to America: The Reception of Rabindranath
      Tagore in the United States, 1912-1941. Ph.D.: Univ. of Pennsylvania,
      1963.

6491 Sen, Nabaneeta. The Reception of Rabindranath Tagore in England, France,
      Germany, and the United States. Ph.D.: Indiana, 1964.

Malaysia and the Philippines

6492 Baksh, Abdul Majin bin Nabi. A Critical History of the Filipino Novel
      in English. M.A.: Malaya, 1969.

6493 Choo, Gladys Saw Gaik. Sir Hugh Clifford: A Literary and Biographical
      Approach. M.A.: Malaya, 1969.

6494 Lava, Josefa C. The Filipino Novel in English from 1940 to the Present.
      M.A.: Philippines, 1955.

6495 Moreno, Virginia R. A Critical Study of the Short Story in English as
      Written by Filipinos from 1910 to 1941 with an Anthology of
      Representative Stories. M.A.: Philippines, 1952.

6496 Ordoñez, Elmer A. The Filipino Short Story in English from the
      Commonwealth Period Through the War Years to the Post War Decade:
      1935-1955. M.A.: Philippines, 1956.

6497 Salleh, Habibah binte Dato Mohammed. Anthony Burgess's Malayan Trilogy.
      M.A.: Malaya, 1969.

6498 Yabes, Leopoldo Y. The Filipino Essay in English--A Critical Study
      with an Anthology of Representative Essays. M.A.: Philippines, 1950.

New Zealand: General

6499 Baxter, J. The New Zealand National Character as Exemplified by Three
      Novelists. M.A.: Wellington, 1952.

6500 Burns, Patricia Mary Frances. The Foundation of the New Zealand Press
      1839-1850. Ph.D.: Victoria Univ. College (Wellington), 1957.

6501 Delautour, C. F. New Zealand and the Novel 1945-1960. M.A.: Otago,
      1964.

6502 Gonley, W. K. J. New Zealand Life in Contemporary Literature. M.A.:
      [New Zealand], 1932.

6503 Gries, J. C. An Outline of Prose Fiction in New Zealand. Ph.D.:
      Auckland, 1951.

6504 Hanlon, P. J. The Development of Literature in New Zealand: A Study
      of Cultural Conditions in New Settlements. Ph.D.: Edinburgh, 1955.

6505 McCormick, E. H. Literature in New Zealand. M.A.: Wellington, 1929.

6506 O'Brien, E. J. A Critical Study of Selected Short Stories Written in
      New Zealand Since 1930. M.A.: Canterbury (NZ), 1949.

6507 Wall, N. The Representation of the Maori in Pakeha Fiction. M.A.:
      Otago, 1963.

6508 Wild, J. M. The Literary Periodical in New Zealand. M.A.: Wellington,
      1951.

New Zealand: Individual Authors

BAXTER, J. K.

6509 Weir, J. E. A Man Without a Mask: A Study of the Poetry of James K.
      Baxter. M.A.: Canterbury (NZ), 1970.

BETHELL, Ursula

6510 Morton, J. M. The Poetry of Ursula Bethell. M.A.: Wellington, 1949.

BUTLER, Samuel

6510a Hislop, J. M. Samuel Butler: The Years in Canterbury. M.A.: Canterbury
      (NZ), 1941.

FAIRBURN, A. R. D.

6511 Ross, J. C. A Study of the Poem "Dominion" by A. R. D. Fairburn.
      M.A.: Wellington, 1962.

MANSFIELD, Katherine

6512 Davies, Ellenor A. The Poet in the Short Story: A Study of Katherine
      Mansfield's Art. M.A.: Guelph, 1970.

6513 Garlington, Jack O'Brien. Literary Theory and Practice in the Short
      Stories of Katherine Mansfield. Ph.D.: Wisconsin, 1953.

6514 Gibbons, Eileen. Techniques Toward Dramatic Intensity in Katherine
      Mansfield's "The Daughters of the Late Colonel." M.A.: Brigham
      Young, 1962.

6515 Greenwood, Lillian B. The Technique of Katherine Mansfield. M.A.:
      British Columbia, 1965.

6516 Hattendorff, Rosemarie. Der Gebraulh der progressiven Form in
      Katherine Mansfields Kurzgeschicten. Ph.D.: Kiel, 1959.

6517 Hofer, E. H. A New Use of Symbolism in English Fiction, Particularly
      as Illustrated in the Works of Henry James, Dorothy Richardson,
      Virginia Woolf, E. M. Forster, and Katherine Mansfield. B.Litt.:
      Oxford (Lincoln), 1953.

6518 Hutchinson, S. A. The Short Story of Katherine Mansfield. M.A.:
      Toronto, 1941.

6519 Kinne, Wisner Payne. The Expression of Katherine Mansfield. M.A.:
      Iowa, 1939.

6520 Kleine, Donald William. Method and Meaning in the Stories of Katherine
      Mansfield. Ph.D.: Michigan,1962.

6521 Kominars, Sheppard B. Katherine Mansfield: The Way to Fontainebleau.
      Ph.D.: Boston, 1966.

6522 Lang, W. Sprach und Stil in Katherine Mansfields Kurz-geschichten.
      Tübingen, 1936.

6523 Larsh, Elisabeth. The Influence of Anton Tchekhov on Katherine
      Mansfield. M.A.: Stanford, 1933.

6524 McLennan, Isabel. Katherine Mansfield Stands Alone. M.A.: Melbourne,
      1941.

6526 Mantz, Ruth Elvish. A Bibliography of the Works of Katherine Mansfield,
      (Mrs. John Middleton Murry, 1888-1923). M.A.: Stanford, 1924.

6527 Marmon, Ina Florence. The Influence of Anton Chekhov on Katherine
      Mansfield. M.A.: Iowa, 1933.

6528 Mitchell, Charles H. The Short Stories of Katherine Mansfield. M.A.: Univ. of Pittsburgh, 1941.

6529 Muffang, May Lilian. Katherine Mansfield, sa vie, son oeuvre, sa personnalité. D.Lett.: Paris, 1937; published Paris: A. C. P., 1940.

6530 Pattinson, P. M. Vision and Design in the Short Stories of Katherine Mansfield. M.A.: Liverpool, 1968.

6531 Stephens, Donald. Aspects of the Growth and Practice of the English Short Story. Ph.D.: Edinburgh, 1960.

6532 Stevenson, Boynton. A Study of Katherine Mansfield. Ph.D.: Southern Methodist (Dallas), 1941.

6533 Weigelmann, T. Das Weltbild der Katherine Mansfield. Ph.D.: Bonn, 1937.

6534 Yen, Yuan-shu. Katherine Mansfield's Use of Point of View. Ph.D.: Wisconsin, 1967.

SARGESON, Frank

6535 Johnston, C. M. Anderson, Hemingway and Sargeson. M.A.: Otago, 1969.

6536 Whelan, D. B. Alienation in the Novels of Sargeson and Davin. M.A.: Canterbury (NZ), 1967.

South Africa: General

6537 Brink, André Philippus. Three South African English Poets: A Critical Study. M.A.: Pretoria, 1959.

6538 Kannemeyer, Margaret. Lady Anne Barnard: A Literary Study of Her Cape Episode. M.A.: Rhodes, 1942.

6539 Millar, C. J. The Contemporary South African Short Story in English. M.A.: Cape Town, 1962.

6540 Mostert, Cornelius Wickaum. The Native in the South African Novel in English. M.A.: Orange Free State, 1955.

6541 Mphahlele, Ezekiel. The Non-European Character in South African English Fiction. M.A.: Univ. of South Africa, 1956.

6542 Robinson, A. M. Lewin. The English Periodical Literature of the Cape Colony, 1824-1835. Ph.D.: Cape Town, 1961.

6543 Snyman, J. P. L. The Achievement of the South African Novel in English from 1880-1930: A Critical Study. D.Litt.: Potchefstroom, 1950.

6544 Stopforth, L. D. M. Drama in South Africa, 1925-1955: A Critical Survey. D.Litt.: Pretoria, 1956.

6545 _____ Some Exponents of the South African Short Story in English. M.A.: Pretoria, 1954.

6546 Taylor, Avis Elizabeth. The Frontier in South African Verse, 1820-1927. Ph.D.: Rhodes, 1960.

6547 Terblancke, J. D. V. H. Rider Haggard: A Critical Study of His Prose Fiction. M.A.: Pretoria, 1956.

6548 Van Zyl, John Andrews. <u>The Afrikaner Way of Life as Depicted in South African English Fiction</u>. M.A.: Orange Free State, 1959.

6549 Weinstock, Donald Jay. <u>The Boer War in the Novel in English, 1884-1966: A Descriptive and Critical Bibliography</u>. Ph.D.: UCLA, 1968.

6550 Wroblewski, Nancy. <u>An Examination of the South African Autobiography</u>. M.A.: Kent State, 1969.

South Africa: Individual Authors

CAMPBELL, Roy

6551 Davis, Reginald Victor. <u>Roy Campbell: A Critical Survey</u>. M.A.: Pretoria, 1957.

GORDIMER, Nadine

6552 Ledbetter, Dorothy E. <u>The Theme of Isolation in the Short Stories of Nadine Gordimer</u>. M.A.: San Diego, 1969.

LESSING, Doris

6553 Carey, Father Alfred A. [John Leonard]. <u>Doris Lessing: The Search for Reality--A Study of the Major Themes in Her Novels</u>. Ph.D.: Wisconsin, 1965.

6554 Cox, Marilyn J. <u>Narrative Technique in Doris Lessing's "The Golden Notebook</u>." M.A.: Queen's (Kingston, Ont.), 1969.

6555 Jarvis, Peter. <u>The Works of Doris Lessing</u>. B.Phil.: St. Andrews, 1970.

6556 Schlueter, Paul George, Jr. <u>A Study of the Major Novels of Doris Lessing</u>. Ph.D.: Southern Illinois, 1968.

PATON, Alan

6557 David, R. <u>South African Prose Fiction of the Past Two Decades (with Special Reference to Nadine Gordimer, Dan Jacobson, and Alan Paton)</u>. M.A.: Liverpool, 1967.

6558 Leopold, Robert Erik. <u>The Contemporary Novel and Its Condensation ["The Blackboard Jungle," "By Love Possessed" and "Too Late the Phalarope"]</u>. Ph.D.: Columbia, 1963.

6559 Nielsen, Lorna. <u>A Critical Evaluation of "Cry, the Beloved Country</u>." M.A.: Brigham Young, 1962.

6560 Walker, Steven. <u>Biblical Elements in the Prose Works of Alan Paton</u>. M.A.: Brigham Young, 1966.

SCHREINER, Olive

6561 Friedman, Marion. <u>Olive Schreiner: An Examination of the Personality of a Writer and Her Material</u>. M.A.: Witwatersrand, 1951.

6562   Postma, Vera Kathleen. The Life and Writings of Olive Schreiner.
       Ph.D.: Cape Town, 1948.

SMITH, Pauline

6563   Haresnape, Geoffrey. A Study of the Works of Pauline Smith. M.A.:
       Cape Town, 1960.

West Indies: General

6564   Birbalsingh, Frank M. Novelists of the British Caribbean, 1940-63.
       M.A.: London (King's), 1967.

6565   Boxill, Anthony. The Novel in English in the West Indies 1900-1962.
       Ph.D.: New Brunswick, 1966.

6566   Davies, Barrie. The Achievement of the West Indian Novel. M.A.:
       Univ. of the West Indies (Mona), 1966.

6567   Ramchand, Kenneth. A Background to the Novel in the West Indies.
       Ph.D.: Edinburgh, 1968.

6568   Sharp, S. A West Indian Literature (Verse-Short Story). M.A.: Leeds,
       1952.

6569   Smith, R. E. A Study of the Correspondence Between the "Roman de
       Renard," Jamaican Anansi Stories, and West African Animal Tales
       Collected in Culture-Area V. Ph.D.: Ohio State, 1971.

6570   Warner, M. Language in Trinidad, with Special Reference to English.
       M.Phil.: York (England), 1968.

6571   Zoller, P. T. Revolt in Jamaica: A Study of Carlyle, Ruskin, Mill,
       and Huxley. Ph.D.: Claremont, 1970.

See also: 6071.

West Indies: Individual Authors

MCKAY, Claude

6572   Conroy, Sister M. James. Claude McKay: Negro Poet and Novelist. Ph.D.:
       Notre Dame, 1968.

NAIPAUL, V. S.

6573   Broughton, G. A Critical Study of the Development of V. S. Naipaul as
       a Novelist as Reflected in His Four West Indian Novels. M.Phil.:
       London Institute of Education, 1967.

6574   Derrick, A. O. The Uncommitted Artist: A Study of the Purpose and
       Methods of Satire in the Novels of V. S. Naipaul. M.Phil.: Leeds,
       1968.

6575 Hamner, Robert D. An Island Voice: The Novels of V. S. Naipaul. Ph.D.: Texas (Austin), 1971.

6576 Ramraj, Victor Jammona. A Study of the Novels of V. S. Naipaul. M.A.: New Brunswick, 1968.

Index of Critics, Editors, Translators

GOPALA, REDDI B.   5540
GOPALAKRISHNAN, ADIGA M.   4949
GOPALAM, VAJJHALA   5541 5542
GORDIMER, NADINE   147 4348 4349   4350 4351 4352
     4353 4573 4574 4713
GORDON, ADAM LINDSAY   1410
GORDON, ALFRED   2409 3533
GORDON, B. K.   3534
GORDON, CHARLES WILLIAM   2913 2914
GORDON, IAN   3878 3878A 3879 3880 4121 4122 4123
GORDON, SUZANNE   4354
GORELIK, MORDECAI   645
GOSE, E. B.   2901 3382
GOSPARD, DAVID   5851
GOSSE, FAYETTE   1442
GOTLIEB, PHYLLIS   3115 3181
GOULD, GERALD   1900
GOWDA,   H.   H.   ANNIAH   4950 4951 4952 4953 5184
     5229 5319 5336 5363 5947 6011
GOWEN, HERBERT   4954
GRAHAM-WHITE, A.   6077
GRAHAM, JEAN   2814
GRAHAM, NEIL   6398
GRAHAM, ROBERT S.   6208
GRAMMATICUS   3881
GRANT, BRUCE   1554
GRANT, DAMIAN   5935
GRANT, DOUGLAS   2410
GRANT, GWENDOLYN MARGARET   6332
GRANVILLE-BARKER, HARLEY   2411
GRATTAN, C. HARTLEY   646 647 648 1349   1350 1901
     1902
GRAUSTEIN, GOTTFRIED   4637
GRAVE, S. A.   3990
GRAY, A.   6136
GRAY, ALAN   4456 4499 4744
GRAY, C.   5852
GRAY, CECIL   6045
GRAY, THOMAS   5579
GREEN, DOROTHY   1109   1480 1481 1579 1903 1904
     1905 1995 2029 2231
GREEN, ELEANOR   1386
GREEN, H. M.   649 650 651 652 653 654 1146 1822
GREEN, PAUL   2412
GREEN, ROBERT J.   4561
GREENBERGER, ALLEN J.   4955
GREENE, DONALD   2413
GREENE, MARGARET LAWRENCE   18
GREENFIELD, STANLEY B.   4124
GREENING, W. E.   2414
GREENOP, FRANK S.   655
GREENWAY, JOHN   656 657
GREENWOOD, LILLIAN B.   6515
GREER, ANNE   3497
GREER, REGINALD THOMAS   6209
GREGG, LYNDALL   4745 4746 4747 4748
GREGOR, IAN   3338
GREGORY, ALYSE   4125
GREGORY, HORACE   1482
GREGORY, R. M.   4749
GRENE, MARJORIE   158
GREVER, RONALD   6210
GRIES, J. C.   6503
GROBLER, P. DU P.   4500
GRONOWSKI, IRENE   658
GROSSKURTH, PHYLLIS   2415 3700 3701
GROVE, FREDERICK PHILIP   2416 2756 3007 3008 3009
     3010
GRUBE, JOHN   3797
GUCKIAN, PATRICK A.   5993
GUEHENNO, JEAN   5543
GUHA, NARESH   5544 5545
GUIBERT, ARMAND   4501 4502
GUILLET, EDWIN CLARENCE   2417
GULLASON, THOMAS H.   4575
GULLETT, H. B.   1073
GUMA, S. M.   4355
GUNASINGHE, SIRI   19
GUNAWARDENA, A. J.   5155 5156
GUNDY, H. P.   2838
GUNN, JOHN   659
GUNSON, NIEL   660
GUNTHER, HELMUT   5969
GUPTA, JOGENDRANATH   5225
GUPTA, NOLINI KANTA   5243 5685
GUPTA, P. C. KABIR   4956
GUPTA, RAMESHWAR   5244
GUPTA, SUBODH BHUSHAN   5546
GURR, A. J.   3882
GUSTAFSON, RALPH   2418 2419 2420 2421 2422   3153
     3552 3565

GUTHRIE, NORMAN G.   3154
GZELL, SYLVIA   2145
H. KOHN   5145
H., R.   4126
HAARHOFF, T. J.   4356
HAAS, CHARLES EUGENE   6105
HABIB, KAMAL MOHAMMED   4957
HADGRAFT, CECIL   661 662 663 664 665 666 827 969
     1242 1658 1742 1804 1906 1907 2146
HAFERKAMP, BERTA   4127
HAGAN, J.   667
HAGERMAN, VERNA B.   6211
HAGOPIAN, JOHN T.   4128
HAIG-BROWN, RODERICK   2423
HALDAR, ARUNA   5547
HALDOR, GOPAL   5548
HALE, FRANCES   6464
HALE, KATHERINE   2920 2921
HALE, NANCY   4129
HALEY, MARTIN   1147
HALL, A. D.   4357
HALL, CHIPMAN   6212
HALL, D.   3883
HALL, DAVID   668
HALL, JAMES   1505
HALL, LESLIE M.   3884
HALL, RODNEY   669
HALL, SANDRA   670 671 1287 1419 1469 1506 1532
HALL, W. F.   2995
HAMBLETON, RONALD   2941
HAMELIN, JEAN   2424
HAMER-JACKSON, CELESTA   3755
HAMER, CLIVE   672 673 674 675 1087 1224 1351 1352
     1544
HAMILTON-GREY, A. M.   1513
HAMILTON, IAN   4008 6018
HAMILTON, JAMES STUART   6144
HAMILTON, L.   2425
HAMILTON, ROBERT M.   2271
HAMILTON, S. C.   3269
HAMILTON, WILLIS DAVID   6439
HAMM, VICTOR M.   4503
HAMMOND, DOROTHY   148 6078
HAMMOND, M. O.   3090
HAMNER, ROBERT D.   4 6575
HANGER, EUNICE   676 677 678 679 680 681 1555 2147
     2148 2149
HANLON, P. J.   6504
HANNAH, DONALD   39
HANSHELL, DERYCK   149
HAQUE, A. S. M. ZAHURUL   6488
HARDER, HELGA IRENE   6213
HARDING, L. A. A.   3057 3058 3059 6344
HARDWICK, ELIZABETH   1996
HARDY, FRANK   682 1580
HARESNAPE, GEOFFREY   4358   4783   4784   4785   4786
     4787 6563
HARKINS, EDWARD F.   3654
HARLOW, ROBERT   2426
HARMEL, MICHAEL   4750
HARNETT, R.   4359
HARPER, G. M.   4130
HARREX, S. C.   5307 5337
HARRINGTON, CHARLES DAVID   6105A
HARRIS, BERNITA HELENA   6296
HARRIS, COLE   2427
HARRIS, FRANK   4751
HARRIS, L. J.   5792
HARRIS, LAWREN   2890
HARRIS, MAX   590 683 684 685 686 687 688 689 690
     1302 1458 1581 1756 1843 1970 2232
HARRIS, MICHAEL   2902
HARRIS, P.   4360
HARRIS, WILSON   5853 5854   5855   5856   5948 5949
     5950 5951 6048 6062
HARRISON-FORD, CARL   691
HARRISON, MRS. J. W. F.   2926
HARRISON, RICHARD T.   2428 6414
HARRISON, RUTH   1757
HARROWER, ELIZABETH   692
HART-SMITH, WILLIAM   3885 3982
HARTE, W. B.   2429
HARTLEY, LOIS   4807 5298 5338
HARTMAN, W.   4537
HARTWIG, DOROTHEA   4638
HARVEY, C. J. D.   4361 4504 4505 4551
HARVEY, D. C.   3060 3376
HARVEY, EVELYN B.   6290
HARVEY, FRANK R.   693
HARWOOD, H. C.   4131
HASLUCK, ALEXANDRA   1285 1286